The Ohio State Football Scrapbook

BY

Richard M. Cohen,
Jordan A. Deutsch,
and David S. Neft

BOBBS-MERRILL

Indianapolis/New York

Copyright © 1977 by Sports Products, Inc.

All rights reserved including the right of reproduction
in whole or in part in any form
Published by the Bobbs-Merrill Company, Inc.
Indianapolis/New York

Manufactured in the United States of America

First printing

Cover photos from the Ohio State University Photo Archives. Photo of Archie Griffin by Malcolm W. Emmons.

Library of Congress Cataloging in Publication Data

Cohen, Richard M   1938-
   The Ohio State football scrapbook.

    1. Ohio. State University, Columbus—Football—History.   I. Deutsch, Jordan A., joint author.
II. Neft, David S., joint author.   III. Title.
GV958.035C65   796.33′263′0977157   77-5260
ISBN 0-672-52334-5

The Ohio State Football Scrapbook

ACKNOWLEDGMENTS

The *Ohio State Football Scrapbook* is one of the first books in a continuing series of major college scrapbooks. The authors are sure you will enjoy this unique and new concept in sports publishing.

    The task of assembling all the material and data contained in this book could not have been accomplished by the three authors alone. In order to make this book a reality, the cooperation of many individuals, institutions, libraries, newspapers and news services was needed. The authors, therefore, would like to express their deep appreciation to the following people, who contributed their time and facilities during the preparation of this book:

    Nancy McCormack, *Visual and Technical Coordinator and Photo Reproduction Consultant*
    Roland T. Johnson, *Research Assistant and Advisor*
    Stan Grosshandler, *Research Advisor*

Ohio State Sports Information Department:
    Marvin Homan, *Sports Information Director*
    D. C. Koehl, *Assistant Sports Information Director*
    Stephen Snapp, *Assistant Sports Information Director*

Ohio State Press:
    Weldon Kefauver, *Ohio State Press*
    William J. Vollmar, *Ohio State Archivist*
    Ruth Jones, *Ohio State Photo Archivist*

Ohio State Publications:
    The Makio
    Ohio State Football Guides
    Ohio State Football Game Programs

Notre Dame International Sports and Games Research Collection:
    Herb Juliano, *Curator/Researcher*

Pro Football Hall of Fame:
    Jim Campbell, *Historian*

Hartford Public Library, Reference and General Reading Department:
    Josephine Sale, *Head*
    Martha Nolan, *Administrative Assistant*
    Dorothy Brickett, Rosalie Fawcett, Carol Fitting, Bhaskararao Kali, Shirley Kiefer, Fernando Labault, Beverly Loughlin, Betty Mullendore, Ann Santos, *Research Assistants*

Library of Congress, Serial Division:
    The staff of the *Reference Section*

Danbury Public Library:
    The staff of the *Reference Section*

New York Public Library Annex:
    The staff of the Newspaper Division

The authors would also like to thank the following news services and newspapers for the use of their material:
    Associated Press News Service
    The Baltimore Sunpapers
    The Cleveland Plain Dealer
    The Hartford Courant
    The New York Times
    The Washington Star News

Production:
    Sally Lifland

The Authors' Wives:
    A special thanks to Nancy Cohen, Thea Deutsch, and Naomi Neft for their continuous faith, understanding, and cooperation throughout all our projects.

All comments and inquiries on this book should be sent to
    Sports Products Inc.
    415 Main Street
    Ridgefield, CT 06877

Foreword

Who was Ohio State's first football opponent? Was it mighty Michigan or powerful Notre Dame? Or maybe Penn State, or Army, the Black Knights of the Hudson? Or perhaps it was Alabama, or Stanford, the scourge of the West during the early days of college football? But, alas, the Ohio State football program had a much more humble beginning. The date was May 3, 1890, and the opponent was Ohio Wesleyan, a tiny church-affiliated school located in Delaware, Ohio, a sleepy little village about twenty miles north of Columbus which is now more famous for its harness racing than for its football. The Buckeyes won the game, but not without a struggle: 20–14. Only a handful of fans gathered for the contest, which started at 9:30 A.M. in order to give the Ohio State team time to get back home before dark. But the seed had been planted. Football had arrived at Ohio State. From that humble beginning, it would grow and grow during the years to come.

What is the most talked about game in Ohio State football history? Unquestionably, the Notre Dame game of 1935, a contest that still brings heated debate anytime alumni of the two great football schools get together. It was the first meeting ever between the Buckeyes and the Fighting Irish, and the game was sold out almost a year in advance. Fittingly, both teams were unbeaten going into the titanic struggle in Ohio Stadium; Notre Dame boasted a 5–0 mark, and Ohio State had won all four of its starts. The first half belonged to the Buckeyes of Coach Francis Schmidt, who looked on with delight as his team built at 13–0 lead before intermission. Even the most ardent Notre Dame followers seemed willing to admit that Schmidt's "team of a thousand plays" was too much for their beloved Irish. But then, to the utter disbelief of the Ohio State following, the roof fell in on the Buckeyes. Schmidt was one of the greatest offensive minds the game has ever known, but in the second half nothing seemed to work for his team, and everything—yes, everything—went right for Notre Dame. Still, the Irish could not manage to cross the goal line in the third period, and even though things were going badly for the hometown favorites, a 13-point lead seemed safe enough. But Schmidt, the Buckeyes and all the OSU fans had forgotten one thing—the luck of the Irish. And never was the Notre Dame magic more evident than in that final quarter. Notre Dame scored early in the fourth period. The point after failed, and Ohio led 13–6. The Irish threatened again almost immediately, but their drive stalled when a fumble on the one-yard line was recovered by the Buckeyes. Ohio State couldn't move the ball and was forced to punt. This time the Irish would not be denied; they marched quickly into the end zone for another score. But again the point after went awry, and Ohio State led 13–12 with just over two minutes to play. Ohio State had only to run out the clock and victory would belong to the Buckeyes. But then the unthinkable happened: an Ohio State player fumbled on the Buckeyes' very first play after the kickoff, and Notre Dame took over at midfield. Three plays later, quarterback Bill Shakespeare, who was filling in for injured regular Andy Pilney, rifled a nineteen-yard scoring pass to tight end Wayne Millner, and the Irish had staged one of the greatest comebacks in college football history. Later, sports writers around the country would vote the 1935 Ohio State–Notre Dame game "the most exciting game of the first half of the twentieth century."

Name the greatest football player ever to play for the Buckeyes. Wow! What a task! The possibilities literally stagger the imagination. You could go all day and never find two people with the same choice. The list of backs reads like a "Who's Who in College Football." There is Charles "Chic" Harley, Gaylord

Stinchcomb, Les Horvath, Howard Cassady, Jim Otis, John Brockington, Rex Kern, Cornelius Greene, Brian Baschnagel and Archie Griffin. And that is just the tip of the iceberg. The list of linemen, All-Americans every one, includes Wesley Fesler, Gust Zarnas, Bill Willis, Jim Parker and John Hicks. If you want to consider linebackers and defensive backs, few schools anywhere can match the likes of Jim Stillwagon, Ike Kelley, Randy Gradishar, Jack Tatum, Arnie Chonko, Mike Sensibaugh, Neal Colzie and Tim Fox. There is no way to choose "the greatest" from that assortment of talent. It would be hard enough just to pick an all-star team of all-time greats.

What Ohio State football team do you remember best? Is it that 1935 team, whose only blemish in eight starts was that disheartening loss to Notre Dame? That was a team worth remembering. So, too, were Paul Brown's 1942 team and Carroll Widdoes's 1944 squad, both of which won Big Ten titles. And the 1944 squad was the mythical national civilian champion. The 1954 team will always be special to a large number of fans, because it was the first great team in the Woody Hayes era. But the tireless Hayes would have many great teams. His unbeaten 1968 team won the national championship. Until it lost its season finale, the 1969 squad was regarded as one of the greatest teams of all time. The 1970 team lost just one game. Hayes put together a brilliant array of talent in 1973—his squad tied the regular season finale at Michigan, but redeemed itself five weeks later by crushing a good Southern California team 42–21 in the Rose Bowl. Each team had a different personality, a different character, but each brought countless hours of delight to innumerable Ohio State fans, who will forever remember their favorite OSU eleven.

What is the greatest rivalry in college sports? Answers Buckeye Coach Woody Hayes, without hesitation, "Why it's the Ohio State–Michigan football game. I don't think anything else even comes close." Hayes has a penchant for being right, and he has hit the proverbial nail right on its proverbial head again this time. Because for sheer drama and emotion, nothing can compare with the annual season finale between the Buckeyes and their dreaded foe from the North, the Wolverines. And why not? The series that began in 1897 has been filled with what can only be described as classic football games. The incredible Snow Bowl Game of 1950 was such a contest. So was the 10–10 tie in 1973. And the 1974 and 1975 games went right down to the final play before a winner could be proclaimed. Individual pride, state pride and school honor are all on the line when Ohio State and Michigan meet on the gridiron. It is college football at its best.

I could ask fifty more questions like those above. And I could provide fifty more answers. But there's really no need to now. All the answers to all the questions are right here in *The Ohio State Football Scrapbook*. All you need to do is flip open the cover and leaf through the pages, and you'll discover all there is to know about Ohio State football.

With painstaking deliberation, the authors of this book, Richard Cohen, Jordan A. Deutsch and David Neft, have put together a vast storehouse of Buckeye grid lore. It begins with that very first game back in 1890 and goes right up to the 1977 Orange Bowl game. In between are clippings of almost every football game the Buckeyes have ever played. In addition to game stories, there are related clippings on many of the Buckeyes' greatest personalities, both players and coaches. Harley, Horvath, Janowicz, Cassady, Griffin, Fesler, Wilce and Hayes—they're all here. So whether you are an avid Buckeye fan or simply a trivia buff, mountains of information are contained herein for you to enjoy.

Ohio State football is college football at its best—and you won't find any better account of it anywhere than right here. Countless hours of fun and relaxation are ahead for you as you reminisce.

Steve Snapp
Assistant Sports Information Director
Ohio State University

First Ohio State Football Team—1890

Front row (seated): Herbert Johnson, Charles W. Foulk. *Back row:* Richard T. Ellis, "Kansas" Miller, Paul Lincoln, Mike Kennedy, Frank W. Rane, Ham H. Richardson, Jesse Jones (C), H. E. Rutan, Ed. Martin, Charles T. Morrey, Dave Aigler, Jack Huggins.

Foot Ball Team.

C. B. MORREY,	Manager.
P. M. LINCOLN,	Captain.

RUSH LINE.

P. M. LINCOLN,	Center Rush.
H. J. WHITACRE,	Right Guard.
H. H. RICHARDSON,	Right Tackle.
W. S. SCOTT,	Right End.
R. O. KEISER,	Left Guard.
J. B. HUGGINS,*	Left Tackle.
R. T. ELLIS,*	Left End.

QUARTER BACK.
C. W. FOULK.

HALF BACKS.
G. C. SCHAEFFER,*
W. A. LANDACRE.

FULL BACK.
F. W. RANE,†
A. P. BRONSON.

SUBSTITUTES.
E. D. MARTIN,
H. E. RUTAN,
H. BEATTY.

* Left College.
† Resigned.

1890
Coaches Alexander S. Lilley
Jack Ryder
Captains: Jesse L. Jones
Paul M. Lincoln

20	Ohio Wesleyan	14
0	*Wooster	64
0	Denison	14
10	*Kenyon	18
30		110

Won 1, Lost 3

Back row: Withoft, Dunlap, Patterson, Ernst, Smith, Zurfluh, Foulk, Walsh, Krumm. *Middle row:* Richardson, Lawrence, Ellis, Powell, Hine, Haas. *Front row:* Kennedy, Pearce, Gillen.

Varsity Eleven

1891-92

CHARLES W. FOULK, *Manager.*

RICHART T. ELLIS, *Captain.*

P. M. LINCOLN,	Right Guard.
J. S. HINE,	Left Guard.
H. H. RICHARDSON,	Right Tackle.
L. C. ERNST,	Left Tackle.
C. S. POWELL,	Center.
CLARENCE WITHOFT,	Right End.
R. E. KRUMM,	Left End.
GEO. D. PEARCE,	Quarter Back.
A. H. KENNEDY,	Right Half Back.
A. P. GILLEN,	Left Half Back.
G. SMITH,	Full Back.

SUBSTITUTES

J. J. WALSH,   M. W. LAWRENCE,
W. N. ZURFLUH,   R. W. DUNLAP,
FRANK HAAS,   F. D. PATTERSON.

1891
Coach: Alexander S. Lilley
Captain: Richard T. Ellis

6	*Western Reserve	50
0	Kenyon	26
8	*Denison	4
6	Akron	0
20		80

Won 2, Lost 2

[1892-1893]

```
          1892
    Coach: Jack Ryder
  Captain: Richard T. Ellis
   0   Oberlin         40
  62  *Akron            0
  80  *Marietta         0
  32   Denison          0
  42  *Dayton YMCA      4
  18   Western Reserve 40
  26  *Kenyon          10
  ---                 ---
  260                  94
       Won 5, Lost 2
```

```
          1893
   Captain A. P. Gillen
  16   Otterbein        22
  36  *Wittenberg       10
  10  *Oberlin          38
   6   Kenyon           42
  16  *Western Reserve  30
  32  *Akron            18
  38  *Cincinnati        0
  40  *Marietta          8
   8  *Kenyon           10
  ---                  ---
  202                  178
       Won 4, Lost 5
```

Varsity Eleven of '92.

W. J. Sears	Manager.
R. T. Ellis,	Captain.
P. M. Griffith,	Right End.
R. Thompson,	Right Tackle.
J. H. Mathers,	Right Guard.
C. S. Powell,	Center Rush.
W. A. Reed,	Left Guard.
J. J. Walsh,	Left Tackle.
R. T. Ellis,	Left End.
Frank Haas,	Quarter Back.
L. C. Ernst, A. H. Kennedy.	Right Half Back.
A. P. Gillen.	Left Half Back.
C. W. Withoft,	Full Back.

Substitutes.

W. F. Genheimer,   W. G. Nagel.

Varsity Eleven of '93.

C. S. Morrey	Manager.
A. P. Gillen,	Capt. and Left Half Back.
W. G. Nagel,	Right End.
A. J. Boynton,	Right Tackle.
G. C. Gibbs,	Right Guard.
W. A. Reed,	Center Rush.
J. H. Mathers,	Left Guard.
A. G. Thurman, G. Smith,	Left Tackle.
R. W. Dunlap,	Left End.
Frank Haas, C. L. Wood,	Quarter Back.
W. J. Foley,	Right Half Back.
F. B. Nicholls,	Left Half Back.
H. C. Howard,	Full Back.

Substitutes.

E. H. French, P. L. Mullay and E. S. Norton, Ends.
W. A. Snedicker, Center Rush.

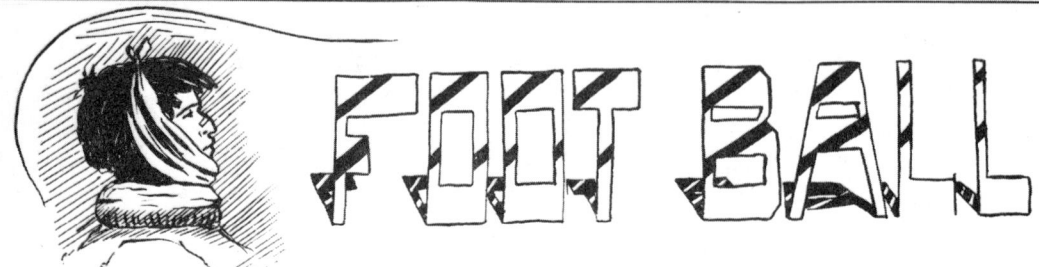

FOOT BALL

'Varsity Eleven of '94.

DUNLAP	Left End.	HUNTINGTON	Right End.
MILLER	Left Tackle.	H. HOWARD	Quarter Back.
CRECILIUS	Left Guard.	GIESSEN AND NICHOLS	Left Half Back.
SNEDAKER	Center.	NAGEL (Captain)	Right Half Back.
CALKINS	Right Guard.	POTTER	Full Back.
BOYNTON AND MATHERS	Right Tackle.		

SUBSTITUTES.

CARSON,   MYERS,   FRAYER.

W. H. RUDGE..................Manager.

```
        1894
    Captain: W. G. Nagel
   6   Akron              12
   0   Wittenberg          6
  32  *Antioch             0
   6   Wittenberg         18
  30   Columbus Barracks   0
   4  *Western Reserve    24
  10  *Marietta            4
   0   Case               38
   6   Cincinnati          4
  46  *17th Regiment       4
  20  *Kenyon              4
  ---                    ---
 160                     114
        Won 6, Lost 5
```

Crecelius, Left Guard. Howard, Quarter. Potter, Full Back. Mathers, R. Guard. Rudge, Manager. Myers, Sub. F.B. Frayer, Sub. End.
Huntington, Right End. Carson, L. Tackle. Nagel, (Capt), Right Half Back. Calkins, Right Guard. Giesson, Left Half. Miller, Sub. Tackle.
Warden, Sub. Dunlap, Left End.

[1895-1896]

Back row: French, Butcher, Thurman, Ryder, Giesson, Bulin, Potter. *Middle row:* Nichols, Johnson, Crecelius, R. W. Dunlap, Calkins, J. H. Dunlap. *Front row:* Howard, Richt, Wasson, De Long.

1896
Coach: Charles A. Hickey
Captains: Edward H. French
William A. Reed

OSU	Opponent	Opp
24	*Ohio Medical	0
6	Cincinnati	8
12	Otterbein	0
0	Oberlin	16
30	*Case	10
4	*Ohio Wesleyan	10
10	*Columbus Barracks	2
0	*Ohio Medical	0
6	*Wittenberg	24
12	*Ohio Medical	0
18	*Kenyon	34
122		104

Won 5, Lost 5, Tied 1

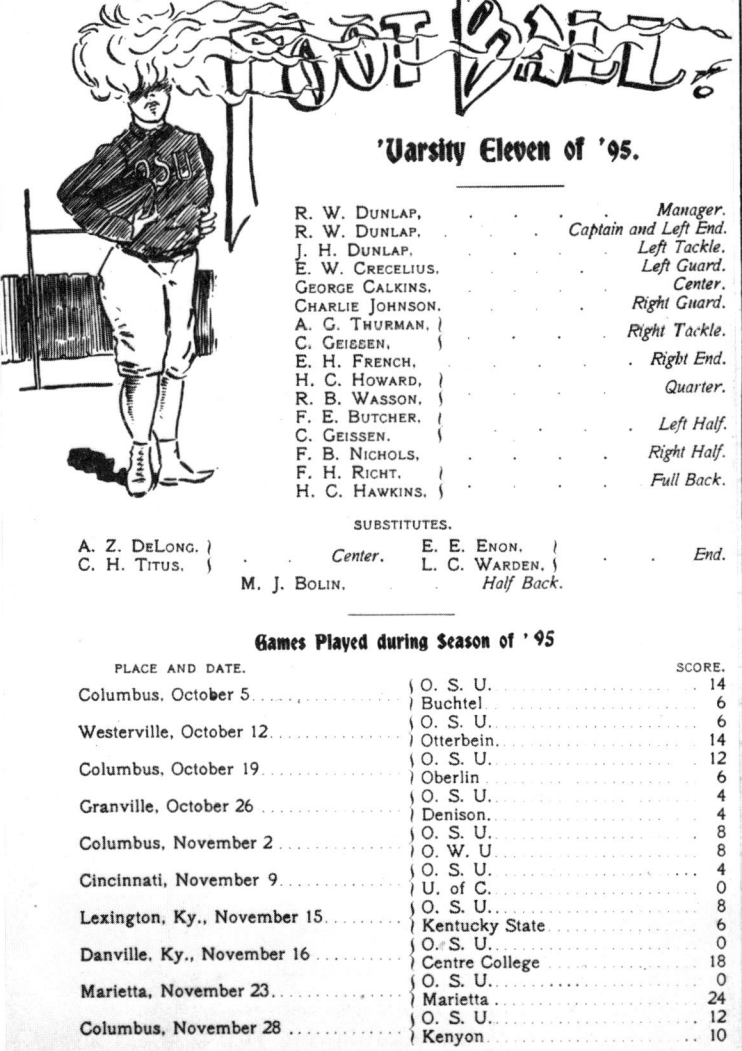

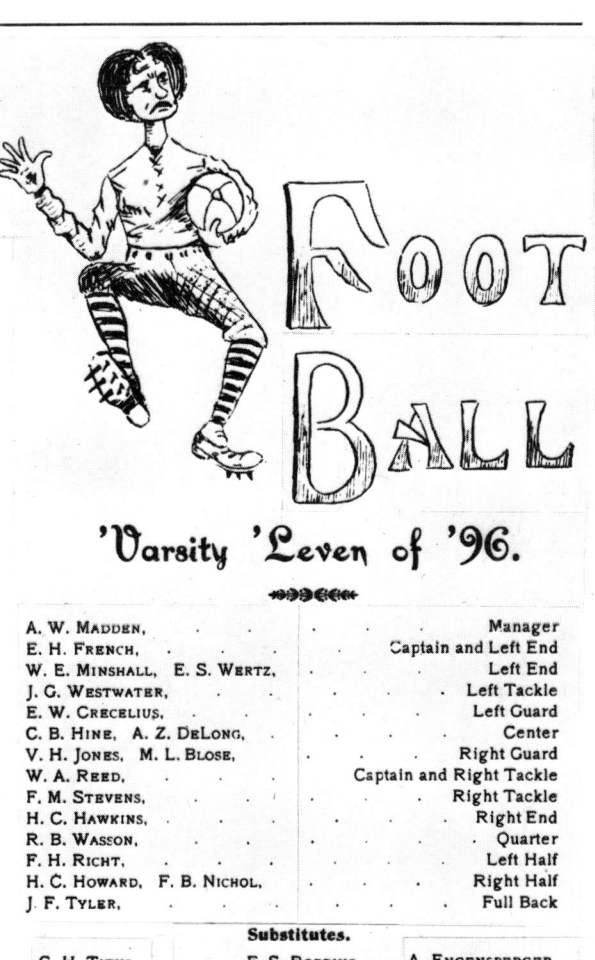

[1897]

1897—Michigan 34, Ohio State 0

Front row (left to right): Brophy, Mackey, Leonard, Engensberger, Richards, Stienie, Waite. *Second row:* Purdy, Urban, Captain Hawkins, Saxby, Scott. *Third row:* Butcher, Benedict, Segrist. *Back row:* Culbertson, King, Sykes, Enos, Dyer, Miller, Segrist.

1897
Coach: David F. Edwards
Captain: Harry C. Hawkins

6	*Ohio Medical	0
0	*Case	14
0	Michigan	34
12	*Otterbein	12
0	*Columbus Barracks	6
0	*Oberlin	44
0	West Virginia	28
0	Cincinnati	24
0	*Ohio Wesleyan	6
18		168

Won 1, Lost 7, Tied 1

Foot Ball Team.

HAWKINS, CAPT.	Full Back
SEGRIST, L. T.	Center
SEGRIST L. T.	Left guard
URBAN	Right guard
MILLER	Right tackle
RICHARDS	Left tackle
SCOTT	Right end
WAITE	Left end
MACKEY	Left tackle
SAXBY	Quarterback
ENGENSBERGER	End and right half-back
BROPHY	Left half-back
BENEDICT	Tackle and half-back
PURDY	Right half-back
BUTCHER	Half-back
LEONARD	End
DYER	Tackle
KING	Guard
SYKES	Tackle
CULBERTSON	Half-back
STEINLE	Half-back
ENOS	Mgr.

The Ohio State University

COLUMBUS

The head of the State System of public and free education
    Maintained by the people for the children of the people

Liberally Co-educational in all Colleges and Courses
    Definite (elective) course for young women, combining
Broad general culture and every detail of Domestic Science

Six distinct and independent Colleges, each with its own
Dean and Faculty
Agriculture, Arts, Engineering, Law, Pharmacy, Veterinary Medicine
THIRTY FOUR DEPARTMENTS
TWENTY SEVEN DISTINCT COURSES
Short courses for those of mature years, not candidates for degrees

EIGHTY THREE INSTRUCTORS
    OVER A THOUSAND STUDENTS
(No art, commercial, music, normal or preparatory students)

Thirteen buildings devoted to instruction (no dormitories)
THE FINEST GYNASIUM AND ARMORY IN THE WEST
Three hundred thousand dollars spent in buildings and equipment during 1896-97

TUITION FREE
The only charges made by the University are
    An incidental fee of $15 per year and usual laboratory fees

[1898]

SCORES.

Oct. 1—O. S. U., 17, Heidelberg, 0.
Oct. 8—O. S. U., 0, O. M. U., 10.
Oct. 15—O. S. U., 34, Denison, 0.
Oct. 22—O. S. U., 0, O. M. U., 10.
Nov. 5—O. S. U., 5, Case, 23.
Nov. 12—O. S. U., 0, Kenyon, 29.
Nov. 22—O. S. U., 0, Adelbert, 49.
Nov. 25—O. S. U., 24, Delaware, 0.

SEASON 1898.

SIGRIST, Captain,	Right End.
MARSHALL,	Left End.
SAYRES,	Left Tackle.
WHARTON,	Left Guard.
TILTON,	Right Guard.
WERTZ,	Right Tackle.
SIGRIST, C.,	Center.
HARDY,	Quarter-back.
HAGER,	Left Half-back.
HARRIS,	Right Half-back.
BLOSE,	Full-back.
STIMSON,	Left Guard.
SNYDER,	Left Tackle.
MINSHALL,	Left End.
STARK,	Right Half-back.
POOLE,	Right Tackle.
SCHREIBER,	Right End.
BROPHEY,	Left Half-back.
RIGHTMIRE,	Right Half-back.
EAGLESON,	Full-back.

Football Team

Season of 1899

J. B. C. Eckstorm — Coach
W. R. Sprague — Manager

Sayers, Captain — Left Tackle	Scott — Left End	
Sigrist J. — Center	Huddleson — Left End	
Sigrist C. — Right Tackle	Westwater — Left Half-back	
Wharton — Left Guard	Hager — Right Half-back	
Tilton — Right Guard	Kittle — Full-back	
Lloyd — Right End	Fay — Left Tackle	
Poole — Right End	Wilson — Left Half-back	
Hardy — Quarter Back	Yost — Right Half-back	

Substitutes

Breese, Center	Fulton	Tilden	Peoples
Davis	Graham	Frechtling	Galloway
Tangemann	Weber	Johnson	Albott
Hauk	McOwen	Jones	Orton

Scores

Sept. 30, O. S. U. 30—Otterbein, 0
Oct. 7, O. S. U. 29—Wittenberg 0
Oct. 14, O. S. U. 5—Case 5
Oct. 21, O. S. U. 41—O. U. 0
Oct. 28, O. S. U. 6—Oberlin 0
Nov. 4, O. S. U. 6—Adelbert 0
Nov. 11, O. S. U. 17—Marietta 0
Nov. 18, O. S. U. 12—O. M. U. 0
Nov. 25, O. S. U. 34—Muskingum 0
Thanksgiving, O. S. U. 5—Kenyon 0

[1900]

1900—Ohio State 0, Michigan 0

Front row (left to right): Lloyd, McLaren, Hardy, Herron, Boothman. *Middle row:* Dr. J. C. B. Eckstorm (coach), C. Sigrist, Wharton, Capt. Tilton, J. Sigrist, Faye, Rightmire. *Back row:* L. W. St. John, Tangeman, Westwater, Coover, Kittle, Bulen, Howland, Hawk, Hager.

1900	
Captain: J. H. Tilton	
20 *Otterbein	0
20 *Ohio University	0
29 Cincinnati	0
47 *Ohio Wesleyan	0
17 *Oberlin	0
27 *West Virginia	0
24 *Case	10
6 *Ohio Medical	11
0 Michigan	0
23 *Kenyon	5
213	26
Won 8, Lost 1, Tied 1	

FOOT BALL TEAM.
1900.

J. B. C. ECKSTORM, Coach.   ROBERT RIGHTMIRE, Manager.   J. H. TILTON, Captain.

TILTON	Right Guard	BULEN	Full Back
J. SEGRIST	Center and End	HAGER	Right Half
C. SEGRIST	Right Tackle	HAWK	Right Half
WHARTON	Left Guard	HOWLAND	Left Half
HARDY	Quarter Back	HERRON	Quarter Back
COOVER	Left Tackle	ST. JOHN	Left Half
LLOYD	Right End	WESTWATER	Left Half
KITTLE	Full Back	FAY	Center
TANGEMAN	Left Guard	McLAREN	Right Half
	BOOTHMAN	Left End	

Substitutes.

SCOTT	Left End
DUBOIS	Full Back
BUTCHER	Left End
ADAMS	Right End
HUDDLESON	Right End
BREESE	Center
FRECHTLING	Right Tackle
WEBER	Left End
SHERMAN	Left End

Foot Ball Team

1901

J. B. C. Eckstorm	Coach
Robert Rightmire	Manager
J. M. Kittle	Captain

Kittle	Full Back	Bulen		Full Back
Fay	Centre	Hardy		Quarter Back
J. Segrist (d'c'd)	Centre	Jackson		Quarter Back
C. Segrist	Right Tackle	McLaren		Right Half
Tangeman	Left Guard	Dill		Left Half
Riddle	Right Guard	Westwater		Left Half
Coover	Left Tackle	Marker		Right Tackle
Tilton	Right Guard	Birdseye		Right Half
Lloyd	Left End	Elder		Right End

Substitutes

Ricketts	Half Back	Rodreiguez	Half Back
Dilts	Centre	Huntington	End
Boothman	Quarter Back	Oliver	Guard
Girard	End	Tillman	End
	Riddle	Guard	

```
            1901
      Captain: J. M. Kittle
   0  *Otterbein           0
  30  *Wittenberg          0
  17  *Ohio University     0
  24  *Marietta            0
   6  *Western Reserve     5
   0  *Michigan           21
   0   Oberlin             6
   6  *Indiana            18
  11  *Kenyon              6
  ──                      ──
  94                      56
    Won 5, Lost 3, Tied 1
```

Back row: McLaren, Birdseye, Dill. *Third row:* Marker, Bullen, Lloyd, Tangeman, Segrist (C), Tilton, Coover, Eckstorm. *Second row:* Elder, Faye, Gerard, Oliver, Jackson, Rightmire. *Front row:* Tillman, Ricketts, Kittle, Boothman.

[1902]

POSTLE MGR TILLMAN CASE HILL LINCOLN   RIDDLE   MARQUARD WALKER DILTZ SURFACE HALE (COACH)
        THROWER   MARKER   FAYE   McCLARREN   CLARKE
BROWNE CORNELL   ELDER   COOVER   FOSS   MAYNARD
                            CAPT.

Foot Ball Team 1902

Perry T. Hale, Coach   W. F. Coover, Captain
                Carl H. Postle, Manager

"Texas" Thrower	Right End	Maynard
"Jim" Marker	Right Tackle	Shearer
"Fat" Diltz	Right Guard	Riddle
"Fatty" Fay	Centre	Malone
Case	Left Guard	Clarke
"Buck" Coover	Left Tackle	Surface
"Mule" Elder	Left End	Ranney
"Pete" McLaren	Right Half-back	Walker
"Frog" Hill	Left Half-back	Brown
"Bo" Foss	Quarter-back	Tillman
"Jim" Lincoln	Full-back	Marquardt

Cornell	End	Hogue	Half-back
Brown	Half-back	Potter	Half-back
Niemeyer	Full-back	Kellough	End
Swan	Half-back	Oliver	End
Wiles	Quarter-back	Andrews	Tackle
Klie	End	Wheeler	End
Van Horn	End	Townsend	Full-back
		Newman	Half-back

Foot Ball Scores 1902

Ohio State	5	Otterbein	0	Ohio State	55	Kenyon	5
Ohio State	17	Ohio	0	Ohio State	12	Case School	23
Ohio State	30	Univ. of W. Va.	0	Ohio State	0	Illinois	0
Ohio State	34	Marietta College	0	Ohio State	17	Ohio Wesleyan	16
Ohio State	0	Michigan	86	Ohio State	6	Indiana	6

[1902]

1902	
Coach: Perry Hale	
Captain: W. F. Coover	
5 *Otterbein	0
17 *Ohio University	0
30 *West Virginia	0
34 *Marietta	0
0 Michigan	86
51 *Kenyon	5
12 *Case	23
0 *Illinois	0
17 Ohio Wesleyan	16
6 *Indiana	6
172	136
Won 6, Lost 2, Tied 2	

J. B. C. Eckstorm
Our Retiring Coach

To future students of the Ohio State University J. B. C. Eckstorm will be named as the man whose ceaseless interest, tireless activity and consistent effort did so much toward placing our teams in their present high position among Western foot ball teams, and toward fostering our, at one time, dormant College Spirit. His name will ever be remembered with the fondest recollections by all.

Perry T. W. Hale
Our New Coach

Perry T. W. Hale, Yale '00, whom the Athletic Board has, with confidence, selected to coach our foot ball team next fall, comes to us not only with the best of recommendations but also with a record strong enough to substantiate all assertions. It is with pleasure that the MAKIO herewith presents his picture, and welcomes to O. S. U. such a coach as Perry Hale.

Ohio State Snowed Under.
SPECIAL TO THE PLAIN DEALER.

ANN ARBOR, Mich., Oct. 25.—Thirty-five car loads of scarlet and gray admirers arrived yesterday morning confident that their team would give the Wolverines their hardest contest of the season if not beating them. The visitors received a very cordial reception owing to the splendid welcome which was accorded to Michigan at Columbus last season.

Over 6,000 people witnessed the game, making it the largest crowd that had assembled on the local gridiron this season. The Wolverines were in fine condition, not a man being on the hospital list. The O. S. U. squad were all well except McLaren, whose leg was not in first-class shape.

Michigan punted O. S. U., who lost the ball, and after three minutes' play, Herrnstein planted the pigskin between the goal posts. Heston, after a brilliant sixty-yard run, throwing the Buckeye off and with his line bucks, carried the ball over for the second touchdown.

Foss and McLaren's playing was splendid, but they could do nothing with the Wolverines' mass plays.

After Michigan got the ball the O. S. U. got into a wrangle with McGuggin and a slugging match was narrowly averted. Lawrence carried the ball over and kicked goal.

Sweeley's punting was of the old-time order, he repeatedly sending the pigskin sixty to seventy-five yards. Heston made another ninety-yard run, dragging three O. S. U. players for ten yards, making another touchdown. The O. S. U. were all discouraged and lost all heart. In vain their admirers rooted, but they could do nothing against the Michigan battering ram.

McLaren, whose leg had been in bad shape before the game, was forced to retire, Walker taking his place. Lincoln was put out of the game for slugging Carter. The first half ended 45 to 0. Herrnstein made the first touchdown in the second half in two minutes' play, and six minutes after he made another.

The O. S. U. players began to show the effects of the hard knocks from the Wolverines and many substitutes had to be called in. Michigan used its tackle back plays to good advantage and, with McGuin, the ball was again forced over. The next touchdown was made by Palmer in forty-five seconds. This ended the half. Line up:

O. S. U.—0.	Position.	Michigan—86.
Ranney, Maynard and Kellough	Left end	Redden
Cover	Right tackle	Palmer
Lincoln and Riddle	Left guard	McGugin
Thrower	Center	Gooding and Gregory
Fay and Chase	Forest, Cole and	
Marker	Right guard	Carter
Cornell	Right tackle	Maddock
Foos	Right end	Sweeley
Hill and Brown	Quarterback	Weeks
McLaren and Walker	Left halfback	Graver and Heston
	Right halfback	Cole and Herrnstein
Townsend	Fullback	Jones and Lawrence

Touchdowns—Michigan, Herrnstein 4, Heston, Lawrence 2, Maddock. Goals from touchdowns—Lawrence 7, Sweeley 4, Jones Palmer 2, McGugin 2. Umpire—Hinckey of Yale. Referee—Hoagland of Princeton. Linesmen—Michigan, Weeks; O. S. U., Tinker. Timers—Michigan, Millard; O. S. U., Rightmire. Head linesman—Biles of Yale. Time of halves—35 and 25 minutes.

Reprinted with permission of the **Cleveland Plain Dealer**

The Varsity, 1903

Hale (Coach), Clark, Surface, Jones, Lincoln, Walker, Maynard, Hagaman, Tilton, McClure, Thrower, Hoyer, Diltz, Marker, Huntington, Case, Hyde, Heekin, Lawrence, Powell, Foss, Swan, Oliver.

Varsity 1903

Thrower	Right End.
Marker (c)	Right Tackle.
Huntington	Left Guard.
{ Powell { Hoyer	Center.
Diltz	Right Guard.
Case	Left Tackle.
{ Hyde { Heekin	Left End.
Foss	Quarter.
Jones	Right Half.
Walker	Left Half.
Lincoln	Full Back

Substitutes

BACK FIELD

Lawrence, Swan, Oliver, Klous, Byrne, Wallace, Hagaman.

LINE

Clark, Maynard, Surface.

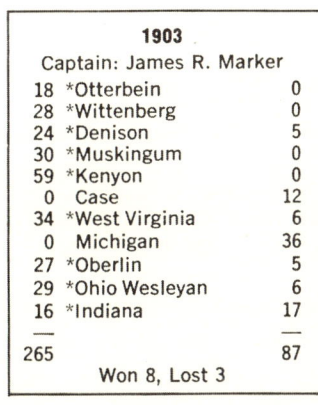

1903
Captain: James R. Marker

18	*Otterbein	0
28	*Wittenberg	0
24	*Denison	5
30	*Muskingum	0
59	*Kenyon	0
0	Case	12
34	*West Virginia	6
0	Michigan	36
27	*Oberlin	5
29	*Ohio Wesleyan	6
16	*Indiana	17
265		87

Won 8, Lost 3

"FAT" HOYER.
Center, 1903.
V. O. A.

[1904]

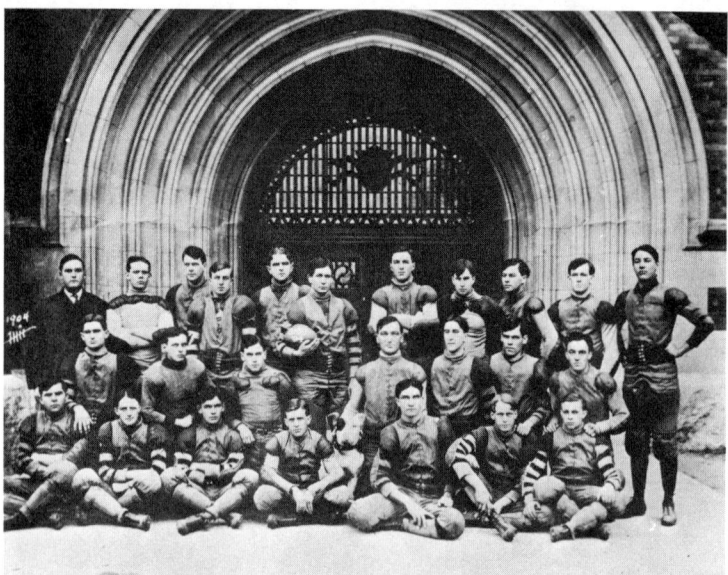

Back row: Smith, Walker, Dunsford, Swan, Hoyer, Thrower, Schorey, Heffelman, Claggett, Lawrence, Oliver. *Second row:* Carver, Waters, Jones, Marker, Marquard, Curran, Gill. *Front row:* Diltz, Reemsnyder, Warwick, Martz, Clarke, Surface, Foss.

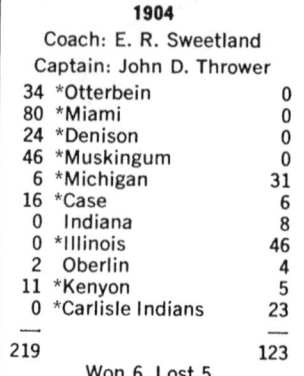

1904
Coach: E. R. Sweetland
Captain: John D. Thrower

34	*Otterbein	0
80	*Miami	0
24	*Denison	0
46	*Muskingum	0
6	*Michigan	31
16	*Case	6
0	Indiana	8
0	*Illinois	46
2	Oberlin	4
11	*Kenyon	5
0	*Carlisle Indians	23
219		123

Won 6, Lost 5

E. R. SWEETLAND, Cornell '01, Coach

NO MATCH FOR THE INDIANS

Ohio State Could Not Win From Even the Carlisle Second Team.

SPECIAL TO THE PLAIN DEALER.

COLUMBUS, O., Nov. 24.—Carlisle Indian coaches ran in their second team against Ohio State this afternoon and saw the scrubs win an easy game, 23 to 0. Ohio State's line was all to the bad in the first half and the fleet Indians ripped big holes and drove through them for three touchdowns.

In the second half they played more of a kicking game. Ohio braced up considerably and held the Indians to a single touchdown and goal.

The Ohio backs and ends played a good defensive game at times. Gill was responsible for the one first down made by Ohio in the first half.

In the second half, Ohio worked the ball up as far as her forty-yard line but holding stopped the advance and made a punt necessary. Marker was put out of the game along with Fremont, an Indian end. This pair had an open field hair pulling match as the climax of a lot of roughhouse. The score:

State—0.	Position.	Carlisle—23.
Walters	Left end	Mount Pleasant, Fremont and Tomahawk
Gill	Left tackle	Eagleman
Dunsford	Left guard	Clark and LaRoque
Hoyer	Center	Kennedy, Jackson and Shouchuk
Diltz	Right guard	Jackson and Lubo
Marker and Curran	Right tackle	Lubo and Leroy
Remsnyder	Right end	P. Kennedy
Thrower and Jones	Quarterback	Baker, Mount Pleasant and Libby
Carver	Left half	Doxtator
Swan and Warwick	Right half	Charles and Fisher
Marquardt and Schory	Fullback	Gardner and Charles

First half: Touchdowns—Doxtator, Gardner 2. Goal from touchdowns—Charles 2. Second half: Touchdown—Gardner. Goal from touchdown—Charles. Referee—Stauffer of Pennsylvania. Umpire—Wrenn of Harvard. Head linesman—Inglis of Washington and Jefferson. Time of halves—25 minutes.

Reprinted with permission of the **Cleveland Plain Dealer**

Scarlet and Gray 1905

Back row: Foss (Manager), Tangeman, Brindle, Lincoln, Gillie, Hoyer (Captain), Schory, Dunsford, Kirby, Thompson (L. W.), Woodbury, Davis (Graduate Manager). Middle row: Surface, Heffleman, Lantry, Segrist, Thompsen (George), Warren, Gillard, Perry. Front row: Barrington, Reemsnyder, Foster, Jones, Leonard, McDonald.

1905		
Captain: Ralph W. Hoyer		
6	*Otterbein	6
28	*Heidelberg	0
40	*Muskingum	0
17	*Wittenberg	0
2	*Denison	0
32	*DePauw	6
0	*Case	0
23	*Kenyon	0
0	Michigan	40
36	*Oberlin	0
15	*Wooster	0
0	*Indiana	11
199		63
Won 8, Lost 2, Tied 2		

O. S. U. Line-up

Left End	Reemsnyder
Left Tackle	Brindle
Left Guard	Dunsford
Center	Capt. Hoyer
Right Guard	Heffleman
Right Tackle	Woodbury
Right End	Leonard
Quarter Back	Jones
Left Half	Stolp
Right Half	Kirby
Full Back	Lincoln

O.S.U. vs INDIANA
THANKSGIVING DAY
UNIVERSITY FIELD.
November 30, 1905.

[1906]

1906: MICHIGAN 6—OHIO STATE 0

Front row, seated (left to right): Carr, Schachtel, Gillie, Capt. Lincoln, Lawrence, ———. *Middle:* Sanzenbacher, Schory, Gibson, Coach Al Herrnstein, Barrington, Bryce, Whipple, Clagget, Segrist, Manager Linhart, Claflin. *Back row:* McDonald, Tracy, Stolp.

1906
Coach: A. E. Herrnstein
Captain: James F. Lincoln

41	*Otterbein	0
52	*Wittenberg	0
16	*Muskingum	0
0	*Michigan	6
6	Oberlin	0
6	*Kenyon	0
9	Case	0
12	*Wooster	0
11	*Ohio Medical	8
153		14

Won 8, Lost 1

OHIO STATE

NAME	AGE	HEIGHT	WEIGHT
Claflin	19	5–7	153
Lincoln	23	6–2	190
Laurence	23	5–10	180
Sheldon	22	5–10	175
Gillie	24	6–3	189
Schory	21	6–1	183
Carr	20	5–9	165
Barrington	19	5–7	145
Gibson	19	6–	168
Tracy	20	6–	170
Stolp	20	5–11	170
Mcdonald	19	5–11	160
Average	20¾	5–11	170⅔

KICKED GOAL FROM FIELD.
Michigan Won Close Game From Ohio State University.

COLUMBUS, Ohio. October 20.—Michigan University's foot ball team today defeated Ohio State University 6 to 0, scoring on a field goal and a safety. The Ohio team, coached by Herrnstein, a former Michigan foot ball star, put up a strong defense.

Unable to carry the ball across Ohio's goal, and with but four minutes of the game remaining, Garrels made his fourth attempt to kick a goal from the field and was successful. After the next kick-off an exchange of punts gave Ohio the ball on her fifteen-yard line. A penalty put the ball back to five yards, and when Gibson dropped back to punt a bad pass sent the oval over his head and he was compelled to fall on it back of the goal line, giving Michigan two more points.

Reprinted with permission of the **Cleveland Plain Dealer**

Coach Herrnstein

STATE FINISHES GREAT SEASON

Prevents Its Goal Line From Being Crossed Throughout the Campaign.

Beats the Medics, 11 to 8, Means Kicking Two Goals From the Field.

SPECIAL TO THE PLAIN DEALER.

COLUMBUS, O., Nov. 29.—The toe of Jack Means, quarterback of the Ohio Medics, scored eight points against Ohio State today in the first game between the Columbus colleges in six years, sending the oval from the fifty-one-yard line over the bar on his second successful place kick. Means, however, was the only mainstay of the Doctors and State played all around their rivals in making two touchdowns.

Means started the scoring twelve minutes after the game commenced, dropping the oval over from the thirty-six-yard line. State on receiving the kick-off started toward the Medics' goal and by terrific line plunges and end runs crossed the Medic line two minutes later. The same style of play took the ball to the Medic twenty-five-yard line seven minutes afterward, from where Secrist made a brilliant end run for his second touchdown.

Means toward the end of the half added the final points of the game by making a clean place kick fifty-one yards from the bar.

In the second half Means appeared to have lost his nerve and missed four place kicks. Two of these were in the last two minutes of play, when he had the chance of winning the game. One attempt was from the forty-five-yard line and the other from the forty-seven. State in the half twice went to the doctors' fifteen-yard line but lost the ball on downs when the Medics' line braced.

The State line was strong on defense though the Medics made a number of long gains through it. State gained nearly all of her ground through and around the line, the forward pass being used successfully once. A number of trick plays were tried but only two or three secured any advances.

Secrist and Barrington were the strong players for State. Secrist was used most in carrying the ball and always brought long gains, while he was great on defense. Referee Wrenn called him the best half in the country. Barrington played a safe, sure game, but had poor interference in returning punts. Means was half of the Medic team, punting brilliantly, in addition to place kicking and returning the oval consistently. Capt. Cann was strong at half.

After the game State raised an Ohio championship pennant on the field.

Line up.

Ohio State—11.	Position.	Ohio Medics—8.
Claflin	Left end	Blue
Lincoln	Left tackle	Hawkins
Lawrence and Schachtel	Left guard	Furnas
Sheldon	Center	Saunders
Gillie	Right guard	Wycker
Lawrence-Schachtel-Schory	Right tackle	Holzer
Carr	Right end	Kershaw
Barrington and Bryce	Quarterback	Means
McDonald	Right halfback	Carter and Brown
Secrist and Stolp	Left halfback	Cann
Tracey and Gibson	Fullback	Mace and Barnes

Touchdowns—Secrist 2. Goals from placement—Means 2. Goals from touchdown—Lincoln. Referee—Wrenn. Umpire—Hougland. Head Linesman—Inglis. Time of halves—30 minutes. Attendance—6,500.

Reprinted with permission of the **Cleveland Plain Dealer**

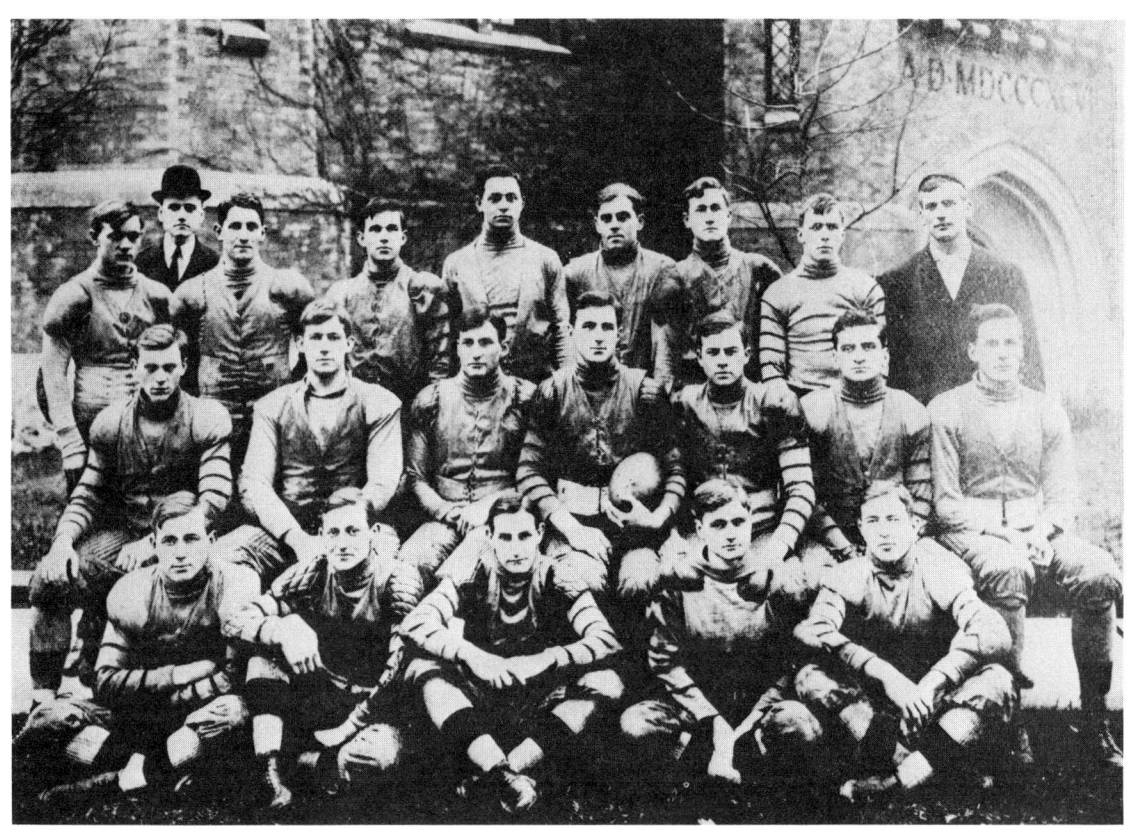

Top: Walker, Boli (Manager), Arnold, Rothrock, Way, Darst, Fraser, Clatlin, Hernstein (Coach). *Second:* Gibson, Van Buskirk, Sanzenbacher, Schory (Captain), Clagett, Schactel, McAllister. *Bottom:* Carr, Bryce, Barrington, Manning, Secrist.

OHIO STATE LINE UP

NOVEMBER 28, 1907

Claflin	Left End
McAllister	Left Tackle
Schachtel	Left Guard
Clagget	Center
Sanzenbacher	Right Guard
Schory	Right Tackle
Carr	Left Tackle
Barrington	Quarter Back
Secrist	Left Half
Bryce	Right Half
Gibson	Full Back

1907
Captain: H. J. Schory

28	*Otterbein	0
16	*Muskingum	0
28	*Denison	0
6	*Wooster	6
0	Michigan	22
12	*Kenyon	0
22	*Oberlin	10
9	*Case	11
23	*Heidelberg	0
16	*Ohio Wesleyan	0
160		49

Won 7, Lost 2, Tied 1

[1908]

1908: MICHIGAN 10—OHIO STATE 6.
Front row (left to right): McCarty, Summers, Hugus, Walker. Second row: Bryce, Eberle, Secrist, Gibson, Capt. Barrington, Jones, Wells, Bachman, Claflin. Third row: Coach Herrnstein, Van Buskirk, Wetzel, Sanzenbacher, Donley, Schachtel, Gillie. Fourth row: Powell, McAllister.

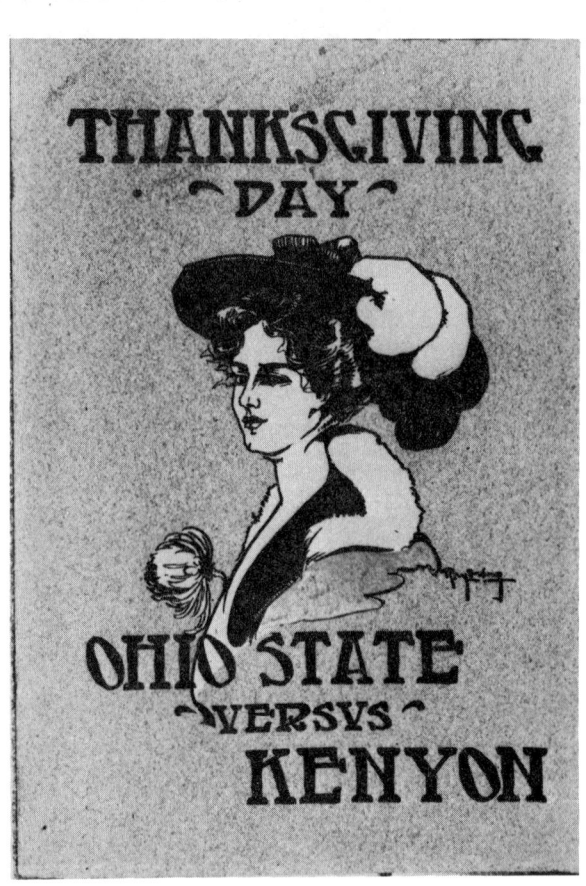

OFFICIAL FOOTBALL SCHEDULE FOR 1908

September 26—Otterbein	20 minute halves
October 3—Wooster	25 and 20 minutes
October 10—Denison	30 and 25 minutes
October 17—Western Reserve	30 minutes
October 24—Michigan	35 minutes
October 31—Ohio Wesleyan	30 and 25 minutes
*November 7—Case at Cleveland	35 minutes
*November 14—Vanderbilt at Nashville	30 minutes
November 21—Oberlin	35 minutes
November 26—Kenyon	35 minutes

*Abroad.

The 1908 Football Season and its Greater Significance to Ohio State

The results of the games throughout the 1908 football season were to a very great extent unexpected. The average observer, looking over the heavy schedule at the beginning of the season, would never have predicted that State would lose the games that were lost, and would scarcely have expected the Varsity to make her most creditable showing against Michigan and Vanderbilt instead of against her natural enemies here in Ohio.

The unexpected reverses in the early part of the season tested to the limit the spirit of the team and its followers; and it was the grit of the boys on the field and the loyalty of the boys in the bleachers that made possible our unlooked for victories.

In our Michigan game, when Gibson started on his long trip to Michigan's goal, he was apparently stopped several times, but shook himself free on each occasion, and went through the entire Michigan team for a touchdown. In the Vanderbilt game, after several substitutions had been made, including that of Jones for Captain Barrington, Vanderbilt expected to more than gain back the ground that they had lost,—the score standing 11 to 6 against them. They had not reckoned with our Tommie, however. In the briefest space of time, while the umpire's whistle was blowing for a foul committed by Vanderbilt, taking advantage of a slight hesitancy on the part of the other team, Tommie carried the ball from well out in the field to within one yard of their goal, and soon converted this gain into a touchdown, bringing certain victory to Ohio State.

"HERRNIE"

"RUBE" SCHORY

These unexpected results, brought about by the fighting spirit of the team, made a success of that part of the season's work which we want to remember. Our victory over Vanderbilt, our fine showing against Michigan, and the complete blotting out of the good records of Oberlin and Kenyon established us in a high position in the football world. The brilliant climax of the season has probably wiped out all recollection of the early reverses from the minds of the rooters, although it still remains in the hearts of the coaches and players. Of the results of the Michigan, Vanderbilt, Oberlin, and Kenyon games we can be justly proud; and of the rest of the season, the least said the better. The unexpected reverses taught us to take our defeats with courage, and our unexpected success in the other games taught us to take our victories with modesty.

At home,—here within the University circle,—we had throughout the season the one thing which every rooter, player, captain, manager, and coach of every university team in the country wishes for most, especially in the moments of saddest defeat,—a perfect demonstration of loyalty, which came direct from the SPIRIT of the men and women of the University.

The granting of a half-holiday by the president and faculty of this university, the co-operation of the Athletic Board, the presence of nearly 1,000 students in the line of the snake dance from the University to the Union Station, on the afternoon the team left Columbus for Nashville to play Vanderbilt, will always stand as a record for Spirit. That display of loyalty and enthusiasm in the face of defeat and adverse conditions has never been equaled anywhere, and can always be pointed to as a standard which future rooters should strive to live up to.

Next year we are going to have a hard row to hoe; but with that spirit always possessing the minds and hearts of all University men, victory should be the only result of our efforts.

Ohio State Line-Up
Nov. 26, 1908

Claflin	L. End
Schachtel	L. Tackle
McAllister	L. Guard
Wetzel	Center
Sanzenbacher	R. Guard
Powell	R. Tackle
Bryce	R. End
Barrington-Jones	Q.-B.
Wells	L. Half
Secrest	R. Half
Gibson	Full Back

1908
Captain: W. D. Barrington

18	*Otterbein	0
0	*Wooster	8
16	*Denison	2
0	*Western Reserve	18
6	*Michigan	10
20	*Ohio Wesleyan	9
8	Case	18
17	Vanderbilt	6
14	*Oberlin	12
19	*Kenyon	9
118		92

Won 6, Lost 4

Ohio Field

FOOTBALL

In reviewing the football season just past, many facts are obvious, the summarization of which, on the whole, give a satisfactory conclusion. Football at Ohio State, as in most of the larger colleges, over towers all other sports in importance and, coming as it does, at a time when the students have returned for the year, full of enthusiasm, Ohio Field becomes a mecca every Saturday for practically the whole college, the effects of which are never really lost before another year rolls around.

Looking at it, however, from the point of view of the man to whom victory is the all-important thing, the past season was only one of moderate success. One must admit that the two most important Ohio games were lost, yet the splendid victory over Vanderbilt, to a certain degree, atoned for those reverses. The men from whom Herrnstein had to select his team were what the "up-state" papers characterized as "a bunch of recruits," and, in a sense, that was undoubtedly true. These men, however, were whipped into a team that was at all times a factor in the race for state honors. Every team of any importance in the state was successfully defeated until the Case game, when on a slippery field the Scientists won undisputed claim to the Trophy Cup. Two out of the three remaining games were victories. The other was the defeat at Oberlin, but the team came back to true form on Thanksgiving Day and gave Kenyon one of the worst drubbings of the year. Among many, at least two things were demonstrated conclusively last fall. In the first place, it became evident that a change was needed in our playing schedule, for we had arrived at the point where we should drop most of the Ohio teams and fill these dates with out of state elevens, or confine our schedule to the colleges within the state. The time was evidently not at hand, in view of the unsettled championship of the last two years, to take the former step, and as a consequence, the latter has been adopted in its entirety. Our schedule for the coming season includes but one out of state game. At present this is commendable, but the time is at hand when finally demonstrating our superiority by one of possibly two championship teams, we shall step out into a broader field and make Ohio State the great Middle Western football power that everyone feels she should be—that everyone knows she can be.

In the second place, no one that witnessed such examples of college spirit as were displayed last fall on more than one occasion, both on the field and from the stands, can but realize that Ohio State has a new fighting spirit. For this we are greatly indebted to the man who, for the past four years has been our coach, and who in all places, at all times, in defeat as well as in victory, has stood for high athletic ideals and absolutely clean sport. This year ends Coach Herrnstein's engagement at Ohio State and the coming season will see the Eastern style of coaching inaugurated. Extremely fortunate, it seems, has the Athletic Board been in securing as Mr. Herrnstein's successor, Mr. Jones, head coach at Yale last season, who will be assisted by Mr. Farrell, present track coach, in the capacity of trainer, and by Mr. Welch, of Ohio Wesleyan, who will have charge of the new men. The outlook for next fall is bright and it must be admitted, that barring none but the very impossible, Howard Jones will give Ohio State one of the very best teams in her history.

Ohio State Line-Up
Nov. 25, '09

L. E.—Summers 10, Beatty.

L. T.—Powell 8, McClain 17.

L. G.—Portz 6.

C.—McCarty 5, Olds 19, Boone.

B. G.—Hall, Perry 9.

B. T.—Boesel 15, VanSwearingen.

R. E.—Schieber 21, Wright 18.

Q. B.—Jones 1, Schaffer 13.

L. H.—Wells 2, Hines 12.

R. H.—Hatfield 3, Clare.

F. B.—Eberle 4, Cox 16.

1909
Captain: Thomas H. Jones

14	*Otterbein	0
39	*Wittenberg	0
74	*Wooster	0
6	Michigan	33
29	*Denison	0
21	*Ohio Wesleyan	6
3	*Case	11
5	*Vanderbilt	0
6	Oberlin	26
22	*Kenyon	0
219		76

Won 7, Lost 3

[1910]

1910: MICHIGAN 3—OHIO STATE 3.
Front row (left to right): Clare, Summers, Foss, Long, Schieber, Smith, Cox. Middle row: Smith, Markley, Boesel, Egbert, Wells, Laybourn, Hall, Barricklow, Pavy. Back row: Manager Kirkpatrick, Wright, Blain, Powell, Coach Jones, Olds, Bachman, Raymond, Farrell.

1910
Coach: Howard Jones
Captain: Leslie R. Wells

14	*Otterbein	5
62	*Wittenberg	0
23	*Cincinnati	0
6	*Western Reserve	0
3	*Michigan	3
5	*Denison	5
10	Case	14
6	*Ohio Wesleyan	0
0	*Oberlin	0
53	*Kenyon	0
182		27

Won 6, Lost 1, Tied 3

HOWARD JONES

With the change of football coaches this year comes a man who is not only well known locally, but who has behind him a reputation throughout the country of being one of the best coaches Old Yale ever had. Jones played on the Yale 'Varsity for three successive years, and finished his career brilliantly, being recognized as one of the best ends in America. His first real coaching experience was at Syracuse University, where he turned out one of the best teams that university ever boasted of, defeating Michigan, as well as several of the larger eastern colleges. This year he was head coach at Yale, and his success can only be exemplified by the fact that Old Eli's goal line was not crossed, nor did she lose a single game throughout the season. We feel that we have been very fortunate in securing him to lead our team, and can only prophesy one of the best seasons in Ohio's history next fall. Already he has shown the earnestness with which he has taken hold of his work by the inauguration of spring practice. A comparatively large squad has been working out under his supervision, and while he has not as yet expressed himself, things are already looking very promising. We welcome Mr. Jones with that spirit of hospitality that only Ohio State students know how to give, and we hope that his stay here will be a pleasant one. It is up to the students now to support him, and there is no doubt but that this will be done to the fullest extent of their ability. Our best wishes go out to our new coach, and we feel certain that the bonds of interest and loyalty that bind coach and student body alike will be as pleasant and as well-knit as is anticipated.

Review of Football Season of 1910

FROM the standpoint of retiring captain, many things might be noted which did not present themselves in the same light to other students around the University. First of all it might be well to bring up the point of available material in the school,—not exactly as a criticism but more as an appeal. We made a good showing last fall but we might have done better had more men been out for positions on our team. Our coaching staff has been the best that money can secure and other facilities are fairly adequate for training a large number of men. A school of our size should have about four times as many men on the squad as were out last year. I earnestly request that more men come out next year.

The last season saw the advent of the Eastern style of football, under the guidance of Coach Jones. During the earlier part of the season all the time and energy of the coach and his assistants was devoted to the development of a strong defense. The success of such tactics was demonstrated beyond a doubt,—even for the Michigan game where we held that University to a 3—3 score; no new plays on the offensive were worked up. After defense was mastered, then offensive play was given attention.

During the season only one game was lost, that being the Case game at Cleveland. In this game every man on the team played brilliantly and the recorded result hardly does us justice. I might add that this game was played under protest of our Athletic Board. The only arrangements that Case would agree to were that they should have sole choice of officials—that these officials did not render the most competent service will be attested to by almost anyone who witnessed the game.

Besides having a tie with Michigan we also played a 0—0 game with Oberlin. In this game we seemed to have the best of the argument but still we couldn't get the necessary count. The other games of the season were all won with fair margins and with one or two of them the scores would seem to indicate that our opponents were rather outclassed. A new game on our schedule this year was Cincinnati; this game, which we won handily, was a very good exhibition of football and was not so easy as the score would indicate. Next Thanksgiving the game at Cincinnati promises to be an interesting contest. Another game worthy of mention is the Denison game, in which the score was 5—5. This game followed the Michigan game and the fellows apparently hadn't got back to real hard work yet.

Our schedule next year includes Syracuse, the school which, under Coach Jones, could beat Michigan. The adding of this game to our schedule is a great step toward extending our athletic relations and prestige to a higher plane, where they rightfully belong.

Another point which I am glad to have an opportunity of mentioning concerns our trainer, Mr. Stephen Farrell. No Ohio State team was ever kept in as good physical condition as the 1910 team; not one man was seriously injured during the whole season. The credit for this should all go to "Steve," who certainly knows how to take care of men. It was his idea that we go to Groveport for a rest-up the night before the Oberlin game.

As a closing word it is not amiss to remark about the rooting at the games. Ohio State is justly proud of the spirit that has marked all the contests on Ohio Field. Rooters on both sides of the field have always applauded both teams and whenever a man on either team is hurt, it certainly cheers him and his fellow players to hear the opposing rooters give him a yell. Besides this sort of cheering the rooting of our own team is a great feature of our games, not only helping out our team but adding interest to the contest in general.

[1911]

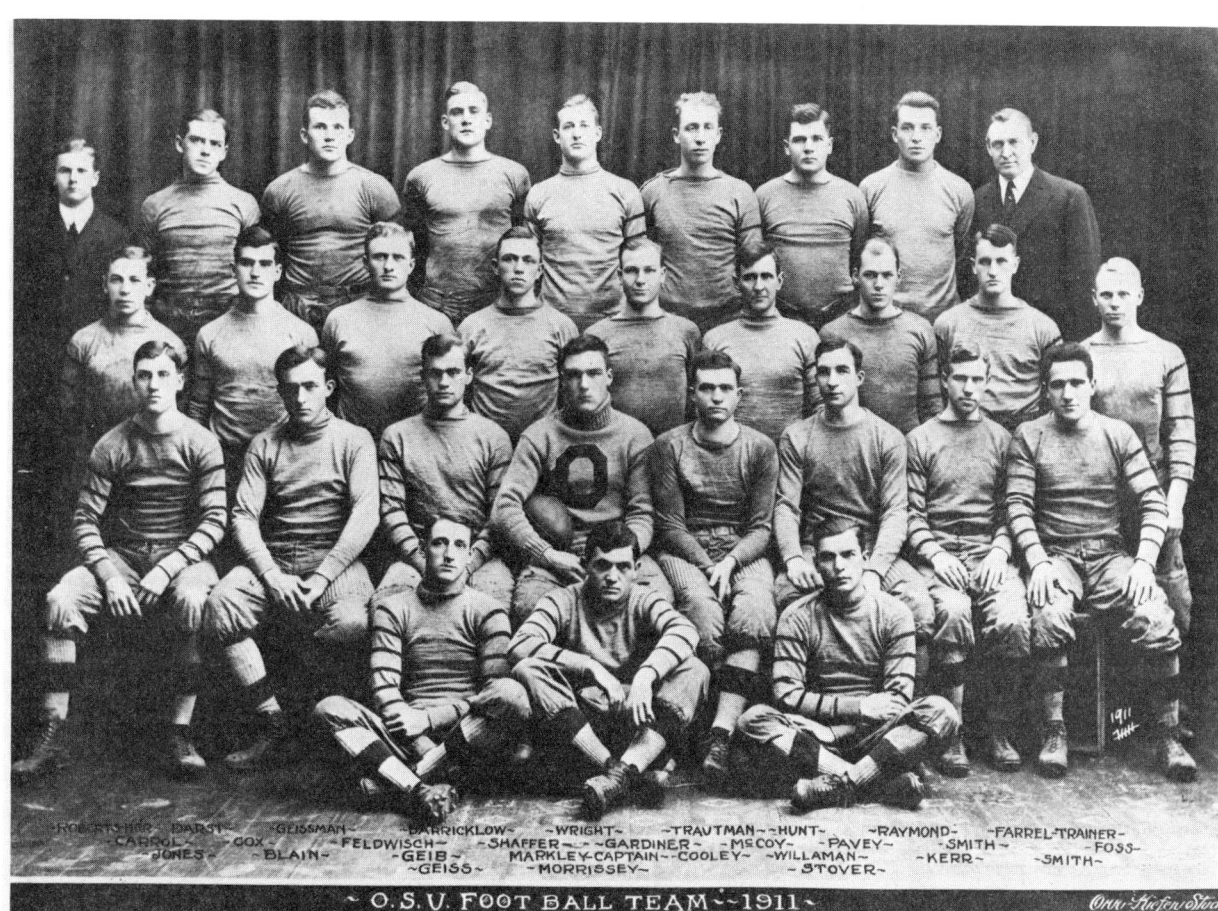

ROBERTSHAW— DARST— GEISSMAN— PARRICKLOW— WRIGHT— TRAUTMAN— HUNT— RAYMOND— FARREL-TRAINER—
CARROL— COX— FELDWISCH— SHAFFER— GARDINER— McCOY— PAVEY— SMITH— FOSS—
JONES— BLAIN— GEIB— MARKLEY-CAPTAIN— COOLEY— WILLAMAN— KERR— SMITH—
GEISS— MORRISSEY— STOVER—

~ O.S.U. FOOT BALL TEAM ~ 1911 ~

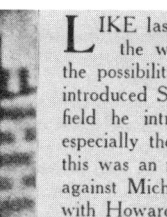

LIKE last year at this time, we are discussing the work done by our retiring coach and the possibilities of our new coach. Coach Jones introduced Spring training for football and on the field he introduced the Eastern style of play, especially the development of a strong defense,— this was an important factor in our great showing against Michigan. We regret very much to part with Howard Jones, who leaves to enter business. In saying farewell to him we know football is losing one of its foremost coaches. However, we all join in wishing him unbounded success in his new field of work.

HARRY W. VAUGHN, our new coach, also comes to us from Yale, and we have reason to expect great things from him. He received his training under the same system that Coach Jones did and for a year was a pupil of our departing coach, who recommends him highly. He is made of All-American material and would probably have been an All-American end had he not been injured in the Yale-Princeton game of the 1909 season. During the early part of the last season he helped coach the Yale eleven and later on when his injuries of the previous year had mended, he got back to his old position and was the running-mate of Kilpatrick. In securing Vaughn we are sure the great work of Coach Jones will be carried on and the greatest team we ever had will be turned out this fall.

Hoss Markley, Captain
Football, 1911

[1911]

```
          1911
     Coach: Harry Vaughn
     Captain: Frank P. Markley
   6  *Otterbein         0
   3  *Miami             0
   0  *Western Reserve   0
   0   Michigan         19
   3  *Ohio Wesleyan     0
   0  *Case              9
  24  *Kenyon            0
   0   Oberlin           0
   0  *Syracuse          6
  11  *Cincinnati        6
  ___               ___
  47                 40
     Won 5, Lost 3, Tied 2
```

1911 ROSTER

Hoss Markley (C.)
C. L. Baer
Don Barricklow
Ernie Blaine
Ike Carroll
———— Cooley
Joe Cox
Lester Darst
Hen Feldwisch
Whitie Foss
Gardy Gardner
Dad Geib
J. R. Geise
Irving Geismann
L. W. Hunt
———— Jones
Stan Kerr
Mac McCoy
Ed Morrissey
Baldy Pavey
Bugs Raymond
Ralph Shafor
Earl Smith
Hack Smith
Dutch Stover
Red Trautman
Willie Willaman
Bill Wright

Football Reflections

THE notable feature of the past football season was the increased spirit shown by the men that did come out for the team. But more men should have come out. The entire squad was made up of willing workers. The Freshmen were especially devoted and worked with the Varsity after their season was over. This enthusiasm was in large measure due to Coach Harry Vaughn. He was at all times with the men and one of them. The team when in battle stood their ground manfully. However that was not sufficient to win games. The rules as they were in 1911 were a great handicap to the Scarlet and Gray. As the season came toward its close an offense that was effective was finally developed. The opening quarter of the Michigan game was a hummer. Ohio State looked like the goods, but the defeat that came, 19-0, was not terrific. Some day when dreams come true Case will lack a Roby and we will win. Let's have a true dream this Fall. The Syracuse game was a revelation to the Eastern delegation. They expected at least an 18-0 victory. They were asked by a St. Louis team not to defeat us too badly. At this point in the season our offense began to get into effective action. The final game at Cincinnati was the test of the season and should have been more overwhelmingly ours. This Fall—1912—we have the hardest schedule yet. We also have the ground work of an excellent team. Our football coach will, as has been so often the case, have the handicap of being a comparative stranger to the men. The permanent coach should increase the team's efficiency tremendously. Next Fall every man of brains should come out for the team. Harry Vaughn had a poster put up in the football room in 1911: "To H——l with weight, it's BRAINS that counts in Football."

Thirty-nine years ago, it was—
Michigan State 35, Ohio State 20

Here are members of the 1912 Ohio State football squad, the only Buckeye gridders to face a Michigan State eleven prior to today. Front row, left to right: Lester Darst, George Trautman (minor league baseball commissioner); E. R. Godfrey, assistant athletic director and assistant Ohio State football coach; Art Raymond, Maurice Briggs, Don Barricklow, captain; Earl Maxwell, James McClure, Lee Ryan, Jay Geib, Charles Swartzbaugh. Second row: King Brady, trainer; George Hoskins, manager; Grant Ward, Dave Derivan, Arthur Jones, Ralph Shafor, Hugh Walker, Irving Geissman, Clovis Holliday, Howard Fritz, Honus Graf, Paul Jones, Ed Morrissey, Jack Richards, head coach. Back row: L. W. St. John, athletic director; Louis Pickrel, Boyd Cherry, R. L. Fetterson, Earl Smith, Percy Radcliff, Henry Feldswich, Art Kiefer, Sol Yassenoff, Howard Neff, Byron Stover.

COACH RICHARDS STATE TEAM OFF FIELD WHEN BEATEN

STATE IS BEATEN AND LEAVES FIELD

Coach Richards Objects to Rough Tackling by Penn State.

Pennsylvanians Have No Trouble in Rolling Up the Score.

COLUMBUS, O., Nov. 16.—Five minutes before the end of the game between Pennsylvania State university and Ohio State university, after the easterners had outplayed the local team by a score of 37 to 0, Coach Richards of Ohio State withdrew his men from the field because of alleged rough playing, and officials awarded Pennsylvania State the game by a score of 1 to 0. Frequently during the game the Ohio coach objected to the "unnecessarily rough playing" of the visitors. When one of his men was tackled hard, Richards became angry and called the Ohio State team from the field and refused to allow the men to continue playing. Pennsylvania

State played fast football and outplayed Ohio State in every point of the game, excepting along the line. Ohio State's line held so good that the eastern team had to make most of its gains around the end. The few gains that the local team did make were through Pennsylvania's line.

Ohio State players could not master the perfect interference of the visitors, who seemed to be able to score at will. Sixteen points were scored in the first quarter, none in the second, 14 in the third and 7 in the fourth, up till the time the game was forfeited. Line-up:

Pennsylvania—27.	Position.	Ohio—0.
Wilson	L. E.	Cherry
Engle	L. T.	Barricklow
Bebout	L. G.	Feldswich
Clark	C.	Ward
Hansene	R. G.	Geissman
Lamb	R. T.	Keifer
Very	R. E.	Stover
Miller	Q.	McClure
Welty	L. H.	Trautman
Berryman	R. H.	Ryan
Mauthe	F.	Graf

Substitutions—Pennsylvania State, Vogel for Bebout, Bebout for Vogel, Tobin for Welty, Kellar for Tobin; Ohio State, Geib for Feldswich, Keifer for Geib, Maxwell for Earl, Raymond for Keifer, Darst for Stover, Gardner for Darst, Godfrey for Gardner, Carroll for McClure, Briggs for Trautman, Snyder for Ryan, Shafer for Graf. Touchdowns—Miller 3, Mauthe, Very, Coatfield—Mauthe. Goals from touchdowns—Mauthe 4. Referee—Dr. Mews, University of Pennsylvania. Umpire—Hineman, Wesleyan. Linesman—Dr. Eckstorm, Dartmouth. Time of periods—15m.

Reprinted with permission of the **Cleveland Plain Dealer**

1912
Coach: John R. Richards
Captain: Don B. Barricklow

55	*Otterbein	0
34	*Denison	0
0	*Michigan	14
45	*Cincinnati	7
31	Case	6
23	*Oberlin	17
0	*Penn State	37
36	Ohio Wesleyan	6
20	*Michigan State	35
244		122

Won 6, Lost 3

Ohio State's First Big Ten Team

Here is the first Ohio State Western Conference team of 1913 which lost to Indiana 7 to 6, likewise the first Big Ten encounter by a Buckeye eleven. Front row, left to right, Sol Yassenoff, Ivan Boughton, George Trautman, Irving Geissman, captain; Art Kiefer, Charles Snyder, Boyd Cherry. Second row:—L. W. St. John, athletic director; Watt Hobt, Ed Morrissey, Louis Pickrel, Honus Graf, Sam Willaman, Maurice Briggs, Earl Maxwell, Jack Wilce, head coach. Third row, Dwight Ewalt, E. R. Godfrey, Elmo Knoll, Hugh Nesbitt, manager; George Springer, Corwin Fergus, James McClure.

Football

John A. McNamara

CONCEDED the Ohio Conference championship by the majority of sport writers and dope experts, Ohio State finished its first season in Western Conference football by a 58 to 0 defeat of Northwestern on November 22. One of the changes brought about by the advent into the conference was the shortening of the schedule from nine to seven games, which is all that is permitted under the Western-Intercollegiate rules. Of these seven, four were victories, two were defeats and one—that with Oberlin—resulted in a scoreless tie. A technical offense, which in no way figured in the play, caused Eddie Morrisey to be called back after a 60-yard run for a touchdown. This alone prevented a Scarlet and Gray victory in this time honored contest.

In the spring of 1913, John W. Wilce, formerly athletic manager at the University of Wisconsin, was appointed head football coach and took up his duties in September. By winning the confidence of both the student body and the public at large, he has secured for himself a high place in their estimation and the success of the team is the best possible testimony of his ability.

Several members of the team were given places on the mythical "All-Ohio" eleven and two were selected by some critics for the "All-Western."

Only four men are lost by graduation and with "Jack" Wilce again at the helm, the prospects for 1914 are exceptionally bright.

1913
Coach: John W. Wilce
Captain: W. Irving Geissman

58	*Ohio Wesleyan	0
14	*Western Reserve	8
0	*Oberlin	0
6	*Indiana	7
0	Wisconsin	12
18	*Case	0
58	*Northwestern	0
154		27

Won 4, Lost 2, Tied 1

Ohio State in the Western Conference

BY L. W. ST. JOHN

HE past year has been an epoch making one in the history of Ohio athletics. After much careful consideration on the part of those who have had the best interests of the University at heart, Ohio State sought and gained admission to the Western Inter-collegiate Conference.

It is a well recognized fact that the athletic life of the University is the one great interest around which to develop a real live college spirit. It is the great enemy of "individualism." Here is the common ground on which all meet and really enthuse. Here we may bring in closest harmony, faculty, students and alumni. While the athletic rivalry Ohio State has had in Ohio has been keen and the competition for the most part worthy, still there has been something lacking. The bounds have seemed too prescribed; the victories gained, to lack something of the true ring. It is not surprising, therefore that our development in whole-souled loyalty to the University has not kept pace with our growth as a great institution of a great State. It is surely fitting that we should have sought for recognition by, and competition with, other universities like our own, where there is similarity of aims and ideals, a real community of interests. Here is indeed that larger center, that broader interest which should fuse and mould our great cosmopolitan University body into a unit that is real, live and efficient. We have here the conditions which should interest and enthuse the individual student and keep him interested, be he player or spectator.

Our State has been well received in the Conference. We have been styled "a new rival well worthy of the steel" of our opponents. One of the greatest Universities says in a recent publication "Ohio State, we welcome you to keen, clean rivalry, which the position and standing of these two Universities should bring forth.

To meet this keen clean rivalry, in a creditable manner, we must have the unqualified support of the whole student body. We must establish and develop sound and definite athletic policies that shall have continuity and merit, the support we desire. We must build right foundations and make each succeeding superstructure stronger and more efficient.

1914
Captain: Campbell J. Graf

16	*Ohio Wesleyan	2
7	Case	6
0	Illinois	37
6	*Wisconsin	7
13	Indiana	3
39	*Oberlin	0
27	*Northwestern	0
108		55

Won 5, Lost 2

NORTON PUTNUM STINSON KNOLL WATT MGR. SILSBY S.YASSENOFF GINN GARVEY
ST.JOHN SORESON HOBT PICKEREL GRAFF CAPT HAVENS GHEEN HOWARD WILSE COACH
S.YASSENOFF BOUGHTON SPRINGER GODFREY KIEFER SNYDER CHERRY

Foot Ball Squad

TOP ROW
Wasson, Bennett, Yerges, Johnson, Boesel, Thomas, Karch, Gwinn, S. Sorensen, Lapp, H. J. Courtney, Assistant Coach Castleman.

SECOND ROW
Assistant Coach St. John, Assistant Coach Pickerel, Van Dyne, Proctor, Stevens, Lieberman, Hoyt, Holliday, Bolen, Steckel, Malm, Dreyer, Schwartz, Coach Wilce.

BOTTOM ROW
Peabody, Putnam, Hobt, Ginn, Knoll, Yassenoff, Captain Boughten, Poe, H. G. Courtney, Silsby, Schweitzer, Healy, Jones, Price, Duddy, Seddon, Garvey, Driscoll, Havens, Hamilton, Trainer Gurney.

	Age	Height	Wt.	High School	No. of Years	Rank
Captain Ivan B. Boughton	22	6' 1"	185	North High	3	Senior
Sorensen, Frank	20	5' 9"	171	Norwood	2	Junior
Hobt, A. Watt	22	5' 9"	163	Wellston Hi.	3	Senior
Knoll, Elmer P.	23	5' 10"	173	Norwalk Hi.	3	Senior
Courtney, Howard G.	21	5' 10½"	180	East Hi., Col.	1	Junior
Karch, Robert H.	21	6' 1"	214	So. Hi., Col.	1	Soph.
Courtney, Harold J.	19	5' 9"	165	East Hi., Col.	1	Soph.
Ginn, Dwight C.	22	6' 1"	178	Piqua High	2	Senior
Bolen, Charles W.	20	6'	175	Lima H. S.	1	Soph.
Peabody, Dwight V.	21	6'	161	Oberlin Hi.	1	Soph.
Yassenoff, Leo	22	6' 1½"	210	Stivers High, Dayton	2	Senior
Yerges, Howard F.	19	5' 9"	145	North High	1	Soph.
Winters, Harold A.	19	5' 9"	175	Norwalk Hi.	1	Soph.
Boesel, Richard E.	21	6'	194	New Bremen H. S.	1	Law
Schwartz, Robert M.	20	6' 1"	175	North High	1	Soph.
Schweitzer, Fred L.	20	5' 6½"	148	Ravenna, O., W. & J.	1	Soph.
Norton, Fred W.	22	5' 8½"	154	Lakeside Hi.	2	Junior
Havens, William F.	21	5' 9"	165	East Hi., Col.	2	Senior

1915
Captain: Ivan B. Boughton

19	*Ohio Wesleyan	6
14	*Case	0
3	*Illinois	3
0	Wisconsin	21
10	*Indiana	9
25	*Oberlin	0
34	Northwestern	0
105		39

Won 5, Lost 1, Tied 1

OFFICIAL PROGRAM
FOOTBALL 1915
Saturday, October 16
OHIO STATE vs. ILLINOIS

Students:

If you did not get to register in Columbus DON'T fail to go home and cast your vote to make OHIO DRY. You have a right to vote somewhere.

To do it MARK your BALLOT like this Nov. 2:

X YES	Prohibition of the sale and manufacture for
NO	sale of intoxicating liquor as a beverage

WORTHINGTON KAUTZMAN,
Chairman County Dry Organizations,
701 Wyandotte Bldg., Columbus, Ohio

Football

(By Ivan B. Boughton)

At the beginning of the football season of 1915, the outlook here at Ohio State was anything but bright. Eight men of the 1914 team had graduated and an almost entirely new team had to be built up.

Wesleyan opened the season on Ohio Field on October 3. The game was ragged on the part of Ohio State, but the team showed promise of developing into a strong aggregation.

Case was played here on October 10. In the first half play was listless and ragged. The second half marked the appearance of Dick Boesel in a new role, that of fullback. No one who saw the game will forget the two wonderful marches for touchdowns made in the third quarter.

The next Saturday, Illinois, the champion of the Western Conference, was *played to a standstill*. The final score was 3—3, Ohio's points coming from a 22-yard place kick by "Fat" Winters, and Bart Macomber's toe being responsible for the points of the Illini. This game was the "Home Coming" game of the season and the team exhibited a brand of teamwork that could hardly be beaten. The superior condition of the Ohio State players showed a noticeable improvement since the two previous games. Ohio's good showing was in no small measure due to the splendid work of "Swede" Sorenson at fullback. It was his first attempt and the fans will never forget his sterling performance that afternoon.

The next week Wisconsin was played on her own grounds at Madison, and Ohio was defeated by a 21—0 score. On that day Wisconsin had probably the best team in the conference. The score does not show the true value of the two teams. During the entire first half Wisconsin was unable to score. Ohio State showed an impregnable defense by twice holding Wisconsin for downs within the five yard line. In the last part of the third quarter Byers broke loose and scored. Again, in the fourth quarter he scored on a long end run. Wisconsin's last score was made two or three minutes before the final whistle when they intercepted a forward pass on the Buckeye ten-yard line.

After a week's lay-off, Indiana was defeated on Ohio Field by a 10—9 score. This was the most thrilling and, in all probability, the hardest game of the season. The playing of the Ohio State team was ragged at times but was an improvement as a whole over previous games. This game was featured by Fred Norton's catching of a long forward pass, and his thirty yard sprint for a touchdown. The forward passing game of Ohio State was still weak and had not yet been worked successfully to any extent.

The following Saturday the ancient rivals from Oberlin were taken into camp to the tune of 25 to 0. This was the second successive victory over Oberlin. The game itself was rather ragged and listless in the first and fourth quarters. In this game "Wattie" Hobt glittered and shone with his cross-bucks and short end-runs. Still the forward passes did not work well.

On November 20 the final game of the season was played with Northwestern at Evanston, and resulted in a 34—0 victory for Ohio State. In the first half the two teams were more or less evenly matched and no scoring was done. In the third and fourth quarters the forward passing game was used almost exclusively. Out of 26 passes by Ohio 22 were completed. Coach Murphy of Northwestern said after the game: "It was the best aerial attack I have ever seen."

The season of 1915 was the most successful since Ohio State has been in the Conference, the team standing in fifth place at the end of the race. Too much cannot be said for the wonderful coaching and splendid personality of Coach John Wilce.

Team Statistics 1916

Name	Position	Weight	Height	Age	Home
("O" Men)					
Boesel, R. E.	F.	187	5' 11"	22	New Bremen
Bolen, C. W.	L.E.	171	5' 10"	21	Cridersville
Courtney, H. J.	L.T.	168	5' 9"	20	Columbus
Courtney, H. G.	R.T.	175	5' 9"	22	Columbus
Dreyer, V. O.	F.	163	5' 9"	22	Middlefield
Harley, C. W.	R.H.	157	5' 9"	19	Columbus
Holtkamp, F. G.	C.	181	6' 1"	22	Cleveland
Hurm, P. W.	L.H.	160	5' 6"	20	Hamilton
Johnson, E. L.	G.	186	6' 3"	21	Painesville
Karch, R. H.	L.G.	212	6' 1"	21	Columbus
Lapp, H. R.	G.	220	6' 3"	21	Akron
MacDonald, C. A.	E.	162	6'	20	Columbus
Norton, F. W.	L.H.	157	5' 8½"	23	Columbus
Peabody, D. V.	R.E.	167	5' 11"	20	Oberlin
Rhodes, G. M.	L.H.	150	5' 8"	19	Columbus
Seddon, C. E.	G.	150	5' 7"	22	Columbus
Sorensen, F. G., Capt.	F.	156	5' 9"	23	Norwood
Turner, I. L.	R.G.	172	6'	21	Columbus
Van Dyne, K.	C.	172	5' 11½"	23	Bellaire
Yerges, H. F.	Q.	162	5' 8½"	20	Columbus
("Oaa" Men)					
Cramer, W. E.	E.	145	5' 5½"	19	Fostoria
Friedman, L. A.	Q.	140	5' 8½"	21	Circleville
Kirk, R. E.	Q.	149	5' 10½"	21	Alliance
Leonard, A. T.	T.	183	6' 1"	21	Salem
Sullivan, D. E.	T.	175	5' 9"	22	Columbus
(Squad)					
Bell, F. J.	T.	157	5' 11"	19	Columbus
Daughters, C. G.	H.	143	5' 7"	19	Milford
Dillon, E. W.	H.	172	5' 11½"	20	Columbus
Fuller, M. A.	E.	150	5' 9"	19	Lima
Hamilton, D.	E.	159	5' 11"	20	Columbus
Lieberman, E. H.	F.	162	5' 11"	20	Cleveland
Metzger, W. E.	H.	148	5' 10"	19	Columbus
Schmidt, F. F.	H.	143	5' 9"	20	Columbus
Wolfe, F. J. L.	G.	162	5' 11½"	20	Fremont

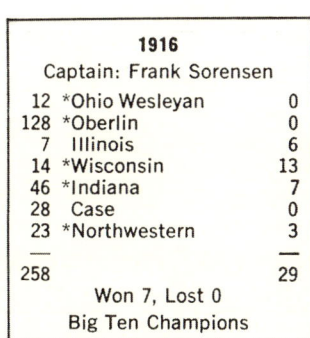

1916
Captain: Frank Sorensen

12	*Ohio Wesleyan	0
128	*Oberlin	0
7	Illinois	6
14	*Wisconsin	13
46	*Indiana	7
28	Case	0
23	*Northwestern	3
258		29

Won 7, Lost 0
Big Ten Champions

"Chic" Harley
All-American Halfback 1916

Football Season

Ohio State has come into its own.

No longer are the Buckeyes the "Babes of the Conference," but rather "OHIO STATE—WESTERN CONFERENCE FOOTBALL CHAMPIONS 1916."

The credit goes to years of conference playing past, to the coaching staff, particularly to Coach Wilce, to the student body attitude and more directly to the 1916 Ohio State Football Team, captained by Frank G. Sorensen and managed by William A. Dougherty.

Directly, it began with the Illinois game, when the Buckeyes, playing with all odds against them, vanquished the 1915 Championship Illinois eleven 7-6.

The name of "Chic" Harley is written in gold in the story of this game. After several splendid defensive stands by Ohio, and after the famed Macomber had scored six points via field goals, passes by Harley to MacDonald, Norton and others carried the ball to Illinois' 13-yard line.

There remained just one minute and ten seconds to play. A pass over the center of the line was covered by Illinois' guarding. Harley realized the state of affairs, faked the pass, "cut" around left end, evaded three tacklers and scored a touchdown. A few moments later, he changed his mud-filled shoes for a dry pair and kicked the goal that won the game.

This was the first conference game that Illinois had lost on its own field for four years. The field, after snows of the day before, was a morass of Illinois clay. The Buckeyes were without the services of End Peabody, who was not able to last two minutes because of an injury to his hip sustained in practice during the week. Several others were in poor condition because of injuries and the team entered this game more seriously handicapped than at any other time in the season.

Two weeks later, on November 4, on Ohio State Homecoming Day, Wisconsin was defeated by the fighting Buckeyes by a 14-13 score. True enough, the one point margin was due to a missed kickout after a touchdown, which might have turned the final score into a tie, but—try to catch a twisting football yourself with eleven opponents running toward you and yelling in true Comanche style—at least that is the best alibi Quarterback Taylor of the Badgers had.

Again in this game were the achievements of Harley vitally instrumental in Ohio's success. "Chic" scored both of the Scarlet and Gray's touchdowns and kicked one of the goals. His first score occurred after Wisconsin had made a touchdown a-la-forward pass. It was Ohio's ball on the Wisconsin 25-yard line, when on a fake punt Harley skirted left end, cut back, eluded the halfback and safety man for a touchdown. Sorensen kicked goal. That was all in the second quarter and the 13,000 people who watched the game saw the rest of that and all of the third quarter pass without a score. In the final quarter, Harley, playing defensive quarterback, received a punt on his own 22-yard line. With a one-man interference, Harley brushed past the oncoming Badger forward line, then dodged, feinted and sped past and away from the remainder of the Wisconsin eleven, making a 78-yard run for a touchdown. Wisconsin's sensational march goalward which ended in a touchdown and the dropped kickout completed what was probably the most significant game in Ohio State football history.

A week later, Indiana was swept away by a cyclonic proof that Ohio was not a one-man team when the Hoosiers discovered that Ohio, playing without Harley, was 46-7 points too good for them. Captain Sorensen, Yerges, Norton, Bolen, Karch and "Hap" Courtney took leading parts in the complete overwhelming of the Hoosiers. Coach Stiehm, of Indiana, said, after the game, "The team is the best I've seen and should win the conference championship."

And Northwestern. The Purple and Ohio, until November 25, were undefeated. On that date 15,000 people watched the Buckeyes win the Western Conference title by defeating Northwestern decisively, 23-3.

A big feature of the championship game was the wonderful defensive play of Ohio State's line. Few people realized that Ohio State was the only team that

(cont.)

Season (continued)

prevented the strong and speedy Northwestern backs from scoring by the touchdown route throughout the season.

Harley again played a leading offensive part, scoring two touchdowns, one after a 63-yard run. Sorensen, playing his last game of collegiate football, was in rare form. For three-quarters of the game Ohio State led, three to nothing, by virtue of Harley's field goal from the 33-yard line.

Shortly after the fourth quarter started, Driscoll, of Northwestern, tied the score with a drop kick from the 40-yard line. That was Harley's cue and receiving the ball on a punt, he ripped off a 67-yard run in his own copyrighted style. After a Northwestern fumble and an Ohio recovery within the Purple's 20-yard zone, Harley streaked around the opposing right end on a fake forward pass and the score was 16-3.

Aided by a beautiful pass received by MacDonald, "Chic," Boesel and Sorensen ploughed through the steadily weakening Purple line for another touchdown. Captain Sorensen carried the ball over for the final touchdown of the championship team.

In addition to winning the Big Nine title, the Buckeyes also won out in the Ohio Conference, having a clear record. Wesleyan was defeated in the season's opener 12-0. In this game, which was played on an extremely hot and sultry day, not a single end run was attempted by Ohio. The team next broke the world's record for collegiate football high score by massacring Oberlin, 128-0.

The game with Case at Cleveland was played on a field of snow, mud and water. Case was overwhelmed 28-0. Stonewall defense, Harley's great running and kicking on the wet field, Hurm's bucking, and the even better team interference than that which had characterized the team's play from the Wisconsin game, impressed Cleveland fans thoroughly. A significant thing during the season was the new spirit of friendly boosting and co-operation shown for the first time in the Cleveland newspapers.

Football Staff

Head Coach..J. W. Wilce
L. W. St. John
F. R. Castleman
Grant Ward

PLAYER SCORING MOST POINTS

	Touchdowns	Goals from Touchdown	Goals from Field	Points
Harley	8	7	1	58

NOTABLE RUNS FROM SCRIMMAGE

Harley	25 yards	Wisconsin	November 4
Norton	36 yards	Indiana	November 18
Harley	63 yards	Northwestern	November 25
Norton	43 and 30 yards	Oberlin	October 14
Boesel	40 yards	Oberlin	October 14
Hurm	45 yards	Oberlin	October 14

[1917]

Team Statistics

"O" MEN

Name	Position	Weight	Height	Age	Home
Boesel, R. E.	F.	165	5' 11"	23	New Bremen
Bolen, C. W.	L.E.	175	5' 10"	22	Cridersville
Courtney, H. J. (Cap.)	L.T.	165	5' 9"	21	Columbus
Courtney, H. G.	R.T.	165	5' 9"	23	Columbus
Harley, C. W.	R.H.	156	5' 9"	20	Columbus
Karch, R. H.	L.G.	228	6' 1"	22	Columbus
Myers, R. L.	G.	197	6' 2"	22	Salem
Peabody, D. V.	R.E.	170	5' 11"	21	Oberlin
Seddon, C. E.	R.G.	150	5' 7"	23	Columbus
Stinchcomb, G. R.	L.H.	146	5' 8"	22	Fostoria
Schweitzer, F. L.	H.	152	5' 7"	22	Ravenna
Van Dyne, K.	C.	165	5' 11"	24	Bellaire
Wieche, R.	G.	198	6' 1½"	20	Hamilton
Willaman, F. R.	F.	176	5' 10"	20	Salem
Yerges, H. F.	Q.	150	5' 9"	21	Columbus

"OAA" MEN

Name	Position	Weight	Height	Age	Home
Cramer, W. E.	E.	148	5' 6"	20	Fostoria
Friedman, L. A.	Q.	142	5' 8"	21	Circleville
Fuller, M. A.	E.	154	5' 8"	20	Lima
Hamilton, H. W.	F.	171	5' 11"	19	Columbus
Metzger, W. E.	H.	148	5' 8"	20	Columbus
Miller, L. E.	H.	154	5' 8"	19	Columbus
Wasson, R. H.	T.	163	5' 10"	20	Barberton
Nemecek, A. J.	C.	185	6' 3"	21	Lorain

SQUAD MEN

Name	Position	Weight	Height	Age	Home
Baldwin, R. H.	H.	153	5' 8"	21	Columbus
Bell, F. J.	T.	165	5' 10"	20	Columbus
Ewart, K. L.	C.	170			Tallmadge
Gross, J. S.	F.	165	5' 10"	20	Cleveland
Harbage, P. O.	E.	150			West Jefferson
Hay, H. L.	E.	158	5' 10"	21	Washington, C. H.
Howenstein, J. A.	G.	175	5' 8"	19	Hicksville
Keunzli, P.	H.	152	5' 6"	21	Upper Sandusky
Johnson, E. Y.	E.	164	5' 11"	19	Lima
Merritt, M. L.	G.	180			Columbus
Moore, J. C.	G.	160	5' 9"	19	Akron
Skimming, L. H.	T.	172	6' 1"	19	Columbus
Wiper, H.	Q.	158	5' 9"	19	Columbus

1917

Captains: Harold J. Courtney
Howard Courtney

49	*Case	0
53	*Ohio Wesleyan	0
40	*Northwestern	0
67	*Denison	0
26	Indiana	3
16	Wisconsin	3
13	*Illinois	0
0	Auburn	0
28	*Camp Sherman	0
292		6

Won 8, Lost 0, Tied 1
Big Ten Champions

One of "Chic's" Four in the Indiana Game

Season Summary

Early last fall it was evident that the team that stopped Jack Wilce's hustling Scarlet and Gray contingent would emerge acknowledged champions of the Western Conference. Minus the services of fighting Fritz Holtkamp at center, Captain Sorensen at fullback and halves Norton, Hurm, Rhodes and Daughters, Ohio State entered upon the season with much the same line as in 1916 but an altered backfield. Kelley Van Dyne soon dispelled any anxiety as to his ability to fill Holtkamp's shoes at center while Stinchcomb and Schweitzer at halfback and Boesel and Willaman at full assumed important roles in the reconstructed backfield. It was this backfield combination, generaled by heady Howard Yerges at quarterback and with "Chic" Harley playing the lead, which was soon in the headlines as the greatest scoring machine in Ohio State gridiron annals.

Conclusive evidence of the superiority of the Scarlet and Gray over its smaller Ohio rivals was produced in a trio of early season games against Case, Ohio Wesleyan and Denison while the rout of Northwestern, from whom the Western Conference title was wrested in 1916, presaged the nature of the problem the leading "Big Ten" teams had to solve in the race for season's honors.

The backfield began to sparkle in the very first game when Case was smothered 49 to 0 on Ohio Field, the Buckeyes rolling up the highest score they had ever made against Case. Case had no punch at all, making but one first down through the rival line of veterans, while on the defensive the Scientist's wings had a tough afternoon of it. Harley, Yerges, Boesel and Stinchcomb were hard men to stop and it was on long runs off tackle and around end with midseason interference that the big score was made possible.

Thirty players were used in the runaway game with Ohio Wesleyan which ended 53 to 0. The Red and Black team fought hard the first half but was worn down by the more experienced Buckeye line, the Champions scoring 39 points during the second half. Late in the second period Boyer recovered a fumble by Schweitzer on the Ohio State 44-yard line and in a series of short forward passes Wesleyan carried the ball to the four-foot line where a quarterback sneak on the fourth down failed. No other team ever got that close to Ohio's goal line during the balance of the season.

Speculation was rife as to the comparative strength of Northwestern and Ohio State when those arch foes of 1916 lined up for the opening gun of the Western Conference season on October 13. The result was not long in doubt. Northwestern fought hard in the first and last periods, holding Ohio to one touchdown in each of these quarters but in the middle periods the Champions did enough damage to run the final score to 40-0. Stinchcomb, playing in his first "Big Ten" game, proved a sensation. Three times he crossed the Purple goal line and was the biggest individual ground-gainer of the day. Harley opened the eyes of critics to a new All-American trait in his wonderful blocking, which paved the way for many of Stinchcomb's long gains. Peabody shone in picking off forward passes, grabbing one over the line for a touchdown. "Chief" played the game of his career.

Denison, back on the schedule after a lapse in athletic relations between the two universities of five seasons' duration, was submerged in a mud battle on a water-soaked field and in a drizzling rain in the last game against an Ohio opponent. The score of 67 to 0 was the record scoring effort of the Scarlet and Gray, and this in spite of the heavy field.

With the minor games gloriously passed, Ohio State turned into the home stretch confronted by Indiana, Wisconsin and Illinois. At Indianapolis the Wilcemen faced a beefy squad, imbued with a fighting spirit which only a deep-seated desire to win this one game of the season can instill in a team. Consequently the Hoosiers, backed by an enthusiastic home-coming crowd, were anything but easy. In fact, not until Harley was called into the game late in the second quarter were they scored on. "Chic" was the only consistent ground-gainer. His long runs resulted in four touchdowns, the only ones made by Ohio State. Fans who came to see the All-American Harley in action never witnessed a more typical exhibition of the All-American brand of football. Harley's open field runs of from 25 to 50 yards, his change of pace, dodging, squirming and diving were nothing short of phenomenal.

But while Harley was counting 26 points, the Hoosiers were living up to tradition in scoring on Ohio. In the fourth period Indiana worked to the 12-yard line but here the Buckeye defense stiffened and in four downs Indiana was hurled back five yards. Here Captain Hathaway dropped back and booted from the 25-yard line, thus producing the first points of the season against Ohio State.

In many respects the week ending November 10 was the critical period of the season for the Champions. Ohio had not played up to form at Indiana while Wisconsin surprised the football world by upsetting the touted Minnesota team 10 to 7. Imagine, then, the fight at Madison when the hopeful Badgers were trimmed 16 to 3 in a wonderful battle. Superior playing won that contest, including the ability to make the breaks as well as the sense to put them to advantage once they were uncovered. There was little to choose in aggressiveness, but in

(CONT.)

Season Summary (cont.)

condition Ohio excelled. The Buckeyes had a much more effective repertoire of plays. Wisconsin had only a forward pass and was dangerous only in the first period.

For the first time Ohio had to come from behind to win. Repulsed by the Scarlet and Gray line in the first period after a series of gains, Simpson was forced to resort to a kick. Dropkicking from the 43-yard line, Simpson booted three points and gave Wisconsin the jump. Then the Buckeyes hit their stride. Harley was a spotted man. The Badger ends stopped his famous end running by sensational individual performances. But "Chic" was not completely stopped. Halted in one direction, he merely directed his energies through another channel. When end runs failed, forward passes were essayed, and there hangs the tale of a splendid victory.

Two tried by Harley had resulted in 10 yards loss and Ohio was on the Badger 44-yard line late in the second period with 20 yards to go and third down. "Chic" dropped back to kick, then wheeled and passed true into the arms of Bolen, who had been lurking in wait for the throw. The big end bore down on the Wisconsin secondary defense, was tackled in front of the goal, but crashed the remaining distance for a touchdown.

Again in the third period Wisconsin stopped the Wilcemen. Again Harley dropped back. This time it was H. G. Courtney who nailed the pass and raced to the one-yard line for a 32-yard gain. Yerges went over on a quarterback sneak. Just to clinch the victory, Harley once more dropped back in the final stanza. This time he did not bluff but put his toe to the ball for three points from a placement kick on the 40-yard line.

Having disposed of Wisconsin, the Buckeyes faced Illinois in the championship game. Neither team's goal line had been crossed. Illinois, two-times champion of the Western Conference before Ohio snatched away that title, scented a strong chance for revenge. For 60 minutes the rivals battled savagely, Ohio emerging the victor by a 13 to 0 count. For three periods the score stood at 3-0. At the outset Harley and Boesel gained 50 yards on two plays. Then Illinois braced and Harley was forced to boot three points from placement. That was all until the last quarter. Illinois gained many yards and twice got inside the 30-yard line, but both time kicks failed. Then came the break. Captain Courtney recovered a fumble on the Illinois 40-yard line and Ohio was off. A series of gains brought the ball within scoring distance and again Courtney leaped into the limelight, this time receiving a forward pass from Harley which brought the only touchdown of the game for Ohio and the only one scored on Illinois during the season. Harley later kicked another field goal and Ohio was again champion by 13 points.

By this time the fame of Harley, Coach Wilce and Ohio State had spread and the Buckeyes were in demand. Two post-season games were arranged for the benefit of soldiers at Camp Sheridan and Camp Sherman. At Montgomery, Ala., on November 24 the Champions played listlessly after the nerve-racking Illinois contest, and allowed the mediocre Auburn Pollytechnical Institute eleven to tie them 0-0 in a scoreless game. Without Yerges, Van Dyne and Seddon and with Harley suffering from an injured hand, the Buckeyes lacked the punch.

Never was such a galaxy of former collegiate heroes seen in action in a single game on Ohio Field as appeared against Ohio State in the first Thanksgiving Day game in five years on Ohio Field when the Buckeyes redeemed themselves for the showing made in Alabama, by trouncing Camp Sherman 28 to 0. Prior to that game the Sherman team, with five former All-American, one All-Western and two All-Ohio stars in the line-up, had been undefeated. But Harley, Stinchcomb, Boesel and company with Yerges back on a furlough to general the team, proved too much for the aggregation of soldier stars. For at least ten "O" men it was the last game in an Ohio State uniform and not a few saw in that day's performance the masterpiece of individual and team play as a happy combination in a well coached championship team.

Charles W. Harley
Captain-elect

Philip M. Foote
Manager-elect

"O" Men

Name	Position	Weight	Height	Age	Home
Addison, E.	R.T.	178	5' 11"	19	Columbus
Davies, T. C.	L.H.	147	5' 8"	20	Ironton
Friedman, M.	C.	156	5' 9"	19	Circleville
Huffman, I.	L.T.	184	5' 11"	20	Chandlersville
Gillam, N.	C.	175	6'	20	Lorain
Myers, C.	R.H.	160	6'	20	Bucyrus
Matheny, O.S.	F.B.	189	6' 1"	19	Columbus
McCune, J.H.	R.T.	175	6'	23	Cando, N. D.
Pixley, L.	L.G.	220	6' 1"	18	Columbus
Rife, R. E.	R.H.	145	5' 8"	21	Columbus
Slyker, W. V.	R.E.	165	6' 1"	19	Huron
Wiper, H. A.	Q.B.	162	5' 9"	20	Columbus
Sneddon, E. R.	R.G.	200	6' 1"	31	Bay Village
Bell, F. J.	R.T.	177	5' 10"	21	Columbus
Farcasin, C.	L.H.	152	5' 10"	20	Cleveland

FOOTBALL COACH of Ohio State University

J. W. WILCE

Chic Harley   **Clarence MacDonald**

1918
Captain:
Clarence A. MacDonald

41	*Ohio Wesleyan	0
34	*Denison	0
0	*Michigan	14
56	*Case	0
0	Illinois	13
3	*Wisconsin	14
134		41

Won 3, Lost 3

Football Season 1918

With two Western Conference Championships in succession to its credit Ohio State started its 1917 season with the most discouraging outlook in the history of the University. Not a single letter man returned and only Wiper, Bell, Metzger and Howenstine of the 1917 squad registered in school. Of these men only Wiper and Howenstine stayed throughout the season. Bell and Metzer both going into the army before the Western Conference games.

From the 1917 freshman team most of the varsity material was drawn. On the line Huffman, Friedman, Addison, Zentmyer and Slyker were sophomores. Farcasin, Davies and Myers were backfield men who had had freshman experience a year ago. Myers, however, had enlisted in the navy before the season opened and was called for duty at the Great Lakes the week of the Illinois game and did not play in any of the Big Ten contests.

The Ohio State stock took a decided brace soon after practice was started when Clarence MacDonald, letter man from 1916, and Roy Rife, who had played on Ohio University in 1917, were sent to the University from the navy to continue their education at Ohio State. MacDonald was appointed acting captain before the Wesleyan game and later elected to take the place of "Chic" Harley who was picked as captain after the 1917 season, but who enlisted in the aviation corps instead of returning to the University. MacDonald was used at end throughout the season with Rife at half and as punter.

In addition to Harley the men on the 1917 squad who would have been eligible this year, but who did not return, doing service for their country instead, were Stinchcomb, Willaman, Schweitzer, Myers, Weiche, Nemecek, Miller, Fuller, Johnson, Cramer and Hamilton. Hamilton was in medical college but did not have time for football practice.

Ohio State was confronted with the same dilemma as all other colleges, as to what action the war department would take on athletics. It was finally decided by the Western Conference to turn control of all intercollegiate athletics over to the Government. The committee on education agreed to allow all members of the Students' Army Training Corps to participate in intercollegiate games, regardless of eligibility or class standing. This ruling allowed the colleges to use freshmen on their football teams, ineligibles or men not in the training corps. The war department also decided to allow each team one overnight trip during the season.

The government ruling caused a revision of the schedules and the Northwestern game was dropped. The date of the Michigan contest was shifted from October 26 to November 30. The matter of practice was left to the military authorities at the different universities to decide in order not to conflict with schedules.

In the matter of practice Ohio State faced its hardest problem. The only opportunity given was an hour after drill until evening mess. This hour coming from 5:00 p. m. to 6:00 p. m., practically all the work was done after dark under electric lights. The Buckeyes faced another difficulty in that Coach Wilce, who attended medical college throughout the season, was also a member of the training corps and had only a short time each day to spend with the team.

Whereas other Western Conference schools were allowed from two to three hours of daylight practice Ohio State was forced to be content with the one hour of after dark work. Not only was Coach Wilce handicapped in developing his candidates, who had had some previous experience, but he had practically no time to work with his freshman material. While Illinois, Wisconsin and Michigan teams were composed almost entirely of first year men, Ohio State used only one as a regular, that being Pixley, who was used at guard all season.

Coach Wilce did get to use three of the men in the veterinary reserve, Sneddon and McCune on the line and Moeller in the backfield. In addition to MacDonald and Rife, Early, substitute center, was sent to the University from the navy. Volzer, who was in the dental reserve, was used occasionally on the line.

Varsity Football Squad

Top Row:
  FOOTE, Manager; MATHENY, WIECHE, FULLER, FRIEDMAN, GURNEY, Trainer; GILLAM, JOHNSON, EWART, BELL, JOHNSON, KIME, Manager.

Second Row:
  ST. JOHN, Athletic Director; WEAVER, D. WIPER, FARCASIN, COTT, SCHWEITZER, STINCHCOMB, WILLAMAN, BLISS, DAVIS, TAYLOR, H. WIPER, WILCE, Coach.

Bottom Row:
  MacDONALD, FLOWER, SPIERS, TROTT, HOLTKAMP, HARLEY, Captain; NEMECEK, PIXLEY, HUFFMAN, SLYKER, MYERS.

Player and Position	Age	Ht.	Wt.	Prep. School
Myers L. E.	21	6.00	170	Bucyrus
Huffman L. T.	21	5.11	181	Chandlersville
Pixley L. G.	19	6.2	230	Columbus
Holtcamp C.	23	6.00	188	Lakewood
Trott R. G.	19	5.11	180	Columbus
Spiers R. T.	23	5.10	183	Freedom Sta.
Flower R. E.	22	6.1	184	Akron
Stinchcomb, Q. B.	22	5.7	150	Fostoria
Davies L. H.	21	5.8	155	Ironton
Harley (C) R. H.	22	5.8	165	Columbus
Willaman F. B.	21	5.10	194	Salem
Slyker E.	20	6.1	171	Huron
MacDonald E.	23	6.2	165	Columbus
Weiche T.	21	6.00	216	Hamilton
Addison T.	20	6.00	181	Columbus
Friedman T.	20	5.8	170	Circleville
Johnson G.	24	6.3	197	Painesville
Churches G.	20	5.9	210	Columbus
Ewart G.	21	5.8	170	Tallmadge
Nemecek C.	22	6.4	196	Lorain
Gillam C.	21	6.00	170	Lorain
Cott Q. B.	22	5.8	152	Columbus
H. Wiper Q. B.	20	5.10	169	Columbus
Bliss H.	21	5.8	155	Butler, Pa.
Taylor H.	20	5.11	165	Martins Ferry
Schweitzer H.	24	5.7	165	Ravenna
Farcasin H.	20	5.10	153	Cleveland
D. Wiper H.	19	5.10	150	Columbus
Matheny F.	20	6.00	194	Columbus
Weaver F.	19	5.9	171	Youngstown

[1919]

Nov. 22 vs. Illinois

In the last period "Chic," who had been unable to get away because of a lame knee, broke loose on one of his dazzling sprints and ran 25 yards before he was downed. Four more plays carried the pigskin within striking distance. Harley then dashed to the side of the field and hurled the ball into the outstretched arms of MacDonald, who was downed on the 2-yard mark. The Buckeye leader then went through tackle for a touchdown and kicked goal. The crowd went wild and continued to do so as the Buckeyes took up another march toward the Illinois goal. Pixley's place kick from the 40-yard line was blocked, however, and Illinois took the ball. Fighting desperately, the visitors cut loose with a puzzling variety of forward passes that terrified the fans. The "Walquist-to-Carney combination" worked the ball to State's 20-yard line and with eight seconds left to play, "Bob" Fletcher booted the oval between the posts spelling defeat for the Wilcemen. Thus ended one of the most sensational gridiron seasons in the history of Ohio State.

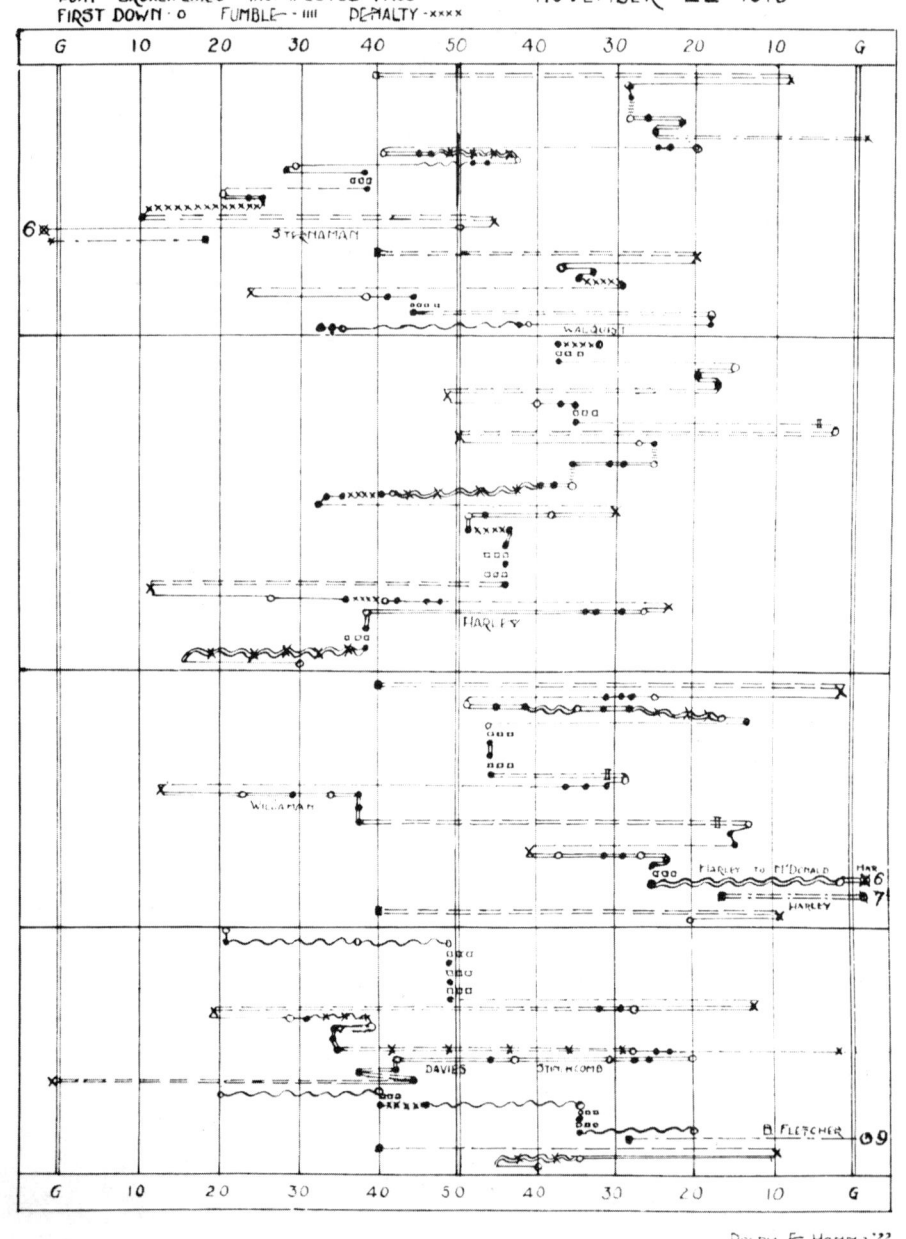

1919	
Captain: Charles W. Harley	
38 *Ohio Wesleyan	0
46 *Cincinnati	0
49 *Kentucky	0
13 Michigan	3
20 *Purdue	0
3 Wisconsin	0
7 *Illinois	9
176	12
Won 6, Lost 1	

Hoskins (Manager), Gurney (Trainer), Ward (Asst. Coach)
Third—Pauley, McGregor, Speed, G. H. Johnson, Jackson, Navin, Doig, Miller, Kaplow, Patchell, Weiss, Lusk.
Second—St. John (Dir. of Ath.), Blair, Weaver, Henderson, Bliss, H. Workman, Stinchcomb, Cott, Wiper, Wilder, Isabel, E. Y. Johnson, Dr. Wilce (Coach).
Bottom—C. A. Taylor, N. Workman, Slyker, Spiers, Trott, Huffman (Capt.), Wieche, Nemecek, J. L. Taylor, Myers, Willaman.

OHIO STATE TEAM

Left Guard	Center	Right Guard
Weiche (4)	Nemecek (1)	Trott (3)
Tayler (5)	Kaplow (2)	C. MacGinnis (36)
	Lusk (30)	Rumer (35)

Left Tackle	Quarterback	Fullback	Right Tackle
Huffman (Capt.) (6)	H. Workman (17)	Willaman (26)	Spiers (7)
Jackson (8)	D. Wiper (18)	Isabell (25)	Johnson (9)
		Weaver (27)	
		Taylor (24)	

Left End	Left Half	Right Half	Right End
Myers (12)	Stinchcomb (19)	Bliss (22)	Slyker (11)
Blair (13)	Cott (20)	Henderson (21)	N. Workman (15)
Weiss (32)	Lakin (37)	Volzer (34)	Albl (46)
McGregor (29)	Early (49)	Blumenthal (51)	D. MacGinnis (53)
Pauley (10)	Osburn (43)	Patchel (31)	DeMore (48)
Craig (44)	Campbell (33)	Lightner (41)	Speed (14)
Duell (55)	Doig (—)	Nesbitt (47)	Failer (54)
Alcorn (40)	Wilder (25)	Miller (24)	Patterson (45)
	Navin (38)	Johnson (16)	Walker (42)
	Miller (39)		

1920
Captain: Iolas M. Huffman

55	*Ohio Wesleyan	0
37	*Oberlin	0
17	*Purdue	0
13	*Wisconsin	7
7	Chicago	6
14	*Michigan	7
7	Illinois	0
0	†California	28
150		48

Won 7, Lost 1
Big Ten Champions
† Rose Bowl

[1920]

Time was speeding past. The game was almost over. It looked as though the Scarlet and Grey of Ohio State and the Orange and Blue of Illinois would close the 1920 drama in a draw.

Only a few minutes were left to play. The two teams had grappled at each other's one-yard line, only to lose the ball, ere making the needed three feet.

The season, filled with nerve racking events for both elevens, was coming to a close. Its life could be counted in seconds — this was the last game and still the title had not been claimed.

And so with the eyes of the western football world turned upon them, Illinois and Ohio State lineup in mid field. From the east, north, south and west, 18,000 voices thundered to the fatigued Urbana men. Four thousand voices chanted a "Fight, Fight, Fight," to the battle scarred Buckeyes.

The press box hummed with the click of the telegraph, as wires buzzed with the words, "nothing to nothing and only seconds left to play."

Again the Scarlet and Grey lined up. For the third time "Pete" Stinchcomb went far out on left end. The ball sped back to "Hoge" Workman. Two Illini tackles raced toward him. He stepped aside and hurled the pigskin. The ball reached mid air. The time keeper dashed upon the field, both arms up. The whistle blew. The game, all but this play, was over.

Seventeen yards away from the goal, "Truck" Myers received the ball. In an instant he had covered the intervening distance and crossed the goal.

The game was won—Ohio State 6, Illinois 0.

The goal was not needed, but "Pete" Stinchcomb, first shaking his fist at the Illini, booted the pigskin over for another point. The last act of the 1920 season had closed.

In silence the Illini stands received the defeat which sent their eleven tumbling back to fourth place in the Big Ten standing; in a wild outburst of joy the Buckeyes rolled over Urbana field, shouting not alone for the 1920 honors, but for the revenge of the "last eight seconds" of 1919.

"PETE" STINCHCOMB
All American Halfback 1920

Perpetuate Your Name on the Ohio Stadium

Immediate and permanent benefits will accrue to those who make the proposed Stadium a reality.

Those who contribute $5,000 or more will be known as Founders. Their names will be inscribed on a bronze tablet on the center pillar of the main entrance to the Stadium. A box off the field will be named in their honor and so marked and an option for the box or as many seats in it as they desire will be open to them.

Those who contribute $1,000 or more up to $5,000 will be known as Patrons. Their names will be inscribed in bronze on tablets to be set in other pillars of the main entrance to the Stadium. Options for six seats will be open to them for the games in the Stadium for ten years after it is completed.

Those who give $200 or more up to $1,000 will be known as Donors. Their names will be inscribed in bronze on tablets to be conspicuously located about the Stadium. Options for four seats will be open to them for ten years after the Stadium is completed.

Those who give $100 or more up to $200 will be known as Subscribers. Their names will be inscribed on bronze tablets prominently located in the Stadium. They will be offered options for two seats for ten years after the Stadium is completed.

Students giving $25 will receive the same benefits as alumni and friends who give $100.

Ohio Stadium Committee,
SAMUEL N. SUMMER, Chairman,
CARL E. STEEB, Treasurer.

Headquarters, Ohio Union Building,
Campus, Columbus, Ohio.

CALIFORNIA'S "WONDER TEAM" DEFEATS OHIO STATE, 28 TO 0

Famed Aerial Attack of "Big Ten" Champions Fails to Work Against Unbeaten Coast Eleven — 42,000 Spectators See Game—Stinchcomb and Muller Star.

SUMMARY OF PASADENA GAME.

California.	Ohio State.
Stephens .... le	Myers
Dean .... lt ..	Huffman (Capt.)
Majors (Capt.) ...lg........	Taylor
Latham ....c........	Nemeck
Cranmer ....rg........	Wiche
McMillan ....rt........	Trott
Muller ....re.....	N. Workman
Erb ....qb.....	H. Workman
Sprott ....lhb.....	Stinchcomb
Toomey ....rhb.....	Blair
Nisbet ....fb.....	C. Taylor

Score by periods:—
California ....7 14 0 7—28
California scoring — Touchdowns, Sprott 2, Stephens, Deeds (substitute for Toomey); goals from touchdowns, Erb, Toomey 3. Officials—George M. Varnell, Chicago, referee; F. E. Birch, Earlham, umpire; W. S. Kienholtz, Minnesota, head linesman; Joseph Magidson, Michigan, field judge.

Pasadena, Cal., Jan. 1.—University of California's "wonder team" outplayed and defeated the "big ten" champions, Ohio State, 28 to 0, today in the annual tournament of roses New Year's Day East-West game. The score was the largest ever rolled up by a Western team against Eastern invaders.

Beaten at Own Game.

Ohio State's famed aerial attack and "last minute drive to victory" fell before the brilliant Blue and Gold defense and the 42,000 spectators saw California take a leaf from the Buckeye's book and beat the Ohio men at their own game of forward passing. California, on the offensive, had a dazzling assortment of passes, long and short, and on the defense got in the way and broke up most of Ohio's throws, intercepting them always when the middle Westerners threatened.

Coupled with the phenomenal California display of passing was an offense as varied as any ever seen in the West. Coach Andy Smith's men slashed the Ohio line at will, circled the Ohio ends and with double passes and criss-cross plays baffled their opponents.

Muller Big Factor.

The story of California's victory, in a large measure was the story of the playing of "Bric" Muller, California's brilliant end. Muller was a stonewall on defense, and on the offense played a remarkable game. Three of California's touchdowns were the direct result of Muller's mastery of the aerial attack, both in passing and receiving.

Stinchcomb Comes Through.

Pete Stinchcomb, Ohio State's representative on the mythical All-American eleven, did everything expected of him and more, but the California defense, which had been perfected to stop him, was impassable and although Stinchcomb gained probably more yardage than any other player today, his work demonstrated that one man cannot win from a trained varsity club.

California's line outcharged its rivals and often opened tremendous holes through which their backs plunged for large gains. The Ohio forwards were unable to cope with the fierceness of this attack and when the secondary defense came into back up the forward wall, California opened up and forward passed their way to victory. "Tarzan" Taylor and Captain Huffman were the stars of the Ohio line while every man on the Berkeley line shone. Captain "Cort" Majors, playing his last varsity contest, put up a great game. On many occasions he broke through the Ohio line and shattered plays at their start.

A southern California sun blazed down on the turf and probably hampered the Buckeyes, who came from a cold climate, but it is doubtful if snow, rain and slush could have halted the Californians.

Statistics Tell Story.

Statistics of the game showed California made eighteen first downs to ten for Ohio and gained considerable more yardage both on straight and open football.

Gains at punting were about even, California was penalized frequently, while Ohio drew but one penalized loss. The game was marked with roughness. Fumbles were about even.

Reprinted with permission of the **Hartford Courant**

Campaign Off Campus

EXECUTIVE COMMITTEE

SAMUEL N. SUMMER	Chairman
CARL E. STEEB	Treasurer
Thomas E. French	Simon Lazarus
W. A. Ireland	J. L. Morrill
John A. Kelley	J. J. Munsell
Charles F. Kettering	T. V. Taylor

Organization to raise funds for the Stadium was divided into three heads—national, district and local. At the head of the national division was the Board of Trustees of the University, of which John F. Cunningham was chairman. An honorary committee, composed of Warren G. Harding, James M. Cox, Atlee Pomerene and other dignitaries was selected to give such assistance as might be needed.

The real head of the campaign was the Executive Committee, with Samuel N. Summer as chairman. This committee formulated the general plans of the enterprise, effected the organization of the various units and exercised supervision over them. Charles F. Kettering headed a founders committee whose duty was to solicit those who could give $5000 or more. J. Lewis Morrill had charge of the Committee on Organization whose duty was to build up local and district organizations.

California Trip

On the morning of December 18, although cold and snappy a delegation of over a thousand students and loyal Ohio State backers assembled at the Union Station to see the team and party of officials and rooters start on their transcontinental trip to clash with the Golden Bears of California on New Years Day as the biggest event of the annual tournament of Roses. With hopes high and full of enthusiasm for a victory, the party pulled out of the train shed on the first lap of the trip.

The first stop was made at Chicago, where a large group of alumni entertained the representatives of Ohio State. At several other places, the boys were given a rousing time and send off. At Ames, Iowa, a crowd from Iowa State greeted them with Ohio State yells, and showed the campus of that university to our athletes and staff. Regretfully the party left and at five o'clock the train stopped at Omaha. An hour's tour of the city had been planned but lateness in arriving prevented it.

Denver was the next stop, here a most cordial welcome was given the team. Although it was snowing heavily, the team dressed and went to a park to stage their first practice session since leaving Columbus.

As the train pulled into Sacramento, a rousing ovation was given by alumni and Easterners wintering in California. The party carried on to Berkeley. Students showed our group around the beautiful campus and expressed their friendliness in dozens of ways to the visitors, who by this time felt that cordiality was the middle name of the West. That evening the party was the guest of the alumni at a sumptuous banquet in the St. Francis Hotel.

The second real practice session came at Stanford University. December 24, the party left for Los Angeles where a committee from the Tournament of Roses met them. That night a Christmas Party was staged at the hotel.

Christmas morning a tour was made through the district, several very famous old places being visited. Again that night came a Christmas party with more gifts.

New Years Day and the deluge came. The Scarlet and Gray followers were heartsick but loyal, as was shown by cheers and songs as the vanquished team left for home the next morning. Although defeated 28 to 0 the team was loyaly greeted at every stop on the way back; Santa Fe, St. Louis and Indianapolis greeted our party with great enthusiasm and welcome and aided in dispelling the gloom clouds spread by the Golden Bears.

Finally the team reached home. A real welcome was given the globe trotters when the train pulled into Columbus by several thousand students and Columbus folk, who followed the boys to the Athletic Club where rousing cheers and songs preceded an informal dinner to the team. Here ends the story of the California trip.

[1921]

Ohio State Team

Left End	Left Tackle	Left Guard	Center	Right Guard	Right Tackle	Right End
10–Myers	1–Huffman	4–Pixley	8–Young	30–Trott	6–Spiers	48–Speed
36–Conklin	2–Dunlap	32–Wallace	3–Pauley	31–Wasson	9–Jackson	42–Slyker
38–Siebert	34–Addison	43–Kruse	12–Kaplow	56–Moseley	7–Steele	35–Friend
45–Hamilton	29–McGregor	11–Gillam		49–Patchell	33–Wormser	37–Gwinn
47–Mesloh	44–Anderson			5–Petcoff	61–Roff	39–Colvin

Left Half	Full Back	Right Half	Quarter-Back
20–Stuart	21–Taylor	17–Isabel	41–Lincoln
14–Cott	13–Blair	50–Kissell	24–Workman
18–Lightner	22–Weaver	16–Honaker	23–Wiper
27–Higgins	26–Oberlin	25–Diamond	40–Metzger
19–Moorehead		28–Harter	
51–Connell			
52–Thompson			

1921: OHIO STATE, 14—MICHIGAN, 0

Front row (left to right): Pauley, Slyker, Spiers, Trott, Capt. Myers, Pixley, Huffman, Young, Taylor. *Second row:* Director L. W. St. John, Conklin, Doig, Isabel, Blair, D. Wiper, C. N. Workman, Cott, Stuart, Honaker, Moorehead, Weaver, Higgins, Dr. J. W. Wilce, head coach. *Third row:* G. P. Ward (coach), Metzger, Oberlin, Jackson, Wasson, Steel, Addison, Gillam, Wallace, Dunlap, Kaplow, W. J. Essman (coach). *Rear:* Johnson, manager; E. G. Gurney, trainer; Ralph Hanna, manager.

Ohio State Loses To Illinois In Big Upset

Columbus, Ohio, Nov. 19.—Illinois today dashed to earth the hopes of Ohio State for a claim to the Western Conference football championship. The Illinois, defeated by every conference team they had met this season, played the Buckeyes to a standstill and raced off the field victors 7 to 0. The feat was accomplished before a homecoming crowd of more than 20,000 which packed all available space on the stands.

Captain Larry Walquist, playing his last game for his alma mater, scored the touchdown in the second period. He had only touched a forward pass tossed to him by Peden, but turned quickly as the ball passed him, and seeing it bound from the chest of Captain Myers of the Buckeyes, snatched it and plunged twenty-five yards for the first touchdown Illinois had scored during the conference season. Sabo kicked the goal.

Reprinted with permission of the **Hartford Courant**

1921
Captain: Cyril E. Myers

28	*Ohio Wesleyan	0
6	*Oberlin	7
27	*Minnesota	0
14	Michigan	0
7	Chicago	0
28	*Purdue	0
0	*Illinois	7
110		14

Won 5, Lost 2

[1921]

Next Year We'll Swarm In the Stadium

You Can Still Perpetuate Your Name

HAVE you reserved your seat?
Your opportunity is at the bottom of this page. Fill it out.

Subscribers of $100 or more up to $200 to the Stadium Building Fund are entitled to options on two seats in the new Stadium for ten years. Even this season they have been given preference in the allotment of seats for the last big games in overcrowded Ohio Field.

Subscribers of $200 or more up to $1000 may reserve four seats in the new Stadium for ten years. Donors of $1000 or more up to $5000 may reserve six seats for ten years. Contributors of $5000 or more will have a box off the field named in their honor and will be entitled to an option on the box or as many seats in it as they desire.

Names of all subscribers of $100 or more will be perpetuated on bronze tablets, to be located prominently in the new Stadium.

Students giving $25 will receive the same benefits as Alumni and friends who give $100.

OHIO STADIUM FUND
OHIO UNION, OHIO STATE UNIVERSITY
COLUMBUS, OHIO

Date..................

Name
Address

I hereby give/pledge the following amount to the Ohio Stadium Fund:

Cash................$ Pledge................$
Securities
(Describe fully or append signed memorandum)

Payable in installments due: 25% cash; 25% January 1, 1922; 25% July 1, 1922; 25% January 1, 1923.

(Signed) ....

BREAKING GROUND

OHIO STATE FOOTBALL SQUAD, 1922 [1922]

Front row (left to right): R. T. Donham, halfback; E. C. Milliken, halfback; D. Klein, halfback; A. V. McNamer, quarterback; C. M. Zaenglein, halfback; F. H. Milliken, quarterback; E. D. Watts, halfback; A. G. Harter, halfback; R. P. Wood, halfback; R. F. Marts, quarterback; J. M. Fox, halfback; J. J. Schaffer, quarterback; W. C. Lincoln, quarterback; P. M. Holmes, halfback.
Second row:— H. L. Hamilton, center; G. S. Kyle, end; C. Farcasin, halfback; W. D. Lightner, halfback; H. H. Workman, halfback; C. N. Workman, quarterback; H. H. Blair, halfback; C. F. Honaker, end; L. S. Moorehead, halfback; Ollie Klee, halfback; G. D. Cameron, quarterback; C. C. Reiser, halfback; C. C. Kissell, halfback.
Third row:— H. G. Olsen, coach; Dean Trott, coach; Eugene Van Scoyk, tackle; ;H. Schweinsberger, end; Alex Klein, center; N. H. Dunlap, guard; R. J. Kutler, guard; Capt. L. A. Pixley, guard; T. N. Long, guard; Boni Petcoff, tackle; Kenneth Pauley, center; E. E. Addison, tackle; M. D. Hollingsworth, guard; F. D. Young, tackle; W. J. Essman, coach; Dr. J. W. Wilce, head coach.
Fourth row:— G. M. Trautman, coach; E. G. Gurney, trainer; G. P. Ward, coach; W. M. Jackson, tackle; W. W. Gwinn, end; R. W. Oberlin, guard; P. A. Lemley, end; Bradley Skeele, tackle; E. S. Elgin, end; R. W. Wallace, guard; B. H. Schulist, end; J. E. Nida, guard; A. H. Sandrock, end; Donald Calhoun, tackle; A. R. Fioretti, end; W. P. Guild, guard; A. O. Myers, end; D. R. Croft, guard; J. B. Wilson, end; R. E. Chambers, guard; G. W. Studabaker, end; J. M. Patchell, center; W. S. Speed, end; L. P. Jisa, tackle; E. J. Kaplow, center; G. A. Scanlon, tackle; L. E. Judy, end; I. M. Huffman, coach; J. M. Vorys, coach; A. J. Nemecek, coach.
Back row:— C. A. MacDonald, coach; N. C. Ervin, senior manager; W. R. Updegraff, senior manager; G. K. Bowman, junior assistant manager; B. W. Williston, fullback; A. C. Michaels, fullback; L. A. Murphy, center; I. B. Hamilton, fullback; P. M. Shepard, guard; G. F. Knickerbocker, fullback; H. R. Butler, guard; Harold Wasson, tackle; S. A. Jenney, junior assistant manager; Raymond Miller, assistant; Harold Eckert, sophomore assistant manager; W. T. Craver, sophomore assistant manager; W. W. Thomen, senior manager.

OHIO STATE

		Michaels		Klee	
Isabel 4		22		9	
Right Half		175 lbs.		Left Half	
167 lbs.		**Fullback**		152 lbs.	
		Blair			
		15			
		171 lbs.			
		H. Workman			
		40			
		Quarterback			
		163 lbs.			

Honaker	Petcoff	Kutler	Pauley	Pixley (C)	Young	Schweinsberger
8	7	17	31	1	5	16
Right End	Right Tackle	Right Guard	Center	Left Guard	Left Tackle	Left End
190 lbs.	210 lbs.	175 lbs.	188 lbs.	242 lbs.	180 lbs.	173 lbs.

Average Weight of Ohio State Team—183 lbs. Line—194 lbs. Backfield—164 lbs.

1922
Captain: Lloyd A. Pixley

5	*Ohio Wesleyan	0
14	*Oberlin	0
0	*Michigan	19
0	Minnesota	9
9	*Chicago	14
9	*Iowa	12
6	Illinois	3
43		57

Won 3, Lost 4

OHIO STATE RESERVES

Ends
10—Kyle
12—Elgin
19—Gwinn
20—Fioretti
30—Wilson
41—Judy
43—Lemley
47—Sandrock
50—Speed
52—Studabaker
69—Myers

Tackles
13—Schulist
23—Wasson
28—Steel
32—Addison
36—Jackson
51—Skeele
55—Van Scoyk
57—Jisa
59—Calhoun
72—Scanlon

Guards
27—Oberlin
29—Hollingsworth
33—Dunlap
34—Long
53—Guild
58—Butler
60—Croft
70—Nida
—Chambers

Quarterbacks
25—Cameron
38—Schaffer
45—McNamer
56—Lindauer
67—Marts
68—F. H. Milliken
—Lincoln

Centers
3—Kaplow
26—A. Klein
48—Patchell
49—Murphy
64—H. L. Hamilton

Halfbacks
6—Lightner
14—Farcasin
18—Harter
24—Moorehead
42—Kissell
44—D. Klein
46—E. C. Milliken
61—Donham
62—Fox
65—Holmes
71—Reiser
74—E. D. Watts
75—R. P. Wood
76—Zaenglein

Fullbacks
11—Hamilton, Ian B.
54—Williston
—Knickerbocker

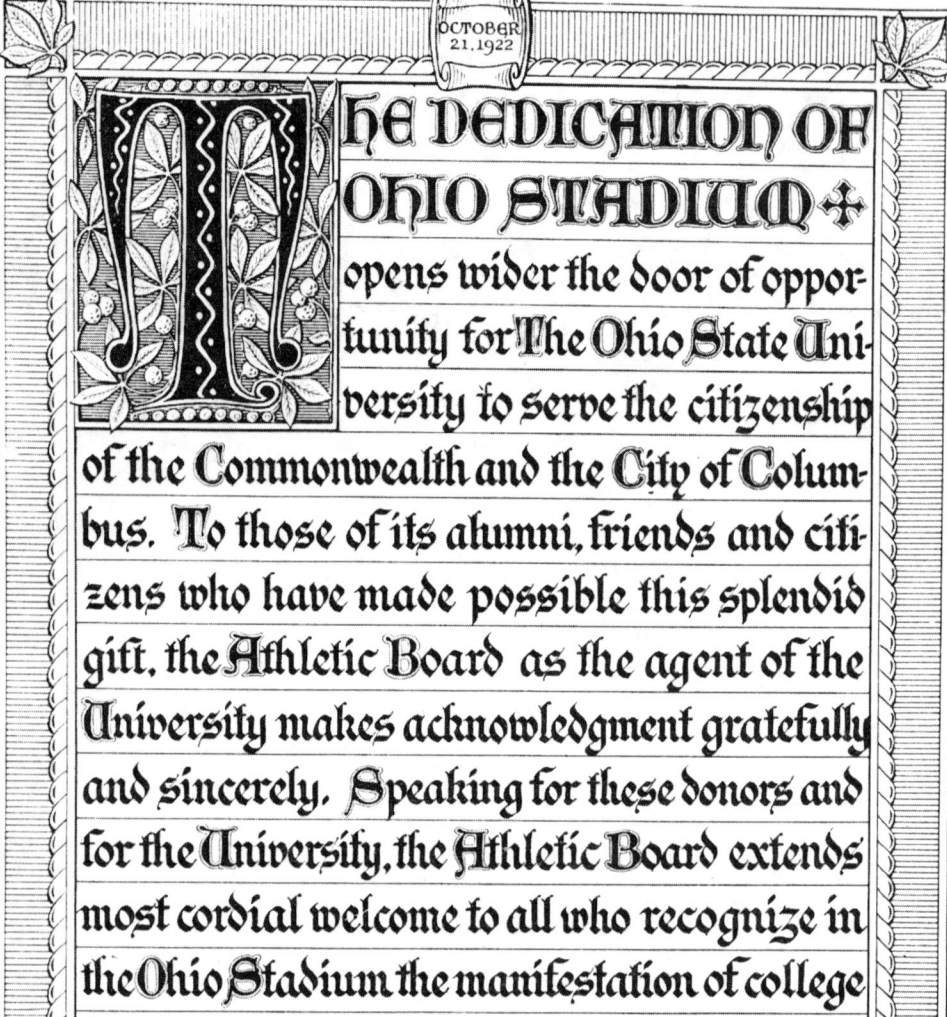

OCTOBER 21, 1922

The Dedication of Ohio Stadium opens wider the door of opportunity for The Ohio State University to serve the citizenship of the Commonwealth and the City of Columbus. To those of its alumni, friends and citizens who have made possible this splendid gift, the Athletic Board as the agent of the University makes acknowledgment gratefully and sincerely. Speaking for these donors and for the University, the Athletic Board extends most cordial welcome to all who recognize in the Ohio Stadium the manifestation of college loyalty, of devotion to the ideals of sportsmanship, of generous support for the cause of higher education, of proud allegiance to Ohio.

STADIUM FACTS

Permanent seats 62,110. Temporary capacity 72,000.

Construction cost $1,341,000. Financed chiefly by gifts aggregating $1,083,000 pledged by 13,000 people.

Seats in lower deck 41,000. Seats in upper deck 21,000. Box seats 3100. Closest seats are 72 feet from the sidelines, farthest seats 231 feet.

Circumference from end to end, one-third mile.

Ground area 10 acres.

Height of wall 98 feet, 3 inches.

Length 754 feet, width 597 feet.

Material: concrete and steel.

Twelve ramps feed 112 aisles.

Tickets may be taken from one to 81 entrances.

Seven hundred ushers are required to handle a capacity crowd.

Advantages of the Ohio Plan:

(1) The upper deck brings rear seats closer to the playing field.

(2) The open end improves ventilation.

(3) The curved sides equalize seat values and are a factor in crowd psychology.

Architectural Features:

(1) Eighty-seven concrete and steel arches, each 13 feet wide and 56 feet high.

(2) Towers at the open end and main entrance, each 109 feet high and 36 feet square.

(3) A half dome 86½ feet high and 70 feet in diameter.

With the preliminary games aside, the Wilce machine concerted its efforts for the important dedication game in the Stadium with Michigan, October 21. Before a throng of more than 70,000 persons—the largest which ever saw a football game in the West and which included many Homecoming alumni—Michigan cleanly defeated the Buckeyes, 19 to 0. From the early moments of the game, when Captain Goebel of the Wolverines toed over a field goal, until the final whistle, Michigan cleanly had the advantage. Only at the outset of the second half did Pixley and his mates seem to have a chance, and this was short-lived. On the other hand, Yost's brilliant eleven gathered 16 more points. Kipke at half was the outstanding star of the contest, his all-round play lifting him upon a high eminence. Goebel and Kirk were also bugbears for the Buckeyes.

IOLAS M. HUFFMAN
Winner Western Conference Scholarship Medal 1922

One of the greatest honors that can come to a varsity athlete at any Western Conferencee University is to win the "Big Ten" medal awarded annually by each member institution to its best scholar-athlete. Iolas M. Huffman, captain of the great 1920 football team, tackle for four years, baseball catcher and slugger extraordinary, was the Ohio State medal winner last spring. "Huffy," now enrolled in the College of Medicine, achieved honor by completing 22 hours of merit work, 43 hours with "G" grade and 34 with "A" while annexing seven varsity "O's" on the football gridiron and baseball diamond.

SOUVENIR DEDICATION PROGRAM
MICHIGAN VERSUS OHIO STATE

[1923]

Name	Home	Age	H't	W't	Year	Position
Bradshaw, Jas. B.	Columbus	19	6'	150	1	
Brashear, Richard	Columbus	20	5' 8"	145	1	Quarterback
Bruck, H. J.	Columbus	19	5' 11"	210	1	
Cameron, Geo. D.	Cleveland	24	5' 10"	150	2	Quarterback
Carlson, Herbert R.	Cleveland	22	6' 1"	166	1	Halfback
Croft, Daniel R.	Elkton	20	6' ½"	176	2	Center
Cunningham, Harold	Mt. Vernon	18	6' 2"	183	1	End
Dobeleit, Richard	Dayton	20	5' 4"	145	1	Halfback
De Voe, Keith E.	Lima	19	5' 10"	179	1	Fullback
Dunlap, Nelson	Columbus	21	5' 10"	196	3	Tackle
Edmiston, Charles	Columbus	19	5' 10"	186	1	
Friend, Dwight	Columbus	23	6'	165	2	End
Fioretti, A. R.	Cleveland	22	5' 11½"	171	2	End
Guild, W. P.	Columbus	19	6' 1"	190	2	Guard
Gorrill, C. V.	Fostoria	20	5' 11"	160	1	End
Hamilton, Ian B.	Louisville, O.	20	5' 11"	155	3	Fullback
Hamilton, Howard	Columbus	20	6'	150	3	Center
Harter, Albert G.	Akron	23	5' 9½"	167	2	Halfback
Hollingsworth, Morris	Columbus	21	5' 10"	214	2	Guard
Hendershott, L. W.	Columbus	19	5' 8½"	148	1	Quarterback
Holmes, Paul M.	Columbus	25	5' 6½"	160	2	
Honaker, Frank	Huntington, W. Va.	23	5' 11"	182	3	Fullback
Howell, Raymond S.	Columbus	24	5' 8½"	144	1	
Judy, Edwin	Martins Ferry	21	5' 10"	161	2	Quarterback
Klee, Ollie	Dayton	23	5' 8"	153	2	Quarterback
Kyle, George S.	Cortland	21	5' 9½"	153	2	End
Kutler, R. J.	Cleveland	21	5' 8½"	180	2	Guard
Lusk, Homer D.	Bainbridge	23	6'	166	1	
Long, Thomas N.	Columbus	24	6'	156	3	Guard
Lang, Robert A.	Muncie, Ind.	26	6' 2"	183	1	Fullback
Mack, Carl	Belle Center		6' 3½"	232	1	Tackle
Marts, R. J.	Middletown	26	5' 7"	142	3	Quarterback
Marion, A. W.	Circleville	19	6' 1½"	180	1	Tackle
Miller, J. B.	Portsmouth	19	5' 9"	146	1	
Miller, E. P.	Lima	19	5' 8"	157	1	Center
Murphy, Loren A.	Columbus	20	6'	186	2	Fullback
NcNamer, A. V.	Columbus	22	5' 7½"	160	2	Halfback
Nichols, John H.	La Grange		6'	183	1	Tackle
Nopper, Arnold	Toledo	24	5' 10"	176	1	Tackle
Oberlin, R. W.	Navarre	23	5' 8"	161	3	Tackle
Ort, Paul	Columbus	18	5' 9"	146	1	
Paul, Charles E.	Columbus	20	5' 8"	140	2	
Petcoff, Boni (Capt.)	Toledo	23	5' 10"	195	3	Tackle
Peterson, Archie	Cedar Rapids, Ia.	23	5' 10½"	168	1	End
Place, Graham	Bowling Green	19	5' 7"	138	1	Halfback
Pothoff, William	Sharonville	22	5' 9"	254	1	Guard
Poling, Luther	Marysville	20	5' 11"	166	1	End
Rader, O. W.	Columbus	19	5' 9"	138	1	
Roesch, Karl O.	Cleveland	19	5' 11½"	195	1	Guard
Rogers, John	Columbus	18	5' 9"	164	1	Guard
Ross, J. G.	Sandusky	22	5' 7"	132	1	
Rogers, R. J.	Cincinnati	20	5' 9"	165	1	
Schulist, B. N.	Cleveland	19	5' 10"	168	2	Guard
Schweinsberger, H.	Columbus	21	5' 10"	175	2	Guard
Southern, Clarence	Evansville, Ind.	22	5' 9"	150	1	Halfback
Snyder, Lawrence	Columbus	26	6'	155	1	Halfback
Sobul, Sanford	Cleveland	20	5' 8"	137	1	Quarterback
Seiffer, Ralph E.	Evansville, Ind.	19	6' 1"	164	1	End
Steel, Harry D.	East Sparta	24	6' 3"	201	3	Tackle
Van Scoyk, E. N.	Dayton	23	6'	171	3	
Walther, L. R.	Canton	21		170	1	Center
Watkins, E. H.	Mansfield	19	5' 8"	164	1	Guard
Watts, R. S.	Columbus	22	5' 7"	145	2	Center
Wasson, Harold	Columbus	21	6' 1"	190	3	Tackle
Wisterman, John M.	Galion	20	5' 8½"	150	1	Quarterback
Wilson, John F.	Milan	20	6' 1"	167	2	End
Workman, Harry	Huntington, W. Va.	23	5' 10½"	166	3	Halfback
Wendler, Harold	Fremont	21	5' 10"	146	1	Halfback
Wood, Rolland P.	Columbus	19	5' 9"	147	2	
Woodruff, Charles	Columbus	25	5' 5"	205	1	Guard
Young, Frank D.	Toledo	24	6'	178	2	Center
Zaenglein, C. M.	Botkins	21	5' 7"	153	2	Halfback

[1923]

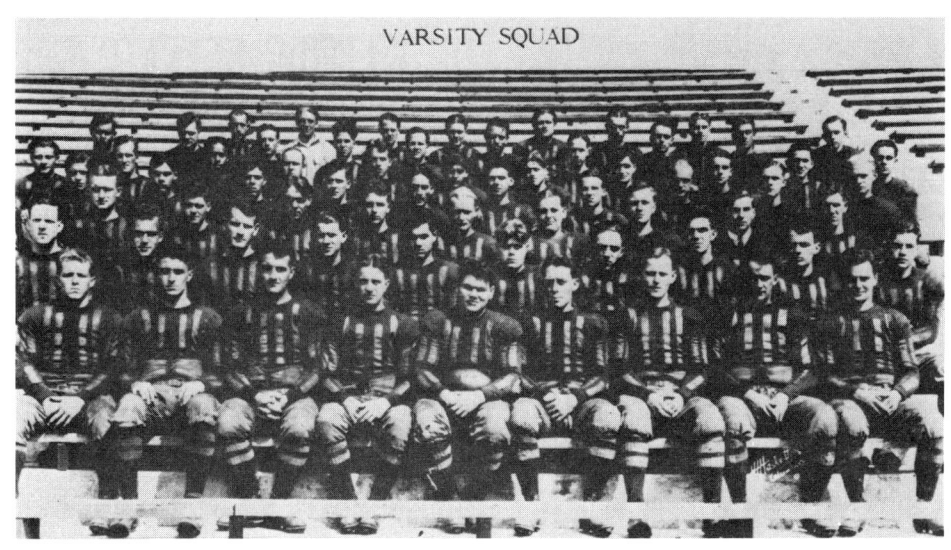

VARSITY SQUAD

1923		
Captain: Boni Petcoff		
24	*Ohio Wesleyan	7
23	*Colgate	23
0	Michigan	23
0	*Iowa	20
42	*Denison	0
32	Purdue	0
3	Chicago	17
0	*Illinois	9
124		99
Won 3, Lost 4, Tied 1		

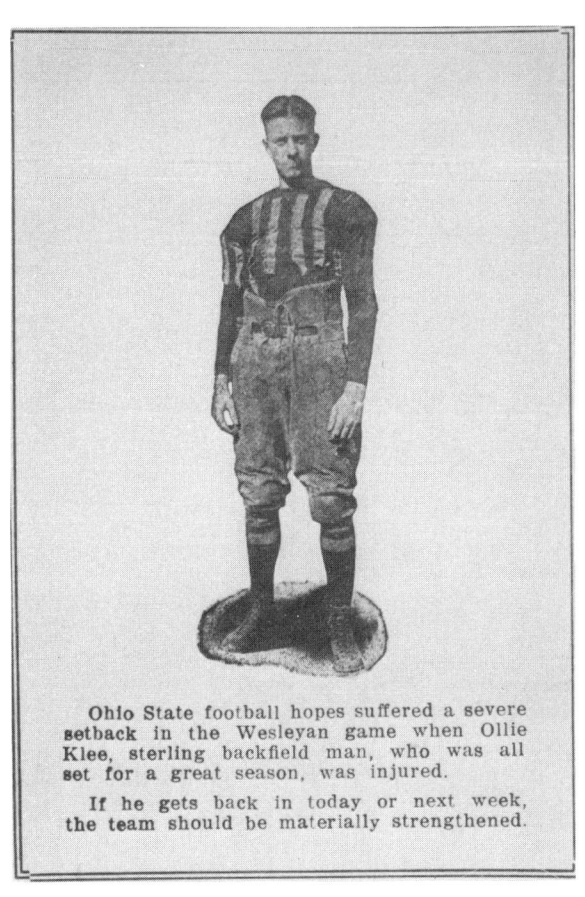

Ohio State football hopes suffered a severe setback in the Wesleyan game when Ollie Klee, sterling backfield man, who was all set for a great season, was injured.

If he gets back in today or next week, the team should be materially strengthened.

[1923]

Touchdown--- *by* Santa Claus

And he will score it with a copy of the

Songs of Ohio State University

official song book of the University,— a volume that every friend, every "oldtimer" and every student of Ohio State will be proud to own.

It Solves the Problem: "What to get someone for Christmas?"

ILLINOIS DEFEATS OHIO STATE, 9-0

45,000 Spectators Look on As Two Teams Wage Typical Struggle.

Ohio Stadium, Columbus, O., Nov. 24.—(By The Associated Press.)—Illinois defeated Ohio State 9 to 0 in the annual game between the two institutions and won a tie with Michigan for the western conference championship here today.

With more than 45,000 spectators looking on, the trailing western conference Buckeyes played the Illinois eleven to a standstill in the first three periods, but weakened in the fourth and permitting a field goal touchdown.

For a time it looked like the tue Buckeyes were going to spoil Illinois championship aspirations. In the third period Ohio rushed and forward passed the ball to the Illinois foot line but Honaker, playing his last game, failed to take it over on three plunges.

Is Typical Battle.

It was a game typical of the memorable battles which have been staged between the two schools in years past. Starting with the odds against them and faced with the necessity of stopping "Red" Grange, Illinois star halfback, the buckeyes not only held him in check for three periods, but outplayed his team, definitely threatening to score on three occasions, but lacking the final punch to put the ball over.

MICHIGAN GAME—WORKMAN (17) STARTS FORWARD PASS

Who's Who on Ohio State Squad

Name	Home	Year	Age	Height	Weight	Position
Beck, Herbert R.	Columbus	1	19	5' 11"	163	End
Blanchard, Bruce	Columbus	1	19	5' 9"	145	Quarterback
Bloser, Parker G.	Columbus	1	21	6'	177	End
Blumer, Gabe	Sandusky	1	19	5' 11"	158	Halfback
Boxwell, Paul	Xenia	1	19	5' 9½"	172	Halfback
Bradley, R. T.	Woodstock	1	19	5' 11"	182	Tackle
Cameron, George D.	Cleveland	3	25	5' 10"	152	Quarterback
Carlson, Herbert R.	Cleveland	2	23	6' 1"	186	Halfback
Cervenka, Laddie F.	Lorain	1	21	5' 11½"	168	End
Clark, Myers A.	Gettysburg	1	20	5' 11½"	168	Halfback
Cook, James M.	West Dover	1	21	5' 9"	150	Halfback
Cunningham, Harold B.	Mt. Vernon	2	19	6' 2"	197	End
De Voe, Keith	Lima	2	20	5' 10"	180	Fullback
Dreyer, Carl A.	Toledo	1	19	6' 1½"	203	Guard
Evans, Benjamin F.	Windham	1	20	5' 11¾"	176	Tackle
Galbraith, M. H.	Columbus	1	23	6' 1½"	160	End
Gorrill, Charles V.	Fostoria	1	21	5' 10¾"	162	End
Griffith, William N.	Bluffton	1	24	5' 8"	168	Guard
Harrison, H. C.	Columbus	1	22	6'	175	Tackle
Hess, Edwin	Chardon	1	19	6'	179	Tackle
Hunt, Howser C.	Richwood	1	19	5' 10"	153	Halfback
Hunt, William	Toledo	1	19	5' 8"	153	Halfback
Jackson, George H.	Columbus	1	24	6'	231	Guard
Jenkins, William R.	Columbus	1	20	6' 2"	188	Guard
Jones, A. D.	Columbus	1	23	5' 10"	164	Guard
Jones, Norman K.	London	1	18	5' 11"	193	Guard
Karow, Marty	Cleveland	1	20	5' 10"	173	Fullback
Klee, Ollie	Dayton	3	24	5' 8"	164	Halfback
Kreglow, James J.	De Graff	1	18	6' 1"	217	Guard
Kromer, Philip F.	Columbus	1	19	5' 9"	166	Tackle
Kutler, Rudolph J.	Cleveland	3	23	5' 8½"	186	Guard
Mackey, F. C.	Galion	1	20	5' 9½"	183	Tackle
Manchester, Frank	Perry	1	21	6'	175	Tackle
Marion, A. W.	Circleville	2	20	6' 1½"	190	Tackle
Marr, Joseph E.	Hamilton	1	21	5' 10"	158	Halfback
McCarthy, Tim	Fremont	1	19	6' 2"	185	Tackle
McNamer, Arthur	Columbus	3	23	5' 6½"	156	Halfback
Meacham, Howard	Atwater	1	20	6' 1½"	198	Guard
Miller, A. R.	Canton	1	24	5' 11½"	177	Center
Murphy, Loren A.	Columbus	3	21	6'	188	Center
Nichols, John H.	La Grange	2	20	6'	193	Tackle
Ort, Paul J.	Columbus	2	19	5' 7½"	149	End
Packard, Ralph	Columbus	1	20	6' 2"	167	Guard
Penrod, James L.	Lewisburg	1	20	5' 10"	192	Guard
Peterson, Archie L.	Cedar Rapids, Iowa	3	24	5' 10¾"	174	Halfback
Poling, Luther	Marysville	2	21	5' 11"	174	End
Pothoff, William	Sharonville	2	23	5' 9"	264	Guard
Price, Charles R.	Dayton	2	21	6'	159	End
Roesch, Karl A.	Cleveland	2	20	5' 11"	191	Guard
Rosofsky, Jacob	Columbus	2	20	5' 8"	146	End
Royer, John	Columbus	2	19	5' 9"	180	Guard
Scheiderer, Paul F.	Columbus	1	19	5' 10"	150	Guard
Schulist, Bernard	Cleveland	3	20	5' 10"	187	End
Schweinsberger, H.	Columbus	3	22	5' 10"	185	Halfback
Seiffer, Ralph E.	Evansville, Ind.	2	20	6'	173	End
Shifflette, Don F.	Columbus	1	19	5' 11"	166	Fullback
Slemmons, R. H.	Columbus	1	19	5' 8"	149	Quarterback
Slough, H. R.	Mansfield	1	18	5' 10½"	177	Center
Smith, R. G.	Columbus	1	18	5' 9"	133	Quarterback
Stewart, William E.	Columbiana	1	19	5' 10"	170	Guard
Tanner, Charles C.	London	1	19	6'	158	End
Watkins, Ed H.	Mansfield	2	20	5' 8"	170	Guard
Wilson, J. B.	Milan	3	20	6'	176	End
Watts, Robert	Columbus	3	23	5' 7"	148	Center
Wendler, Harold	Fremont	2	22	5' 10"	153	Halfback
Wentz, Burke	Kenton	1	19	5' 8½"	158	Halfback
Winters, Paul C.	Briggsdale	1	19	5' 9"	169	End
Wisterman, John M.	Galion	2	21	5' 9"	161	Quarterback
Woerlein, George	Groveport	1	20	5' 10½"	157	Halfback
Woods, G. C.	Port William	1	21	5' 11"	183	Tackle
Young, Frank D.	Toledo	3	24	6'	188	Center

1924	
Captain: Francis D. Young	
7 *Purdue	0
0 Iowa	0
10 *Ohio Wesleyan	0
3 *Chicago	3
7 *Wooster	7
7 *Indiana	12
6 *Michigan	16
0 Illinois	7
40	45
Won 2, Lost 3, Tied 3	

OHIO STATE TO PAY TRIBUTE TO SIX OLYMPIC MEN TODAY

With a sense of gratitude for the honor they have done the University along with their country and themselves, Ohio State today pays tribute to the six members of her athletic teams who were members of the American contingent which competed in the Olympic games in 1912 and 1924.

Two Ohio State men won places on the team of a dozen years ago which competed at Stockholm. The other four bore the Yankee shield at Paris last summer. A number of others won the right to compete in the final tryouts for places on the American team.

The two 1912 stars, the first Buckeyes to win places on an American team which competed in the Olympiad, are Clement C. Cooke, Columbus, and Garnet Wikoff, Columbus. Cooke, now a contractor here, was a sprinter in his college days of nearly a decade and a half ago, Wikoff was a distance runner.

The four athletes of the recent generation who will be honored are George P. Guthrie, Elyria, hurdler; Russell Payne, Cincinnati, steeplechase and distance runner, and Perry Martter, Los Angeles, and Harry Steel, East Sparta, wrestlers. So far as available records show Ohio State had more men actually participating in the 1914 Olympics than any other Western Conference school. A number of other Ohio State athletes qualified for the final tryouts but were not picked for the team.

WOOSTER 7	OHIO STATE 7
INDIANA 12	OHIO STATE 7

THE third tie of the season resulted November 1 when Wooster surprised Ohio State in the fourth quarter and scored a touchdown when Halfback Smith tallied on a 38-yard run through the Buckeye team and made the score 7 to 7. Though constantly striking at the Wooster goal line, the Ohioans were unable to put over but one touchdown, that coming in the second quarter when thirty-seven yards were gained on passes from "Jake" Cameron to "Cookie" Cunningham, and bucks by Clark and Wentz. Clark smashed through from the seven-yard line for the touchdown.

Taking the ball from its own four-yard line and driving the entire length of the field, but stopped three yards from a touchdown by the final whistle, Ohio State received the first set-back of the season from Indiana, 12 to 7, November 8. Marks counted both touchdowns for the visitors, the first after catching a pass, and the second on a 55-yard run. From the 33-yard mark, Ohio fought down the field until reaching an advantageous position from which Ollie Klee drove over the line. "Cookie" Cunningham again played a brilliant all-around game.

WOOSTER—CLARK SMASHES 7 YARDS FOR TOUCHDOWN

Special Trains to Illinois!

An annual football classic, the Ohio State-Illinois game at Urbana next week closes the spectacular 1924 season, for both teams.

The Athletic Department has chartered a number of special trains over the Big Four route for the trip. As many special trains will be run as are needed. Railroad and game tickets will be on sale Monday morning, November 17th, at the Athletic House. Accommodations will be available either for individuals or groups. Special attention will be given to parties.

Round trip ticket, good for special train only, including LOWER berth, ticket to game, breakfast and dinner on diner Saturday, and armband—$25.00.

Round trip ticket good for special train only, with ticket to game, UPPER berth, and breakfast and dinner on diner Saturday, and armband—$23.50.

Round trip fare in day coach only*—$11.00.

Special trains will leave Union Station, Columbus, at 10 p. m., Friday, November 21st. Arrive in Urbana by 8 a. m., Saturday, November 22nd. Leave Urbana about 7 p. m., Saturday, November 22nd. Reach Columbus, by 9 a. m., Sunday, November 23rd.

Seventy-five hundred seats have been set aside for Ohio State in the Illinois Memorial Stadium for next week's game.

*Does not include ticket to game nor meals.

ILLINOIS 7   OHIO STATE 0

ALTHOUGH "Red" Grange was not in the lineup when the Buckeyes met Illinois in the last conference game of the season, November 22 at Champaign, thrills were not lacking for the spectators. The game ended with the Scarlet and Gray eleven on the small end of a 7 to 0 score.

The Illini started with Gallivan and Green doing most of the business. Run after run through the Buckeye line made the 3000 Ohio State followers sink low in their seats. But a touchdown was averted by sudden strengthening of the line.

Illinois scored a touchdown in the second quarter after a series of passes when a line buck was good for six points. Britton added the final point with his educated toe.

The game closed the football careers of Captain "Tee" Young, "Bobby" Watts, "Rudy" Kutler, Ollie Klee, "Bernie" Schulist and "Johnny" Wilson.

[1925]

Who's Who on Ohio State's Squad

Name	Home	Age	Height	Weight	Year	Position
Ackerman, Cornelius	Wauseon	18	5' 10"	164	1	End
Bell, Bob	Columbus	20	5' 9"	185	1	Fullback
Bell, Robin	Erie, Pa.	19	6'	173	1	Quarterback
Blanchard, Bruce	Columbus	20	5' 9"	144	2	Quarterback
Brobeck, John	Richwood	19	5' 8"	152	1	Halfback
Bradley, Bob	Woodstock	20	6'	188	2	Center
Brumbaugh, Carl L.	West Milton	19	5' 10"	155	1	Halfback
Boyer, Dan	Canal Winchester	21	5' 10"	160	1	Back
Bloser, Parker	Columbus	22	6'	175	2	End
Clark, Myers	Gettysburg	21	5' 11½"	170	2	Halfback
Cunningham, Harold	Mt. Vernon	20	6' 3"	193	3	End
DeVoe, Keith	Lima	21	5' 10"	188	3	Fullback
Diehl, Richard C.	Defiance	21	5' 11"	172	2	
Freeman, Eddie	Canal Winchester	22	5' 8"	143	1	Quarterback
Gorrill, Charles	Fostoria	22	5' 10¾"	165	3	End
Grim, Fred	Toledo	20	5' 10½"	160	1	Halfback
Griswold, F. H.	Erie, Pa.	20	5' 11"	170	1	Halfback
Hall, Charles C.	Columbus	20	5' 10½"	165	1	Center
Hamilton, Clarence	Louisville	21	5' 11"	150	1	Halfback
Harrison, Henry C.	Columbus	22	6'	173	2	Tackle
Hess, Edwin	Chardon	20	6'	185	2	Guard
Hieronymus, Ted	Columbus	19	6' 3"	202	1	Fullback
Hunt, William	Toledo	20	5' 8½"	160	2	Halfback
Jeffrey, Gordon	Toledo	22	6'	178	1	End
Jenkins, William	Columbus	22	6' 1"	188	2	Tackle
Joseph, Chalmer	Columbus	19	6' 2¾"	175	1	End
Karow, Marty	Cleveland	22	5' 10"	175	2	Fullback
Karow, Joe	Cleveland	21	5' 10½"	155	1	Halfback
Klein, Alex	Lorain	23	5' 11"	175	2	Center
Kates, Paul	Columbus		5' 10"	163	1	
Koch, John	Columbus	19	6' 2½"	177	1	Tackle
Kopp, Harold	Chicago	21	5' 11"	167	1	Halfback
Kreglow, Julius	DeGraff	19	6' 1½"	220	2	Guard
Lacksen, Frank	Ashtabula	22	6' 4¼"	194	1	Tackle
Lawrence, Harold	Lancaster	22	6'	175	2	Center
Llewellyn, Sam	Cleveland	19	5' 9½"	170	1	End
Mackey, Fred	Galion	21	5' 10"	178	2	Tackle
Moler, William	Columbus	21	5' 11"	190	1	Guard
Marek, Elmer	Cedar Rapids, Ia.	21	5' 10½"	170	1	Halfback
Meyers, Ted	Cleveland	20	5' 10"	190	1	Guard
Mitchell, Paul	Lima	21	5' 11"	162	1	Halfback
Mitchell, Jordan	Columbus	19	5' 11"	165	1	Quarterback
Moellenkamp, Henry	Wapakoneta	20	6' 1½"	205	1	Tackle
McCarthy, Tim	Fremont	20	6' 2"	180	2	Tackle
Nichols, John	La Grange	21	6'	190	3	End
Olander, Ed.	Columbus	21	5' 11"	174	1	Guard
Ort, Paul	Columbus	20	5' 7"	150	3	Quarterback
Oster, Harvey	Cleveland	18	5' 11"	175	1	
Penrod, James L.	Lewisburg	21	5' 10½"	190	1	
Reed, William	Columbus	20	5' 8"	180	1	Guard
Rosenthal, Alex	Cleveland	20	6'	183	1	
Rowan, Everett	Chillicothe	22	6' 1"	180	1	End
Seiffer, Ralph E.	Evansville, Ind.	21	6'	170	3	End
Shapiro, H. L.	Columbus	25	5' 10"	181	3	
Shields, Roy	Cleveland	23	5' 11½"	198	1	Guard
Shifflette, Don	Columbus	20	6'	165	2	Halfback
Slemmons, Robert H.	Columbus	20	5' 8"	150	2	Quarterback
Slough, Herbert	Mansfield	20	5' 11"	180	2	Center
Sobul, Sanford	Cleveland	22	5' 10"	143	2	Quarterback
Schweinsberger, Harold	Columbus	23	5' 10"	185	3	Fullback
Ullery, Jack	Bradford	18	6' 1½"	184	1	Center
Uridil, Leo	Cedar Rapids, Ia.	21	6'	174	1	Tackle
Watkins, Edward	Mansfield	21	5' 8½"	177	3	Guard
Wendler, Harold	Fremont	23	5' 10"	152	3	Halfback
Wentz, Burke	Kenton	20	5' 8½"	165	2	Halfback
Willaman, Dan	Cleveland	22	5' 7½"	157	3	Halfback
Wisterman, John	Galion	22	5' 8½"	160	3	Quarterback
Wiswell, Owen	Columbus		6' 2"	185	1	Tackle
Woerlein, George	Groveport	21	5' 11"	168	2	Halfback
Wood, Rolland P.	Columbus	21	5' 8½"	150	1	Halfback
Young, William	Kenton	23	5' 10"	180	1	Tackle
Zuber, John	Columbus	18	5' 10"	150	1	Halfback

```
              1925
            Captain:
       Harold B. Cunningham
  10  *Ohio Wesleyan        3
   9  *Columbia             0
   3   Chicago              3
   0  *Iowa                15
  17  *Wooster              0
   7  *Indiana              0
   0   Michigan            10
   9  *Illinois            14
  ___                     ___
  55                       45
      Won 4, Lost 3, Tied 1
```

Ohio State's Third All-American

EDWIN A. HESS

THE third in Ohio State's family of All-American football players is "Ed" Hess, of Chardon, Ohio. Ohio's other All-American stars, Harley and Stinchcomb, were backfield players, but Hess lends his talent to the line at guard. Last year was Ed's second on the Scarlet and Gray eleven. He did not flash until the closing games of the 1924 season, but in 1925 his brilliance was not dimmed once throughout the season, and in two games, the Columbia and Illinois contests, he rose to the heighth of his colorful playing. Football is Hess's only sport.

COLUMBIA OHIO STATE
OHIO STADIUM • OCTOBER 17 1925 • 25¢

Who's Who on Ohio State's Squad

Name	Home	Age	Height	Weight	Year	Position
Ackerman, Cornelius	Wauseon	19	5' 10"	170	2	End
Alber, George	Toledo	21	5' 10"	175	1	End
Bell, Robert	Columbus	21	5' 9"	170	2	Fullback
Bell, Robin	Erie, Pa.	20	6'	176	2	End
Blanchard, Bruce	Columbus	21	5' 10"	148	3	Quarterback
Bloser, Parker	Columbus	23	6'	175	3	End
Bonser, Thomas	Dayton	20	5' 7½"	138	1	End
Carlin, Oscar E.	Bryan	20	5' 11"	170	1	Guard
Carter, Dave	Springfield	18	6'	175	1	Guard
Chambers, H. E.	Sold. Summit, Utah	21	5' 8"	140	1	Quarterback
Clark, Myers	Gettysburg	22	5' 11½"	170	3	Halfback
Conklin, Robert	Chicago, Ill.	22	6' ½"	170	1	Halfback
Cox, Joe	Dayton	20	6' 2"	177	1	Tackle
Dunlap, John	Williamsport	21	5' 11½"	170	1	Guard
Eby, Byron	Chillicothe	21	6'	170	1	Halfback
Fenner, Harry	Dayton	20	5' 10"	149	1	End
Freeman, Eddie	Canal Winchester	22	5' 8½"	152	2	Quarterback
Glenn, C. L.	Columbus	19	6' 4"	195	1	End
Grim, Fred	Toledo	21	5' 10½"	163	2	Halfback
Griswold, Francis	Erie, Pa.	21	5' 10"	168	2	Halfback
Hamilton, Clarence	Louisville	21	5' 11"	150	2	Halfback
Hardway, L. E.	Columbus	20	6' 1½"	185	1	Tackle
Hess, Ed.	Columbus	21	6' ½"	178	3	Guard
Hunt, William	Toledo	21	5' 8½"	160	3	Halfback
Jeckell, Charles	Youngstown	19	6' 2½"	157	1	End
Karow, Marty	Cleveland	22	5' 10½"	170	3	Fullback
Klein, Alex	Lorain	24	5' 11"	175	3	Center
Kreglow, Julius	DeGraff	20	6' 2"	223	3	Guard
Kriss, Howard	East Cleveland	20	5' 7½"	164	1	Quarterback
Kruskamp, Harold	Wellston	20	6'	185	1	Halfback
Lacksen, Frank	Ashtabula	23	6' 4"	195	2	Tackle
McCarthy, Tim	Fremont	21	6' 2"	185	3	Tackle
McMillen, Harold	Bellpoint	20	6'	205	1	Tackle
Mackey, Fred	Galion	22	5' 10"	175	3	Tackle
Marek, Elmer	Cedar Rapids, Ia.	23	5' 10½"	165	2	Halfback
Meacham, H. C.	Atwater	22	6' 1½"	200	1	Tackle
Meyer, Ted	Cleveland	21	5' 11"	180	2	Guard
Moler, William	Columbus	22	5' 11"	193	2	Guard
Nesser, John	Columbus	21	6'	187	1	Guard
Ohsner, Clarence	Columbus	19	5' 10"	175	1	Halfback
Preston, Fred	Lancaster	19	5' 10"	184	1	Center
Raskowski, Leo	Cleveland	20	6' 3"	199	1	Tackle
Reed, William	Columbus	21	5' 9"	178	2	Guard
Roshon, Ray	Basil	22	5' 10½"	180	1	Guard
Rowan, Deb	Chillicothe	23	6' 1"	181	2	End
Schmidt, Walter	Cleveland	19	6' 2"	177	1	End
Shifflette, Don	Columbus	21	6'	167	3	Halfback
Slemmons, Robert	Columbus	21	5' 8"	153	3	Quarterback
Slough, Herb	Mansfield	20	5' 11½"	183	3	Center
Surina, Cyril	Cleveland	19	5' 10½"	167	1	End
Thone, Franklin	Columbus	20	5' 11"	175	1	Guard
Trombetti, Raymond	Steubenville	21	5' 10"	220	1	Guard
Ullery, Jack	Bradford	19	6' 1"	185	2	Center
Uridil, Leo	Cedar Rapids, Ia.	23	6'	180	2	Tackle
Wiswell, Owen	Columbus	23	6' 1"	181	2	Tackle
Woerlein, George	Groveport	22	5' 11"	166	3	Halfback
Yingling, Walter	Lima	18	5' 8"	154	1	Center

Front row, left to right:—Slough, Robin Bell, Shifflette, Rowan, Ullrey, Klein, Meyer, Ackerman, Kraglow. Second row, Eby, Clark, Hunt, Robert Bell, Blanchard, Karow (captain), Grim, Marek, Ed Hess, Mackey, Ohsner. Third row, Al Hess, McMillen, Cox, Preston, Nesser, Raskowski, Kruskamp, Alber, Carter, Trombetti, Woerlein, Griswold. Fourth row, Plesko, Moler, Freeman, Wiswell, Dunlap, Carlin, McClain, Oster, Hardway, Surina, Glenn. Fifth row, Cole, Peacocke, Jones, Meacham, Bonser, Fenner, Slemmons, Yingling, Schmidt, Prince. Sixth row, Uridil, Riggs, manager, Oberlander, coach; Wieche, coach; Seddon, coach; Yerges, coach; Willaman, coach; Dr. J. W. Wilce, head coach; Chambers, trainer, Kriss, Metz, manager.

The Columbia secondary defense stops Karow

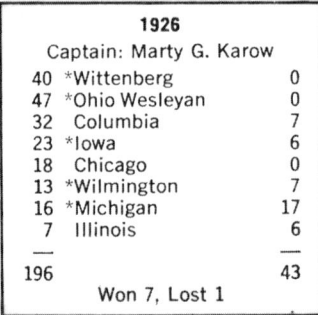

1926
Captain: Marty G. Karow

40	*Wittenberg	0
47	*Ohio Wesleyan	0
32	Columbia	7
23	*Iowa	6
18	Chicago	0
13	*Wilmington	7
16	*Michigan	17
7	Illinois	6
196		43

Won 7, Lost 1

OHIO STATE 32, COLUMBIA 7

THE first invasion of an Ohio State football team into the east gave Dr. John W. Wilce's already famous eleven the second triumph in as many seasons over Coach George Crowley's Columbia Lions, when on October 16, in the Polo Grounds, it trounced the eastern outfit by a 32-7 count.

A new star loomed on the Western Conference gridiron horizon when Freddy Grim, who replaced Byron Eby early in the first period, electrified the 30,000 fans who had assembled on a drizzling, rainy day, by scoring three touchdowns after runs of 65, 28 and five yards. Grim broke into the contest following the opening score of the tussle, a dropkick by Myers Clark from the 15 yard stripe.

The game was full of unusual occurrences on a football field. The first freak play of the game came when Truck Meyer recovered a fumbled punt by Madden, captain of the Lions, on Columbia's nine yard line. It was following Meyer's fine play that Clark made his score. Grim made the longest run of the game when he intercepted a Columbia pass and ran the 65 yards to the goal line for a touchdown. In the final few minutes of the game, Marty Karow duplicated Grim's feat and dashed 50 yards for six more points.

Clark, Karow and Kruskamp were uncanny with their fine blocking play which aided Grim materially on his long runs. The combination excited more comment on eastern sport pages than any demonstration of the year. On the line Ed Hess and Alex Klein vied for honors, which were later to give them mythical recognition, while Raskowski and Cox played great games at the tackle posts.

MICHIGAN
OHIO STATE
OHIO STADIUM
NOVEMBER 13·26
HOMECOMING
50¢

OHIO STATE 16, MICHIGAN 17

A THRILLING page in athletic history was written when Michigan, traditional rivals of Ohio State, invaded the sanctity of the Stadium on Saturday, November 13, and, playing a superhuman style of football, defeated the Buckeyes 17-16, following a comeback which was preceded by a sturdy vision of a big Ten championship for Dr. John W. Wilce and his team of eleven players.

The game opened with Ohio kicking to Michigan. Starting a drive which had made them a threat in every game of the season preceding, the Wilcemen forced the visitors back to their own twelve yard line, following an exchange of punts by Robin Bell and Gilbert, Ann Arbor halfback. The first break of the game came then, when Gilbert let slip the ball on a dash through tackle, and it was recovered by Meyer of Ohio. Smashes by Karow and Grim netted the ball six yards and from that point, Clark dropped back to the fifteen yard line and sent over 90,000 fans into a heart attack with a boot over the goal bar for three points.

Less than five minutes later, Ohio got its second score and seven points when Michigan lost the ball on its own fifty yard line and the powerful Buck drive started. Catching the Maize and Blue secondary offense off balance, Robin Bell hurled a pass nearly 50 yards, which Myers Clark caught on the dead run. He was downed on Michigan's five yard line, and leaping, scrambling, twisting and turning, he worked himself to the one foot line with two Michigan backs on him. The next play was a punch over the goal line by Marty Karow. Clark dropkicked for the extra point.

With the score 10-0 against them, the Wolverines came back and in the second quarter played football, alone which was worthy of a Big Ten championship. With Benny Friedman on the throwing end of an aerial attack, which made the Ohio secondary defense look almost as helpless as London during a German Zeppelin raid, the Michiganders advanced the ball to Ohio's forty yard line. Two passes to Benny Oosterbaan, end, placed the ball across the line for Michigan's first touchdown. Friedman place kicked for the added point and three minutes later, with ten seconds to go, he place kicked the ball, which was taken from Ohio on its 45 yard line, right between the two goal posts. The gun cracked and the half had ended with Michigan in the middle of one of the greatest comebacks ever seen. The score was 10-10.

Ten seconds before the third period had ended, Elmer Marek got the worst break of the game, when a punt from Gilbert took a bad bound as he was about to pick it up, and it dropped into Baer's arms. The ball was Ann Arbor's at the start of the fourth period on Ohio's six yard line. The third play which followed was a bullet pass from Friedman over the line to Hoffman for Michigan's six points. Friedman kicked the added point.

With the score 17-10, Byron Eby entered the game. The sophomore flash advanced the ball from midfield to the 12 yard line with daring runs and from that point scampered around Flora's end for Ohio's touchdown. Myers Clark missed the kick and, two minutes later, a sharp bark from the timer's pistol piled 90,000 sad fans out of the gray concrete stands.

Eby eludes the Michigan tacklers on a twisting jaunt through right tackle.

Who's Who on Ohio State's 1927 Squad

Name	Home	Age	Height	Weight	Year	Position
Ackerman, Cornelius	Wauseon	20	5' 10¼"	170	3	End
Alber, George	Toledo	22	5' 10"	177	2	End
Bell, Robert	Columbus	22	5' 9"	173	3	Fullback
Bell, Robin	Erie, Pa.	21	6'	182	3	End
Brozic, Andrew	Midland, Pa.	23	5' 7½"	197	1	Tackle
Buechsenschuss, Albert	Toledo	21	5' 11"	176	1	Tackle
Bruck, John	Columbus	22	6'	224	1	Guard
Barklow, Carson	Portsmouth	21	5' 10"	177	1	Guard
Carlin, Oscar E.	Bryan	20	5' 10½"	167	2	Guard
Chambers, H. E.	Summit, Utah	22	5' 8"	135	2	Quarterback
Cox, Joe	Dayton	21	6' 2"	177	2	Tackle
Cory, Lincoln	Coon Rapids, Ia.	22	5' 10"	176	1	Fullback
Coffee, Chas. Byron	Salem	18	5' 10½"	159	1	Halfback
Dunn, D. L.	Curtice	19	5' 5"	150	1	Fullback
Eby, Byron	Chillicothe	22	6'	179	2	Halfback
Fouch, George	Columbus	18	5' 7¾"	160	1	Quarterback
Fry, Edgar Allen	Columbus	20	5' 7"	172	1	Guard
Grim, Fred	Toledo	22	5' 11"	163	3	Halfback
Glasser, Chester	Youngstown	21	6' 1"	185	3	Tackle
Griswold, Francis	Erie, Pa.	22	5' 10"	167	3	Halfback
Hieronymus, Theo.	Columbus	21	6' 2"	190	2	Fullback
Huston, Arthur	Findlay	21	5' 10½"	160	1	Halfback
Heppberger, C. E.	Akron	20	5' 10"	162	1	Quarterback
Harris, George	Cleveland	21	5' 10"	148	1	Halfback
Hess, Albert	Cincinnati	20	5' 11"	162	1	Halfback
Henninger, Willard	Cleveland	21	5' 10½"	158	1	End
Idle, Ralph	Wapakoneta	21	5' 9"	160	1	End
Kriss, Howard	East Cleveland	20	5' 7¾"	166	2	Quarterback
Marek, Elmer	Cedar Rapids, Ia.	24	5' 7½"	167	3	Halfback
Meyer, Theodore	Cleveland	22	5' 11½"	182	3	Guard
Moler, William	Columbus	23	5' 11¾"	195	3	Guard
Mitchel, Joe	Van Wert	19	6'	198	1	Guard
McClure, Donald	Toledo	20	5' 10"	165	1	Halfback
Moore, James H.	Struthers	20	6'	160	1	
Nesser, John P.	Columbus	22	6'	180	2	Tackle
Ohsner, Clarence	Columbus	20	5' 10½"	171	2	Halfback
Penrod, James L.	Lewisburg	23	5' 10¾"	205	2	Tackle
Popp, Milton F.	Fort Wayne	20	5' 11"	179	2	Tackle
Raskowski, Leo	Cleveland	21	6' 2"	212	2	Tackle
Rowan, Deb	Chillicothe	23	6' 1¾"	181	3	End
Redman, F. A.	Chillicothe	23	5' 10½"	160	1	Quarterback
Ray, Ernest	Akron	24	5' 10"	222	1	Guard
Schmidt, Walter	Cleveland	20	6' 2"	180	2	End
Surina, Cyril	Cleveland	20	5' 10½"	165	2	End
Schear, Herbert	Dayton	19	5' 8"	174	1	Center
Sandman, Russell	Cincinnati	20	6' ½"	170	1	
Tarr, Robert	Orchard Island, Russell Pt.	19	5' 11"	168	1	Tackle
Uridel, Leo	Cedar Rapids, Ia.	24	6' 1"	173	3	Tackle
Ullery, Jack	Bradford	20	6' 1½"	187	3	Center
Walker, Gordon	Columbus	19	6'	168	2	Center
Weaver, Wm.	Cleveland	20	6' ½"	160	2	Center
Weprin, Abram	Dayton	20	6' ¼"	185	1	Tackle
Wiswell, Owen	Columbus	24	6' 2"	181	2	Guard
Yingling (Bud) Walter	Lima	19	5' 8"	151	2	Center
Young, William	Kenton	25	5' 10"	189	2	Guard

1927
Captain: Theodore R. Meyer

31	*Wittenberg	0
13	Iowa	6
13	*Northwestern	19
0	Michigan	21
13	*Chicago	7
0	Princeton	20
61	*Denison	6
0	*Illinois	13
131		92

Won 4, Lost 4

OHIO-MICHIGAN

OHIO hoped to be aided by the "Stadium jinx" that was present when Ohio stadium was opened by Michigan in 1922. But the bowl of our traditional enemy is not spotted by records of defeat in the opening game.

The new Michigan bowl is circular, with but one deck. The playing field is small, being but 135 yards long. It is not suited for track events and so will be used only for football.

It was Michigan's sixth consecutive victory in as many years over Ohio. The game was the second Big Ten loss in the season for Ohio and was bitter medicine for the team and the thousands of Ohio followers, who prefer not to remember the 21 to 0 score.

Ooosterbaan and Gilbert of Michigan made three passes which resulted in touchdowns. The Ohio line seemed stronger than in the Northwestern game, but the Michigan play could not be broken up.

Raskowski stood out on the Ohio line as did Uridil and Young. The Ohio football crowd experienced much anxiety because of the criticism of over-zealous alumni of this game, but all finally sat back to wait for another year.

OHIO-CHICAGO

STILL biting under the Michigan defeat of the week before, Ohio drug the University of Chicago from first place in the Big Ten race by a 13 to 7 win at Ohio Stadium, October 29.

The game was full of thrills, and the team looked better in action than at any time during the season. For this game Rowan was changed from his old position of end to fullback, where he played the rest of the season.

The Buckeyes held the lead until the second half, when the Maroons, aided by a fumble in Ohio territory and short punting, punctured the line for a touchdown. Just before this score Ohio made a valiant stand on its six-inch line, holding for downs. A short punt, two running plays, and the ball was again in position to push over, but the line held for two more plays. A pass scored, finally, after the fans got weak from the suspense. These few minutes were some of the most interesting of the season.

Kriss, by scoring on a 50-yard pass from Robin Bell, provided thrills in the last stages of the game that gave Ohio its second victory of the season.

Who's Who for Ohio

Name	Address	Age	Height	Weight	Year	Position
Alber, George	Toledo	23	5' 11"	177	3	End
Barratt, F. W.	Lansing, Mich.	22	6' 1½"	236	1	Center
Beck, P. E.	Columbus	22	5' 10"	180	1	Center
Buechsenschuss, A.	Toledo	22	5' 11"	174	2	Tackle
Carlin, Oscar	Bryan	21	5' 10½"	166	3	Guard
Cahen, Herman	Cleveland Heights	24	5' 10"	158	1	Halfback
Carter, David W.	Springfield	20	6' 1"	172	2	Tackle
Cory, Lincoln	Coon Rapids, Ia.	22	5' 10"	171	2	Fullback
Coffee, Chas.	Salem	19	5' 10½"	161	2	Halfback
Cox, Joe	Dayton	22	6' 2"	184	3	Tackle
Dill, M. R.	Lakewood	22	6' 1"	171	1	End
Eby, Byron	Chillicothe	23	6'	175	3	Halfback
Evans, Robert	Columbus	19	6'	170	1	End
Ferral, Walter	Columbiana	22	6'	181	2	Tackle
Fesler, W.	Youngstown	20	5' 11½"	173	1	End
Fisher, Max M.	Salem	20	6' 1"	168	2	Center
Fivaz, Robert	Sunbury	20	5' 10"	157	1	Halfback
Fouch, George	Columbus	19	5' 10"	159	2	Quarterback
Freppel, F.	Napoleon	20	5' 7"	145	1	Quarterback
George, Samuel	Youngstown	26	5' 10"	168	2	Fullback
Gerhard, Maurice	Hamilton	22	5' 11½"	181	1	Fullback
Glasser, Chester	Youngstown	22	6' 1½"	186	2	Tackle
Griffith, Wm.	Cleveland	18	5' 11½"	218	1	Tackle
Hess, Albert	Cincinnati	21	5' 11"	162	2	Halfback
Hieronymous, Theo.	Columbus	22	6' 3"	200	3	Tackle
Holman, Allen	Fairfield, Ia.	23	5' 10½"	171	1	Quarterback
Horn, R.	Columbus	19	6'	175	1	Halfback
Hudson, A. M.	Columbus	20	6' 1"	172	1	End
Humberstone, H. J.	Columbus	18	6' 1"	177	1	Guard
Huston, Arthur	Findlay	22	5' 10½"	161	2	Halfback
Idle, Ralph	Wapakoneta	22	5' 10½"	166	2	End
Kriss, Howard	Cleveland	21	5' 8"	168	3	Halfback
Kruskamp, Harold	Wellston	22	6'	189	2	Fullback
Larkins, R.	East Liverpool	19	6'	180	1	Tackle
Lemon, George D.	Toledo	21	6' 2"	189	2	Guard
McConnell, A. L.	Massillon	21	6' 1½"	174	1	Halfback
McClure, Donald	Toledo	21	5' 10½"	167	2	Fullback
Neidert, John	Akron	21	5' 9"	158	2	Center
Nesser, John	Columbus	23	6'	191	3	Tackle
Nesser, Wm.	Columbus	19	5' 7"	158	1	Halfback
Neubreckt, K.	Toledo	22	5' 10½"	170	1	Halfback
Nichlaus, F. E.	Columbus	17	6' 2½"	175	1	Tackle
North, D. W.	Groveport	20	6'	171	1	Guard
O'Shaughnessy, J. J.	Columbus	19	6' 1"	182	2	End
Oster, Harvey	Cleveland	21	6'	190	1	Tackle
Popp, Milton	Fort Wayne, Ind.	21	5' 11"	182	3	Tackle
Ray, Ernest	Akron	25	5' 10"	225	2	Guard
Raskowski, Leo	Cleveland	22	6' 3"	208	3	Tackle
Reboulet, Laverne	Dayton	21	5' 10½"	173	1	Tackle
Reese, D.	Findlay	23	6'	177	1	Tackle
Rose, Milton	Cleveland	21	5' 10½"	170	3	Tackle
Sack, Irving A.	Toledo	21	5' 7"	164	1	Quarterback
Sattler, C. L.	Findlay	19	5' 9½"	188	1	Guard
Schear, Herbert	Dayton	20	5' 8"	170	2	Center
Selby, Sam	Middletown	20	5' 11"	174	1	Guard
Sundra, John	Cleveland	22	5' 11"	175	3	End
Surina, Cyril	Cleveland	21	5' 10¾"	175	3	End
Taylor, R. E.	Sandusky	19	5' 10½"	157	1	Fullback
Tuttle, George	Columbus	22	5' 10"		1	Halfback
Ujhelyi, Joe	Lorain	21	5' 11"	191	3	Guard
Van Heyde, Geo.	Columbus	21	6' 3"	164	1	End
Walker, Gordon	Columbus	20		170	3	Center
Walkup, Mos. K.	Columbus	19	5' 10½"	156	2	Halfback
Weprin, Abram	Dayton	21	6' 1"	196	2	Tackle
Wiragos, Lewis	Cleveland	23	5' 10½"	175	1	Fullback
Wilson, Franklin	Dayton	20	5' 8"	153	2	Quarterback
Wyer, P. H.	Orrville	20	5' 10½"	169	1	Quarterback
Yingling, Walter	Lima	20	5' 8"	153	3	Center
Young, Wm.	Kenton	26	5' 10½"	190	3	Guard

1928
Captain Leo Raskowski

41	*Wittenberg	0
10	Northwestern	0
19	*Michigan	7
13	Indiana	0
6	*Princeton	6
7	*Iowa	14
39	*Muskingum	0
0	Illinois	8
135		35

Won 5, Lost 2, Tied 1

FOOTBALL SQUAD OHIO STATE UNIVERSITY 1928

Left to right:

Front row: Wyer, Wiragos, Sack, Taylor, McClure, Cory, W. Nesser and Hall.

Second row: Freppel, Hess, Horn, McConnell, Fouch, Kruskamp, Eby, Holman, Huston, Coffee.

Third row: S. S. Willaman, Coach; John Tayler, Coach; Popp, Schear, Dill, Fesler, Fontaine, Alber, Surina, Idle, O'Shaughnessy, Glasser, Charles Seddon, Coach.

Fourth row: Robert Watts, Coach; Gamble, Mgr.; Evans, Oster, Reboulet, Griffith, Young, Ujhelyi, Barratt, Raskowski, Cox, Hieronymous, Beck, Zinke, Mgr.; Howard Yerges, Coach.

Fifth row: Dr. Walter Duffee, Team Physician; Roemer, Mgr.; Jim Oberlander, Coach; Tuttle, Reese, Selby, Larkins, Yingling, Carlin, J. Nesser, Ray, Bueschenschuss, Carter, Mike Chambers, Trainer; Tony Aquila, caretaker; Dr. John W. Wilce, Director of Football.

Sixth row: Nichol, Sattler, Nicklaus, Gerhard, Walkup, Fivaz, Rose, Neidert, Ahrens, Van Heyde.

Back row: Hudson, Lemon, Fisher, Weprin, Robt. Brunson, Mgr.; Cahen, Humberstone, Sundra and North.

OHIO STATE

Yea Team! Yea Team! Yea Team!
Fight! Fight! Fight!

Ohio, Rah; Ohio Rah;
Rah, Rah, Ohio.

O—, Ohio; O—, Ohio;
Rah, Rah, Rah, Rah, Ohio.

LOCOMOTIVE

S-s-s-s (3 times)
Rah, Rah, Rah, Rah;
Ohio State, Ohio State.
 (Repeat three times, very slowly,
  faster, very fast, all cheer at end.)

THE SKYROCKET

A prolonged rising whistle—
Boom—, Hurrah, Ohio.

E————ee, Coma—Lioh,
Gee————ee———Wah!
Ohio.

Eee—————ee, Yah.
Eee—————ee, Yah.
Fight!—Fight!—Fight!—Fight—FIGHT!
Ohio! Ohio! Ohio!
O O O-HI-O (Repeat indefinitely)

THE DIVIDED OHIO

O—O—O—O
H—H—H—H
I—I—I—I
O—O—O—O
OHIO

O—Ohio, Ohio,
The hills send back the cry,
We're here to do or die
For Ohio, Ohio.
We'll win the game or know the reason why!
And when we've won the game 'tell you what we'll do.
We'll yell for old Ohio
'Till we wobble in our shoes.
 (Repeat first 5 lines)

OHIO DRAG

O————HIO
O————HIO
O—H—I—O
O————HIO
A—H-H-H-H (prolonged)
(Everyone rise)
BEAT MICHIGAN

THE BUCKEYE BATTLE CRY

Words and Music by
Frank Crumit

In old Ohio there's a team,
That's known throughout the land;
Eleven warriors, brave and bold,
Whose fame will ever stand,
And when the ball goes over,
Our cheers will reach the sky,
Ohio Field will hear again
The Buckeye Battle Cry.

Drive! Drive on down the field,
Men of the Scarlet and Gray;
Don't let them thru that line,
We have to win this game today,
Come on, Ohio! Smash thru to victory,
We cheer you as we go;
Our honor defend
So we'll fight to the end
For Ohio

CARMEN OHIO

Words and Music by Fred Cornell, ex-'06
(Hats off, standing)

O, come, let's sing Ohio's praise
And songs to Alma Mater raise;
While our hearts rebounding thrill
With joy that death alone can still.
Summer's heat or winter's cold,
The seasons pass, the years will roll;
Time and change will truly show
How firm thy friendship—Ohio.

These jolly days of priceless worth
By far the gladdest days on earth,
Soon will pass and we not know
How dearly we love Ohio.
We should strive to keep thy name
Of fair repute and spotless fame;
So in college halls we'll grow
And love thee better—Ohio.
    Alumni Chorus
Tho' age may dim our mem'ry's store,
We'll think of happy days of yore,
True to friend and frank to foe,
As sturdy sons of O-hi-o.
If on seas of care we roll,
'Neath blackened sky, o'er barren shoal,
Thots of thee bid darkness go,
Dear Alma Mater—O-hi-o.
    (All in on last Ohio)

ACROSS THE FIELD

Words and Music by
W. A. Dougherty, Jr., '17

Fight that team across the field,
Show them Ohio's here
Set the earth reverberating with a mighty cheer
Hit them hard and see how they fall;
Never let that team get the ball.
Hail! Hail! the gang's all here,
So let's beat that Michigan now.
Oh, Ohio! Oh, Ohio! Wa-hoo! Wa-hoo! for Ohio.

[1928]

Wilce Will Leave Ohio State As Football Coach Next Year

COLUMBUS, Ohio, June 2 (P).—Dr. John W. Wilce, coach of Ohio State University's football teams for the last fourteen years, tendered his resignation today, effective June, 1929, to take up the practice of medicine and teaching. The University Athletic Board accepted the resignation with "sincere regret" and indicated that no successor would be named until the close of the 1928 season. In 105 games played since he took charge, his elevens won sixty-nine games, lost twenty-eight and were tied eight times. He is a graduate of the University of Wisconsin.

Buckeyes Triumph Over Michigan, 19-7 After Six Lean Years

Columbus, Ohio, Oct. 20.—(AP.)—Buckeye boosters waited a long time to give the mighty cheer, "Ohio's", the Buckeyes' famous song, but there was plenty of excuse for it today.

The Buckeyes' 19 to 7 defeat of Michigan unloosed the pent up yelling of six years and there was no Michigan man in the 72,723 spectators willing to cry "silence."

It was all Ohio. The Wolverines led for 14 minutes by a point, but Byron Eby had not been heard from then, and after the backfield ace put his team out in front, there was no heading the Ohio outfit. Eby gained more ground than any player on the field but he had more opportunity, in 17 chances he carried the ball 74 yards.

The visitors made only one first down, Captain Rich contributing the major part of this brief offensive, while Ohio ran up 13, nine by rushing and four through the medium of forward passes.

It was a great day for Dr. J. W. Wilce and his pupils. In 24 games since the intense rivalry started between the two universities in 1897, Ohio State has been returned the winner only three times.

Ohio Buckeyes Rally

Rushing And Passing Spurt Saves Conference Eleven

Wilce Team Drives Through Air and Along Ground From Midfield to Score Tieing Touchdown—Bengals Superior in First Half

Columbus, Ohio, Nov. 3.—(AP.)—Two other teams will have to decide the question of football supremacy between the East and West. Princeton and Ohio State could not do it today when their thrilling intersectional battle ended in a dead heat six to six.

After a first half made up of threats and promises but no results, the Tigers from the East jumped into a 6 to 0 lead at the close of the third period, only to stand by and see the western Buckeyes run and pass themselves into a deadlock in the final quarter.

Bennett Misses Goal.

It was not a good day for kicking goals to add points after touchdowns. Trix Bennett missed his shot that would have given his team seven points instead of six, and later, with the decision resting on his toe, the gigantic Fred Barratt failed to get his placement between the posts.

Princeton outplayed and outthought the Buckeyes in the first half, but had not decided advantage in the second half in spite of the Tiger score.

Princeton had an edge in the rushing game. Ohio realized a greater profit in number of completed passes although the invaders gained more ground from their overhead attack.

In the third period Kriss fumbled and Miles picked the ball off the ground. With Wittmer bearing the brunt of the burden, assisted by good interference, the Tigers marched to the six-yard line from where Wittmer went the rest of the way to break the scoring ice.

Ohio State went from midfield to tie the score in the next period. Eby caught a kick on the 50 yard line and ran to Princeton's 43 yard line. Holman passed to Alber for a gain of 13 yards and then Fessler caught a toss from Holman for 16 more. Eby slipped outside Princeton's right end and behind good interference, went over for the touchdown that knotted the count.

The paid admissions were 72,496 but many more than this number saw the game. Summary:

Ohio		Princeton
Surina	le	Lawler
Raskowski	lt	Whyte
Selby	lg	Moore
Barratt	c	Howe
Young	rg	Mestres
Larkins	rt	Berflid
Fesler	re	Stinson
Holman	qb	Norman
Eby	lh	Wittmer
Kriss	rh	Lowry
Cory	fb	Miles

Princeton ....0 0 6 0—6
Ohio State ....0 0 0 6—6

Princeton scoring, Touchdown, Wittmer; Ohio State scoring, touchdown, Eby.

Officials—Walter Eckersall, Chicago, referee; Fred D. Murphy, Brown, umpire; W. D. Knight, Dartmouth, field judge; E. W. Carson, Penn State, head linesman.

McLain, Indian Fullback, Stars In Iowa Victory, 14-7

Hawkeyes Practically Clinch Big Ten Championship by Conquering Ohio State Before 47,000—Holman Scores For Buckeyes

Ohio Stadium, Columbus, O., Nov. 10.—(AP.)—Iowa defeated Ohio State 14 to 7 in the last minute of their game played before 47,000 in the Ohio State horseshoe this afternoon.

The Hawkeyes, undefeated in the Western Conference race, ruined whatever chances Ohio State had by chalking up a dramatic victory. Mayes McLain, the giant Indian fullback, scored both of Iowa's touchdowns. He plunged over in the second period then came back for the winning touchdown in the fourth.

Ohio State		Iowa
Alber	le	Moore
Raskowski	lt	Musgrave
Selby	lg	Westra
Barratt	c	Brown (c)
Young	rg	Roberts
Larkins	rt	Jessen
Fesler	re	Reedquist
Holman	qb	Armil
Eby	lh	Glasgow
Kriss	rh	Farroh
Cory	fb	McLain

Iowa ....0 7 0 7—14
Ohio State ....0 0 7 0— 7

Ohio State scoring: Touchdown, Holman. Point after touchdown, Barratt, (placement). Iowa's scoring, touchdowns, McLain 2. Points after touchdown, Nelson 2, (substitute for Glasgow), by dropkicks.

Officials, James Masker, Northwestern, referee; A. H. Haines, Yale, umpire; Fred Young, Illinois Wesleyan; field judge; Lion Gardiner, Illinois, head linesman.

[1929]

Name	Home Town	Age	Year	Position	Weight	Height
Atkinson, Robert M.	Trenton, N. J.	26	3	Guard	176	6'
Baker, Morgan W.	Youngstown	24	3	Quarter	171	5'10"
Barratt, Fred W.	Lansing, Mich.	23	4	Center	239	6' 2"
Bell, William	Akron	20	2	Tackle	177	6' 1"
Benis, Joseph	Cleveland	19	2	Quarter	164	5'10"
Bogert, Paul J.	Sandusky	20	2	End	160	6'
Buechsenschuss, Albert	Toledo	23	3	Tackle	170	5'11½"
Campbell, Charles A.	Coshocton	19	2	Guard	165	5' 9"
Cancik, Charles	Cleveland	23	2	Halfback	160	5'10"
Carlin, Oscar	Bryan	22	4	Guard	166	5'10½"
Carter, David	Springfield	21	3	Center	175	6' 1"
Clymer, Roy B.	Findlay	24	4	Halfback	174	6'
Cochran, E. L.	Mt. Vernon	19	2	Center	184	6'
Combs, Alton	Middletown	19	2	Guard	175	6'
Corcoran, Joseph T.	Holyoke, Mass.	19	2	Tackle	195	6' 3"
Dick, Earl H.	Cleveland	19	2	End	179	5'10½"
Dill, M. Reese	Lakewood	23	3	End	175	6' 1½"
Doyle, Burton L.	Mishawaka, Ind.	21	2	Halfback	170	6' 1"
Dunn, Donald L.	Curtice	21	4	Halfback	162	5' 5"
Farrier, Marvin E.	Dayton	21	2	End	180	6' 1½"
Fesler, Wesley E.	Youngstown	21	3	End	183	5'11½"
Fisher, Max	Cleveland	21	3	Center	175	6' 1½"
Fivaz, Robert	Sunbury	21	3	Halfback	165	5'10"
Fontaine, Lawton J.	Akron	24	3	End	184	6'
Fouch, George	Columbus	20	4	Quarter	170	5'10"
Glasser, Chester	Youngstown	24	4	Tackle	192	6' 2"
Grady, Robert	Columbus	22	2	Halfback	160	5'10"
Griffith, William A.	E. Cleveland	19	3	Guard	212	6'
Hall, John E.	Mansfield	20	2	Center	180	6' 1"
Haubrich, Robert C.	Columbus	19	2	Tackle	190	6'
Heppberger, C. E.	Atwater	22	3	Quarter	162	5'11"
Hess, Albert F. Jr.	Cincinnati	22	4	Halfback	166	5'11"
Hinchman, William J.	Columbus	22	4	Quarter	166	6'
Hindulak, John A.	Cleveland	18	2	Guard	182	5'11½"
Holan, J. R.	Cleveland	22	2	Guard	174	5' 8"
Holcomb, Stuart K.	Erie, Pa.	19	2	Fullback	165	5'10½"
Holman, Allen	Fairfield, Iowa	23	4	Halfback	177	5'10½"
Horn, Robert L.	Columbus	20	3	Halfback	181	6'
Hudson, Addison M.	Columbus	21	2	End	180	6' 2"
Humberstone, H. J.	Columbus	19	3	Guard	180	6' 1"
Huston, Arthur	Findlay	23	4	Halfback	163	5'10"
Kabealo, Charles L.	Youngstown	21	2	Guard	176	5'10½"
Kile, Eugene M.	Marysville	21	2	Guard	185	5'10"
Lake, Albert E.	Cleveland	19	3	End	150	5'9"
Lanzendorfer, George A.	Cleveland	19	3	Center	201	5'10"
Larkins, Richard C.	E. Liverpool	21	3	Tackle	184	6'
Larson, Harry E.	Bridgeport, Ct.	23	2	Guard	206	5' 9½"
Lemon, George H.	Toledo	22	4	Tackle	197	6' 2"
McClure, Donald L.	Toledo	22	4	Fullback	172	5'11"
McConnell, Arden L.	Massillon	22	3	Halfback	170	6' 1½"
Makres, George	Youngstown	23	4	Tackle	185	5'10½"
Marsh, George C.	Cleveland	24	2	Tackle	208	6' 1"
Modica, I. R.	Cleveland	18	2	Halfback	140	5'10"
Nesser, William H.	Reynoldsburg	21	3	Halfback	163	5' 7"
Newart,	Lower Salem	21	3	Tackle	155	5'8"
Nicklaus, Frank E.	Columbus	19	3	Tackle	190	6' 2½"
O'Shaughnessy, Joseph J.	Columbus	20	4	End	184	6' 1"
Peterson, L. B. Jr.	Steubenville	20	2	End	171	6'
Plesko, Stanley	Norwalk	25	4	Guard	187	5' 8½"
Prachar, Frank	Cleveland	19	2	Halfback	180	6'
Rabenstein, Howard P.	Lockland	20	2	End	160	5'11"
Reboulet, Laverne	Dayton	22	3	Guard	170	5'11"
Rentschler, Carl G.	Cleveland	20	2	Tackle	182	6'
Roth, Michael	Bridgeport, Ct.	20	2	Halfback	155	5'9"
Sattler, Charles L.	Mansfield	20	3	Guard	195	5' 9½"
Selby, Sam	W. Middletown	21	3	Guard	180	5'11"
Slaughter, David R.	Louisville, Ky.	20	2	Guard	170	6'
Stout, C. E.	Dayton	19	2	Center	183	5'11½"
Taylor, Russell E.	Sandusky	20	3	Fullback	168	5'10½"
Thompson, Carl R.	Columbus	19	2	Guard	184	5'10"
Ujhelyi, Joseph	Lorain	23	4	Fullback	198	5'10"
Von Derau, John	Dayton	20	2	Center	168	5' 9"
Walkup, Joseph K.	Columbus	20	3	Halfback	164	5'11"
Weaver, J. Edward	Lima	18	2	End	185	6' 3"
White, Robert	Columbus	19	2	Guard	237	6' 1"
Worstell, Hillis	Bloomdale	19	2	Tackle	178	6' 2½"
Wyer, Paul H.	Orrville	21	3	Halfback	175	5'10½"
Zeckhauser, Joseph M.	Columbus	19	2	Tackle	206	5'11"

NOTE: The figure in the year column denotes year in school and not number of years on squad.

1929

Coach: Sam S. Willaman
Captain: Alan M. Holman

19	*Wittenberg	0
7	*Iowa	6
7	Michigan	0
0	*Indiana	0
2	Pittsburgh	18
6	*Northwestern	18
54	*Kenyon	0
0	*Illinois	27
95		69

Won 4, Lost 3, Tied 1

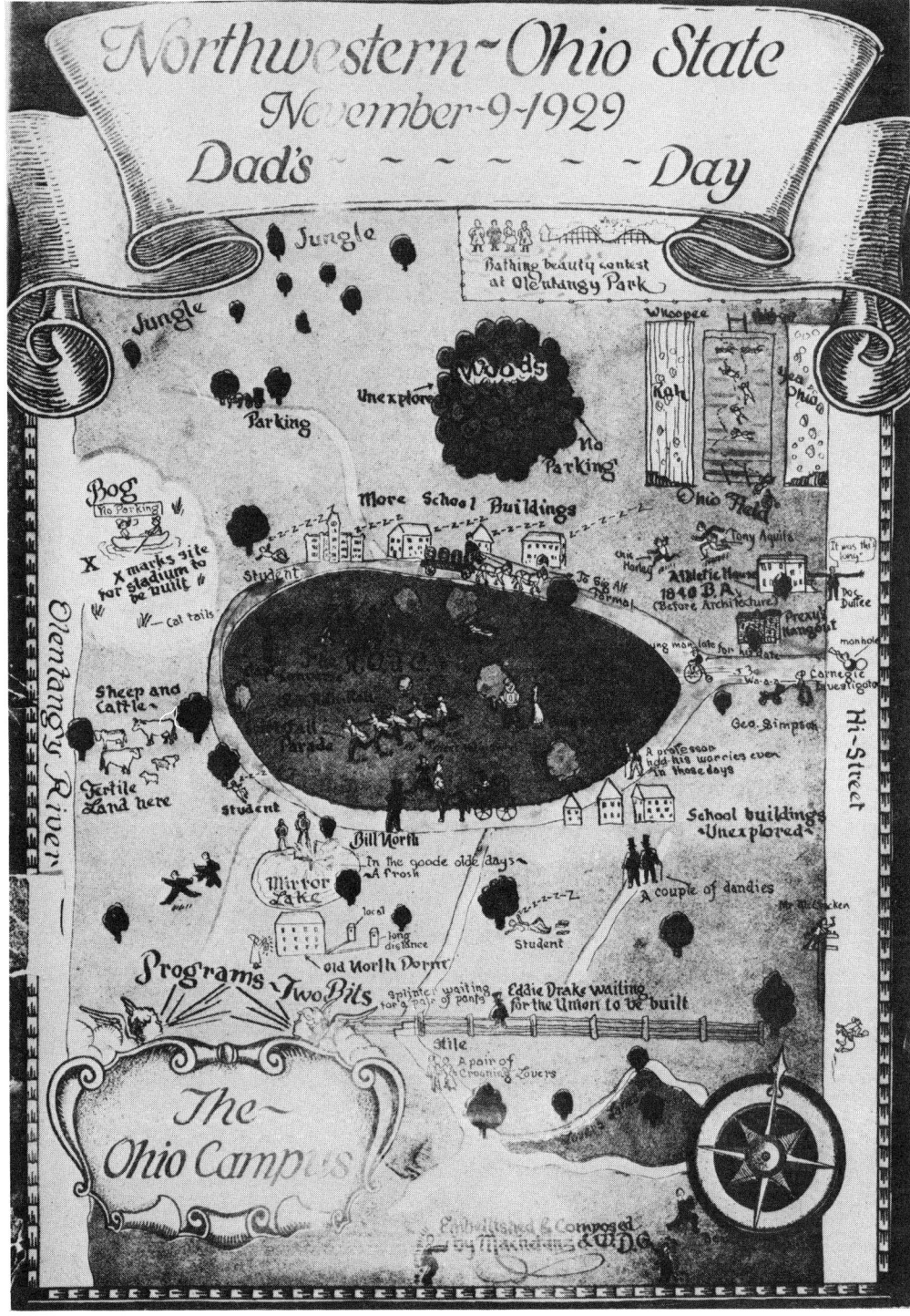

Last summer Sam Willaman rather inauspiciously became the Ohio State Football Coach. Some were enthusiastic, some were dubious, and others were quite pessimistic about Ohio's football future.

Now that the first season is history we can resume and judge.

Sam is giving everything that he has for the football success of our university and in his first attempt he went to Michigan and returned with a scalp. That in itself is indicative enough that Sam is getting what Ohio Staters demand.

This next year we hope that Willaman will repeat and we know that he will do all in his power to lengthen the victory string.

OHIO 7
MICHIGAN 0

Led by the driving play of Wes Fesler, the Buckeyes duplicated their performance of 1929 by downing their Wolverine rivals to the tune of 7 to 0. "Fes" was on the end of the touchdown pass and many times cut through to spill the Michigan backs for a loss.

In the first half, the Scarlet and Gray predominated in all departments of the game and made its 15,000 followers feel confident of a victory. The story was reversed in the final frame and the Michigan drive repeatedly threatened the Ohio goal. The Wolverine attack became null and void, however, when met by the sturdy and impregnable band of Ohio linemen.

The opening minutes of play found the fast moving offense of the Willaman lads carrying the ball to the 10 yard marker before it was checked by the Michigan linemen.

The second quarter was but a minute and a half old, when Fesler hooked a pass from Hoffman and slipped over the line for the games only touchdown. Graf Barratt added the extra point with his big but trusty toe.

Willie Heston, son of Michigan's "only one", started out the second half, to set the world on fire, but, fortunately, because of a few Scarlet boys, had to go home for more matches. He did, however, worry the Ohioans for some thirty minutes and displayed some shifty running tactics. Truskowski, pulled from the line to serve in the backfield, although playing a good game, was not quite acclimated to his new role.

OHIO 2
PITTSBURGH 18

In the first battle ever waged between Ohio and the highly touted Panthers, the latter, led by Toby Uansa, kept their slate clean by a 16 point margin. The gridiron was a mass of mud and water but Uansa defied the elements and remained unstopable throughout the afternoon. Parkinson, Pitt's powerful fullback, was also a big factor in Ohio's defeat. The game was still in its youth when Uansa slipped through the Ohio line and, cutting to the sideline, raced 65 yards for a touchdown. A second touchdown came as the result of a twenty yard pass from Rooney to Uansa, who ran the additional 17 yards across the line.

Rooney added three more points in the second period by a field goal from the 16 yard line. Each team scored a safety, which brought the total to 18-2.

The duel waged between the two Youngstown All-Americans, Fesler and Donchess, was declared a draw according to the opinions of most sport scribes who covered the game.

McConnell outpunted the Pitt efforts until Rooney was ushered in, who displayed booting par excellence.

The Pitt machine displayed a powerful offense and a stubborn defense, the two coupling together to form a team capable of standing up against the strongest in the country. The Ohioans put up a spirited fight but the efforts of Fesler, Nesser, Dill, Horn and Holcomb were to little avail.

OHIO 6
NORTHWESTERN 18

The previous scoreless backfield of Ohio remained as such after the trouncing handed them by the Wildcats, with Fesler garnering the lone touchdown. From an Ohio standpoint the game seems to possess only two important items: the evercrushing, always scoring offense of Northwestern and the way our Wesley acquired those lonely six points. In the second period the touchdown-bound Wildcats were but a yard from the Ohio goal when the century dash took place. Fesler, picking up a fourth down fumble, was off, it seemed, before the men in Purple (and Sarlet too) realized what had happened. A single man took up the chase, but the fleet legs of Fesler carried him over the line with a substantial lead.

Bob Grady, playing his first Big Ten game, was the mainspring in the Buckeye offense, displaying a host of fight and drive. Stew Holcomb, Reese Dill, and Sam Selby played good football but seemed below the caliber of Northwestern's stellar play.

With Bergherm, Moore, and Burnstein at the helm of their attack, the Purple displayed a precise, well coached team, which played smoothly and cleanly. The Hanley coached crew turned in seventeen first downs to Ohio's five. The visitors used a wing back formation and from it ran many spinner plays. Bergherm accounted for two touchdowns, while Moore made the other tally.

The game certainly ran true to the old saying—the better team won.

THE OHIO STATE ROSTER

Name	Home Town	Age	Year	Position	Weight	Height
Adkins, David	Columbus	20	So.	Guard	238	6' 1"
Allen, Robert	Columbus	20	So.	Guard	168	5'10"
Bauer, Robert	Upper Sandusky	22	So.	Full	184	6'
Baumgarten, Eugene	Louisville, Ky.	20	So.	Tackle	204	6' 4"
Bell, William M.	Akron	21	Jr.	Tackle	189	6' 1"
Benis, Joseph V.	Cleveland	20	Jr.	Quarter	163	5'10"
Bough, Clifford A.	E. Liverpool	22	Jr.	Tackle	190	6' 3"
Bryant, John C.	Cincinnati	21	So.	Full	175	5'11"
Campbell, Charles D.	Washington C. H.	19	So.	Guard	195	5'11"
Carroll, William	Columbus	20	So.	Half	171	5'10"
Chizek, David	Cleveland	19	So.	Quarter	161	5' 9"
Cochran, Kenneth	Mt. Vernon	20	So.	Center	190	5' 7"
Craig, G. Ralph	Columbus	21	So.	Half	165	5' 7"
Cremer, Martin	Parkersburg, W. Va.	19	So.	End	176	6'½"
DeMelker, Bert	Geneva	20	So.	Full	183	5'10"
Dick, Earl	Cleveland	20	Jr.	End	184	5'10"
Diehl, William	Columbus	20	So.	Guard	189	5'11"
Ehrensberger, Carl	Columbus	19	So.	Center	190	5'11"
Ferrall, Junius B.	Canton	19	So.	End	173	5'11"
Fesler, Wesley E.	Youngstown	22	Sr.	End	180	5'11"
Fox, Morris	Columbus	22	Sr.	Quarter	135	5' 5"
Ford, Robert	Springfield	21	So.	End	162	5' 9"
Fried, Lawrence	Lakewood	20	So.	Tackle	200	6'
Gardner, James	Warren	20	So.	Half	182	6' 2"
Garshman, Lewis	Wadsworth	21	So.	Guard	173	6'
Gilsdorf, Albert	Columbus	20	Jr.	End	154	5'10"
Grady, Robert	Columbus	23	Jr.	Half	160	5'10"
Greenberg, Jack	Detroit, Mich.	20	So.	Half	163	5' 8"
Griffith, William	Cleveland	20	Jr.	Guard	225	6'
Hall, John	Mansfield	21	Jr.	Center	181	6' 1"
Haubrich, Robert	Columbus	20	Jr.	Tackle	194	6'
Hinchman, Lewis	Columbus	19	So.	Quarter	170	5'10"
Hindulak, John A.	Cleveland	19	Jr.	Tackle	188	5'11"
Hodnick, Paul	Canton	20	So.	Full	167	5' 8"
Hoffer, Joseph	Youngstown	23	So.	Quarter	163	5'11"
Holcomb, Stuart	Erie, Pa.	20	Jr.	Full	170	5'10"
Holan, Joseph	Cleveland	23	Jr.	Guard	170	5' 9"
Horn, Robert L.	Columbus	21	Sr.	Half	184	6'
Hudson, Addison	Columbus	22	So.	Guard	181	6' 2"
Idle, Ralph H.	Wapakoneta	24	Sr.	End	163	5'10"
Kazmerchak, Chas.	Nanticoke, Pa.	25	Jr.	Full	174	5'10"
Kabealo, Charles	Youngstown	22	Jr.	Guard	182	5'10"
Keller, C. P.	Mechanicsburg	18	So.	Guard	180	5'10"
Kile, Eugene M.	Marysville	22	Jr.	Guard	185	5'10"
Krumm, Tahlman	Columbus	18	So.	End	168	5'10"
Larkins, Richard	E. Liverpool	22	Sr.	Tackle	180	6'
Lukz, Frank	Niles	22	So.	Guard	180	5' 9"
Mandula, George	Cleveland	20	So.	Half	190	6'½"
Marshall, Max	Xenia	21	So.	End	170	5'11"
Mazaika, John	Spring Valley, Ill.	19	So.	Tackle	176	5'11"
Meek, Robert	Youngstown	20	So.	End	155	5'11"
Meincer, John H.	Fremont	20	So.	End	164	6' 1"
Miller, Walter	Columbus	19	So.	Guard	175	6'
Modica, Robert	Cleveland	19	Jr.	Half	142	5'10"
Nasman, Bert	Youngstown	20	So.	Center	180	6'
Nicklaus, Frank	Columbus	20	Sr.	Tackle	194	6' 2½"
Peppe, Louis	Columbus	22	Jr.	Quarter	150	5' 7"
Peterson, L. B.	Steubenville	21	Jr.	End	173	6'
Rabenstein, Howard	Lockland	21	So.	End	162	5'11"
Rentschler, Carl G.	Cleveland	21	Sr.	Tackle	189	6' 1"
Richardson, Sherman	Mansfield	21	So.	Tackle	172	6' 3"
Roth, Michael	Bridgeport, Conn.	21	Jr.	Half	154	5' 9"
Sattler, Chas. L.	Mansfield	21	Sr.	Guard	203	5' 9½"
Scherer, Belden D.	Cleveland	21	So.	End	169	6'½"
Schorr, George	Columbus	19	So.	Guard	165	5'11"
Selby, Sam	W. Middletown	22	Sr.	Guard	180	5'11"
Smith, Richard	E. Chicago, Ind.	18	So.	Center	188	6' 2½"
Sola, Olavi	Erie, Pa.	20	So.	Full	184	5'11½"
Taylor, Russell E.	Sandusky	21	Sr.	Half	165	5'10½"
VanBlaricom, Robt.	Salem	20	So.	Tackle	183	6'
Van Derau, John N.	Dayton	21	Jr.	Center	168	5' 9"
Varner, Martin	Lima	19	So.	Half	200	5'11"
Vilela, Joseph	Gary, Indiana	22	So.	Half	148	5' 7½"
Weaver, Edward	Columbus	22	Jr.	End	186	6' 3"
Werner, Irvin	Newark, N. J.	21	So.	End	171	5'10"
White, Robert J.	Columbus	20	Jr.	Guard	232	6' 1"
Williams, Paul	Columbus	20	So.	Half	151	5' 9"
Wingert, Charles	New Lexington	21	So.	Tackle	194	5'11"
Worstell, Hillis M.	Bloomdale	20	Jr.	End	180	6' 2½"
Worcester, Benj. D.	Middletown	21	So.	Half	165	5' 9"
Zeckhauser, Milton	Columbus	20	Jr.	Tackle	206	6'

[1930]

1930
Captain: Wesley E. Fesler

59	*Mt. Union	0
23	*Indiana	0
2	Northwestern	19
0	*Michigan	13
0	*Wisconsin	0
27	Navy	0
16	*Pittsburgh	7
12	Illinois	9
139		48

Won 5, Lost 2, Tied 1

OHIO STATE 27...NAVY 0

THE SCARLET AND GRAY eleven rises to its full height ... playing almost perfect football ... winning its biggest intersectional battle in years ... overpowering the strong Navy team ... scoring in every period ... showing great superiority in every department of the game ... Fesler is the sparkplug ... leading the Buckeyes' smooth running attack and fighting defense ... Navy receives ... has to punt ... the Bucks take the ball ... off-tackle plays from double wing back formation carry the ball to Navy's 23 yard line ... Stu Holcomb takes the ball off left tackle ... he's smothered by six tacklers ... he breaks through ... twists ... turns ... pivots ... shifts ... cuts back to his right ... he's free ... he romps 23 yards for the score ... a great run ... the kick is no good ... Fesler and Hagberg in a punting duel ... Navy fumbles on its 27 yard line ... Dick Larkins recovers ... Fesler passes to Larkins in the end zone after dodging two tacklers ... touchdown ... Tubby Ehrensberger placekicks the extra point ... second half ... the punting duel again ... Hinchman scoops a Navy pass off the receiver's finger tips ... he races 25 yards for a touchdown ... Bob Haubrich kicks the goal ... Bob Grady intercepts another Navy pass ... and tears to Navy's 39 yard line ... Buckeye backs crack the Navy line down to the 14 yard stripe ... Fesler tears off 20 yards at one crack ... Benis passes to Bob Horn ... Bob makes a great running catch in the end zone ... the Bucks' fourth tally of the afternoon ... Navy is offside on the kick ... the point goes to Ohio ... Navy's big threat comes after an Ohio fumble ... Navy recovers on its own 11 yard line ... Navy takes the ball to Ohio State's 25 yard line ... Grady intercepts a Navy pass ... the threat is over ... the one and only Fesler plays the game of a century ... Larkins plays a great defensive end ... the bulwark of the line, Sam Selby, stands off the Navy offense like a sea wall ... Holcomb does some great offensive work ... Gene Baumgarten is outstanding on the defense ... the entire Buck team plays a game for history ... Lou Kirn, the Navy's white hope, is never allowed to get away for long ... Capt. Bowstrom of the Navy is a tower of strength at left tackle ... the Bucks make 13 first downs to the Navy's 8 ... and outgain the gobs throughout ... it's a great day for the Scarlet and Gray aggregation.

OHIO STATE 0...WISCONSIN 0

HOMECOMING ... a heavily favored Badger team ... the Bucks put up a great defensive fight ... almost inspired football ... they outbattle the confident visitors ... outscrap them from start to finish ... but lack the final drive that scores touchdowns ... a slashing attack in the center of the gridiron but impotence when within reach of a touchdown ... Ohio threatens time and again ... once has victory almost in its grasp ... Bob Horn blocks a Badger pass behind the line of scrimmage ... Bill Bell grabs the ball ... he's downed on Wisconsin's 33 yard line ... a lateral pass, Hinchman to Fesler nets 14 yards ... Fesler passes to Hinchman ... Lew tears to the 5 yard line ... the Bucks are stopped ... Fesler plays a great game ... calling signals ... doing the punting ... and passing ... carrying the ball ... all over the field ... always on top of the ball ... one of football's truly greats ... in action ... Gantenbein downs a punt on the Scarlet's 1 yard line ... Fesler punts out of danger ... Fesler chases Behr as he's trying to pass ... Marty Varner spills the Badger back for a 10 yard loss ... Fesler does some great kicking ... then an injury forces him out of the game ... for the first time since 1928 ... he trots limpingly to the bench ... head hanging ... tears in his eyes ... the crowd cracks the skies ... one of those things you never forget.

OHIO STATE 12...ILLINOIS 9

FESLER'S last game ... and it's almost a one-man triumph ... Wes kicks Illinois back to their 8 yard line ... Illinois fumbles ... Tubby Ehrensberger recovers on the 10 yard line ... Fesler, switching from end to fullback, takes the ball for 4 yards ... then flips a beautiful pass ... over right end ... to Bob Grady ... who falls over the goal line ... Ehrensberger's kick for the extra point is blocked ... Fesler turns loose the passing attack again ... after kicking deep into Illini territory ... Fesler heaves a pass to Grady that nets 10 yards ... he flips one to Horn that's good for 18 more ... putting the ball on the 1 yard line ... Varner goes over in two line plunges ... Ehrensberger's kick is blocked ... Illinois takes advantage of a heavy wind ... Berry and his teammates fight their way to the Bucks' 30 yard line ... the Scarlet defense stiffens and holds there ... with a powerful wind aiding him, Bodman outkicks Fesler ... Illinois has the ball on its own 48 yard line ... Berry fakes a punt and tosses a short pass to Yanuskus ... Yanuskus catches it on Ohio's 37 yard line ... he races around right end for a touchdown ... his place kick is good ... Illinois breaks through and blocks one of Fesler's punts ... an Illinois jersey covers it beyond the end zone ... scoring two points for the Illini ... the Scarlet and Gray eleven puts up a great defensive fight for the remainder of the game ... stopping the Illini advance ... time after time ... as they get inside the danger zone ... the Bucks fight gallantly for their slim lead ... and hold it.

A first down against Wisconsin

THE OHIO SQUAD

No.	Name	Class	Position	Weight	Age	*Experience	Home
1	HOFFER, JOSEPH	'33	HB	160	23	0	Youngstown, O.
2	FISHER, JEROME	'34	HB	168	19	0	Cleveland, O.
3	VIDIS, MARTIN	'34	HB	158	21	0	Youngstown, O.
4	RABENSTEIN, HOWARD	'32	E	168	22	2	Lockland, O.
5	FUGGIT, JOHN	'34	HB	157	20	0	Portsmouth, O.
6	CRON, ROBERT	'34	HB	153	21	0	Piqua, O.
7	HOLCOMB, STUART	'32	HB	174	21	2	Erie, Pa.
8	RAMSEY, ROBERT	'34	HB	167	21	0	Columbus, O.
9	HINCHMAN, LEWIS	'33	HB	172	20	1	Columbus, O.
10	CRAMER, CARL	'34	HB	168	20	0	Dayton, O.
12	WELEVER, WATSON	'34	FB	186	21	0	Toledo, O.
13	WILSON, DONALD	'34	E	184	19	0	Garfield Heights, O.
14	GRADY, ROBERT	'32	HB	162	25	2	Columbus, O.
15	BENIS, JOSEPH	'32	HB	165	21	2	Cleveland, O.
16	GREENBERG, JACK	'33	HB	163	21	0	Detroit, Mich.
17	EMBREY, RUSSELL	'34	HB	165	23	0	Dayton, O.
18	VAUCHINICH, MICHAEL	'33	HB	190	23	0	Southwest, Pa.
19	RUSS, DONALD	'34	E	168	21	0	Toledo, O.
20	CARROLL, WILLIAM	'33	HB	173	21	1	Columbus, O.
21	KULL, HERBERT	'34	HB	179	21	0	Columbus, O.
22	OLIPHANT, MARSHALL	'34	HB	164	21	0	Cleveland Heights, O.
23	KEEFE, THOMAS	'34	HB	176	23	0	Toledo, O.
24	McKINNEY, WILLIAM	'34	T	185	19	0	New Rochelle, N. Y.
25	VAN BLARICOM, ROBERT	'33	T	190	21	0	Salem, O.
26	KIRK, JAMES	'34	E	179	19	0	Canton, O.
27	GILLMAN, SIDNEY	'34	E	180	20	0	Minneapolis, Minn.
28	KILE, EUGENE	'32	G	170	23	2	Marysville, O.
29	ALLEN, ROBERT	'33	G	176	21	0	Columbus, O.
30	DELICH, PETER	'33	C	180	20	0	Gary, Ind.
31	FERRALL, JUNIUS	'33	E	167	20	1	Canton, O.
32	GALIUS, JOSEPH	'33	G	188	21	0	Vandergrift, Pa.
33	FITZGERALD, FRED	'33	E	168	21	0	Detroit, Mich.
34	CONRAD, FREDERICK	'34	E	200	20	0	Wooster, O.
35	WEAVER, EDWARD	'33	E	186	23	0	Columbus, O.
36	BAUMGARTEN, EUGENE	'32	T	215	21	2	Louisville, Ky.
37	HAUBRICH, ROBERT	'32	T	195	21	2	Columbus, O.
38	LUKZ, FRANK	'33	G	180	23	0	Niles, O.
39	SMITH, RICHARD	'33	C	204	19	1	E. Chicago, Ill.
40	VARNER, MARTIN	'33	G	198	20	1	Lima, O.
41	COCHRAN, KENNETH	'32	C	205	21	0	Mt. Vernon, O.
42	BELL, WILLIAM	'32	T	192	21	2	Akron, O.
45	NASMAN, BERT	'33	E	175	21	1	Youngstown, O.
46	MANDULA, GEORGE	'33	HB	190	21	1	Cleveland, O.
47	ROSEQUIST, TED	'34	T	208	23	0	Warrensville, O.
50	DRAKULICH, SAMUEL	'34	HB	133	18	0	Salem, O.
51	BOMPEIDI, CARL	'34	G	160	20	0	Cleveland, O.
54	TANSKI, VICTOR	'34	G	188	22	0	Cleveland, O.
57	DIEHL, WILLIAM	'33	G	185	20	0	Columbus, O.
58	HOSKET, WILMER	'34	E	194	20	0	Dayton, O.
60	JOHNSON, EARL	'34	G	178	20	0	Mount Iron, Minn.

[1931]

1931	
Captain: Stuart K. Holcomb	
67	*Cincinnati	6
21	*Vanderbilt	26
20	Michigan	7
0	*Northwestern	10
13	Indiana	0
20	*Navy	0
6	Wisconsin	0
40	*Illinois	0
7	Minnesota	19
194		68
Won 6, Lost 3	

Ohio State Crushes Illinois In Worst Loss

Columbus, Ohio, Nov. 21 (AP)—Ohio State ambled up and down Touchdown street here this afternoon and as a result, the University of Illinois eleven was handed the worst licking it ever received from an Ohio team. The final score was 40 to 0.

It was a three-fold victory for the Buckeyes. It marked the first time Illinois had ever been beaten in the Ohio horseshoe and the first time since 1917 that it has been subdued on Ohio soil. Also it was the first time Ohio ever defeated Illinois and Michigan in the same season.

Not only was this the worst defeat ever handed the Illini by Ohio, but the worst given Illinois by any team in the twenty years that Bob Zuppke has guided the destinies of football at that institution.

Ohio State In Surprise Victory Over Michigan

Co-Champions of 1930 'Big Ten' Swept Off Feet Early in Game

Ann Arbor, Mich., Oct. 17.—(AP.)—Rated as underdogs, a husky Ohio State eleven took Michigan by surprise today, swept them off their feet from the start, and delivered a major blow to the Wolverine championship hopes. The final score, 20 to 7, was as unexpected to the 70,000 spectators as it was to Coach Harry Kipke's 1930 co-champions.

Michigan's running attack was stopped on nearly every occasion, and her vaunted aerial attack failed to function until too late to be effective.

A series of costly fumbles brought trouble to the Michigan line early in the game. One, by Jack Heston, sophomore fullback, second son of the famed Willie Heston of a generation ago, contributed directly to the first Ohio touchdown. Even Michigan's famous scoring play "old 83" developed years ago by Field H. Yost, failed when an official became entangled in the play, and Ohio recovered the ball.

Summary:

Ohio State	Pos.	Michigan
Nasman	le	Hewitt
Bell	lt	Aur
Varner	lg	LaJeunesse
Smith	c	Morrison
Gailus	rg	Kowalik
Haubrich	rt	Samuels
Gillman	re	Williamson
Cramer	qb	Newman
Hinchman	lhb	J. Heston
Holcomb	rhb	Fay
Vuchinich	fb	Hudson

Ohio State ...... 7 0 6 7—20
Michigan ...... 0 7 0 0— 7

Ohio State touchdowns — Carroll (substitute for Holcomb) 2; Cramer. Points after touchdown — Haubrich (place kick); Peppe (sub for Haubrich drop kick).

Michigan touchdown—Williamson. Point after touchdown—Goldsmith (sub for Samuels), place kick.

Referee: Frank Birch, (Earlham); umpire: John Schommer, (Chicago); field judge: Fred Young (Illinois Wesleyan); head linesman: Arlie Mucks (Wisconsin).

OHIO—20   MICHIGAN—7

To DEFEAT Michigan is generally regarded by Ohio followers to be ample compensation for losing the balance of the games of the season, so it goes without saying that it was a happy group of Ohio fans that left the Wolverine stadium on last October 17th. Entirely rejuvenated, the Buckeyes showed even more spirit than had been exhibited in the last half of the Vanderbilt game. Bill Carroll and Carl Cramer vied for the day's honors and the end of the game found them even. Carroll scored the first two touchdowns and Cramer scored the last by a beautiful 46-yard return of a Michigan punt. Vuchinich, Haubrich and Gilman were the defensive stars, the players who made possible the effective work of the backfield. Williamson proved to be the savior of the Ann Arborites when he recovered a blocked Ohio State punt behind the Ohio goal. The passing ability of Harry Newman is not to be discounted, for this great passer was responsible for most of the 105 yards gained by the Michigan team on aerial plays.

The Ohio State Roster

Name	Home Town	Age	Year	Position	Weight	Height
Allen, Robert	Columbus	22	Sr.	Guard	176	5' 10"
Bompiedi, Carl	Cleveland	21	Jr.	End	170	5' 9"
Burger, Carl	Columbus	21	Sr.	End	150	5' 11"
Carmody, Clarence	Middletown	22	So.	End	180	5' 11½"
*Carroll, William	Columbus	22	Sr.	Half	173	5' 10"
*Conrad, Frederick	Wooster	20	Jr.	Tackle	208	6' 4"
Cox, Budd	Springfield	19	So.	End	165	5' 10"
*Cramer, Carl	Dayton	21	Jr.	Quarter	168	5' 10"
Cron, Robert	Piqua	22	Jr.	Half	164	5' 9½"
*Delich, Peter	Gary, Ind.	21	Jr.	Guard	180	5' 10"
Diehl, William	Columbus	21	Sr.	Guard	195	5' 11½"
Drakulich, Sam	Salem	19	Jr.	Quarter	132	5' 7"
*Ferrall, Junius	Canton	21	Sr.	End	168	5' 10"
Fisher, Jerome	Cleveland	20	Jr.	Half	172	6'
Ford, Samuel	Columbus	20	So.	End	180	6' ½"
Fugitt, John	Portsmouth	21	Jr.	Half	170	5' 11½"
*Gailus, Joseph	Vandergrift, Pa.	22	Jr.	Guard	192	6' 1"
*Gillman, Sidney	Minneapolis, Minn.	21	Jr.	End	185	5' 11"
Granger, Ralph	Columbus	19	So.	End	196	6' 3"
*Greenberg, Jack	Detroit, Mich.	22	Sr.	Half	173	5' 9"
Greenblatt, Louis	Massena, N. Y.	20	Jr.	Center	182	5' 11½"
Griffith, Eugene	No. Baltimore	19	So.	Half	182	6'
Heekin, Richard	Cincinnati	20	So.	Half	193	6'
Heyman, Joseph	Toledo	19	So.	Center	175	5' 11"
*Hinchman, Lewis (C)	Columbus	21	Sr.	Half	178	5' 11"
Hosking, John	Ft. Thomas, Ky.	19	So.	Tackle	206	5' 11½"
Johnson, Earl	Prospect	23	Jr.	Tackle	243	6' 3"
Jones, Dave	Jackson	20	So.	Half	164	5' 10"
Kabealo, Charles	Youngstown	23	Sr.	Full	178	5' 10"
Kabealo, George	Youngstown	21	So.	Center	180	5' 9¾"
Karcher, James	Forest	18	So.	Full	188	5' 11"
*Keefe, Tom	Toledo	23	Jr.	Half	172	6'
Kirk, James	Canton	20	Jr.	End	183	6'
Livorno, Joseph	Bellaire	19	So.	Guard	170	5' 10"
*Lukz, Frank	Niles	24	Sr.	Guard	180	5' 10"
*Mandula, George	Cleveland	22	Jr.	Full	190	6' ½"
McAfee, John	Ironton	20	So.	Quarter	168	5' 9½"
McCombs, Alton	Middletown	22	Jr.	Tackle	202	6' 1"
McKenney, John	Cleveland	20	So.	Quarter	180	5' 11"
McKinney, William	New Rochelle, N. Y.	20	Jr.	Tackle	200	6'
Monahan, Regis	Lorain, O.	21	So.	Tackle	209	5' 11"
*Nasman, Bert	Youngstown	22	Sr.	Center	178	6' 1"
Neal, George	Dayton	19	So.	Guard	187	6'
Nelson, Harry	Gary, Ind.	19	So.	Tackle	220	6'
*Oliphant, Marshall	Cleveland	21	Jr.	Quarter	171	6'
O'Shaughnessey, Tom	Columbus	20	Jr.	Guard	218	6'
Padlow, Max	Dayton	21	So.	End	190	6'
Ramsey, Robert	Bloomfield, Ind.	21	So.	Half	162	5' 10½"
Reilly, Robert	Columbus	19	So.	Quarter	171	5' 8"
Rose, James	Wilmington	19	So.	Quarter	155	5' 9"
Rosequist, Ted	Warrensville	24	So.	Tackle	207	6' 4½"
Salvaterra, Joe	Bellaire	23	Sr.	End	165	6'
Scherer, Belden	Cleveland	23	Sr.	Half	155	6'
Scott, James	Toledo	20	So.	End	185	6' 2"
Smith, Jack	Hamilton	19	So.	Half	182	6'
*Smith, Richard	E. Chicago, Ind.	20	Sr.	Center	204	6' 2"
Tanski, Victor	Cleveland	23	Jr.	Guard	188	5' 10"
*Thies, Wilford	Norwood	20	Jr.	Tackle	196	6' 4"
Thomas, Joe	Columbus	20	Sr.	Half	170	5' 11"
Van Blaricom, Robert	Salem	22	Sr.	Tackle	190	6' 1"
*Varner, Martin	Lima	21	Sr.	Guard	212	5' 11"
Vidis, Martin	Youngstown	22	Jr.	Half	158	5' 8"
*Vuchinich, Michael	Southwest, Pa.	22	Jr.	Full	192	6'
Weaver, J. H.	Hilliards	20	So.	Center	163	6'
Werner, Irving	Newark, N. J.	22	Sr.	End	168	5' 10"
Wetzel, Damon	Columbus	21	So.	Full	188	5' 10½"
Yards, Ludwig	Gary, Ind.	20	So.	Tackle	195	6' 3"

*Indicates lettermen.

1932 - OHIO STATE FOOTBALL SQUAD - 1932

Row I—Willaman (Coach), Gillman, Conrad, Nasman, Delich, Varner, Oliphant, Vuchinich, Hinchman (Captain), Gailus, R. Smith, Carroll, Ferrall, Keefe, Cramer, Lukz, Miller (Coach).

Row II—Godfrey (Coach), Vidis, Bompiedi, Allen, Greenblatt, Van Blaricom, Tanski, McKenney, Greenberg, Kirk, Wetzel, Monahan, Hosking, Yards, Stahl (Coach).

Row III—Larkins (Coach), Scott, Cox, Thomas, J. Smith, McAfee, McKinney, Thies, Fisher, Heekin, Johnson, Neal, Diehl, Padlow, Granger, Drakulich, Fesler (Coach).

Row IV—Haubrich (Coach), Cron, Livorno, Reilly, Fugitt, Carmody, McComb, Nelson, Rudy, Weaver, Heyman, Griffith, Whinnery, G. Kabealo, C. Kabealo, Werner, Surington (Coach).

Row V—Burger, Bennett, Ford, Karcher, Bakke (Trainer), Smith (Trainer), James (Manager), Dixon (Manager), Mahaffey (Manager), Rose, Jones, McDaniel, O'Shaughnessy.

[1932]

	1932	
	Captain: Lewis G. Hinchman	
34	*Ohio Wesleyan	7
7	*Indiana	7
0	*Michigan	14
0	Pittsburgh	0
7	*Wisconsin	7
20	Northwestern	6
19	*Pennsylvania	0
3	Illinois	0
90		41
	Won 4, Lost 1, Tied 3	

Ohio — 7
Indiana — 7

OFFERING fandom its first chance of the season to view Coach Willaman's pigskin chasers under fire in the Big Ten, the Hoosiers enter the game as the underdogs . . . the Scarlet and Gray collect their lone tally in the second quarter when Bill Carroll, the Blond Express, skirts around left end for a score . . . Vuchinich's place-kick is good, giving the Buckeyes a total of seven points . . . a pass from Hinchman to Cramer accounts for 25 yards . . . several line plays and a lateral pass put the ball on Indiana's 18 . . . but State's offensive drive stops there . . . Indiana seriously threatens to score in the second quarter but the Buckeye line holds fast on the one-foot line . . . the Hoosiers' score comes after Opasik intercepts a pass, romps down the field for fifty yards . . . three more plays and then Veller, substitute halfback, plunges eleven yards for the score . . . Cramer and Hinchman play good ball for the Scarlet and Gray . . . the latter making twenty-four yards from scrimmage and the former chalking up thirty-nine yards . . .

Ohio — 0
Michigan — 14

THE Michigan game . . . . always drawing the largest crowd of the year, is certainly an aerial scrimmage . . . . Harry Newman, the All-American quarterback, accounts for both Wolverine touchdowns . . . . this is the same Newman that spelled defeat for Ohio State in 1930 . . . . his pass from Ohio's 28 to the 15 line marker in the first 3 minutes of play puts the ball in dangerous territory . . . . another pass zips through the air accounting for the first score . . . . the second Michigan touchdown comes midway in the second quarter when Williamson receives a pass and gallops fifteen yards to score . . . . during the second half the Buckeyes continually outplay the Kipke men aided greatly by brilliant playing by Oliphant and Captain Hinchman . . . . the Wolverines never seriously threaten to score in the second half . . . . statistics, if they mean anything, show that Ohio State made eight first downs to Michigan's seven . . . . and gained 144 yards from scrimmage to the Wolverine's 46 . . . . over nineteen thousand fans were in attendance . . . .

Ohio — 0
Pittsburgh — 0

SMOKY CITY . . . . pre-game predictions . . . . Pitt, said to be one of the best teams in the east . . . . Ohio State, a disappointment to the critics . . . . the first half is mostly Pitt's . . . . several long drives made by the Panther are stopped by State's forward wall . . . . the biggest thrill is when the Buckeye's line holds Pitts on the one-yard line . . . . Rosequist stops Heller on the thirteen-yard line with only a half-yard needed for first down . . . . the second half is State's . . . . Ohio threatens to score several times but lacks the final punch . . . . the first chance comes when Gillman recovers Pitt's bad center pass on the Gold and Blue thirteen-yard line . . . . but their opportunity ends when the try for first down fails by inches . . . . first downs are plentiful with each team getting eleven . . . . Salvaterra, Rosequist, and Vuchinich are outstanding in this scoreless game . . . . from the fan's viewpoint as well as from the player's viewpoint this is one of the most spectacular battles ever played in the Gold and Blue Stadium . . . .

THE OHIO STATE ROSTER

No.	Name	Home Town	Pos.	Wt.	Ht.	Age	Yr.
59	Barrows, Arthur	Columbus	G.	175	5' 10"	19	So.
9	Beltz, Richard H.	Findlay	HB.	163	5' 9"	21	So.
57	Benton, Julian	Columbus	HB.	160	6'	21	So.
56	Bompeidi, Carl J.	Cleveland	E.	170	5' 9"	22	Sr.
8	Boucher, Franklin A.	Kent	HB.	172	6' 1"	18	So.
25	Brungard, Geo. H.	North Lima	FB.	170	5' 11"	19	So.
31	Busich, Sam	Lorain	C.	185	6' 2½"	19	So.
55	Cashell, Jack	Columbus	C.	195	6' 1"	18	So.
34	*Conrad, Frederick B.	Wooster	T.	208	6' 4"	21	Sr.
28	Cox, M. Budd	Springfield	E.	168	5' 10"	20	Jr.
10	*Cramer, Carl F.	Dayton	QB.	163	5' 10"	22	So.
30	*Delich, Pete B.	Gary, Ind.	C.	185	5' 10"	22	Sr.
50	Drakulich, Sam	Salem	QB.	155	5' 7"	20	Sr.
24	Fisch, Frank	Mansfield	HB.	182	6'	20	Sr.
40	Fisher, Jerome	Cleveland	HB.	176	6'	21	Sr.
46	Fleming, Mark	Columbus	T.	190	6' 1½"	19	So.
32	*Gailus, Joseph T. (Capt.)	Vandergrift, Pa.	G.	197	6' 1"	23	Sr.
27	*Gillman, Sidney (Capt.)	Minneapolis, Minn.	E.	188	5' 11"	22	Sr.
51	Greenblatt, Louis	Massena, N. Y.	C.	170	5' 11½"	21	Sr.
48	Harre, Gilbert	Toledo	T.	207	6' 1"	19	So.
6	Heekin, Richard F.	Cincinnati	HB.	195	6'	21	So.
26	Heyman, Joseph	Toledo	E.	170	5' 11"	21	Sr.
44	Johnson, Earl	Prospect	T.	240	6' 3"	24	Sr.
2	Jones, David L.	Jackson	HB.	168	5' 10"	21	Jr.
33	Jones, Gomer T.	Cleveland	G.	200	5' 8"	19	So.
19	Karcher, James M.	Forest	FB.	198	5' 11"	19	Jr.
54	Kabealo, George	Youngstown	C.	185	5' 10"	22	Jr.
16	Kabealo, John	Youngstown	FB.	183	5' 10"	21	So.
23	*Keefe, Thomas C.	Toledo	HB.	182	6'	24	Sr.
45	Kleinhaus, John L.	Maumee	C.	190	6' 3"	19	So.
5	Lightburn, Robert	Crestline	E.	172	6' 1"	21	So.
52	Livorno, Joseph	Bellaire	G.	170	5' 10"	20	Sr.
11	Liptak, Steve	Cleveland	E.	178	5' 10"	20	So.
14	McAfee, John N.	Ironton	FB.	170	5' 9½"	21	Jr.
58	Miller, Robert	Cleveland	C.	175	5' 11"	18	So.
41	*Monahan, J. Regis	Lorain	G.	210	5' 11"	22	Jr.
36	Neal, George V.	Dayton	C.	205	6'	20	Jr.
22	*Oliphant, Marshall T.	Cleveland	QB.	170	6'	22	Sr.
29	*Padlow, Max	Dayton	E.	187	6'	22	Jr.
37	Phillips, Clyde	Columbus	QB	160	5' 11"	19	So.
1	Pincura, Stanley	Lorain	QB.	157	5' 11"	20	So.
20	Pipoly, James E.	Struthers	E.	170	5' 9"	20	So.
12	Rees, Trevor J.	Dover	E.	180	5' 11½	18	So.
38	Romoser, James W.	Lorain	G.	185	6'	22	So.
47	*Rosequist, Theodore	Cleveland	T.	209	6' 4½"	25	Sr.
42	Roush, Ernest	Black Lick	G.	200	5' 10½"	20	So.
35	Scott, James	Toledo	T.	190	6' 2"	21	Jr.
4	Smith, Jack E.	Hamilton	HB.	189	6'	20	Jr.
53	Thies, Wilfred	Norwood	T.	200	6' 4"	21	Sr.
7	Thomas, Joseph A.	Columbus	HB.	175	5' 11"	21	Sr.
3	Vidis, Martin S.	Youngstown	HB.	160	5' 8"	23	Sr.
15	Vogelgesang, James	Lima	HB.	174	6'	20	So.
18	*Vuchinich, Michael	Southwest, Pa.	C.	190	6'	23	Sr.
17	*Wetzel, Damon H.	Columbus	FB	182	5' 10½"	22	Jr.
21	Whinnery, Glenn	Salem	HB.	170	5' 11"	20	Sr.
13	*Wilson, Don A.	Garfield Hts.	E.	185	6' 1"	21	Sr.
43	*Yards, Ludwig	Gary, Ind.	T.	182	6' 3"	21	Jr.
49	Zirkle, Lewis G.	Defiance	T.	210	6' 4"	18	So.

* Lettermen.

OHIO STATE	75
VIRGINIA	0

In a demonstration of hurricane force—scoring eleven touchdowns—Ohio State's giant, versatile football squad started the season against a little band of Virginia Cavaliers, who were outweighed and outclassed from the beginning. The score was the largest seen in the Buckeye stadium, with forty-eight players being used.

The first touchdown came two minutes after the initial whistle, due to some beautiful running by Cramer and Wetzel; the second 6 points soon followed; with Smith taking major honors. A reserve team played the next period and scored 16 points. Then came the third quarter rant, with the staggering sum of 34 points being run up, while the fourth quarter was played by reserve men, who scored 13 points.

Heekin did well on the receiving end of passes; Oliphant and Keefe flashed great form, both giving exhibitions of great football; while Smith and McAfee tore off some long runs and proved extremely slippery in the open.

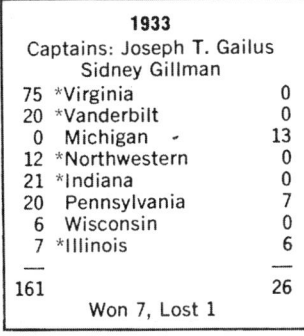

1933
Captains: Joseph T. Gailus
Sidney Gillman

75	*Virginia	0
20	*Vanderbilt	0
0	Michigan	13
12	*Northwestern	0
21	*Indiana	0
20	Pennsylvania	7
6	Wisconsin	0
7	*Illinois	6
161		26

Won 7, Lost 1

CO-CAPTAINS GAILUS AND GILLMAN

SID GILLMAN

JOSEPH GAILUS

[1933]

OHIO STATE 0
MICHIGAN 13

Playing before the largest crowd ever to jam itself into the Wolverine Bowl—approximately 90,000—Ohio State met the Maize and Blue warriors in the first Big Ten game of the season for either team. There is nothing to elaborate on with the exception of mentioning that an offensiveless Ohio State team played a great Michigan eleven on a day when the Wolverines were clicking. There were extremely few, if any, flaws which an observer could find in Michigan's play, everything the Ann Arbor boys attempted appearing to work with plenty of finesse.

The Wolverine tallies came at the last of each half, one when Renner, faking a lateral, raced around left end to score and, again, after a series of line-plunges by Everhardus.

Kabealo, Sophomore fullback, turned in his greatest game, being the only Scarlet and Gray player who could find the Michigan line for gains. Kabealo continually played a smart kicking game, often out-punting Regeczi, Michigan's great kicker.

Ohio State Edges 'Fighting Illini,' 7-6

Columbus, Ohio, Nov. 25.—(AP)—Mickey Vuchinich again proved his right to rate considerable respect in an around Champaign, Ill., today when his toe provided the winning point for Ohio State in a battle with Illinois. The score was 7 to 6.

By those who watched the Ohio-Illinois tussle a year ago at Champaign, it will be recalled that Mickey Vuchinich kicked a field goal to permit the Buckeyes to win 3-0.

Mickey Vuchinich didn't kick a field goal today, but his conversion of the extra point after the Buckeyes had managed a touchdown in the third period—after a scoreless first half—was the margin of victory.

OHIO STATE 12
NORTHWESTERN 0

Two timely fumbles paved the way for the 12-0 defeat of the silk-clad Northwestern by the hard-driving Ohio eleven in the 1933 Homecoming game. Willaman's gridders rolled up their initial six tallies in the first period when Leeper, safety man, touched one of Kabealo's mighty kicks and failed to hold it. Racing over his own goal, he attempted to return the ball onto the field but was tackled hard and the ball slipped from his grasp to be recovered by Pincura for a touchdown.

The second break was nothing short of phenomenal. Duvall juggled a bad pass from center and while smashing the line, the ball bounded from his arms into the eager hands of Gillman, who dashed unscathed 52 yards for the second tally.

Kabealo was the stellar attraction through his superb punting. With the excellent support of the entire front wall, backs Heekin, Pincura, Smith and McAfee piled up a total of 77 yards by plunging.

Sam Willaman Signs To Coach Football At Western Reserve

Columbus, O., Jan. 31.—(AP.)— The coaching situation at two Ohio universities was changed completely today when Sam Willaman resigned as director of football at Ohio State and Western Reserve announced he had signed a three-year contract to replace Tom Keady.

Unconfirmed reports said Cleark Shaughnessy, coach at the University of Chicago, would replace Willaman. The Ohio State Board of Athletic Control, however, appointed a committee to investigate the records of several coaches, whose names it withheld.

L. W. St. John, Ohio State athletic director, announced the remainder of his staff would not be affected by Willaman's resignation.

Willaman had been at Ohio State for seven years.

SCHMIDT NAMED COACH.
Succeeds Willaman as Football Mentor at Ohio State.

COLUMBUS, Ohio, March 2 (AP).— Francis Schmidt today was appointed head football coach at Ohio State University, succeeding Sam Willaman, resigned.

The Texan received a three-year contract, beginning June 1, when Willaman's term expires. The new coach will assume his duties in time to take charge of Spring football practice the first of next month. The salary was not announced.

1934
Coach Francis A. Schmidt
Captain: J. Regis Monahan

33	*Indiana	0
13	Illinois	14
10	*Colgate	7
28	Northwestern	6
76	Western Reserve	0
33	*Chicago	0
34	*Michigan	0
40	*Iowa	7
267		34

Won 7, Lost 1

Speculate On Successor To Willaman
Gossip Leans Heavily on Clark Shaughnessy, Present Grid Coach at Chicago

Columbus, Ohio, Feb. 1.—(AP.)— Followers of the gridiron fortunes of Ohio State University went into a "stove league" huddle today to speculate on the successor to Sam Willaman, who resigned yesterday after five years as football director to accept a three-year contract at Western Reserve University in Cleveland, replacing Tom Keady.

While a committee appointed by Ohio State's board of athletic control began considering several coaches without disclosing their names, gossip leaned heavily on Clark Shaughnessy, coach at the University of Chicago.

Shaughnessy was a star at Minnesota, where he played end, tackle and half-back for the Gophers, and has coached one season at Chicago without winning a Big Ten game.

Also mentioned in the unconfirmed reports were Gus Dorais of Detroit, Don Peden of Ohio University, Jock Sutherland of Pitt, Robert Zuppke of Illinois, and Wesley Fesler, a recent Ohio State stellar player.

Francis Schmidt

1934 SQUAD ROSTER 1934
OHIO STATE

No.	Name	Home Town	Pos.	Weight	Height	Year
7	Antenucci, Frank	Niles	HB.	176	5' 9"	So.
9	Beltz, Dick	Findlay	HB.	167	6' 1"	Jr.
10	Bettridge, John	Toledo	FB.	178	5' 10"	So.
56	Bittel, Robert	Cleveland	G.	177	6' ½"	So.
8	Boucher, Frank	Kent	HB.	177	6' 1"	Jr.
15	Boston, William	Cleveland	C.	185	6'	So.
25	Brungard, George	North Lima	HB.	191	6'	Jr.
31	Busich, Sam	Lorain	E.	187	6' 2"	Jr.
28	Cox, Budd	Springfield	E.	174	5' 11"	Sr.
27	Cumiskey, Frank	Youngstown	E.	186	6' 1"	So.
11	Dobbs, Bennie	Columbus	E.	180	6' ½"	Jr.
5	Dorris, Victor	Bellaire	FB.	178	5' 9"	So.
50	Dye, William	Pomeroy	QB.	138	5' 6"	So.
24	*Fisch, Frank	Mansfield	QB.	189	6' ½"	Jr.
46	Fleming, Mark	Columbus	G.	190	6'	Jr.
47	George, August	Dayton	T.	224	6' 4½"	So.
60	Georgepoulos, Tom	Cleveland	C.	181	6' 1½"	Jr.
26	Greider, Robert	Cleveland	T.	202	6' 2"	So.
59	Haddad, George	Toledo	G.	161	5' 5½"	So.
34	Hamrick, Charles	Gallipolis	T.	230	6' ½"	So.
48	Harre, Gilbert	Toledo	T.	213	6' 2½"	Jr.
6	*Heekin, Dick	Cincinnati	HB.	196	6' 1"	Jr.
51	Heiser, Vern	Mansfield	C.	175	5' 11"	So.
37	Horwitz, Sam	Columbus	QB.	147	5' 8½"	So.
2	Jones, Dave	Jackson	HB.	162	5' 10"	Sr.
33	Jones, Gomer	Cleveland	C.	207	5' 8½"	Jr.
54	Kabealo, George	Youngstown	C.	195	5' 9"	Jr.
16	*Kabealo, John	Youngstown	FB.	203	5' 9"	Jr.
19	Karcher, James	Forest	G.	192	5' 10"	Sr.
45	Kleinhans, John	Maumee	E.	195	6' 1½"	Jr.
39	Lightburn, Robert	Crestline	E.	166	6'	Jr.
55	Luckino, Angelo	Wellsville	G.	175	5' 6"	Jr.
14	*McAfee, John	Ironton	FB.	165	5' 10"	Sr.
53	Miller, James	Shelby	HB.	178	5' 11"	So.
58	Miller, Robert	Cleveland	C.	180	5' 11"	Jr.
41	*Monahan, Regis (Capt.)	Lorain	G.	203	5' 10½"	Sr.
40	Nagy, John	Cleveland	HB.	160	5' 11"	So.
36	Neal, George	Dayton	G.	219	6'	Sr.
52	Novotny, George	Elyria	T.	193	5' 11¾"	So.
1	Pincura, Stan	Lorain	QB.	163	5' 11"	Jr.
20	Pipoly, James	Struthers	E.	176	5' 9"	Jr.
12	*Rees, Trevor	Dover	E.	183	6'	Jr.
30	Roberts, Vernell	Wellsville	G.	195	5' 11"	So.
42	Roush, Ernest	Blacklick	G.	210	5' 9"	Jr.
44	Scholl, Millard	Lorain	T.	224	5' 9"	So.
35	Scott, James	Toledo	T.	201	6' 1½"	Sr.
29	Smith, Inwood	Mansfield	G.	191	5' 11"	So.
4	*Smith, Jack	Hamilton	HB.	183	6'	Sr.
3	Stump, Wilson	Alliance	QB.	153	5' 8"	So.
21	Thomas, Earl	Ashland	E.	186	6' 1"	So.
32	Torrance, James	Cleveland	E.	186	6' 1"	So.
18	Wendt, Merle	Middletown	E.	191	5' 10"	So.
17	*Wetzel, Damon	Columbus	C.-FB.	185	5' 10"	Sr.
43	*Yards, Ludwig	Gary, Ind.	T.	188	6' 3"	Sr.
49	Zirkle, Lewis	Defiance	T.	214	6' 4½"	Jr.

*Denotes Letterman.

[1934]

OHIO STATE – 34
MICHIGAN – 0

Eleven vengeful Bucks pulled the Michigan jinx around the home field by the tail until that venerable personage yielded to a 34-0 trimming, the worst a Wolverine eleven has ever suffered at the hands of an Ohio State team. As a result, Michigan tumbled from the Big Ten cellar to the grave. The Scarlet squad showed everything: magnificent power, rapid-fire passing, deception, and rugged all around football. A capacity crowd, 68,000, jammed the stadium for the season's highlight. In the first five minutes of the contest, Heekin and Wetzel worked the ball from midfield on successive first downs, the former going over for a touchdown. Wetzel and Boucher accounted for the second tally with the help of Tippy Dye's passing. Antenucci recovered Smith's fumble over the goal line to account for the third score. Wendt converted Fisch's heave into a fourth marker after a 44-yard run. Busich took a pass from Dye for the final score. Four out of five tries for extra points were made good. The game came as a climax to the largest rally and Homecoming celebration Ohio has ever seen.

Stahl

OHIO STATE – 13
ILLINOIS – 14

Bewildered by the drive of the Zuppkemen, the Buckeyes were slow in finding their bearings, but once on firm ground they displayed running and passing attacks never before displayed by an Ohio team.

Illinois, aided by breaks, converted touchdowns by means of beautifully executed passes. Conversions after both touchdowns were good, bringing the score to 14-0 in favor of the Illini.

The Scarlet Wave rolled down the field in the final quarter when Wetzel, who was removed from center to fullback tore the Illini to shreds. He scored two touchdowns but Ohio converted once, bringing their total to 13 points. The final minutes were played with Ohio vainly trying to score, which was climaxed when Capt. Monahan attempted placement, which was short, from the Illinois 48 yard stripe. Wetzel was the outstanding player of the game, plunging for repeated gains.

The 1934 Football Season at a Glance

Game	Score	Touchdowns	Field Goals	Safeties	Points After T.	First Downs	Yards Rushing	Attempted Passes	Completed Passes	Yards Passing	Intercepted By	Number of Punts	Distance	Average	Runback of Punts	Fumbles	Own Recovered	Penalties	Yards Lost	Attendance
INDIANA	0	0	0	0	0	2	81	18	5	48	1	12	398	33	42	12	7	5	30	
OHIO	33	5	0	0	3	7	182	22	7	80	5	12	478	40	62	11	4	1	5	47,785
ILLINOIS	14	2	0	0	2	10	51	13	8	159	1	5	228	46	11	2	1	5	30	
OHIO	13	2	0	0	1	13	145	15	9	129	2	4	188	47	56	2	1	1	15	20,130
COLGATE	7	1	0	0	1	2	33	18	9	113	1	11	407	42	42	2	2	3	15	
OHIO	10	1	1	0	1	7	71	23	10	132	2	9	364	40	64	3	1	1	25	29,139
NORTHWESTERN	6	1	0	0	0	3	39	8	1	0	3	15	580	38	39	3	1	1	15	
OHIO	28	4	0	0	4	12	192	18	9	125	2	10	456	41	144	6	3	3	20	25,360
W. RESERVE	0	0	0	0	0	3	72	13	5	37	2	11	373	34	10	2	0	1	5	
OHIO	76	11	0	0	10	17	313	22	8	230	3	3	139	45	109	1	1	6	40	11,890
CHICAGO	0	0	0	0	0	7	55	10	2	27	1	12	450	37	48	4	3	2	10	
OHIO	33	5	0	0	3	14	114	16	5	121	3	9	384	42	66	4	3	3	15	32,279
MICHIGAN	0	0	0	0	0	3	6	15	2	34	0	12	547	45	46	9	0	1	5	
OHIO	34	5	0	0	4	24	319	13	5	141	2	10	372	37	58	5	2	2	20	68,678
IOWA	7	1	0	0	1	3	95	10	0	0	2	17	655	39	65	6	6	5	45	
OHIO	40	6	0	0	4	16	119	17	9	230	2	11	429	39	180	3	2	2	10	27,214
OPPONENTS	34	5	0	0	4	34	432	105	32	418	11	95	3638	38.29	303	31	20	23	155	
OHIO	267	39	1	0	30	110	1455	136	62	1188	21	68	2810	41.32	739	35	19	21	150	262,475

1935 - OHIO STATE FOOTBALL ROSTER - 1935

No.	Name	Home	Pos.	Yr. on Squad	Wgt.	Height	High School Coach
*7	Antenucci, Frank	Niles	FB.	2	174	5' 10"	O. Smith
*9	Beltz, Richard	Findlay	HB.	3	171	6'	R. T. Knode
14	Belli, Roxie	Martins Ferry	G.	1	176	5' 10½"	J. Marks
*10	Bettridge, John	Toledo	HB.	2	177	5' 8½"	D. Mills
15	Boston, William	Lakewood	C.	2	185	5' 10"	Schupp
*8	Boucher, Frank	Kent	HB.	3	180	6' 1"	L. Moorhead
25	Brungard, George	North Lima	G.	3	187	5' 10½"	M. Atkins
*31	Busich, Sam	Lorain	E.	3	178	6' 1"	M. E. McCaskey
51	Chrissinger, Warren	Springfield	G.	1	185	5' 9"	A. Mansfield
52	Cook, Donald	Columbus	HB.	1	185	5' 11"	M. Hagley
23	Crow, Fred	Pomeroy	E.	1	180	6' 4"	R. Farnom
*27	Cumiskey, Frank	Youngstown	E.	2	185	6'	H. Lansing
5	Dorris, Victor	Bellaire	FB.	1	175	5' 8"	B. Rutan / C. M. Wright
*50	Dye, William H. H.	Pomeroy	QB.	2	142	5' 8"	R. Farnom
*24	Fisch, Frank	Mansfield	QB.	3	189	6' ½"	J. R. Murphey
20	Gales, Charles	Niles	T.	1	190	5' 11"	O. Smith
47	George, August	Dayton	T.	2	208	6' 4"	Cuthbert
60	Georgopoulos, Tom	Cleveland	E.	3	185	6' 1"	Schupp
59	Haddad, George	Toledo	G	2	169	5' 6"	J. Aitken / Rettig
*34	Hamrick, Charles	Gallipolis	T.	2	216	6' 1"	Myers / Lutz
44	Hargraves, William	Akron	E.	1	190	6' 2"	Rus Beichly
*48	Harre, Gilbert	Toledo	T.	3	205	' 2"	R. Bevan
*6	Heekin, Richard	Cincinnati	HB.	3	189	6'	E. Brooks
*33	Jones, Gomer (C)	Cleveland	C.	3	200	5' 8"	Brubaker / Shallcross
*16	Kabealo, John	Youngstown	FB.	3	188	5' 10"	C. H. McPhee
*19	Karcher, James	Forest	G.	3	189	6'	Baum
40	Maggied, Sol	Columbus	G.	1	189	5' 10"	Webster
35	McDonald, James	Springfield	FB.	1	181	6' 1"	A. Mansfield
53	Miller, James	Shelby	HB.	1	170	5' 11½"	J. J. Young
58	Miller, Robert	Cleveland	C.	3	181	5' 10½"	D. Carter
41	Monahan, Thomas	Lorain	G.	1	174	5' 8"	P. Scanlon
39	Nardi, Richard	Cleveland	HB.	1	182	5' 10"	P. S. Yost
*1	Pincura, Stanley	Lorain	QB.	3	167	5' 10"	McCaskey / J. L. Marks
57	Ream, Charles	Navarre	T.	1	191	6' 2"	Briedwiser
*12	Rees, Trevor	Dover	E.	3	182	6'	M. Rimieck
49	Ross, Robert	Troy	T.	1	223	6' 2"	W. P. Howald
*42	Roush, Ernest	Blacklick	T.	3	198	5' 10½"	Rosenthal
*29	Smith, Inwood	Mansfield	G.	2	189	5' 11"	J. R. Murphy
3	Stump, Wilson	Alliance	QB.	1	156	5' 7"	Wilcoxen
17	Van Meter, Howard	Struthers	E.	2	176	6' 1"	R. Schill
22	Vuchinich, Walter	Cleveland	E.	2	170	5' 11"	
37	Wasylik, Nicholas	Astoria, L. I.	QB.	1	147	5' 10"	Raskin
*18	Wendt, Merle	Middletown	E.	2	188	5' 11"	E. Lingrel
4	West, Edward	Springfield	E.	1	181	6' 1"	A. Mansfield
13	Williams, Joseph	Barberton	HB.	1	165	5' 5"	J. Price
46	Wolf, Ralph	Youngstown	C.	1	187	6' 2"	H. W. Lansing
26	Zarnas, Gus	Youngstown	G.	1	190	5' 10"	O. D. Williams / J. L. Marks

* Denotes Letterman.

OHIO COACHING STAFF

Francis A. Schmidt, Head Coach, Nebraska.
Ernest R. Godfrey, Line Coach, Ohio State.
Floyd S. Stahl, Assistant Coach, Illinois.
Gaylord R. Stinchcomb, Assistant Coach, Ohio State.
Joseph Galius, Assistant Coach, Ohio State.
Frederick C. Mackey, Freshman Coach, Ohio State.

1935 - OHIO SQUAD - 1935

BACK ROW: Pete Stinchcomb, Varsity Ass't.; 22, Vuchinick; 49, Ross; 44, Hargraves; 4, West; 45, Kleinhans; 46, Wolf; 47, George; 23, Crow; 57, Ream; 17, Van Meter; 52, Cook; 11, Waller; Mason, Ted Hieronymus.

THIRD ROW: 20, Gales; 40, Maggied; 3, Stump; 51, Chrissinger; 39, Nardi; 41, Mcnahan; 60, Georgopoulos; 21, Thomas; 14, Belli; 26, Zarnas; 15, Boston; 30, Seaman; Luchino; 59, Haddad; Tucker Smith, Trainer; Senior Manager, Koegele.

SECOND ROW: Francis Schmidt; 34, Hamrick; 19, Karcher; 6, Heekin; 16, Kakealo; 31, Busich; 42, Roush; 1, Pincura; 33, Jones (C.); 12, Rees; 24, Fisch; 48, Harre; 8, Boucher; 9, Beltz; 58, R. Miller; Ernie Godfrey, Varsity Line Coach.

FIRST ROW: Joe Gailius, Ass't Coach; 37, Waslik; 5, Dorris; 35, McDonald; 13, Williams; 7, Antenucci; 18, Wendt; 50, Dye; 29, Smith; 10, Bettridge; 27, Cumiskey; 53, J. Miller; 25, Brungard; Floyd Stahl, Ass't Coach.

1935	
Captain: Gomer T. Jones	
19 *Kentucky	6
85 *Drake	7
28 *Northwestern	7
28 Indiana	6
13 *Notre Dame	18
20 Chicago	13
6 *Illinois	0
38 Michigan	0
237	57
Won 7, Lost 1	
Big Ten Co-Champions	

[1935]

How High Hoosier Hopes Were Shattered

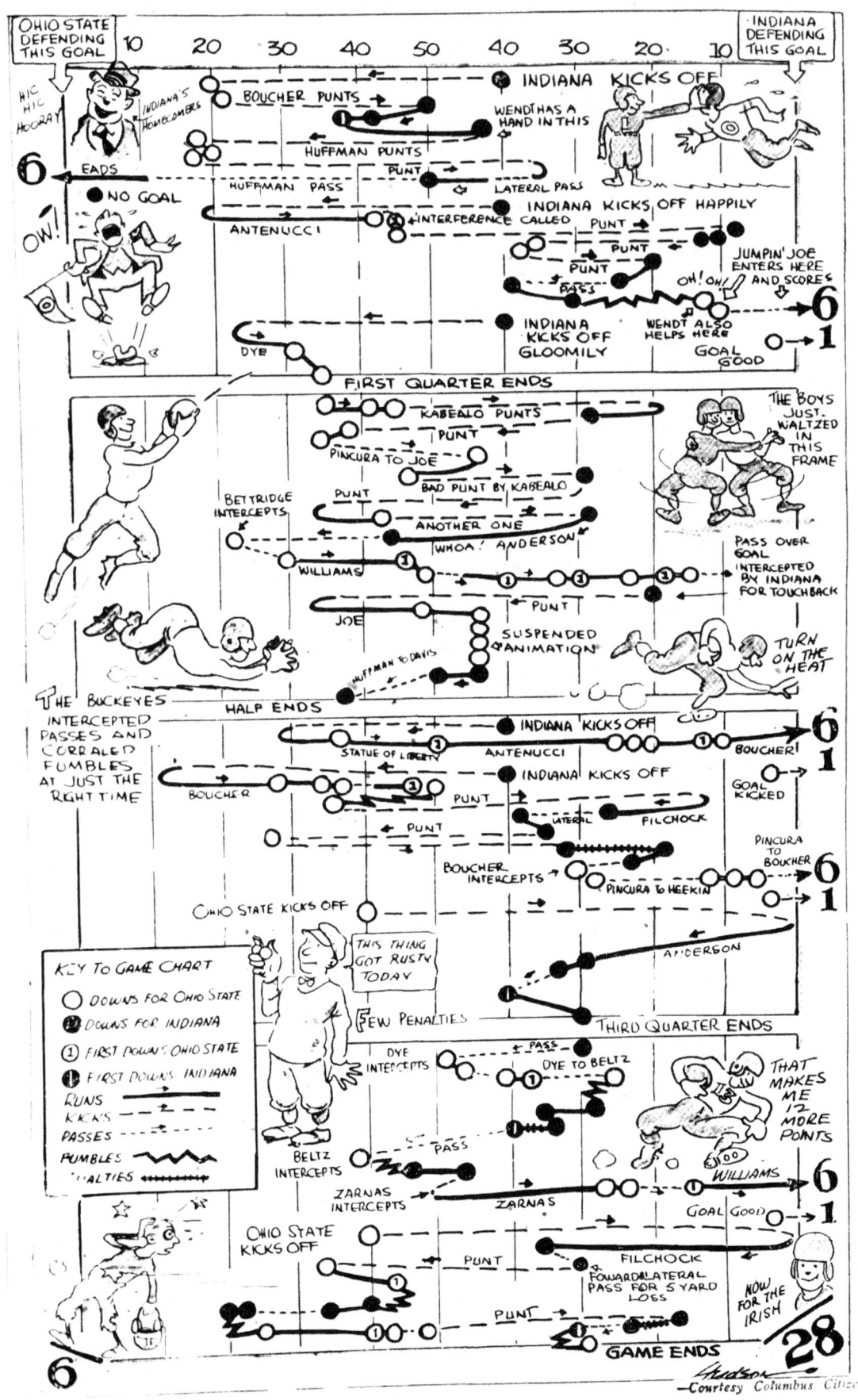

[1935]

vs. Notre Dame

CAME the game of the year, the game Ohio fans had awaited for years—Notre Dame! Columbus went stark raving mad on the subject of football with the city hotels jammed to the doors and even outlying towns feeling the pressure of the crowd that was making its way toward the Ohio Stadium. Sports writers and critics from every paper and sports magazine in the country attended. It was given to thousands of others via the NBC hookup with Ted Husing, radio's best, giving the play by play description to those reclining in their easy chairs.

The Columbus fans were back of the great Scarlet and Gray combine with every ounce of spirit they possessed and every drop they could buy. The town resembled an American Legion convention with all the color necessary for a successful rally. Posters, small signs, decorations, all urging the team to greater heights and putting forth the hope that they would wipe the South Bend Irish off the map. The students banded together in a huge rally to show Schmitty and the team that they were behind him and his boys, win, lose, or draw. But all the excitement and furor before the game was incidental to the game itself.

With 81,018 persons jammed into the stadium to watch them perform, the teams finally lined up and Ohio kicked off. From this point it was thrill after thrill until the final minute and the crack of the gun.

It started off like an Ohio State run-away. An intercepted pass, followed by a lateral from Antenucci to Boucher, gave the Buckeyes their first touchdown before the game was three minutes old. This was the perfect play. It was a perfect set-up and showed what exact coaching could do to make it perfectly executed. But then, shortly after the second quarter the Bucks marched to another touchdown. The Buckeye running attack tore huge holes in the Irish defense and split the team wide open; then Joe Williams scored the second touchdown. The rest of the second quarter the Bucks still held the upper hand; they threatened again but failed to make it.

With the start of the second half, Coach Elmer Layden sent in his entire second string line with the first string backfield and from then on it was a different story with Notre Dame.

The fourth period was a nightmare. It has been recounted so many times that only Tunney's "long count" outdoes it in record. It is indelibly imprinted upon the minds of every one of the 80,000 who witnessed it and even greater numbers that read and heard about it.

It was intestinal fortitude and the spirit of a team that "wouldn't be beaten" that gave Notre Dame the victory. Ohio was a good ball club for a half but they made their mistake by coasting on their 13 points in the last period. Shakespeare, Pilney, 3 touchdowns and Ohio's National Championship hopes fell just as Tony Aquila's goal posts fell with the onslaught of the Irish rooters. Ohio fans didn't protest, they sat rooted to their seats, heart broken. A once great Ohio team trudged into the showers where even the supposed soothing cold water failed to bring them to the reality that the game was over and they had lost.

vs. Michigan

A crowd of 43,000 braved the elements to see the 1935 edition of Ohio State after the N. D. had finished with it. After dragging through the uninteresting game with Illinois, the Buck outfit still had to cope with Michigan at Ann Arbor. The Wolverines had lost to Minnesota's powerful grid machine by a top heavy 40-0 score and Ohio was out to equal that or better it if possible.

FROM the opening gun there was no doubt as to the outcome, as "No mercy" Schmidt's improved ball club used terrific line smashes, sweeping end runs, laterals—single, double and even triple to pile up an unbelievable

CUMISKEY

high yardage total. The slaughter was terrific. Forty Buckeye gridmen saw service in the contest and it seemed to be the aim of Schmidt to use them all, rather than to pile up a big score. But the more players he sent in, the higher mounted the total.

Tippy Dye featured the big show with a spectacular 73 yard "traffic directing" jaunt much the same as in the Illinois game. As he ran he pointed and as he pointed the Ohio interference cut down the Michigan men like a huge scythe sweeping before him. "Jumpin' Joe" Williams also had a brilliant 44 yard run only to be pulled down from behind with the goal in sight. Every department of the Ohio offense worked to perfection and the defense was even more brilliant when it was known that Michigan gained but 12 yards from the scrimmage all afternoon.

The humiliation was even greater than the 38-0 score indicated, as 3 touchdowns were called back, all long running plays or passes.

Official 1936 Ohio State Varsity Football Roster

NAME	POSITION	WEIGHT	HEIGHT	YRS ON SQUAD
Hull, James	Quarterback	165	5'10"	1
*Wasylik, Nicholas	Quarterback	151	5'8"	2
Rabb, John	Fullback	175	5'11"	1
Birkholtz, Paul	Left Halfback	179	6'	1
Dorris, Victor	Right Halfback	180	5'10"	2
*Bettridge, John	Right Halfback	182	5'10"	3
*Antenucci, Frank	Right Halfback	178	5'10"	3
*McDonald, James	Fullback	186	6'	2
Booth, William	Left Halfback	177	5'11"	1
Phillips, Thomas	Quarterback	176	5'10"	1
Nardi, Richard	Right Halfback	183	5'11"	2
Cartwright, Ernest	Right Halfback	175	6'	1
*Williams, Joseph	Left Halfback	166	5'7"	2
Wedebrook, Howard	Right Halfback	139	6'1"	1
Springer, Fred	Fullback	187	6'	1
Kabealo, Michael	Left Halfback	161	5'9"	1
Knecht, John	Left Halfback	175	5'10"	1
*Wendt, Merle (Capt.)	Left End	190	5'10"	3
Bliss, Keith	Fullback	170	5'11"	1
*Gales, Charles	Right Tackle	192	5'11"	2
Kleinhans, John	Left End	195	6'2"	3
Aleskus, Joseph	Center	190	6'2½"	1
Crow, Fred	Left End	189	6'3"	2
Rutkay, Nicholas	Left Guard	189	6'	1
Kleinfelder, Kenneth	Right End	188	6'1"	1
*Zarnas, Gust	Right Guard	193	5'10"	2
*Cumiskey, Frank	Right End	187	6'	3
West, Edward	Right End	195	6'	2
*Smith, Inwood	Left Guard	190	5'11"	3
Young, Louis	Left Guard	193	5'10½"	1
Lind, Jack	Left End	183	6'	1
Masoner, Robert	Right End	175	5'11½"	1
Wolfe, Ralph	Center	191	6'2"	2
*Hamrick, Charles	Left Tackle	243	6'	3
Wendt, Emerson	Right End	191	6'1"	1
*Maggied, Sol	Left Guard	192	5'10"	2
Monohan, Thomas	Fullback	176	5'10"	2
Schoenbaum, Alex	Right Tackle	210	5'11"	1
Kaplanoff, Carl	Right Tackle	215	5'10"	1
Hargreaves, William	Right Tackle	196	6'2"	1
*George, August	Left Tackle	212	6'3"	3
Hohenberger, Clarence	Right Tackle	218	5'11"	1
Ross, Robert	Left Tackle	239	6'1"	2
*Dye, William	Quarterback	145	5'7½"	3
Chrissinger, Warren	Right Guard	192	5'11"	2
Boughner, Richard	Left End	172	5'11"	1
Bullock, William	Quarterback	167	5'10"	1
Hofmayer, Edward	Right Guard	175	5'10"	1
Lohr, Wendell	Right End	174	6'	1
*Ream, Charles	Left Tackle	196	6'	2
*Miller, Robert	Center	182	5'11"	3
Haddad, George	Right Guard	170	5'6"	2
Belli, Roxie	Right Guard	182	5'11"	2
Kinel, Tony	Quarterback	143	5'7"	1
Novotny, George	Left Guard	187	5'11"	1
Robinson, James	Center	184	6'1"	1
Welbaum, Thomas	Left Halfback	165	5'10"	1
Wuellner, Richard	Center	180	5'11"	1
Stump, Wilson	Quarterback	157	5'9"	2

* Major Monogram.

1936
Captain: Merle E. Wendt

60	*New York University	0
0	*Pittsburgh	6
13	Northwestern	14
7	*Indiana	0
2	Notre Dame	7
44	*Chicago	0
13	Illinois	0
21	*Michigan	0
160		27

Won 5, Lost 3

Buckeye Passes Defeat Michigan

Columbus, Ohio, Nov. 21.—(AP.)—Ohio State combined power and "razzle-dazzle" today to defeat Michigan's Wolverines 21 to 0, giving the Bucks a second place tie in the Western Conference race, in which they tied for the title with Minnesota a year ago.

The invaders were unable to match power with the Ohioans, but it was the devastating Buckeye aerial attack which proved the deciding factor. The Wolverines played the Bucks to a standstill in the opening period, once rushing the ball to the Ohio three-yard line, but they faded rapidly in the closing sessions and the Bucks rammed over three touchdowns and added a field goal. A 12-yard boot by Sophomore Bill Booth, for good measure. The Wolves blocked each of the three tries for extra points, as well as two other place-kick attempts by Booth.

A crowd of 56,202 witnessed the fray, and few of them left as a drenching rain fell through the closing period.

The Bucks, after an impotent first period, opened up in the second, starting a drive on their own 24 and not stopping until Dye tossed a 14-yard pass to Cumiskey for the first touchdown.

During the day the Bucks completed 11 of 19 aerials for 143 yards, and completed three laterals in as many attempts for 30 more yards. On the other hand the Wolverines clicked on but two of 12 passes, gaining 39 yards, and made five more yards on their lone lateral.

The second Ohio touchdown came in a hurry in the third period, Dye running a punt back from his 15 to the 31 to start the long jaunt. Johnny Rabb, the Akron sophomore fullback, led the attack which carried the ball down the field, and he climaxed it by cutting over tackle, reversing his field and sprinting 31 yards for the marker. A few minutes later Bill Booth booted a field goal from placement on the 12-yard line.

The last touchdown was the result of a long Ohio march ending in a 15-yard sprint around right end by Nick Wasylik, substitute quarterback.

1936 Ohio State Football Squad

READING LEFT TO RIGHT

FIRST ROW—Fritz Mackey (Ass't Coach), Nardi, Rabb, Dorris, Wasylik, Dye, Bettridge, Williams, McDonald, Haddad, Kabealo, Monahan, Knecht, Birkholtz, Kinel, Boughner.

SECOND ROW—Godfrey (Line Coach), Gales, Hamrick, George, Maggied, Kleinhans, Miller, Antenucci, Smith, Wendt (Capt), Cumiskey, West, Zarnas, Ream, Schoenbaum, Chrissinger, Wedebrook, Stahl (Ass't Coach).

THIRD ROW—Schmidt (Head Coach), Hieronymus (Ass't Coach), Masoner, E. Wendt, Lohr, Springer, Hull, Mitchell, Wolf, Wuellner, Bullock, Belli, Ross, Rutkay, Cook, Kleinfelder, Young, Cunningham, Blair, McQuaig (Manager).

FOURTH ROW—Kaplanoff, Hohenberger, Bliss, Cartwright, Hargreave, Jackson, Lind, Crow, Hyman, Booth, Novotny, Hofmayer, Welbaum, Kopach, Smith, Tucker (Trainer).

IRISH BEAT BUCKEYES IN THRILLING GAME BY 7-2 SCORE

By Al Bride

The largest crowd ever to push its way into the local stadium witnessed an alert Notre Dame team triumph, 7-2, over the tricky ball-handling outfit from Ohio State. Led by California's speedy "Bunny" McCormick and the hard driving sophomore fullback Simonich the Fighting Irish dominated the Ohioans in every department with the exception of punting.

Rain which showered at intervals did not dim the enthusiasm of the capacity crowd which was brought to its feet in the closing minutes by a determined Ohio State drive that was reminiscent of last year's contest. Taking the ball deep in its own territory Ohio State passed its way to the Irish 12 yard line before losing the ball on two incomplete passes into the end zone.

Ohio State scored first, capitalizing on a fumble early in the second period. From near his own goal line Miller, on a fake kick, broke through the line only to lose the ball when he was tackled hard by the Scarlet secondary. Ohio State registered a first down, but was then stopped with a touchdown in sight. A safety was good for two points, and the Irish were trailing, 2-0.

After an exchange of kicks the Laydenmen started to move. A pass to McCormick was good on the two yard line, and on the next play McCormick started swiftly to the left, cut in sharply over tackle, and dashed into the end zone for a touchdown. Wojcihovski was rushed in to hold the ball for Danbom, who booted a perfect placement to make the score 7-2.

The second half found Ohio State using every trick in its "razzle dazzle" in an attempt to break loose for a score, but the hard charging Irish line broke up most of the plays before they could get under way. In the closing minutes red shirted receivers managed to elude the Notre Dame secondary, and several completed passes brought the ball to the Irish 12 yard line. In a desperate attempt to score before the gun went off the Ohioans threw two passes into the end zone, both of which were incomplete. According to the new rules Notre Dame received the ball, and for the remaining seconds they held on to it.

One of the features of the game was the performance of Simonich. This husky 200 pounder was given his chance, and he came through in a manner that ought to give the other fullbacks something to worry about. Time after time he crashed through the powerful Ohio line for gains. When not advancing the ball through sheer power this second year man was clearing the way with some of the best blocking displayed by an Irish player to date.

Reprinted with permission from the **Notre Dame Scholastic**

1937 - OHIO STATE ROSTER - 1937

No.	Name	Pos.	Yr. on Squad	Wgt.	Ht.	Home
22	Aleskus, Joe	LT	2	197	6' 2"	Columbus, Ohio
36	Andrako, Steve	C	1	184	6'	Trinway, Ohio
48	Barren, Henry	LT	1	215	6'	Shaker Hts., Ohio
17	Bartschy, Ross	LE	1	185	6'	Orrville, Ohio
19	Bliss, Keith	RE	2	180	5' 11"	Columbus, Ohio
52	Boughner, Richard	LE	2	178	5' 11"	Akron, Ohio
54	Bullock, William	QB	2	174	5' 10"	Kent, Ohio
*51	Chrissinger, Warren	RG	3	196	5' 11"	Springfield, Ohio
29	Clair, Frank	LE	1	193	6'	Hamilton, Ohio
61	Coyer, William	QB	1	157	5' 8"	Orrville, Ohio
*23	Crow, Fred	LE	3	189	6' 3"	Pomeroy, Ohio
5	Dorris, Victor	FB	3	185	5' 10"	Bellaire, Ohio
7	Fordham, Forrest	FB	1	172	5' 8"	Toledo, Ohio
*20	Gales, Charles	RT	3	205	5' 11"	Niles, Ohio
53	Graf, Campbell	RG	1	170	5' 9"	Columbus, Ohio
59	Haddad, George	LG	3	173	5' 6"	Toledo, Ohio
44	Hargreaves, William	RT	2	192	6' 3"	Akron, Ohio
55	Hofmayer, Edward	LG	2	180	5' 10"	Columbus, Ohio
58	Howe, Frank	RH	1	190	5' 10"	Columbus, Ohio
*16	Kabealo, Michael	LH	2	170	5' 9"	Youngstown, Ohio
*43	Kaplanoff, Carl	RT	2	235	5' 11"	Bucyrus, Ohio
64	Kopach, Stephen	RG	1	160	5' 8"	Youngstown, Ohio
56	Lohr, Wendell	RE	2	178	6'	Massillon, Ohio
71	Madro, Joseph	LG	1	175	5' 7"	Wellington, Ohio
*40	Maggied, Sol	LG	3	197	5' 10"	Columbus, Ohio
50	Marino, Victor	LG	1	178	5' 7"	Youngstown, Ohio
46	Mastako, Frank	RT	1	190	6'	New Philadelphia, Ohio
*8	McDonald, James (Co-Capt.)	QB	3	190	6'	Springfield, Ohio
12	Miller, James	LH	3	182	5' 11"	Shelby, Ohio
21	Moloney, Robert	LH	1	173	6'	Columbus, Ohio
41	Monahan, Thomas	FB	3	180	5' 10"	Lorain, Ohio
11	Nardi, Richard	RH	3	193	5' 11"	Cleveland, Ohio
62	Novotny, George	RT	2	198	6' 1"	Elyria, Ohio
10	Phillips, William	QB	2	180	5' 10"	Columbus, Ohio
*3	Rabb, John	FB	2	178	5' 11"	Akron, Ohio
*57	Ream, Charles	RE	3	208	6'	Navarre, Ohio
24	Rutkay, Nicholas	RG	1	212	6'	Youngstown, Ohio
25	Sarkkinen, Esco	LE	1	176	6'	Fairport Harbor, Ohio
*42	Schoenbaum, Alex	LT	2	215	5' 11"	Huntington, W. Va.
34	Shaffer, Bernard	LT	1	265	6' 2"	Cincinnati, Ohio
15	Simione, John	QB	1	162	5' 8"	Youngstown, Ohio
18	Smith, Francis L.	FB	1	190	5' 10"	Quincy, Mass.
31	Smith, Frank	RG	1	190	5' 10"	Columbus, Ohio
27	Spears, Jerry	RE	1	191	6' 1"	Columbus, Ohio
49	Tucci, Amel	RG	1	186	5' 9"	Zanesville, Ohio
*2	Wasylik, Nicholas	LH	3	160	5' 9"	Astoria, L. I.
*14	Wedebrook, Howard	RH	2	191	6' 1"	Portsmouth, Ohio
65	Welbaum, Thomas	LH	2	156	5' 10"	Akron, Ohio
35	Wendt, Emerson	LT	1	195	6' 1"	Middletown, Ohio
37	White, Claude	C	1	181	5' 11"	Portsmouth, Ohio
28	Whitehead, Stuart	RE	1	196	6' 1"	Columbus, Ohio
*33	Wolf, Ralph (Co-Capt.)	C	3	194	6' 2"	Youngstown, Ohio
66	Wuellner, Richard	C	2	181	5' 11"	Columbus, Ohio
30	Young, Louis	LG	2	199	5' 11"	Massillon, Ohio
6	Zadworney, Frank	RH	1	195	5' 10"	Cleveland, Ohio
*26	Zarnas, Gust	RG	3	198	5' 10"	Brackenridge, Pa.

*Indicates Letterman.

1937	
Captains: Ralph C. Wolf	
James A. McDonald	
14 *Texas Christian	0
13 *Purdue	0
12 Southern California	13
7 *Northwestern	0
39 Chicago	0
0 *Indiana	10
19 *Illinois	0
21 Michigan	0
125	23
Won 6, Lost 2	

55,000 See Southern California Conquer Ohio State by a One-Point Margin

This pictures the instant Ohio State failed to kick the tieing point at Southern California.

Scrappy Indiana Hoosiers Defeat Ohio State Team

Played Inspired Game to Conquer Buckeyes in Surprise Result, 10-0

Columbus, Ohio, Nov. 6.—(AP.)—Ohio State's Big Ten championship hopes were trampled into the cleat-torn turf of Buckeye Stadium today by the golden toe of Center George Miller and the flying feet of Halfback Frank Petrick as Indiana's Hoosiers won 10 to 0.

A crowd of 47,056 watched the inspired Hoosiers turn back two Buckeye threats in the shadow of the goal posts in the opening minutes and then go on to win a victory as startling as it was impressive.

Miller, who played a great defensive game, stepped back to the 21 yard mark in the second period as an Indiana thrust was halted on the 12, and place kicked a field goal for three points.

Quarterback Frank Filchock faded back in the next period, following a long drive down the field, and fired a 12-yard pass to Petrick who lunged over the goal from the four-yard line.

Lineup and summary:

INDIANA		OHIO STATE
Kenderdine	le	Crow
McDaniel	lt	Schoenbaum
Sirtosky	lg	Magvied
Miller	c	Wolf
Olmstead	rg	Zarnas
Haak	rt	Kaplanoff
Petrick	re	Ream
Filchock	qb	McDonald
Graham	lh	Kabealo
Heistand	rh	Nardi
Davis	fb	Rabb
Indiana	0 3 7 0—10	

Score by periods:
Indiana scoring: touchdown, Petrick; goal from field, Miller (placement); points from try after touchdown, Miller (placement).
Substitutions: Indiana: end, Birr; tackles, Stevenson and Stevens; guards, Logan and Szabo; center, Sloss; backs, Tanner and Fowler. Ohio State: ends, Bliss, Bartschy, Sarkkinen, Lohr; tackle, Aleskus; guards, Marino, Chrissinger; center, Andrako; backs, Wasylik, Wedebrook, Dorris, Zadworney, Fordham, Phillips, Miller.

SO. CALIF. (13)		OHIO STATE (12)
Coleman	L.E.	Crow
McNeil	L.T.	Schoenbaum
Thomassin	L.G.	Magvied
Tonelli	C.	Wolf
Radovich	R.G.	Zarnas
George	R.T.	Kaplanoff
Williams	R.E.	Ream
Schindler	Q.B.	McDonald
Hoffman	L.H.	Kabealo
Morgan	R.H.	Nardi
Day	F.B.	Rabb

SCORE BY PERIODS
So. Calif. .... 0 6 0 7—13
Ohio State .... 0 0 6 6—12

Touchdowns—McDonald, Nardi, Schindler, Anderson (sub for Morgan). Point after touchdown—Stanley (sub for Williams) (placement).

SUBSTITUTES
Ohio State—Ends, Bartschy, Whitehead, Lohr, Bliss, Sarkkinen; tackles, Aleskus, Novotny; guards, Chrissinger, Marino; quarterback, Phillips; halfbacks, Wasylik, Miller, Wederbrook, Zadworney; fullback, Fordham.
Southern California—Ends, Stanley, Hibbs, Fiske, Slatter; tackles, Gaspar, Fisher; guards, Hamsen, Norton; quarterback, Lansdell, Pappas, Keller; halfback, Anderson; fullback, Sangster, Shell.

Ohio State Aerials Turn Back Michigan For Fourth Successive Year

OHIO STATE VICTOR AS 65,000 LOOK ON

Buckeyes' Forward Pass Plays Bring About Downfall of Michigan, 21 to 0

MILLER SHOWS THE WAY

Plunges Across After Aerial Sets Stage and Also Snares Toss for Score

STATISTICS OF THE GAME

	O.S.	Mich.
First downs	9	4
Yards gained rushing	194	3
Forward passes	12	12
Forwards completed	4	4
Yards gained, forwards	91	38
Forwards intercepted by	3	4
*Av. dist. of punts, yds.	37	33
†Run-back of kicks, yds.	116	72
Opponent's fumb. recov.	1	2
Yards lost, penalties	35	35

*From line of scrimmage.
†Includes punts and kick-offs.

By The Associated Press.

ANN ARBOR, Mich., Nov. 20. — Ohio State's Scarlet Tide rolled relentlessly over Michigan's hopes of a winning football season today, vanquishing the Wolverines for the fourth successive year, 21 to 0.

The victory provided some balm for the Buckeyes' Western Conference title aspirations, blasted when Minnesota defeated Wisconsin today to win the championship, and gave them a record for the season of six games won and two lost.

For the Wolverines and their followers among the 65,000 spectators who shivered in freezing temperature and snow, the defeat ended the season on a dismal note. It snapped a four-game winning streak and left Michigan with a record of four victories and four defeats.

Ohio State, paced by Jim Miller, brilliant halfback, scored two touchdowns through the air and reached scoring position for its third touchdown by the aerial route.

Michigan Braces Valiantly

Its first two points, however, came from a safety scored when Norm Purucker, Michigan punter, was tackled by Charles Ream, Buckeye end, behind the Michigan goal line. The safety came on the first play of the second period, after Michigan had braced valiantly to take the ball on downs on its 3-yard line.

Another Buckeye scoring chance was frustrated when the timer's gun ended the game with the ball on Michigan's 1-yard stripe.

Michigan's only scoring threat ended at the Buckeye 12, where the Wolverines lost the ball on downs. So tight was the Ohio State defense that Michigan had a net gain of only 3 yards from scrimmage and 38 yards from forward passes. The Buckeyes made 194 yards from scrimmage and 91 yards from passes and collected nine first downs to the Wolverines' 3.

Miller scored two of the Ohio touchdowns. Late in the second period he intercepted a Michigan pass, returned it 29 yards, then lateraled to Quarterback Nick Wasylik, who ran another 7 yards to the Michigan 33. On the next play, Miller rifled a pass to Dick Nardi, who was brought down on the 4. Miller plunged over three plays later and Jim McDonald placekicked the extra point.

Takes Ball on Dead Run

Midway in the third period, Wasylik intercepted a Michigan pass on the Wolverine 44. Then Wasylik faded back and shot the ball across the field to Miller, who took the ball on the Michigan 15 on the dead run and raced across the goal line.

In the fourth period Purucker sliced a punt that went out of bounds on the Michigan 29. Wasylik passed to Nardi for a first down on the 13. Then Nardi gathered in Wasylik's fourth-down pass on the 7 and went over for the final touchdown.

The line-up:

OHIO STATE (21)		MICHIGAN (0)
Crow	L.E.	Nicholson
Aleskus	L.T.	Siegel
Maggied	L.G.	Brennan
Wolf	C.	Kodros
Zarnas	R.G.	Heikkinen
Kaplanoff	R.T.	Smith
Ream	R.E.	Sinick
Wasylik	Q.B.	Farmer
Wederbrook	L.H.	Purucker
Miller	R.H.	Ritchie
McDonald	F.B.	Stanton

SCORE BY PERIODS
Ohio State .... 0 9 6 6—21
Michigan .... 0 0 0 0— 0

Touchdowns—Miller 2, Nardi (sub for Wederbrook). Point after touchdown—McDonald (placement). Safety—Purucker.

SUBSTITUTES

Ohio State—Ends: Bartschy, Lohr, Bliss, Sarkkinen, Whitehead. Tackles: Novotny, Hargreaves. Guards: Marino, Chrissinger, Rutkay, Haddad, Young. Centers: Andrakow, White. Backs: Nardi, Kabealo, Zadworney, Phillips, Fordham, Dorris, Bullock, Monahan.

Michigan—Ends: Valpey, Gedeon. Tackles: Janke, Savilla. Guards: Vandewater, Penderson. Center: Rinaldi. Backs: Trosko, Levine, Barclay, Campbell, Renda, Kinsey.

Referee—Fred Gardner, Cornell. Umpire—Anthony Haines, Yale. Field judge—Frank Lane, Detroit. Linesman—Don Hamilton, Notre Dame.

1938 « OHIO STATE ROSTER » 1938

Name	No.	Pos.	Year of Competition	Wgt.	Ht.	Home
*Aleskus, Joseph	22	LT	3	230	6' 2"	Columbus, Ohio
Andrako, Steve	36	C	2	185	6'	Trinway, Ohio
Arnold, James	52	RG	1	184	5' 8"	Akron, Ohio
*Bartschy, Ross	17	LE	2	187	6'	Orrville, Ohio
Bennet, William	41	RT	1	204	6'	Willoughby, Ohio
*Bliss, Keith	19	RE	3	192	5' 10"	Columbus, Ohio
Bolser, Harvey	60	RT	1	228	6' 2"	Lockland, Ohio
Bullock, William	54	QB	3	184	5' 11"	Kent, Ohio
Clair, Frank	29	RE	1	200	6'	Hamilton, Ohio
Coyer, William	61	QB	1	170	5' 8"	Orrville, Ohio
Crabbe, Jack	68	FB	1	186	5' 8"	Columbus, Ohio
Elliott, Roy	11	RH	1	176	5' 11"	Grindstone, Pa.
*Fordham, Forrest	7	RH	2	170	5' 9"	Toledo, Ohio
*Gales, Charles	20	LG	3	202	5' 10"	Niles, Ohio
Graf, Campbell	53	LG	1	168	5' 9"	Columbus, Ohio
Grundies, Jerry	34	LT	1	235	6' 2"	Cleveland, Ohio
Hofmayer, Edward	55	RG	2	191	6'	Columbus, Ohio
Hodick, Mike	70	C	1	173	5' 11"	Martins Ferry, Ohio
Howe, Frank	58	RH	1	176	5' 10"	Columbus, Ohio
*Kabealo, Michael, (Co-Captain)	16	QB	3	175	5' 8"	Youngstown, Ohio
*Kaplanoff, Carl, (Co-Captain)	43	RT	3	245	5' 11"	Bucyrus, Ohio
Langhurst, James	8	FB	1	187	5' 10"	Willard, Ohio
*Lohr, Wendell	56	RE	3	186	5' 10"	Massillon, Ohio
Maag, Charles	33	C	1	206	6' 3"	Sandusky, Ohio
Madro, Joseph	71	LG	1	185	5' 9"	Wellington, Ohio
*Marino, Victor	50	LG	2	189	5' 7"	Youngstown, Ohio
Masoner, Robert	69	LE	2	185	5' 11"	Middletown, Ohio
Monas, Alfons	48	LT	1	265	6' 3"	Dayton, Ohio
Newlin, John	72	LE	1	192	6'	St. Clairsville, Ohio
Nosker, William	26	RG	1	200	5' 11"	Columbus, Ohio
Oman, Donald	44	RT	1	190	6'	Richwood, Ohio
Rosen, Andy	40	RT	1	204	6' 1"	Isabella, Pa.
*Rutkay, Nicholas	24	RG	2	220	6'	Youngstown, Ohio
Santschi, John	32	LE	1	180	6'	Akron, Ohio
Sarkkinen, Eino	35	LE	1	172	6'	Fairport Harbor, Ohio
*Sarkkinen, Esco	25	LE	2	191	6'	Fairport Harbor, Ohio
*Schoenbaum, Alex	42	LT	3	219	5' 11"	Huntington, W. Va.
Scott, Donald	9	LH	1	200	6' 1"	Canton, Ohio
Sexton, James	5	QB	1	184	5' 10"	Middletown, Ohio
Simione, John	15	QB	1	168	5' 8"	Youngstown, Ohio
Smith, Francis	18	RE	2	190	5' 10"	Quincy, Mass.
Smith, Frank	31	RG	2	203	5' 10"	Columbus, Ohio
Strausbaugh, James	4	LH	1	172	5' 10"	Chillicothe, Ohio
Spears, Jerry	27	LG	1	219	6'	Columbus, Ohio
Tobik, Andy	51	RG	1	175	5' 10"	Cleveland, Ohio
Tucci, Amel	49	RG	1	195	5' 9"	Zanesville, Ohio
Vittek, Paul	63	LG	1	185	5' 10"	Columbus, Ohio
*Wedebrook, Howard	14	RH	3	196	6' 1"	Portsmouth, Ohio
Welbaum, Thomas	65	FB	2	165	5' 9"	Akron, Ohio
White, Claude	37	C	2	190	6'	Portsmouth, Ohio
Whitehead, Stuart	28	LE	2	195	6'	Columbus, Ohio
Wuellner, Richard	66	C	2	186	5' 11"	Columbus, Ohio
Young, Lewis	30	RT	3	220	5' 10"	Massillon, Ohio
*Zadworney, Frank	6	RH	2	190	5' 11"	Cleveland, Ohio
Zuchegno, Albert	2	FB	1	166	5' 8"	Dover, Ohio

*INDICATES LETTERMAN.

[1938]

```
              1938
       Captains: Michael Kabealo
             Carl G. Kaplanoff
    6   *Indiana               0
    7   *Southern California  14
    0    Northwestern          0
   42   *Chicago               7
   32    New York University   0
    0   *Purdue               12
   32    Illinois             14
    0   *Michigan             18
   ---                       ---
   119                        65
         Won 4, Lost 3, Tied 1
```

Ohio State 6, Indiana 0

Ohio State, with an unbalanced and inexperienced lineup, entered the game as the underdog. Oliver, Nickolson, and Harris were the main thorns that troubled the Bucks. Sexton, Welbaum and Scott were the headliners for the Bucks by constantly breaking up the Hoosier deadly aerial attack. The Indiana game proved one thing to the Bucks — they lacked game experience.

Ohio 7, Southern California 14

Playing superb football but lacking the necessary punch, Ohio State bowed to Howard Jones' Trojans in one of the most thrilling games of the football season. The Bucks literally outplayed the Trojans in the first half, but Southern California redeemed themselves in the second half.

Lansdell took Mike Kabealo's punt on the fourth play of the game, tore for the sidelines, and behind perfect interference, zig-zagged down the field for a touchdown.

In the second period, the Bucks had the ball on the 23-yard line. The Jones' boys, gaining the ball on downs, attempted to kick out of danger but Ohio blocked the ball and recovered on the one-yard line. Jim Langhurst battered through the Trojans for the touchdown. Charlie Maag kicked the extra point.

The Buck advance then took the ball up past the mid-field stripe where two passes to Scott and Langhurst put the ball on the two-yard line. With 16 seconds remaining in the period, the Bucks called time. Co-captain Kaplanoff's attempted field goal failed.

The Trojans scored their winning touchdown in the third period with two long heaves. In the last quarter, the Bucks attempted to get into the scoring zone, but the Trojans held them at bay.

Ohio State 32, Illinois 14

Pulling out of the Ohio Stadium once again, the Buck squad journeyed to meet the Illini. With Jimmy Langhurst at the controls, a revamped Ohio State team made history when they rolled over a strong Illinois team, 32-14.

In the first period, Langhurst and Scott crossed the goal line for two Buck scores. In the second period, however, the home team retaliated with two touchdowns.

Langhurst scored again early in the second half, after the Orange and Black had fumbled deep in their own territory. In the final quarter, Chillicothe's Jimmy intercepted an enemy pass and raced for a score. Charlie Maag scored the final touchdown after a blocked kick.

Ohio State 0, Michigan 18

Finally the day of days had arrived; Michigan had come to town. Filled not only with traditional rivalry, but also with high spirits, a crowd of 75,000 people jammed the stadium to witness the battle.

With effectiveness rarely seen by Ohio fans, Michigan completely unseated the Buck's chances for a Big Ten title. Michigan, for the first time in five years, came from behind, and defeated a Buck team.

The Bucks had more first downs and net yardage than the Wolves in the first half, but lost their stamina. A score was inevitable. Michigan again scored in the fourth period, when Harmon passed to Frutig on the Buck's 18. Another pass with the same combination, scored the second tally. The Bucks attempted to score with an aerial attack but it failed. Two plays later, Michigan romped unscathed for another touchdown.

1939--OHIO STATE ROSTER--1939

Name	No.	Pos.	Years on Squad	Weight	Height	Home
Anderson, Charles	22	E	1	189	5' 11"	Massillon, Ohio
*Andrako, Stephen (Capt.)	36	C	3	192	6'	Trinway, Ohio
*Bartschy, Ross	17	E	3	185	6'	Orrville, Ohio
Bell, William	20	C	1	195	5' 11"	Steubenville, Ohio
Bennet, William	41	T	2	210	6'	Willoughby, Ohio
Bruckner, Edwin	30	G	1	193	5' 11"	Sandusky, Ohio
Carlin, Earl	21	G	1	182	5' 10"	Bryan, Ohio
*Clair, Frank	29	E	2	198	6'	Hamilton, Ohio
Cornsweet, Harold	70	HB	1	175	5' 8"	Cleveland, Ohio
Coyer, William	61	HB	2	172	5' 8"	Orrville, Ohio
Daniell, James	1	T	1	210	6' 1"	Mt. Lebanon, Pa.
Dixon, Thornton	44	T	1	212	5' 11"	Toledo, Ohio
Eastlake, Charles	67	E	1	180	5' 11"	Youngstown, Ohio
Fisher, Richard	2	HB	1	185	5' 10"	Columbiana, Ohio
Fox, Sam	38	E	1	188	6'	Washington, D. C.
Graf, Campbell	53	G	2	170	5' 9"	Columbus, Ohio
Graf, Jack	11	QB	1	196	6'	Columbus, Ohio
*Grundies, Jerome	34	T	2	228	6' 2"	Cleveland, Ohio
Gustavson, Carl	48	T	1	230	6' 2"	Erie, Pa.
Hallabrin, John	12	FB	1	194	5' 10"	Mansfield, Ohio
Hecklinger, Harold	47	E	1	181	6'	Toledo, Ohio
Heffelfinger, Clifford	45	E	1	184	5' 10"	Martins Ferry, Ohio
Hershberger, Pete	56	E	1	185	6'	Columbus, Ohio
Howard, Fritz	23	G	1	194	5' 11"	Toledo, Ohio
Howe, Frank	58	HB	2	180	5' 10"	Columbus, Ohio
Karvasales, James	62	HB	1	160	5' 8"	Columbus, Ohio
Kinkade, Thomas	16	HB	1	190	6' 1"	Toronto, Ohio
*Langhurst, James	8	FB	2	191	5' 11"	Willard, Ohio
Lindsey, Jean	69	E	1	182	5' 11"	Columbus, Ohio
*Maag, Charles	33	T	2	210	6' 3"	Sandusky, Ohio
Madro, Joseph	71	G	2	180	5' 9"	Wellington, Ohio
*Marino, Victor	50	G	3	178	5' 7"	Youngstown, Ohio
Moloney, Robert	19	HB	2	185	6'	Columbus, Ohio
Newlin, John	72	E	2	190	5' 11"	St. Clairsville, Ohio
*Nosker, William	26	G	2	194	6'	Columbus, Ohio
Oman, Donald	39	T	2	189	6'	Richwood, Ohio
Parry, Ward	68	HB	1	171	6'	Augusta, Kan.
Piccinini, James	42	T	1	229	6'	Cleveland, Ohio
*Rabb, John	3	FB	3	178	5' 10"	Akron, Ohio
Rosen, Andy	40	T	2	210	6' 1"	Isabella, Pa.
Santschi, John	32	E	1	178	6'	Akron, Ohio
Sarkkinen, Eino	35	HB	1	172	6'	Fairport, Ohio
*Sarkkinen, Esco	25	E	3	192	6'	Fairport, Ohio
Scarberry, William	52	C	1	193	6' 1"	Columbus, Ohio
*Scott, Don	9	QB	2	208	6' 1"	Canton, Ohio
*Sexton, James	5	QB	2	185	5' 10"	Middletown, Ohio
Simione, John	15	QB	2	170	5' 9"	Youngstown, Ohio
*Smith, Frank	31	G	2	195	5' 10"	Columbus, Ohio
*Spears, Jerry	27	G	2	204	6'	Columbus, Ohio
Stephenson, Jack	43	T	1	214	6' 1"	Marion, Ohio
Terry, Carl	10	HB	1	212	6' 2"	Ironton, Ohio
Thom, Leonard	46	T	1	196	6'	Sandusky, Ohio
Tobik, Andy	51	G	2	180	5' 10"	Cleveland, Ohio
Tucci, Amel	49	G	2	190	5' 9"	Zanesville, Ohio
Wansack, Andy	18	HB	1	171	5' 10"	Campbell, Ohio
*Wedebrook, Howard	14	HB	3	195	6' 1"	Portsmouth, Ohio
*Welbaum, Thomas	65	FB	3	165	5' 9"	Akron, Ohio
*White, Claude	37	C	3	196	6'	Portsmouth, Ohio
*Whitehead, Stuart	28	G	3	192	6'	Columbus, Ohio
Williams, Quentin	57	E	1	187	6' 2"	Cincinnati, Ohio
*Wuellner, Richard	66	C	3	190	5' 11"	Columbus, Ohio
*Zadworney, Frank	6	HB	3	190	6'	Cleveland, Ohio
Zavistoske, George	24	HB	1	160	5' 10"	Racine, Wis.

* denotes lettermen.

[1939]

```
         1939
Captain: Steven F. Andrako
 19  *Missouri         0
 13  *Northwestern     0
 23   Minnesota       20
 14  *Cornell         23
 24  *Indiana          0
 61   Chicago          0
 21  *Illinois         0
 14   Michigan        21
---                  ---
189                   64

      Won 6, Lost 2
     Big Ten Champions
```

49,583 Shivering Fans Watch Stunning Setback

Staters Grab Pair of Early Scores; Walter Scholl Starts Big Red Rally With 78-Yard Touchdown Romp in Second Period

Columbus, O., Oct. 28.—(AP.)—Courageous Cornell spotted Ohio State a pair of touchdowns today, and then roared from behind with a dazzling display of gridiron legerdemain to win, 23 to 14, before 49,583 half-frozen fans.

The Ivy League champions, winning their fourth straight contest, butted the bucks off the road to football fame and rolled up more points than any team has been able to score against Ohio since Francis A. Schmidt became coach here six years ago.

The stunning setback was Ohio's first of the year, and came as a decided upset on the heels of Buckeye victories over Missouri, Northwestern and mighty Minnesota.

Ohio started strong, marching 87 yards to a touchdown in the opening period. Jimmy Strausbaugh, Buck halfback, plunged two yards for the score after a mighty power drive.

The second period was just getting under way when the Bucks grabbed another marker, following an air and ground attack that gained 73 yards. Quarterback Don Scott scooted seven yards for the score, after fumbling the pass from center and appearing trapped far behind the line.

Scholl Runs 78 Yards.

After the second Buck touchdown, Landsberg, Cornell fullback, carried the kickoff back to his 22-yard line, and on the first play substitute halfback Walter Scholl slipped over his right tackle for 78 yards and a touchdown. Perfect blocking paved Scholl's way, but he did plenty of hip-wiggling to elude tacklers not cleared away by his mates.

Two minutes after the kickoff, Scholl passed to substitute halfback Jack Borhman for the second Cornell touchdown. The play went for 64 yards. Borhman, sneaking behind the Ohio secondary, ran 30 yards unmolested. Tackle Nick Drahos placekicked the extra point, and Ohio clung to 14-13 edge at the half.

Halfback Harold McCullough set up and then scored Cornell's third and deciding marker. His punt early in the third session died on Ohio's two-yard line, putting the bucks in a hole. Ohio punted out, but McCullough passed to end Alva Kelly for a first down on the 21. Cornell drove through the line the rest of the way, with McCullough scoring from the three-yard line.

In the middle of the final period, with Cornell thwarting Ohio's aerial attack with interceptions, Drahos booted a perfect place kick from the 12 yard line, clinching the victory. The invaders were on Ohio's 23, going strong, as the game ended.

Ohio had 16 first downs to Cornell's eight, each getting three through the air and the others by rushing.

Cornell-Ohio State Game Statistics

Columbus, Ohio, Oct. 28.—(AP.)—Statistics of the Cornell-Ohio State game:

	Cornell	Ohio State
First downs	8	16
Yards gained rush. (net)	172	203
Forw'd passes attempted	9	14
Forw'd passes completed	6	4
Yards for forw'd passing	121	85
Yards lost, attempted forward passes	21	15
Forward passes intercepted by	3	0
Yards gained, run-back of int. passes	7	0
Punting average (from scrimmage)	39	43
Total yards, all kicks returned	173	98
Opp. fumbles recovered	0	0
Yards lost by penalties	5	20

The lineups:

CORNELL		OHIO STATE
Schmuck	le	Sarrkinen
Blasko	lt	Dixon
Dunbar	lg	Marino
Finneran	c	Andrako
Conti	rg	Nosker
Drahos	rt	Stephenson
Jenkins	re	Clair
Matuszczak	qb	Scott
McCullough	lh	Strausbaugh
Baker	rh	Zadworney
Landsberg	fb	Langhurst

Cornell .... 0 13 7 3—23
Ohio State .... 7 7 0 0—14

Scoring summary: Cornell scoring, touchdowns, Scholl (sub for Baker), Borhman (sub for McCullough), McCullough; points from try after touchdown, Drahos 2 (placekicks); field goal, Drahos (placekick); Ohio State scoring, touchdowns, Strausbaugh, Scott; points from try after touchdown, Scott 2 (placekicks); Cornell substitutions, ends, Kelley, Burke, Hershey; tackles, West, Lafey; guards, Cohn; backs, Bohrman, Murphy, Scholl, Brown, Ruddy; Ohio State substitutions, ends, Anderson, Bartschy; tackles, Maag, Thom; guards, Howard, Spears, Tucci, Whitehead; center, Wuellner; backs, Rabb, Graff, Hallabrin, Wedebrook, Simione, Welbaum, Fisher; officials, referee, Frank Lane, Cincinnati; umpire, Russ Finsterwald, Ohio University; field judge, R. H. Rupp, Lebanon Viley; head linesman, Boyd Chambers, Denison.

OHIO STATE NORTHWESTERN
OCTOBER 14·1939
OHIO STADIUM
TWENTY FIVE CENTS

Tom Harmon Sparks Michigan To Second Half Rally That Beats Ohio State, 21-14

Mighty Back Passes, Runs Team To Victory

Wolverines Duplicate Recent Cornell Feat by Spotting Buckeyes Two Scores Before Coming Back to Win; Staters to Share Crown

Ann Arbor, Mich., Nov. 25.—(AP.)—Ohio State University won at least a share of the Western Conference football championship today in much the same manner that Max Schmeling won the world's heavyweight title—flat on its back.

Michigan's wily Wolverines wrecked the Buckeye hopes of a "clean" conference season by spotting Ohio two first-period touchdowns and then roaring back to win by 21 to 14, the second time this year that Ohio State surrendered a two-touchdown edge. Cornell came from behind earlier in the campaign to hand the Buckeyes their only previous loss.

Tom Harmon, Michigan's mighty halfback, stood head and shoulders above the rest of the field, his passing and running constituting a one man victory parade—but Buckeye mistakes cost Ohio State the laurels. Twice the alert Wolves turned Ohio fumbles into touchdowns.

A crowd of 80,227 crammed every corner of the Michigan Stadium to witness one of the most thrilling duels in the 37-year history of the Buckeye-Wolverine grid feud.

Scott Passes Good.

Ohio State started like a powerhouse, ramming across two touchdowns in the first 10 minutes, both on passes by Don Scott, quarterback, after intercepted aerials had started the Bucks goalward.

Ohio dipped deep into its bag of tricks to score the first, guard Vic Marino lining up at an end and then taking Scott's five-yard heave in the end zone. Three minutes later Scott passed 17 yards to end Frank Clair for the second marker, Clair taking it in scoring territory.

Scott booted both extra points, and that ended Ohio. Early in the second session Harmon and end Joe Rogers connected on a 49-yard aerial, down to the Buckeye six, and on the second play Harmon flipped a touchdown pass to Quarterback Forest Evashevski.

In the third period Guard Ralph Fritz snatched Scott's fumble on the Ohio 35, and Harmon followed with a pass to Rogers on the 16. Then Michigan pulled "old 83" out of the sack, and Harmon, after a bit of backfield "Dipsy Doo," skirted his right end for the touchdown that evened the count. Harmon kicked both extra points.

Hallabrin Fumbles.

Scott took the next kick-off on his ten and raced to the 24, from where halfback Jimmy Strausbaugh went off tackle for 37 yards, the longest run of the contest, but John Hallabrin, fullback filling in for injured Jim Langhurst, fumbled on the 11, with Bob Westfall recovering for the Wolves.

The game-clinching touchdown came with 50 seconds to play, and was a personal as well as an artistic triumph for Coach Fritz Crisler of the Wolverines. Michigan started its march on its own 33, where Westfall recovered Strausbaugh's fumble. Harmon's runs, and his passes to Ed Czak and Evashevski, put the ball on the Ohio six, but the Bucks pushed them back to the 24 in three plays.

Then Crisler sent Bob Ingalls, a sophomore center, in at the quarterback spot with instructions. The Wolves lined up in placekick formation with Halfback Fred Trosko holding the ball, and Harmon in kicking position. Harmon faked the kick and ran ahead as Trosko picked up the pigskin and raced behind him for 24 yards into the end zone. Harmon booted the perfectly useless extra point.

That bit of payoff strategy gave Crisler his second win over Ohio's Francis Schmidt in as many starts, the Wolves having taken last year's struggle by 18 to 0 after suffering four straight setbacks at Schmidt's hands before Crisler took over the reins.

OHIO STATE		MICHIGAN
Sarkkinen	e	Rogers
Daniell	t	Savilla
Marino	g	Fritz
Andrako	c	Kodros
Nosker	g	Sukup
Maag	t	Smith
Clair	e	Nicholson
Scott	q	Evashevski
Strausbaugh	h	Trosko
Zadworney	h	Harmon
Hallabrin	b	Westfall

Michigan .... 0 7 7 7—21
Ohio State .... 14 0 0 0—14

Ohio State scoring: Touchdowns, Marino, Clair; points from try after touchdown, Scott 2 (placements).

Michigan scoring: Touchdowns, Evashevski, Harmon, Trosko; points from try after touchdown, Harmon 3 (placements).

Referee, James Masker, Northwestern; umpire, Anthony Haines, Yale; field judge, E. C. Krieger, Ohio University; head linesman, Perry Graves, Illinois.

Ohio State-Michigan Game Statistics

	O.S.	M.
First downs	11	11
Yards gained by rushing (net)	172	119
Forward passes attempted	13	20
Forward passes completed	5	12
Yards by forward passing	36	146
Yards lost attempted forward passes	2	12
Forward passes intercepted by	4	2
Yards gained, runback of int. passes	79	8
Punting average (from scrimmage)	44	41
Total yards, all kicks returned	86	94
Opponents' fumbles recovered	1	4
Yards lost by penalties	0	20

1940 — OHIO STATE ROSTER — 1940

Name	No.	Pos.	Years on Squad	Wt.	Ht.	Home
Adams, William	27	E	1	191	6' 1"	Steubenville, Ohio
Alexinas, Edward	19	B	1	171	6' 1"	Dayton, Ohio
*Anderson, Charles	22	E	2	189	5' 11"	Massillon, Ohio
Bell, William	20	C	2	190	5' 11"	Steubenville, Ohio
Bruckner, Edwin	30	G	2	191	5' 11"	Sandusky, Ohio
Carlin, Earl	21	G	2	180	5' 10"	Bryan, Ohio
*Clair, Frank	29	E	3	198	6'	Hamilton, Ohio
Cornsweet, Harold	70	B	2	175	5' 8"	Cleveland, Ohio
Correll, John	68	B	1	172	5' 11"	Canton, Ohio
*Daniell, James	1	T	2	209	6' 1"	Mt. Lebanon, Pa.
*Dixon, Thornton	44	T	2	212	5' 11"	Toledo, Ohio
*Fisher, Richard	2	B	2	181	5' 10"	Columbiana, Ohio
Fox, Sam	38	E	2	188	6'	Washington, D. C.
*Graf, Jack	11	B	2	190	6'	Columbus, Ohio
*Grundies, Jerry	34	T	3	210	6'	Cleveland, Ohio
Gustavson, Carl	48	T	1	215	6'	Erie, Pa.
*Hallabrin, John	12	B	2	187	5' 10"	Mansfield, Ohio
Hecklinger, Harold	47	E	2	182	6'	Toledo, Ohio
Heffelfinger, Clifford	45	G	2	184	5' 10"	Martins Ferry, Ohio
Hershberger, Peter	56	E	2	185	6'	Columbus, Ohio
Horvath, Leslie	53	B	1	169	5' 10"	Parma, Ohio
*Howard, Fritz	23	G	2	193	5' 11"	Toledo, Ohio
Howe, Frank	58	B	3	180	5' 9"	Columbus, Ohio
*Kinkade, Thomas	16	B	2	184	6' 1"	Toronto, Ohio
*Langhurst, James (Captain)	8	B	3	193	5' 11"	Willard, Ohio
Linkins, Arthur	54	C	1	180	5' 11"	Middletown, Ohio
Lynn, George	6	B	1	185	5' 11"	Niles, Ohio
*Maag, Charles	33	T	2	208	6' 3"	Sandusky, Ohio
Massie, Edmund	14	E	1	192	5' 11"	Wellston, Ohio
McCafferty, Don	25	E	1	198	6' 2"	Cleveland, Ohio
Mires, David	63	T	1	204	5' 11"	Liberty Center, Ohio
Newlin, Jack	72	E	1	192	5' 11"	St. Clairsville, Ohio
Nichols, Harold	17	B	1	177	5' 11"	Marietta, Ohio
*Nosker, William	26	G	3	191	5' 11"	Columbus, Ohio
Novak, Joseph	18	B	1	178	5' 9"	Chardon, Ohio
*Piccinini, James	42	T	2	215	6'	Cleveland, Ohio
Pitton, Robert	59	T	1	194	6'	Columbus, Ohio
Placas, John	66	T	1	197	5' 11"	Cleveland, Ohio
Richey, Frank	13	B	1	151	5' 10"	Columbus, Ohio
Roman, Nicholas	28	E	1	198	6'	Canton, Ohio
*Rosen, Andy	40	G	3	199	6'	Isabella, Pa.
Santschi, John	32	E	2	178	6'	Akron, Ohio
Sarkkinen, Eino	35	B	3	173	6'	Fairport Harbor, Ohio
Sayers, Peter	31	G	1	193	5' 11"	Columbus, Ohio
Schimke, Louis	50	G	1	190	5' 9"	Massillon, Ohio
*Scott, Donald	9	B	3	208	6' 1"	Canton, Ohio
*Sexton, James	5	B	3	184	5' 10"	Middletown, Ohio
Siferd, Charles	67	G	1	187	5' 11"	Wapakoneta, Ohio
*Simione, John	15	B	3	170	5' 9"	Youngstown, Ohio
Staker, Loren	65	B	1	167	5' 10"	Columbus, Ohio
Stephenson, Jack	43	T	2	214	6' 1"	Marion, Ohio
*Strausbaugh, James	4	B	3	180	5' 10"	Chillicothe, Ohio
Sweeney, Paul	3	B	1	179	5' 9"	Cleveland, Ohio
*Thom, Leonard	46	G	2	196	6'	Sandusky, Ohio
Tobik, Andy	51	G	3	179	5' 10"	Cleveland, Ohio
Vickroy, William	36	C	1	182	5' 11"	Toledo, Ohio
*White, Claude	37	C	3	196	6'	Portsmouth, Ohio
Williams, Quent	57	E	2	190	6' 2"	Cincinnati, Ohio
Wynn, Herbert	7	B	1	182	5' 11"	Canton, Ohio
Zavistoske, George	24	B	2	161	5' 10"	Racine, Wis.

denotes lettermen.

First Row: Left to right—Blickle (Backfield Coach), Jones (Center Coach), 34 Grundies, 51 Tobik, 15 Simione, 5 Sexton, 37 White, 4 Strausbaugh, 9 Scott, 8 Langhurst (Capt.), 33 Maag, 46 Thom, 26 Nosker, 29 Clair, 72 Newlin, 1 Daniell, 40 Rosen, 58 Howe, Gillman (End Coach), Mackey (Freshman Coach).

Second Row: Left to right—Dr. Duffee (Team Physician), Schmidt (Head Coach), St. John (Athletic Dir.), 35 Sarkkinen, 52 Scarberry, 16 Kinkade, 2 Fisher, 60 Arnold, 43 Stephenson, 20 Bell, 22 Anderson, 21 Carlin, 12 Hallabrin, 11 Graf, 50 Schimke, 56 Hershberger, 18 Novak, 44 Dixon, 48 Gustavson, 23 Howard, Godfrey (Line Coach), Smith (Trainer).

Third Row: Left to right—15 Heffelfinger, 17 Nichols, 30 Bruckner, 47 Hecklinger, 57 Williams, 24 Zavistoske, 25 McCafferty, 53 Horvath, 67 Siferd, 3 Sweeney, 14 Massie, 59 Pitton, 54 Linkins, 68 Correll, 27 Adams, 70 Cornsweet, 42 Piccinini.

Fourth Row: Left to right—Zieske (Mgr.), 39 Lewis, 63 Mires, 32 Santschi, 38 Fox, 66 Placas, 62 Vittek, 19 Alexinas, 65 Staker, 10 Greenler, 6 Lynn, 36 Vickroy, 31 Sayers, 28 Roman, 7 Wynn, 13 Richey.

Cornell Beats Ohio State In Impressive Fashion

Big Red Comes From Behind After Buckeyes Score in First Period to Make Runaway of Contest, Gaining Triumph, 21 to 7

```
           1940
    Captain: E. James Langhurst

    30  *Pittsburgh          7
    17  *Purdue             14
     3   Northwestern        6
     7  *Minnesota          13
     7   Cornell            21
    21  *Indiana             6
    14   Illinois            6
     0  *Michigan           40
    ---                    ---
    99                     113
         Won 4, Lost 4
```

Ithaca, N. Y., Oct. 26—(AP)—Cornell's fine football team had to come from behind today to keep its record intact, but was tremendously impressive in doing so as it walloped Ohio State, 21-7, in the big Red's first and only intersectional game of the year.

In its first three games this season, Cornell was able to get off in front and keep rolling. But this afternoon, before a capacity crowd of 34,500 in Schoellkopf Stadium, the Ithacans were rocked right back on their heels by the Buckeyes' powerful opening drive, yet had poise, power and all-around proficiency enough to make it a runaway in the second half.

Of these three, poise probably was the most important. Almost any other team might have been thrown completely off stride by the 89-yard scoring march Ohio State put on the first time it got the ball.

Cornell Rallies.

But not this team, now unbeaten in 16 straight games. Cornell came back to go 47 yards for the tying touchdown in the second quarter, and in the second half not only throttled the Ohio State attack down to 44 yards but drove 61 yards once, to go out in front and capitalized on a break for the final score.

The victory was at a price, however, Kirk Hershey, fine end who had returned to action after a two-game absence, went out for the rest of the year with an aggravation of his knee injury, and Howard Dunbar, playing with a mask to protect his broken nose, had it broken again.

Ohio, after its opening march, couldn't do anything. The big, bruising Buckeyes got inside the Cornell 35 only once again, on a recovered fumble a few minutes after their touchdown. From then on they got to the 35, and no further, twice.

On that scoring drive, the Buckeyes looked as if they could keep rolling all day. Tom Kinkade, Jim Langhurst and Hard-W Don Scott, who played without relief, pounded into and around the Cornell line. Without throwing a single pass, they hammered to six straight first downs, the last of them on the Cornell 1, and sent Langhurst driving through the middle from there.

Cornell-Ohio State Game Statistics

Ithaca, N. Y., Oct. 26—(AP.)—Statistics of the Ohio State-Cornell football game:

	OS	Cornell
First downs	10	15
Yds. gain. by rush. (net)	149	184
Forw'd pass. attempted	14	16
Forw'd pass. completed	7	7
Yds. gained forw'd pass	43	92
Yds. lost att. forw'd pass	8	4
Forw'd pass. intercept. by	1	5
Yds. gained runback of int. passes	13	45
Punt. ave. (from scrim.)	43	31
xTot. yds. kicks returned	82	61
Opp. fumbles recovered	2	0
Yds. lost by penalties	50	5

x—Includes punts and kickoffs.

Francis Schmidt Resigns As Head Football Coach At Ohio State University

Withdraws After Poor Grid Year

Resignations of Other Members of Staff Also Accepted; Makes Little Comment

OHIO STATE 14, ILLINOIS 6

Another Big Ten victory was obtained by the Scarlet at Illinois. Don Scott, playing up to his pre-season reputation, scored all the Ohio points and starred as line-backer on defense. The Bucks crossed the Illinois goal after the first ten plays. In the third quarter Kinkade pounded the tackles relentlessly and fought his way to the two-yard line. Scott went over on the first attempt. Bob Zuppke's eleven kept fighting till the final whistle. They threatened continually in the last quarter, completing nine passes. Illinois made 13 first downs against nine for Ohio, but were outgained heavily in total yardage.

OHIO STATE 0, MICHIGAN 40

No rosy verbiage can gild the memory of the 1940 Ohio-Michigan football game.

Seventy-four thousand Homecoming Day fans stuck through intermittent rain and sleet to the horrible end. They saw probably the most brilliant individual exhibition of football since Chic Harley ended his grid career in 1919. Thomas Dudley Harmon, Michigan's great All-American halfback, played 59 minutes and 22 seconds, during which he did everything but steal the southwest tower of the Stadium. He scored three touchdowns and passed for two others (breaking Red Grange's conference scoring record). He kicked four extra points and had a punting average of fifty yards; tackled like a demon on defense and blocked excellently on offense; and rolled up a staggering amount of yardage from his running and passing. The entire Wolverine team contributed superb assistance.

The scoring started with an 80-yard Michigan march in the first quarter, Harmon going over from the 7-yard line.

Columbus, Ohio, Dec. 16.—(AP.)—Francis A. Schmidt, the tall, greying Texan who made football a spectacle with his wide-open "razzle-dazzle" style of play, stepped out tonight as head coach at Ohio State University.

The Board of Athletic Control announced it had accepted the resignation of Schmidt and five other members of the coaching staff.

Submits Resignation.

Schmidt submitted his resignation earlier today because, he commented dryly, "the board is dissatisfied." He did not amplify, but an investigation of the "football situation" at Ohio State was launched by the athletic board a week ago tonight following a four-won, four-lost season—the first for the Bucks in 10 years.

The assistant coaches who also resigned were Ernie Godfrey, line coach, Sil Gillman, end coach, Ed Blickle, backfield coach, and Gomer Jones, a scout and assistant line coach.

Fritz Mackey resigned as coach of the freshman squad, but will remain as baseball coach. The board said that Blickle also would remain as assistant basketball coach.

The resignations are effective next June 30, when the coaching contracts expire. Ohio State employs its athletic staff on a year-to-year basis.

The board's announcement, which terminated Schmidt's seven-year reign at Ohio State, came after a two and one-half hour session. Rumors were rife earlier that Schmidt had resigned, but he did not confirm this until after the board met in a specially-called session.

Has Winning Record.

In his seven years at Columbus, rated as one of the toughest coaching towns in the country, Schmidt's teams won 39 games, lost 16 and tied one. In 1934 the Bucks tied for the Big Ten title, and in 1939 they won it outright—their first since 1920.

Schmidt, who came here from Texas Christian, did not attend the board meeting because "the board doesn't want anything more from me. Mrs. Schmidt and I are going out for the evening."

Paul Brown Is 'Drafted' To Ohio State Position

High School Coach Approved by Athletic Board and University Trustees; Receives Full Support of Fans Throughout State

Columbus, Ohio, Jan. 14.—(AP.)—Paul Brown, who was too small to play with Ohio State University's freshman football team 13 years ago, today became the biggest gridiron figure on the Buckeye campus.

A "draft Brown" movement which started a couple of minutes after Francis Schmidt had resigned the head coaching job December 16 swept the Massillon High School miracle man into the vacant berth today as the athletic board and university trustees stamped him with their official okeh.

Never In History.

Never in the history of Buckeye athletics has a man received the state-wide support of fans, alumni and other coaches as did Brown, whose Massillon High teams lost only eight games in his nine years of scholastic mentorship. They lost only one in the last 60 contests.

With practically everyone in Ohio on the Brown band-wagon, the athletic board's unanimous decision today was a mere formality.

Brown, informed of his appointment while addressing a joint meeting of Columbus luncheon and sports clubs, declared:

"I am a very happy man. I have been running this football business on a basis of merit and right and wrong. I'll continue to run it that way, no matter where the chips may fall. I say this is the expectation and conviction that I will receive the utmost cooperation from the university officials and the youngsters.

"I have made no commitments relative to my staff. That will take a lot of serious thought, but I expect to have my assistants lined up in about three weeks. But you may say this, the staff will be my own, of my own choosing. And I alone will answer for it."

Not Certain.

The new Buckeye mentor, the first to jump straight from a high school job to the fifth largest university in the country, was not certain when he would take over his new chores. He will confer with Athletic Director L. W. St. John on that point.

Brown will get a one-year contract, with a three-year gentleman's agreement. The first year, it was understood, he will receive $6500, with a $500 increase the second and third season. On top of that a summer school teaching session will add about $500 annually to his earnings.

Brown's appointment gives the Western Conference two head coaches from the town of Massillon (pop. 26,000). The other is Harry Stuhldreher of Wisconsin, who was the smallest quarterback in Massillon High School history. Brown was the second smallest ever to play with that scholastic juggernaut.

1941
Coach: Paul E. Brown
Captain: Jack W. Stephenson

12	*Missouri	7
33	Southern California	0
16	*Purdue	14
7	*Northwestern	14
21	Pittsburgh	14
46	*Wisconsin	34
12	*Illinois	7
20	Michigan	20
167		110

Won 6, Lost 1, Tied 1

Name	No.	Pos.	Wt.	Ht.	Exp.	Home Town
*Anderson, Charles	22	E	196	6'	2	Massillon
*Bruckner, Ed	80	G	188	5'11"	2	Sandusky
Burgett, Richard	24	FB	178	5'11"	0	Columbus
Coleman, Kenneth	26	E	180	6'	0	Brooklyn, N. Y.
Cheroke, George	28	G	183	5'9"	0	Shadyside
Csuri, Charles	60	T	197	6'1"	0	Cleveland
*Daniell, James	99	T	219	6'2"	2	Mt. Lebanon, Pa.
Dean, Harold	84	G	185	6'	0	Wooster
*Dixon, Thornton	86	T	202	5'11"	2	Toledo
*Fisher, Dick	33	HB	188	6'	2	Columbiana
*Fox, Sam	34	E	197	6'1"	2	Washington, D. C.
Frye, Robert	36	FB	180	6'	0	Crestline
*Graf, Jack	44	FB	190	6'	2	Columbus
*Hallabrin, John	55	QB	190	5'10"	2	Mansfield
Hecklinger, Robert	42	FB	185	5'11"	0	Toledo
*Hershberger, Peter	70	E	187	6'1"	2	Columbus
*Horvath, Leslie	48	HB	157	5'10"	1	Cleveland
*Howard, Fritz	72	G	195	6'	2	Toledo
Houston, Lindell	96	G	192	6'	0	Massillon
*Kinkade, Thomas	66	HB	190	6'2"	2	Toronto
Lynn, George	11	QB	191	6'	0	Niles
McCafferty, Don	98	T	200	6'3"	1	Cleveland
Martin, Earl	50	C	200	6'3"	0	Massillon
McCormick, Robert	52	T	202	6'	0	Columbus
Novak, Joe	58	HB	175	5'9"	0	Chardon
Palmer, Richard	62	QB	190	5'10"	0	Cleveland
Placas, John	68	QB	195	5'10"	0	Cleveland
Roe, John	74	C	180	5'11"	0	Steubenville
Rosen, John	10	C	185	5'11"	0	Isabella, Pa.
Sarringhaus, Paul	88	HB	190	6'	0	Hamilton
Schneider, Wilbur	12	G	175	5'8"	0	Gahanna
Schoenbaum, Leon	82	E	187	6'	0	Huntington, W. Va.
Sedor, William	14	E	188	6'2"	0	Shadyside
Shaw, Robert	40	E	198	6'3"	0	Fremont
Steinberg, Don	46	E	190	6'	0	Toledo
*Stephenson, Jack	90	T	212	6'1"	2	Marion
Sweeney, Paul	16	HB	178	5'9"	1	Cleveland
Staker, Loren	32	HB	180	5'10"	0	Columbus
Vickroy, William	18	C	190	6'	1	Toledo
Zavistoske, George	20	HB	172	5'10"	2	Racine, Wisconsin
Zimmerman, Dick	30	T	210	6'1"	0	Columbus

(*) Lettermen

MISSOURI

Coach Paul Brown had a happy debut into college football as his Buckeye eleven gained a hard-fought 12-7 victory over Missouri. By using few more than ten plays Ohio played a straight forward football game and showed a much keener knowledge of football fundamentals than has most previous Buck teams.

Tom Kinkade, Buckeye right halfback, broke loose for what looked like a spectacular thirty-four yard touchdown run in the first quarter, but the officials ruled that Tom had stepped out on the seventeen yard line. The first score came in the second quarter, after a long march down the field, when Jack Graf plunged two yards on a fourth down to give the Scarlet their first six points. In the third quarter Graf got off a beautiful punt that led to Ohio's second tally. After a few short line smashes Graf again scored—this time from the one yard line. Late in the last period Missouri fullback Wade took the ball without first shifting, and ran twelve yards straight through the center of the line for the Tigers' only score.

Jack Graf displayed a fine offensive drive as he consistently made good gains through the line. The whole line was excellent in stopping the Tiger offense, with big Jim Daniell carrying most of the burden. Kinkade was as good defensively as always.

12-7

SOUTHERN CAL.

Ohio State's 33-0 triumph over the University of Southern California was so unexpected that the entire football world was upset. Over 15,000 people stormed the Union Station to pay tribute to the Buckeye gridders.

Ohio State's entire squad saw action. In no quarter was there a letdown. It was the same fighting team throughout the game. Les Horvath, in his first real varsity chance, played a whale of a game at halfback. Jack Graf equalled his brilliant performance against Missouri. Tom Kinkade and Dick Fisher both reeled off terrific gains. Johnny Hallabrin's quarterbacking was close to flawless. The whole line was sensational in smearing the Trojan running attack.

Three thousand miles away from home the Ohioans scored two touchdowns after one quarter of play. Graf plunged two yards for the first score after a rambling drive down the field. Anderson romped seventeen for the next one. In the second period Graf recovered his own fumble on the California's 29 and Fisher ran the intervening 29 yards without being touched. Score at the half: Ohio State, 20—Southern California, 0. A 48 yard pass from Graf to end Bob Shaw accounted for the fourth score in the third quarter. Late in the last period Fisher smashed through tackle after a Buck drive to the opponents' four yard line which accounted for the last score.

33-0

Ohio pulls their famous "End-Around" play to score six points against the Trojans of Southern California.

NORTHWESTERN

Before a sellout crowd of 71,896 people, Ohio State lost their only game of the season to the highly favored and powerful team of Northwestern. The Wildcats displayed a well balanced team with plenty of spirit, and well deserved to win.

Northwestern scored in the second half on a pass from Graham to Hasse. A few minutes later State responded with a touchdown set up by a 30 yard pass from Fisher to Shaw. Sophomore Hecklinger plunged over for the score. The winning tally came after an Ohio State fumble and a pass from Graham to Molte.

Outplayed in every department of the game the Bucks had that determination to fight which goes a long way in making a great team. Not once did they give up. They were in there fighting until the last play but lost to a more powerful adversary.

7-14

WISCONSIN

Two favorite sons of Massillon sent their teams into Ohio Stadium and presented football fans with one of the most thrilling battles ever fought in the history of the Western Conference. Harry Stuhldreher, captain of the famous "Four Horsemen" from Notre Dame, saw his Badgers chalk up 34 points; but Paul Brown witnessed his Scarlet Gridders run, pass and punt to pile up 46 points and win their fifth victory of the year.

By the end of the first half the score stood 20-14 in favor of Ohio. After the intermission the Badgers took the ball and marched 80 yards for the tieing score. But, a series of Ohio drives saw Graf cross the goal line often enough to raise the Scarlet score to 40. When the game was over, the scoreboard read 46-34 and Ohio rooters went home exhausted but exceedingly happy.

46-34

MICHIGAN

Much more exciting than last year's game, just as many points—and Ohio got half of them. Everything happened as the Buckeyes finished a successful season by surprising the highly rated Wolverines with a tie.

It was a thrilling game with both teams scoring three touchdowns and missing their third conversion. Kuzma and Westfall sparked the drive for the Wolverines as they either scored or passed for all of Michigan's points.

Jack Graf and Dick Fisher, Ohio's two great running backs, climaxed their careers with impressive performances. Graf's running and passing — Fisher's running and pass receiving — were the Ohio State attack. Tom Kinkade, also playing his last game, turned in a brilliant defensive job while the line held the highly esteemed Michigan forward wall to a standstill.

20-20

Coach Paul Brown
Captain Jack Stephenson

1942... Ohio State ...ROSTER

No.	Name	Pos.	Wt.	Ht.	Class	High School
50	Appleby, Gordon	C	181	5' 11"	So.	Massillon
92	Amling, Martin	G	180	5' 9"	So.	Parma, Ill.
82	Antennucci, Thomas	E	178	5' 11"	So.	Niles
78	Cleary, Thomas	HB	188	5' 11"	So.	Clev. St. Ignatius
26	Coleman, Kenneth	C	185	6' 1"	Jr.	Brooklyn, N. Y.
60	Csuri, Charles	T	195	6'	Jr.	Clev. W. Tech.
84	Dean, Hal	G	190	6'	Jr.	Wooster
68	Drake, Phillip	QB	185	6'	So.	Columbus North
94	Dugger, Jack	T	205	6' 4"	So.	Canton McKinley
20	Durtschi, William	HB	172	5' 8"	Jr.	Galion
48	Eichwald, Kenneth	E	181	6' 4"	So.	Lakewood
44	Fekete, Gene	FB	192	6' 1"	So.	Findlay
36	Frye, Robert	HB	161	5' 10"	Jr.	Crestline
28	Hackett, William	G	185	5' 9"	So.	London
22	Horvath, Leslie	HB	160	5' 11"	Sr.	Cleveland Rhodes
96	Houston, Lindel	G	198	5' 11"	Jr.	Massillon
72	Jabbusch, Robert	G	187	5' 10"	So.	Elyria
66	James, Thomas	HB	155	5' 9"	So.	Massillon
76	Lipaj, Cyril	FB	180	5' 10"	So.	Lakewood
33	Lavelli, Dante	E	185	6' 1"	So.	Hudson
11	Lynn, George (C)	QB	195	6'	Jr.	Niles
98	McCafferty, Don	T	202	6' 4"	Sr.	Cleveland Rhodes
52	McCormick, Bob	T	198	5' 10"	Jr.	Columbus South
24	MacDonald, W.	G	182	5' 10"	So.	Detroit
10	Matus, Paul	E	178	5' 11"	So.	Wakeman
86	Naples, Carmen	G	185	5' 11"	Jr.	Youngstown
62	Palmer, Richard	FB	192	5' 10"	Jr.	Cleveland Shaw
30	Priday, Paul	QB	180	5' 10"	So.	W. Jefferson
90	Rees, James	T	199	6'	So.	Greenville
74	Roe, Jack	C	180	5' 11"	Jr.	Steubenville
88	Sarringhaus, Paul	HB	190	5' 10"	Jr.	Hamilton
12	Schneider, Wib	G	175	5' 8"	Jr.	Gahanna
14	Sedor, William	E	188	6' 2"	Jr.	Shadyside
54	Selby, Paul	QB	198	5' 10"	So.	Upper Arlington
40	Shaw, Robert	E	199	6' 3"	Jr.	Fremont Ross
42	Slusser, George	HB	170	5' 11"	So.	Massillon
80	Souders, Cecil	E	189	6'	So.	Bucyrus
32	Staker, Loren	HB	160	5' 11"	Sr.	Columbus East
46	Steinberg, Don	E	190	6'	Jr.	Toledo Scott
55	Vickroy, William	C	190	6'	Sr.	Toledo Scott
99	Willis, William	T	202	6' 2"	So.	Columbus East
70	White, John	E	190	6' 3"	So.	River Rouge, Mich.
64	Taylor, Tom	T	195	6' 1"	So.	Lancaster

(*) Lettermen

1942
Captain: George M. Lynn

59	*Fort Knox	0
32	*Indiana	21
28	*Southern California	12
26	*Purdue	0
20	Northwestern	6
7	Wisconsin	17
59	*Pittsburgh	19
44	Illinois (Cleveland)	20
21	*Michigan	7
41	*Iowa Seahawks	12
337		114

Won 9, Lost 1
Big Ten Champions

1942
A.P. POLL

1. OHIO STATE
2. Georgia
3. Wisconsin
4. Tulsa
5. Georgia Tech
6. Notre Dame
7. Tennessee
8. Boston College
9. Michigan
10. Alabama

Those wide open spaces. George Slusser races across the line way into the Purdue backfield. The Boilermakers only had the ball twice in Ohio territory and one of those resulted from a fumble.

Wisconsin Knocks Off Ohio State

Underdog Badgers Arise to Gridiron Heights to Blast Buckeyes From Top

Madison, Wis., Oct. 31.—(AP.)—Underdog Wisconsin, arising to gridiron heights, blasted Ohio State's Buckeyes from football's number one ranking today.

After 60 minutes of hair-raising football, the Badgers trotted off Camp Randall Field to the cheers of most of the 45,000 bulging-eyed spectators with a 17 to 7 triumph. And the score just about tells the story. Wisconsin threatened three times and scored three times. The Buckeyes had one good scoring chance, and cashed it in.

The headline makers were big Marlin (Pat) Harder, fleet Elroy Hirsch and All-America End Dave Schreiner, but it was a brilliant team victory for Wisconsin. Ohio State's vaunted running attack, which had mauled out triumphs over Fort Knox, Southern California, Indiana, Purdue and Northwestern, piled up a lot of yardage, but when danger threatened, Badger linemen and secondary defenders combined to take charge.

When the Badgers had the ball, fierce charging by the forwards and solid blocking down field gave the backs all the help they needed.

The triumph, which sent Wisconsin to the heights, was Wisconsin's sixth in seven games. After whipping Camp Grant, Wisconsin fought a 7 to 7 tie with Notre Dame, then conquered Marquette, Missouri, Great Lakes and Purdue, to come up to today's all important test undefeated.

OHIO STATE		WISCONSIN
Sedor	le	Manzlik
Willis	lt	Baumann
Dean	lg	Negus
Vickroy	cg	Vogds
Houston	rg	Currier
Csuri	rt	Hirsbrunner
Shaw	re	Schreiner
Lynn	qb	Wink
Sarringhaus	lh	Hirsch
Horvath	rh	Hoskins
Fekete	fb	Harder

Score by periods:
Wisconsin   0 10 0 7—17
Ohio State   0   0 0 7— 7

Ohio State scoring: Touchdown, Sarringhaus, point after touchdown, Fekete (placement).
Wisconsin scoring: Touchdowns, Harder, Schreiner, points after touchdown, Harder 2 (placements). Field goal, Harder (place kick).

Substitutions: Ohio State—Ends, Lavelli, Squires, White; guards, Jabbusch, Schneider, centers, Roe, backs, James, Clery, Frye, Slusser, Priday.
Wisconsin—Ends, Lyons, tackles, Thornally, Wasserbach, guards, Boyle, Roberts, Frei, centers, McKay, backs, Calligaro, Seelinger, Ray, McFadzean.

[1942]

OSU gains 587 yards

OHIO STATE 59; PITTSBURGH 19.

	OSU.	PITT.
Total first downs	21	11
Net yds gained by rushing	348	168
Net yds gained by passing	239	158
Forward passes attempted	20	19
Forward passes completed	11	6
Number of fumbles	5	4

INDIVIDUALS

	TCB	YG	YL	PTS	PT	Comp	YG	HI
Fekete*	3	139	0	10	0	0	0	0
Sarringhaus	5	36	0	12	1	1	37	0
Horvath	4	34	2	0	3	2	33	0
James	4	32	0	6	2	1	21	0
Slusser	6	37	0	0	8	4	119	1
Palmer	4	14	0	6	1	1	20	0
Frye	2	10	0	7	0	0	0	0
Lipaj	5	15	11	6	3	0	0	0
Selby	1	17	0	0	0	0	0	0
Staker	5	24	10	6	3	1	11	0
Eichwald	0	0	0	6	0	0	0	0
Drake	1	5	0	0	0	0	0	0
Amling	1	1	0	0	0	0	0	0

*Ran 83 yards for a touchdown.

Legend: TCB—Times carried ball; YG—Yds. gained; YL—Yds. lost; PTS—Points scored; PT—Passes thrown; Comp—Completed; HI—Had intercepted.

1st home game ever not on OSU campus

OHIO STATE ROUTS ILLINOIS, 44 TO 20

68,656 See the Buckeyes Gain Undisputed Lead in Western Conference

JAMES TALLIES TWICE

Scores on 76 and 33 Yard Runs—Sarringhaus and Horvath Also Shine

By The Associated Press.

CLEVELAND, Nov. 14 — Ohio State, attacking with devastating fury, trounced its old rival, Illinois, 44 to 20, today to take over undisputed first place in the Western Conference football race before 68,656 chilly fans.

The loss eliminated Illinois, with one of its strongest teams since the boom gridiron days of the '20s, from the title chase. Iowa, which had been in a three-way tie for the lead with Ohio and the Illini, was toppled by Minnesota 27 to 7.

From the time little Leslie Horvath, Ohio halfback, sprinted 36 yards for a touchdown, in the first Conference game ever staged here, the Bucks held the edge.

Play in Stadium

Horvath, hard driving Paul Sarringhaus, the other half back, and Sarringhaus's alternate, red-haired Tommy James, held the spotlight in the high scoring game at Cleveland's Lake front stadium.

Horvath's first run came after seven minutes of play. He scored again in the third period by slipping around end for six yards.

But it was Sarringhaus, who uses contact lens because of poor vision, who was largely responsible for the Buckeyes' success. Besides scoring touchdowns on a 1-yard plunge and a 47-yard pass from Horvath, the hard-driving Sarringhaus turned in sensational punting.

Make Two Brilliant Runs

James, given a chance to become Ohio's climax runner, swept wide around end twice for touchdown runs of 76 and 33 yards.

Horvath's and James's long runs and a 15-yard field goal by Fullback Gene Fekete gave Ohio a 23-to-0 lead, but Illinois was still in the game in the second period.

Tony Botkovitch raced a kickoff back 77 yards to the Ohio 3 and scored on the next play. The Illini came booming back with an aerial attack spearheaded by a sub-halfback, Art DeFilippo, that resulted in another touchdown to Sub-Halfback Steve Sucic.

With their lead whittled down at the half, Ohio took advantage of two Illinois fumbles to score twice in the third period after the Illini braced once on the 2½-yard line.

Short Plunge Scores

Sarringhaus got one on his one-yard plunge and Horvath the other on his short sprint. Ohio's last touchdown came on the Horvath-to-Sarringhaus pass.

Illinois scored in the waning minutes against the Buckeye second and third stringers on a 13-yard pass from Don Griffin to sub end Bob Gibbs.

The victory was Ohio's seventeenth in the team's thirty-one years of rivalry. Two games have been tied. The triumph also was Ohio's fourth in the conference against one defeat—to Wisconsin.

While Illinois led in passing, 157 yards to 102, Ohio's power attack rolled up 297 yards to 58. Ohio had a 12-to-9 edge in first downs.

The line-up:

OHIO STATE (44)		ILLINOIS (20)
Steinberg	L.E.	McCarthy
Csuri	L.T.	Genis
Dean	L.G.	Pawlowski
Vickroy	C.	Wenskunas
Houston	R.G.	Agase
McCafferty	R.T.	Kasap
Shaw	R.E.	Engel
Lynn	Q.B.	Florek
Sarringhaus	L.H.	Griffin
Horvath	R.H.	Correll
Fekete	F.B.	Smith

SCORE BY PERIODS
Ohio State .... 13 10 14 7—44
Illinois .... 0 13 0 7—20

Touchdowns—Horvath 2, James (sub for Sarringhaus) 2, Sarringhaus 2, Butkovich (sub for Smith), Sucic (sub for Correll), Gibbs (sub for Engel). Points after touchdown—McCarthy, Wilson (sub for Agase), Fekete 4, Palmer (sub for Fekete) (placekicks). Goal from field—Fekete.

SUBSTITUTES

Ohio State—Ends: White, Souders, Eichwald, Lavelli, Matus. Tackles: Willis, Rees, Dugger. Guards: Schneider, Jabbusch, Amling, Hackett, MacDonald. Centers: Appleby, Roe. Backs: Pfiday, Slusser, James, Palmer, Staker, Lipaj, Drake. Illinois—Ends: Gibbs, Grierson. Tackles: Wallin, Butt. Guards: Smerdel, Wilson. Center: MacArthur. Backs: Butkovich, Sucic, Dufelmeier, Pfeifer.

[1943]

No.	Name	Pos.	Wt.	Home Town	High School Coach
90	Warren Amling	LG	187	Pana, Ill	Ken Chittum
50	Gordon Appleby	C	175	Massillon	Paul Brown
40	Matthew Brown	FB	162	Canton McKinley	John Reed
85	Jim Campbell	RH	174	Huron	Mel Clark
82	Gene Clark	RE	170	Columbus Central	Dave Parks
75	Lee Cunningham	RG	180	Revere, Mass.	Tim Collins
32	Paul Davis	LH	171	Middletown	Elmo Lingrell
55	Jack Dugger	LE	189	Canton McKinley	John Reed
68	Bill Dunivant	C	157	Cuyahoga Falls	Carl Spessard
95	Jerry Fedderson	LE	190	Sandusky	Wal. Glenwright
64	Bob Hall	LG	182	Toledo Libbey	Bill Orwig
96	Bill Hackett	RG	177	London, Ohio	Jacob Von Kanel
20	Bob Hecker	RH	160	Olmsted Falls	Norm Schoen
60	Ronnie Hefflinger	RG	174	Napoleon	Cliff Nelson
30	Jasper Harris	LH	162	Canton McKinley	Herman Rearick
80	Don Kay	LT	186	Marion Harding	Vic Dorris
84	Bud Kessler	RE	181	Worthington	Frank Howe
34	Ernest Lehman	RT	190	Toledo Waite	Jack Mollenkopf
38	Bill Lonjak	C	165	Cleveland W. Tech.	Charles Blickle
86	Paul Maltinsky	C	180	Wheeling, W. Va.	Everett Brinkman
24	Jim Marker	LT	188	Columbus Rosary	Pete Beck
26	Bill McCarty	QB	158	Hilliards	Mr. Tarnholtz
36	Bob McQuade	LH	157	Columbus Aquinas	Frank Zadworney
28	Dick Meinke	LT	187	Elyria	Roy Clymer
70	William Miller	LG	174	Wapakoneta	Paul Schafer
94	George Neff	RG	184	Bellaire	John Neimic
44	Glen Oliver	FB	162	Cols. Univ. H. S.	Bill Williams
65	Frank Parenti	RG	164	Dayton	Bill Stover
22	Ernest Parks	RH	190	Canton McKinley	Herman Rearick
21	Ernest Plank	LE	189	Bexley	Carlton Smith
35	Jack Redd	LG	170	Columbus North	Mike Hagely
33	Dean Sensenbaugher	LH	175	Uhrichsville	Chic Maurer
45	Gene Slough	LH	155	Findlay	Carl Bachman
27	Emil Slovak	FB	158	Oak Harbor	Sam Owen
66	Cecil Souders	RE	188	Bucyrus	Elden Armbrust
92	Ray Stackhouse	RT	199	Dayton Roosevelt	Bobby Coburn
93	Joe Stora	RH	152	Shadyside	Bill Ellis
72	John Stungis	QB	180	Powhatan Point	Dan Piloseno
74	Jack Swartzbaugh	RT	187	Toledo Scott	Robert Retigg
76	Howard Tiefke	C	174	Fremont	Les Binkley
98	Russell Thomas	RT	199	Charleston, W. Va.	Lyle Rich
11	Albert Williams	QB	184	Canton McKinley	T. Swartzwalder
99	Bill Willis	LT	199	Columbus East	Ralph Webster
25	Howard Yerges	QB	160	Grandview	George Hood

1943

Captains: John R. Dugger
Charles A. Csuri

13	*Iowa Seahawks	28
27	*Missouri	6
6	*Great Lakes	13
7	*Purdue (Cleveland)	30
0	*Northwestern	13
14	*Indiana	20
46	*Pittsburgh	6
29	*Illinois	26
7	*Michigan	45
149		187

Won 3, Lost 6

Top row: Brown, P., Head Coach; Stora, Souders, Parks, Kessler, Fedderson, Mackey, Asst. Coach; Miller, Williams, Kay, Oliver, Davis, Dugger, Capt.; Willis, Stungis, Lonjak, Maltinsky, Dunivant, Mayer, Mgr. *Third row:* Appleby, Neff, Lehman, Swartzbaugh, Tiefke, Godfrey, Asst. Coach. *First row:* Bixler, Asst. Coach; Yerges, McCarthy, Slough, McQuade, R.; Parenti, McGranahan, Asst. Coach; Harris, Hecker, Hull, Meinke, Stackhouse, Thomas, Clark, Marker, Plank, Komer, Redd, Biggs, Trainer. *Second row:* Hefflinger, Sensenbaugher, Hackett, Brown, M.; Widdoes, Asst. Coach.

[1943]

OSU 14 — INDIANA 20

"When greater heartbreakers are made, this game will make them." The score read Ohio State 14, Indiana 13. There were only 39 seconds left to play, when a penalty and a sensational passer by the name of Bob (Hunchy) Hoernschemeyer altered the state of affairs completely.

Indiana dominated the offense during the whole first half of the game. Early in the game, Hunchy climaxed a 72-yard drive with a 17-yard aerial to Cannady who went over for the first tally of the game. Cannady scored again during the second quarter when Hunchy picked up 20 yards on a run and passed to Pihos for 20 more.

During the third quarter, Sensenbaugher, Parks, and Brown began to blast through Indiana's line. McQuade then came in for Sensy and tossed a pass to Parks who scampered to Indiana's 29. After working the ball to the 12-yard line, the Bucks gave it to Sensy who dashed around his own end for a tally. Stungis converted the extra point. The Bucks scored again in the final quarter when the trio of Parks, Sensenbaugher, and Brown ripped the Hoosier line to shreds. Stungis again converted, and the Bucks led 14 to 13.

During the close of the game, the Bucks were forced to punt to safety. Hunchy then began his aerial attack. McQuade intercepted one, but a penalty called the play back. It was at this point that Hunchy heaved his game-winning aerial to end the contest.

Sensy skirts around end as Indiana's secondaries close in.

OSU 29—ILLINOIS 26

This game brought forth a new oddity to be recorded in the annals of football. The "fifth quarter" was the most dramatic event in the history of the Big Ten. It is comparable to the Notre Dame-Carnegie Tech game of 1938 when the Irish were allowed to have five downs to score due to the referee's error.

Johnny Stungis was our hero for the day. The score was 26-26, there were only ten seconds to play. Bobby McQuade fired a pass that eluded Ernie Parks' fingertips in the end zone, and the gun cracked. Both teams rushed off the field to their dressing rooms. But Head Linesman Paul Goebel remained in the middle of the field waving his hands frantically. An Illinois man was offside. The play was called back after the gun had sounded. Johnny Stungis went in and booted the ball over the placements with only inches to spare. Those *Dick Merriwell* stories are very exciting and dramatic, but let's see them top this event.

McQuade held it, and Stungis kicked it.

Ohio State Swamped By Wolverines

Michigan Completes Undefeated Western Conference Season With 45-7 Win; Wiese Stars

Statistics.	OS	M
First downs	2	23
Yds. gained rushing (net)	68	426
Forward passes attempted	11	11
Forward passes completed	3	7
Yds. by forward passing	27	105
Forward passes inter. by	1	3
Yards gained runback of int. passes	15	51
Punting average (from scrimmage)	39	27
Total yards, all kicks returned	134	8
Opponents fumbles recovered	1	4
Yards lost by penalties	0	65

Ann Arbor, Mich., Nov. 20.—(AP.)—Michigan's Navy-Marine studded Wolverines trounced the "Baby Buckeyes" of Ohio State, 45-7, to clinch a share of the western conference football championship with Purdue in a season finale witnessed by 45,000 here, today.

The victory, with its second largest point total in a feud started in 1897, gave Michigan its first title claim since 1933. The Wolverines and the Boilermakers each finished undefeated in six league starts, while over the season Michigan was beaten only by Notre Dame.

Michigan's seven-touchdowns splurge was fashioned mainly in the second half when the Wolverines rolled up 32 points against the scrappy but outmanned Ohio State youngsters.

Lead Shaved to 13-7.

The Wolverines, held scoreless in the second period, led only 13-0 at half time and then had their lead shaved to 13-7 when Ernie Parks, rangy Negro star, sprinted 36 yards for the only Buckeye touchdown and Johnny Stungis kicked the point.

But then the Wolverines caught fire and savagely ripped the tiring Buckeye line to score almost at will. Fullback Bob Wiese, whose spinning thrusts bewildered the Buckeyes, led the scoring with two touchdowns, both on short bucks.

Four other Wolverines counted a touchdown apiece, Bob Nussbaumer's 31-yards sweep around end, and a 20-yards sprint by Fullback Don Lund providing the most spectacular scoring.

Gets Team's Second Touchdown.

Wally Dreyer, 158-pounds halfback from Wisconsin, plunged two yards for Michigan's second touchdown, while Earl Maves, another ex-Badger, pounded eight yards for another in Michigan's 19-points final period. Vince Mroz, former Michigan State end, snared a 10-yards pass from Quarterback Jack Wink, former Wisconsin player, for the seventh Michigan touchdown.

Guard Rex Wells booted two conversions and injured Elroy Hirsch, ex-Wisconsin star, kicked one point to wind up as Michigan's leading scorer this season with 63 points.

Largest score in the 40-game series is Michigan's 86-0 victory in 1902.

OHIO STATE		MICHIGAN
Dugger	le	Smeja
Willis	lt	Hanzlik
Neff	lg	Gallagher
Appleby	c	Negus
Hackett	rg	Wells
Thomas	rt	Derleth
Souders	re	Renner
Williams	qb	Wiese
Sensanbaugher	lh	Nussbaumer
Parks	rh	Dreyer
Davis	fb	Lund

Michigan   13 0 13 19—45
Ohio State   0 0   7   0— 7

Ohio State scoring: Touchdown, Parks. Point after touchdown, Stungis (for Williams) (placekick).

Michigan scoring: Touchdowns, Wiese 2, Dreyer, Nussbaumer, Mroz (for Smeja), Lund, Maves (for Dreyer). Points after touchdown, Wells 2, Hirsch (for Nussbaumer) (placekicks).

Substitutions: Ohio State — Ends, Plank, Clark; tackles, Stackhouse, Swartzbaugh, Key; guards, Neff, Heffinger; backs, Brown, Stungis, McQuade, Hecker, Oliver.

Michigan—Ends, Olshanski, Johnson, Mroz, Rennebohm, Crame, Cook, Hilkene; tackles, Greene, Bryan, Kennedy; guards, Kraeger, Myll, Sigler, Sturges, Trump; center, Kern; backs, Maves, Hirsch, Kikel, Powers, Wink, Ponsetto, Aliber.

[1943]

Ohio State Roster

No.	Name	Pos.	Wt.	Home Town	Class
90	Warren Amling	RT	196	Pana, Ill.	Soph.
*50	Gordon Appleby	C	182	Massillon, O.	Senior
28	Kenneth Boxwell	FB	178	Xenia, O.	Fresh.
*40	Matthew Brown	FB	168	Canton, O.	Soph.
11	Robert Brugge	HB	188	Parma, O.	Fresh.
33	Ollie Cline	FB	194	Fredericktown, O.	Fresh.
92	Ernest Cottrell	LT	214	Curtice, O.	Fresh.
82	Traian Dendiu	RE	182	Campbell, O.	Fresh.
73	Charles Diamond	LT	194	Ashtabula, O.	Fresh.
68	Ray DiPierro	LG	192	Toledo, O.	Fresh.
45	Robert Dove	QB	165	Ashland, O.	Fresh.
*55	Jack Dugger	LE	210	Canton, O.	Senior
26	John Ehrsam	FB	168	Toledo, O.	Fresh.
27	Richard Flanagan	HB	189	Sidney, O.	Fresh.
46	George Gordon	QB	153	Maumee, Ohio	Fresh.
88	Frank Graper	RT	204	Maumee, O.	Fresh.
*96	William Hackett	RG	191	London, O.	Junior
84	M. N. Hamilton	RE	174	Toledo, O.	Fresh.
52	Kendall Herron	C	183	Willoughby, O.	Fresh.
*22	Leslie Horvath	RH	167	Parma, O.	Senior
87	Richard Jackson	LE	181	Wellsville, O.	Fresh.
36	Gene Janecko	LH	156	Campbell, O.	Fresh.
44	Tom Keane	QB	178	Bellaire, O.	Fresh.
34	Dan T. Klofta	FB	178	Toledo, O.	Fresh.
*86	Paul Maltinsky	LG	188	Wheeling, W. Va.	Junior
14	Joe Mascio	RH	192	Ravenna, O.	Fresh.
80	John Motejzik	LE	188	Parma, O.	Fresh.
72	Norman McElheny	RT	194	Tiffin, O.	Fresh.
74	Robert McGinnis	LT	194	Wyoming, O.	Fresh.
*94	George Neff	LG	198	Bellaire, O.	Soph.
12	Myron Powelson	RH	158	Zanesville, O.	Fresh.
*60	Jack Redd	RG	181	Columbus, O.	Junior
54	Charles Renner	C	178	Akron, O.	Fresh.
56	Robert Ryan	C	185	Columbus, O.	Soph.
58	Max Schnittker	C	188	Sandusky, O.	Fresh.
64	Tom Snyder	LG	187	Upper Sandusky, O.	Fresh.
10	Tony Stranges	RH	157	St. Clairesville, O.	Fresh.
*98	Russell Thomas	RT	220	Huntington, W. Va.	Soph.
65	George Toneff	RG	175	Barberton, O.	Fresh.
42	Jerry Tuttle	QB	176	Kent, O.	Fresh.
85	Robert Wallace	LE	167	Massillon, O.	Fresh.
24	Richard Wandke	LH	185	Toledo, O.	Fresh.
*99	William Willis	LT	205	Columbus, O.	Senior

* Denotes letterman

BROWN NAVY LIEUTENANT
Football Coach at Ohio State Ordered to Great Lakes

COLUMBUS, Ohio, April 13 (P) —Paul Brown is going to Great Lakes Naval Training Station as a lieutenant (jg)—just at a time when the Bluejackets may be looking for a gridiron coach. The 35-year-old head coach at Ohio State University received notice yesterday that he had been commissioned in the Navy and ordered to report to Great Lakes Monday.

Great Lakes officials were mum on whether Brown might enter into the station's football picture, but Lieut. Paul D. (Tony) Hinkle, who has been directing the Bluejacket football and basketball teams, has been made athletic officer. There has been no word, however, whether he will give up active coaching.

1944
Coach: Carroll C. Widdoes
Captain: Gordon Appleby

54	*Missouri	0
34	*Iowa	0
20	Wisconsin	7
26	*Great Lakes	6
34	*Minnesota	14
21	*Indiana	7
54	*Pittsburgh	19
26	Illinois (Cleveland)	12
18	*Michigan	14
287		79

Won 9, Lost 0
Big Ten Champions

1944 A.P. POLL
1. Army
2. OHIO STATE
3. Randolph Field
4. Navy
5. Bainbridge
6. Iowa Pre-Flight
7. Southern Cal.
8. Michigan
9. Notre Dame
10. 4th AAF

Francis Schmidt, Famed Football Coach, Dies

Spokane, Wash., Sept. 19.—(AP.) —Francis A. Schmidt, head football coach at the University of Idaho until last March and famous for his "razzle dazzle" grid teams at Ohio State University and in the southwest, died tonight.

Schmidt's physician said the coach had been in failing health several months and he had been in a hospital here since early this month.

He was signed at Idaho in 1941, coming west from Ohio State with a 24-year coaching record of 170 victories, 47 losses and 12 ties. A year ago Idaho joined other Pacific northwest colleges in suspending football due to a war-prompted manpower shortage and last March Schmidt's contract was not renewed.

William Willis

OHIO STATE 26 — GREAT LAKES 6

If there were ever a game that was a natural attraction, it was the Great Lakes game. Lt. Paul Brown returned to the giant Buckeye stadium for the first time since he went in the Navy. On Ohio State's bench sat the man who had taken over his job directing an all-civilian squad against his power-laden Navy team. The game was jam-packed with all the thrills that can take place in a contest and they started with Dick Flanagan's sixty-one yard run in the opening minutes. The Sailors were set on bottling up Les Horvath and so Flanagan carried the brunt of the attack in the first half and scored the first touchdown. Horvath started to click in the last half and turned the tide of the game in the closing minutes of the third quarter. His toss to J. Dugger accounted for twenty-five yards and he skirted end for thirty-three on the next play. Three plays later, Les was over for the second score and soon the Bucks had the game on ice.

Meet Carroll Widdoes, new head coach for the coming football season and a person who, as acting head coach this year, achieved the goal in his first year that many fail to attain in a lifetime— "Coach of the Year." Widdoes was born in Manila in the Philippines and obtained his schooling at Otterbein College in Westerville. After graduation, he began his career in Massillon as an assistant to Paul Brown. When Brown came to Ohio State, Wid came too, and is now head man of the Buckeye Bruisers.

Ohio State
Stages Sensational Rally To Overhaul Wolverines, 18 To 14
Crowd Of 71,958 Sees Bucks Win Big 10 Title

Horvath's Fourth Period Score Clinches Struggle, Climaxing Buckeyes' 52-Yard March; Rose Bowl Appearance Now Looms for Victors

Columbus, Ohio, Nov. 25.—(AP.)—Ohio State's All-Civilian football team roared from behind in the closing minutes today to defeat Michigan, 18 to 14, and thus win the Big Ten football championship, finish an unbeaten and untied season and put itself in a spot to go to the Rose Bowl if the western conference lifts its ban on post-season games.

A crowd of 71,958 screaming fans watched the Bucks get up off the floor to march 52 yards late in the fourth period and score the winning touchdown with only 3 minutes and 16 seconds to go.

And then a leaping pass interception by Dick Flanagan finally sealed Michigan's doom a moment later. That gave the Bucks the ball again and they stalled away the time remaining.

The victory gave Ohio State a season record of nine straight triumphs and brought the Big Ten championship to the Bucks for the second time in three years. This was their first unbeaten and untied regular season since 1920.

It was a terrific battle all the way, one team and then the other taking the lead, but the gentleman who eventually produced the payoff was the great Leslie Horvath. The Buck veteran literally leaped over the line of scrimmage from the one-yard line to score the winning touchdown.

It climaxed an Ohio drive that had its inception immediately after Michigan's last touchdown. A bad kickoff that went out of bounds on the Ohio 48-yard line set the stage for that irresistible Buck march.

MICHIGAN		OHIO STATE
Hilkene	le	Dugger
Lazetich	lt	Willis
Burg	lg	Snyder
Watts	c	Appleby
Sickles	rt	Thomas
Bauman	rg	Hackett
A. Renner	re	Dendiu
Derricotte	lb	Horvath
Ponsetto	qh	Flanagan
Chubb	rh	Brugge
Lund	fb	Cline

Michigan   0 7 0 7—14
Ohio State   6 0 6 6—18

Michigan scoring: touchdowns, Culligan 2. Points after touchdown, Ponsetto 2.

Ohio State scoring: touchdowns, Cline, Horvath 2.

Substitutions: Michigan, ends, Greer; tackle, Brielmair; guards, Mahaffey, Chaeverni; center, Lintol; backs, Weisenburger, Yerges, Culligan.
Ohio State, end, Jackson; tackle, Amling; center, C. Renner; backs, Brown, Keane.

STATISTICS.

	M	OS
First downs	10	17
Yds. gained rush. (net)	162	225
Forward passes at.	7	4
F'ward passes completed	1	0
Yds. by f'ward passing	1	1
Forward passes int. by	2	0
Yds. gained run-back int. passes	35	0
Punt. av. (from scrim.)	34	40
Total yds., all kicks ret.	115	73
Opp. fumbles recov.	1	3
Yards lost penalties	5	15

Ohio Rushing and Scoring

Player	TC	YG	AV	Pts.
Gordon	6	80	13.3	6
Brugge	59	384	6.5	42
Horvath	163	924	5.7	72
Janecko	33	150	4.7	24
Keane	36	164	4.6	20
Ehrsam	4	17	4.2	0
Brown	8	34	4.2	0
Flanagan	103	406	3.9	24
Dove	12	46	3.8	2
Cline	65	221	3.4	39
Wandtke	14	43	3.1	0
Stranges	11	27	2.6	6
Boxwell	17	37	2.2	0
Powelson	3	6	2.0	1
Klofta	2	4	2.0	0
Mascio	3	4	1.3	0
Tuttle	2	−5	−2.5	0
Dugger	0	0	0	25
Hamilton	0	0	0	12
Motejzik	0	0	0	6
Souders	0	0	0	6

Passing

Player	PA	Comp	AV	YG
Gordon	2	2	1.000	42
Brugge	1	1	1.000	49
Janecko	1	1	1.000	15
Flanagan	2	1	.500	13
Horvath	32	14	.437	344
Dove	12	4	.333	99
Keane	35	9	.257	164
Tuttle	4	1	.250	17
Wandtke	4	1	.250	16
Stranges	1	0	.000	0
	94	34	.362	

Team Statistics for 1944

	Ohio State	Opponents
Net gain rushing	2496	1152
Total first downs	131	71
Net gain passing	756	706
Passes attempted	94	142
Passes completed	34	46
Total points	287	79

HEISMAN TROPHY

LES HORVATH

"He's an All-American all the way." Those are the words that best describes the Bucks' Heisman trophy winner, Les Horvath. You don't have to take the word of sports writers and coaches to prove this statement. Here are some of his records: He played more total time than any other Buck gridder; he carried the ball more than any other; he had the most total points, the most yards by rushing, and the most completed passes for the greatest yardage. Les was always the loudest and most spirited player on the field. He becomes the first Buckeye to ever win the Heisman trophy.

Action on the field

PAUL BROWN SIGNS TO COACH PRO TEAM

Gets Five-Year Contract With Cleveland of All-America Football Conference

ALSO IS GENERAL MANAGER

Great Lakes Mentor to Start New Duties After Release From Navy Service

CHICAGO, Feb. 8 (P)—Lieut. Paul Brown, football coach at Great Lakes Naval Training Center and former Ohio State University mentor, today signed a five-year contract as head coach and general manager of the Cleveland professional team in the new All-America Conference.

The 36-year-old Brown, whose 1942 Ohio State team won the mythical national championship, thus will not return to Ohio State, from which he had leave of absence.

Arthur McBride, Cleveland taxicab magnate who owns the All-America franchise in that city, did not disclose terms of the contract, but asserted it was the best ever given to a football coach. From another source, however, it was reported Brown's annual salary would exceed $15,000. McBride also disclosed that his team would use Municipal Stadium, which seats 83,000.

Brown, replaced at Ohio State last season by Carroll Widdoes, his former assistant, who directed the Buckeyes to the Western Conference championship, followed Lieut. Comdr. Jack Meagher of the Iowa Seahawks and Buck Shaw of Santa Clara in signing coaching contracts in the proposed league. Meagher, former Auburn mentor, was signed by Miami and Shaw by San Francisco.

Reluctant to Leave Ohio State

Brown, who will report at Cleveland when he has completed Navy service, declared: "I leave Ohio State reluctantly. I appreciate the whole-hearted support I enjoyed during my three years there from the fans of Ohio and especially from Athletic Director St. John and members of the athletic board.

"The time arrived for me to decide whether I was to continue as a professor or a business man. In addition to a generous salary I have been offered a share in the profits of the Cleveland club. I simply couldn't turn down the deal in fairness to my family."

Ohio State Roster

No.	Name	Pos.	Wt.	Age
*90	Amling, Warren	LG	197	20
55	Baker, Ray	C	182	18
64	Barna, Joseph	RG	197	17
12	Biel, William	RHB	177	18
*40	Brown, Matt	FB	169	24
*33	Cline, Ollie	FB	195	19
56	Crane, James	LE	183	19
46	Daugherty, Harold	LHB	164	17
*73	Dixon, Thornton	RT	204	24
*45	Dove, Robert	QB	162	19
*26	Ehrsam, John	QB	178	19
72	Fazio, Charles	RT	203	19
*17	Fisher, Richard	RHB	198	26
28	Fout, James	QB	174	17
18	Galbraith, James	C	159	17
34	Gandee, Charles	FB	188	18
30	Gorby, Herbert	LE	193	17
93	Gunther, Don	LE	188	20
*96	Hackett, William (C)	RG	189	21
76	Hamilton, Forrest	LT	204	17
*87	Jackson, Richard	LE	182	22
89	Keane, Michael	RE	175	17
95	Kelsey, Thomas	RE	172	17
*80	Kessler, Bud	LE	189	20
44	Krall, Jerry	LHB	179	18
54	Lininger, Jack	C	193	18
*74	McGinnis, Robert	LG	200	19
14	McKenna, James	RHB	174	17
*86	Maltinsky, Paul	RT	195	25
16	Marshall, Clyde	RHB	181	17
94	Merrell, Bob	RE	181	17
92	Nicolls, Donald	LE	182	18
50	O'Dea, Stephen	C	196	16
*27	Priday, Robin	QB	190	23
*60	Redd, Jack	RG	177	22
66	Roe, Jack	LG	204	26
52	Ryan, Robert	C	191	21
78	Santora, Ernest	LG	207	19
*88	Sarringhaus, Paul	LHB	184	25
70	Schnittker, Max	LT	209	18
42	Smith, Harley	LHB	183	20
*85	Steinberg, Don	RE	190	23
*98	Thomas, Russell	LT	223	20
11	Verdova, Alex	RHB	177	17
65	Walbolt, George	LG	192	20
24	Wambold, Ed	FB	184	21
82	Watson, Thomas	RE	188	17
67	Wible, Cal	RG	170	17
75	Winters, Samuel	LT	198	18
83	Wright, Ward	RE	201	18
68	Zangara, Don	LG	191	19

*Denotes letterman.

[1945]

1945
Captain: William C. Hackett

47	*Missouri	6
42	*Iowa	0
12	*Wisconsin	0
13	*Purdue	35
20	Minnesota	7
16	*Northwestern	14
14	Pittsburgh	0
27	*Illinois	2
3	Michigan	7
194		71

Won 7, Lost 2

Boilermakers Run Wild In Racking Up 35-13 Win

Ed Cody, New Britain Star, Scores Three Touchdowns for Victors; Passing Attack Too Much for Buckeyes in Day's Big Game

	P	OS
First downs	13	9
Yards gained rushing (net)	258	175
Passes attempted	13	11
Passes completed	9	3
Yards by passing	138	75
Passing int. by	2	1
Yards gained, runback int. passes	12	24
Punting average (from scrimmage)	40	22
Total yards, all kicks returned	85	84
Opp. fumbles recovered	2	3
Yards lost, penalties	45	35

PURDUE		OHIO STATE
Heck	le	Kessler
O'Brien	lt	Thomas
Crowe	lg	Amling
Kodba	c	Lininger
Logan	rg	Redd
Hughes	rt	Dixon
Maloney	re	Watson
DeMoss	qb	Priday
Canfield	lh	Krall
Adams	rh	Fisher
Cody	fb	Cline

Purdue   6 16 6   7—35
Ohio State   0   0 0 13—13

Purdue scoring: Touchdowns, Cody 3, Canfield 2; points after touchdown, Hughes 3; safety, Hughes.
Ohio State scoring: Touchdowns, Kessler, Verdova (sub for Fisher); point after touchdown, Schnittker (sub for Cline); attendance (actual) 73,858.
Purdue substitutions: Ends, Fox, Gilbelt; tackle, O'Bryan; guards, Clymer, Lenczyk; center, Lockwood; backs, Mihal, Dobrzykowski, Adams, Dale.
Ohio substitutions: Ends, Steinberg, Gorby, Wright; tackles, Hamilton, Fazio, Winters; guards, McGinnis, Roe; centers, O'Dea, Oaker; backs, Daugherty, Sarringhaus, Verdova, Ehrsam, Fout, Dove, Gandee, Schnittker.

Columbus, Ohio, Oct. 20.—(AP.)—Purdue's unbeaten and untied boilermakers wrote "the end" today to Ohio State's football winning streak with a masterful exhibition which produced a 35 to 13 victory over the Bucks, who had won their last 12 games.

A huge outpouring of 73,585 fans saw the boilermakers blast the Bucks from the opening whistle, and it wasn't until the final period that Ohio State was able to score.

The Boilermakers were almost letter perfect, ripping gaping holes in the Ohio line and operating their deadly passing combination of Bob DeMoss, to Bill Canfield with such precision they had the Bucks hanging on the ropes all the way.

vs. Northwestern

Michigan Wolverines Stage Rally To Defeat Buckeyes 7-3 Before 85,132

STATISTICS.

	OhioS.	Mich.
First downs	11	11
Yds. gained rush.	143	105
Forwards attempted	6	12
Forwards completed	1	4
Yds. forwards	35	63
Forwards intercepted	2	2
Yds. gained run-back intercepted passes	28	5
Punting avg. scrim.	31.8	29.7
Total yds. kicks ret.	33	56
Oppo. fumbles recov.	1	2
Yds. lost penalties	14	15

Ann Arbor, Mich., Nov. 24.—(AP.)—Michigan's dogged Wolverines, coming from behind for a capacity crowd of 85,132 fans, punched over a fourth period touchdown for a 7 to 3 victory over Ohio State here today after tackle Max Schnittker had put the Buckeyes ahead, 3 to 0, with a 17-yard field goal in the third period.

The hard-earned victory gave Michigan second place in the final big ten standings behind unbeaten Indiana, which won the title by pasting Purdue, 26 to 0.

Less than seven minutes of play remained when Michigan sent halfback Henry Fonde diving through Ohio State's right tackle from the one-yard line for the winning touchdown. The 18-years-old Navy trainee had made the opportunity himself by going 25 yards with a pass from Pete Elliott.

Fonde side-stepped Buckeye halfback Dick Fisher as he caught the pass on the Ohio State 35-yard line and pedalled 16 yards farther before being hauled down by Ollie Cline on the Ohio 19.

From there Elliott drove to the 10 in two plays and Howard Yerges lateraled to Fonde for a first down on the Buckeye 5. An Off-side penalty set Ohio on its one-yard line and Fonde hit through right tackle on the second play for the winning touchdown.

George Cniames' first conversion attempt was nullified by a penalty against the Wolverines and his second try from the seven-yard line split the uprights.

Ohio's field goal, Schnittker's second of the season, was a beautiful angle boot from the 17-yard line after the Buckeyes had moved to the Michigan 12 on Hal Daugherty's 35-yard pass to Tom Watson and Michigan braced.

The ball was in Michigan territory throughout the third period. Ohio once punched to the Wolverine 15-yard line but lost the ball on downs.

OHIO STATE		MICHIGAN
Crane	le	McNeill
Thomas	lt	Johnson
McGinnis	lg	Tomasi
Lininger	c	Momsen
Amling	rg	Wilkins
Schnittker	rt	Hinton
Watson	re	Renner
Priday	qb	Yerges
Daugherty	lh	Elliott
Fisher	rh	Nussbaumer
Cline	fb	Dworsky

Michigan   0 0 0 7—7
Ohio State   0 0 3 0—3

Ohio State scoring: Field goal, Schnittker (placement). Michigan scoring: Touchdown, Fonde (sub for Nussbaumer; point after touchdown, Cniames (sub for Dworsky).

Substitutes:—Ohio State—end, Steinberg; tackles, Dixon, Maltinsky, Fazio, Winters; guards, Roe, Redd; center, O'Dea; backs, Ehrsam, Krall, Verdova, Sarringhaus, Gandee. Michigan—ends, Ford, Hershberger; tackles, Derleth, Prashaw, Callahan; guards, Lintol, Soboleski, Smith; center, Teninga; backs, Muelder, Bentz, Fonde, Cniames.

OHIO STATE 14
NORTHWESTERN 13

The Junior Bucks showed their fathers a game long to be remembered in the hearts of Buckeye fans. In the first quarter Farrar and Whan of Northwestern crashed through, over and around the Buckeye line with terrific speed. In the second quarter a long pass from Fisher to Kessler set up the first Buckeye touchdown. The third quarter was scoreless as the Buckeyes rebuilt their team. In the first minutes of the last quarter Cline and Sarringhaus drove in eight plays for the second touchdown. This run made the score 12 to 13, Northwestern. With a minute and a half to go "automatic" Max Schnittker kicked a field goal from a difficult angle on the 21 yard line. The final score was 14 to 13, Ohio.

Season Statistics

RUSHING

Name	Games	Carried Ball	Yds. Gained	Yds. Lost	Net Yds.	Avg.	Pts.
Cline	9	181	939	3	936	5.1	54
Sarringhaus	9	84	467	53	414	4.9	36
Fisher	8	70	321	61	260	3.7	12
Daugherty	9	54	291	33	258	4.7	12
Krall	8	47	205	51	154	3.0	0
Verdova	9	33	127	34	93	2.8	12
Gandee	9	17	51	5	46	2.7	6
Marshall	5	11	25	10	15	1.3	6
Wambold	4	3	6	0	6	2.0	0
Priday	9	3	4	4	0	0.0	0
Fout	4	2	3	1	2	1.0	0
Ehrsam	8	1	3	0	3	3.0	0
Dove	8	1	0	0	0	0.0	0
Totals		507	2442	255	2184	2.4	138

ADDITIONAL SCORES

Name and Pos.	Games	Touchdowns	Field Goals	Extra Pts.	Total
Schnittker, Tackle	8	0	2	20	26
Watson, End	9	2	0	0	12
Kessler, End	9	2	0	0	12
Steinberg, End	9	1	0	0	6
Totals		5	2	20	194

PASSING

Name	Att. Passes	Completions	Yds. Gained	Had Intercepted
Fisher	28	9	245	3
Daugherty	31	8	188	4
Sarringhaus	17	6	133	2
Krall	2	1	12	0
Marshall	2	0	0	0
Biel	1	0	0	0
Totals	81	24	578	9

SCORE BY PERIODS

Ohio State	28	31	50	85	—194
Opponents	29	23	8	20	— 70

OHIO STATE UNIVERSITY FOOTBALL ROSTER—1946

*One Letter **Two Letters ***Three Letters SR Service Returnee

Pos.		Name	High School	Home Town	Age	Weight	Height	Class
C	(SR)	Adamle, Anthony	Collinwood	Cleveland	22	215	6'	Sophomore
G	(SR)	Alban, Richard	West	Columbus	20	192	6' 1"	Freshman
T		Amling, Warren**	Pana Twp.	Pana, Illinois	21	200	5' 11½"	Senior
G		Barna, Joseph	Benedictine	Cleveland	19	220	5' 11"	Sophomore
E	(SR)	Biber, Paul	Lorain	Lorain	26	198	6' 3"	Sophomore
HB	(SR)	Brugge, Robert*	Parma	Parma	20	192	6'	Sophomore
HB	(SR)	Cannavino, Michael	Collinwood	Cleveland	21	169	5' 11"	Sophomore
QB	(SR)	Cokor, Matthew	Orange	Cleveland	21	195	5' 11"	Freshman
T	(SR)	Cox, Martin	Junior Home	Tiffin	22	215	6' 3"	Freshman
E	(SR)	Crane, James*	Upper Arlington	Columbus	20	195	5' 10"	Sophomore
T	(SR)	Csuri, Charles**	West Tech	Cleveland	25	202	6' ½"	Senior
FB	(SR)	Culbertson, James	Barberton	Barberton	21	217	6'	Freshman
T		Dawson, Jack	Waite	Toledo	17	195	6' 1"	Freshman
G	(SR)	Dean, Hal**	Wooster	Wooster	24	201	5' 11"	Senior
E	(SR)	Dendiu, Traian*	Campbell	Campbell	20	191	6'	Sophomore
E	(SR)	Dierker, Richard	East	Columbus	23	196	5' 11"	Freshman
G	(SR)	DiPierro, Raymond*	Libbey	Toledo	20	195	5' 9"	Sophomore
E	(SR)	Dixon, Stanley	Wyoming	Wyoming	22	215	6' 1"	Sophomore
QB	(SR)	Doolittle, William	Mansfield	Mansfield	23	202	5' 9"	Sophomore
C	(SR)	Duncan, Howard	Lakewood	Lakewood	22	220	6' 3"	Freshman
T	(SR)	Fazio, Charles*	Marion	Marion	20	210	6' 3"	Sophomore
QB		Fout, James*	Portsmouth	Portsmouth	18	180	5' 11"	Sophomore
FB		Gandee, Charles*	Berea	Berea	19	200	5' 10"	Sophomore
G		Gaudio, Robert	Shaw	Cleveland	21	210	6'	Freshman
E		Gorby, Herbert*	East Palestine	East Palestine	19	205	6' 1"	Sophomore
QB	(SR)	Gordon, George*	Maumee	Bexley	20	160	5' 9"	Sophomore
E	(SR)	Guenther, Donald	LaCrosse, Wisc.	LaCrosse, Wisc.	23	185	6' 2"	Sophomore
T		Hamilton, Forrest*	John Adams	Cleveland	19	210	6' 3"	Sophomore
G	(SR)	Jabbusch, Robert*	Elyria	Elyria	23	196	5' 10"	Junior
E		Jackson, Richard**	Wellsville	Wellsville	23	187	5' 10"	Junior
HB		James, Thomas*	Massillon	Massillon	23	176	5' 9"	Junior
T	(SR)	Jevnikar, Warren	Euclid Shore	Cleveland	20	195	6'	Freshman
E	(SR)	Kessler, Carlton**	Worthington	Worthington	21	190	6' 2"	Junior
HB		Krall, Gerald*	Libbey	Toledo	19	185	5' 10"	Sophomore
T	(SR)	Lashley, Richard	Steubenville	Steubenville	20	230	5' 11"	Freshman
FB	(SR)	Lucas, Robert	Paulding	Paulding	22	210	5' 10"	Freshman
FB	(SR)	Martens, John	Wickliffe	Wickliffe	20	195	6' 1"	Freshman
G	(SR)	Mattey, George	East	Cleveland	19	215	5' 11"	Freshman
HB	(SR)	McQuade, Robert*	Aquinas	Columbus	22	160	5' 10"	Sophomore
G	(SR)	Miller, Wilbur*	Blume	Wapakoneta	21	185	5' 10"	Sophomore
E	(SR)	Morrison, Fred	Upper Arlington	Columbus	19	210	6' 1"	Freshman
HB	(SR)	Nelson, Neal	Euclid Shore	Cleveland	21	185	5' 11"	Freshman
C		O'Dea, Stephen*	Campbell	Campbell	17	219	5' 11"	Sophomore
T		O'Hanlon, Richard	E. Liverpool	E. Liverpool	17	212	6' 2"	Freshman
FB	(SR)	Oliver, Glenn*	University	Columbus	20	191	5' 11"	Sophomore
T		Palcich, Joseph	Warren	Warren	22	220	6' 1"	Freshman
E	(SR)	Palmer, James	Springfield	Springfield	22	183	6'	Sophomore
QB	(SR)	Palmer, Richard*	Shaw	Cleveland	24	215	5' 10"	Senior
E	(SR)	Parks, Ernest*	McKinley	Canton	21	210	6' 2"	Sophomore
T	(SR)	Perrotti, Michael	Collinwood	Cleveland	23	240	6' 2"	Sophomore
QB	(SR)	Phillips, Thomas	Berea	Berea	22	180	5' 9"	Sophomore
E	(SR)	Plank, Ernest*	Bexley	Columbus	22	195	5' 11"	Sophomore
QB	(SR)	Priday, Robin**	West Jefferson	West Jefferson	23	193	5' 11"	Senior
G		Quattrone, Joseph	Steubenville	Steubenville	21	200	5' 11"	Freshman
C		Renner, Charles*	Kenmore	Akron	20	186	5' 11½"	Sophomore
T	(SR)	Santora, Ernest	East	Cleveland	20	210	6'	Sophomore
G	(SR)	Schneider, Wilbur*	Gahanna	Gahanna	24	175	5' 6"	Junior
T		Schnittker, Max*	Sandusky	Sandusky	19	209	6' 2"	Junior
G	(SR)	Schuster, George	McKinley	Canton	22	192	5' 11"	Sophomore
C	(SR)	Seremetis, William	Fairview	Dayton	23	200	5' 10"	Freshman
E		Sedor, William*	Shadyside	Shadyside	22	190	6' 3"	Senior
HB	(SR)	Slough, Gene	Findlay	Findlay	21	160	5' 11"	Sophomore
G	(SR)	Snyder, Thomas*	Upper Sandusky	Upper Sandusky	20	205	5' 11"	Sophomore
E	(SR)	Souders, Cecil***	Bucyrus	Bucyrus	26	200	6' 1"	Senior
QB	(SR)	Spencer, George	Bexley	Columbus	21	195	5' 11"	Freshman
QB	(SR)	Stungis, John*	Powhatan Point	Powhatan Point	21	195	6' 1"	Sophomore
HB	(SR)	Swinehart, Rodney	Wooster	Wooster	20	175	5' 9"	Freshman
C	(SR)	Teifke, Howard*	Ross	Fremont	21	190	6'	Sophomore
T	(SR)	Templeton, David	Mansfield	Bedford, Ind.	25	200	5' 11"	Sophomore
HB		Verdova, Alex*	Lakewood	Lakewood	18	184	5' 10"	Sophomore
FB	(SR)	Wambold, Ed	Perrysburg	Perrysburg	22	185	5' 11"	Sophomore
FB	(SR)	Whisler, Joseph	Willard	Willard	22	219	5' 11"	Sophomore
G		Wible, Calvin*	Lakewood	Lakewood	18	185	5' 9"	Sophomore
T		Wilson, Jack	Xenia	Xenia	21	210	6' 4"	Freshman
T		Winters, Samuel*	East Liverpool	East Liverpool	20	212	5' 11"	Sophomore
FB	(SR)	Wippel, Samuel	Grandview	Columbus	22	195	5' 11"	Freshman
HB	(SR)	Wolfe, Russell	Upper Sandusky	Upper Sandusky	22	160	5' 9"	Sophomore
T	(SR)	Zeigler, Andrew	Euclid Shore	Cleveland	20	220	6' 3"	Freshman
HB	(SR)	Zorn, Paul	Niles	Niles	21	195	5' 9"	Freshman

*One Letter **Two Letters ***Three Letters SR Service Returnee

BIXLER WILL COACH OHIO STATE ELEVEN

Named Successor of Widdoes, Who Asked to Be Relieved —Latter to Be Assistant

COLUMBUS, Jan. 2 (AP) — Ohio State University's athletic board tonight unanimously approved the appointment of Paul Bixler as head football coach to succeed Carroll Widdoes, who asked to be relieved of his duties after directing the Buckeyes to sixteen victories in eighteen games.

The change was unprecedented in Ohio State football annals. Both Bixler, 39, and Widdoes were assistants under the former coach, Paul E. Brown, and Bixler served as Widdoes' assistant during the last two years.

The athletic board announced that Widdoes, at Bixler's request, would remain on the staff as an assistant coach.

The board said there was a "gentleman's agreement" that Bixler's contract would run for three years, starting as of yesterday. The salary was not given.

Assistant to Brown

Widdoes had been one of Brown's assistants in creating the fabulous teams at Massilon High School. Bixler had been coach at Canton McKinley High School and also had served at Colgate and Akron Universities.

They aided Brown in the development of the 1942 national champion team.

Early in 1944 Brown entered the Navy. Widdoes was named acting head coach. That fall his team blasted its way to nine straight victories, Ohio State's first unbeaten and untied regular season since 1920, and won the Big Ten championship. Gridiron coaches throughout the nation voted Widdoes "coach of the year."

1946
Coach: Paul O. Bixler
Captain: Warren Amling

13	*Missouri	13
21	Southern California	0
7	Wisconsin	20
14	*Purdue	14
39	*Minnesota	9
39	Northwestern	27
20	*Pittsburgh	13
7	Illinois	16
6	*Michigan	58
166		170

Won 4, Lost 3, Tied 2

PAUL O. BIXLER
HEAD FOOTBALL COACH
OHIO STATE UNIVERSITY

Paul Orlando Bixler, 39-year-old head football coach of Ohio State University, assumed charge of the grid forces January 2, 1946, succeeding Carroll C. Widdoes, who asked to be returned to the role of assistant after two years as chief of the staff.

Bixler came to Ohio State from Colgate University in 1941 as coach of the ends and wingbacks. During the 1941-45 period he also served as scout, both from the Ohio stadium press box and those of rival institutions. He proved so adept in making accurate and comprehensive reports of opposing teams that his scouting activities brought as much praise as his coaching ability.

During Bixler's five-year period as assistant, Ohio State won the Western Conference and national titles in 1942 and the Big Ten crown in 1944. The latter team was undefeated and untied and was acclaimed the No. 1 civilian eleven of the war-time season.

Bixler was born in Louisville, Ohio, where he attended high school and played football. He enrolled at Mt. Union College, where he played guard and fullback on the football team and where he also was a member of the basketball team.

After being graduated from Mt. Union in 1929, he was named coach at Central Junior High School in Canton but in 1932 was selected as line coach and head basketball coach at Canton McKinley. James Aiken was McKinley's football coach and when the latter went to Akron University in 1935, Bixler accompanied him as head basketball coach and assistant football coach.

Bixler was named freshman football coach at Colgate in 1937, later being elevated to the varsity staff under Andy Kerr as end and wingback coach. He also was named head basketball coach before coming to Ohio State.

Bixler is a member of Phi Kappa Tau fraternity and the father of five children—Dennis, Jack, Jane, William and Susan.

O.S.U. 20
Pittsburgh 13

Dads of nearly every Buckeye player got a greater thrill than they had bargained for when a scrappy Pittsburgh eleven forced Ohio State to battle hard for a 20-13 triumph in the annual Dad's Day classic that was to be a pushover according to pre-game predictions. Although outweighed at nearly every position, the Panthers fought on even terms with State most of the contest, displaying football skill that comes only with experienced coaching. This exceptional performance undoubtedly was a contributing factor in the University Athletic Board's decision to bring Coach Wesley Fesler to Ohio State after Paul Bixler's resignation. It was the closest Pitt had come to upsetting Ohio since 1936. Early in the second quarter, after haulting several Buckeye drives, Pittsburgh completed a pass in the end-zone to open the scoring. A few minutes later and again in the third period, George Spencer tossed scoring passes that pushed State into the lead. Both teams added six-pointers in the final quarter.

O.S.U. 6
Michigan 58

The fourth largest crowd in the history of Ohio stadium saw a mighty Michigan combine rout the hapless Buckeyes by an almost unbelievable score of 58-6 in the saddest homecoming spectacle in many a year. Nearly 79,000 jammed the oval to see Ohio take its worst beating since 1902 when another Michigan eleven trounced them 86-0. It was the second consecutive year that the Buckeyes closed their season by bowing to the Wolverines. Ohio State was completely paralized by an uncanny Michigan passing attack that accounted for half its touchdowns. The Wolverines opened the scoring early in the first quarter with a single six-pointer, then really hit their stride in the second to compile a 27-0 lead at halftime. Michigan added two more in the third period and contributed the seventh and eighth along with a subtle field goal in the final canto. State accounted for its lone score in the last 59 seconds of play.

O.S.U. 7
Illinois 16

Ohio State's dream of a Big Nine championship and a possible bid to the Rose Bowl ended abruptly in a barrage of rain, sleet, mud and Illinois strategy as the battling Buckeyes bowed to the fighting Illini, 16-7, at Champaign. Preceding the game, a three-way race existed for the conference title with Ohio, Illinois and Michigan as competitors. The victory was Illinois' first over Ohio in twelve years. It was a heart-breaking defeat for the Buckeyes who had outplayed the Illini in every department but the final score. The turning point of the game occurred in the third period when an Illinois back, Jules Rykovick, snatched an intended Spencer-to-Brugge aerial on Ohio's two-yard line and scampered 98 yards for the score that broke the Buckeyes' back. State opened the scoring in the first quarter when Joe Whisler smashed over. Soon after, Illinois retaliated with a safety after blocking an Ohio punt. In the second quarter the Illini tallied their first touchdown to grab a 9-7 lead at the half.

OHIO STATE INDIVIDUAL STATISTICS, 1946

RUSHING

Player	G	TC	G	L	Net	Ave.
Whisler	9	129	553	9	544	4.2
James	9	93	459	56	403	4.3
Brugge	9	73	378	66	312	4.3
Krall	7	29	165	5	160	5.5
Verdova	9	50	209	49	160	3.2
Perini	9	30	120	9	111	3.7
Swinehart	5	15	61	19	42	2.8
Phillips	5	11	41	1	40	3.6
Spencer	8	13	34	17	17	1.3
Gandee	2	6	12	..	12	2.0
Cannavino	8	2	6	..	6	3.0
Wolfe	4	3	7	..	7	2.3
Dave Bonnie	4	1	2	..	2	2.0
R. Palmer	3	3	9	16	—7	—2.3
Doolittle	6	1	..	7	—7	—7.0
Totals	9	560	2056	261	1795	199.4

PASSING

Player	G	Att.	Comp.	Int.	Yds.	Pct.
Spencer	8	51	25	4	398	.490
James	9	19	7	3	125	.368
Verdova	9	8	3	1	90	.375
Brugge	9	6	2	0	71	.333
Phillips	5	21	3	3	31	.143
Slager	2	4	1	1	22	.250
Krall	7	7	1	1	20	.143
Swinehart	4	2	1	0	15	.500
R. Palmer	3	5	2	0	13	.400
Doolittle	6	4	1	1	63	.250
Totals	9	127	46	14	848	.362

PASS RECEIVING

Player	G	Catch	Yds.
Brugge	9	8	193
Souders	9	9	157
Parks	8	6	79
Verdova	9	3	67
Kessler	6	4	63
Swinehart	5	1	63
Krall	7	2	62
James	9	4	57
Whisler	9	2	41
Dendiu	3	2	20
Crane	8	2	15
Wolfe	4	1	15
Gandee	2	1	11
Perini	9	1	5
Totals	9	46	848

PUNTING

Player	K	YK	Ave.
Perini	30	1193	39.8
James	11	418	38.0
Phillips	3	129	43.0
Spencer	7	249	35.6
Swinehart	1	37	37.0
Verdova	1	20	20.0
Totals	53	2046	38.5

SCORING

Player	G	TD	CA	Pat	Tp
Whisler	9	10	0	0	54
Brugge	9	5	0	0	30
James	9	2	0	0	12
Krall	7	2	0	0	12
Stungis	5	0	18	12	12
Verdova	9	1	0	0	6
Dave Bonnie	4	1	0	0	6
Parks	8	1	0	0	6
Perini	9	1	0	0	6
Souders	9	1	0	0	6
Swinehart	5	1	0	0	6
Schnittker	5	0	7	4	4
Totals	9	25	25	16	166

OHIO STATE TEAM STATISTICS, 1946

	Ohio State	Opp.
First Downs		
Total	111	101
By Rushing	83	60
By Passing	24	35
By Penalties	4	6
Rushing		
Number of Rushes	460	383
Yards Gained	2056	1799
Yards Lost	261	207
Net Yards Gained	1795	1592
Average per Game	199.4	176.9
Forward Passing		
Number Attempted	127	153
Number Completed	46	61
Number had Intercepted	14	16
Net Yards Gained	848	959
Average per Game	94.2	106.6
Percentage Completions	.362	.399
Total Plays		
Rushes and Passes	587	536
Total Net Yards Gained	2643	2551
Average Net Yards Gained per Game	293.7	283.3
Punts		
Number	53	62
Average, Yards	38.5	36.1
Had Blocked	1	4
Kickoffs		
Number	35	35
Average, Yards	49.4	44.0
Kick Returns		
Punt Returns, Number	35	27
Punt Returns, Yards	370	257
Kickoff Returns, Number	33	33
Kickoff Returns, Yards	603	683
Interception Returns		
Number	16	14
Yards Returned	223	250
Fumbles		
Number	33	41
Ball Lost, Fumbles	20	15
Penalties		
Number	48	41
Yards Penalized	388	354

Score by Quarters

	1	2	3	4	Final
Opponents	27	52	47	44	170
Ohio State	35	52	33	46	166

OHIO STATE UNIVERSITY FOOTBALL ROSTER, 1947

Name	Pos.	Age	Weight	Height	Home Town	High School	Class
Anderson, Thomas	E	18	184	6' 1"	St. Marys	St. Marys	Soph'mr
Benjamin, Robert	C	19	194	6'	Conneaut	Conneaut	Soph'mr
Bevan, Daniel	G	20	207	6'	Warren	Harding	Soph'mr
Beyland, Richard	T	21	210	6'	Dayton	Roosevelt	Soph'mr
Bonnie, Dale	E	20	193	6'	Columbus	North	Soph'mr
Bonnie, David*	E	20	195	6'	Columbus	North	Soph'mr
Brugge, Robert*	HB	20	194	6'	Parma	Parma	Junior
Burkholder, Robert	QB	21	185	5' 10"	Bluffton	Bluffton	Soph'mr
Cannavino, Michael*	HB	22	168	5' 11"	Cleveland	Collinwood	Junior
Chabek, Jack	QB	24	185	5' 10"	Cleveland	Canton McKinley	Soph'mr
Cheney, John	QB	19	175	5' 11"	Richwood	Richwood	Soph'mr
Clark, James	HB	22	175	6'	Columbus	North	Soph'mr
Cline, Ollie**	FB	20	200	5' 11"	Fredericktown	Fredericktown	Junior
Cox, Martin	T	23	210	6' 1"	Middletown	Middletown	Soph'mr
Crane, Jameson**	E	21	190	5' 10"	Upper Arlington	Upper Arlington	Senior
Davis, Lawrence	C	23	205	5' 11"	Xenia	Central	Soph'mr
Dawson, Jack	T	19	196	6'	Toledo	Waite	Soph'mr
Demmel, Robert	HB	21	180	5' 10"	Fremont	Ross	Soph'mr
Dendiu, Traian**	E	21	183	6'	Campbell	Campbell	Junior
DiPierro, Ramon**	G	21	194	5' 10"	Toledo	Libbey	Junior
Dixon, Stanley	E	23	202	6' 1"	Wyoming	Wyoming	Junior
Doolittle, William*	QB	24	188	5' 9"	Mansfield	Mansfield	Junior
Dorsey, Robert	E	23	195	5' 10"	Houston, Tex.	Wheatley	Junior
Duncan, Howard*	C	22	220	6' 3"	Lakewood	Lakewood	Junior
Eberle, Michael	HB	19	170	5' 7"	Columbus	Aquinas	Soph'mr
Edwards, William	T	21	225	6' 4"	Willoughby	Mentor	Soph'mr
Fazio, Charles**	T	21	212	6' 3"	Marion	Harding	Junior
Fedderson, Jerold	E	21	208	6' 1"	Sandusky	Sandusky	Soph'mr
Fritzsche, James	T	19	232	6' 5"	Bedford	Bedford	Soph'mr
Gilbert, Charles	G	20	185	6'	Columbus	North	Soph'mr
Gordon, George*	HB	23	155	5' 8"	Columbus	Maumee	Soph'mr
Gray, William	E	20	198	6' 2½"	Cleveland	East Tech	Junior
Hague, James	E	19	195	6'	Rocky River	Rocky River	Soph'mr
Hale, George	C	21	168	5' 10"	Columbus	East	Soph'mr
Hamilton, Forrest**	T	19	219	6' 3"	Cleveland	John Adams	Junior
Henry, Joseph	QB	22	193	5' 11"	Columbus	Lakewood	Junior
Hickman, Dale	T	20	210	5' 9"	Utica	Utica	Soph'mr
Houser, Robert	E	19	170	5' 11"	Upper Sandusky	Upper Sandusky	Soph'mr
Jabbusch, Robert**	G	24	195	5' 10½"	Elyria	Elyria	Senior
Jackson, Paul	FB	21	185	5' 10"	Newark	Newark	Soph'mr
Jackson, Richard**	E	24	186	5' 11"	Wellsville	Wellsville	Senior
Jennings, Jack	T	20	222	6' 3"	Columbus	North	Soph'mr
Jesko, Howard	E	21	225	6' 3"	Lorain	Lorain	Soph'mr
Jolliffe, John	G	19	200	5' 11"	Bexley	Bexley	Soph'mr
Kay, Charles	E	19	185	6' 1"	Youngstown	South	Soph'mr
Kessler, Carlton**	E	22	190	6' 2"	Worthington	Worthington	Senior
Kirk, Brenton	T	22	216	6' 2"	New Philadelphia	New Philadelphia	Soph'mr
Krall, Gerald**	HB	20	181	5' 10"	Toledo	Libbey	Junior
Krieger, George	QB	21	191	5' 11"	Bexley	Bexley	Junior
Layne, Richard	E	21	210	6' 2"	Columbus	West	Junior
Lininger, Jack*	C	20	197	5' 11"	Van Wert	Van Wert	Soph'mr
Mattey, George	G	20	208	5' 10"	Cleveland	East	Soph'mr
Morrison, Fred*	E	21	205	6' 2"	Columbus	Upper Arlington	Soph'mr
Newell, William	HB	19	180	5' 11"	Columbiana	Columbiana	Soph'mr
O'Hanlon, Richard*	G	19	225	6' 2"	East Liverpool	East Liverpool	Soph'mr
Oliver, Glenn*	FB	21	195	5' 11"	Columbus	University	Junior
Orth, Vernoll	T	21	204	6' 1"	Marion	Harding	Soph'mr
Palmer, James	E	23	185	6' 2"	Springfield	Springfield	Junior
Perini, Pete*	QB	19	220	5' 10"	Washington, N.J.	Washington, N.J.	Soph'mr
Phillips, Richard	C	21	205	6'	Berea	Berea	Soph'mr
Phillips, Thomas*	HB	23	182	5' 9"	Berea	Berea	Junior
Prchlik, Richard	T	19	205	6' 3"	Cleveland	West Tech	Soph'mr
Renner, Charles*	C	21	190	6'	Akron	Buchtel	Junior
Rothchild, Max	G	19	195	5' 7"	Toledo	Libbey	Soph'mr
Savic, Pandel	QB	22	185	6'	Girard	Girard	Soph'mr
Scarvelli, Charles	HB	19	182	5' 11"	Cleveland	Cathedral Latin	Soph'mr
Sensanbaugher, Dean*	HB	22	192	5' 10"	Uhrichsville	Uhrichsville	Junior
Shannon, Richard	E	21	211	6' 1½"	Akron	Garfield	Soph'mr
Sheets, Carl	G	18	204	5' 8"	Columbiana	Columbiana	Soph'mr
Singley, Alfred	HB	19	185	5' 11"	Washington, N.J.	Washington, N.J.	Soph'mr
Slager, Richard	QB	19	185	5' 11"	Columbus	West	Soph'mr
Snyder, Thomas*	G	21	196	5' 10"	Upper Sandusky	Upper Sandusky	Soph'mr
Spencer, George*	QB	21	205	5' 11"	Bexley	Bexley	Soph'mr
Stackhouse, Ray*	T	21	235	6' 2"	Dayton	Roosevelt	Soph'mr
Stungis, John**	QB	21	190	6' 1"	Powhatan Point	Powhatan Point	Junior
Swinehart, Rodney*	HB	21	178	5' 10"	Wooster	Wooster	Soph'mr
Taylor, Lloyd	C	20	170	5' 9"	Barberton	Barberton	Soph'mr
Teifke, Howard**	C	21	193	6'	Fremont	Ross	Junior
Templeton, David*	G	26	210	5' 11½"	Bedford, Ind.	Mansfield	Junior
Thomas, James	G	23	200	5' 6"	Bellaire	Bellaire	Soph'mr
Toneff, George*	G	20	190	5' 9"	Barberton	Barberton	Soph'mr
Verdova, Alex**	HB	19	183	5' 10"	Lakewood	Lakewood	Junior
Wertz, George	HB	20	164	5' 9"	Piqua	Piqua	Soph'mr
Whisler, Joseph*	FB	23	210	5' 11"	Willard	Willard	Junior
Wilson, Jack*	T	22	205	6' 4"	Xenia	Central	Soph'mr
Wippel, Samuel	FB	23	195	6'	Columbus	Grandview	Soph'mr

* One Letter ** Two Letters

1947
Coach: Wesley E. Fesler
Captain: Robert O. Jabbusch

13	*Missouri	7
20	Purdue	24
0	*Southern California	32
13	*Iowa	13
0	Pittsburgh	12
0	*Indiana	7
7	*Northwestern	6
7	*Illinois	28
0	Michigan	21
60		150

Won 2, Lost 6, Tied 1

OHIO STATE 0 — INDIANA 7

Again it was the lack of any substantial offensive threat that cost the Buckeyes another victory. Indiana only needed its first period touchdown to hand Ohio a 7-0 defeat. It was the first meeting of the two teams since 1944 when Ohio State registered a 21-0 victory. According to the statistics, the Buckeyes were superior in every department but passing and it was here that the game was decided. The Indiana touchdown was a direct result of a long pass from the brilliant George Taliferro to Mel Groomes who was finally downed on the Ohio 12 yard line. Taliferro picked up the remaining yards on two plays to score standing up. Ohio State had four scoring chances. One was culminated by an attempted field goal, another was halted when State lost the ball on downs, the third was stopped by a pass interception, and the fourth ended with a fumble.

Taliferro crosses goal line standing up for game's only touchdown.

[1947]

WESLEY E. FESLER
Head Football Coach, Ohio State University

Wesley E. Fesler, a nine-letter winner in varsity athletics, was graduated from Ohio State University in the College of Commerce in 1932. A three-time all-American football selection, Fesler played with the Buckeye elevens in 1928, 1929 and 1930 and served as captain his third season.

Fesler, an end and fullback on the gridiron, also was versatile on the baseball field, playing first base, second base and center field. He played guard for three seasons on the basketball team and was honored as an all-conference selection. In 1930, he was named the most valuable player to his football team in the Western Conference.

Because Fesler began his college career in engineering, a course he followed for more than one year before transferring to commerce, his graduation was delayed until 1932. In the fall of 1931, and for one season following his graduation, Fesler was a member of the Ohio State football coaching staff. In 1933 he went to Harvard University as head basketball coach and assistant in football.

In 1942, Fesler joined the staff of Connecticut Wesleyan University as head football and basketball coach and freshman baseball coach.

During 1944, Fesler received a leave of absence to join the Office of Strategic Services, but in February of 1945, became head basketball and assistant football and baseball coach at Princeton University. In the spring of 1946, Fesler was named head football coach at the University of Pittsburgh.

Fesler is 39 years of age, married and the father of two sons and one daughter.

OHIO STATE INDIVIDUAL STATISTICS, 1947

RUSHING

Player	G	TC	G	L	Net	Ave.
Cline	9	80	346	14	332	4.15
Clark	9	52	294	61	233	4.5
Whisler	8	51	238	19	219	4.3
Sensanbaugher	9	41	222	54	168	4.1
Verdova	7	30	135	12	123	4.1
Swinehart	7	14	122	14	108	6.3
Cannavino	5	19	97	5	92	4.8
Brugge	5	19	60	2	58	3.1
Crane	7	5	21	..	21	4.2
Morrison	9	5	15	2	13	2.6
Demmel	6	28	70	31	39	1.5
Newell	5	3	6	..	6	2.0
Dave Bonnie	9	2	4	..	4	2.0
Hague	9	2	4	..	4	2.0
Perini	8	4	7	6	1	0.25
Doolittle	4	1	..	2	-2	-2.0
Dorsey	5	2	7	10	-3	-1.5
Dale Bonnie	5	1	...	10	-10	-10.0
Slager	9	18	25	48	-23	-3.2
Savic	8	13	9	51	-42	-3.2
Totals	9	390	1682	341	1341	148.9

PASSING

Player	G	Att.	Comp.	Int.	Yds.	Pct.
Slager	9	69	19	10	236	.275
Savic	8	41	16	5	193	.390
Whisler	8	11	4	0	40	.364
Verdova	7	5	2	1	57	.400
Doolittle	4	4	1	0	24	.250
Cline	9	4	1	0	15	.250
Perini	8	2	1	1	12	.500
Clark	9	1	0	0	0	.000
Totals	9	137	44	17	577	.321

PASS RECEIVING

Player	G	Catches	Yds.
Morrison	9	7	113
Clark	9	6	104
Demmel	6	5	97
Sensanbaugher	9	4	47
Hague	9	4	36
Cline	9	4	-10
Dave Bonnie	9	3	39
Cannavino	5	2	32
Crane	7	2	28
Slager	9	2	7
Newell	5	1	30
Brugge	5	1	24
Dale Bonnie	5	1	13
Verdova	7	1	9
Shannon	7	1	8
Totals	9	44	577

PUNTING

Player	K	YK	Ave.
Swinehart	2	99	49.5
Perini	48	1876	39.1
Whisler	13	425	32.7
Cline	1	19	19.0
Totals	64	2419	37.8

PUNT RETURNS

Player	No.	Yards	Ave.
Brugge	5	85	17.0
Cannavino	5	54	10.8
Clark	11	113	10.3
Demmel	3	26	8.7
Newell	1	8	8.0
Verdova	2	12	6.0
Swinehart	3	11	3.7
Duncan	1	3	3.0
Teifke	1	1	1.0
Totals	32	313	9.8

SCORING

Player	G	TD	CA	Pat	Tp
Whisler	8	2	0	0	12
Sensanbaugher	9	2	0	0	12
Cline	9	2	0	0	12
Verdova	7	1	0	0	6
Morrison	9	1	0	0	6
Moldea	9	0	8	6	6
Stungis	1	0	1	0	0
Totals	9	9	9	6	60

OHIO STATE 7
NORTHWESTERN 6

Ohio State football fans have seen a lot of thrilling finishes, but none more exciting than the one that gave the Buckeyes a 7-6 victory over Northwestern—a victory which was not determined until the third play after the prescribed time had elapsed. When the Wildcats took the ball on downs with less than two minutes to play, most of the 70,203 hopeful fans had conceded the contest and had started for the exits. But when seven penalties were called on the visitors before they finally punted, everyone began to wonder. Taking over on the 35, the Bucks engineered a Savic-to-Demmel pass that put the ball on the 7 with time for only one more play. Rod Swinehart failed on a reverse but an offside penalty gave State another chance although time had run out. This time Savic passed to Clark in the end zone to tie the score, 6-6. Emil Moldea's first place-kick was blocked but another offside penalty was called. As the ball split the uprights for the winning point on his second try, the fans went wild. The Wildcats' lone touchdown came early in the final period after a hard battle.

OHIO STATE 0
MICHIGAN 21

Ohio State turned in its best performance of the season in its last game at Ann Arbor when it tackled the nation's top-ranking gridiron eleven and held them to an unimpressive 21-0 victory. After this game the Michigan Wolverines dropped to second place in the nation's polling. It was a far cry from the humiliating 58 to 7 defeat suffered at the hands of Michigan last year. Most surprising of all to the 86,000 fans who jammed Michigan Stadium was the close 7-0 halftime score. Michigan's first six-pointer came in the initial period when Chalmers Elliott climaxed a 68 yard drive with a touchdown. In the third quarter All American Bob Chappius sparked an 80 yard march by completing three brilliant aerials and then bucked the line for the touchdown. After recovering a Buckeye fumble on the Ohio 35 in the last quarter, Michigan drove to the Ohio 7 and Jack Weisenburger scored. The Buckeye's only scoring threat came late in the last quarter when Tom Snyder recovered a Michigan fumble on its 10 yard line. However, a fumble on the first play halted the threat abruptly.

[1948]

OHIO STATE UNIVERSITY FOOTBALL ROSTER, 1948

Name	Pos.	Age	Weight	Height	Home Town	High School	Class
Anderson, Thomas	QB	19	190	6-1	St. Marys	St. Marys	Junior
Basinger, Edward	E	20	178	6-1	Lima	South	Soph'mr
Biltz, John	G	21	210	6-0	Bedford	Bedford	Soph'mr
Bonnie, Dale*	E	21	188	6-2	Columbus	North	Junior
Bonnie, David**	HB	21	197	6-0	Columbus	North	Junior
Brickman, Robert	G	19	192	6-0	Lima	Central	Soph'mr
Cannavino, Michael**	HB	23	168	5-11½	Cleveland	Collinwood	Senior
Clark, James*	HB	23	175	6-0	Columbus	North	Junior
Dawson, Jack	T	20	204	6-1	Toledo	Waite	Junior
Demmel, Robert*	HB	20	181	5-10	Fremont	Ross	Junior
DiPierro, Ray***	G	22	196	5-11	Toledo	Libbey	Senior
Dorsey, Robert*	E	24	191	5-10	Houston, Tex.	Wheatley	Senior
Edwards, William	T	22	225	6-4	Willoughby	Mentor	Junior
Ellwood, Richard	HB	19	180	5-10	Dover	Dover	Soph'mr
Endres, George	G	19	190	5-10	Cincinnati	Hughes	Soph'mr
Fazio, Charles***	T	22	212	6-3	Marion	Harding	Senior
Gandee, Charles*	FB	20	200	5-10	Berea	Berea	Junior
Gandee, Sherwin	E	19	185	6-0	Akron	Garfield	Soph'mr
Gilbert, Charles	E	21	185	6-0	Columbus	North	Junior
Hague, James*	E	20	190	6-0	Rocky River	Rocky River	Junior
Hasselo, Albert	E	20	197	6-1	Cleveland	Latin	Soph'mr
Henry, Joseph	FB	23	194	5-11	Columbus	Lakewood	Junior
Jennings, Jack*	T	21	228	6-3	Columbus	North	Junior
King, Dale	E	19	185	6-0	Columbus	North	Soph'mr
Kirk, Brenton	G	23	215	6-2	New Philadelphia	New Philadelphia	Senior
Krall, Gerald**	HB	21	181	5-10	Toledo	Libbey	Junior
Lininger, Jack**	C	21	200	5-11	Van Wert	Van Wert	Junior
Manz, Jerry	G	19	210	5-10	Toledo	Libbey	Soph'mr
Marshall, Clyde*	FB	20	190	5-10	Mingo Junction	Mingo Junction	Soph'mr
Mattey, George	G	21	218	5-10	Cleveland	East	Junior
McCleery, Tony	HB	21	185	6-0	Delaware	Willis	Soph'mr
McCullough, Robert	C	19	170	6-1	Uhrichsville	Uhrichsville	Soph'mr
Miller, William	T	20	195	6-2	Fremont	Ross	Soph'mr
Momsen, Robert	T	19	200	6-2	Toledo	Libbey	Soph'mr
Morrison, Fred**	FB	22	207	6-2	Columbus	Upper Arlington	Junior
Newell, William*	HB	20	175	5-11	Columbiana	Columbiana	Junior
O'Hanlon, Richard**	T	20	234	6-2	East Liverpool	East Liverpool	Junior
Palmer, James	E	24	185	6-2	Springfield	Springfield	Senior
Perini, Peter**	QB	20	220	5-11	New Village, N.J.	Washington, N.J.	Junior
Renner, Charles**	C	22	190	6-½	Akron	Buchtel	Senior
Savic, Pandel*	QB	23	188	6-0	Girard	Girard	Junior
Shannon, Richard*	T	22	217	6-1½	Akron	Garfield	Junior
Slager, Richard*	HB	20	193	6-0	Columbus	West	Junior
Snyder, Thomas**	G	21	203	5-10	Upper Sandusky	Upper Sandusky	Junior
Sturtz, Karl	HB	19	178	5-11½	Coshocton	Coshocton	Soph'mr
Swinehart, Rodney**	HB	22	178	5-10	Wooster	Wooster	Junior
Tabener, Joe	G	18	220	5-9	Toledo	Libbey	Soph'mr
Teifke, Howard***	C	22	190	6-0	Fremont	Ross	Senior
Templeton, David**	G	27	216	5-11½	Bedford, Ind.	Mansfield	Senior
Thomas, James	G	24	195	5-6	Bellaire	Bellaire	Soph'mr
Toneff, George*	G	21	190	5-9	Barberton	Barberton	Junior
Trautwein, William	T	22	235	6-4	Athens	Athens	Soph'mr
Verdova, Alex***	HB	20	186	5-10½	Lakewood	Lakewood	Senior
Watson, Thomas*	E	21	195	6-2	Urbana	Urbana	Soph'mr
Wertz, George	QB	21	166	5-9	Piqua	Piqua	Junior
Whisler, Joseph**	FB	24	220	5-11½	Willard	Willard	Senior
Widdoes, Richard	QB	19	165	5-8	Columbus	North	Soph'mr
Wilson, Jack**	T	23	217	6-4	Xenia	Central	Junior
Wulf, Ronald	C	21	200	6-1	Ludlow, Ky.	Ludlow, Ky.	Soph'mr

* One Letter ** Two Letters *** Three Letters

1948
Captain: David I. Templeton

21	*Missouri	7
20	*Southern California	0
7	*Iowa	14
17	Indiana	0
34	*Wisconsin	32
7	Northwestern	21
41	*Pittsburgh	0
34	Illinois	7
3	*Michigan	13
184		94

Won 6, Lost 3

Ohio State Edges Badgers In Wild Scoring Contest

Columbus, Ohio, Oct. 23.—(AP.)
In one of the most hair-raising games ever staged in Buckey Stadium, Ohio State came from behind twice today to nose out a "fired up" Wisconsin eleven, 34 to 32, before 77,205 fans.

The Bucks, blocked on the ground by the Badger forward wall, took to the air lanes for all five of their touchdowns. Wisconsin stayed on the ground for its five markers.

The point after-touchdown department decided the issue, the Bucks getting four of five while the Badgers converted only two.

Determined to win this one for harassed Coach Harry Stuhldreher, and to turn those "Goodbye Harry" signs into "Good Boy Harry,'" the invaders started explosively by shoving over two touchdowns in the opening period.

The first came on an eight-yard run over tackle by halfback Bob Petruska after tackle Harold Otterback recovered Jimmy Clark's fumble on the Ohio 22. The second was the result of a 58-yard drive, fullback Gene Evans taking a pitchout around right end for 25 yards.

Wally Dreyer fumbled both passes from center on the extra point attempts as the Badgers built up their 12-0 edge.

The Bucks went overhead for three touchdowns in the second period, while Wisconsin was getting one. The Bucks led 20-19 at the half.

Wisconsin took the third period kickoff and rolled 72 yards in eight plays, with Gene Evans skirting end for nine yards and the touchdown. Seconds later John Pinnow intercepted a Savic pass on Ohio's 40 and ran to the 24, from where Calvin Vernon went the rest of the way around end to put the Badgers out front 32 to 20.

Ohio needed 12 plays for an 84-yard touchdown drive in the same session, Savic climaxing it with a 25-yard pass to Mike Cannavino in the end zone.

Then Wisconsin's Vernon fumbled on his own 25, Cannavino recovering. The Bucks moved right in and Jerry Krall tossed a three-yarder on fourth down to Verdova for the final score, seconds after the last period opened.

The second biggest crowd in the history of Ohio Stadium—82,845—on hand for the 1948 Michigan game.

Michigan Air Attack Beats Bucks, 13 To 3

Wolverines Overtake Ohio State to Wrap Up Perfect Campaign

Columbus, Ohio, Nov. 20. — (AP.)—Mighty Michigan's Wolverines, their ground attack stymied by a stalwart Ohio State team, took to the airways today and came from behind to win a 13-3 victory.

hTe second largest crowd ever to throng the Ohio stadium, 82,-754, saw the Ohioans rise to their greatest heights of the season, take the lead with a first-period field goal, and win everything but the ball game.

The victory, the wolves' ninth straight of the season and twenty-third in a row, wrapped up their second consecutive Western Conference championship and gave them an outstanding claim on the national title. It was their fourth straight conquest over the Bucks. The game ended the season for both teams.

The Bucks, not the Wolves, looked like the champions in the early going as they allowed the invaders only three first downs in the first half, one on a pass, one by rushing and one on a penalty. Overall, the Ohioans had a 14-9 edge in first downs. The Wolves got two on pass interference penalties, four through the air and only three by rushing.

Ohio ripped the Michigan line apart for nine first downs and passed for five others.

Ohio scored first, a field goal from the 16-yard line by End Jimmy Hague. Ohio had picked up the ball on the Wolverine seven as Halfback Chuck Ortmann's lateral went awry, Center Jack Lininger recovering. An offside penalty and two cracks at the line lost nine, setting the stage for Hague's kick.

The Wolves, who failed to gain a yard on the ground the first half, never got beyond their own 40 in the opening quarter, but scored with a flash in the second.

After Fullback Joe Whisler punted out on the Michigan eight, Ortmann flipped a pass to End Dick Rifenburg who bumped the umpire and dropped the ball. Jimmy Clark recovered for Ohio on the Michigan 23, but after three plays the Bucks were back to the 30.

Again Whisler booted out on the eight, but this time Ortmann's pas to Rifenburg was ruled complete on the 44 because of interference. Then Quarterback Pete Elliott passed 13 to Ortmann. Two Ortmann passes failed, and then he smacked one to End Harry Allis who toko it on the 20 and raced over for the touchdown. The play covered 44 yards and the scoring surge went 92 yards in five plays, all passes, of which three were completed.

Early in the third session the Bucks roared from their own 21 to Michigan's 30, a Pandel Savic to Sonny Gandee pass for 22 yards featuring the drive, but Elliott intercepted Dick Slager's pass to halt the threat.

The Wolves surged 62 yards in eight plays for their fourth-period touchdown which clinched the verdict. Once again the airlanes were used for the distance-eating maneuvers. Walt Teninga passing 21 to Leo Koceski, and Elliott repeating to the same receiver for 13 and to Allis for 12 to reach the Ohio 11.

Koceski hit center for one. Teninga faked a pass and skirted end for eight, and then fullback Tom Peterson rolled over center for the score. Allis, who booted the first extra point, missed the second.

Ohio rolled up 130 yards on the ground to 54 for Michigan, but the Wolves were out front, 116 yards to 73, through the air. Each side completed seven passes, Michigan in 16 attempts and Ohio in 20.

OHIO STATE INDIVIDUAL STATISTICS, 1948

RUSHING

Player	G	TC	G	L	Net	Ave.
Whisler	9	132	589	10	579	4.4
Krall	9	113	560	43	517	4.6
Clark	9	89	421	41	380	4.3
Morrison	8	27	133	..	133	4.9
Verdova	9	32	105	17	88	2.75
Slager	8	20	97	27	70	3.5
Swinehart	8	11	50	9	41	3.7
Cannavino	7	11	39	8	31	2.8
Wertz	8	6	29	3	26	4.3
Sturtz	4	8	26	..	26	3.25
Henry	4	4	16	..	16	4.0
Ellwood	2	7	17	2	15	2.1
S. Gandee	9	1	6	..	6	6.0
Widdoes	8	2	4	..	4	2.0
Demmel	4	4	6	5	1	0.25
Dave Bonnie	1	4	6	5	1	0.25
Perini	7	2	1	2	-1	-0.5
Newell	6	2	..	3	-3	-1.5
Savic	9	8	7	35	-28	-3.5
Totals	9	483	2112	210	1902	3.9

PASSING

Player	Att.	Comp.	Int.	Yds.	TD's	Pct.
Savic	69	36	7	486	5	.522
Slager	34	11	5	177	..	.324
Wertz	6	2	..	66	1	.333
Clark	8	3	..	33	..	.375
Krall	3	3	..	24	3	1.000
Verdova	1	1	..	16	1	1.000
Sturtz	2	1	..	15	..	.500
Widdoes	1	1	..	10	..	1.000
Anderson	1	0	..	..	..	.000
Swinehart	1	0	1	..	..	.000
Total	127	58	13	827	10	.457

SCORING

Player	TD	FG	CA	PAT	TP
Whisler	8	..	..	..	48
Verdova	5	..	..	..	30
Krall	5	..	..	..	30
Hague	1	2	20	17	29
Clark	2	..	..	..	12
Morrison	2	..	..	..	12
S. Gandee	2	..	..	..	12
Cannavino	1	..	..	..	6
Widdoes	0	..	5	3	3
Trautwein	0	..	1	0	0
SAFETY					2
Totals	26	2	26	20	184

PUNTING

Player	K	YK	Ave.
Perini	29	1125	38.6
Morrison	13	490	37.7
Whisler	16	550	34.4
Totals	58	2165	37.3

PASS RECEIVING

Player	Catches	Yds.	TD's
Verdova	12	117	5
S. Gandee	8	130	1
Watson	7	147	..
Krall	6	56	2
Clark	6	53	..
Cannavino	4	51	1
Dorsey	3	74	..
Hague	3	73	1
Wertz	2	30	..
Whisler	2	27	..
Morrison	1	17	..
Savic	1	16	..
Widdoes	1	15	..
Dave Bonnie	1	11	..
Henry	1	10	..
Totals	58	827	10

OHIO STATE TEAM STATISTICS, 1948

	Ohio State	Opp.
First Downs		
Total	136	86
By Rushing	97	48
By Passing	35	29
By Penalties	4	9
Rushing		
Number of Rushes	483	337
Yards Gained	2112	1225
Yards Lost	210	218
Net Yards Gained	1902	1017
Average Yards Gained per Game	211.3	113.0
Average Yards Gained per Rush	3.9	3.0
Forward Passing		
Number Attempted	127	139
Number Completed	58	52
Number Had Intercepted	13	22
Net Yards Gained	827	683
Average Yards Gained per Game	91.9	75.9
Percentage Completions	.457	.374
Scoring Passes	10	3
Average Net Yards Gained per Game	303.2	187.8
Punts		
Number	58	57
Yards Kicked	2165	2311
Average, Yards	37.3	40.5
Had Blocked	1	1
Kick Returns		
Punt Returns, Number	38	29
Punt Returns, Yards	384	426
Kickoff Returns, Number	22	34
Kickoff Returns, Yards	363	820
Interception Returns		
Number	22	13
Yards Returned	276	125
Fumbles		
Number	22	23
Ball Lost, Fumbles	13	15
Penalties		
Number	51	44
Yards Penalized	389	386

[1949]

OHIO STATE UNIVERSITY FOOTBALL ROSTER, 1949

No.	Name	Pos.	Age	Wgt.	Hgt.	Home Town	High School	Class
82	Anderson, Richard	LE	19	180	6-1	Portsmouth	Portsmouth	So.
23	Arledge, Richard	QB	19	184	6-0	Chillicothe	Chillicothe	So.
81	Armstrong, Ralph	LE	19	189	6-4	Cleveland	James Rhodes	So.
87	Basinger, Edward	LE	20	188	6-1	Lima	South	Jr.
83	Behrens, Lawrence	RE	19	181	6-4	Middletown	Middletown	So.
91	Bell, Robert	LH	19	195	6-1	Worthington	Mt. Lebanon, Pa	So.
92	Bilkie, Edward	LE	21	175	6-0	Detroit	Campbell, O.	Jr.
66	Biltz, John	RG	22	206	6-0	Bedford	Bedford	Jr.
34	Blubaugh, Park	FB	20	196	6-1	Lima	Central	So.
43	Bonnie, David**	RH	22	198	6-0	Columbus	North	Sr.
72	Campanella, Joseph	RT	19	223	6-2	Cleveland	Cathedral Latin	So.
15	Chiappini, Albert	LH	21	172	5-9	Jeannette, Pa.	Val. Forge Mil. Aca.	So.
12	Clark, James**	LH	21	188	6-0	Columbus	North	Sr.
56	Cox, Donald	C	20	207	6-0	Pittsburgh	Mt. Lebanon, Pa.	So.
78	Dawson, Jack*	RT	21	226	6-2	Toledo	Waite	Sr.
47	Demmel, Robert*	RH	23	180	5-10	Fremont	Ross	Sr.
14	Doyle, Richard	LH	19	180	6-0	Rochester, Pa.	Rochester, Pa.	So.
75	Edwards, William	RT	23	225	6-4	Willoughby	Mentor	Sr.
24	Elwood, Richard	QB	20	192	5-10	Dover	Dover	Jr.
63	Endres, George	LG	20	190	5-10	Cincinnati	Hughes	Jr.
77	Endres, Robert	LT	18	204	6-1	Cincinnati	Hughes	So.
68	Fachl, Paul	LG	22	214	5-11½	Piqua	Piqua	So.
32	Gandee, Charles*	FB	22	198	5-10½	Berea	Berea	Jr.
84	Gandee, Sherwin*	LE	20	195	6-0	Akron	Garfield	Jr.
89	Gilbert, Charles*	LE	22	193	6-0	Columbus	North	Sr.
80	Hague, James**	RE	21	198	6-1	Rocky River	Rocky River	Sr.
10	Hamilton, Ray	RH	19	176	5-11	Canton	McKinley	So.
54	Heid, Robert	C	19	188	6-1	Fremont	Ross	So.
48	Henry, Joseph	RH	24	194	5-11	Columbus	Lakewood	Sr.
31	Janowicz, Victor	FB	19	180	5-9	Elyria	Elyria	So.
71	Jennings, Jack**	LT	22	235	6-3	Columbus	North	Sr.
85	King, Dale	LE	20	201	6-1	Columbus	North	Jr.
16	Klevay, Walter	RH	19	166	5-10	Independence	Independence	So.
44	Krall, Gerald***	LH	22	180	5-10	Toledo	Libbey	Sr.
53	Lininger, Jack***	C	22	201	5-11	Van Wert	Van Wert	Sr.
90	Logan, Richard	LT	19	205	6-1	Mansfield	Mansfield	So.
62	Manz, Jerry*	LG	20	220	5-10	Toledo	Libbey	Jr.
57	Marold, John	C	19	195	5-10	Hempstead, N. Y.	Williston Park	So.
64	Mattey, George*	LG	22	221	5-10	Cleveland	East	Sr.
52	McCullough, Robert	C	20	187	6-1	Uhrichsville	Uhrichsville	Jr.
70	Miller, William*	LT	22	230	6-4	Fremont	Ross	Jr.
73	Momsen, Robert	LT	20	218	6-3	Toledo	Libbey	Jr.
40	Morris, Robert	RH	20	185	5-10½	Columbus	Grandview	Jr.
33	Morrison, Fred***	FB	23	210	6-2	Columbus	Upper Arlington	Sr.
41	Newell, William*	RH	21	175	5-11	Columbiana	Columbiana	Sr.
74	O'Hanlon, Richard**	LT	21	220	6-2	East Liverpool	East Liverpool	Sr.
36	Perini, Peter***	FB	21	220	6-0	New Village, N. J.	Washington, N. J.	Sr.
21	Petersen, William	QB	18	190	6-0	Cleveland	Cathedral Latin	So.
55	Rath, Thomas	C	20	205	5-10	Defiance	Defiance	So.
59	Ronemus, Thor	LG	18	190	5-9½	Springfield	Public	So.
86	Ruzich, Steve	LT	21	205	6-2	Madison	Madison	So.
25	Savic, Pandel**	QB	24	197	6-0	Girard	Girard	Sr.
65	Smith, Carroll	RG	19	186	5-11½	Sebring	Sebring	So.
11	Sturtz, Karl	RH	21	178	6-0	Coshocton	Coshocton	Jr.
42	Swinehart, Rodney***	LH	23	178	5-10	Wooster	Wooster	Sr.
61	Taberner, Joseph	RG	19	225	5-10	Toledo	Libbey	Jr.
69	Thomas, James	RG	25	200	5-7½	Bellaire	Bellaire	Jr.
60	Toneff, George**	RG	22	190	5-8½	Barberton	Barberton	Sr.
76	Trautwein, Bill*	RT	23	236	6-4	Athens	Athens	Jr.
30	Wagner, Jack	FB	19	188	6-1	Piqua	Piqua	So.
88	Watson, Thomas**	RE	22	205	6-2	Urbana	Urbana	Jr.
26	Wertz, George*	QB	22	172	5-5½	Piqua	Piqua	Sr.
28	Widdoes, Richard*	QB	20	174	5-8	Athens	Columbus North	Jr.
79	Wilson, Jack*** (C)	RT	24	216	6-4	Xenia	Central	Sr.
67	Wittman, Julius	RT	19	209	6-1	Massillon	Massillon	So.

*—Denotes Letters.

1949
Captain: A. Jack Wilson

35	*Missouri	34
46	*Indiana	7
13	Southern California	13
0	*Minnesota	27
21	Wisconsin	0
24	*Northwestern	7
14	Pittsburgh	10
30	*Illinois	17
7	Michigan	7
17	†California	14
207		136

Won 7, Lost 1, Tied 2
Big Ten Co-Champions
† Rose Bowl

OHIO STATE 35
MISSOURI 34

On September 24, Ohio State launched its 1949 season by defeating Missouri's alert and powerful team 35-34. The largest opening crowd in the nine game series, 66,510 fans, was in attendance.

Missouri was first to score and was in the lead until late in the third quarter when Lininger ended a Tiger drive on a pass interception that gave Ohio two TD's in succession.

From a 21-21 tie in the third quarter, the Bucks went ahead 28-21 on Hamilton's touchdown-pass catch and Hague's conversion. After the Tigers brought the score to read 28-27 in the fourth period, the Bucks once again scored on a Savic-to-Hamilton pass combination which ended a 74-yard drive. Hague's fifth straight extra conversion ended Ohio's scoring for the day.

Ohio's first two TD'S came in the second quarter after Morrison's two yard power drive and Krall's seven yard jaunt to make the half-time score read 14-14.

The Bucks third score came in the third period when Hague caught a nine yard pass in the end zone. He then booted the extra point.

OHIO STATE 13
SO. CAL. 13

The Trojans of Southern California and the Bucks battled to a 13-13 tie as they both made touchdowns in the first period and then came back to make TD's in the third period, each missing a conversion. The squads were stout representatives from their respective Big Ten and Pacific Coast conferences and, at the time, proved to be likely contenders for the Rose Bowl invitation come New Year's Day.

Ohio's first score came when Krall passed to Hamilton in the end zone. Hague converted. The score was set up by a 35-yard gain on a combination lateral play by Morrison and Krall.

Southern Cal scored after recovering a Buck fumble on the Ohio five. Martin scored and the try for extra point failed, giving Ohio a 7-6 lead, which it held throughout the half.

After intermission, the Bucks capitalized on an 80-yard drive including Morrison's 66-yard sprint through the entire secondary. The try for extra point by Hague was blocked.

Not to be outdone, the Trojans came back on the next series of plays and, with the combination of Martin's runs and Powers' passes, scored. Gifford made his kick good to tie the score 13-13 where it stayed the rest of the game. In statistics, the Bucks had a decisive advantage, but they were beaten as far as Lady Luck was concerned.

Minnesota Romps To Easy Win Over Ohio State, 27-0

Billy Bye and Dick Gregory Spark Gophers to Important Western Conference Triumph; Buckeyes' Attack Smothered by Powerful Rivals

Columbus, Ohio, Oct. 15.—(AP.) —Minnesota moved a lengthy piece down the Rose Bowl road today by belting Ohio State, 27-0, in a Western Conference football game before 82,111 fans.

The running of halfbacks Billy Bye and Dick Gregory, with the help of savage blocking, sparked the Golden Gophers' four-touchdown parade.

The result never was much in doubt after the first few plays.

Minnesota's giant line took command of the situation almost immediately. Led by center Clayton Tonnemaker and tackle Leo Nomellini, the Minnesota forwards simply smothered any Ohio State attack that became even slightly dangerous.

Bye counted the first Minnesota touchdown late in the first period, going 14 yards over Ohio State's right guard. End Gordon Soltau kicked the first of three straight conversions.

Gregory set up the second touchdown with a 51-yard run around his own right end and another 20-yard scamper. He scored it on his second plunge from the eight-yard line.

Balked on the ground, Bye tossed a 20-yard pass to quarterback Jim Malosky in the Ohio end zone early in the fourth quarter. The final marker came a few minutes later after Ohio's halfback Jim Clark fumbled on his own 13. Fullback Ken Beiersdorf threw to end Bud Grant on the Ohio one, then dived over two plays later.

OHIO STATE 7
MICHIGAN 7

Ohio State's battling Bucks hit the jack pot as they tied the mighty Wolverines of Michigan 7-7, grabbing a share of the Big Nine grid title and the right to represent the conference in the famed Rose Bowl game at Pasadena, Jan. 2. It was the Bucks first conference title since 1944 and was their second trip to the Rose Bowl. The Buckeyes lost a 28-0 decision to California in 1921.

The Maize and Blue capitalized on a first quarter break in order to score a TD on a desperation pass from Teninga to Koceski. End Allis kicked the extra point and as the game wore on the seven point lead seemed larger and larger to the 97,239 fans who filled the Michigan stadium.

However, the Bucks were not finished. With only ten minutes remaining, Janowicz dropped a Michigan punt on his 36 and recovered it on the 20. From there, it took only six plays for the 80-yards. Morrison plunged for fifteen yards. Krall then added two around end and ten more yards through the middle to make a first down on the 47. Hamilton then hauled in an aerial from Savic on Michigan's 40 and headed for the sidelines. Teninga finally forced him out of bounds on the four. Morrison picked up the final yards in two powerful plunges into the line. Hague needed two tries to tie up the game. His first one was wide, but Michigan was offside. His second one split the uprights.

Coach Fesler declared of the victory: "It's certainly a great tribute to a great bunch of boys. They are the greatest bunch of boys a coach ever had to work with".

INDIVIDUAL STATISTICS, 1949
(Regular Season)

RUSHING

Player	G	TC	G	L	Net	TD
Krall	9	128	679	73	606	4
Morrison	9	130	559	65	494	8
Clark	7	66	372	37	335	1
Hamilton	9	41	270	53	217	1
Janowicz	5	30	121	9	112	1
Klevay	8	13	73	2	71	0
Gandee	8	11	40	0	40	0
Sturtz	8	1	24	0	24	0
Chiappini	1	1	21	0	21	0
Swinehart	7	3	20	0	20	0
Schnittker	7	1	5	0	5	0
Armstrong	6	3	8	3	5	0
Perini	9	1	3	0	3	0
Doyle	2	4	6	11	-5	1
Blubaugh	1	1	0	9	-9	0
Savic	9	15	20	51	-31	1
Totals	9	449	2221	313	1908	17

PASSING

Player	Att	Comp	Int	Yds	TD
Savic	84	35	4	581	6
Krall	39	17	3	257	3
Clark	29	10	4	172	0
Janowicz	4	2	0	50	0
Doyle	5	2	1	45	1
Swinehart	2	2	0	30	0
Ellwood	2	2	0	26	0
Hamilton	3	1	0	8	0
Petersen	2	0	0	0	0
Gandee	1	0	0	0	0
Totals	171	71	12	1169	10

SCORING

Player	TD	FG	CA	CM	TP
Morrison	8	0	0	0	48
Hague	1	1	24	21	30
Hamilton	5	0	0	0	30
Krall	4	0	0	0	24
Janowicz	2	0	3	2	14
Savic	2	0	0	0	12
Clark	1	0	0	0	6
Armstrong	1	0	0	0	6
Schnittker	1	0	0	0	6
Klevay	1	0	0	0	6
Doyle	1	0	0	0	6
				SAFETY	2
Totals	27	1	27	23	190

PUNTING

Player	Punts	T. Yds.	Ave.
Perini	5	202	40.4
Morrison	49	1869	38.1
Janowicz	4	137	34.9
Totals	58	2206	38.0

PASS RECEIVING

Player	Catches	Yds.	TD's
Hamilton	15	347	4
Armstrong	9	166	1
Schnittker	9	156	1
Hague	4	100	1
Klevay	5	82	1
Watson	1	65	0
Morrison	9	65	0
Gilbert	6	60	0
Savic	7	44	1
Janowicz	1	24	1
Clark	3	23	0
Basinger	1	22	0
Gandee	1	15	0
Totals	71	1169	10

PUNT RETURNS

Player	No.	Yds.	Ave.
Janowicz	10	120	12.0
Newell	7	87	12.4
Clark	7	84	12.0
Widdoes	3	36	12.0
Swinehart	2	20	10.0
Klevay	1	15	15.0
Sturtz	1	14	14.0
Totals	31	376	12.1

OHIO STATE TEAM STATISTICS, 1949
(Regular Season)

	Ohio State	Opp.
First Downs		
Total	137	109
By Rushing	90	75
By Passing	41	31
By Penalties	6	3
Rushing		
Number of Rushes	449	449
Yards Gained	2221	1728
Yards Lost	313	234
Net Yards Gained	1908	1494
Average Yards Gained per Game	212	166
Average Yards Gained per Game	4.2	3.3
Forward Passing		
Number Attempted	171	172
Number Completed	71	65
Number Had Intercepted	12	14
Net Yards Gained	1169	846
Average Yards Gained Per Game	129.9	94
Percentage Completion	41.5	37.8
Scoring Passes	10	4
Total Plays		
Rushes and Passes	620	621
Total Net Yards Gained	3077	2340

	Ohio State	Opp.
Average Net Yards Gained per Game	341.9	160
Punts		
Number	58	64
Yards Kicked	2206	2440
Average Yards per Kick	37.8	38.1
Had Blocked	1	0
Kick Returns		
Punt Returns, Number	31	32
Punt Returns, Yards	376	285
Kickoff Returns, Number	27	37
Kickoff Returns, Yards	514	680
Interception Returns		
Number	14	12
Yards Returned	168	82
Fumbles		
Number	34	32
Ball Lost, Fumbles	15	18
Penalties		
Number	43	32
Yards Penalized	364	354

Score by Quarters:

	1	2	3	4	Final
Ohio State	34	23	75	58	190
Opponents	34	31	31	26	122

HAGUE'S GOAL CRACKS TIE IN LAST TWO MINUTES

Ohio State scored a history-making field goal in the final two minutes to defeat the California Bears 17-14 in the annual Rose Bowl classic at Pasadena. Once again the banners of the Big Ten triumphed over the Pacific Coast Conference for the fourth straight year.

Right End Jim Hague, whose place-kick against Michigan brought the Bucks to this thirty-sixth classic, brought his team through. There was one minute and 55 seconds left in the game and the score was tied at 14-14 as Hague got ready for his team's last chance to win the game. As a record crowd of 106,052 looked on, Center Lininger centered the ball from the California ten-yard line. Widdoes placed the ball on the 17½-yard mark as Hague's toe met the pigskin. The ball split the uprights as it was kicked at a slight angle to the left and made it the first time in the history of the Rose Bowl that a game had been decided by a field goal.

California was the first to score. Mid-way in the second quarter the Bears recovered a fumble on their own 25-yard line. On the next play Bob Celeri passed 55 yards to Brunk on the Buck 19. The score came when Monachino whirled around his own left end for six and the TD. Cullom converted.

The Bucks then slammed back in the third period for two TD's and a 14-7 lead. Janowicz intercepted Celeri's pass and raced back 43 yards to California's 31-yard line. Ten plays later Morrison plunged over and Hague placekicked for a tie.

A bit later, Bill Trautwein, Buck tackle who stood out on the defensive play, burst in to block Celeri's punt and Lininger pounced on the ball on the Bear six yard line. Four plays later Krall slashed over for the TD. Hague again converted.

The Bears took the kickoff to their 41-yard line. Five plays later Monachino smashed through tackle on a pitchout and down the sidelines on a 44-yard run to score. Cullom's conversion tied the score at 14-14.

The all important field goal was set-up after Celeri bobbled a pass from center on his own five on fourth down. An attempted boot, while running, went out of bounds on the Bears 13-yard line.

The kick that won the game.

Kroll goes over for Ohio's second touchdown.

1949
A.P. POLL
1. Notre Dame
2. Oklahoma
3. California
4. Army
5. Rice
6. OHIO STATE
7. Michigan
8. Minnesota
9. L.S.U.
10. Coll. of Pacific

Wes Fesler Remains As Grid Coach

Ohio State Trustees Give Mentor Raise In Pay to Retain Him

Columbus, Ohio, Jan. 9.—(AP.)—Wes Fesler decided today to remain as Ohio State University's head football coach.

In making his decision, Fesler accomplished three things:

1. Set at rest a six-week rumor that he would desert the Bucks for a $25,000 per year job in the business world;
2. Killed "on the vine" a series of prospective booms for possible successors; and
3. Assured his future welfare and security by getting a $1500 raise to $15,000 a year, and a board of trustees promise of a full professorship in the physcial education department, if and when he gives up the coaching job.

Fesler talked the whole thing over last Saturday with university president Howard L. Bevis and three members of the board of trustees. The result was announced today in statements by the coach and prexy, a few minutes after a board meeting.

1950
Captain: Henry Bill Trautwein

27	*Southern Methodist	32
41	*Pittsburgh	7
26	Indiana	14
48	Minnesota	0
83	*Iowa	21
32	Northwestern	0
19	*Wisconsin	14
7	Illinois	14
3	*Michigan	9
286		111

Won 6, Lost 3

OHIO STATE UNIVERSITY FOOTBALL ROSTER, 1950

No.	Name	Pos.	Age	Wgt.	Hgt.	Home Town
82	Anderson, Richard	LE	20	194	6-1	Portsmouth
23	Arledge, Richard	QB	20	183	6-0	Chillicothe
81	Armstrong, Ralph*	LE	20	196	6-4	Cleveland
87	Basinger, Edward	RE	21	184	6-1	Lima
48	Beekley, Marts	RH	19	181	5-9	Sharonville
92	Bilkie, Edward	RE	22	187	6-1	Detroit
66	Biltz, John*	RG	23	208	6-0	Bedford
46	Bruce, Earle	LH	19	160	5-8	Cumberland, Md.
12	Bruney, Fred	LH	18	163	5-11	Martins Ferry
72	Campanella, Joseph	RT	20	226	6-2	Cleveland
25	Curcillo, Tony	QB	19	188	6-1	Elyria
47	Demmel, Robert*	RH	24	185	5-11	Fremont
14	Doyle, Richard	LH	20	183	6-0	Rochester, Pa.
24	Ellwood, Richard*	QB	21	189	5-10	Dover
63	Endres, George	LG	21	189	5-10	Cincinnati
77	Endres, Robert	LT	20	200	6-1	Cincinnati
68	Faehl, Paul	RG	22	207	5-11	Piqua
61	Fischer, Lou	LG	20	198	5-11	Charleston, W.Va.
43	Gambill, David	RH	19	177	5-11	Portsmouth
32	Gandee, Charles**	FB	23	200	5-10	Berea
84	Gandee, Sherwin*	RE	21	191	6-0	Akron
56	Geib, Gene	C	20	178	5-11	Fremont
42	Gentile, Earle	LH	21	182	5-10	Cleveland
80	Grimes, Robert	RE	19	194	6-1	Middletown
74	Guthrie, George	RT	18	207	6-0	Columbus
10	Hamilton, Ray*	RH	20	177	6-0	Canton
54	Heid, Robert*	C	20	181	6-0	Fremont
75	Hietikko, James	RT	19	220	6-3	Conneaut
86	Hinebaugh, Kenneth	LE	19	178	6-3	East Chicago, Ind.
36	Hlay, John	FB	20	212	6-1	Niles
31	Janowicz, Victor*	QB	20	186	5-9	Elyria
16	Klevay, Walter*	RH	20	164	5-10	Independence
33	Koepnick, Robert	FB	19	192	6-0	Dayton
71	Logan, Richard	LT	20	208	6-1	Mansfield
83	Lytle, John	RE	21	195	6-0	Indianapolis
91	Manyak, John	LE	20	188	6-1	Warren
62	Manz, Jerry**	LG	21	216	5-10	Toledo
57	Marold, John	C	21	205	6-0	Hempstead, N.Y.
52	McCullough, Robert*	C	21	188	6-1	Uhrichsville
70	Miller, William**	LT	23	225	6-4	Fremont
73	Momsen, Robert	RT	21	218	6-3	Toledo
34	Moritz, Roger	FB	19	198	6-1	Columbus
85	Moshier, William	RE	19	196	6-2	Montpelier
21	Petersen, William	QB	20	182	6-0	Cleveland
55	Rath, Thomas	C	21	197	5-10	Defiance
64	Ronemus, Thor	RG	19	185	5-9	Springfield
53	Ruehl, James	C	20	200	6-2	Cumberland, Md.
60	Ruzich, Steve	LG	22	209	6-2	Madison
69	Savic, George	LG	19	186	5-10	Girard
44	Skvarka, Bernie	LH	20	182	5-9	Struthers
22	Slager, Richard**	QB	22	192	6-0	Columbus
65	Smith, Carroll	RG	21	185	5-11	Sebring
11	Sturtz, Karl*	RH	22	182	5-10	Coshocton
59	Ternent, William	LG	18	195	6-0	Columbus
90	Thomas, Richard	LE	19	183	6-1	Martins Ferry
76	Trautwein, William**	RT	24	237	6-4	Athens
79	Vavroch, William	LT	19	210	6-1	Cleveland
30	Wagner, Jack	FB	20	189	6-1	Piqua
89	Walther, Richard	RE	21	187	5-10	Dayton
88	Watson, Thomas***	LE	23	201	6-2	Urbana
28	Widdoes, Richard**	QB	21	174	5-8	Athens
67	Wittman, Julius*	LT	20	212	6-1	Massillon
58	Wolter, Robert	RG	19	187	5-11	South Euclid

Ohio State Smothers Iowa Under 83-21 Score

Columbus, Ohio, Oct. 28.—(AP)—Touched off by the sparkling Vic Janowicz, Ohio State's Rose Bowl champions exploded for 12 touchdowns today to smother Iowa's Hawkeyes under an 83-21 score, largest since 1939 in Western Conference play.

A crowd of 82,174, third largest ever to fill the Buckeye Stadium, sat stunned as Janowicz, a junior from Elyria, Ohio, piloted the Bucks to three touchdowns in the first five minutes.

From then on, it was all Ohio, the Hawkeyes showing none of the form they displayed a week ago in defeating Purdue 33-21.

The Bucks, who picked up four Iowa fumbles in the first period, rolled an astounding five-touchdown lead in that session and picked up three more touchdowns in the second period before Iowa made an offensive move.

Illinois Downs Buckeyes By 14-7 Margin

Tricky Aerials Score Both Touchdowns in Big Ten Grid Battle

Campaign, Ill., Nov. 18.—(AP)—Illinois, the great running team, sprung two aerial touchdowns off trick plays in the second period to surprise mighty Ohio State 14-7 today and shoot ahead in the Big Ten Rose Bowl race.

It was the first Big Ten loss for Ohio State, ranked last week as the nation's top team in the AP poll.

Muffled on the ground as never before this season, the Illini pecked at the Buckeyes' weakest spot, pass defense, and clicked superbly before a capacity throng of 71,119 wild fans.

The win, the Illini's fourth in five league games, shoved them ahead of Wisconsin in their torrid duel for the bowl bid. Each has one more game to play.

Little Fred Major, wearing a chin mask to protect a broken jaw bone, faked a jump pass in the first two minutes of the second quarter and finally fired the ball to Don Stevens. The former Youngstown, Ohio, prep star snared it on the Ohio State 28 and, as defender Fred Bruney lunged at his heels, skipped loose to flee for a touchdown. The play was good for 52 yards and the tally was Stevens' first in two years at Illinois.

Spread Formation

Six minutes later the Illini thrust again through the air to what became the clinching marker. The drive was touched off by Illini Joe Hall's recovery of Chuck Gandee's bobble on the Illinois 47. With hobbled Johnny Karras streaking 12 yards, the Illini covered the distance goalward in seven plays with Major finally pitching the last five yards to Stevens in the end zone.

The payoff pass came on a spread formation off a fake punt, a play nursed along in secrecy all season to be used today.

Just before the touchdown, Major's toss to end Tony Klimek on the same spread alignment was fumbled by the great end, but Stevens snapped it up in midair to make it count and set up the touchdown on the next down.

Sam Rebecca converted both times.

With three and one half minutes left in the explosive second period, Ohio State became the first team of the season to score on the ground against Illinois' steeled defense.

Ohio State's Viv Janowicz, every bit an All-American today, and Tony Curcillo, the injured Buckeye quarterback who played brilliantly, used end Tom Watson as their passing target on three plays that gained 59 yards.

Janowicz Scores

Janowicz eventually slammed over from the four to end an 83 yard surge in ten plays. He also converted.

Two intercepted passes and a recovered fumble quelled Ohio State just as it appeared that the Buckeyes were wound up for touchdowns. Herb Neatherly filched a Curcille pitch in the third, and Al Brosky minutes later stole a Janowicz aerial. Both times the Bucks were striving to piece midfield and seemed to be rolling.

In the finale, Walt Klevay's 22 yard run ignited a 70 yard Buckeye blast that ended on the Illinois 10 when Eli Popa, a defensive fullback from Canton, Ohio, recovered his second fumble as sophomore Klevay bobbled. Later Chuck Gandee led a spurt to the Illini 28 before Ohio State was stalled.

Ohio State Barely Edges Wisconsin To Near Title

Badgers Gamble Twice in Game and Lose Both Times As Buckeyes Come From Behind for 19-14 Victory in Vital Big Ten Encounter

Columbus, Ohio, Nov. 11.—(AP)—Wisconsin's gambling Badgers slowed Ohio State's vaunted offense down to a walk today, but the brilliant Bucks pulled out a 19-14 victory before 81,535 fans to practically clinch the Western Conference championship.

A victory over either Illinois or Michigan in remaining games would give the undisputed title to Ohio State.

The underdog Badgers gambled twice today, lost both times, and the gambles cost them the contest. The first gamble came in the third period with Wisconsin leading 7-6. The Badgers stopped a 52-yard Ohio drive on the one-foot line, taking the ball on downs, and tried two plunges at the line, which failed to gain an inch.

Each time the ball carrier was almost nabbed in the end zone for a safety. The Badgers gambled on a quick kick on third down, the ball going out of bounds on Wisconsin's 28. Walt Klevay plunged for six and then Tony Curculo, Ohio quarterback, hit end Tom Watson on the goal line with a 22-yard touchdown pass.

Early in the fourth session, Wisconsin gambled again, trying to make half a yard on fourth down on its own 22-yard line. The play missed by inches. Ohio took over and moved the 22 yards in five plays with halfback Vic Janowicz skirting right end for the touchdown which won the contest.

Late in the period, the Badgers zoomed down to Ohio's 14-yard line on the sensational passing of quarterback John Coatta, but Ray Hamilton of Ohio intercepted on Ohio's four to stop the threat.

Janowicz fumbled on the next play, however, and Ed Withers recovered on the four for Wisconsin.

Jimmy Hammond, Wisconsin fullback, plunged a yard on second down for the touchdown to bring the Badgers up to a 19-14 deficit, with about 3½ minutes to go. But Ohio ran the time out with ground plays after taking the kickoff.

Wolverines Block Punts To Upset Buckeyes, 9-3

Michigan Gains Probable Rose Bowl Shot Without Making First Down on Wind Swept, Snow Blanketed Gridiron at Columbus

Columbus, O., Nov. 25.—(AP)—Michigan's wily Wolverines wrapped up the Western Conference championship and a probable Rose Bowl bid today, blocking two attempted punts to defeat Ohio's favored Buckeyes 9 to 3 on a snow-covered, storm-swept gridiron.

Michigan failed to make a first down in fighting its way into the king row, but turned a pair of breaks into the nine points needed to give it the title.

Playing on a field on which several inches of snow hid the yard lines and made ball-handling treacherous, Michigan was able to gain only 27 yards by rushing. Ohio's vaunted offense was held to 16 yards on the ground and a total of 41 as the Bucks picked up 25 yards on three successful passes in 18 attempts.

A 28-mile wind swept across the Buckeye Stadium and the athletes played like they were wearing boxing gloves as Michigan took advantage of a weird set of circumstances to annex the title and take the favored role for the Rose Bowl invitation.

Michigan had to couple a victory over Ohio State with a Northwestern win over Illinois today, and both came to pass.

Chuck Ortmann, Michigan's brilliant halfback, was the difference in today's climatic contest. Known mostly for his fine passing, Ortmann's nine aerial attempts today failed to find a mark, but his unerring kicking kept the Buckeyes deep in their own territory.

Eleven times in 24 attempts, Ortmann punted out of bounds inside the Ohio 15-yard line, and the Buckeyes failed to fight their way out of the hole at any time.

Bucks Score First

Ohio drew first blood in the opening five minutes, when Vic Janowicz booted a field goal through the swirling snow flakes from 22 yards out.

The break on that one came the first time Michigan had the ball. Joe Campanella, Ohio tackle, blocked Ortmann's attempted quick kick from the six-yard line, and Bob Momsen fell on it there.

Janowicz was thrown for a loss and an intentional grounding penalty moved the ball back to the 35, but Janowicz hit Tom Watson with a pass to the 22. From that point the Ohio halfback booted his three-pointer to wind up the Buckeye scoring.

Late in the same period, Ortmann booted out of bounds on Ohio's three, from which point Michigan's Captain, R. Allen Wahl, broke through to block Janowicz' kick, the ball rolling out of the end zone for an automatic safety.

A bit of quick thinking and another blocked kick gave Michigan its winning touchdown in the second period. Ortmann had punted out on Ohio's eight, with less than a minute to go, and Ohio attempted to run line plays to use up the time rather than kick from its own end zone.

Brooms Needed

After each play, however, Michigan called time out. Ohio was forced to kick with 20 seconds to play. Tony Momsen, brother of Ohio's Bob, rushed through the line, blocked Janowicz' kick in the slippery footing, and fell on the ball in the end zone for the score.

Harry Allis booted the extra point and Michigan was on its way to the Big Ten title and the Tournament of Roses.

The last half was a scoreless duel, with Janowicz and Ortmann continuing their punting exchanges.

Ortmann booted 24 times for a 30-yard average, and Janowicz kicked 21 times for a 32-yard average.

Both were phenomenal marks in view of the slippery going and the heavy wind. So heavy was the snow that at times it was impossible to see the players from the pressbox, and when measurements for first downs were necessary, brooms were used to sweep off the gridiron to find the yard markers.

Although 82,300 tickets—third largest amount ever sold for an Ohio game—were disposed of before the contest, only 50,503 braved the elements to see the game.

Only two weeks ago Ohio State was rated the No. 1 team in America, but today after successive defeats by Illinois and Michigan, the Buckeyes find themselves as also-ran in their own conference.

Chuck Gandee was Ohio's top ground gainer, with 15 yards in 11 tries, while Ralph Straffon, substitute fullback, topped the Wolverines on the ground with 14 yards in 12 tries.

All of Straffon's running was in the closing periods, when Michigan used ground plays to runout the clock and relied on Ortmann's fine punting to keep the Buckeyes from scoring.

Ohio State Back Named For Award

Vic Janowicz Winner Of Heisman Trophy, Rote Places Second

New York, Dec. 5. — (AP) —Vic Janowicz, a standout on offense and defense for Ohio State, has been chosen as the 1950 winner of the Heisman Memorial Trophy, awarded annually to the "outstanding college football player in the United States."

The announcement was made today by the trophy committee which polled sports writers and sportscasters from coast to coast.

The 20-year old junior from Elyria, Ohio, received a total of 633 votes to win decisively over a sterling list of eligibles.

Kyle Rote of Southern Methodist was second with 280 followed in order by Reds Bagnell, Pennsylvania, 231; Babe Parelli, Kentucky, 214; Bobby Reynolds, Nebraska, 174; Bob Williams, Notre Dame, 159; Leon Heath, Oklahoma, 125, and Dan Foldberg, 103.

In the sectional voting, Janowicz was named first in the east, midwest and far west. Parelli was rated tops in the south and Rote in the southwest.

Leon Hart, Notre Dame's fine end, was the winner last year. Ohio State had another winner in 1944 when Les Horvath was selected.

Janowicz, a workhorse on offense and defense, divided his duties between left half and quarterback on the attack, and at safety when defending. He handled all the kickoffs, booted 26 points after touchdown, three field goals, completed 32 of 77 passes for 561 yards and 12 touchdowns, did the punting, and led the team in scoring with 65 points.

Vic played more than any other Buckeye. He saw action in all nine games for a total of 277.5 minutes. The 5-9, 185-pounder led the Big Ten in scoring with 48 points and in total offense with 703 yards.

He will be awarded the trophy next Tuesday.

OHIO STATE INDIVIDUAL STATISTICS, 1950
(Regular Season)

RUSHING

Player	G	TC	G	L	Net	Av.	TL
Klevay	9	66	547	27	520	7.9	3
C. Gandee	9	99	362	3	359	3.6	3
Janowicz	9	114	439	125	314	2.8	4
Curcillo	9	35	202	44	158	4.5	1
Doyle	5	29	125	18	107	3.7	1
Koepnick	6	18	84	0	84	4.7	0
Wagner	4	24	70	6	64	2.7	1
Bruney	9	23	66	8	58	2.5	2
Hlay	9	16	49	0	49	3.1	0
Sturtz	9	18	56	22	34	1.9	1
Widdoes	9	3	21	0	21	7.0	0
Skvarka	4	8	29	10	19	2.4	1
Hamilton	9	5	13	3	10	2.0	0
Gambill	2	4	0	4	-4	-1.0	0
Totals	9	462	2063	270	1793	3.9	17

PASSING

Player	Att.	Comp.	Int.	Yds.	TD's
Janowicz	77	32	7	561	12
Curcillo	38	18	5	337	2
Doyle	26	14	2	190	2
Bruney	6	4	0	38	0
Gentile	1	1	0	26	0
Skvarka	6	2	1	13	0
Ellwood	4	1	0	7	1
Widdoes	1	0	0	0	0
Totals	159	72	13	1172	17

PASS RECEIVING

Player	Catches	Yards	TD's
Watson	23	463	4
Curcillo	13	226	6
Klevay	9	128	0
Armstrong	9	127	2
Grimes	2	57	1
Anderson	2	33	1
Arledge	1	26	0
Widdoes	3	21	0
Janowicz	1	17	0
Sturtz	2	15	0
Bilkie	1	15	0
Hamilton	2	14	2
Doyle	1	10	0
S. Gandee	1	7	1
Ellwood	1	7	0
Bruney	1	6	0
Totals	72	1172	17

PUNTING

Player	Punts	Yards	Blocked	Avg.
Janowicz	54	1960	4	36.5
Hamilton	9	277	1	30.8
Bruney	2	76	0	38.0
Curcillo	1	46	0	46.0
Totals	66	2368	5	35.8

PUNT RETURNS

Player	No.	Yds.	Avg.	TD's
Bruney	14	97	6.9	0
Demmel	8	62	7.8	1
Hamilton	6	58	9.7	0
Janowicz	7	46	6.6	1
Totals	35	263	7.5	2

SCORING

Player	TD's	FG	CA	CM	TP
Janowicz	5	3	36	26	65
Curcillo	7	0	0	0	42
Watson	4	0	1	1	25
Klevay	4	0	0	0	24
C. Gandee	3	0	0	0	18
S. Gandee	2	0	0	0	12
Armstrong	2	0	0	0	12
Hamilton	2	0	0	0	12
Bruney	2	0	0	0	12
Demmel	2	0	0	0	12
Doyle	1	0	0	0	6
Wagner	1	0	0	0	6
Sturtz	1	0	0	0	6
Widdoes	1	0	0	0	6
Skvarka	1	0	0	0	6
Grimes	1	0	0	0	6
Anderson	1	0	0	0	6
Manz	1	0	0	0	6
Trautwein	0	0	3	2	0
Arledge	0	0	1	0	0
SAFETY					2
Totals	41	3	41	29	286

KICKOFF RETURNS

Player	No.	Yds.	Avg.	TD's
Sturtz	10	303	10.3	0
Klevay	4	154	36.0	1
C. Gandee	3	80	26.7	0
Skvarka	1	21	21.0	0
Watson	1	14	14.0	0
Walther	1	14	14.0	0
Grimes	1	8	8.0	0
Ronemus	1	0	.0	0
Totals	22	594	27.0	1

INTERCEPTION RETURNS

Player	Number	Yards	TD's
Widdoes	4	71	1
Demmel	2	36	1
Hamilton	4	25	0
S. Gandee	1	24	1
Janowicz	1	18	0
C. Gandee	2	11	0
Bruney	3	7	0
Walther	1	3	0
Watson	1	0	0
Totals	19	195	3

Wes Fesler Quits Ohio State Berth

Chicago, Dec. 9.—(AP) Wes Fesler, on the verge of a nervous breakdown during the football season, resigned as head football coach of Ohio State University in a surprise move tonight at the annual Big Ten winter meetings.

Giving his reason for quitting as "poor health," Fesler presented his resignation to Athlet Director Dick Larkins. Larkins, in turn, handed it to Ohio State president, Dr. Howard L. Bevis. It was accepted.

Fesler told a friend that "I was in the training room during the football season more often than the players—getting treatment for my head and neck."

OHIO STATE TEAM STATISTICS, 1950

	Opp.	OSU
First Downs		
Total	99	139
By Rushing	34	95
By Passing	59	43
By Penalty	6	1
Rushing		
No. of Rushes	341	462
Yards Gained	875	2063
Yards Lost	299	270
Net Yds. Gained Rushing	576	1793
Average Yards Gained Per Game	64	199
Average Yards Gained Per Rush	1.4	3.9
Forward Passing		
Number Attempted	234	159
Number Completed	111	72
Number Had Intercepted	19	1172
Touchdown Passes	11	17
Average Yards Gained Per Game	162	130
Percentage Completed	47.4	45.3
Total Net Yards Gained	2031	2965
Average Yards Gained Per Game	225.7	329.5
Punts		
Number	85	66
Yards Kicked	3088	2368
Average Yards Per Kick	36.3	35.8
Had Blocked	2	5
Kick Returns		
Punt Returns, No.	29	35
Punt Returns, Yards	238	263
Kickoff Returns, No.	43	22
Kickoff Returns, Yards	844	594
Interception Returns		
Number	15	19
Yards Returned	158	195
Fumbles		
Number	43	31
Ball Lost, Fumbles	25	16
Penalties		
Number	38	52
Yards Penalized	302	409

An All-American Leaves "Home"...

THE all-American end who liked to call Ohio State his home, called it quits in December, 16 days after the 1950 season ended. His name was Wesley Eugene Fesler, head football coach since 1947.

For Fesler resignation was a mighty big step and meant movement into employment far removed from the practice field, Ohio Stadium, and a crowd of young football players.

But, less than two months after he announced his resignation, Fesler returned to football—as head football coach at the University of Minnesota. The curly-headed Ohioan had a new job, a new environment, and most of all, a new start.

1,500 AT OHIO STATE CHEER BROWN VISIT

Placards of Cleveland Youth, Urging Coach to Stay With Pros, Burned on Campus

COLUMBUS, Ohio, Jan. 27 (Æ) —Paul E. Brown went into a huddle with Ohio State University's coach-seeking athletic board tonight, as a student crowd estimated at 1,500 by campus policemen milled around the faculty club.

The throng started chanting "we want Brown" as the mentor of Cleveland's five-time professional champions left his car and started up the steps to meet the board. A four-piece drum corps added to the din. Only one dissenting voice was heard, and that was long before Brown, who coached the Bucks from 1941 through 1943, appeared on the conference scene. An automobile, with a scarlet and gray clad football dummy perched on top, rolled by with its horn blaring. It bore placards, fore and aft, which said:

"There's no place like home. Cleveland wants you. Go back!"

Dummy Torn From Auto

The student driving the car, halted by the crowd, explained he was from Cleveland and that he wanted Brown to stay with the professional team there. The crowd failed to agree, tore the placards and dummy from the auto and burned them in the middle of the street while three campus policemen stood by and directed traffic.

Another "hot-rod," plastered with "We want Brown" signs, was cheered every time it backfired past the crowd. At least ten students were in the ancient car.

Woody Hayes Named Coach At Ohio State

Columbus, Ohio, Feb. 18.—(Æ)— Wayne Woodrow (Woody) Hayes, 38-years-old Miami (Ohio) University football mentor, tonight was named Ohio State University's football coach, succeeding Wesley E. Fesler, who resigned December 9.

The appointment was approved unanimously by the board of trustees after Hayes had been recommended by a screening committee, the athletic board, Athletic Director Richard C. Larkins, and University President Howard L. Bevis.

The appointment was approved in a meeting lasting about an hour and a half.

The original meeting scheduled for 4 p. m. (EST) was held up more than two hours and a half until Senator John W. Bricker, Republican, Ohio, flew here from St. Louis.

Six of the seven trustees attended the session.

One Year Contract

Hayes was given a one-year contract at a salary of $12,500, with the general understanding that it would be a continuing contract. Hayes also was appointed a full professor in physical education and will be permitted to name his own staff of assistants.

The contract is effective March 1.

The following statement on Hayes' appointment was issued by the trustees:

"The nomination by the President (Bevis) of Mr. Wayne W. Hayes to be head football coach has been confirmed by the board of trustees by unanimous vote.

"Such action is not to be considered as a reflection upon the other candidates, as there were a number of well-qualified persons considered by the screening committee and the athletic board. Considering all the factors involved, Mr. Hayes appeared to be the best choice.

"The board wishes to announce that there is absolutely nothing of any kind of character to disqualify any of the other candidates interviewed by the screening committee and the athletic board."

Hayes' first coaching job was at Mingo Junction, Ohio, in 1935-36, as assistant to John Muth. The next year he moved to New Philadelphia, Ohio as assistant to Johnny Brickles, current athletic director and basketball coach at Miami.

Becomes Head Coach

Hayes took over as head coach at New Philly in 1938 when Brickles moved to Huntington, W. Va., and had two outstanding seasons—winning 17, losing two and tying one before a disastrous won 1-lost 9 campaign in 1940-41.

He enlisted in the Navy in July, 1941, five months before Pearl Harbor, as a chief specialist in Gene Tunney's physical education branch. He came out in 1946 as a lieutenant commander, having commanded the PC 1251 in the Palau Islands invasion and the destroyer escort Rinehart in both Atlantic and Pacific operations.

Denison University, which had discontinued football during the war, called in Hayes as head coach in 1946—and he failed to win until the final game. That started him on a 19-game winning streak, however, carrying him through his first game at Miami U., to which he had shifted in 1949.

Salad Bowl Winner

He won five of nine his first year with the Redskins, and came back last fall with nine wins in 10 starts, including one over Arizona State in the Salad Bowl. His overall record as head coach is 51 victories, 23 losses and one tie.

He shocked some of the Denison and Miami fans by refusing to drag out the crying towel. His pre-game speeches run something like this:

"We expect to win. I'm not predicting that we will win, but we enter every game expecting to win. We play to win. I'll never come out moaning about how we don't have a chance, because I don't think it's fair to boys who have been doing their best for me."

1951 OHIO STATE FOOTBALL ROSTER

No.	Name	Pos.	Wgt.	Hgt.	Age	Home Town and High School	Class
10	**Hamilton, Ray	RE	178	5-11	21	Canton (McKinley)	Sr.
11	Ernst, Richard	RH	169	5-9	19	Cincinnati (Withrow)	So.
12	*Bruney, Fred	LH	161	5-11	21	Martins Ferry	Jr.
14	*Doyle, Richard	LH	183	6-0	21	Rochester, Pa.	Jr.
15	Deeks, Harry	RH	168	5-9	19	Cleveland (Orange)	So.
16	**Klevay, Walter	RH	164	5-9	21	Independence	Sr
17	Bruce, Earle	RH	160	5-8	20	Cumberland, Md. (Allegheny)	So.
23	Arledge, Richard	QB	188	6-0	21	Chillicothe	Sr.
24	Hague, Tom	QB	191	6-0	19	Rocky River	So.
25	*Curcillo, Tony	QB	188	6-1	20	Elyria	Jr.
28	Wilks, William	QB	182	6-2	20	Hamilton (Public)	Jr.
30	*Wagner, Jack	FB	189	6-1	21	Piqua	Sr.
31	**Janowicz, Victor	LH	186	5-9	21	Elyria	Sr.
32	Bechtel, Earl	FB	194	6-2	19	Fredericktown	So.
33	*Koepnick, Robert	FB	185	6-0	20	Dayton (Chaminade)	Jr.
34	Moritz, Roger	FB	200	6-1	20	Columbus (North)	Jr.
36	*Hlay, John	FB	212	6-1	21	Niles (McKinley)	Jr.
42	Gentile, Earle	LH	185	5-11	21	Cleveland (Cathedral Latin)	Jr.
43	Gambill, David	RH	177	5-11	20	Portsmouth	Jr.
44	*Skvarka, Bernie	LH	184	5-9	21	Struthers	Jr.
47	Rosso, George	RH	172	5-10	21	Pittsburgh, Pa. (Langley)	So.
48	Beekley, Marts	LH	181	5-9	20	Sharonville	Jr.
52	Andrews, Lawrence	C	185	5-11	21	Toledo (DeVilbiss)	Jr.
53	Merrell, James	C	225	6-3	19	Geneva	So.
54	**Heid, Robert (Capt.)	C	203	6-0	21	Fremont (Ross)	Sr.
55	*Rath, Thomas	C	200	5-10	22	Defiance	Sr.
56	Epps, Robert	C	191	5-11	18	Columbus (West)	So.
58	Wolter, Robert	RG	188	5-11	20	Hubbard	Jr.
59	Ternent, William	LG	197	6-0	19	Columbus (North)	Jr.
60	*Ruzich, Steve	LT	209	6-2	21	Madison	Sr.
61	*Fischer, Louis	RG	191	5-10	21	Charleston, W. Va. (Catholic)	Jr.
62	Takacs, Michael	LG	192	6-0	21	Massillon	So.
63	Tice, Richard	LG	196	5-10	20	Columbus (Arlington)	So.
64	*Ronemus, Thor	RG	186	5-9	20	Springfield (Public)	Jr.
65	*Smith, Carroll	LG	187	5-11	22	Sebring	Sr.
66	Roberts, Robert	LG	188	5-11	19	Zanesville (Lash)	So.
67	**Wittman, Julius	RT	221	6-1	21	Massillon	Sr.
68	*Faehl, Paul	LG	216	5-11	22	Piqua	Sr.
69	Savic, George	RG	190	5-10	20	Girard	Jr.
71	*Logan, Richard	RT	221	6-2	21	Mansfield	Sr.
72	*Campanella, Joseph	LT	226	6-2	21	Cleveland (Cathedral Latin)	Sr.
73	Jacoby, George	LT	206	5-10	19	Toledo (Libbey)	So.
74	Guthrie, George	LT	215	6-1	19	Columbus (Arlington)	Jr.
75	*Hietikko, James	LT	220	6-3	20	Conneaut	Jr.
76	Denker, Irv	RT	224	6-1	20	New York, N. Y. (DeWitt Clin.)	So.
77	Endres, Robert	RT	200	6-1	21	Cincinnati (Hughes)	Sr.
78	Edgington, Harry	RT	207	6-3	20	Toledo (DeVilbiss)	So.
80	*Grimes, Robert	RE	194	6-1	20	Middletown	Jr.
81	**Armstrong, Ralph	LE	198	6-4	21	Cleveland (Rhodes)	Sr.
84	**Gandee, Sherwin	LE	197	6-0	22	Akron (Garfield)	Sr.
85	Joslin, Robert	LE	182	6-0	20	Middletown	So.
87	Knapic, Bernie	LE	192	6-2	20	Youngstown (Chaney)	So.
89	*Walther, Richard	RE	191	5-10	21	Dayton (Fairmont)	Jr.
90	Thomas, Richard	RE	183	6-1	20	Martins Ferry	Jr.
91	Manyak, John	LE	188	6-1	21	Warren (Harding)	Jr.
93	Katula, Ted	RE	192	6-1	20	Campbell (Memorial)	So.

* Indicates Letter.

Vic Janowicz

1951
Coach: W. W. "Woody" Hayes
Captain: Robert C. Heid

7	*Southern Methodist	0
20	*Michigan State	24
6	Wisconsin	6
10	*Indiana	32
47	*Iowa	21
3	*Northwestern	0
16	Pittsburgh	14
0	*Illinois	0
0	Michigan	7
109		104

Won 4, Lost 3, Tied 2

Hoosier Team Routs Buckeyes by 32 to 10

Columbus, Ohio, Oct. 20 —(P)— Indiana's underdog Hoosier's buried Ohio State's Rose Bowl and Big Ten championship hopes today with a startling 32-10 upset victory before 74,265 amazed fans.

The Hoosiers, struck like lightning for three touchdowns in the opening period and then hung on to win an easy and convincing victory.

The Hoosiers romped out front in the first three minutes when Bob Inserra recovered a fumble on Ohio's 14 by All-American Vic Janowicz. Two plays later Lou D'Achille passed 14 yards to Don Luft, 6 foot, 4-inch, 205 pound end. D'Achille missed the extra point, but from there on it was all Indiana.

82,640 See Michigan State Down Ohio State With Late Rally, 24-20

STATISTICS OF THE GAME

	Mich. State	Ohio State
First downs	17	17
Yards gained, rushing	234	186
Forward passes	16	18
Forwards completed	12	10
Yards gained, forwards	167	184
Forwards intercepted by	1	1
Number of punts	6	6
Punting average	42.5	40
Fumbles lost	0	2
Yards lost, penalties	113	36

By The Associated Press.

COLUMBUS, Ohio, Oct. 6—Michigan's State's sparkling Spartans proved their right to the ranking as the nation's No. 1 football power today when they surged back from a 10-point deficit in the final quarter to defeat seventh-ranked Ohio State, 24-20, before 82,640 fans. It was the third largest crowd ever to jam the Ohio Stadium.

In a wild finish reminiscent of Notre Dame's three-touchdown last-quarter surge which whipped Ohio in 1935, the Spartans came to life with scoring marches covering 74 and 46 yards within a three and one-half minute span in the final session after Ohio had taken a 20—10 lead.

The pay-off punch was a beauty, a 27-yard pass from sophomore halfback Tom Yewcic to quarterback Al Dorow on fourth down. Dorow, under center on the T-formation, lateraled to Yewcic, who cut off to his right, while Dorow headed for the left sideline and scooted toward the goal. Yewcic's long pass across the field hit Dorow around the 10-yard line, where he shook off two tacklers and fell into scoring territory with the points his team needed.

The pass was the first ever thrown in a college game by Yewcic, and it marked the first time he had been in an offensive play for the Spartans. He had been used exclusively as a punter.

Coach Biggie Munn said the winning play had been concocted on the bench just a couple of seconds before it was used. The play was outlined to Yewcic on the bench, Munn said, and the sophomore went in, relayed the strategy to his huddled team-mates and they worked it to perfection.

Although he did not figure in the scoring, much of the credit for the Spartans' victory must go to Leroy Bolden, a shifty 165-pound replacement halfback.

The yearling caught passes all over the field and ran over, around and through the Ohio State defenders.

MICHIGAN STATE (24)

Left Ends—R. Carey, Dekker.
Left Tackles—Coleman, Purcell, Fowler.
Left Guards—Garner, Serr.
Centers—Creamer, Hughes, Neal, Tamburo.
Right Guards—Kaoral, Kuh, Kush.
Right Tackles—McFadden, Frank, Klein.
Right Ends—W. Carey, Luke, Doheney, Mazza.
Quarterbacks—Dorow, Wilson.
Left Halfbacks—McAuliffe, Yewcic, Bolden, Corles.
Right Halfbacks—Picano, Vogt, Ellis, Wells.
Fullbacks—Panin, Timmerman, Slonac.

OHIO STATE (20)

Left Ends—Hamilton, Gandee, Armstrong.
Left Tackles—Hietikko, Campanella.
Left Guards—Takacs, Fischer.
Center—Merrill, Reid.
Right Guards—Roseboro, Ruzich, Wittman.
Right Tackles—Ecker, Logan, Jacoby.
Right Ends—Joslin, Walther, Thomas, Grimes.
Quarterbacks—Curcillo, Alleder.
Left Halfbacks—Janowicz, Skvarka.
Right Halfbacks—Klevay, Bruney, Borton, Rosso.
Fullbacks—Koepnick, Beekler.

SCORE BY PERIODS

Michigan State .... 3 7 0 14—24
Ohio State .... 6 7 0 7—20

Michigan State touchdowns—Dekker, Dorow. Points after touchdowns—R. Carey 2. Field Goal: R. Carey. Ohio State touchdowns—Hamilton 2, Janowicz. Points after touchdowns—Janowicz 2.

Ohio State Conquers Pitt, 16-14, On Janowicz' 20-Yard Field Goal

Boot in Third Period Decides Struggle Before 34,747—Panthers Make Gallant but Futile Bid in Last Session

PITTSBURGH, Nov. 10 (AP)—Ohio State made good on three of four scoring opportunities today to beat Pitt, 16-14, but it was the underdog Panthers, who have yet to win a game, who walked off the field with a moral victory.

The deciding points of the battle came in the third quarter on a 20-yard field goal by Vic Janowicz, a boot that provided just enough cushion to offset Pitt's two last-quarter touchdowns.

Ohio State took the opening kick-off 56 yards for a touchdown then in the second quarter went 52 yards for another. In the third stanza a pass interception set up Janowicz' winning field goal.

A homecoming day Pitt crowd of 34,747 saw the luckless Panthers threaten five times before scoring with six and a half minutes to play.

Pitt put on a 74-yard drive for its second touchdown, Quarterback Bob Bestwick plunging over from inches out with thirty-eight seconds left. Time ran out before Pitt could get the ball again.

Pitt piled up 21 first downs to 13, gained a net 205 yards by rushing to 157 for Ohio State and made 127 yards by passing to 39. But nevertheless, the Panthers went down to their seventh straight defeat of the season.

Halfback Fred Bruney played what was perhaps the most decisive role for the victorious Buckeyes. In the second half when Pitt threatened time and time again, Bruney thwarted the Panthers on three occasions.

Statistics of the Game

	Oh. St.	Pitt.
First downs	13	21
Rushing yardage	157	205
Passing yardage	39	127
Passes attempted	15	30
Passes completed	6	16
Passes intercepted by	2	0
Number of punts	10	7
Punting average, yds.	45.2	35.5
Fumbles lost	0	2
Yards penalized	102	35

Pitt tried a short kick-off at the game's start in an effort to get the ball. But the attempt failed and Ohio State got the pigskin on its own 44. Janowicz and Quarterback Tony Curcillo alternated in lugging the ball to the Pitt 1. From there, Curcillo went over on a quarterback sneak.

A 68-yard quick kick by Janowicz put O. S. U. on its way to a second score. After Janowicz missed a field goal from the 34, Ohio State regained the ball on its own 48. The Buckeyes made it a first down on the Pitt 26 then Curcillo ran 26 for a touchdown. Janowicz converted.

Pitt dominated the play for the rest of the game. The Panthers drove to the Ohio State 10, 6, 9 and 29 before the fifth drive ended with Epps plunging over from the 1.

SCORE BY PERIODS

Ohio State .... 6 7 3 0—16
Pittsburgh .... 0 0 0 14—14

Touchdowns—Ohio State, Curcillo 2; Pittsburgh, Bestwick, Epps. Points after touchdowns—Ohio State, Janowicz 2; Pittsburgh, Wrabley 2. Field Goal—Ohio State, Janowicz.

1951 OHIO STATE TEAM STATISTICS

Teams	First Downs	Rush	Net Gain Pass	Total	Total Plays	Att.	Passing Comp.	No. had Int.	Punting Average	Fumbles Lost	Yards Penalized	Points
SOUTHERN METHODIST	14	38	211	249	52	31	21	4	45.0	4	25	0
OHIO STATE	18	172	87	259	75	14	6	2	40.2	2	81	7
MICHIGAN STATE	17	234	167	401	80	16	12	1	42.7	0	113	24
OHIO STATE	18	186	184	370	56	18	10	1	40.2	2	36	20
WISCONSIN	19	174	172	346	76	27	17	2	36.9	2	59	6
OHIO STATE	7	61	45	106	58	20	6	2	43.8	2	30	6
INDIANA	12	137	146	283	60	17	10	1	47.8	1	60	32
OHIO STATE	19	279	79	358	83	24	11	1	37.4	4	60	10
IOWA	23	172	170	342	91	31	16	2	47.2	1	89	21
OHIO STATE	18	91	308	399	57	18	11	3	40.5	1	15	47
NORTHWESTERN	11	83	119	202	83	30	12	4	22.3	0	69	0
OHIO STATE	10	103	92	195	67	25	7	2	36.1	2	75	3
PITTSBURGH	21	205	127	332	86	30	16	2	35.6	2	33	14
OHIO STATE	13	157	39	196	58	15	6	0	45.2	0	102	16
ILLINOIS	11	48	119	167	64	25	9	4	38.8	2	65	0
OHIO STATE	10	86	105	191	65	12	5	1	43.5	4	43	0
MICHIGAN	14	135	80	215	87	29	12	2	31.6	2	55	7
OHIO STATE	14	120	102	222	63	26	9	4	26.9	4	15	0
SEASON TOTALS												
OPPONENTS	142	1226	1311	2537	679	236	125	22	36.6	14	568	104
OHIO STATE	127	1255	1041	2296	582	172	71	16	39.3	21	457	109

FINAL 1951 INDIVIDUAL STATISTICS

RUSHING

Player	Tries	Gain	Lost	Net	Ave.	TD's
Janowicz	106	424	48	376	3.5	1
Wagner	54	235	3	232	4.3	0
Curcillo	104	411	185	226	2.2	4
Klevay	56	185	53	132	2.4	0
Skvarka	31	138	18	120	3.9	1
Koepnick	17	102	8	94	5.5	0
Goodsell	21	67	4	63	3.0	0
Hamilton	6	24	0	24	4.0	0
Bruney	2	20	0	20	10.0	0
Armstrong	1	5	0	5	5.0	0
Howell	1	4	0	4	4.0	0
Grimes	1	1	0	1	1.0	0
Joslin	2	1	3	-2	-1.0	0
Ernst	1	0	8	-8	-8.0	0
Wilks	3	0	15	-15	-5.0	0
Leggett	4	1	18	-17	-4.2	0
Totals	410	1618	363	1255	3.1	6

FORWARD PASSING

Player	Att.	Comp.	Int.	Yds.	Comp. %	TD's
Curcillo	133	58	11	912	43.6	6
Janowicz	25	7	3	74	28.0	2
Wilks	10	5	2	52	50.0	0
Skvarka	3	1	0	3	33.3	1
Bruney	1	0	0	0	00.0	0
Totals	172	71	16	1041	42.3	9

SCORING

Player	TD's	PAT Att.	PAT Made	FG	Total
Curcillo	4	..	..	..	24
Janowicz	1	14	9	3	24
Joslin	3	..	..	..	18
Armstrong	2	..	..	..	12
Hamilton	2	..	..	..	12
Skvarka	1	..	..	..	6
Grimes	1	..	..	..	6
Goodsell	1	..	..	..	6
Logan	..	1	1	0	1
Totals	15	15	10	3	109

PUNTING

Player	Number	Yards	Blocked	Ave.
Janowicz	62	2446	0	39.4
Shelton	9	344	0	38.2
Totals	71	2790	0	39.3

PASS RECEIVING

Player	Caught	Yards	TD's
Joslin	18	281	3
Hamilton	13	185	2
Grimes	9	164	1
Janowicz	7	126	0
Skvarka	9	108	0
Armstrong	4	58	2
Goodsell	3	51	1
Klevay	5	48	0
Wagner	1	16	0
Curcillo	1	9	0
Koepnick	1	-5	0
Totals	71	1041	9

INTERCEPTIONS

Player	Number	Yards
Bruney	7	81
Rosso	4	29
Arledge	2	29
Hoffman	1	13
Borton	2	12
Beekley	4	12
Walther	1	0
Janowicz	1	0
Totals	22	176

PUNT RETURNS

Player	Number	Yards
Skvarka	8	146
Goodsell	5	49
Janowicz	4	32
Bruney	1	4
Totals	18	231

KICKOFF RETURNS

Player	Number	Yards
Skvarka	9	160
Bruney	3	76
Klevay	3	38
Janowicz	1	34
Koeknick	2	19
Totals	18	327

1952 OHIO STATE FOOTBALL ROSTER

No.	Name	Pos.	Wgt.	Hgt.	Home Town	Class
11	Ernst, Richard	RH	168	5-9	Cincinnati	Jr.
12	**Bruney, Fred	LH	172	5-10	Martins Ferry	Sr.
14	*Doyle, Richard	FB	189	6-0	Rochester, Pa.	Sr.
15	Knecht, Gilbert	LH	180	5-10	Lima	So.
16	Skelly, Jack	RH	170	5-11	Rocky River	So.
17	Bruce, Earle	RH	164	5-8	Cumberland, Md.	Jr.
19	Howell, Carroll	LH	167	5-9	Portsmouth	So.
20	*Borton, John	QB	197	6-1	Alliance	So.
21	Petersen, William	QB	200	6-0	Cleveland	Sr.
22	Leggett, David	QB	196	6-0	New Philadelphia	So.
23	Koder, Robert	QB	185	5-10	Toledo	Jr.
24	Weed, Thurlow	QB	128	5-5	Columbus	So.
26	**Curcillo, Tony	RH	192	6-1	Elyria	Sr.
28	*Wilks, William	QB	182	6-2	Hamilton	Sr.
29	Edwards, Frank	QB	178	6-1	Columbus	So.
30	Ludwig, Paul	FB	212	6-3	Marion	Fr.
32	Bechtel, Earl	FB	192	6-2	Fredericktown	Jr.
33	**Koepnick, Robert	RH	194	6-0	Dayton	Sr.
34	Morse, James	FB	190	6-0	Columbus	So.
36	**Hlay, John	FB	212	6-1	Niles	Sr.
40	Cassady, Howard	LH	168	5-10	Columbus	Fr.
42	*Goodsell, Douglas	FB	192	6-2	Columbus	Sr.
43	Gambill, David	RH	177	5-9	Portsmouth	Sr.
44	**Skvarka, Bernie	LH	182	5-9	Struthers	Sr.
45	Watkins, Robert	RH	182	5-9	New Bedford, Mass.	So.
46	Bond, Robert	RH	182	6-1	Akron	Fr.
47	*Rosso, George	RH	174	5-10	Pittsburgh, Pa.	Jr.
48	*Beekley, Marts	RH	183	5-9	Sharonville	Sr.
50	Ruehl, James	C	210	62-	Cumberland, Md.	So.
51	*Krisher, Jerry	C	227	6-0	Massillon	So.
53	*Merrell, James	C	222	63-	Geneva	Jr.
55	Thornton, Robert	C	196	6-0	Willard	Jr.
56	Dawdy, Donald	C	200	6-1	Cincinnati	Jr.
58	Mott, William	C	190	6-2	Proctorville	So.
59	Ternent, William	LG	197	6-1	Columbus	Sr.
60	Sidell, Rollo	LG	209	6-0	Oak Harbor	So.
61	**Fischer, Louis	RG	197	5-11	Charleston, W. Va.	Sr.
62	*Takacs, Michael	LG	208	6-0	Massillon	Jr.
63	*Reichenbach, James	RG	203	5-10	Massillon	So.
64	Williams, David	LG	204	5-11	Pittsburgh, Pa.	So.
65	Hamilton, Walter	RG	192	5-11	Columbus	So.
66	Roberts, Robert	LG	188	5-11	Zanesville	Jr.
68	Riticher, Ray	RG	212	5-10	Toledo	So.
70	Schiller, Richard	RT	228	6-2	Bellaire	So.
71	Myers, Robert	RT	225	6-5	Springfield	So.
72	Schumacher, James	RT	210	6-0	Massillon	So.
73	*Jacoby, George	RT	222	5-11	Toledo	Jr.
74	*Guthrie, George	RT	221	6-1	Columbus	Sr.
75	**Hietikko, James	LT	221	6-3	Conneaut	Sr.
76	Denker, Irv	LT	219	6-1	New York, N. Y.	Jr.
77	Swartz, Donald	LT	230	6-1	Newark	So.
78	Edgington, Harry	LT	209	6-3	Toledo	Jr.
79	Vavroch, William	LT	203	6-1	Cleveland	Sr.
80	**Grimes, Robert	LE	196	6-1	Middletown	Sr.
82	*Anderson, Richard	RE	192	6-1	Portsmouth	Sr.
83	Dugger, Dean	RE	216	6-2	Charleston, W. Va.	So.
84	Croy, Jack	LE	181	6-1	Dayton	So.
85	*Joslin, Robert	RE	187	6-0	Middletown	Jr.
86	Campbell, Jack	RE	185	5-11	New Philadelphia	So.
87	Corbitt, Walter	LE	190	6-1	Portsmouth	So.
88	Hague, Thomas	LE	192	6-0	Rocky River	Jr.
90	*Thomas, Richard	LE	181	6-1	Martins Ferry	Sr.
91	Manyak, John	LE	191	6-1	Warren	Sr.
92	Ashton, William	LE	190	6-1	Piqua	So.
93	Katula, Theodore	RE	182	6-1	Campbell	Jr.

* Indicates letter.

1952
Captain: Bernie G. Skvarka

33	*Indiana	13
14	*Purdue	21
23	*Wisconsin	14
35	*Washington State	7
0	Iowa	8
24	Northwestern	21
14	*Pittsburgh	21
27	Illinois	7
27	*Michigan	7
197		119

Won 6, Lost 3

33-13 TRIUMPH TO OHIO STATE

Freshman Cassady Scores 3 Times To Provide Margin

Columbus, Ohio, Sept. 27 — Howard Cassady, 168-pound freshman, scored three touchdowns to provide the victory margin today as Ohio State defeated Indiana, 33 to 13, in the season's opening Western Conference football game.

Cassady was the difference in the bitterly contested fray which Ohio broke wide open in the final quarter with a three-touchdown barrage, two by Cassady.

13-13 Until Fourth

The outweighed and undermanned Hoosiers gave the favored Buckeyes a tussle through the first three periods and were on even terms at 13-13 well into the fourth session. The Buckeyes turned two intercepted passes and a recovered fumble into three quick touchdowns to avenge last year's 32-10 loss to Indiana.

As the fourth opened, Ohio went 49 yards in six plays, finally sending 18-year-old Cassady over left tackle for six yards and a touchdown which put the Bucks out front to stay.

Fumble Leads To Score

Late in the game, with Indiana fighting to even the count, Jerry Ellis fumbled on his own 35 and Bill Vavroch recovered for Ohio. Casady made 12 and Fullback John Hlay picked up the other 24 over tackle without being touched.

The final one came when Marts Beekley intercepted Lou D'Achille's pass on Indiana's 46 and ran it back to the 3, from where Cassady squirted through the line for the final points.

Indiana......... 7 6 0 0—13
Ohio State...... 6 7 0 20—33
Indiana scoring: Touchdowns—Borden, Ellis. Conversion—D'Achille. Ohio State scoring: Touchdowns—Bruney, Cassady (3), Hlay. Conversions—Weed (3).

OHIO STATE FOOTBALL SQUAD

Front row, left to right: George Guthrie, John Manyak, Marts Beekley, Bill Vavroch, Bob Grimes, Jim Hietikko, Richard Doyl Fred Bruney, Bernie Skvarka, captain; Tony Curcillo, John Hlay, Dick Anderson, Dick Thomas, Bill Wilks, Bob Koepnick, Bill Petersen Bill Ternent, Bill Koder, David Gambill, E. R. Godfrey, assistant coach; second row, Head Coach W. W. (Woody) Hayes, John Borton Jim Reichenbach, Doug Goodsell, Jerry Krisher, Harry Edgington, Jimmy Hague, George Rosso, Bob Joslin, Jim Merrell, Mike Takacs George Jacoby, Dick Nosky, Don Dawdy, Dick Ernst, Irv Denker, Earl Bechtel, Bob Thornton, Bob Roberts, William Hess, freshman coach third row, Bob Watkins, Thurlow Weed, Jim Schumacher, Jack Croy, Bill Damsel, Jack Standard, Jervis McEntee, Don Swartz, Richard Young, Carroll Howell, Gilbert Knecht, Bill Ashton, Dean Dugger, Dave Leggett, Ray Riticher Rollo Sidell, Jerry Williams, Howard Cassady, Jim Ruehl, Harry Strobel, assistant coach; fourth row, Hal Martin, co-manager, Doyt Perry, assistant coach; Bill Arnsparger assistant coach; William O'Hara, assistant coach; Gene Fekete, assistant coach; Esco Sarkkinen, assistant coach, Bob Myers, Paul Ludwig, Dick Schiller, Bill Mott, Joel Maddox, Walter Corbitt, Jack Campbell, Robert Bond, Jerry Schwartz, co-manager.

PURDUE 21 — OHIO STATE 14

The Boilermakers from Purdue journeyed into town on Friday, Oct. 3, and left the following day with a 21-14 victory packed tightly under their belts. Capitalizing on the Buck's weaknesses, the engineers scored in the first four minutes of play after recovering a fumble on Ohio's 25-yard line. Before the Buckeyes could catch their breath, Purdue scored again in the second period when End John Kerr raced through the Ohio forward wall to block Bill Petersen's punt on the 19-yard line. Boilermaker Guard Tom Bettis picked up the loose pigskin and raced into the end zone for the second Purdue tally. The Bucks, behind 14 points, scored a TD in the waning minutes of the second period after Marts Beekley had recovered a Purdue bobble. Both teams managed to push one more touchdown across the opponents goal in the second half. Purdue went ahead 21-7 on a series of pass play completions by Quarterback Dale Samuels. Ohio countered with a second, but much too late, touchdown in the final three minutes to be on the short end of a 21-14 score. Fullback John Hlay was outstanding for the Buckeyes as he passed the individual ground gainers for the day with 133 yards in 22 tries for a six yard average.

OHIO STATE 23 — WISCONSIN 14

The number one team in the country was playing in the Ohio Stadium on the afternoon of Oct. 11th. But the inspired Buckeyes paid no heed to the press raves of the mighty Wisconsin Badgers once the opening whistle blew. Some 80,000 fans crammed the huge horseshoe to roar themselves hoarse as the underdog Ohio State team raced to a convincing lead and time after time threw the Badger offensive out of gear. The Bucks, a pre-game two touchdown underdog, took the field in the peak of condition and slowly but surely wore the men from the dairyland to a grinding halt. The Rose Bowl bound Badgers played good football, but just couldn't meet the challenge offered by a well-trained Buckeye unit that wouldn't settle for less than a victory. Spectacular runs by Fred Bruney, Hop Cassady, and big John Hlay, plus some superb defensive work by linebackers Tony Curcillo, Bud Bond and Dick Doyle paved the way for the best upset in many a year. Quarterback John Borton was invincible with his needle threaded passing and generalship of the new Split-T formation. When the final 23-14 Ohio State victory was posted on the scoreboards, and Coach Woody Hayes was lifted triumphantly to the shoulders of his victorious Bucks, the Buckeye followers were convinced they had seen the Split-T executed to perfection. It was one of those games to be remembered for a lifetime.

Ohio State Overwhelms Washington State, 35-7

COLUMBUS, O., Oct. 18 (P) — Ohio State's sophomore quarterback, Big John Borton, unleashed one of the most devastating aerial attacks ever seen in Buckeye Stadium today as Ohio smothered Washington State's Cougars under a 35-7 score in an intersectional contest.

A crowd of 71,280 watched the contest.

Borton, 197-pound, six-foot, one-inch 19-year-old from Alliance, O., passed for all five touchdowns. Senior End Bob Grimes of Middletown, O., took four of the scoring tosses.

The West Coast Club, sticking to a nine-two defense most of the day to handle Ohio's running attack, had to answer to the Buckeyes' long passing game. Borton's touchdown heaves went for 11, 54, 14, 70 and 25 yards.

OHIO STATE 24 — NORTHWESTERN 21

Making a fourth quarter comeback was the theme for the television game of the week when the Bucks traveled to Northwestern. Some 19 million football fans gathered around their TV sets to see the Buckeye gridders post a 7-0 first period score, but go to the locker room behind 21-7 at the halftime intermission. Failing to score in the third quarter, the Ohio State hopes sank to a new low as the Wildcats held on downs on their own one-yard line at the beginning of the final stanza. Northwestern was forced to kick and the Bucks took advantage of a bad punt which went out of bounds on the Wildcat 18-yard line. Hammering their way to the one yard line once again, it took four tries before Fred Bruney skirted right end for the six-marker. After holding the Cats on their own 42 following the kickoff, the Buckeye offensive machine started to roll goalward once again. Quarterback John Borton flipped a 30-yard pass to Bruney who cut behind three Wildcat defenders and faked for the third Ohio score. Tad Weed, with nerves of steel, booted the ball squarely through the uprights for the tying 21-21 score. Following the kickoff, the Buck defensive team pushed the fading Northwestern team back to their 5-yard line. Tackle Irv Denker broke through the Wildcat forward wall to block a slow punt, and the Bucks took over on Northwestern's 6-yard line. Ohio was penalized back to the 22-yard line for clipping, and after four desperate tries found itself on the 11-yard line with fourth and goal to goal. Once again little Tad Weed came off the bench, and this time booted Ohio State to a brilliant 24-21 victory with a difficult field goal. 17 points in the last fifteen minutes. One of the greatest football comebacks in Buckeye history.

OHIO STATE 27 — MICHIGAN 7

The Ohio State football season ended in a blaze of glory as an inspired Buckeye team derailed the Rose Bowl bound Michigan Wolverines before a jam-packed Ohio Stadium 27-7. Playing the regular Michigan game on Saturday instead of the usual Thursday night practice the relaxed Bucks took the field full of confidence, something missing in the eight previous years of bad games. The pattern was set in the initial quarter when Fred Bruney, playing his last and most brilliant game in a Buckeye uniform, intercepted two Wolverine passes to put the skids under sustained drives. His second interception resulted in a Buckeye march that carried to the Michigan 4-yard line as the quarter ended. As the second quarter began, the Bucks hammered to the Michigan 1-yard line where a fumble ended the scoring threat. The Wolves punted out and George Rosso returned 37 yards to the Michigan 26. With Koepnick, Hlay, and Watkins providing the ground punch, the Bucks came back down to the Michigan 6-yard line. Quarterback John Borton, calling his best game of the year, crossed up the Wolves with a TD pass to End Bob Joslin in the end zone. After the kick off, Michigan pulled its favorite quick kick, but Safety George Rosso was ready again and returned 19 yards to the Michigan 28. Hlay and Watkins hammered the line several times before Borton faded deep to uncork a sensational pass to Bob Joslin who made an equally sensational catch as he was falling in the end zone. The Bucks were leading 14-0 as Michigan put in its bid for a TD. With 18 seconds remaining in the first half, the Wolves tried a touchdown pass that was snatched up by Fred Bruney for his third interception of the day, and thus ended the Wolverines scoring threat. The Bucks came back in the second half with that air of confidence and determination to win. After a series of ball exchanges, Ohio's vicious tackling caused a Michigan to fumble. The Bucks recovered and four plays later, Borton scooted inside the Michigan right end for another score. With a commanding 21-point lead, Ohio racked up its fourth and final score in the fourth quarter. George Jacoby dropped back to intercept a Michigan pass, and 6 plays later Borton hit End Bob Grimes who carried three Michigan defenders into the end zone with him. After the kick off, the Wolves marched 71 yards for a token score to give a final reading of 27-7 in favor of Ohio State. The win was strictly a team victory. Seventeen seniors played the greatest ball game of their collegiate career. An eight year drought had ended, and Columbus, Ohio rocked with the victorious rhythm.

HOWARD CASSADY, 18, 5-10, 168, freshman . . . entered Ohio State in March of 1952 . . . a fierce competitor, who is certain to play plenty of football at Ohio State . . . looked good in the spring football game with only 19 days of practice . . . has good speed and excellent determination . . . attended Central high school in Columbus . . . father works as an interior decorator . . . Howard was a construction worker last summer . . . may not see too much action on offense this year with two experienced men in front of him, Bruney and Skvarka, but he is certain to be in the fight for a defensive post . . . played defensive safety in the spring game and ran a punt back 60 yards . . . of Irish descent . . . nicknamed "Hoppie" . . .

1952 OHIO STATE TEAM STATISTICS

	First Downs	Net Gain Rush	Net Gain Pass	Net Gain Total	Total Plays	Passing Att.	Passing Comp.	Passing Int.	Punting No.	Punting Ave.	Fumbles Lost	Yards Penalized	Points
INDIANA	14	141	164	305	63	23	14	3	8	40.1	1	52	13
OHIO STATE	21	286	139	425	73	22	9	1	6	35.7	1	65	33
PURDUE	13	216	56	272	63	18	9	0	7	41.1	5	52	21
OHIO STATE	18	171	149	320	77	20	11	2	10	29.8	2	45	14
WISCONSIN	18	166	184	350	72	27	18	3	2	30.0	1	5	14
OHIO STATE	16	254	141	395	66	12	8	0	4	32.7	2	55	23
WASHINGTON STATE	14	164	35	199	67	15	4	1	7	35.9	3	52	7
OHIO STATE	21	113	375	488	66	21	18	0	6	28.3	2	80	35
IOWA	9	194	18	212	78	12	3	1	8	37.0	1	40	8
OHIO STATE	14	42	173	215	71	38	19	1	9	36.2	2	35	0
NORTHWESTERN	9	133	145	278	54	14	6	3	7	27.6	0	50	21
OHIO STATE	19	236	201	437	87	25	15	2	4	34.0	1	65	24
PITTSBURGH	11	143	94	237	69	18	6	0	8	37.5	3	77	21
OHIO STATE	22	51	282	333	79	44	25	1	6	40.8	4	99	14
ILLINOIS	16	111	254	365	60	35	19	6	2	33.5	2	103	7
OHIO STATE	19	252	98	350	73	17	8	2	4	35.7	1	45	27
MICHIGAN	14	188	134	322	68	19	8	4	5	40.0	4	51	7
OHIO STATE	12	120	151	271	68	18	11	0	9	36.3	2	65	27
OPPONENTS	118	1456	1084	2540	594	181	87	21	54	36.0	20	482	119
OHIO STATE	162	1525	1709	3234	660	217	124	9	58	34.0	17	554	197

FINAL 1952 OHIO STATE INDIVIDUAL STATISTICS

RUSHING

Player	Tries	Gain	Lost	Net	Avg.	TD's
Hlay	133	554	19	535	4.0	2
Bruney	91	359	17	342	3.8	2
Cassady	65	327	34	293	4.5	4
Watkins	59	262	9	253	4.3	0
Koepnick	9	51	0	51	5.7	0
Gambill	4	46	0	46	11.5	0
Leggett	5	31	0	31	6.2	0
Goodsell	9	22	6	16	1.7	0
Bechtel	1	9	0	9	9.0	0
Doyle	3	2	0	2	.7	0
Joslin	1	0	5	5	−5.0	0
Petersen	1	0	5	5	−5.0	0
Borton	62	115	158	43	−.8	4
Totals	443	1778	253	1525	3.4	12

FORWARD PASSING

Player	Att.	Comp.	Int.	Yds.	Comp. Pct.	TD's
Borton	196	115	6	1555	58.6	15
Bruney	11	4	2	70	36.3	1
Wilks	1	1	0	45	100.0	0
Petersen	5	4	0	39	80.0	0
Gambill	1	0	0	0	00.0	0
Goodsell	2	0	0	0	00.0	0
Leggett	1	0	1	0	00.0	0
Totals	217	124	9	1709	57.1	16

SCORING

Player	TD's	PAT Att.	PAT	FG	Total
Cassady	6	0	0	0	36
Bruney	6	0	0	0	36
Grimes	6	0	0	0	36
Weed	0	26	23	2	29
Borton	4	0	0	0	24
Hlay	2	0	0	0	12
Dugger	2	0	0	0	12
Joslin	2	0	0	0	12
Krisher	0	2	0	0	0
Totals	28	28	23	2	197

PUNTING

Player	Number	Yards	Avg.
Petersen	57	1	34.3
Borton	1	0	22.0
Totals	58	1	34.0

PASS RECEIVING

Player	No.	Yds.	TD's
Grimes	39	534	6
Bruney	21	379	4
Joslin	27	329	2
Cassady	13	192	2
Dugger	13	157	2
Hague	3	63	0
Watkins	4	33	0
Goodsell	2	13	0
Beekley	1	8	0
Krisher	1	1	0
Totals	124	1709	16

PUNT RETURNS

Player	Number	Yards	Avg.
Rosso	12	82	6.8
Bruney	5	29	5.8
Goodsell	1	12	12.0
Cassady	1	7	7.0
Curcillo	1	2	2.0
Beekley	1	0	0.0
Totals	21	132	6.3

KICKOFF RETURNS

Player	Number	Yards	Avg.
Bruney	10	185	18.5
Cassady	8	146	18.2
Watkins	1	27	27.0
Goodsell	1	22	22.0
Hlay	1	12	12.0
Beekley	1	10	10.0
Joslin	1	6	6.0
Hague	1	0	0.0
Totals	24	408	17.0

INTERCEPTION RETURNS

Player	Number	Yards	Avg.
Bruney	7	124	17.7
Beekley	3	53	17.6
Goodsell	1	28	28.0
Howell	2	18	9.0
Curcillo	1	5	5.0
Rosso	2	4	2.0
Doyle	2	3	1.5
Cassady	1	3	3.0
Jacoby	1	3	3.0
Roberts	1	2	2.0
Totals	21	243	11.6

OHIO STATE ROSTER

No.	Name	Pos.	Wgt.	Hgt.	Age	Class
11	Boudrie, James	LH	182	5-11	20	Junior
12	Auer, John	RH	178	5-7	18	Sophomore
14	Augenstein, Jack	FB	192	5-10	19	Sophomore
15	Knecht, Gilbert	FB	185	5-10	20	Junior
19	*Howell, Carroll	LH	168	5-9	20	Junior
20	**Borton, John	QB	196	6-1	20	Junior
22	*Leggett, David	QB	192	6-0	20	Junior
23	Gage, Ralph	QB	170	5-10	19	Sophomore
24	*Weed, Thurlow	QB	145	5-5	20	Junior
28	Booth, William	QB	180	6-0	19	Sophomore
30	Hans, Joseph	LH	165	5-8	22	Sophomore
33	Brilliant, George	FB	189	5-7	19	Sophomore
34	Spears, Thomas	FB	197	6-0	18	Sophomore
35	Gibbs, Jack	FB	180	5-10	22	Junior
36	Campbell, Jack	FB	194	6-2	19	Sophomore
40	*Cassady, Howard	LH	172	5-10	19	Sophomore
42	Robson, Charles	QB	168	5-10	19	Sophomore
44	Harkrader, Jerry	RH	172	5-9	19	Sophomore
45	*Watkins, Robert	FB	190	5-9	21	Junior
46	*Bond, Robert	RH	184	5-11	20	Sophomore
47	**Rosso, George	RH	176	5-10	23	Senior
48	Shedd, Jan	RH	168	5-10	19	Sophomore
49	Young, Richard	RH	164	5-10	21	Junior
50	*Ruehl, James	RT	218	6-3	23	Junior
51	**Krisher, Jerry	C	221	6-0	20	Junior
54	Nosky, Richard	LG	200	6-1	21	Senior
55	*Thornton, Robert	C	189	6-0	21	Senior
56	Dawdy, Donald	C	220	6-1	22	Senior
57	Nestich, Martin	C	194	5-11	19	Sophomore
58	Mott, William	C	213	6-4	21	Junior
59	Vargo, Kenneth	C	190	6-1	19	Sophomore
60	Weaver, David	RG	190	5-8	19	Sophomore
61	Ramser, Richard	LG	197	5-10	19	Sophomore
62	**Takacs, Michael	LG	209	6-0	23	Senior
63	**Reichenbach, James	RG	202	5-10	20	Junior
64	Williams, David	LG	198	5-11	20	Junior
65	Jones, Herbert	LG	182	5-10	20	Sophomore
66	*Roberts, Robert	LG	188	5-11	21	Senior
67	Stewart, Roland	LT	205	6-1	19	Sophomore
68	*Riticher, Raymond	RG	225	5-10	20	Junior
69	Slagle, William	RG	200	5-10	21	Senior
70	Hilinski, Richard	LT	230	6-2	22	Junior
71	Rader, Ted	LT	216	6-3	24	Sophomore
72	*Schumacher, James	RT	208	6-0	21	Junior
73	**Jacoby, George (CC)	RT	210	5-11	21	Senior
74	Stoeckel, Donald	LT	206	6-0	19	Sophomore
75	Whetstone, Robert	LT	199	5-11	19	Sophomore
76	Verhoff, Jack	RT	250	6-4	18	Sophomore
77	*Swartz, Donald	LT	224	6-1	20	Junior
78	Ebinger, Elbert	RT	235	6-3	19	Sophomore
79	Machinsky, Francis	RT	209	6-0	19	Sophomore
80	Brubaker, Richard	RE	198	6-0	21	Junior
82	*Ludwig, Paul	LE	206	6-3	19	Sophomore
83	*Dugger, Dean	LE	204	6-2	20	Junior
84	Hesler, Robert	RE	193	6-0	19	Sophomore
85	**Joslin, Robert (CC)	RE	188	6-0	22	Senior
87	Collmar, William	LE	170	6-2	19	Sophomore
88	*Hague, Thomas	LE	198	6-0	21	Senior
89	Guzik, Frank	LE	194	6-3	21	Sophomore
92	Ashton, William	RE	190	6-2	20	Junior

* Indicates Letter

1953
Captains: Robert V. Joslin
George Jacoby

36	*Indiana	12
33	California	19
20	*Illinois	41
12	Pennsylvania	6
20	Wisconsin	19
27	*Northwestern	13
13	*Michigan State	28
21	*Purdue	6
0	Michigan	20
182		164

Won 6, Lost 3

---

northwestern
bucks rise to 27-13 victory before capacity homecoming crowd

Saturday, October 31, 1953, was homecoming not only for many thousands of Ohio State alumni, but also for Coach Woody Hayes' football team. After two straight road engagements, the Bucks returned to the stadium to oust Northwestern's Wildcats, 27-13, much to the delight of the 80,567 fans in attendance.

No one actually ever determined whether the reason was homecoming or not, but Ohio was a revitalized ball club against the Wildcats. Although again trailing the opposition 6-0 at the outset, the Ohio eleven soon began to roll with precision.

The 27 points recorded was the best offensive output since the California win. Every Buckeye backfielder got into the scoring act. Howard Cassady uncorked his first pass of the season to Tommy Hague for 25 yards and 6 points. Cassady later scampered 65 yards through the Wildcat defenses for another TD, his fourth distance scoring jaunt of the season. Bobby Watkins entered the point column once from the five, and increased his string of games without a yardage loss to six. Dave Leggett's expert passing (six out of ten for 110 yards) aided the already proven ground game.

Coach Woody Hayes handed out the most praise, however, to the Buckeye forward wall. Ends Dick Brubaker, Tommy Hague, and Bob Joslin completely destroyed the effectiveness of the heretofore terrific passing of Wildcat quarterback Dick Thomas. Brubaker, in answering his first call to a starting position, showed all the assets of a veteran. George Jacoby, Mike Takacs, Ken Vargo, Jim Reichenbach, Francis Machinsky, and Dick Hilinski all played great football—one reason why Wildcat runners had difficulty going up the middle.

With the Michigan State game coming up, Coach Hayes' only words after the Northwestern win were, "That will be a terrific ball game Saturday."

wisconsin
bucks' 20-19 win is thriller of the year

The drive, drive of the Bucks in the thrilling Wisconsin tilt is exemplified here when it takes two Badgers to halt Buckeye Dave Leggett.

Junior Bobby Watkins plunges through the Badger forward wall with head low and knees high before a capacity crowd in Camp Randall Stadium.

A Dave Leggett to Howard Cassady pass, with but 2½ minutes remaining, climaxed an uphill battle that gave Ohio State a 20-19 win over Wisconsin in one of the most exciting games in Buckeye annals. A missed field goal just as the gun sounded by the Badgers' Bill Miller was anticlimactic as far as the victorious Hayes' men were concerned.

After Ohio opened the tilt with a 55 yard scoring march, the home team Badgers took over and it was strictly their game until the fourth quarter. Bobby Watkins helped shave six points off a 19-7 deficit with a 3 yard off-tackle slant just as the fourth period got underway.

Ohio's hopes of victory were still slim as Wisconsin began a time-consuming possession type of game. However, the Bucks held for downs on their own forty yard line. On the very next play Ohio's Dave Legett, with all the poise in the world, hurled a perfect thirty yard pass to Cassady, and the latter proceeded to outrun all defenders to the goal. The Bucks led, 20-19.

Ohio still almost let victory slip away, but time ran out on Wisconsin's last ditch bid to score.

Bolden Paces Mich. State To Victory Over Ohio State

Columbus, Ohio, Nov. 7 (AP)—Leroy Bolden, 157-pound halfback, personally knocked Ohio State out of the Big Ten championship contention today as he led Michigan State to a 28-to-13 victory.

Bolden scored three Michigan State touchdowns, two of them on runs of 20 and 37 yards on which he repeatedly shook off the heavy Ohio State tacklers.

The victory, achieved before 82,328 fans in cold and gloomy weather, gave Michigan State a Big Ten standing of four wins against one defeat, and kept alive their championship hopes.

On Long Marches

Ohio State's two touchdowns were made on explosive marches powered by Howard Cassady and Bobby Watkins.

Michigan State scored first on a steady march down the field with Bolden carrying over from the 3. Ohio State struck back at the start of the second quarter with Watkins smashing 16 yards through the line for the touchdown.

A few moments later Bolden burst away for 37 yards and a touchdown, carrying three Ohio State men the last 15 yards.

A Pretty Pass

Cassady made it 14 to 13 at the start of the second half with a pretty 18-yard pass to Tom Hague, but Bolden led a fourth-period march down the field and crashed his way for 20 yards and the touchdown—although hit by six or seven tacklers.

In the closing moments Tom Yewcic tossed a 15-yard pass to Ellis Duckett for the fourth and final touchdown.

Statistics

Michigan State		Ohio State
17	First downs	14
309	Rushing yardage	199
52	Passing yardage	47
12	Passes attempted	17
4	Passes completed	4
1	Passes intercepted by	3
5	Punts	6
34.2	Punting average	35.1
1	Fumbles lost	1
30	Yards penalized	17

Michigan State 7 7 0 14—28
Ohio State 0 6 7 0—13

Michigan State scoring: Touchdowns—Bolden (3), Duckett. Conversions—Slonac (4).

Ohio State scoring: Touchdowns—Watkins, Hague. Conversion—Hague.

The Story of Illi-Buck

THE history of the Illibuck—the wooden turtle trophy for which Illinois and Ohio State football teams compete each year—began back in 1925, when the Illini and Buckeye junior men's honorary societies decided that it would be a good idea to inaugurate a trophy to commemorate their historic but friendly rivalry in the annual game.

A live turtle—dubbed "Illibuck" to combine both the Illini and Buckeye names—was first chosen as a suitable trophy, partly because it was supposed that the marine reptile would display suitable longevity. The trophy's originators envisioned the same turtle fifty years hence, hoary but hearty, with the scores of fifty historic Illini-Buckeye games carved on his back.

After the 1925 game, Illibuck's first, the trophy went right back to Illinois along with the famous "Red" Grange, who had played his last game at Columbus that year. Illinois had won 14-9.

However, after the wear and tear of a few years traveling back and forth between games in a suitcase and spending the rest of the year in the basement of some fraternity house, Illibuck quietly expired. He was replaced, more pessimistically, with a wooden replica—a faithful reproduction of its live predecessor in his prime. Since the untimely end of Illibuck I, the teams have competed for a succession of wooden replicas, of which the present is the third.

Although Illibuck has gone back and forth between Champaign and Columbus many times through the years, he has spent 19 of these years at Ohio State and only eight at Illinois.

The ceremony of transferring Illibuck to his new owner traditionally occurs during the half-time of the game. Members of Bucket and Dipper, the Ohio State junior men's honorary, and Sachem, the Illinois honorary (the latter draped in their Indian blankets), parade out on the field and solemnly pass the peace pipe around to participants. Illibuck is then given over to the winner of the previous year's game, which, today, will be Ohio State, on the strength of last year's 27-7 victory.

1953 TEAM STATISTICS

	First Downs	Net Gain Rush	Net Gain Pass	Total	Total Plays	Passing Att.	Passing Comp.	Passing Int.	Punting No.	Punting Ave.	Fumbles Lost	Yards Penalized	Points
INDIANA	12	69	176	245	61	31	12	4	5	37.4	1	25	12
OHIO STATE	20	192	139	331	65	20	13	1	5	32.6	0	24	36
CALIFORNIA	18	164	170	334	61	25	13	2	2	38.0	1	30	19
OHIO STATE	17	255	111	366	69	19	9	1	1	30.0	3	15	33
ILLINOIS	19	432	15	447	66	6	1	1	3	25.7	2	139	41
OHIO STATE	16	106	119	225	54	24	12	3	2	25.0	4	25	20
PENNSYLVANIA	10	103	89	192	63	21	8	2	3	48.3	3	45	6
OHIO STATE	15	199	127	326	65	18	7	2	3	39.0	4	45	12
WISCONSIN	17	153	137	290	62	13	8	0	6	38.8	1	74	19
OHIO STATE	15	217	106	323	60	16	5	1	5	36.6	1	86	20
NORTHWESTERN	19	223	79	302	76	21	8	1	5	38.4	2	94	13
OHIO STATE	22	238	238	476	64	27	14	3	4	20.5	2	85	27
MICHIGAN STATE	17	309	52	361	70	12	4	3	5	34.4	1	30	28
OHIO STATE	14	199	47	246	55	12	4	1	6	35.2	1	17	13
PURDUE	10	110	84	194	53	12	4	1	7	32.0	3	40	6
OHIO STATE	19	150	131	281	69	24	11	4	2	27.0	2	40	21
MICHIGAN	15	285	19	304	67	12	2	2	5	37.2	1	74	20
OHIO STATE	10	95	107	202	57	21	10	5	5	33.0	1	10	0
OPPONENTS	137	1848	821	2669	579	153	60	16	41	35.1	15	551	164
OHIO STATE	148	1651	1125	2776	558	181	85	21	33	31.9	18	347	182

[1953]

FINAL 1953 OHIO STATE INDIVIDUAL STATISTICS

PASS RECEIVING

Players	No.	Yards	TD's
*Hague	19	275	4
Cassady	16	273	2
Dugger	11	139	0
Brubaker	7	114	0
*Joslin	9	110	0
Watkins	5	74	1
*Rosso	6	49	0
Howell	4	45	0
Guzik	3	43	0
Bond	1	8	0
Harkrader	4	—5	0
Totals	85	1125	7

PUNTING

Player	Number	Yards	Blocked	Ave.
*Rosso	24	804	0	33.5
Borton	6	182	0	30.3
Ludwig	3	68	0	22.7
Totals	33	1054	0	31.9

PUNT RETURNS

Player	Number	Yards	Ave.
Howell	3	43	14.3
Cassady	6	43	7.2
Brubaker	1	24	24.0
Bond	2	24	12.0
*Rosso	4	15	3.7
Leggett	2	6	3.0
Totals	18	155	8.6

KICKOFF RETURNS

Player	Number	Yards	Ave.
Cassady	15	343	22.9
Watkins	5	87	17.5
Howell	2	71	35.5
Leggett	3	56	18.7
Harkrader	1	22	22.0
*Hague	1	9	9.0
Borton	1	9	9.0
Brubaker	1	7	7.0
Totals	29	604	20.8

INTERCEPTION RETURNS

Player	Number	Yards	Ave.
Cassady	3	74	24.7
Leggett	5	63	12.6
*Rosso	2	38	19.0
Vargo	1	33	33.0
Borton	1	8	8.0
Watkins	1	2	2.0
*Takacs	1	0	0.0
*Roberts	1	0	0.0
Boudrie	1	0	0.0
Totals	16	218	13.6

* graduated

RUSHING

Player	Tries	Gain	Lost	Net	Ave.	TD's
Watkins	153	891	16	875	5.7	10
Cassady	86	537	23	514	5.9	6
Leggett	69	207	103	104	1.5	2
Howell	19	69	3	66	3.5	1
Harkrader	8	57	1	56	7.0	0
*Rosso	14	34	6	28	2.0	0
Spears	2	27	0	27	13.5	0
Auer	6	21	8	13	2.2	0
Bond	7	15	5	10	1.4	0
Augenstein	1	4	0	4	4.0	0
Shedd	1	4	0	4	4.0	0
Borton	8	3	37	—34	—4.2	1
Booth	3	0	16	—16	—5.3	0
Totals	337	1869	218	1651	4.4	20

FORWARD PASSING

Player	Att.	Comp.	Int.	Yds.	Comp. Pct.	TD's
Borton	86	45	9	522	52.2	4
Leggett	81	35	10	468	43.2	2
*Rosso	7	2	0	71	28.6	0
Booth	5	2	2	39	40.0	0
Cassady	2	1	0	25	50.0	1
Totals	181	85	21	1125	47.0	7

TOTAL OFFENSE

Player	Plays	Rush	Pass	Total	Ave.	TD's
Watkins	153	875	0	875	5.7	10
Leggett	150	104	468	572	5.1	4
Cassady	88	514	25	539	6.1	7
Borton	94	—34	522	488	5.2	5
*Rosso	21	28	71	99	4.7	0
Howell	19	66	0	66	3.5	1
Harkrader	8	56	0	56	7.0	0
Spears	2	27	0	27	13.5	0
Booth	8	—16	39	23	2.9	0
Auer	6	13	0	13	2.2	0
Bond	7	10	0	10	1.4	0
Augenstein	1	4	0	4	4.0	0
Shedd	1	4	0	4	4.0	0
Totals	558	1651	1125	2776	5.0	27

SCORING

Players	TD's	PAT Att.	PAT Made	FG	Total
Watkins	11	0	0	0	66
Cassady	8	0	0	0	48
*Hague	4	8	4	0	28
Weed	0	19	13	1	16
Leggett	2	0	0	0	12
Borton	1	0	0	0	6
Howell	1	0	0	0	6
Totals	27	27	17	1	182

* graduated

1954 OHIO STATE FOOTBALL ROSTER

No.	Name	Pos.	Wgt.	Hgt.	Home Town	Class
14	*Augenstein, Jack	FB	188	5-10	Loudonville	Jr.
16	Archer, Jack	LH	177	5-10	Dayton	So.
18	Williams, Lee	LH	174	5-10	Springfield	So.
19	**Howell, Carroll	LH	171	5-9	Portsmouth	Sr.
20	***Borton, John (CC)	QB	200	5-1	Alliance	Sr.
21	Okulovich, Andrew	QB	187	5-11	Cleveland	So.
22	**Leggett, David	QB	192	6-1	New Philadelphia	Sr.
24	**Weed, Thurlow	QB	151	5-5	Columbus	Sr.
26	Theis, Franklyn	QB	195	5-10	Nyack, N.Y.	So.
27	Lilienthal, Robert	QB	174	6-0	Cambridge	So.
28	*Booth, William	QB	178	6-0	Youngstown	Jr.
30	Young, James	FB	192	6-0	Van Wert	So.
33	Vicic, Donald	FB	209	6-1	Euclid	So.
34	Nussbaum, Lee	FB	212	6-1	Massillon	So.
40	**Cassady, Howard	LH	177	5-10	Columbus	Jr.
42	Bobo, Hubert	FB	192	6-0	Chauncey Dover	So.
43	Roseboro, James	RH	173	5-9	Ashland	So.
44	*Harkrader, Jerry	LH	176	5-9	Middletown	Jr.
45	**Watkins, Robert	RH	196	5-9	New Bedford, Mass.	Sr.
46	Thompson, Kenneth	RH	184	6-0	Dayton	So.
48	Shedd, Jan	RH	173	5-10	Columbus	Jr.
49	*Young, Richard	RH	168	5-10	Columbus	Sr.
50	Dillman, Thomas	C	192	6-2	Middletown	So.
52	**Bond, Robert	C	186	5-11	Akron	Jr.
53	Slicker, Richard	C	193	6-3	Toledo	So.
54	Sommers, Karl	C	215	6-2	Martins Ferry	So.
55	**Thornton, Robert	C	192	6-0	Willard	Sr.
59	*Vargo, Kenneth	C	192	6-1	Martins Ferry	Jr.
60	*Weaver, David	LG	191	5-8	Hamilton	Jr.
61	Ramser, Richard	LG	191	5-11	Shadyside	Jr.
62	Parker, James	LG	248	6-3	Toledo	So.
63	***Reichenbach, James	RG	200	5-10	Massillon	Sr.
64	*Williams, David	RG	206	6-0	Dormont, Pa.	Sr.
65	Wassmund, James	LG	200	6-0	Toledo	So.
66	Cole, Robert	LG	200	5-10	Carey	So.
67	Quinn, Thomas	LG	190	5-10	Portsmouth	So.
68	*Riticher, Raymond	RG	198	5-10	Toledo	Sr.
69	Keller, John	LT	210	6-0	Fremont	So.
70	*Hilinski, Richard	LT	240	6-2	Cleveland	Sr.
71	***Krisher, Jerry	RT	230	6-0	Massillon	Sr.
72	Thomas, Aurelius	RT	197	6-1	Columbus	So.
73	Cummings, William	LT	247	6-2	Toledo	So.
74	*Stoeckel, Donald	LT	214	6-0	Hamilton	Jr.
75	Guy, Richard	LT	206	6-3	Mansfield	So.
76	Verhoff, Jack	RT	250	6-4	Columbus	Jr.
77	**Swartz, Donald	LT	226	6-1	Newark	Sr.
78	Ebinger, Elbert	RT	238	6-3	Hamilton	Jr.
79	*Machinsky, Francis	RT	212	6-0	Uniontown, Pa.	Jr.
80	*Brubaker, Richard (CC)	RE	198	6-0	Shaker Heights	Sr.
81	Kriss, Frederick	RE	193	5-11	El Paso, Texas	So.
82	**Ludwig, Paul	RE	208	6-3	Marion	Jr.
83	**Dugger, Dean	LE	206	6-2	Columbus	Sr.
84	Trabue, Jerry	LE	203	6-3	Columbus	So.
85	Shingledecker, William	RE	181	5-10	Springfield	So.
86	Campbell, Jack	LE	204	6-2	Lima	Jr.
87	Collmar, William	RE	170	6-1	Martins Ferry	Jr.
88	*Spears, Thomas	RE	193	6-0	Wheeling, W. Va.	Jr.
89	Michael, William	LE	204	6-1	Hamilton	So.
92	Blazeff, Lalo	RE	187	6-0	Akron	So.
93	Ellwood, Frank	LE	192	5-11	Dover	So.

* Indicates letter.

1954
Captains:
C. Richard Brubaker
John R. Borton

28	*Indiana	0
21	*California	13
40	Illinois	7
20	*Iowa	14
31	*Wisconsin	14
14	Northwestern	7
26	*Pittsburgh	0
28	Purdue	6
21	*Michigan	7
20	†Southern California	7
249		75

Won 10, Lost 0
Big Ten Champions

62—PARKER, James, 20, 6-3, 248, sophomore . . . may be a starting guard this season . . . one of the biggest guards in Ohio State grid history . . . from Toledo . . . played tackle as a frosh last season but has been shifted to guard . . . very quick for his size . . . movies are his hobby . . . majoring in physical education . . . once blocked two kicks in a high school game and ran both back for touchdowns . . . will battle Dave Williams for the left guard berth . . . has four brothers and two sisters . . . was born in Georgia but moved to Toledo, attending Scott High School . . . may be used as a linebacker . . . one of the top line prospects on last year's frosh team . . .

Wisconsin 14
Ohio State 31

The week following the Iowa scare, Wisconsin, ranked number two in the nation at the time, came to Columbus. The game was very close through the third quarter. At this time the Bucks found themselves trailing 3-7, with Wisconsin threatening another score. Then came the play that will long be remembered by Ohio fans. Hop Cassady intercepted a Badger pass and romped 88 yards for a TD. This turned the tide. The animated Bucks went on to score three more touch-downs. The final score read Ohio 31, Wisconsin 14.

Four Wisconsin players are preparing to play "London Bridge Is Falling Down" with Hoppy.

DR. WILCE and WES FESLER IN THE FOOTBALL HALL OF FAME

THE election of 12 coaches to the National Football Hall of Fame in 1954 includes the name of Dr. John W. Wilce, who, for 16 years, guided the gridiron fortunes of Ohio State University. Wilce's name will be enshrined in the Football Hall of Fame as one of the greatest coaches of all time and today's halftime ceremonies are intended to add significance to the occasion.

The 12 coaches selected to the Hall of Fame were screened from scores of candidates and only those mentors retired from active coaching at least five years were eligible for consideration. The 1954 election marks the second in the National Football Hall of Fame's history.

Dr. Wilce's 16-year tenure at Ohio State is the longest in Buckeye football lore. His teams, 1913 through 1928, won 78 games, lost 33, and tied nine, a winning percentage of .687. Wilce-coached Buckeye elevens were unbeaten in 1916 and 1917, lost but one game during four different seasons (1915, 1919, 1920 (Rose Bowl), and 1926), and captured three Western Conference championships (1916, 1917, and 1920).

Dr. Wilce is the only Ohio State coach to have more than one perfect season. Wilce's feat of four seasons in which his teams lost but one contest likewise never has been equaled and no other Ohio State coach has guided his teams to three Big Ten titles.

Wilce is significant in Ohio State's rise to football prominence. His first year at Ohio State marked the University's initial season as a Western Conference member and three years later, in 1916, the Buckeyes won the conference championship with their first of two successful unbeaten seasons under Dr. Wilce.

Dr. Wilce has the distinction of coaching nine All-American players, representing 13 selections to All-American teams. Ohio State's first, and probably greatest, All-American was Charles (Chic) Harley, who made the mythical team in 1916, 1917 and 1919 as a sparkling back. Dr. Wilce coached Harley throughout his fabulous career.

Robert Karch, tackle, and Charles Bolen, end, were the next Ohio State All-Americans in 1916 and 1917, respectively, both under the leadership of Wilce. Wilce coached two players who gained All-America stature in duplicate, Iolas Huffman in 1920 and '21, and Edwin Hess, 1925 and 1926.

One time All-Americans under Dr. Wilce were Gaylord (Pete) Stinchcomb (1920), Marty Karow, present Ohio State Baseball Coach, (1926), Leo Raskowski (1927), and Wesley Fesler, who is being honored today along with Dr. Wilce. Dr. Wilce's identification with nine All-American football players ranks him high among the all-time coaching greats. This is indeed a noteworthy accomplishment. Ohio State has had 31 All-America choices through its entire football history.

The three Big Ten titles won under Dr. Wilce represents one-third of Ohio State's total championships.

The late L. W. St. John, athletic director of Ohio State University when Dr. Wilce first arrived, and himself an all-time great figure in Ohio State athletic history, wrote the following:

"His first year as Director of the Gridiron activities has stamped him as much more than a master of football science. He brings to the staff an enthusiasm, a breadth of vision and a degree of efficiency which spell SUCCESS in large letters. To meet him is to feel the qualities of leadership; to know him is to be certain that he has richly deserved all the honors he has recived. We are proud to introduce his name to the pages of the Ohio State University History."

The words of Mr. St. John in 1913 may well be applied to today's occasion. Ohio State University is proud to introduce the name of Dr. John W. Wilce to the National Football Hall of Fame and consequently into the national history of the great gridiron sport.

* * *

WESLEY E. FESLER, a three-time All-American at Ohio State University, joins 39 other playing greats of the gridiron in the National Football Hall of Fame this year.

Fesler came to Ohio State from Youngstown, O., where he established a reputation as an outstanding all-around athlete. During his athletic activities at Ohio State, "Wes" won nine varsity letters, reaching the highest possible attainment in football and also earning honors as an All-Western Conference guard in basketball. He played three different positions during a standout career in baseball.

Fesler today is being honored for his achievements as a football player. He was an All-America end all three seasons he played at Ohio State, 1928, 1929, and 1930. In 1930, "Wes" captained the Buckeyes. His versatile athletic ability again was shown as he performed on the gridiron at both end and fullback. Fesler turned in a 99-yard run against Northwestern in 1929, the longest ever made in Ohio Stadium. He was named the most valuable player on the 1930 squad. When Fesler played football at Ohio State, the Buckeyes won 14 games, seven, and tied three.

Richard C. Larkins, Ohio State director of athletics, was Fesler's teammate in both football and basketball.

Fesler returned to his alma mater in 1947 as head football coach. He served through the 1950 season during which his teams won 21 games, lost 13, and tied three. His 1949 team defeated California in the Rose Bowl, 17 to 14.

Thousands of candidates have been screened for the National Football Hall of Fame, and the 40 players selected in 1954 were deemed the "greatest and most obvious," according to William Cunningham, chairman of the Honors' Court.

"Chic" Harley, Ohio State's immortal half back of 1916-'17-'19, became the first former Buckeye to reach Hall of Fame stature last year. Now, "Wes" joins this highly select class of football immortals.

Fesler has the distinction of being the only Ohio State gridder other than Harley to achieve the honor of being named an All-American for three seasons. His achievements on the football field have brought fitting honors to his person and likewise to the university for which he played.

Ohio State Wins 21-7 To Take Big Ten Title, Finish Unbeaten
Buckeyes Top Wolverines To Secure Rose Bowl Trip

COLUMBUS, Ohio, Nov. 20 (P)—Ohio State's unbeaten Buckeyes made good on a four-way bid for gridiron glory here today, coming from behind with two long touchdown drives in the final period to defeat Michigan 21-7. A crowd of 82,438, and a national television audience saw the game.

The conquest gave the brilliant Buckeyes the undisputed Big Ten championship, a berth in the Rose Bowl, a hefty claim to the national title, and their first unbeaten, untied season in 10 years.

In beating Michigan for only the third time in 12 seasons, Ohio became only the second Western Conference team in history to win seven straight games in the rugged league. Only Chicago's 1913 team had done it before.

The Bucks came from nowhere to climb back on the football throne. Held to only four first downs in the first three periods, Ohio came to life after holding Michigan on the 6-inch line to take the ball just as the third session ended.

99 Yards, 2 Feet, 6 Inches

With the score deadlocked at 7-7, the Wolverines had a first down on the 4, but four cracks at the line served only to turn the ball over to the Bucks, who promptly marched 99 yards, 2 feet and 6 inches in 12 plays, climaxed by Dave Leggett's 8-yard touchdown toss to end Dick Brubaker.

Late in the session, Howard (Hopalong) Cassady, Ohio's outstanding star of the day, intercepted a pass and ran it back to his own 38, and 11 plays later he ended the 62-yard drive with a 1-yard plunge for the final score.

Little Tad Weed, 145-pound placekicking specialist, booted all three placements for Ohio.

Michigan marched 68 yards in 12 plays at the start of the game for its only touchdown, an intricate buck lateral play sending left halfback Dan Cline into the end zone for the score. Ron Kramer, Michigan's great sophomore end, who played a fine game on both offense and defense booted the extra point.

A.P. POLL	U.P.I. POLL
1. OHIO STATE	1. U.C.L.A.
2. U.C.L.A.	2. OHIO STATE
3. Oklahoma	3. Oklahoma
4. Notre Dame	4. Notre Dame
5. Navy	5. Navy
6. Mississippi	6. Mississippi
7. Army	7. Army
8. Maryland	8. Arkansas
9. Wisconsin	9. Miami (Fla.)
10. Arkansas	10. Wisconsin

Michigan   7 0 0 0— 7
Ohio State   0 7 0 14—21
 Michigan scoring: Touchdowns, Cline. Conversion, Kramer.
 Ohio scoring: Touchdowns, Kriss, Brubaker, Cassady. Conversions, Weed 3.

NATIONAL TITLE TROPHY ACCEPTED FROM NOTRE DAME

Ohio State University's undefeated Buckeyes of 1954 are possessors of the Rev. J. Hugh O'Donnell trophy, Notre Dame University's award to the national championship team. The presentation was made to Coach "Woody" Hayes by Notre Dame Assistant Coach William Earley (left).

Ohio State Pounds Trojan Eleven 20-7

SC's Dandoy On 86 Yard Run In Rain

PASADENA, Calif., Jan. 1 (CP) — Ohio State's smooth-clicking Buckeyes, led by master magician Dave Leggett at quarterback, ploughed through the mud of the Rose Bowl in a rainstorm to a 20 to 7 victory today over Southern California before 89,191 fans.

Exploding for scores when they were given the breaks, the Buckeyes demonstrated their championship caliber although the record individual performances were all on the side of Southern California as tailback Armais Dandoy set a new Rose Bowl punt return mark of 86 yards for a touchdown.

But that brilliant broken field run and two superlative near-record efforts by his substitute, Jon Arnett, were not enough to turn the tide of Buckeye might as All-America halfback Howard Cassady, aided by Bobby Watkins and Jerry Harkrader ran up big yardage to keep their lead throughout the game after their initial score.

Worst Going Since 1934

The game was played under the worst conditions since the 1934 Rose Bowl contest between Stanford and Columbia. Columbia won that game in an upset, 7-0. Rain fell throughout today's game and by the second period the numobliterated.

The potent power of the Buckeyes was displayed from the opening kickoff when they drove to the Southern Cal 14, were penalized back to the SC 19 and Tad Weed missed a field goal attempt from the 27.

The Buckeyes' next took the ball on their 31 when guard Jim Parker recovered Jin Contratto's fumble. Cassady and Harkrader alternated in driving all the way, with Legett scoring from the three. The touchdown came at the start of the second period.

A fumble by SC sub quarterback Frank Hall set up the second Ohio State score. Leggett recovered and after Watkins made 14, Leggett threw a 21-yard scoring pass to Watkins.

Arnett Kicks 70 Yards

The picture was grim at that point but Southern California came back with five minutes left in the period. Fullback Hubert Bobo went back from his 32 to kick, got a bad pass from center, but was able to get off a boot to Dandoy on the 14.

The Southern Cal tailback was sprung by a key block from tackle George Belotti and ducked and weaved his way through the entire Ohio State team to score. His 86-yard run set a new record for a Rose Bowl punt runback to a touchdown. It shattered the mark of 62 yards set last year by Billy Wells of Michigan State in the game against UCLA.

It was in the third period that Southern California's Arnett covered himself with individual glory although his efforts were not enough to give the Trojans another score and possibly tie up the game.

The brilliant 19-year-old sophomore got off a quick kick from his own nine that was good for 70 yards to come within two yards of the bowl record and later in the same period the young star broke loose for 70 yards from scrimmage to the Ohio State 26, where Ohio held on downs. The run came within a yard of the Rose Bowl record of 71 yards set by Frank Aschenbrenner of Northwestern against California in 1949.

Bucks Stopped At Four

But after holding the Buckeyes on the four, Southern California had shot its bolt and the Buckeyes came back in the last period to march 77 yards in 12 plays with Harkrader going the final nine to score.

In addition to its backs, individual brilliant performances were turned in by Buckeye center Bob Thornton, guard Jim Parker, end Dean Dugger and tackle Dick Hilinski.

The difference in the teams was best illustrated by the first downs as Ohio State made 21 to Southern California's six.

Despite that superiority, the Trojans fought savagely throughout, with guard Orlando Ferrante showing special brillance in the line along with center Marvin Goux and nd Leon Clarke.

The 13-point margin while proving Ohio State was as good as the two-touchdown margin it rated in pre-game predictions, did not settle whether the Buckeyes were any better than the mythical national champions, UCLA, because of the poor playing conditions. UCLA beat Southern California, 34 to 0.

1954 TEAM STATISTICS

	First Downs	Rush	Net Gain Pass	Total	Total Plays	Att.	Passing Comp.	Had Int.	Punting No.	Ave.	Fumbles Lost	Yards Penalized	Points
INDIANA	19	149	104	253	75	30	11	2	3	30.0	2	34	0
OHIO STATE	15	196	64	260	49	7	4	0	4	40.0	1	43	28
CALIFORNIA	12	101	88	189	51	13	7	0	4	38.2	3	25	13
OHIO STATE	18	285	89	374	56	12	7	1	5	30.0	3	60	21
ILLINOIS	8	83	40	123	42	13	4	2	4	38.5	2	71	7
OHIO STATE	24	313	166	479	79	17	9	2	1	12.0	0	101	40
IOWA	13	153	79	232	56	14	6	1	5	34.0	1	49	14
OHIO STATE	15	212	29	241	67	7	4	2	5	35.0	0	18	20
WISCONSIN	19	87	270	357	74	36	22	2	4	38.2	2	47	14
OHIO STATE	12	172	69	241	56	17	6	1	5	40.2	1	50	31
NORTHWESTERN	14	100	100	200	66	22	6	3	4	42.0	1	20	7
OHIO STATE	14	178	73	251	64	16	6	1	4	40.8	2	40	14
PITTSBURGH	5	118	19	137	53	14	3	2	6	39.2	2	37	0
OHIO STATE	20	242	83	325	70	14	7	0	6	30.2	0	71	26
PURDUE	18	88	217	305	65	40	21	1	3	37.8	1	35	6
OHIO STATE	21	407	41	448	73	15	7	1	4	41.7	1	100	28
MICHIGAN	15	229	74	303	64	14	6	3	3	42.7	2	86	7
OHIO STATE	13	196	58	254	54	9	4	1	5	24.6	1	35	21
SOUTHERN CALIFORNIA	6	177	29	206	36	8	3	0	5	46.6	3	60	7
OHIO STATE	22	305	65	370	80	11	6	1	4	38.2	0	40	20
OPPONENTS	129	1285	1020	2305	582	204	89	18	41	38.7	19	464	75
OHIO STATE	174	2506	737	3243	648	125	60	10	43	34.7	9	558	249

FINAL 1954 OHIO STATE INDIVIDUAL STATISTICS

RUSHING

Player	Tries	Gain	Lost	Net	Ave.	TD's
Cassady	123	764	63	701	5.7	6
*Watkins	119	668	8	660	5.5	8
Bobo	69	401	0	401	5.7	3
Leggett	116	393	91	302	2.6	4
Harkrader	33	219	3	216	6.5	3
Roseboro	26	99	12	87	3.3	0
Howell	9	41	2	39	4.3	0
Thompson	2	34	0	34	17.0	1
Booth	6	24	0	24	4.0	0
Vicic	6	23	0	23	3.8	0
L. Williams	2	18	0	18	9.0	0
*Gibbs	4	8	0	8	2.0	0
Shedd	1	2	0	2	2.0	0
*R. Young	1	1	0	1	1.0	0
Okulovich	2	4	7	—3	—1.5	0
*Borton	4	3	10	—7	—1.7	1
Totals	523	2702	196	2506	4.8	26

FORWARD PASSING

Player	Att.	Comp.	Int.	Yds.	Comp. Pct.	TD's
*Leggett	106	52	7	643	49.1	8
*Borton	11	7	3	52	63.6	0
Booth	5	1	0	42	20.0	0
Cassady	1	0	0	0	00.0	0
*R. Young	1	0	0	0	00.0	0
Robson	1	0	0	0	00.0	0
Totals	125	60	10	737	48.0	8

SCORING

Player	TD'S	PAT Att.	PAT Made	FG	Total
*Watkins	10	4	4	0	64
Cassady	8	0	0	0	48
*Weed	0	26	24	1	27
*Leggett	4	0	0	0	24
Bobo	3	0	0	0	18
*Brubaker	3	0	0	0	18
Harkrader	3	0	0	0	18
Michael	2	0	0	0	12
*Borton	1	0	0	0	6
Thompson	1	0	0	0	6
Kriss	1	0	0	0	6
*Krisher	0	4	2	0	2
Booth	0	1	0	0	0
(Team)	0	1	0	0	0
Totals	36	36	30	1	249

PASS RECEIVING

Player	No.	Yards	TD's
Cassady	13	148	0
*Dugger	9	144	0
*Brubaker	12	120	3
*Watkins	8	93	2
Michael	3	43	2
Harkrader	5	42	0
*Ludwig	1	42	0
Roseboro	2	33	0
Kriss	2	31	1
Spears	4	30	0
*Howell	1	11	0
Totals	60	737	8

PUNTING

Player	No.	Yards	Blocked	Ave.
Bobo	37	1287	1	34.8
Trabue	3	134	0	44.7
*Borton	3	72	1	24.0
Totals	43	1493	2	34.7

PUNT RETURNS

Player	Number	Yards	Ave.
Cassady	11	85	7.7
*Leggett	12	84	7.0
L. Williams	1	7	7.0
*Howell	1	0	0.0
Totals	25	176	7.0

INTERCEPTION RETURNS

Player	No.	Yards	Ave.
Cassady	4	109	27.2
*Gibbs	1	45	45.0
Bobo	1	31	31.0
*Howell	2	30	15.0
*Leggett	3	27	9.0
*Thornton	1	16	16.0
*Watkins	1	6	6.0
*R. Young	3	4	1.3
Harkrader	1	3	3.0
Thompson	1	0	1.0
Totals	18	271	15.1

KICKOFF RETURNS

Player	No.	Yards	Ave.
Cassady	9	179	19.9
*Leggett	3	51	17.0
*Watkins	1	24	24.0
*Howell	1	16	16.0
Vicic	1	14	14.0
*Dugger	1	13	13.0
Bobo	1	12	12.0
*Brubaker	2	11	5.5
Totals	19	320	16.8

* Graduated

1955 OHIO STATE FOOTBALL ROSTER

No.	Name	Pos.	Wgt.	Hgt.	Class	Home Town
12	Walters, Ronald	LH	165	5-7	So.	Lima
14	Beerman, Raymond	RH	174	5-11	So.	Toledo
15	Disher, Larry	LH	178	5-11	So.	Waterville
16	Cannavino, Joseph	LH	177	5-11	So.	Cleveland
18	Williams, Lee	LH	176	5-10	Jr.	Springfield
19	Peggs, Carl	LH	180	5-9	Jr.	Fostoria
23	Crawford, Thomas	QB	175	5-11	So.	Toledo
24	Ellwood, Franklin	QB	188	5-11	Jr.	Dover
25	Karow, Robert	QB	180	5-11	So.	Columbus
26	Theis, Franklyn	QB	191	5-10	Jr.	Nyack, N. Y.
27	Lilienthal, Robert	QB	174	6-0	Jr.	Cambridge
28 **Booth, William	QB	184	6-0	Sr.	Youngstown
29	Lepley, John	QB	172	5-11	So.	Bellevue
30	Young, James	FB	196	6-0	Jr.	Van Wert
33 *Vicic, Donald	FB	214	6-1	Jr.	Euclid
34	Nussbaum, Lee	FB	212	6-1	Jr.	Massillon
35	Trivisonno, Joseph	FB	194	5-11	So.	Cleveland
36	Cisco, Galen	FB	194	5-11	So.	St. Marys
40 ***Cassady, Howard	LH	172	5-10	Sr.	Columbus
41	Shindledecker, William	RH	181	5-10	So.	Springfield
43 *Roseboro, James	RH	176	5-9	Jr.	Ashland
44 **Harkrader, Jerry	RH	182	5-9	Sr.	Middletown
45	Sutherin, Donald	RH	198	5-10	So.	Toronto
46	Thompson, Kenneth	RH	188	6-0	Jr.	Dayton
47	Wable, Robert	RH	171	5-10	So.	Sistersville, W.Va.
48	Shedd, Jan	RH	173	5-10	Sr.	Columbus
49	Richards, David	RH	166	5-9	Jr.	Barnesville
50 *Dillman, Thomas	C	200	6-2	Jr.	Middletown
52 ***Bond, Robert	C	187	5-11	Sr.	Akron
54	Sommers, Karl	C	215	6-2	Jr.	Martins Ferry
55	Breehl, Edward	C	182	6-0	So.	New Philadelphia
56	Palmer, Bradley	C	190	6-1	So.	Bellevue
57	Martin, John	LG	210	5-11	So.	Waverly
58	Quinn, Thomas	RT	190	5-10	Jr.	Portsmouth
59 **Vargo, Kenneth	C	194	6-1	Sr.	Martins Ferry
60 **Weaver, David	RG	191	5-8	Sr.	Hamilton
61 *Ramser, Richard	RG	196	5-11	Sr.	Shadyside
62 *Parker, James	LG	242	6-3	Jr.	Toledo
63 *Jobko, William	LG	192	6-1	Jr.	Lansing
64	Thomas, Aurelius	RG	204	6-1	So.	Columbus
65	Wassmund, James	LG	200	6-0	Jr.	Toledo
66	Cole, Robert	LG	200	5-10	Jr.	Carey
67	Baldacci, Thomas	LG	190	6-0	Jr.	Akron
68	Provenza, Russell	LG	187	5-10	So.	Lorain
69	Facchine, Richard	RG	205	5-9	So.	Vandergrift, Pa.
70	Nagy, Alex	LT	236	6-2	So.	Warren
71	Perry, Charles	RT	212	5-11	So.	Columbus
72 *Whetstone, Robert	RT	199	5-11	Jr.	Barberton
73	Cummings, William	RT	240	6-2	Jr.	Toledo
74 **Stoeckel, Donald	LT	214	6-0	Sr.	Hamilton
75 *Guy, Richard	LT	214	6-3	Jr.	Mansfield
76	Zawacki, Charles	RT	210	6-2	So.	Uniontown, Pa.
77	Humbert, Stanley	LT	200	6-2	Jr.	Cincinnati
78	Ebinger, Elbert	LT	233	6-3	Sr.	Hamilton
79 **Machinsky, Francis	RT	209	6-0	Sr.	Uniontown, Pa.
80	Bowermaster, Russell	LE	196	6-2	So.	Hamilton
81 *Kriss, Frederick	RE	191	5-11	Jr.	El Paso, Tex.
83	Niederhauser, Donald	RE	212	6-5	So.	Toledo
85	Brown, Leo	RE	168	5-10	So.	Portsmouth
86	Trittipo, John	RE	183	6-0	So.	Gambier
87 *Collmar, William	LE	184	6-1	Sr.	Martins Ferry
88 **Spears, Thomas	LE	197	6-0	Sr.	Wheeling, W.Va.
89 *Michael, William	LE	212	6-1	Jr.	Hamilton
92	Goodwin, Roy	LE	190	6-0	So.	Jackson

* Indicates letter.

Front row, left to right: Tackle Coach Bill Hess, Zawacki, Cannavino, Niederhauser, Baldacci, Beerman, Barnes, Karow, Wassmund, Holdren, Perry, Cole, Lepley, Palmer, Floyd, Crawford, Cook, Guard-Center Coach Harry Strobel. *Second row:* Head Coach Woody Hayes, Roseboro, Parker, Collmar, Shedd, Ebinger, Weaver, Bond, Cassady, Vargo, co-captain; Machinsky, co-captain; Spears, Harkrader, Booth, Ramser, Dillman, Guy, Kriss, Freshman Coach Ernie Godfrey. *Third row:* Asst. Freshman Coach Jim Hietikko, Brown, Richards, Quinn, Theis, Whetstone, Jobko, Cummings, Vicic, Michael, Williams, Young, Ellwood, Sommer, Trivisonno, Humbert, Lilienthal. *Fourth row:* End Coach Esco Sarkkinen, Faachine, Sutherin, Cisco, Martin, Thompson, Thomas, Trittipo, Provenza, Disher, Nagy, Breehl, Wable, Backfield Coach Gene Fekete, Asst. Backfield Coach Clive Rush, Defensive Line Coach Lyal Clark.

1955
Captains: Frank C. Machinsky
Kenneth W. Vargo

28	*Nebraska	20
0	Stanford	6
27	*Illinois	12
14	*Duke	20
26	Wisconsin	16
49	*Northwestern	0
20	*Indiana	13
20	*Iowa	10
17	Michigan	0
201		97

Won 7, Lost 2
Big Ten Champions

A.P. POLL
1. Oklahoma
2. Michigan State
3. Maryland
4. U.C.L.A.
5. T.C.U.
6. OHIO STATE
7. Georgia Tech
8. Notre Dame
9. Mississippi
10. Auburn

Amazing Stanford Indians Upset Ohio State's Buckeyes On Coast

PALO ALTO, Calif., Oct. 1 (P)—Stanford's upstart Indians living up to their chief's Blythe midweek prediction, clamped the shackles on All America Hopalong Cassady today and made a first period touchdown stand up for a 6-0 upset victory over eighth-ranked Ohio State in an Intersectional football game.

It was nationally televised.

A slim crowd of 28,000 saw the Indians score the first time they had the ball. A sneaker pass from Jerry Gustafson to Paul Camera climaxed a 72-yard drive.

Stanford completely outplayed the bewildered Buckeyes throughout the first half.

Chunky Chuck Taylor, the optimistic Stanford coach and himself a former All-America guard for the Indians, said early in the week he felt Cassady "could be had," and that he had devised a "gambling" defense which he figured would turn the trick. It did.

Cassady, an All America halfback as a junior last year, was held to only 11 yards in the first half and 26 in the second. The Indians hamstrung him virtually every time he had the ball.

Showing nothing in the first half, the Buckeyes came to life in the second with four scoring threats, but lacked the punch to cross the fighting Indians' goal line.

Tough Indians

Jerry Harkrader and Don Vicic were unable to take up the Cassady slack although Ohio State controlled the ball most of the second half. The Indians were tough in the clutch and stopped all threats.

The Stanford touchdown came from the opening kickoff on a 12-play 72-yard march. Gustafson, sharp as a razor with his passes, was masterful in his team direction. He used the bull-like rushes of fullback Bill Tarr, last year's Pacific Conference running champion, to complement his aerial game with outstanding success.

Tarr, stocky 190-pound senior, tripped the Buckeye tackles and guards and Gustafson passed as though equipped with a bomb sight throughout the drive.

The payoff was a perfectly executed deceptive pass to Camera, all alone in the corner of the end zone, for the final yard. Tarr ripped through the middle of the line without the football, completely fooling the Bucks. The nearest defender was a good 15 yards away when Camera caught the ball.

Mike Raftery's conversion try was blocked.

Stanford   6 0 0 0—6
Stanford scoring: touchdown—Camera. (1, passed from Gustafson.)

U.P.I. POLL
1. Oklahoma
2. Michigan State
3. Maryland
4. U.C.L.A.
5. OHIO STATE
6. T.C.U.
7. Georgia Tech
8. Auburn
9. Notre Dame
10. Mississippi

Duke Overcomes Ohio State 20-14 After 14-0 Deficit

COLUMBUS, Ohio, Oct. 15 (P) — Duke's Blue Devils spotted Ohio State a 14-point lead today, then roared back with a late surge of power and passing to defeat the National champion Bucks 20-14.

A crowd of 82,254 watched the intersectional struggle, first between the two gridiron powerhouses.

It looked like an easy victory for Ohio State as substitute halfback Jim Roseboro swept end for a 44-yard touchdown in the first quarter, and his all-America running mate Howard (Hopalong) Cassady returned a punt 38 yards in the second session. Fred Kriss converted both times for Ohio's 14-0 lead.

One Second to Play

Right there the undefeated Dukes too charge and the Buckeyes never reached Confederate territory the rest of the way. Duke scored with only one second to play in the first half on a five-yard pass from halfback Bob Pascal to 159-pound halfback Bernie Blaney.

The Blue Devils tied it at the start of the third session, marching 43 yards in 11 plays with Pascal plunging one yard for the score. The Southerners clinched it with an 82-yard drive which started late in the third session and ended in the fourth with quarterback Sonny Jurgensen sneaking a yard on the 17th play for the winning touchdown.

Jim Nelson, Duke guard, who had converted 12 of 14 attempts this season, missed after Jurgensen's score, but the six-point margin was plenty.

Duke   0 7 7 6—20
Ohio State   7 7 0 0—14

Duke scoring 8 touchdowns: Blaney (5-yard pass from Pascal); Pascal (1-foot plunge); Jurgensen (1-foot plunge); conversions: Nelson 2.

Ohio scoring — touchdowns: Roseboro (44-yard run); Cassady (38-yard punt return); conversions: Kriss 2.

[1955]

hoppy breaks record as bucks down iowa 20-10

Ohio Stadium's third largest crowd—82,701 cheering fans—the score 20-10—All-American "Hop" Cassady breaking the all time Ohio State scoring record—what more could one ask? Yes, it was a magnificent show as the Buckeyes, led by the stalwart linemen and ever-ready backs defeated a very stubborn Iowa team. The victory was highlighted by the brilliant showing of Howard Cassady, whose three touchdowns totally shattered the long-standing Ohio scoring record set by Chic Harley in 1919. The first touchdown, a beautiful run of forty-five yards was the one that did it. Iowa took the opening kickoff and drove to the Ohio nineteen yard line before they were held for three downs. From that spot they kicked a field goal to lead 3-0. The Bucks took the ball on the 50 as Iowa twice kicked out of bounds. On the second play from scrimmage, Cassady carried for the touchdown. Iowa scored once, then State added two more markers to end the game 20-10. The win gave the Bucks a 5-0 Western Conference mark and set the stage for the big show of the year at Michigan.

Heisman Trophy Goes To Cassady

New York, Nov. 29 (P)—Hopalong Cassidy, the redheaded Ohio State University speedster who has been called by his coach "the greatest player of this century," was selected today as 1955 winner of the Heisman Memorial Trophy.

The Heisman Trophy is awarded annually by the Downtown Athletic Club of New York to the "outstanding college football player in the United States." Cassady was chosen by a landslide vote of 1,324 sports writers and broadcasters.

The trophy is named in honor of John W. Heisman, one of football's great coaches, who was athletic director at the Downtown A.C. at the time of his death in 1936. Heisman, inventor of the spin play, the direct snap from center and many other features of modern football, coached at eight different colleges from 1892 through 1927 and was twice president of the American Football Coaches Association.

The trophy will be presented to Cassady at a dinner here early in December.

Ohio State Knocks Michigan Out Of Rose Bowl

Buckeyes Win, 17 To 0; Capture Big Ten Title

ANN ARBOR, Mich., Nov. 19 (P) — Howard (Hopalong) Cassady, climaxing a fabulous collegiate career, set up a freakish field goal, scored one touchdown and led Ohio State to a 17-0 victory today over crestfallen Michigan, which lost its Rose Bowl bid before its largest crowd in history—97,369 sepctators.

The dramatic shutout — Ohio State's first victory in Ann Arbor since 1937 — gave the Buckeyes their second straight Big Ten championship and clinched the Rose Bowl nomination for Michigan State.

Big Ten rules prohibit a team from going to the Rose Bowl two seasons in a row thus closing the door on Ohio State which played in the Bowl New Year's Day. The Big Ten will conduct its formal vote tomorrow, but it was a foregone conclusion they would now pick Michigan State for the trip.

Michigan State closed its season today by whipping Marquette 33-0 in a non-conference game.

The hard-fought game turned into as especially bruising battle in the last four minutes during which six penalties were meted out to Michigan and two to Ohio, plus two double penalties which offset each other.

Penalties Aid Ohio

Ohio State's final touchdown in the closing minutes was set up by three successive penalties to Michigan on one play. Michigan was penalized to its six when tackle Lionel Sigman was called for a personal foul. When he protested, a second penalty set the ball on Michigan's one and Sigman was ejected from the game.

Michigan's big end, Ron Kramer, carried on the protest and he too left the game after Michigan was penalized to its 18-inch line. Fullback Don Vicic dove over from there for the OSU score.

Michigan head coach Benn Oosterbaan commented aft the game, "maybe it was too e citing. Things may have gotte out of hand."

Michigan freshman coa Wally Weber, interviewed on radio program (WJR) after t game said about sportsmanshi "Perhaps we were a little r miss in it today. I abjectly apol gize to football fans everywhe but I trust it was due to ov exuberance."

Cassady, an All - America ha back from Columbus, Ohi ripped Michigan's veteran l i n from start to finish. He carrie 28 times for 146 yards.

Cassady nailed down the vi tory for the ninth -ranked Buc eyes by diving across from th two shortly after the final qua ter started.

It gave the red - haired senio 15 touchdowns this season a n pushed his four - year point tota to 222 — highest in Ohio Stat history.

As a result the top of the B Ten standings wound up thi way:

	Won	Lost	Pc
Ohio State	6	0	.1000
Michigan State	5	1	.833
Michigan	5	2	.714

It was Ohio State's 13 straig conference victory, just two sho of the record piled up by Mich gan in 1946-47-48.

Score by quarters
Ohio State   0 3 0 14—1
Scoring summary:
Touchdowns: Cassady (Plunge) Vicic (1, run). F i e l goal: Kriss (7). Safeties: Michae (tackled Barr in end zone).

1955 TEAM STATISTICS

	First Downs	Rush	Net Gain Pass	Total	Total Plays	Passing Att.	Comp.	Int.	Punting No.	Ave.	Fumbles Lost	Yards Penalized	Points
NEBRASKA	16	138	189	327	62	26	11	1	1	29.0	3	35	20
OHIO STATE	17	321	17	338	64	3	1	0	4	34.2	1	43	28
STANFORD	13	152	66	218	54	13	6	0	5	38.6	1	35	6
OHIO STATE	17	187	41	228	69	12	5	1	4	34.0	1	40	0
ILLINOIS	17	196	175	371	66	15	7	1	3	39.7	2	45	12
OHIO STATE	16	334	17	351	64	9	4	0	6	28.8	0	76	27
DUKE	20	218	125	343	78	13	9	1	4	30.0	3	23	20
OHIO STATE	8	138	27	165	44	10	2	2	3	43.7	4	1	14
WISCONSIN	20	284	94	378	68	18	7	1	4	36.2	2	10	16
OHIO STATE	16	272	32	304	63	4	2	0	5	41.7	1	26	26
NORTHWESTERN	14	166	75	241	65	19	8	3	4	38.7	1	20	0
OHIO STATE	20	395	24	419	70	5	2	0	3	32.3	0	10	49
INDIANA	16	159	142	301	65	18	11	0	4	39.7	1	55	13
OHIO STATE	13	251	9	251	54	2	0	0	4	39.2	2	17	20
IOWA	16	171	101	272	59	14	9	1	3	42.0	1	40	10
OHIO STATE	16	273	0	273	56	3	0	0	3	35.3	0	15	20
MICHIGAN	5	95	14	109	40	9	3	2	6	43.2	0	70	0
OHIO STATE	20	333	4	337	75	3	1	0	3	34.7	2	50	17
OPPONENTS	557	1579	981	2560	557	145	71	10	34	38.2	14	333	97
OHIO STATE	559	2504	162	2666	559	51	17	3	35	34.6	11	278	201

FINAL 1955 OHIO STATE INDIVIDUAL STATISTICS

RUSHING

Player	Tries	Gain	Lost	Net	Avg.	TD's
*Cassady	161	984	26	958	5.9	14
Roseboro	62	388	9	379	6.1	2
Vicic	63	269	0	269	4.3	1
Ellwood	84	305	40	265	3.1	5
Cannavino	19	156	5	151	7.9	1
*Harkrader	22	160	13	147	6.7	1
Williams	24	131	8	123	5.1	1
Cisco	26	106	2	104	4.0	0
Sutherin	18	75	0	75	4.2	0
Booth	14	34	6	25	2.0	0
*Lilienthal	1	4	0	4	4.0	0
Trivisonno	1	4	0	4	4.0	0
Thompson	1	0	0	0	0.0	0
Theis	12	29	32	−3	−0.2	0
Totals	508	2645	141	2504	4.9	25

* Not returning.

FORWARD PASSING

Player	Att.	Comp.	Int.	Yds.	Comp. Pct.	TD's
Ellwood	23	9	0	60	39.1	2
*Cassady	10	2	2	39	20.0	0
*Booth	6	4	0	36	66.7	0
Theis	11	2	1	27	18.1	0
*Lilenthal	1	0	0	0	00.0	0
Totals	51	17	3	162	33.3	2

* Not returning.

PUNTING

Player	Number	Yards	Blocked	Avg.
Ellwood	23	834	0	36.3
Sutherin	4	133	0	33.2
Theis	7	227	0	32.4
*Cassady	1	16	0	16.0
Totals	35	1210	0	34.6

* Not returning.

PASS RECEIVING

Player	Number	Yards	TD's
Michael	4	50	0
Roseboro	3	40	0
Kriss	2	29	1
*Harkrader	2	17	0
Brown	2	15	1
*Cassady	1	6	0
Vicic	1	4	0
*Williams	2	−8	0
Totals	17	162	2

* Not returning.

SCORING

Player	TD's	PAT Att.	PAT Made	FG	Total
*Cassady	15	0	0	0	90
Ellwood	5	0	0	0	30
Kriss	1	25	20	1	29
Roseboro	2	0	0	0	12
Cannavino	1	1	1	0	7
Vicic	1	0	0	0	6
Parker	1	0	0	0	6
Brown	1	0	0	0	6
*Williams	1	0	0	0	6
*Harkrader	1	0	0	0	6
Sutherin	0	3	1	0	1
(Safety)	0	0	0	0	2
Totals	29	29	22	1	201

* Not returning.

PUNT RETURNS

Player	Number	Yards	Ave.	TD's
*Cassady	17	205	12.1	1
Michael	0	25	25.0	0
*Vargo	1	14	14.0	0
*Harkrader	1	10	10.0	0
Roseboro	1	3	3.0	0
Totals	20	257	12.8	1

* Not returning.

INTERCEPTION RETURNS

Player	Number	Yards	Ave.	TD's
Cisco	2	57	27.5	0
*Cassady	2	44	22.0	0
Parker	1	42	42.0	1
Roseboro	1	24	24.0	0
Theis	1	9	9.0	0
Vicic	1	7	7.0	0
*Vargo	1	3	3.0	0
Thomas	1	0	0.0	0
*Jobko	1	0	0.0	0
Totals	11	196	17.8	1

* Not returning.

KICKOFF RETURNS

Player	Number	Yards	Ave.	TD's
*Cassady	10	313	31.3	0
*Williams	1	36	36.0	0
*Harkrader	1	31	31.0	0
Vicic	2	30	15.0	0
Ellwood	2	29	14.5	0
Cisco	1	18	18.0	0
Roseboro	1	17	17.0	0
Michael	1	7	7.0	0
*Collmar	1	0	0.0	0
Totals	20	481	24.0	0

* Not returning.

N.C.A.A. Puts 4 Schools On Probation For Violations

Hayes Acts Bring Bowl Game Ban

CHICAGO, April 26 (P)—Ohio State University, winner of the Big Ten football championship for the last two years, was put on probation for one year by for giving excessive financial assistance to football players.

The principal penalty in the disciplinary action is that Ohio State will not be permitted to represent the Big Ten in the Rose Bowl football game next New Year's Day if the team should qualify by winning the conference title.

Football Coach Woodrow (Woody) Hayes was the main target of the statement issued from Big Ten offices in Chicago by Commissioner Kenneth L. (Tug) Wilson.

"Football Coach Woodrow Hayes has acknowledged assistance to unnamed members of Ohio State football squads from his personal funds in amounts which are said to total approximately $400 annually over a period of five years," Wilson's statement said.

It went on to say Hayes has refused to name the beneficiaries of this assistance.

Unrecorded Aid

"It is represented by him to have been unsystematic and unrecorded aid of a purely personal nature as a result of individuals' appeals based on need and hardship, and that where granted the help was usually understood to be a loan" the statement added.

The document also stated that "a serious irregularity was discovered in the off-campus work program for certain football players."

This program, Wilson said, is administered by the football staff under an agreement with certain Columbus, Ohio, employers.

Wilson said the practice was to make an exception "in New work standards" for some players, while the standards were enforced for other Ohio State athletes.

This was especially true, Wilson said, where the State was the employer.

"In effect," the statement said, "these boys were being advanced monthly wages for either two or three months with no enforceable liability to repay in king or in services."

Wilson said, however, he is satisfied the athletes involved have repaid, or intend to repay over a period time, the wage advances.

No players were declared ineligible or even named in the statement.

However, it did say that "none of the athletes who were beneficiaries of the irregularities in the work program which permitted them to draw pay in advance of performing work therefore shall be presented for eligibility until I have approved satisfactory evidence they have actually repaid fully in services the wages received."

This means, for instance, that such players as Ohio State's all-American Howard (Hopalong) Cassady, a member of the baseball squad as well as others must satisfy the commissioner that he is all up on his work, if an employer has paid him in advance.

The terms of the probation set forth by Wilson:

1. Ohio State cannot under any circumstances represent the Big Ten in the Rose Bowl football game until probation is lifted.
2. The University must supervise the work program of athletes diligently.
3. Coach Hayes must comply with all rules of the Big Ten regarding financial assistance to athletes.

The Big Ten rule on compensation for athletes states:

"No student shall be eligible for athletes states:

"No student shall be eligible who receives compensation from any employer unless, 1. He is performing useful work, 2. He is being paid at the going rate in his locality for the work performed, and 3. He is working on the job all the time for which he is being paid."

The accusation against Ohio State, Wilson said, is that it has been "lax" in enforcing this rule.

"Hayes' teams have won the conference title the last two years and the Rose Bowl in 1954, thumping the University of Southern California, 20 to 7. He came to Ohio State after fine records at Denison and Miami Universities in Ohio.

N.C. STATE'S TEAMS FACE 4-YEAR BAN

Ohio State, California And Southern California Also Hit

Detroit, Nov. 13 (P)—Four major schools were placed on probation tonight by the powerful council of the National Collegiate Athletic Association. Two others were refused reprieves which would permit them to compete in post-season football bowl games.

North Carolina State, Southern California, California and Ohio State drew probations ranging from nine months to four years.

All but California are prohibited from entering athletes or teams in any of the 14 N.C.A.A. sponsored events or 25 co-operating events during the length of the probation.

Ohio State's probation runs until next August 21, Southern California's to July 1, 1958, and California's to next November 13.

The council also voiced support of the Pacific Coast and Big Ten conferences in their previous probationary action against those three schools.

Unauthorized Financial Aid

The N.C.A.A. backed the Big Ten in barring Ohio State from participating in the Rose Bowl game next January 1 after it was revealed that certain athletes had received unauthorized financial aid from "the head football coach" (Woody Hayes).

1956 OHIO STATE FOOTBALL ROSTER
(Alphabetical)

No.	Name	Pos.	Wgt.	Hgt.	Class	Home Town
61	Bailey, Ralph	LG	198	6-0	So.	Springfield
67	*Baldacci, Thomas	LG	195	6-0	Jr.	Akron
38	Ballinger, Gary	FB	180	5-10	So.	Marion
68	Ballmer, Paul	LG	180	5-10	So.	Lancaster
14	Beerman, Raymond	LH	188	5-11	Jr.	Toledo
42	*Bobo, Hubert	B-E	198	6-0	Jr.	Chauncey
87	Bowermaster, Russell	LE	204	6-2	So.	Hamilton
63	Bowsher, Gerald	RG	195	5-10	So.	Toledo
55	Breehl, Edward	C	180	6-0	Jr.	New Philadelphia
85	*Brown, Leo	RE	168	5-10	Jr.	Portsmouth
16	*Cannavino, Joseph	LH	168	5-11	Jr.	Cleveland
36	*Cisco, Galen	FB	204	5-11	Jr.	St. Marys
18	Clark, Donald	LH	191	5-11	So.	Akron
66	Cole, Robert	LG	208	5-10	Sr.	Carey
77	*Cook, Ronald	RT	209	6-1	Jr.	Lima
15	Craig, George	LH	195	6-1	So.	Clairton, Pa.
78	Crawford, Albert	RT	226	6-0	So.	Canton
23	Crawford, Thomas	QB	176	5-11	Jr.	Toledo
73	Cummings, William	LT	242	6-2	Sr.	Toledo
41	Curtis, John	RH	165	5-8	So.	Toledo
50	**Dillman, Thomas	C	208	6-2	Sr.	Middletown
82	Disher, Larry	LE	182	5-11	Jr.	Waterville
24	*Ellwood, Franklin	QB	194	5-11	Sr.	Dover
28	Exline, Robert	QB	182	5-10	So.	Jackson
69	*Facchine, Richard	RG	205	5-9	Jr.	Vandergrift, Pa.
58	Fronk, Daniel	LG	180	5-11	Jr.	Dover
75	**Guy, Richard	RT	214	6-3	Sr.	Mansfield
71	Hammons, Roger	RT	225	6-1	So.	Hamilton
51	Holdren, Richard	RG	198	5-8	Jr.	West Liberty
74	Humbert, Stanley	LT	209	6-2	Sr.	Cincinnati
53	James, Daniel	C	268	6-2	So.	Cincinnati
59	Jones, Herbert	LG	192	5-10	Jr.	Columbus
89	Katula, Theodore	RE	191	6-1	Jr.	Campbell
32	Karow, Robert	FB	180	5-11	Jr.	Columbus
22	Kremblas, Frank	QB	203	6-1	So.	Akron
81	**Kriss, Frederick	LE	187	5-11	Sr.	El Paso, Texas
44	LeBeau, Richard	RH	182	6-0	So.	London
19	Lord, James	RH	177	5-10	So.	Columbus
34	Lord, John	FB	180	5-10	So.	Columbus
30	McCarthy, Patrick	FB	178	6-0	So.	Detroit, Mich.
17	McMurry, Preston	RH	173	5-9	So.	Pittsburgh, Pa.
72	*Martin, John	LT	205	5-11	Jr.	Waverly
79	*Michael, William	T-E	227	6-1	Sr.	Hamilton
57	Miller, Gary	LG	203	6-1	So.	New Philadelphia
88	Morgan, Thomas	RE	196	6-2	So.	Hamilton
70	Nagy, Alex	LT	230	6-2	Jr.	Warren
62	**Parker, James	LG	251	6-3	Sr.	Toledo
37	Peggs, Carl	FB	180	5-9	Jr.	Fostoria
52	Provenza, Russell	C	186	5-11	Jr.	Lorain
49	Richards, David	RH	154	5-9	Jr.	Barnesville
48	Robinson, Philip	RH	180	5-9	So.	Columbus
43	**Roseboro, James	RH	178	5-9	Sr.	Ashland
84	Schafrath, Richard	RE	203	6-2	So.	Wooster
83	Schenking, Fred	LE	204	6-4	So.	Coldwater
54	Sommer, Karl	C	227	6-2	Sr.	Martins Ferry
60	Spychalski, Ernest	RG	243	6-2	So.	Toledo
45	*Sutherin, Donald	LH	198	5-11	Jr.	Toronto
26	*Theis, Franklyn	QB	193	5-10	Jr.	Nyack, N. Y.
64	*Thomas, Aurelius	RG	202	6-1	Jr.	Columbus
46	**Thompson, Kenneth	RH	189	6-0	Sr.	Dayton
86	Trittipo, John	RE	182	6-0	Jr.	Gambier
35	*Trivisonno, Joseph	FB	208	5-11	Jr.	Cleveland
33	**Vicic, Donald	FB	211	6-1	Sr.	Euclid
47	Wable, Robert	RH	167	5-10	Jr.	Sistersville, W. Va.
65	Wassmund, David	RG	205	6-0	Sr.	Toledo
76	Wilson, Clifford	RT	215	6-2	So.	Newcomerstown
80	*Zawacki, Charles	LE	208	6-2	Jr.	Hightstown, Pa.

* Indicates letter.

1956
Captains:
Franklin D. R. Ellwood
P. William Michael

34	*Nebraska	7
32	*Stanford	20
26	Illinois	6
6	*Penn State	7
21	*Wisconsin	0
6	Northwestern	2
35	*Indiana	14
0	Iowa	6
0	*Michigan	19
160		81

Won 6, Lost 3

Jim Parker
Outland Trophy Winner

[1956]

Hawks Cinch To Share 'Big 10' Championship
Crucial 6-0 Victory Over Ohio Sends Iowa To Rose Bowl

IOWA CITY, Iowa, Nov. 17 (P) —Iowa's Hawks soared right into football heaven today with a 6-0 victory over Ohio State for at least a share of the Big Ten championship and a Rose Bowl appearance.

Not since 1922 has an Iowa team shared the title and never has Iowa shown in a bowl game.

The tremendous victory, which sent a crowd of 57,732 slightly mad at the finish gave Iowa a 5-1 Big Ten record. The Hawks would get an undisputed championship if Michigan defeats Ohio State next Saturday.

Pass Brings Score

Ohio State came into the contest with a 4-0 season mark and a record-breaking string of 17 conference victories. But the defending conference champions, shooting for an unprecedented third straight undisputed title were licked by an Iowa squad that refused to lose.

The only score of the bruising battle was a 17-yard pass in the third period from Kenny Ploen to Jim Gibbons just inside the end zone. The touchdown climaxed an Iowa spurt from its 37 after the kickoff.

Iowa got a big lift on a pass interference ruling against halfback Don Clark that landed Iowa on the Ohio State 20. The Hawks made the most of it two plays later on Ploen's arrow-straight throw to Gibbons, the big end.

Iowa was unbeatable after that touchdown. The Iowa defense confined the normally hard-punching Ohio backs, who had rolled up an average of 308 yards a game, to only three first downs in the last half after getting six in the first half.

Spectators Jump Gun

The Buckeyes had only 147 yards by rushing at the finish.

Iowa fans by the hundreds poured onto the field in a confusing ending in which Iowa had driven the desperate Buckeyes back to their three-yard line. The excited Iowans, thinking the game was over, went pell mell for their heroes. Officials managed to restore order, the fans retreated and Ohio State was called for offside. Iowa refused the penalty and the game, the most important in Iowa history, was done.

Iowa   0 0 6 0—6

Iowa scoring — Touchdowns: Gibbons (17, pass from Ploen).

Buckeyes Beaten By Nittany Lions

COLUMBUS, Ohio, Oct. 20 (P) —Penn State knocked much of the luster off Ohio State's Buckeyes today as the three-touchdown underdog Nittany Lions beat the two-time Big Ten champions at their own game and won a 7-6 football victory before a sell-out crowd of 82,584.

It was a game of lost opportunities with all the scoring packed in a thrilling, final four minutes.

Ohio State's vaunted ground attack, which had averaged 333 yards per game in victories over Nebraska, Stanford and Illinois, was held to 188 yards by the stubborn defense of the Easterners.

Ohio, which has featured control ball all season, lost out on that end, too. The Lions held the ball for 75 plays to the Buckeyes' 58.

After three quarters of frustrations, in which Penn State lost the ball three times inside Ohio's 20—twice on pass interceptions and once on a fumble—Penn State struck suddenly late in the fourth.

A 73-yard punt by quarterback Milton Plum died on Ohio's 3, and the Bucks, unable to dig out of the coffin corner, punted to the 45.

Thirteen plays later sophomore Bruce Gilmore banged over from the 1-foot line and Plum converted to give the Lions a 7-0 lead.

The Bucks, noted for their grinding ground assault, took to the airways in the fading minutes and Jimmy Roseboro and Don Clark hit end Leo Brown with consecutive tosses covering 64 yards to the Lions' 3. From there Clark plunged into the end zone.

As the teams lined up for the conversion, Brown dashed back on the field and Ohio was penalized 5 yards for having too many men in play.

Frank Kremblas, sophomore quarterback from Akron, who previously had missed an 18-yard field goal attempt in the second period, booted the conversion try wide of the goalpost. That gave Penn State its big upset.

Penn State   0 0 0 7—7
Ohio State   0 0 0 6—6

Penn State scoring—touchdown: Gilmore (1, plunge). Conversion: Plum.

Ohio State scoring—touchdown: Clark (3, plunge).

1956 TEAM STATISTICS

	First Downs	Rush	Net Gain Pass	Total	Total Plays	Passing Att.	Comp.	Int.	Punting No.	Avg.	Fumbles Lost	Yards Penalized	Points
NEBRASKA	12	185	68	253	62	11	5	3	5	29.4	2	35	7
OHIO STATE	19	416	62	478	72	6	2	0	5	30.0	0	50	34
STANFORD	25	145	269	414	79	39	22	3	4	28.2	1	46	20
OHIO STATE	17	302	18	320	58	2	1	0	4	42.5	0	10	32
ILLINOIS	15	190	99	289	66	14	8	2	4	34.0	2	15	6
OHIO STATE	16	282	29	311	57	3	2	0	3	43.7	0	55	26
PENN STATE	18	173	115	288	75	17	9	2	5	40.8	2	30	7
OHIO STATE	15	188	89	277	58	10	3	2	6	38.7	0	30	6
WISCONSIN	14	202	44	246	66	10	4	1	3	19.7	4	26	0
OHIO STATE	19	293	28	321	72	5	1	1	3	35.7	0	21	21
NORTHWESTERN	10	152	79	231	60	16	9	2	4	41.7	1	100	2
OHIO STATE	11	193	19	212	59	5	2	0	7	28.6	0	15	6
INDIANA	16	142	147	289	49	17	8	3	2	24.0	2	1	14
OHIO STATE	24	465	5	470	78	3	1	0	1	47.0	2	37	35
IOWA	14	176	63	239	63	12	5	0	5	36.0	2	10	6
OHIO STATE	9	147	18	165	61	11	2	0	6	34.0	1	61	0
MICHIGAN	14	127	156	283	68	21	10	2	6	37.7	0	25	19
OHIO STATE	12	182	10	192	59	5	1	2	4	33.8	4	10	0
OPPONENTS	138	1492	1040	2532	588	157	80	18	38	33.7	16	286	81
OHIO STATE	142	2468	278	2746	574	50	15	5	39	35.7	7	288	160

1956 OHIO STATE INDIVIDUAL STATISTICS

RUSHING

Player	Tries	Gain	Lost	Net	Avg.	TD's
Clark	139	824	27	797	5.7	7
*Roseboro	152	754	42	712	4.6	5
Cisco	64	438	0	438	6.8	0
*Ellwood	78	307	53	254	3.3	6
Sutherin	35	124	20	104	2.9	0
*Vicic	21	93	1	92	4.4	0
Robinson	4	23	0	23	5.7	0
Cannavino	8	26	6	20	2.5	0
*Theis	2	12	0	12	6.0	0
Kremblas	10	27	18	9	.9	0
*Bobo	4	12	8	4	1.0	0
LeBeau	7	16	13	3	.4	0
Totals	524	2656	188	2468	4.7	18

FORWARD PASSING

Player	Att.	Comp.	Int.	Yards	Pct.	TD's
Clark	7	3	1	88	.429	1
*Ellwood	20	7	3	86	.350	4
Sutherin	4	2	0	59	.500	0
*Roseboro	11	3	0	45	.273	0
Kremblas	6	0	0	0	.000	0
LeBeau	1	0	0	0	.000	0
*Bobo	1	0	1	0	.000	0
Totals	50	15	5	278	.300	5

PUNTING

Player	Number	Yards	Avg.
Sutherin	14	553	39.5
*Ellwood	23	841	37.2
(Team)	2	0	0.0
Totals	39	1394	35.7

PASS RECEIVING

Player	Number	Yards	TD's
Brown	8	151	2
*Roseboro	4	82	2
*Kriss	1	27	1
Cisco	2	18	0
Totals	15	278	5

SCORING

Player	TD's	PAT Att.	PAT Made	Total
Clark	7	0	0	42
*Roseboro	7	0	0	42
*Ellwood	6	4	3	39
Brown	3	0	0	18
*Kriss	1	11	7	13
Kremblas	0	8	5	5
Sutherin	0	1	1	1
Totals	24	24	16	160

PUNT RETURNS

Player	Number	Yards	Avg.	TD's
*Roseboro	5	26	5.2	0
Brown	1	18	18.0	1
*Vicic	2	9	4.5	0
Clark	2	9	4.5	0
*Ellwood	3	5	1.7	0
Sutherin	1	0	0.0	0
Totals	14	67	4.8	1

INTERCEPTION RETURNS

Player	Number	Yards	Avg.	TD's
Clark	1	35	35.0	0
*Roseboro	2	16	8.0	0
Cisco	1	14	14.0	0
Sutherin	3	13	4.3	0
*Ellwood	2	11	5.5	0
Cannavino	1	11	11.0	0
*Dillman	3	10	3.3	0
*Vicic	1	7	7.0	0
Bowermaster	2	6	3.0	0
Morgan	1	2	2.0	0
*Bobo	1	1	1.0	0
Totals	18	126	7.0	0

KICKOFF RETURNS

Player	Number	Yards	Avg.	TD's
Clark	7	165	23.6	0
*Roseboro	4	87	21.7	0
*Ellwood	4	66	16.5	0
Sutherin	1	0	0.0	0
*Parker	1	0	0.0	0
Totals	17	318	18.7	0

SCORE BY QUARTERS

	1	2	3	4	—T
Opponents	27	7	27	20	81
Ohio State	53	41	20	46	160

* Not returning for 1957

1957 OHIO STATE FOOTBALL ROSTER
(Alphabetical)

No.	Name	Pos.	Wgt.	Hgt.	Class	Home Town
66	Anders, Richard	LG	180	5-8	So.	Washington C.H.
74	Arnold, Birtho	RT	269	6-2	So.	Columbus
61	Bailey, Ralph	RG	198	6-0	Jr.	Springfield
67	**Baldacci, Thomas	RG	200	6-0	Sr.	Akron
41	Ballinger, Gerry	LH	178	5-10	Jr.	Marion
28	Ballmer, Paul	QB	186	5-10	Jr.	Lancaster
50	Beam, William	C	197	6-1	So.	Moundsville, W.Va.
14	Beerman, Raymond	LH	191	5-11	Sr.	Toledo
87	*Bowermaster, Russell	LE	202	6-2	Jr.	Hamilton
63	Bowsher, Gerald	LG	198	5-10	Jr.	Toledo
55	Breehl, Edward	C	192	6-0	Sr.	New Philadelphia
85	**Brown, Leo (CC)	RE	171	5-10	Sr.	Portsmouth
69	Bryant, Eugene	LT	222	6-2	So.	Ironton
16	**Cannavino, Joseph	LH	172	5-11	Sr.	Cleveland
43	Carr, Leroy	RH	186	6-1	So.	Portsmouth
36	**Cisco, Galen (CC)	FB	203	5-11	Sr.	St. Marys
18	*Clark, Donald	LH	191	5-11	Jr.	Akron
77	*Cook, Ronald	RT	204	6-1	Sr.	Lima
62	Cowans, Leroy	RG	207	5-10	So.	Cleveland
78	*Crawford, Albert	LT	228	6-0	Jr.	Canton
23	Crawford, Thomas	QB	178	5-11	So.	Toledo
54	Crowl, Don	C	216	5-11	So.	Malvern
82	Disher, Larry	RE	182	5-11	Sr.	Waterville
46	Dresser, John	RH	192	6-1	So.	Toledo
51	Fields, Jerry	C	206	6-1	So.	Coal Grove
58	Fronk, Daniel	C	189	5-11	Jr.	Dover
30	Gage, Ralph	FB	174	5-10	Jr.	Painesville
84	Houston, James	LE	216	6-2	So.	Massillon
53	*James, Daniel	C	258	6-2	Jr.	Cincinnati
65	**Jobko, William	LG	212	6-1	Sr.	Lansing
59	*Jones, Herbert	LG	192	5-10	Sr.	Columbus
89	Katula, Theodore	LE	193	6-1	Sr.	Campbell
19	Kilgore, David	PK	160	5-9	So.	Dayton
79	Kreakbaum, Thomas	LT	233	6-0	So.	Akron
22	*Kremblas, Frank	QB	198	6-1	Jr.	Akron
44	*LeBeau, Richard	LH	183	6-0	Jr.	London
81	Lord, John	LE	177	5-10	Jr.	Columbus
76	Marshall, James	RT	232	6-3	So.	Columbus
72	**Martin, John	RT	214	5-11	Sr.	Waverly
68	Matz, James	RT	222	6-0	So.	Chillicothe
17	McMurray, Preston	RH	178	5-9	Jr.	Pittsburgh, Pa.
86	Michael, Richard	LE	221	6-2	So.	Hamilton
42	Moran, John	RH	186	5-10	So.	Bellevue
88	*Morgan, Thomas	RE	202	6-2	Jr.	Hamilton
70	Nagy, Alex	LT	230	6-2	Sr.	Warren
25	Okulovich, Andy	QB	188	5-11	Jr.	Cleveland
32	Provenza, Russell	FB	186	5-11	Sr.	Lorain
48	*Robinson, Philip	RH	176	5-9	Jr.	Columbus
92	Rowland, James	LE	200	6-4	So.	Beckley, W.Va.
21	Samuels, James	QB	186	6-0	So.	Eaton
71	*Schafrath, Richard	LT	216	6-2	Jr.	Wooster
83	Schenking, Fred	RE	206	6-4	Jr.	Coldwater
75	Schram, Bruce	RT	206	6-0	So.	Massillon
57	Seilkop, Kenneth	LT	202	5-11	So.	Columbus
60	*Spychalski, Ernest	RG	248	6-2	Jr.	Toledo
45	**Sutherin, Donald	RH	194	5-11	Sr.	Toronto
64	**Thomas, Aurelius	RG	204	6-1	Sr.	Columbus
35	*Trivisonno, Joseph	FB	214	5-11	Sr.	Cleveland
24	Vitatoe, Ronald	QB	186	6-0	So.	Hamilton
73	Wagner, David	LT	234	6-2	So.	Portsmouth
15	Wentz, William	LH	176	5-11	So.	Canton
33	White, Robert	FB	207	6-2	So.	Covington, Ky.
80	*Zawacki, Charles	RE	208	6-2	Sr.	Uniontown, Pa.
47	Zuhars, David	LH	178	6-1	So.	Columbus

* Indicates letter.

76—MARSHALL, James, 19, 6-3, 232, sophomore . . . from Columbus . . . the tackle with the most potential on last year's freshman team . . . has an unusual combination of speed, agility and strength . . . is a great shot put specialist in track, when, without any practice, tossed the discus 150 feet to win the 1957 Ohio Relays event . . . majoring in physical education . . . will start the 1957 football season as a third stringer, but could finish as a regular . . . ambition is to coach football . . . high school coach, Ralph Webster, compares Marshall favorably with Bill Willis, another East High and Buckeye great . . .

1957
Captains: Galen B. Cisco
Leo M. Brown

14	*Texas Christian	18
35	Washington	7
21	*Illinois	7
56	*Indiana	0
16	Wisconsin	13
47	*Northwestern	6
20	*Purdue	7
17	*Iowa	13
31	Michigan	14
10	†Oregon	7
267		92

Won 9, Lost 1
Big Ten Champions
† Rose Bowl

A.P. POLL	U.P.I. POLL
1. Auburn	1. OHIO STATE
2. OHIO STATE	2. Auburn
3. Michigan State	3. Michigan State
4. Oklahoma	4. Oklahoma
5. Navy	5. Iowa
6. Iowa	6. Navy
7. Mississippi	7. Rice
8. Rice	8. Mississippi
9. Texas A. & M.	9. Notre Dame
10. Notre Dame	10. Texas A. & M.

T.C.U. SETS BACK OHIO STATE, 18-14

Texas Eleven Rallies Twice—Shofner Returns Punt 90 Yards to Score

STATISTICS OF THE GAME

	T.C.U.	Ohio St.
First downs	15	17
Rushing yardage	184	242
Passing yardage	0	20
Passes attempted	3	3
Passes completed	0	2
Passes intercepted by	0	1
Punts	4	5
Av. dist. of punts, yds.	38	35
Fumbles lost	1	2
Yards penalized	20	19

Ohio State's only loss

Texas Christian .... 6 6 6 0—18
Ohio State .... 0 7 7 0—14
  Texas Christian scoring—Touchdowns: Lasater (7 run), Shofner (90 punt return), Spikes (8 run).
  Ohio State scoring—Touchdowns: Lebeau (2 run), Clark (2 plunge). Conversions: Sutherin 2.

GRANDEUR OF THE GREAT HORSESHOE STADIUM IS REFLECTED IN THIS UNUSUAL VIEW FROM A SEAT LOCATED HIGH IN C-DECK.

Ohio State Victor Over Michigan

OHIO LINEMEN OPEN A GAPING HOLE IN THE PURDUE FORWARD WALL AS BOB WHITE DRIVES.

ANN ARBOR, Mich., Nov. 23 (ℙ) — Ohio State's bowl-bound Buckeyes overcame gallant but outgunned Michigan 31-14 today in a tense Big Ten football struggle witnessed by 101,001 spectators who saw the powerful Buckeyes gallop to their third perfect conference record in four seasons.

Twice the Ohio team had to come from behind to win this tradition-packed duel and only because of the Bucks' superior second half power were they able to roll up their eighth straight triumph.

Ohio's stout defense rallied from a 14-10 halftime deficit and blanked Michigan the rest of the way for victory, which always has been so elusive on Michigan ground.

Sophomore fullback Bob White, whose relentless line smashes wore down Iowa a week ago for the victory that sent the Buckeyes to the Rose Bowl, was just as outstanding against Michigan although the 207-pound bulldozer never scored.

Late Fumbles Costly

Two costly fumbles and a pass interception in the late stages helped crush the Wolverines, who since 1937 had lost to Ohio teams only once before on home ground.

Playing the same type of ground-eating ball control offense that has carried them to 24 victories in 26 Big Ten games over four seasons, the Buckeyes blasted Michigan's upset hopes in almost methodical fashion.

They swept to a pair of third-period touchdowns and added another score in the final period while crushing every Michigan comeback try.

Officials had to stop the drama-packed contest in the final three minutes as enthusiastic Ohio supporters tried to rip down the Michigan goal posts.

Halfback Jim Pace, winding up a brilliant career at Michigan, was his team's whole offense and tried gamely to keep the Wolverines in the contest. He scored one touchdown and won the individual scoring championship from Ohio's Don Clark, who stayed on the sidelines today with a groin injury.

Michigan Scores Early

Michigan's miracle men stunned Ohio in the early going with two touchdowns.

The first one came in the first six minutes. Pace set it up with a 23-yard run and romped over from the 16. The Buckeyes charged back with a 70-yard drive all on the ground with junior halfback Dick Le Beau scoring from the five. Ohio went ahead on Don Sutherin's second-period field goal from the Michigan 29. But the Wolverines fought back with a sparkling 75-yard assault that took only three plays.

Pace went 46 yards on an old-fashioned double reverse and quarterback Jim Van Pelt passed 25 yards to halfback Brad Myers for the score.

58-Yard Drive

Ohio never lost its poise and marched 58 yards with the third period kickoff for the tie-breaking touchdown. Quarterback Frank Kremblas kept the drive alive with a fourth down fake pass that gained 10 yards.

Le Beau went eight yards for this touchdown. Fullback White recovered a Michigan fumble on the Buckeye 33 and personally led the touchdown drive that followed. It took 14 plays, including another fourth-down gamble by Kremblas, who skirted end for the final 16 yards.

Ohio used Kremblas' pass interception to spring a 72-yard touchdown drive in the final period. It was Mike Cannavino who scored the touchdown on a 13-yard lateral from Kremblas.

O.S.U.   7 3 14 7—31
Michigan   7 7 0 0—14

Ohio State scoring — Touchdowns: LeBeau 2 (5, run; 8, run); Kremblas (16, run); Cannavino (13, lateral from Kremblas). Field goal: Sutherin (32). Conversions: Sutherin, Kremblas 3.

Michigan scoring — Touchdowns: Pace (16, run); Myers (25, pass-run from Van Pelt). Conversions: Van Pelt 2.

Ohio State Turns Back Oregon In Rose Bowl, 10-7

FIELD GOAL OF 34 YARDS BREAKS TIE

Webfoots Not Forced To Punt; 98,202 Jam Bowl

Pasadena, Cal., Jan. 1 (AP)—An under-rated University of Oregon team yielded to a mauling Ohio State Buckeye eleven in the final period today and the Big Ten champions got away with a 10-7 victory in the Rose Bowl.

The Buckeyes, favored by three touchdowns over the lighter but faster Webfoots, broke a 7-7 tie early in the fourth quarter when Don Sutherin kicked a field goal with the ball traveling 34 yards.

The kick, which came with the ball on the 17-yard line of scrimmage mark and held on the 24, was the difference in a game that was amazing for its closeness.

No Oregon Punts

The Buckeyes had traveled 80 yards, with their sophomore fullback star, Bob White, smashing the Oregon line in nine of the 14 plays for a gain of 49 yards to set the stage for the winning field goal.

Oddly enough, Oregon did not punt a single time, while Ohio State punted only twice. Both Buckeye punts were short ones. It was the first time all year that Oregon did not punt.

A crowd of 98,202 jammed the famous bowl on one of the nicest, balmiest days in the history of the game.

The fans gave the underdog Oregon squad a tremendous hand for a gallant game as the final gun sounded.

Webfoots Battle Back

This was Oregon's first appearance in the Tournament of Roses since 1920 and since the Ducks were considered so far outclassed by Ohio State off their respective season records, they were the sentimental favorites.

Ohio State scored the first time they got the ball on the opening kickoff, driving 79 yards with Quarterback Frank Kremblas making the final yard and kicking the extra point.

The Webfoots battled back in the second quarter with an 80-yard drive that ended in a touchdown when Right Halfback Jim Shanley scored on a 5-yard play.

Fullback Jack Morris's place kick for the conversion tied the score at 7-7 and the two teams rocked and socked through a scoreless third quarter.

Fumbles Hurt Losers

The result was the eleventh triumph for the Big Ten against one victory by the Pacific Coast Conference since the present series was inaugurated in 1947.

This was the third victory for Ohio State in the Big Ten-P.C.C. series and the second for the Buckeyes' present coach, Woody Hayes.

Ohio State had too many troops but a pair of Oregon fumbles and two pass interceptions by Ohio State were major errors which hurt Coach Len Casanova's Webfoots.

Buckeyes' Hayes 'Coach of Year'

New York, Dec. 7 (AP)—Woody Hayes, coach of Ohio State's Big Ten champion football team, today was winner of the National Football Writers' Assn., designation as the coach of the year. It is the first time the writers' group has named the year's outstanding coach.

Five hundred and 70 writers participated in the nationwide poll and 122 voted for the Buckeye's mentor, whose team will represent the Big Ten in the Jan. 1 Rose Bowl clash with Oregon.

Terry Brennan, young Notre Dame coach, was second with 99 first place votes and Ralph (Shug) Jordan of Auburn's unbeaten team, was third with 74. Thirty-seven coaches received first place votes.

[1957]

1957 TEAM STATISTICS

	First Downs	Rush	Net Gain Pass	Total	Total Plays	Passing Att.	Comp.	Int.	Punting No.	Avg.	Fumbles No.	Lost	Yards Penalized	Points
TEXAS CHRISTIAN	15	184	0	184	57	3	0	1	4	38.7	3	1	20	18
OHIO STATE	17	242	20	262	65	3	2	0	5	35.2	3	2	19	14
WASHINGTON	8	161	60	221	51	8	3	0	6	20.2	4	3	62	7
OHIO STATE	20	290	63	353	73	12	7	0	2	45.5	1	0	60	35
ILLINOIS	16	120	208	328	51	18	12	1	1	28.0	5	2	8	7
OHIO STATE	23	299	26	325	85	9	3	0	2	34.0	1	0	5	21
INDIANA	6	24	122	146	47	21	9	5	2	39.5	9	4	55	0
OHIO STATE	24	392	66	458	87	13	8	0	1	41.0	6	1	39	56
WISCONSIN	16	271	3	274	70	3	1	1	4	45.0	3	3	5	13
OHIO STATE	8	203	48	251	53	4	3	0	6	30.8	3	1	10	16
NORTHWESTERN	16	157	125	282	64	19	10	2	4	41.2	4	3	55	6
OHIO STATE	24	386	111	497	66	8	5	0	1	22.0	1	1	27	47
PURDUE	16	173	121	294	76	19	10	1	4	45.0	7	1	10	7
OHIO STATE	14	202	25	227	52	3	2	0	8	44.2	3	3	25	20
IOWA	18	155	94	249	53	16	9	3	1	50.0	5	3	5	13
OHIO STATE	18	295	37	332	67	11	2	1	5	39.6	2	0	45	17
MICHIGAN	16	270	107	377	54	12	5	1	2	46.5	3	2	6	14
OHIO STATE	19	372	49	421	79	9	3	0	4	31.2	0	0	21	31
OREGON	21	160	191	351	63	21	14	2	0	.0	3	2	25	7
OHIO STATE	19	245	59	304	67	6	2	0	2	19.0	0	0	15	10
OPPONENTS	148	1675	1031	2706	586	140	73	17	28	37.5	46	24	251	92
OHIO STATE	186	2926	504	3430	694	78	37	1	36	36.0	21	10	266	267

1957 OHIO STATE INDIVIDUAL STATISTICS
(Includes Rose Bowl)

RUSHING

Player	Tries	Gain	Lost	Net	Avg.	TD's
Clark	132	760	23	737	5.6	8
White	114	657	12	645	5.6	1
LeBeau	85	384	24	360	4.2	7
*Cisco	70	356	6	350	5.0	2
*Trivisonno	34	275	0	275	8.1	2
Kremblas	79	302	64	238	3.0	8
*Cannavino	39	208	10	198	5.1	3
*Sutherin	26	95	20	75	2.9	0
Robinson	9	33	2	31	3.4	0
Dresser	2	7	0	7	3.5	0
*Carr	2	6	0	6	3.0	0
*Ballinger	2	6	0	6	3.0	0
*Zuhars	5	9	5	4	.8	0
Samuels	1	4	0	4	4.0	0
*Provenza	1	4	0	4	4.0	0
Gage	1	3	0	3	3.0	0
*T. Crawford	1	2	0	2	2.0	0
*Okulovich	13	26	45	-19	-1.5	1
Totals	616	3137	211	2926	4.7	32

FORWARD PASSING

Player	Att.	Comp.	Int.	Yards	Pct.	TD's
Kremblas	47	20	1	337	.425	3
*Okulovich	12	7	0	94	.583	0
Clark	6	5	0	51	.833	1
LeBeau	5	2	0	12	.400	0
Wentz	1	1	0	7	1.000	0
*Zuhars	1	1	0	3	1.000	0
*T. Crawford	4	1	0	0	.250	0
*Sutherin	1	0	0	0	.000	0
Dresser	1	0	0	0	.000	0
Totals	78	37	1	504	.474	4

PUNTING

Player	Number	Yards	Avg.
Kremblas	25	929	37.2
*Sutherin	10	345	34.5
*Trivisonno	1	22	22.0
Totals	36	1296	36.0

SCORE BY QUARTERS

	1	2	3	4	—T
Opponents	32	27	27	6	92
Ohio State	71	74	63	59	267

* Not returning for 1958

SCORING

Player	TD's	PAT Att.	PAT Made	FG	Total
Kremblas	8	9	7	0	55
Clark	9	0	0	0	54
LeBeau	8	0	0	0	48
*Sutherin	2	20	18	4	42
*Cannavino	4	1	0	0	24
*Cisco	2	0	0	0	12
*Trivisonno	2	0	0	0	12
White	1	0	0	0	6
*Okulovich	1	0	0	0	6
Spychalski	0	3	3	1	6
Kilgore	0	4	2	0	2
Totals	37	37	30	5	267

PASS RECEIVING

Player	Number	Yards	TD's
Houston	4	126	1
LeBeau	7	91	1
*Brown	7	83	0
Clark	5	63	1
*Cannavino	3	49	0
Bowermaster	3	38	0
*Sutherin	2	19	1
Morgan	1	11	0
Michael	1	9	0
Robinson	1	7	0
Dresser	1	5	0
*Ballinger	1	3	0
*Zuhars	1	0	0
Totals	37	504	3

PUNT RETURNS

Player	Number	Yards	Avg.	TD's
*Sutherin	4	96	24.0	1
Clark	5	65	13.0	0
*Cannavino	5	50	10.0	0
LeBeau	4	18	4.5	0
*Brown	1	0	.0	0
Totals	19	229	12.0	1

INTERCEPTION RETURNS

Player	Number	Yards
*Cannavino	3	46
LeBeau	2	19
*Okulovich	2	12
Kremblas	2	0
*Brown	1	29
White	1	21
*Provenza	1	8
*Baldacci	1	4
Robinson	1	3
*Cisco	1	0
*Jobko	1	0
McMurry	1	0
Totals	17	142

KICKOFF RETURNS

Player	Number	Yards
LeBeau	6	134
Clark	6	107
*Cannavino	4	88
Kremblas	2	39
*Sutherin	2	32
White	2	26
*Cisco	1	12
*Trivisonno	1	6
Totals	24	444

[1958]

1958 OHIO STATE FOOTBALL ROSTER
(Alphabetical)

No.	Name	Pos.	Wgt.	Hgt.	Age	Class	Home Town
26	Adulewicz, Casimir	QB	177	5-9	22	Jr.	Steubenville
56	Altomare, Louis	LG	196	6-0	18	So.	Leetonia
66	Anders, Richard	C	180	5-9	20	Jr.	Washington, C.H.
37	Armstrong, Jack	FB	203	6-0	19	So.	Huron
68	*Arnold, Birtho	RT	290	6-2	19	Jr.	Columbus
85	Azok, Frank	RE	187	6-2	20	So.	Lorain
61	Bailey, Ralph	RG	198	6-0	26	Sr.	Springfield
28	Ballmer, Paul	QB	186	5-10	21	Sr.	Lancaster
50	Beam, William	C	197	6-1	19	Jr.	Moundsville, W.Va.
25	Benis, Michael	QB	184	6-0	19	So.	Columbus
87	**Bowermaster, Russell	RE	202	6-2	22	Sr.	Hamilton
64	Bowsher, Jerry	LG	198	5-10	21	Jr.	Toledo
69	Bryant, Gene	RG	222	6-2	20	So.	Ironton
18	**Clark, Donald	LH	191	5-11	21	Sr.	Akron
78	**Crawford, Albert	RT	234	6-0	22	Sr.	Canton
89	Deyo, Charles	RE	204	6-2	20	So.	Columbus
46	Dresser, John	FB	192	6-1	20	Jr.	Toledo
36	Emelianchik, Robert	FB	206	5-11	20	Jr.	Brooklyn, N.Y.
35	Farrall, John	FB	210	5-11	19	So.	Canton
24	Fields, Jerry	QB	203	6-1	20	So.	Coal Grove
80	Fiers, Alan	RE	202	6-1	19	So.	Indianapolis, Ind.
34	Fontes, Leonard	FB	176	5-8	21	Jr.	Wareham, Mass.
58	*Fronk, Daniel	C	186	5-11	22	Sr.	Dover
30	Gage, Ralph	FB	178	5-10	23	Sr.	Painesville
43	German, William	RH	182	5-10	19	So.	Shaker Heights
67	Hartman, Gabriel	LG	211	5-9	19	So.	Troy
65	Hauer, Oscar	LG	212	6-2	19	So.	Hamilton
45	Herbstreit, James	LH	166	5-8	19	So.	Reading
90	Herrmann, Harvey	RT	220	6-2	19	Jr.	Cincinnati
84	*Houston, James	LE	216	6-2	20	Jr.	Massillon
53	**James, Daniel	LG	235	6-2	21	Sr.	Cincinnati
72	Jentes, Charles	LT	205	6-2	18	So.	Wooster
19	Kilgore, David	PK	164	5-9	20	Jr.	Dayton
22	**Kremblas, Frank	QB	196	6-1	21	Sr.	Akron
91	Langermeier, George	RE	192	6-0	20	So.	Cleveland
44	**LeBeau, Richard	RH	182	6-0	21	Sr.	London
70	Leshner, Robert	LT	218	5-11	19	So.	Hamilton
32	Lindner, James	FB	198	5-10	19	So.	Enon Valley, Pa.
81	Lord, John	RE	181	5-10	20	Sr.	Columbus
76	*Marshall, James	RT	232	6-3	20	Jr.	Columbus
59	Martin, James	LG	208	5-11	24	So.	Columbus
41	Matte, Thomas	LH	190	6-0	19	So.	East Cleveland
74	Matz, James	LT	215	6-1	20	Jr.	Chillicothe
17	McMurry, Preston	LH	178	5-9	22	Sr.	Pittsburgh, Pa.
86	Michael, Richard	LE	221	6-2	19	Jr.	Hamilton
88	**Morgan, Thomas	RE	200	6-2	21	Sr.	Hamilton
48	**Robinson, Philip	RH	184	5-9	21	Sr.	Columbus
92	Rowland, James	LE	207	6-4	21	Jr.	Beckley, W. Va.
71	**Schafrath, Richard	LT	216	6-2	21	Sr.	Wooster
83	Schenking, Fred	RE	208	6-4	21	Sr.	Coldwater
75	Schram, Bruce	RT	211	6-0	22	Sr.	Massillon
57	Seilkop, Kenneth	LG	202	5-11	20	Jr.	Columbus
60	**Spychalski, Ernest	RG	242	6-2	22	Sr.	Toledo
82	Tidmore, Samuel	LE	208	6-0	19	So.	Cleveland
77	Tyrer, James	LT	251	6-5	19	So.	Newark
51	Varner, Thomas	C	193	5-10	19	So.	Saginaw, Mich.
55	Vogelgesang, Don	C	190	6-0	20	So.	Canton
73	Wagner, David	LT	234	6-2	21	Jr.	Portsmouth
15	Wentz, Williams	RH	176	5-10	20	Jr.	Canton
79	Whitaker, Larry	RT	222	6-1	18	So.	St. Johns
33	*White, Robert	FB	212	6-2	20	Jr.	Covington, Ky.
42	*Williams, Lee	LH	178	5-10	24	Sr.	Springfield
63	Wright, Ernest	RG	248	6-3	18	So.	Toledo
62	Young, Don	LG	207	6-0	20	So.	Dayton

* Indicates Letter

Jim Marshall

Thomas Matte

41—MATTE, Thomas, 19, 6-0, 190, sophomore . . . from East Cleveland . . . an ideal split-T back, even though he was a tailback in high school . . . was an outstanding high school athlete, being all-Ohio in football, qualifying for the state high school track meet two years, and was an all-league basketball player two years . . . captained his high school football and basketball teams . . . of French-Canadian ancestry . . . hobbies are hockey and baseball . . . works as an apprentice millwright during the summer . . . enrolled in the College of Commerce, majoring in general business . . . his top football thrill came in high school, when he took the opening kickoff and ran 100 yards for a score . . . will likely be used at left halfback this year . . .

A.P. POLL	U.P.I. POLL
1. L.S.U.	1. L.S.U.
2. Iowa	2. Iowa
3. Army	3. Army
4. Auburn	4. Auburn
5. Oklahoma	5. Oklahoma
6. Air Force	6. Wisconsin
7. Wisconsin	7. OHIO STATE
8. OHIO STATE	8. Air Force
9. Syracuse	9. T.C.U.
10. T.C.U.	10. Syracuse

1958
Captains:
Francis T. Kremblas
Richard P. Schafrath

23	*Southern Methodist	20
12	*Washington	7
19	Illinois	13
49	*Indiana	8
7	*Wisconsin	7
0	Northwestern	21
14	*Purdue	14
38	Iowa	28
20	*Michigan	14
182		132

Won 6, Lost 1, Tied 2

Ohio State Subdues Illinois Team, 19-13, Halting Late Drive

By the Associated Press.

CHAMPAIGN, Ill., Oct. 11 — Undefeated Ohio State scored twice in the third quarter and put down a last-minute Illinois rally today to slip through to a 19-13 Big Ten victory.

Trailing 19-6 in the last quarter, Illinois' Bob Hickey came off the bench, threw one touchdown pass and sparked another drive that almost led to a touchdown.

Bob White dives over for the clinching touchdown against Iowa.

BUCKS TIE WISCONSIN

Playing before a record-breaking Homecoming crowd of 83,412, the Bucks and Wisconsin dueled to a 7-7 tie. Fighting back after a 64-yard touchdown punt return by Wisconsin's Dale Hackbart, the Buckeyes drove 65 yards with fullback Bob White carrying the ball for thirty of those precious yards. The Bucks were aided on this score-tying drive by a pair of "breaks." One of these was a diving recovery of a fumble by Jimmy Herbstreit, who literally stole the pigskin from two Wisconsin defenders. The other was a holding penalty called against the Badgers which put the ball on the one foot line. Bob White plunged over for the score.

STATE UPSETS IOWA

Playing the role of spoilers, the Buckeyes exploded Iowa's dream of an undefeated season and a possible National Championship with a stunning 38-28 upset of the Hawkeyes at Iowa City. Bob White ground out 206 yards, including a 71 yard touchdown gallop. Don Clark added 152 yards with scoring runs of 25 and 37 yards. This, coupled with Dave Kilgore's seven conversions and game-clinching field goal, was enough to top the offensive-minded Hawkeyes who matched the Buckeyes touchdown for touchdown until the final quarter. Jerry Fields, engineering his team like a veteran, did an outstanding job in only his second start.

GRIDMEN TIE PURDUE

The combination of end Jimmy Houston and tackle Jim Marshall for two touchdowns in the first half wasn't enough to hold a determined Boilermaker team. Purdue roared back in the second half to tie the Bucks, 14-14. The heroics of Houston, who blocked a Purdue punt and deflected a pass, and Marshall, who recovered the blocked punt and intercepted the deflected pass to turn both into touchdowns, were bright spots for the Bucks on an otherwise gloomy day at Buckeye Stadium. The second half was all Purdue, as State's offense failed again to score from scrimmage for the second consecutive Saturday.

BUCKS TAME WOLVES

Overcoming a dangerous Wolverine passing attack, the Buckeyes downed an inspired Michigan team by a 20-14 score. The Wolves scored first on a Ptacek to Prahst pass, but the Bucks tallied the equalizer on a seven yard touchdown run by Richard Lebeau. Michigan again took the lead on another touchdown pass by Ptacek. Jerry Fields then struck on a twenty-five yard scoring pass to Jim Herbstreit which left Michigan leading 14-12. In the third period the Buckeyes marched eighty yards to score the winning touchdown with Bob White, an All-American candidate, plunging over to score his twelfth touchdown of the season.

[1958]

1958 TEAM STATISTICS

	First Downs	Rush	Net Gain Pass	Total	Total Plays	Passing Att.	Comp.	Int.	Punting No.	Avg.	Fumbles No.	Lost	Yards Penalized	Points
SOUTHERN METHODIST	18	129	233	362	53	31	21	2	2	42.5	1	0	81	20
OHIO STATE	18	209	78	287	69	9	6	0	4	34.5	1	0	45	23
WASHINGTON	14	174	93	267	73	31	12	3	7	32.3	5	2	75	7
OHIO STATE	10	183	13	196	63	3	2	0	13	29.8	3	0	86	12
ILLINOIS	11	119	102	221	53	21	7	1	6	34.2	3	1	25	13
OHIO STATE	16	246	44	290	71	9	4	1	4	35.5	1	0	50	19
INDIANA	8	125	44	169	53	17	5	3	7	40.9	6	4	114	8
OHIO STATE	19	236	150	386	76	8	5	0	5	33.0	3	3	61	49
WISCONSIN	12	182	45	227	56	8	3	1	4	28.0	2	1	10	7
OHIO STATE	18	208	13	221	67	3	1	0	4	36.2	3	1	5	7
NORTHWESTERN	14	234	122	356	65	10	5	0	6	37.3	5	2	35	21
OHIO STATE	9	156	51	207	62	14	2	1	7	37.3	1	0	15	0
PURDUE	22	161	213	374	83	30	13	4	3	24.0	0	0	36	14
OHIO STATE	11	165	15	180	51	5	1	1	5	40.0	3	3	15	14
IOWA	22	178	249	427	72	33	22	1	2	37.0	4	3	25	28
OHIO STATE	16	397	65	462	59	2	1	0	1	15.0	1	1	20	38
MICHIGAN	24	118	258	376	76	39	25	2	4	37.5	4	4	40	14
OHIO STATE	12	187	75	262	61	10	5	1	5	42.2	1	1	5	20
OPPONENTS	145	1420	1359	2779	584	220	113	17	41	35.0	30	17	441	132
OHIO STATE	129	1987	504	2491	579	63	27	4	48	34.7	17	9	302	182

1958 OHIO STATE INDIVIDUAL STATISTICS

RUSHING

Player	Tries	Gain	Lost	Net	Avg.	TD's
White	218	859	0	859	3.9	12
*Clark	114	613	31	582	5.1	6
*Kremblas	56	241	22	219	3.9	0
*LeBeau	48	170	7	163	3.4	1
Herbstreit	13	54	0	54	4.1	1
Fontes	13	49	0	49	3.8	1
Fields	28	68	38	30	1.1	1
*Williams	6	21	0	21	3.5	0
Lindner	3	15	0	15	5.0	0
*Gage	7	17	8	9	1.3	0
*Dresser	2	5	0	5	2.5	0
Benis	1	3	0	3	3.0	0
Matte	5	5	9	−4	−.8	0
Adulewicz	1	0	5	−5	−5.0	0
(Team)	1	0	13	−13		
Totals	516	2120	133	1987	3.8	22

FORWARD PASSING

Player	Att.	Comp.	Int.	Yards	Pct.	TD's
*Kremblas	42	16	3	281	.381	0
Fields	18	9	1	171	.500	1
*Gage	3	2	0	52	.667	1
Totals	63	27	4	504	.428	2

SCORING

Player	TD's	Conv. Att. R.	P.	K.	Conv. Made R.	P.	K.	FG	Total
White	12	1	0	0	0	0	0	0	72
*Clark	6	0	0	0	0	0	0	0	36
Kilgore	0	0	0	17	0	0	15	1	18
*Marshall	2	0	0	0	0	0	0	0	12
Herbstreit	2	0	0	0	0	0	0	0	12
*LeBeau	1	0	0	0	0	2	0	0	10
Fields	1	2	1	0	1	0	0	0	8
*Tidmore	1	0	0	0	0	0	0	0	6
Fontes	1	0	0	0	0	0	0	0	6
*Kremblas	0	0	2	2	0	0	1	0	1
*Spychalski	0	0	0	1	0	0	1	0	1
Totals	26	3	3	20	1	2	17	1	182

PUNTING

Player	Number	Yards	Avg.
*Kremblas	27	964	35.7
White	11	383	34.8
*Bowermaster	10	318	31.8
Totals	48	1665	34.7

PASS RECEIVING

Player	Number	Yards	TD's
Houston	4	127	0
*Clark	8	110	0
*LeBeau	8	110	0
Schafrath	3	83	0
*Bowermaster	2	33	0
*Tidmore	1	26	1
Herbstreit	1	25	1
Totals	27	504	2

INTERCEPTION RETURNS

Player	Number	Yards	Avg.	TD's
*LeBeau	4	48	12.0	0
White	3	42	14.0	0
*Kremblas	3	1	.3	0
*Bowermaster	1	45	45.0	0
Matte	1	36	36.0	0
*Marshall	1	25	25.0	1
Fontes	1	2	2.0	0
Banis	1	1	1.0	0
*Fronk	1	0	0.0	0
Herbstreit	1	0	0.0	0
Totals	17	200	11.2	1

PUNT RETURNS

Player	Number	Yards
*LeBeau	6	57
†Marshall	1	30
Matte	4	30
*Clark	1	23
Herbstreit	2	16
Houston	1	13
Gage	1	11
Haver	1	10
*Williams	1	2
Totals	17	192

KICKOFF RETURNS

Player	Number	Yards
*Clark	8	181
*Kremblas	4	88
*LeBeau	4	85
Herbstreit	2	46
*Williams	1	21
White	1	15
*Schafrath	1	12
Houston	1	7
Fontes	1	0
Totals	23	455

† Scored a touchdown after blocked punt.
* Not returning for 1959.

SCORE BY QUARTERS

	1	2	3	4	—T
Opponents	20	42	21	49	132
Ohio State	48	47	57	30	182

ILLINOIS DEFEATS OHIO STATE, 9 TO 0

Buckeyes Blanked for 2d Straight Game—73-Yard Aerial Play Clicks

COLUMBUS, Ohio, Oct. 10 (AP)—A 73-yard pass play and a fourth-period field goal enabled Illinois to upset Ohio State, 9—0, today in a Western Conference football game that attracted 82,980 fans.

The Buckeye attack, once the scourge of the Big Ten, foundered on the Rocky Illinois defense as the Bucks lost the ball on downs on the 28 and 11 yard lines and on pass interceptions on the Illinois 11 and 12.

The first-quarter touchdown settled the issue as the Bucks suffered their second straight shutout and Coach Woody Hayes' fourth Conference loss in six years.

Counts Takes Pass

Mel Meyers, the sophomore quarterback from Dallas, was apparently down far behind the 27-yard line of scrimmage on the big play, but eluded three Ohio attackers, broke loose from an ankle tackle and arched the ball far down field. John Counts, a sophomore halfback from New Rochelle, N. Y., took the ball from between two Ohio State defenders on the Illinois 45 and raced the rest of the way untouched.

The clincher was scored in the fourth period when Don Yeazel, a senior tackle from Dayton, Ohio, booted a 27-yard field goal with less than five minutes to go.

Bob White, Ohio State's huge fullback, was stopped almost cold by the rugged Illini defense. The Bucks were able to gain only 76 yards on the ground and 84 yards on the completion of seven of twenty passes. The Illini, with Counts, Meyers and the fullback brothers, Bill and Jim Brown, gained 195 yards on the ground and 174 through the air.

Hayes Blanked 9th Time

Only twice previously in his nine-year regime has Hayes gone two straight games without scoring. Iowa and Michigan shut out his teams at the close of the 1956 season and Illinois and Michigan did the same at the end of the 1951 campaign. He has been blanked only nine times in nine years.

Using a lonesome end offense in which tackles were sometimes eligible for a pass and with a man in motion, Illinois tore the Ohio State defense to shreds. The Illini climbed back even in the Conference race with a 1-1 record.

```
Illinois...............6 0 0 3—9
Ohio State.............0 0 0 0—0
```
Counts, 73, pass from Meyers (kick failed).
FG, Yeazel 27.

1959 FOOTBALL ROSTER
(Alphabetical)

No.	Name	Pos.	Wgt.	Hgt.	Age	Class	Home Town
26	Adulewicz, Casimir	QB	173	5-9	23	Sr.	Steubenville
53	*Anders, Richard	C	190	5-9	21	Sr.	Washington C. H.
43	Armstrong, Jack	RH	189	5-11	20	So.	McArthur
68	*Arnold, Birtho	RT	306	6-2	20	So.	Columbus
85	Azok, Frank	RE	183	6-2	21	Jr.	Lorain
60	Banks, John	RG	210	5-10	19	So.	Hamilton
50	Beam, William	C	216	6-0	20	Sr.	Moundsville, W.Va.
21	Benis, Mike	QB	185	6-0	20	Jr.	Columbus
52	Bowsher, Jerry	LG	211	5-11	22	Sr.	Toledo
88	Bryant, Charles	LE	209	6-1	19	So.	Zanesville
71	Bunnell, Paul	RT	223	6-2	19	So.	Bradford
59	Coburn, Michael	C	209	6-1	19	So.	Akron
73	DeBruin, Walter	LT	235	6-5	21	Jr.	Columbus
32	Detrick, Roger	FB	198	5-9	19	So.	Dayton
89	Deyo, Charles	LE	197	6-2	21	Jr.	Columbus
36	Emelianchik, Robert	FB	205	5-10	21	Sr.	Brooklyn, N.Y.
69	Ehrensberger, Fred	LG	205	5-9	19	So.	Dayton
56	Farrall, John	LG	207	5-10	20	Jr.	Canton
46	Ferguson, Robert	LH	217	6-0	20	So.	Troy
24	*Fields, Jerry	QB	209	6-1	21	Jr.	Coal Grove
80	Fiers, Alan	RE	209	6-1	20	Jr.	Indianapolis, Ind.
34	*Fontes, Leonard	FB	182	5-8	22	Sr.	Wareham, Mass.
66	Foreman, Charles	LG	187	5-9	19	So.	Dayton
47	Hansley, Gary	RH	198	5-9	19	So.	Cleveland
44	Hansley, Terence	LH	195	6-0	21	Sr.	Cleveland
61	Harbin, Jerry	RG	210	5-10	18	So.	Marion
18	Hardman, Von Allen	LH	177	6-0	22	So.	Spencer, W.Va.
67	*Hartman, Gabriel	RG	214	5-9	20	Jr.	Troy
65	*Hauer, Oscar	LG	217	6-2	20	Jr.	Hamilton
12	Haupt, Richard	RH	172	5-11	19	So.	Sumner, Iowa
45	*Herbstreit, James	RH	168	5-8	20	Jr.	Reading
90	Herrmann, Harvey	LT	235	6-2	20	Jr.	Cincinnati
14	Hess, Brice	LH	178	5-11	19	So.	Mt. Vernon
49	Houck, Ronnie	LH	180	5-10	19	So.	Troy
84	**Houston, James (C)	RE	216	6-2	21	Sr.	Massillon
64	Ingram, Michael	LG	219	5-9	20	So.	Bellaire
72	Jentes, Charles	LT	212	6-2	19	Jr.	Wooster
19	*Kilgore, David	PK	174	5-9	21	Sr.	Dayton
17	Lambert, Howard	RH	178	5-7	19	So.	Bellefontaine
54	Lindner, James	C	200	5-11	20	Jr.	Enon Valley, Pa.
23	Lister, Robert	QB	190	6-2	19	So.	Marion
91	Martin, Paul	RE	190	6-2	20	So.	Canton
41	*Matte, Thomas	QB-LH	190	6-0	20	Jr.	East Cleveland
74	*Matz, James	LT	215	6-1	21	Sr.	Chillicothe
70	*Michael, Richard	RT	218	6-3	20	Sr.	Hamilton
83	Niesz, Dale	RE	198	6-2	20	Jr.	East Sparta
87	Perdue, Thomas	LE	197	5-11	18	So.	Huntington, W.Va.
75	Roberts, Jack	LT	237	6-0	18	So.	Strongsville
92	Rowland, James	LE	213	6-4	22	Sr.	Beckley, W.Va.
57	Seilkop, Kenneth	LG	207	5-11	21	Sr.	Columbus
25	Spicheck, Willie	QB	176	5-11	19	So.	Elbert, W.Va.
81	Stephens, Larry	RE	190	6-0	20	So.	Coshocton
42	Strait, Lynn	LH	178	6-11	19	So.	Logan
16	Tingley, David	RH	181	5-9	21	So.	London
78	Tolford, George	RT	225	6-0	21	Jr.	Swanton
77	*Tyrer, James	LT	248	6-5	20	Jr.	Newark
51	Varner, Thomas	C	202	5-10	20	Jr.	Saginaw, Mich.
55	Vogelgesang, Don	C	190	6-0	21	Jr.	Canton
22	Wallace, Jack	QB	212	6-3	20	So.	Middletown
94	Warner, Duane	LE	175	6-0	20	Jr.	Arlington
58	Watkins, Jene	C	197	6-0	19	So.	Smithfield
76	Weldy, Ronald	RT	251	6-3	19	So.	Piqua
15	Wentz, William	RH	175	5-10	21	Sr.	Canton
79	Whitaker, Larry	RT	225	6-0	19	Jr.	St. Johns
33	**White, Robert	FB	214	6-2	21	Sr.	Covington, Ky.
82	Wittmer, George	RE	193	6-1	19	So.	Cincinnati
63	*Wright, Ernest	RG	242	6-3	19	Jr.	Toledo
62	*Young, Don	LG	222	6-1	21	Jr.	Dayton

* Indicates Letter

1959

Captain: James E. Houston

14	*Duke	13
0	Southern California	17
0	*Illinois	9
15	*Purdue	0
3	Wisconsin	12
30	*Michigan State	24
0	*Indiana	0
7	*Iowa	16
14	Michigan	23
83		114

Won 3, Lost 5, Tied 1

TROJANS BLANK BUCKEYES

Woody Hayes Punches Brother of Newsman

LOS ANGELES, Oct. 3 (AP).—Southern California's Trojans supplied the punch on the football field and Ohio State's fiery coach, Woody Hayes, reportedly furnished one in a stormy post-game episode.

The unbeaten Trojans dealt a smashing 17-0 blow to the Buckeyes last night, and made a bid for a place in the top 10 teams of the Nation.

Eyewitnesses said Hayes took a swing at one sports writer, missed but landed a blow on the back of the brother of another as a group waited outside the Buckeye dressing room for the post-game interview.

Denies Swinging

Cooled down 30 minutes later, Hayes denied he swung at anyone. He said he may have shoved someone.

"We didn't say a word," said Dick Shafer, whose brother Bob is sports editor of the Pasadena Independent.

"All of a sudden Hayes barged out of the dressing room like a mad bull.

"The next thing I knew he hit me in the back. It's still sore."

Al Bine of the Los Angeles Examiner gave much the same account. He said Hayes swung at him but missed. "I got out of the place quick," Bine announced.

Praises Trojans

Later Hayes came out of the dressing quarters and chatted amiably enough and extended kind words for the Trojan football team.

The scene in the quarters under the coliseum apparently was more dramatic than most of the football game.

For the most part, the rivals huffed and puffed up and down the turf.

It was left for a Southern California sophomore quarterback, Ben Charles, to supply the excitement.

The 180-pounder from Lancaster, Pa., threw one touchdown pass, set up another via the air, and scored himself and set the stage for a field goal.

Charles' main target was End Luther Hayes. He hit him with a 38-yard scoring throw and one for 33 yards which put USC in position for Charles to carry the ball the final 4 yards.

Charles passed to Glenn Wilder for 21 yards that led to a 27-yard field goal by Don Zachik, which opened the scoring for the 49,592 on hand.

Fullback Bob White was not at his best, according to Hayes, but he was the main gun in rushing the ball for 56 of the net 84 yards the Buckeyes gained against a big Trojan line.

Ohio State did not penetrate past the 20 until the final minutes. White led them to the five, but was twice thrown back for one-yard losses and USC took over on downs.

The win over Ohio State was the first for the Trojans since 1947. The intersectional series dating back to 1937 is now 4-5-1 in favor of Ohio State.

```
OHIO STATE      0  0  0  0— 0
USC             3  0  6  8—17
```
USC—Field goal, Zachik, 27; Hayes, 37, pass from Charles (kick failed); Charles, 4, run (Wilder, pass from Charles).

MICHIGAN DOWNS OHIO STATE, 23-14

Noskin's Passes Pave Way for 2 Tallies—90,093 See 56th Meeting of Rivals

STATISTICS OF THE GAME

	Mich.	O.S.U.
First downs	20	20
Rushing yardage	198	228
Passing yardage	108	130
Passes attempted	11	16
Passes completed	8	11
Passes intercepted by	3	1
Punts	2	1
Av. dist. of punts, yds.	34	30
Fumbles lost	2	2
Yards penalized	10	10

ANN ARBOR, Mich., Nov. 21 (AP)—Michigan, with some of the power of its storied past, defeated Ohio State, 23—14, today before 90,093 chilled spectators.

This fifty-sixth meeting of the Big Ten teams, meaningless except for prestige, turned into a personal tug of war between Michigan's Stan Noskin and Ohio State's Roger Detrick.

Noskin wound up his spotty career with flawless direction of the spirited Wolverines. He passed for Michigan's first score, ran for the second and set up the third with a pair of daring third-down passes.

Darrell Harper provided the insurance with a 29-yard field goal with five and a half minutes to play.

Everything the sagging Buckeyes had was wrapped up in Detrick, a bulldozing sophomore fullback who has been operating in the shadow of burly Bob White, who sat this one out with an injury.

Detrick rumbled for 139 yards in thirty-three carries, only five carries short of the Big Ten record.

The defeat meant the first losing season for Ohio State in the nine-year tenure of Woody Hayes, who provided a full measure of excitement today in a running verbal bout with the officials.

```
Michigan ........7  7  6  3—23
Ohio State ......6  0  8  0—14
```
Mich.—Rio, 8, pass from Noskin (Harper, kick).
O. S. U.—Houston, 1, pass from Field (kick failed).
Mich.—Noskin, 1, run (Harper, kick).
O. S. U.—Detrick, 1, run (Herbstreit, pass from field).
Mich.—Rio, 1, run (kick failed).
Mich.—F. G., Harper, 29.

1959 TEAM STATISTICS, BY GAME

	First Downs	Rush	Net Gain Pass	Total	Total Plays	Passing Att.	Comp.	Int.	Punting No.	Avg.	Fumbles No.	Lost	Yards Penalized	Points
DUKE	12	189	38	227	64	8	5	1	7	30.0	2	1	16	13
OHIO STATE	14	170	100	270	65	13	6	1	4	31.5	3	2	10	14
SOUTHERN CALIFORNIA	23	301	166	467	83	14	9	1	1	44.0	3	2	38	17
OHIO STATE	11	80	59	139	55	12	7	0	6	37.5	3	1	15	0
ILLINOIS	18	195	174	369	74	18	8	2	4	38.7	1	1	61	9
OHIO STATE	10	76	84	160	57	20	7	2	7	35.0	1	0	10	0
PURDUE	19	207	81	288	70	27	8	3	4	36.5	1	0	25	0
OHIO STATE	19	266	24	290	70	3	1	0	5	48.0	1	1	37	15
WISCONSIN	13	235	2	237	69	5	1	0	10	34.0	4	1	52	12
OHIO STATE	9	168	56	224	56	16	4	2	9	33.3	6	2	62	3
MICHIGAN STATE	16	173	149	322	60	14	6	0	5	37.5	3	2	24	24
OHIO STATE	18	260	160	420	66	9	6	0	5	41.0	2	2	10	30
INDIANA	11	179	0	179	67	2	0	0	7	41.4	4	0	38	0
OHIO STATE	7	77	50	127	44	7	3	0	8	41.4	2	0	5	0
IOWA	17	303	35	338	65	10	3	0	4	34.5	7	4	27	16
OHIO STATE	13	123	58	181	62	12	5	0	9	33.5	2	1	15	7
MICHIGAN	20	198	108	306	60	11	8	1	2	34.0	2	2	10	23
OHIO STATE	20	228	130	358	73	16	11	3	1	30.0	2	2	10	14
OPPONENTS	149	1980	753	2733	612	109	48	8	44	35.8	27	13	291	114
OHIO STATE	121	1448	721	2169	548	108	50	8	54	37.1	23	11	174	83

1959 OHIO STATE INDIVIDUAL STATISTICS

RUSHING

Player	Tries	Gain	Lost	Net	Avg.	TD's
Ferguson	61	374	3	371	6.1	2
*White	96	314	2	312	3.2	0
Detrick	55	231	0	231	4.2	2
Matte	92	312	122	190	2.1	1
Fields	69	234	78	156	2.3	0
Houck	10	50	0	50	5.0	0
Wentz	16	44	1	43	2.7	0
*Tingley	6	32	0	32	5.3	0
*T. Hansley	8	24	0	24	3.0	0
Herbstreit	14	27	3	24	1.7	0
*Fontes	2	6	0	6	3.0	0
Martin	2	5	0	5	2.5	0
Wallace	9	14	10	4	0.4	0
Totals	440	1667	219	1448	3.3	5

FORWARD PASSING

Player	Att.	Comp.	Int.	Yards	Pct.	TD's
Matte	51	28	2	439	.549	4
Fields	53	20	6	260	.377	1
Wallace	4	2	0	22	.500	0
Totals	108	50	8	721	.463	5

SCORING

Player	TD's	Conv. Att. Kick	Conv. Att. Pass	Conv. Made Kick	Conv. Made Pass	FG	Total
*Kilgore	0	8	0	7	0	4	19
**Houston	3	0	0	0	0	0	18
Detrick	2	0	0	0	0	0	12
Ferguson	2	0	0	0	0	0	12
Matte	1	0	0	0	0	0	6
Bryant	1	0	0	0	0	0	6
Wentz	1	0	0	0	0	0	6
Herbstreit	0	0	0	0	1	0	2
(Safe'y)	0	0	0	0	0	0	2
Fields	0	0	1	0	0	0	0
Team	0	1	0	0	0	0	0
Totals	10	9	1	7	1	4	83

PUNTING

Player	Number	Yards	Avg.
*White	25	1017	40.7
Fields	21	809	38.5
Matte	5	145	29.0
Ingram	1	33	33.0
Team	2	0	0.0
	54	2004	37.1

PASS RECEIVING

Player	Number	Yards	TD's
*Houston	11	214	3
Bryant	11	153	1
Herbstreit	6	102	0
Perdue	7	74	0
Wentz	5	69	1
Houck	4	39	0
*White	1	30	0
German	2	22	0
*T. Hansley	2	15	0
Ferguson	1	3	0
Totals	50	721	5

INTERCEPTION RETURNS

Player	Number	Yards
Houck	2	54
Ingram	2	16
Hauer	1	12
*White	1	4
Matte	1	0
German	1	0
Totals	8	86

PUNT RETURNS

Player	Number	Yards
Herbstreit	10	109
Fields	3	34
Houck	5	15
Matte	1	15
*Strait	1	10
Wentz	2	7
Ferguson	1	3
Totals	23	193

KICKOFF RETURNS

Player	Number	Yards
Herbstreit	7	116
Fields	5	96
Ferguson	4	78
Matte	4	66
Wentz	2	41
Houck	2	35
*T. Hansley	1	23
*Houston	1	8
Perdue	1	8
Bryant	1	5
Totals	28	476

SCORE BY QUARTERS

	1	2	3	4	—T
Opponents	35	26	6	47	—114
Ohio State	32	19	15	17	— 83

* Not returning for 1960.

[1960]

1960 OHIO STATE FOOTBALL ROSTER
(Alphabetical)

No.	Name	Pos.	Wgt.	Hgt.	Age	Class	Home Town
53	Armstrong, William	C	195	5-11	20	So.	Huron
38	Baffer, Stewart	PK	215	6-4	19	So.	Painesville
21	Benis, Michael	QB	185	6-0	21	Sr.	Columbus
88	*Bryant, Charles	E	209	6-1	20	Jr.	Zanesville
52	Butts, Robert	C	212	6-1	18	So.	Benwood, W. Va.
57	Clymer, William	C	180	5-9	19	So.	Dayton
59	Coburn, Michael	C	209	6-1	20	Jr.	Akron
32	*Detrick, Roger	FB	198	5-9	20	Jr.	Vandalia
42	Eckard, David	HB	164	5-9	19	So.	Akron
56	Farrall, John	G	207	5-10	21	Sr.	Canton
46	*Ferguson, Robert	FB	217	6-0	21	Jr.	Troy
24	**Fields, Jerry	QB	209	6-1	22	Sr.	Coal Grove
71	*Fiers, Alan	T	204	6-1	21	Sr.	Indianapolis, Ind.
66	Foreman, Charles	G	185	5-9	20	Jr.	Dayton
69	Foster, Rodney	G	220	6-0	20	So.	Cleveland
33	Francis, David	FB	205	6-0	19	So.	Columbus
35	*German, William	HB	174	5-10	21	Sr.	Shaker Heights
47	Hansley, Gary	HB	195	5-9	20	Jr.	Cleveland
18	Hardman, Von Allen	HB	177	6-0	23	Jr.	Spencer, W. Va.
67	**Hartman, Gabriel	G	214	5-9	21	Sr.	Troy
65	**Hauer, Oscar	G	217	6-2	21	Sr.	Hamilton
12	Houpt, Richard	HB	172	5-11	20	Jr.	Sumner, Iowa
45	**Herbstreit, James	HB	164	5-8	21	Sr.	Reading
14	Hess, Brice	HB	174	5-11	20	Jr.	Mt. Vernon
28	Hess, William	HB	165	5-10	19	So.	Springfield
49	*Houck, Ronald	HB	169	5-10	20	Jr.	Troy
64	*Ingram, Michael	G	219	5-9	21	Jr.	Bellaire
72	Jentes, Charles	T	212	6-2	20	Sr.	Wooster
16	Johnson, Kenneth	HB	162	5-9	18	So.	New Concord
20	Jones, Ben	PK	169	5-11	19	So.	Salem
30	Katterhenrich, David	FB	212	6-1	19	So.	Bucyrus
19	Klein, Robert	HB	170	5-8	24	So.	Athens, Mich.
61	Krstolic, Raymond	T	210	6-1	19	So.	Mentor
48	Kumler, Karl	HB	190	6-0	19	So.	Columbus
17	Lambert, Howard	HB	177	5-7	20	Jr.	Bellefontaine
70	Laskoski, Richard	T	214	6-4	19	So.	Shamokin, Pa.
60	Lehr, Frederick	T	228	6-4	19	So.	Mansfield
54	*Lindner, James	C	206	5-11	21	Sr.	Enon Valley, Pa.
36	Lindner, Robert	FB	200	6-0	22	So.	Nitro, W. Va.
23	Lister, Robert	QB	190	6-2	20	Jr.	Marion
43	Mangiamelle, Richard	HB	161	5-11	18	So.	Crafton, Pa.
91	*Martin, Paul	E	194	6-2	21	Jr.	Canton
41	**Matte, Thomas	QB	190	6-0	21	Sr.	East Cleveland
74	*Matz, James	T	215	6-1	22	Sr.	Chillicothe
80	Middleton, Robert	E	214	6-3	19	So.	Marion
68	Moeller, Gary	G	205	6-1	19	So.	Lima
26	Mrukowski, William	QB	190	6-3	19	So.	Elyria
25	Mummey, John	QB	197	6-0	19	So.	Painesville
87	*Perdue, Thomas	E	192	5-11	19	Jr.	Huntington, W. Va.
89	Rayford, Elwood	E	175	5-10	20	So.	Toledo
79	Risch, Robert	T	212	6-3	19	So.	Logan
75	Roberts, Jack	T	237	6-0	19	Jr.	Strongsville
76	Sanders, Daryl	T	226	6-4	19	So.	Mayfield Heights
81	Stephens, Larry	E	192	6-0	20	So.	Coshocton
63	Swartz, Aaron	G	207	6-0	19	So.	Newark
85	Tidmore, Sam	E	215	6-0	22	Jr.	Cleveland
78	*Tolford, George	T	225	6-0	22	Sr.	Swanton
77	**Tyrer, James	T	248	6-5	21	Sr.	Newark
44	Ulmer, Ed	HB	184	6-2	20	So.	Brookfield
50	Vanscoy, Jerry	C	200	5-11	19	So.	Harrisville
51	Varner, Thomas	C	202	5-10	21	Sr.	Saginaw, Mich.
73	Vogel, Robert	T	225	6-5	19	So.	Massillon
55	Vogelgesang, Don	C	190	6-0	22	Sr.	Canton
22	Wallace, Jack	QB	212	6-3	21	Jr.	Middletown
58	Watkins, Jene	C	198	6-0	20	Jr.	Smithfield
15	*Wentz, William	HB	172	5-10	22	Sr.	Canton
82	*Wittmer, George	E	193	6-1	21	Jr.	Cincinnati
62	**Young, Don	G	214	6-1	22	Sr.	Dayton

* Indicates Letter.

Bob Ferguson

1960
Captains: James Tyrer
James Herbstreit

24	*Southern Methodist	0
20	*Southern California	0
34	Illinois	7
21	Purdue	24
34	*Wisconsin	7
21	Michigan State	10
36	*Indiana	7
12	Iowa	35
7	*Michigan	0
209		90

Won 7, Lost 2

A.P. POLL
1. Minnesota
2. Mississippi
3. Iowa
4. Navy
5. Missouri
6. Washington
7. Arkansas
8. OHIO STATE
9. Alabama
10. Duke

U.P.I. POLL
1. Minnesota
2. Iowa
3. Mississippi
4. Missouri
5. Washington
6. Navy
7. Arkansas
8. OHIO STATE
9. Kansas
   Alabama

Ohio State Buckeyes Crush Illinois, 34-7

CHAMPAIGN, Ill. (AP) — Ohio State's undefeated Buckeyes, sparked by a 100-yard kickoff return by Bill Wentz and excellent quarterbacking of Tom Matte, crushed Illinois 24-7 Saturday in a Big Ten battle of national football powers.

An Illinois homecoming crowd of 71,119 sat quietly through the first half and watched fullback Bob Ferguson pound out a 13-0 Ohio State lead and then gave up all hope when Wentz took the opening kickoff of the second half and went all the way for a touchdown.

It was the third consecutive victory for Ohio State, the nation's fifth-ranked team in the AP weekly poll, while Illinois — rated No. 4 — suffered its first setback of the season.

OHIO STATE UPSET BY PURDUE, 24-21

Jones Scores 3 Touchdowns and Allen Kicks Remaining Points for Boilermakers

By The Associated Press.

LAFAYETTE, Ind., Oct. 15—Bernie Allen of Purdue kicked a 32-yard field goal and 3 extra points, passed brilliantly and ran the clutch yardage today in a 24-21 upset of previously-unbeaten Ohio State, the nation's third-ranked team.

Willie Jones, a senior Purdue fullback, scored two touchdowns on short plunges and then scored the third-quarter clincher on a 26-yard sprint. He had never before made a collegiate touchdown. Ohio State had given up only one touchdown in three previous games.

Jones outdid the 220-pound Ferguson of the Buckeyes. The Purdue fullback picked up 72 yards in eleven carries to Ferguson's 70 yards in nineteen rushes. Jones also ran back two kick-offs a total of 57 yards.

Allen threw only six passes, completing five for 85 yards. Matte connected on eight of thirteen for 145 yards. Neither had a pass intercepted.

Coach Woody Hayes of Ohio State declined to open his dressing room to newsmen and came out and commented, "Both teams moved the ball well, but Purdue moved it better." He said it was an entertaining example of open play, if you like that type of play. He apparently doesn't.

Jack Mollenkopf, the Purdue coach, said, "I was most satisfied with that win. We certainly deserved it." He said it was definitely Purdue's best performance this year. He thought the Purdue second unit wore down the Buckeyes and the Purdue first unit was fresher than the Buckeye first unit at the end of the game.

```
Purdue ............7   7  10  0—24
Ohio State ........0  14   7  0—21
```
Pur.—Jones, 2, run (Allen, kick).
Pur.—Jones, 3, run (Allen, kick).
O. S. U.—Ferguson, 6, run (Jones, kick).
O. S. U.—Perdue, 31, pass from Matte (Jones kick).
Pur.—FG, Allen, 32.
O. S. U.—Ferguson, 1, run (Jones, kick).
Pur.—Jones, 26, run (Allen, kick).
Attendance—46,284.

Iowa Hawkeyes Beat Ohio State by 35-12

Recapture Big Ten Lead In Televised Encounter

IOWA CITY, Iowa, (P)—Gouging chunks of yardage in a furious running attack, Iowa shot back into the Big Ten lead and contention for the national football title with a 35-12 conquest of Ohio State Saturday.

Junior halfback Larry Ferguson's flashy 91-yard scoring dash down the sidelines and sophomore fullback Joe William's 49-yard touchdown burst highlighted the Hawkeyes' nationally-televised victory.

The stunning triumph assured the Hawks at least a tie for the Big Ten crown with a 5-1 record as previously unbeaten Minnesota was upset 23-14 by Purdue today. The Gophers must beat Wisconsin next week to share the championship.

The Hawkeyes—fifth ranked in the latest Associated Press poll—displayed their crispest attack of the season in turning back powerful Ohio State, which had lost only one game and was ranked third this week.

Iowa was performing in its last home game under head coach Forest Evashevski. And the players shot the works, building a 28-6 halftime lead and using a stubborn defense to turn back the Buckeyes' second half bids.

Williams also scored on a two-yard plunge in the route.

Quarterback Wilburn Hollis added a 12-yard touchdown and his understudy, Matt Szykowny scored on a sneak to thrill the dad's day crowd.

Ohio State quarterback Tom Matte—who had a brilliant day for the Buckeyes but alone couldn't turn the tide—and fullback Bob Ferguson scored Ohio State's touchdowns.

```
Ohio State .........0   6   6  0—12
Iowa ...............7  21   0  7—35
```
Iowa—Williams 49 run (Moore kick).
OS—Bob Ferguson 1 run (kick failed).
Iowa—Hollis 12 run (Moore kick).
Iowa—Szykowny 1 run (Moore kick).
Iowa—Williams 2 run (Moore kick).
OS—Matte 22 run (pass failed).
Iowa—Larry Ferguson 91 run (Moore kick).

IOWA		OHIO STATE
21	First Downs	17
361	Rushing Yardage	220
126	Passing Yardage	124
8-13	Passes	9-23
1	Passes Intercepted by	0
4-30	Punts	6-35.9
1	Fumbles Lost	1
40	Yards Penalized	25

Buckeyes Win Final Over Wolverines, 7-0

COLUMBUS, Ohio (P) — Battering Bob Ferguson broke up a tight defensive duel with a 17-yard fourth-quarter touchdown run Saturday to give Ohio State a 7-0 victory over Michigan in the season's final for both Big Ten teams.

Held at bay by a tenacious Wolverine defense, the Bucks called on their most potent weapon as the final session started. Ferguson, the league's leading scorer and ground-gainer, carried four straight times for 37 yards, including the pay-off punch.

The Bucks, battling for their seventh win in nine starts this season, recovered a fumble and intercepted two passes after Ferguson had scored to save the conquest and white-wash the Wolverines for only the second time in 23 years.

1960 TEAM STATISTICS, BY GAME

	First Downs	Rush	Net Gain Pass	Total	Total Plays	Passing Att.	Comp.	Int.	Punting No.	Avg.	Fumbles No.	Lost	Yards Penalized	Points
SOUTHERN METHODIST	10	25	97	122	52	17	7	2	5	29.2	2	2	25	0
OHIO STATE	17	231	85	316	70	13	6	0	5	39.4	2	1	70	24
SOUTHERN CALIFORNIA	8	69	105	174	58	22	7	4	5	39.2	4	1	25	0
OHIO STATE	15	274	78	352	71	13	6	1	5	35.2	3	2	20	20
ILLINOIS	13	181	52	233	62	13	4	1	6	37.5	4	2	10	7
OHIO STATE	17	330	33	363	57	4	2	1	4	46.0	3	2	15	34
PURDUE	17	189	85	274	59	7	5	0	3	36.3	2	1	33	24
OHIO STATE	14	140	145	285	55	13	8	0	5	33.6	0	0	45	21
WISCONSIN	13	122	154	276	58	29	13	3	6	34.6	1	0	10	7
OHIO STATE	17	300	75	375	60	8	6	1	5	37.6	0	0	30	34
MICHIGAN STATE	19	191	134	325	67	25	10	1	5	27.4	2	2	55	10
OHIO STATE	25	248	63	311	61	12	6	1	5	32.2	3	0	58	21
INDIANA	4	2	58	60	38	12	3	1	7	31.4	4	1	55	7
OHIO STATE	29	223	171	394	91	23	12	1	3	19.0	5	2	22	36
IOWA	21	361	126	487	64	13	8	0	4	30.2	3	1	40	35
OHIO STATE	17	220	124	344	70	23	9	1	6	37.5	2	1	25	12
MICHIGAN	17	132	86	218	68	18	10	2	5	33.4	5	2	15	0
OHIO STATE	9	128	40	168	49	7	2	0	7	31.7	3	1	13	7
OPPONENTS	122	1272	897	2169	526	156	67	14	46	33.0	27	12	268	90
OHIO STATE	160	2094	814	2908	584	116	57	6	45	35.0	21	9	298	209

RUSHING

Player	Tries	Gain	Lost	Net	Avg.	TD's
Ferguson	160	854	1	853	5.3	13
*Matte	161	833	151	682	4.2	2
Detrick	55	235	0	235	4.3	3
Klein	20	159	7	152	7.6	3
*Wentz	10	35	2	33	3.3	0
Katterhenrich	7	31	0	31	4.4	0
Francis	9	29	0	29	3.2	0
*Herbstreit	5	24	0	24	4.8	0
Johnson	7	27	7	20	2.8	0
Mangiamelle	3	15	0	15	5.0	0
Ulmer	10	19	4	15	1.5	0
Mummey	3	15	2	13	4.3	0
Houck	4	12	0	12	3.0	0
Lambert	1	2	0	2	2.0	0
Mrukowski	3	5	3	2	.6	0
Kumler	1	0	2	−2	−2.0	0
Wallace	9	22	44	−22	−2.4	0
Totals	468	2317	223	2094	4.5	21

FORWARD PASSING

Player	Att.	Comp.	Int.	Yards	Pct.	TD's
*Matte	95	50	4	737	.526	8
Mrukowski	7	3	0	52	.428	0
Wallace	11	4	1	25	.363	0
Mummey	1	0	0	0	.000	0
*Benis	2	0	1	0	.000	0
Totals	116	57	6	814	.491	8

SCORING

Player	TD's	Conv. Att. Kick	Pass	Conv. Made Kick	Pass	FG	Total
Ferguson	13	0	0	0	0	0	78
Klein	5	0	0	0	1	0	32
Jones	0	28	0	22	0	1	25
Bryant	4	0	0	0	0	0	24
Detrick	3	0	0	0	0	0	18
*Matte	2	0	2	0	0	0	12
*Wentz	1	0	0	0	0	0	6
Perdue	1	0	0	0	0	0	6
Middleton	1	0	0	0	0	0	6
(Safety)							2
Totals	30	28	2	22	1	1	209

KICKOFF RETURNS

Player	Number	Yards	Average	TD's
*Wentz	6	189	31.5	1
Klein	9	182	20.2	0
Ulmer	1	16	16.0	0
*Herbstreit	1	12	12.0	0
Mangiamelle	1	5	5.0	0
Middleton	1	4	4.0	0
*Stephens	1	2	2.0	0
Sanders	1	0	0.0	0
Totals	21	410	19.5	1

SCORE BY QUARTERS

	1	2	3	4	—T
Opponents	14	38	10	28	— 90
Ohio State	34	38	44	43	—209

PASS RECEIVING

Player	Caught	Dropped	Yards	TD's
Bryant	17	0	336	4
Klein	10	1	110	2
Middleton	7	3	104	1
Perdue	4	1	65	1
Ferguson	3	1	42	0
Detrick	4	1	40	0
*Wentz	4	0	35	0
Stephens	1	0	31	0
Wittmer	2	0	21	0
Tidmore	2	1	20	0
Ulmer	1	1	6	0
Houck	1	2	5	0
Johnson	1	0	−1	0
Martin	0	1	0	0
Totals	57	12	814	

PUNTING

Player	Number	Yards
*Matte	29	1021
Ulmer	14	514
Hess	1	41
(Team)	1	0
Totals	45	1576

INTERCEPTION RETURNS

Player	Number	Yards	Average	TD's
*Herbstreit	3	80	26.7	0
Houck	1	23	23.0	0
Mummey	1	23	23.0	0
*Wentz	1	23	23.0	0
*German	1	16	16.0	0
*Lindner	2	12	6.0	0
Hess	1	10	10.0	0
Ingram	2	4	2.0	0
Mrukowski	1	2	2.0	0
Katterhenrich	1	0	0.0	0
Totals	14	193	13.8	0

PUNT RETURNS

Player	Number	Yards	Average	TD's
*Herbstreit	11	65	5.9	0
Hess	4	39	9.2	0
Klein	3	24	8.0	0
Mrukowski	1	19	19.0	0
Perdue	1	11	11.0	0
Johnson	1	8	8.0	0
Totals	21	166	7.9	0

OPPONENT FUMBLES RECOVERED

Player	Number	Player	Number
Ingram	4	*Wentz	1
Mrukowski	2	*German	1
*Young	1	Tidmore	1
Moeller	1	*Fiers	1

Ohio State recovered a total of 12 opponent fumbles in 1960

* Not returning for 1961

[1961]

1961 OHIO STATE FOOTBALL ROSTER
(Alphabetical)

No.	Name	Pos.	Wgt.	Hgt.	Age	Class	Home Town
53	*Armstrong, William	C	187	5-11	21	Jr.	Huron
18	Baffer, Stewart	PK	215	6-4	20	So.	Painesville
71	Bearss, James	LT	212	6-3	18	So.	Toledo
55	Betz, Wayne	RG	206	6-1	19	Jr.	Cuyahoga Falls
12	Bruney, Robert	LH	172	5-9	19	So.	Martins Ferry
88	**Bryant, Charles	LE	211	6-2	21	Sr.	Zanesville
34	*Butts, Robert	FB	220	6-1	19	Jr.	Benwood, W. Va.
54	Carter, Dennis	RT	220	6-2	18	So.	Springfield
93	Clotz, Dennis	RT	208	6-1	20	So.	Amherst
77	Connor, Dan	LT	203	6-3	22	Jr.	Columbus
32	**Detrick, Roger	FB	192	5-9	21	Sr.	Vandalia
46	**Ferguson, Robert	FB	217	6-0	22	Sr.	Troy
66	Foreman, Charles	LG	185	5-10	21	Sr.	Dayton
69	Foster, Rodney	LG	220	6-0	21	Jr.	Cleveland
33	*Francis, David	FB	205	6-0	20	Jr.	Columbus
58	Fronk, Dean	C	194	6-1	19	So.	Dover
15	Hall, Tony	RH	184	5-10	19	So.	Kettering
35	Hall, William	FB	205	6-1	19	So.	Ironton
47	Hansley, Gary	LH	195	5-9	21	Sr.	Cleveland
28	Hess, William	LH	164	5-10	20	Jr.	Springfield
49	**Houck, Ronald	RH	174	5-10	21	Sr.	Troy
62	Hullinger, Dennis	RG	203	6-3	19	So.	Lima
64	**Ingram, Michael	LG	219	5-9	22	Sr.	Bellaire
65	Jenkins, Thomas	RG	222	6-1	19	So.	Dayton
21	*Johnson, Kenneth	LH	162	5-9	19	Jr.	New Concord
20	*Jones, Ben	PK	169	5-11	20	Jr.	Salem
45	Jones, William	RH	185	5-11	19	So.	Warren
67	*Katterhenrich, David	RG	212	6-1	20	Jr.	Bucyrus
19	*Klein, Robert	RH	170	5-8	25	Jr.	Athens, Mich.
61	Krstolic, Raymond	LT	210	6-1	20	Jr.	Mentor
48	Kumler, Karl	LH	190	6-0	20	Jr.	Columbus
17	Lambert, Howard	FB	177	5-7	21	Sr.	Bellefontaine
70	Laskoski, Richard	LT	217	6-4	20	Jr.	Shamokin, Pa.
23	Lister, Robert	QB	190	6-2	21	Sr.	Marion
79	Mamula, Charles	RT	224	6-3	19	So.	Martins Ferry
43	Mangiamelle, Richard	LH	161	5-11	19	Jr.	Crafton, Pa.
27	Marmie, Larry	QB	182	6-1	19	So.	Barnesville
91	*Martin, Paul	RE	191	6-2	22	Sr.	Canton
80	*Middleton, Robert	RE	214	6-3	20	Jr.	Marion
60	Mirick, Wesley	RG	217	6-0	19	So.	Columbus
68	*Moeller, Gary	RG	205	6-1	20	Jr.	Lima
56	Morgan, Richard	C	198	5-10	22	So.	Shreve
26	*Mrukowski, William	QB	190	6-3	20	Jr.	Elyria
25	Mummey, John	QB	197	6-0	20	Jr.	Painesville
90	Nourse, Joseph	LE	214	6-3	19	So.	Springfield
63	Parker, Albert	LG	217	6-1	19	So.	Dover
87	**Perdue, Thomas	LE	184	6-0	20	Sr.	Wellston
89	Rayford, Elwood	RE	175	5-10	21	Jr.	Toledo
83	Ricketts, Ormonde	LE	197	6-1	19	So.	Springfield
75	Roberts, Jack	RT	233	6-0	20	Sr.	Strongsville
76	*Sanders, Daryl	RT	227	6-5	20	Jr.	Mayfield Heights
84	Smith, Keith	LE	214	6-3	19	So.	Dayton
41	Snell, Matthew	RH	208	6-2	20	So.	Locust Valley, N.Y.
24	Sparma, Joseph	QB	190	6-2	19	So.	Massillon
72	Stanley, Bernie	RT	230	6-0	18	So.	Proctorville
85	*Tidmore, Samuel	RE	210	6-0	23	Sr.	Cleveland
16	*Tingley, David	RH	195	5-9	23	Sr.	London
78	*Tolford, George	LT	215	6-0	23	Sr.	Swanton
44	*Ulmer, Ed	LH	184	6-2	21	Jr.	Brookfield
86	VanRaaphorst, Richard	LE	207	6-1	18	So.	Ligonier, Pa.
50	*Vanscoy, Jerry	C	200	5-11	20	Jr.	Harrisville
73	*Vogel, Robert	LT	228	6-5	20	Jr.	Massillon
22	*Wallace, Jack	QB	205	6-3	22	Sr.	Middletown
42	Warfield, Paul	LH	182	6-0	18	So.	Warren
82	**Wittmer, George	RE	190	6-1	22	Sr.	Cincinnati
51	Zima, Albert	C	195	6-0	22	Jr.	Youngstown

* Indicates Letter.

Paul Warfield

42—WARFIELD, Paul, 18, 6-0, 18.. sophomore . . . from Warren . . . All-Ohio and All-America performer in high school . . . blessed with outstanding speed and a rare sense of balance . . . Ohio State's best break-away threat in recent years . . . without practice ran an indoor 60 yard dash in 6.3 seconds . . . was tried briefly at quarterback early in spring drills, but was moved back to left halfback to take advantage of his running ability . . . is an excellent defensive player and will likely be used some both ways . . . high school coach was Gene Slaughter, Buckeye backfield coach last year . . . scored 30 touchdowns in high school, many on long runs . . . gave an exhibition of his broken field running in the spring game, when he caught a screen pass and raced 80 yards to score . . . hobby is reading sports magazines. . . .

41—SNELL, Matthew, 20, 6-2, 208, sophomore . . . from Locust Valley, New York . . . was an All-Metropolitan, All-New York and All-America halfback in high school, scoring 17, 14 and 16 touchdowns per year . . . is a rare blend of speed and power . . . is another ideal two-way player, but will battle Bob Klein for the starting right halfback berth on offense . . . can be used as a corner linebacker on defense . . . is taking pre-dentistry . . . hobbies are dancing and attending movies . . . admires Jimmy Brown, Cleveland professional great . . . captained his high school football and track team . . . does construction work during the summer . . . ambition is to become a dentist . . .

A.P. POLL	U.P.I. POLL
1. Alabama	1. Alabama
2. OHIO STATE	2. OHIO STATE
3. Texas	3. L.S.U.
4. L.S.U.	4. Texas
5. Mississippi	5. Mississippi
6. Minnesota	6. Minnesota
7. Colorado	7. Colorado
8. Michigan State	8. Arkansas
9. Arkansas	9. Michigan State
10. Utah State	10. Utah State

1961
Captains: Thomas Perdue
Michael Ingram

7	*Texas Christian	7
13	*U.C.L.A.	3
44	*Illinois	0
10	Northwestern	0
30	Wisconsin	21
29	*Iowa	13
16	Indiana	7
22	*Oregon	12
50	Michigan	20
221		83

Won 8, Lost 0, Tied 1

Big Ten Champions

[1961]

FOOTBALL TEAM—*Row 1:* Wallace, Connor, Clotz, Wittmer, Ferguson, Houck, Tolford, Bryant, Tidmore, Perdue, Ingram, Detrick, Stephens, Martin, Roberts, H. Lambert. *Row 2:* Hayes (head coach), Johnson, B. Jones, Katterhenrich, Foster, Ulmer, Moeller, Armstrong, Vogel, Middleton, Mrukowski, Sanders, Hess, Klein, Hardman, Haupt, Godfrey. *Row 3:* Tingley, Betz, Krstolic, Mummey, Francis, Vanscoy, Jenkins, Fronk, Bearss, Ricketts, Mamula, Snell, Sparma, Warfield, W. Jones, Bruney. *Row 4:* Rayford, Laskowski, Butts, Baffer, Kumler, Lister, Mangiamelle, VanRaaphorst, Mirick, Hullinger, Lyons, Marmie, Parker, R. Carter, Zima, Fortney. *Top Row:* Strobel, Fiers, Gunlock, Sarkkinen, Sunderhaus, Unger, Stanley, Hall, D. Carter, Schembechler, Herbstreit, Clark, Wentz, Biggs (trainer).

Buckeyes Tied By Horn Frogs

COLUMBUS, Ohio — Guy (Sonny) Gibbs, Texas Christian's 230-pound, 6-7 quarterback was the offensive - defensive star Saturday as the Horned Frogs held Ohio State to a 7-7 deadlock before a crowd of 82,878.

The "eye-full tower" passed 62 yards to halfback Pete Hill in the fourth quarter to set up the tying touchdown and then climaxed the 84-yard drive with a 12-yarder to Dale Glascock to draw up even.

Ohio, which had scored the first time it got the ball on a 56-yard drive in which Bob Ferguson ate up 41 yards in 14 smashes, made two great, but futile attempts to make it up in the late going.

After the TCU score, the Bucks marched from their own 18 to the Horned Frog 11, but Gibbs squelched the drive by intercepting Bill Mruskowi's pass on the goal line.

It was the tall fellow's second interception.

Ohio State Rolls over Michigan

ANN ARBOR, Mich. (AP) — Ohio State, supplied with raw power by Bob Ferguson and electrifying running by Paul Warfield, completed a perfect Big Ten season Saturday by jolting arch-rival Michigan 50-20.

The second-ranked Buckeyes, who now have won or tied for 12 Western conference titles, finished with only an opening game tie with non-conference Texas Christian marring an otherwise untarnished nine-game season. They won all six of their Big Ten games.

Ferguson, last year's All America fullback and a leading candidate to repeat, bore the burden of Ohio State's predominantly ground attack. He scored four touchdowns as a crowd of 80,444 and a regional television audience watched his awesome display.

The 214-pound bulldozer relied on his crunching strength to ram through the heavy Wolverine line for 152 yards in 30 carries. Ferguson scored the first two Buckeye touchdowns by rumbling 19 yards and battering one yard. Then, after Michigan scored to pull within nine points midway in the third period, Ferguson led a march that put the game out of Michigan's reach.

He capped the 80-yard drive by again scoring from the one.

OSU used passes infrequently but an 80-yard pass play from Joe Sparma to Bob Klein produced the Buckeyes fifth touchdown. Then Ferguson added an insurance tally on another one yard burst in the final five minutes. OSU scored another touchdown in the final seconds on a Sparma to Tom Tidmore pass for 10 yards.

STATISTICS

OHIO STATE		MICHIGAN
22	First downs	16
312	Rushing yardage	162
200	Passing yardage	109
7-10	Passes	10-17
2	Passes intercepted by	1
1-40	Punts	2-36
0	Fumbles lost	1
20	Penalties	40

Ohio State Faculty Says No on Rose Bowl Invite

COLUMBUS, Ohio (AP) — Ohio State's dream of playing in another Rose Bowl game was shattered Tuesday when the school's powerful faculty council rejected a bid to the Pasedena classic.

The council's decision culminated a drama-packed 90-minute session that dealt Buckeye football followers a severe jolt.

By a close 28-25 vote, the faculty body refused to approve the report of the university's athletic council which yesterday agreed to accept a Rose Bowl invitation by a 6-4 decision.

The faculty council has 57 members eligible to vote, but four were absent from today's session.

The second-ranked Buckeyes last Saturday walloped Michigan and clinched the Big Ten championship when Wisconsin upset Minnesota.

Ohio State, Illinois, Northwestern and Wisconsin are opposed to playing in the post-season classic. Big Ten schools in favor are Indiana, Purdue, Iowa, Minnesota, Michigan and Michigan State.

There has been some indication that the second-place Gophers would be receptive to a bowl bid as a replacement for the Buckeyes.

Today's rejection left the most glamorous of all post-season games in somewhat doubtful status. UCLA, winner of the Athletic Association of Western Universities (AAWU), is the host school for the Jan. 1 contest.

In essence, the faculty group's "no bowl" verdict came as a reaffirmation of its stand in 1959 when it nixed by voice vote any bowl trip.

Under Big Ten regulations, the council is the final authority in athletic matters and a majority vote was required to send the Bucks to Pasadena.

The Buckeye gridders voted unanimously last night, prior to the annual appreciation dinner, to play in the Rose Bowl.

Chief objections appeared to be:
1. A trip would disrupt the normal academic life of the school.
2. The university has become known as a "football school" and this has hurt the university's academic standing.
3. Absence from campus of faculty members hampers the operation of the administration.
4. The Rose Bowl is a commercial enterprise.
5. The council already had expressed a decision on the matter and a change in that decision would hurt the school's prestige.
6. The bowl game would only be a rehash of a game played earlier in the season when Ohio beat UCLA, 13-3.

Ohio State	7 14 0 21—50
Michigan	0 6 6 8—20

OSU—Ferguson 19 run (Van Raaphorst kick).
OSU—Ferguson 1 run (Van Raaphorst kick).
MICH—Raimey 90 kickoff return (pass failed).
OSU—Warfield 69 run (Van Raaphorst kick).
MICH—McLenna 1 run (pass failed).
OSU—Ferguson 1 run (Van Raaphorst kick).
OSU—Klein 80 pass from Sparma (Van Raaphorst kick).
MICH—Ward 1 run (Ward run).
OSU—Tidmore 10 pass from Sparma (Tidmore pass from Sparma).

Protest By Students

Columbus, Ohio, Nov. 28 (AP)—Ohio State University students poured out onto the campus here tonight in a demonstration against the school's faculty council decision to reject a Rose Bowl bid.

Soon after the decision was announced an effigy of Jack Fullen, secretary of the alumni association, and a long-time opponent of postseason games, was swinging from a tree in the fraternity district of the campus.

[1961]

1961 TEAM STATISTICS, BY GAME

	First Downs	Rush	Net Gain Pass	Total	Total Plays	Att.	Passing Comp.	Int.	Punting No.	Avg.	Fumbles No.	Lost	Yards Penalized	Points
TEXAS CHRISTIAN	10	94	142	236	51	17	8	1	4	39.5	2	1	10	7
OHIO STATE	16	205	44	249	72	12	7	2	4	40.7	3	2	5	7
U.C.L.A.	8	113	53	166	45	6	4	0	7	42.4	0	0	60	3
OHIO STATE	17	196	86	282	66	11	10	0	5	29.6	1	0	42	13
ILLINOIS	11	129	51	180	61	16	5	2	6	33.7	6	2	49	0
OHIO STATE	22	301	123	424	75	15	8	0	1	38.0	3	2	20	44
NORTHWESTERN	11	119	59	178	49	10	6	2	5	36.8	1	1	0	0
OHIO STATE	16	297	52	349	73	8	2	1	5	25.2	3	1	5	10
WISCONSIN	15	86	219	305	49	23	13	0	6	41.1	0	0	35	21
OHIO STATE	26	357	17	374	76	3	2	0	1	35.0	0	0	4	30
IOWA	21	168	206	374	73	23	12	3	3	36.7	1	1	47	13
OHIO STATE	17	194	94	288	59	14	4	0	3	44.3	2	0	31	29
INDIANA	14	101	156	257	56	20	12	2	6	30.5	2	1	50	0
OHIO STATE	16	215	67	282	65	11	6	0	5	38.0	2	2	76	16
OREGON	19	142	173	315	73	29	13	2	6	34.0	5	0	21	12
OHIO STATE	18	370	12	382	65	6	1	0	6	32.3	0	0	0	22
MICHIGAN	16	162	109	271	62	17	10	2	2	36.0	1	1	40	20
OHIO STATE	22	312	200	512	61	10	7	1	1	40.0	0	0	20	50
OPPONENTS	125	1114	1168	2282	519	161	83	14	45	36.8	18	7	312	83
OHIO STATE	170	2447	695	3142	612	90	47	4	31	34.4	14	7	203	221

RUSHING

	Tries	Gain	Lost	Net	Avg.	TD's
*Ferguson	202	940	2	938	4.6	11
Warfield	77	432	12	420	5.4	5
Mummey	69	420	28	392	5.7	0
Snell	50	213	16	197	3.9	1
Klein	26	181	4	177	6.8	2
Katterhenrich	30	150	0	150	5.0	1
Mrukowski	39	140	29	111	2.8	1
*Ulmer	7	38	4	34	4.8	0
Francis	5	15	0	15	3.0	0
Johnson	4	12	0	12	3.0	0
Lyons	3	7	3	4	1.3	0
Sparma	5	8	4	4	.8	0
*Lambert	1	1	0	1	1.0	0
Hess	1	1	0	1	1.0	0
*Wallace	3	6	15	—9	—3.0	0
Totals	522	2564	117	2447	4.7	21

FORWARD PASSING

Player	Att.	Comp.	Int.	Yards	Pct.	TD's
Sparma	38	16	2	341	.421	6
Mrukowski	35	23	2	231	.657	1
Mummey	14	6	0	106	.429	1
*Wallace	3	2	0	17	.667	0
Totals	90	47	4	695	.522	8

SCORING

Player	TD's	Conversion Att. Kick	Pass	Run	Conversions Made Kick	Pass	Run	FG	Total
*Ferguson	11	0	0	1	0	0	1	0	68
Warfield	6	0	0	0	0	0	0	0	36
VanRapphorst	0	27	0	0	23	0	0	4	35
*Bryant	4	0	0	0	0	0	0	0	24
Klein	3	0	0	0	0	0	0	0	18
*Tidmore	1	0	0	0	0	1	0	0	8
*Perdue	1	0	0	0	0	0	0	0	6
Snell	1	0	0	0	0	0	0	0	6
Mrukowski	1	0	1	0	0	0	0	0	6
Katterhenrich	1	0	0	0	0	0	0	0	6
Johnson	1	0	0	0	0	0	0	0	6
Sparma	0	0	1	0	0	0	0	0	0
(Safety)									2
Totals	30	27	2	1	23	1	1	4	221

KICKOFF RETURNS

	Number	Yards	Average	TD's
Warfield	10	196	9.6	0
Klein	2	43	21.5	0
*Bryant	3	27	9.0	0
*Ulmer	1	22	22.0	0
Middleton	1	13	13.0	0
Mummey	1	12	12.0	0
*Tingley	1	9	9.0	0
*Jones	1	8	8.0	0
Snell	1	2	2.0	0
*Ingram	1	0	.0	0
Totals	22	332	15.1	

PASS RECEIVING

Player	Caught	Dropped	Yards	TD's
*Bryant	15	0	270	4
Warfield	9	0	120	1
Klein	4	0	112	1
Snell	5	1	61	0
Middleton	6	1	52	0
Ricketts	2	0	39	0
Johnson	2	0	14	1
*Tidmore	1	1	10	0
Hess	1	0	10	0
*Ulmer	1	0	7	0
*Ferguson	1	1	0	0
Totals	47	4	695	8

PUNTING

Player	Number	Yards	Avg.
*Hardman	14	540	38.6
*Ulmer	14	476	34.0
*Ingram	2	52	26.0
(Team)	1	0	0.0
Totals	31	1068	34.4

PUNT RETURNS

Player	Number	Yards	Average	TD's
Warfield	11	88	8.0	0
Klein	2	46	23.0	0
*Tidmore	1	40	40.0	0
Hess	5	37	7.4	0
*Ulmer	6	35	5.8	0
*Houck	1	10	10.0	0
Totals	26	256	9.8	0

INTERCEPTION RETURNS

Player	Number	Yards	Average	TD's
*Tidmore	3	6	2.0	0
*Houck	2	16	8.0	0
Moeller	1	54	54.0	0
Bruney	1	29	29.0	0
*Bryant	1	21	21.0	0
*Tingley	1	17	17.0	0
Hess	1	13	13.0	0
Warfield	1	9	9.0	0
*Ulmer	1	7	7.0	0
Snell	1	0	.0	0
*Perdue	1	0	.0	0
Totals	14	172	12.3	0

OPPONENT FUMBLES RECOVERED

Player	Number	TD's
Betz	2	0
*Tidmore	1	0
*Tolford	1	0
*Bryant	1	0
*Perdue	1	1
Krstolic	1	0
Totals	7	1

* Not Returning for 1962

[1962]

1962 OHIO STATE FOOTBALL ROSTER
(Alphabetical)

No.	Name	Pos.	Wgt.	Ht.	Age	Cl.	Home Town
53	**Armstrong, William	C	189	5-11			Huron
14	Barnett, Tyrone	RH	171	5-8	19	So.	Orrville
67	Bearss, James	LG	211	6-3	19	So.	Toledo
55	*Betz, Wayne	RG	209	6-1	20	Sr.	Cuyahoga Falls
16	Bodenbender, Geo.	RH	185	6-0	19	So.	Bellefontaine
12	Bruney, Robert	RH	168	5-9	20	Jr.	Martins Ferry
34	*Butts, Robert	FB	225	6-1	20	Sr.	Benwood, W.Va.
54	Carter, Dennis	C	221	6-2	19	Jr.	Springfield
23	Chonko, Arnold	QB	192	6-2	19	So.	Parma
59	Cummins, Thomas	C	188	5-10	19	So.	London
85	Davidson, James	RE	212	6-4	19	So.	Alliance
58	Dreffer, Stephan	C	197	5-9	19	So.	Montpelier
32	Drenik, Douglas	FB	190	6-1	19	So.	Wickliffe
47	Espy, Bennie	RH	175	6-0	19	So.	Sandusky
50	Federle, Thomas	LG	200	5-11	19	So.	Cincinnati
11	Fortney, Douglas	LH	162	5-9	20	Jr.	West Liberty
69	*Foster, Rodney	RG	228	6-0	22	Sr.	Cleveland
33	*Francis, David	FB	209	6-0	21	Sr.	Columbus
56	Goering, William	RG	205	5-11	19	So.	Cleveland
35	Hall, William	RE	197	6-1	20	Jr.	Ironton
46	Harkins, Don	LH	182	6-1	19	So.	Urbana
38	Hartley, Robert	FB	200	5-11	19	So.	Covington
84	Housteau, Joseph	LE	207	6-2	19	So.	Girard
62	Hullinger, Dennis	RT	215	6-3	20	Jr.	Lima
28	**Hess, William	RH	168	5-10	21	Sr.	Springfield
65	*Jenkins, Thomas	LG	230	6-1	20	Jr.	Dayton
21	**Johnson, Kenneth	LH	155	5-9	20	Sr.	New Concord
87	Jones, David	LE	198	6-3	19	So.	Euclid
71	Kasunic, Gerald	RT	210	6-1	20	So.	Cleveland
30	**Katterhenrich, David	FB	209	6-1	21	Sr.	Bucyrus
27	Kaylor, Ronald	QB	180	6-3	19	So.	Canton
88	Kiehfuss, Thomas	RE	205	6-3	19	So.	Cincinnati
19	**Klein, Robert	RH	170	5-8	26	Sr.	Athens, Mich.
75	Kohut, William	LT	236	6-4	19	So.	Youngstown
61	*Krstolic, Raymond	RG	213	6-1	21	Sr.	Mentor
48	Kumler, Karl	LH	196	6-0	21	Sr.	Columbus
70	*Laskoski, Richard	LT	222	6-4	21	Sr.	Shamokin, Pa.
49	Lindsey, Leon	LH	182	5-10	20	So.	Steubenville
36	Lyons, Douglas	FB	200	6-2	21	Jr.	Parma
79	Mamula, Charles	LT	228	6-3	20	Jr.	Martins Ferry
43	Mangiamelle, Richard	LH	163	5-11	20	So.	Crafton, Pa.
81	Meyer, Terry	RE	215	6-4	19	So.	Dayton
80	**Middleton, Robert	RE	215	6-3	21	Sr.	Marion
60	*Mirick, Wesley	LG	225	6-0	20	Jr.	Columbus
68	**Moeller, Gary	C	212	6-1	21	Sr.	Lima
72	Morehead, Lee	LT	220	6-3	19	So.	Greenfield
26	**Mrukowski, William	QB	200	6-3	21	Sr.	Elyria
25	**Mummey, John	QB	197	6-0	21	Sr.	Painesville
77	Orazen, Ed	LT	218	6-0	19	So.	Euclid
63	Parker, Albert	LG	212	6-1	20	Jr.	Dover
78	Porretta, Daniel	RT	220	6-0	18	So.	Clairton, Pa.
20	Price, Charles	QB	192	6-0	19	So.	Middletown
83	*Ricketts, Ormonde	LE	194	6-1	20	Jr.	Springfield
64	Snyder, Larry	RG	198	6-2	19	So.	Wooster
18	Scott, Robert	FB	203	6-2	19	So.	Connellsville, Pa.
41	Snell, Matthew	RE	212	6-2	21	Jr.	Locust Valley, N.Y.
76	**Sanders, Daryl	RT	235	6-5	21	Sr.	Mayfield Heights
82	Spahr, William	LE	184	6-2	19		Columbus
24	*Sparma, Joseph	QB	190	6-1	20		Massillon
74	Unger, William	RT	229	6-0	20		Morris, Ill.
86	*VanRaaphorst, Richard	LE	208	6-1	19		er, Pa.
73	**Vogel, Robert	LT	232	6-5	21		Massillon
42	*Warfield, Paul	LH	188	6-0	19		Warren
22	Yonclas, Nicholas	QB	180	5-10	18		N.Y.
51	Zima, Albert	C	198	6-0	23		Youngstown

* Indicates Letter.

1962
Captains: Gary Moeller, Robert Vogel

41	*North Carolina	7
7	U.C.L.A.	9
51	Illinois	15
14	*Northwestern	18
14	*Wisconsin	7
14	Iowa	28
10	*Indiana	7
26	*Oregon	7
28	*Michigan	0
205		98

Won 6, Lost 3

UCLA Field Goal Upsets Buckeyes

LOS ANGELES (AP)—The remarkable Bruins of UCLA, after stopping mighty Ohio State three times on the one-yard line, produced the first shocking upset of the 1962 football season Saturday by defeating the Buckeyes 9-7 on a 24-yard field goal with one minute, 35 seconds to go.

Sophomore Quarterback Larry Zeno kicked the goal that spelled defeat for the nation's top-ranked college football power. Zeno guided the inspired Bruins 70 yards in 17 plays in the final seven minutes of the intersectional struggle and climaxed the march on fourth down with the ball on the Buckeye seven.

Ohio State 14-7

COLUMBUS, Ohio (AP) — Ohio State's twice beaten Bucks battled their way back into the Big Ten title race Saturday, knocking Wisconsin's Badgers out of the undefeated class by a 14-7 score before a crowd of 82,540 in a regionally televised game.

The loss dropped Wisconsin to a 4-1 record, moved Ohio up to 3-2 and maintained the Buckeye record of never having lost to the Badgers here since 1918.

It was a rugged struggle all the way, with surprise maneuvers paying off until Ohio ground out the victory with a fourth-quarter 57-yard 8-play drive to clinch it.

Buckeyes 51-15

CHAMPAIGN, Ill (AP) — Ohio State's Buckeyes, sticking mainly to their fearsome ground attack, opened defense of their Big Ten football championship Saturday, battering Illinois 51-15.

Still smarting from a 9-7 loss to UCLA last week which cost them their No. 1 national ranking, the Buckeyes really turned on the stream after a mediocre Illinois team scored a touchdown in the early seconds of the second quarter to pull to a 7-7 tie.

From then on Ohio State showed no mercy and kept hammering away to a one-sided triumph.

Ohio State 10-7

COLUMBUS, Ohio (AP) — Dick Van Raaphorst, 19-year-old junior, gave faltering Ohio State a 10-7 victory over 18-point underdog Indiana Saturday with a 27-yard field goal in the last eight seconds.

The Hoosiers in losing their 18th straight Western Conference game, played the Bucks to a standstill until the final seconds, and had all the edge in the statistics.

Paul Warfield, speedy Buckeye junior from Warren, Ohio, put the Bucks in front with a scintillating 75-yard touchdown run in the second period, and Indiana matched it with a 72-yard, 19-play drive at the start of the third session. Hoosier quarterback Woody Moore sneaked six inches for the counter.

[1962]

Woody's Actions Tell The Score

Carolina . . . . . . 41 to 7
U.C.L.A. . . . . . . 7 to 9
Illinois . . . . . . 51 to 15
Wisconsin . . . . . . 14 to 7
Northwestern . . . . . . 14 to 18
Michigan . . . . . . 28 to 0
Iowa . . . . . . 14 to 28
Indiana . . . . . . 10 to 7
Oregon . . . . . . 26 to 7

FORWARD PASSING						
Player	Att.	Comp.	Int.	Yards	Pct.	TD's
*Sparma	71	30	5	288	.422	2
Mrukowski	18	7	0	42	.389	0
*Mummey	4	1	0	42	.250	1
Yonclas	10	2	1	28	.200	0
Totals	103	40	6	400	.388	3

PUNTING			
Player	Number	Yards	Avg.
*Mummey	12	424	35.3
*Hess	12	401	33.4
*Sparma	2	72	36.0
Totals	26	897	34.5

* Not returning for 1963

1962 TEAM STATISTICS, BY GAME

	First Downs	Rush	Net Gain Pass	Total	Total Plays	Att.	Passing Comp.	Int.	Punting No.	Avg.	Fumbles No.	Lost	Yards Penalized	Points
NORTH CAROLINA	8	58	98	156	47	23	10	4	5	35.0	1	1	60	7
OHIO STATE	25	314	110	424	76	13	7	3	0	0.0	2	2	6	41
U.C.L.A.	8	162	24	186	38	6	2	0	6	37.5	0	0	25	9
OHIO STATE	18	229	47	276	72	11	5	0	3	32.3	2	2	20	7
ILLINOIS	16	107	252	359	64	31	12	2	6	32.7	1	0	25	15
OHIO STATE	24	517	9	526	63	7	2	0	2	40.5	1	1	5	51
NORTHWESTERN	21	137	177	314	71	30	18	2	3	27.3	0	0	56	18
OHIO STATE	18	197	76	273	75	18	8	1	1	34.0	2	2	40	14
WISCONSIN	12	106	111	217	56	22	7	0	4	37.5	2	2	20	7
OHIO STATE	16	213	33	246	71	10	3	1	7	35.4	2	0	42	14
IOWA	14	243	36	279	60	4	3	0	5	33.6	0	0	52	28
OHIO STATE	14	174	20	194	62	10	3	1	3	31.3	3	3	25	14
INDIANA	17	186	39	225	74	10	6	1	4	38.7	2	1	20	7
OHIO STATE	11	220	49	269	49	13	5	0	5	32.8	0	0	22	10
OREGON	14	107	117	224	50	18	10	1	5	29.2	2	2	25	7
OHIO STATE	27	316	49	365	93	15	4	0	2	32.5	1	0	31	26
MICHIGAN	9	74	68	142	47	11	5	1	6	33.8	1	0	10	0
OHIO STATE	19	330	7	337	70	6	3	0	3	38.0	3	1	0	28
OPPONENTS	119	1180	922	2102	507	155	73	11	44	34.1	9	6	293	98
OHIO STATE	172	2510	400	2910	631	103	40	6	26	34.5	16	11	191	205

RUSHING

Player	Tries	Gain	Lost	Net	Avg.	TD's
*Francis	119	626	2	624	5.2	7
*Mummey	66	383	13	370	5.6	4
Warfield	57	370	3	367	6.4	2
Butts	72	312	2	310	4.3	3
*Klein	52	293	26	267	5.1	1
*Katterhenrich	61	252	0	252	4.1	3
*Scott	21	144	2	142	6.7	1
Espy	17	72	4	68	4.0	0
Barnett	12	65	2	63	5.2	1
*Mrukowski	16	56	14	42	2.6	2
Drenik	4	34	0	34	8.5	0
Lindsey	4	15	4	11	2.7	0
Yonclas	1	10	0	10	10.0	0
*Hess	1	6	0	6	6.0	0
Lyons	1	5	0	5	5.0	0
Kaylor	1	1	0	1	1.0	0
Dreffer	1	1	0	1	1.0	0
*Sparma	22	39	102	—63	—2.8	0
Totals	528	2684	174	2510	4.7	24

SCORING

Player	TD's	Conversions (Kick) Att.	Made	Blocked	Field Goals Att.	Made	Total Points
*Francis	7	0	0	0	0	0	42
VanRaaphorst	0	21	19	1	3	2	25
*Mummey	4	0	0	0	0	0	24
Warfield	0	0	0	0	0	0	24
*Katterhenrich	3	0	0	0	0	0	18
*Butts	3	0	0	0	0	0	18
*Klein	2	0	0	0	0	0	12
*Mrukowski	2	0	0	0	0	0	12
Mamula	0	7	6	1	4	2	12
*Scott	1	0	0	0	0	0	6
Snell	1	0	0	0	0	0	6
Barnett	1	0	0	0	0	0	6
Totals	28	28	25	2	7	4	205

PASS RECEIVING

Player	Caught	Dropped	Yards	TD's
Warfield	8	2	139	2
Ricketts	9	0	79	0
Snell	8	2	66	1
*Klein	4	0	40	0
*Middleton	2	2	24	0
Barnett	1	0	19	0
*Vogel	1	0	14	0
Spahr	3	0	13	0
*Scott	1	1	5	0
Espy	3	1	1	0
Totals	40	8	400	3

* Not returning for 1963

KICKOFF RETURNS

Player	Number	Yards	Average	TD's
*Klein	9	269	29.9	1
Warfield	4	123	30.7	0
*Scott	3	51	17.0	0
*Mummey	2	22	11.0	0
Espy	1	20	20.0	0
Barnett	1	16	16.0	0
*Butts	1	5	5.0	0
Orazen	1	0	0.0	0
Totals	22	506	23.0	1

PUNT RETURNS

Player	Number	Yards	Average	TD's
Warfield	14	99	7.1	0
*Klein	7	53	7.6	0
*Hess	5	28	5.6	0
Chonko	1	14	14.0	0
*Scott	1	9	9.0	0
Totals	28	203	7.2	0

INTERCEPTION RETURNS

Player	Number	Yards	Average	TD's
Chonko	2	0	0.0	0
Harkins	1	17	17.0	0
Mirick	1	9	9.0	0
*Moeller	1	6	6.0	0
Parker	1	4	4.0	0
Kiehfuss	1	4	4.0	0
*Armstrong	1	3	3.0	0
Warfield	1	0	0.0	0
*Scott	1	0	0.0	0
*Mangiamelle	1	0	0.0	0
Totals	11	43	3.9	0

OPPONENT FUMBLES RECOVERED

Player	Number	Player	Number
Porretta	2	Spahr	1
Dreffer	1	Snell	1
Warfield	1		

SCORE BY QUARTERS

	1	2	3	4	—T
Opponents	20	47	7	24	—98
Ohio State	49	52	48	56	—205

1963 OHIO STATE FOOTBALL ROSTER
(Alphabetical)

No.	Name	Pos.	Wgt.	Hgt.	Age	Class	Home Town
18	Adderley, Nelson	LH	180	5-11	19	So.	Philadelphia
21	Allen, Richard	QB	175	6-1	19	So.	Sidney
72	Anderson, Richard	RT	232	6-5	19	So.	Medina
61	Andrick, Theodore	LG	209	5-11	19	So.	Cuyahoga Falls
14	*Barnett, Tyrone	LH	166	5-8	20	Jr.	Orrville
25	Barrington, Thomas	QB	208	6-1	19	So.	Lima
67	Bearss, James	RG	211	6-3	20	Jr.	Toledo
16	Bodenbender, Geo.	RH	177	6-0	20	Jr.	Bellefontaine
12	*Bruney, Robert	RH	168	5-9	21	Sr.	Martins Ferry
66	Bugel, Thomas	LG	200	6-0	18	So.	W. Homest'd, Pa.
23	*Chonko, Arnold	LH	194	6-2	20	Jr.	Parma
59	Cummins, Thomas	C	190	5-10	20	Jr.	London
73	Davidson, James	RT	215	6-4	20	Jr.	Alliance
15	Derbyshire, John	RH	167	5-9	19	So.	Edon
30	*Dreffer, Stephan	FB	197	5-9	20	Jr.	Montpelier
32	*Drenik, Douglas	RH	186	6-1	20	Jr.	Wickliffe
47	*Espy, Bennie	RH	177	6-0	20	Jr.	Sandusky
98	Fair, Robert	LG	190	5-11	22	Sr.	Cincinnati
50	Federle, Thomas	C	200	5-11	20	Jr.	Cincinnati
52	Fitz, Thomas	C	208	6-2	19	Jr.	Cuyahoga Falls
11	Fortney, Douglas	RH	162	5-9	21	Sr.	West Liberty
55	Fraraccio, James	RT	227	6-1	19	So.	Alliance
62	Funk, Robert	RG	224	6-1	19	So.	Lakewood
56	Goering, William	RG	206	5-11	20	Jr.	Cleveland
35	Hall, William	LE	201	6-1	21	Sr.	Ironton
46	*Harkins, Donald	LH	188	6-1	20	Jr.	Urbana
38	Hartley, Robert	FB	200	5-11	20	So.	Covington
84	Housteau, Joseph	RE	205	6-2	20	So.	Girard
92	Howman, Dennis	FB	205	6-1	20	Jr.	Wooster
70	Hullinger, Dennis	RT	215	6-3	21	Sr.	Lima
65	**Jenkins, Thomas	LG	226	6-1	21	Sr.	Dayton
71	Kasunic, Gerold	RT	210	6-1	21	Jr.	Cleveland
27	Kaylor, Ronald	QB	185	6-3	20	Jr.	Canton
53	Kelley, Dwight	C	212	5-11	19	So.	Bremen
88	*Kiehfuss, Thomas	LE	205	6-3	20	Jr.	Cincinnati
75	Kohut, William	RT	233	6-4	20	Jr.	Youngstown
90	Ladwig, Eric	LE	210	6-0	20	Jr.	Cleveland
87	Lashutka, Gregory	LE	214	6-5	19	So.	Cleveland
49	Lindsey, Leon	RH	180	5-10	21	Jr.	Steubenville
48	Lykes, Robert	RH	180	6-1	19	So.	Akron
36	Lyons, Douglas	FB	203	6-2	22	Sr.	Parma
79	*Mamula, Charles	RT	220	6-3	21	Sr.	Martins Ferry
81	Meyer, Terry	RE	212	6-4	20	Jr.	Dayton
58	Miller, Gary	LG	200	6-0	19	So.	Bellevue
60	*Mirick, Wesley	RG	220	6-0	21	Sr.	Columbus
77	*Orazen, Ed	RT	218	6-0	20	Jr.	Euclid
76	Palmer, John	LT	212	6-1	19	So.	Kettering
63	*Parker, Albert	LG	212	6-1	21	Sr.	Dover
78	*Porretta, Daniel	LT	218	6-0	19	Jr.	Clairton, Pa.
20	Price, Charles	QB	193	6-0	20	Jr.	Middletown
83	*Ricketts, Ormonde	RE	200	6-1	21	Sr.	Springfield
69	Ridder, William	RG	217	5-9	18	So.	Springfield
54	Rogovin, Jon	LT	222	6-3	20	So.	Cambridge
33	Sander, Willard	FB	210	6-2	19	So.	Cincinnati
41	**Snell, Matthew	LE	214	6-2	22	Sr.	Locust Valley, N.Y.
64	Snyder, Larry	LG	207	6-2	20	Jr.	Wooster
82	*Spahr, William	RE	182	6-2	20	Jr.	Columbus
57	Stanley, Bernie	RT	230	6-0	20	Jr.	Proctorville
80	Stock, Robert	LE	197	6-1	20	So.	Washington, Pa.
74	Unger, William	LT	229	6-0	21	Sr.	Mt. Morris, Ill.
26	Unverferth, Donald	QB	205	6-3	19	So.	Dayton
68	Van Horn, Douglas	RG	226	6-2	19	So.	Columbus
86	**VanRaaphorst, Richard	LE	210	6-1	20	Jr.	Ligonier, Pa.
42	*Warfield, Paul	LH	182	6-0	20	Sr.	Warren
22	Yonclas, Nicholas	QB	177	5-10	19	Jr	Delhi, N.Y.

* denotes letter

1963
Captains: Ormonde Ricketts
Matthew Snell

17	*Texas A. & M.	0
21	Indiana	0
20	*Illinois	20
3	Southern California	32
13	Wisconsin	10
7	*Iowa	3
7	*Penn State	10
8	*Northwestern	17
14	Michigan	10
110		102

Won 5, Lost 3, Tied 1

Ohio State 13-10

MADISON, Wis. (AP)—Ohio State roared 80 yards for a touchdown on the passing of Don Unverferth and the power running of Matt Snell in the closing minutes and knocked Wisconsin from the unbeaten ranks 13-10 Saturday in a Big Ten football upset.

Unverferth, who is a sophomore quarterback who rode the bench most of the game, took charge and completed four passes in a drive which Snell, a pile-driving fullback, capped by plunging into the end zone from two yards out with just 2:13 to play.

The Buckeyes had been shackled by Wisconsin's mighty defense in the second half before rallying behind Unverferth. The Badgers made one last gasp, but the game ended with Ohio State's Paul Warfield intercepting a pass.

[1963]

Michigan Postponed

Sports Events Virtually at Standstill As Shocked Nation Mourns President

Ohio State Checks a Late Drive and Preserves 14-10 Victory

WOLVERINES FAIL TO HOLD 10-0 LEAD

Unverferth Dashes for One Score, Passes for Another —Purdue Whips Indians

STATISTICS OF THE GAME

	Ohio St.	Mich.
First downs	17	11
Rushing yardage	192	188
Passing yardage	105	35
Passes	5-13	7-1
Interceptions by	1	1
Punts	5-35	5-32
Fumbles lost	1	0
Yards penalized	29	30

ANN ARBOR, Mich., Nov. 30 (AP)—Don Unverferth passed for one touchdown and ran for another, but Ohio State had to fight off a late Michigan attack today to preserve a 14-10 Big Ten football victory.

A crowd of 36,424, the smallest at Michigan Stadium in 20 years, saw Unverferth roll 5 yards around left end for the deciding touchdown in the final quarter.

The Ohio State quarterback passed to Paul Warfield for 35 yards and the first Ohio State touchdown with 41 seconds remaining in the first half.

Michigan had held a 10-0 lead. With time running out, Michigan marched to the Buckeye 7. But a fourth-down pass into the end zone fell out of the hands of Dick Rindfuss. However, Ohio State couldn't advance and punted. Michigan then tried to win with sideline passes, but an interception ended the threat.

The normally ground-minded Buckeyes tried 14 passes and completed seven for 105 yards.

Michigan, more of a passing team, threw 13 times and completed five for 35 yards.

Michigan opened the scoring with four minutes gone in the game on Bob Timberlake's 28-yard field goal. Jack Clancy had recovered a fumble by Matt Snell at the Buckeye 27 on the second play from scrimmage to set up the score.

The Wolverines marched 63 yards in 10 plays at the start of the second quarter with Rindfuss going the last 2.

Ohio State then threatened when it marched to the Michigan 6. Unverferth passed to Warfield in the left corner of the end zone on fourth down, but the Buckeye halfback dropped the ball.

Ohio State ..... 0 7 0 7—14
Michigan ..... 3 7 0 0—10

Mich.—FG, Timberlake, 28.
Mich.—Rindfuss, 1, run (Timberlake, kick).
O.S.U.—Warfield, 35, pass from Unverferth (Van Raaphorst, kick).
O.S.U.—Unverferth, 5, run (Van Raaphorst, kick).
Attendance—36,424.

1963 TEAM STATISTICS, BY GAME

	First Downs	Rush	Net Gain Pass	Total	Total Plays	Passing Att.	Comp.	Int.	Punting No.	Avg.	Fumbles No.	Lost	Yards Penalized	Points
TEXAS A. & M.	6	70	40	110	49	12	6	1	8	44.1	4	1	35	0
OHIO STATE	17	220	60	280	74	16	5	0	5	40.4	1	1	20	17
INDIANA	12	89	90	179	64	18	11	2	4	42.5	3	1	27	0
OHIO STATE	11	134	92	226	54	13	8	1	6	40.3	0	0	20	21
ILLINOIS	11	79	150	229	57	26	11	3	6	39.0	2	1	36	20
OHIO STATE	13	209	67	276	65	13	5	1	6	41.7	1	1	50	20
SOUTHERN CALIFORNIA	18	215	192	407	65	18	11	0	2	51.0	3	3	20	32
OHIO STATE	8	119	59	178	61	17	3	4	6	38.5	3	1	31	3
WISCONSIN	19	263	64	327	67	16	6	2	3	32.0	1	1	37	10
OHIO STATE	12	147	98	245	56	11	7	0	4	44.0	4	1	35	13
IOWA	11	137	29	166	57	13	2	2	6	47.7	3	2	3	3
OHIO STATE	10	207	13	220	59	9	2	0	7	39.3	2	1	37	7
PENN STATE	17	154	168	322	70	24	14	1	6	31.3	2	0	35	10
OHIO STATE	15	138	54	242	63	11	5	2	4	40.5	1	1	5	7
NORTHWESTERN	24	273	63	336	82	14	7	1	3	27.3	2	1	35	17
OHIO STATE	16	92	143	235	68	32	12	1	4	39.5	0	0	0	8
MICHIGAN	14	188	35	223	62	13	5	1	5	31.6	0	0	30	10
OHIO STATE	17	192	105	297	66	14	7	1	5	34.8	1	1	29	14
OPPONENTS	132	1468	831	2299	573	154	73	13	43	39.6	20	10	258	102
OHIO STATE	119	1508	691	2199	566	136	54	10	47	39.8	13	7	227	110

1963 OHIO STATE INDIVIDUAL STATISTICS

RUSHING

Player	Tries	Gain	Lost	Net	Avg.	TD's
*Snell	134	491	0	491	3.7	5
Barrington	61	288	24	264	4.3	0
*Warfield	62	261	1	260	4.2	1
Harkins	30	169	1	168	5.6	0
Sander	41	144	1	143	3.5	1
Barnett	17	72	6	66	3.9	0
Unverferth	47	136	96	40	0.8	1
Espy	13	38	7	31	2.4	0
Dreffer	8	23	0	23	2.9	0
Drenik	8	21	2	19	2.5	0
Chonko	5	13	1	12	2.4	0
*Bruney	2	1	1	0	0.0	0
Yonclas	2	0	9	—9	—4.5	0
Totals	430	1657	149	1508	3.5	8

FORWARD PASSING

Player	Att.	Comp.	Int.	Yards	Comp. Pct.	TD's
Unverferth	117	48	6	586	.410	4
Yonclas	12	4	3	73	.333	0
*Warfield	2	1	0	25	.500	0
Chonko	2	1	0	7	.500	0
Barrington	3	0	1	0	.000	0
Totals	136	54	10	691	.397	4

PASSING ANALYSIS

Player	Att.	Comp.	Had Dropped	Deflected	Out of Reach	Had Int.	% Well Thrown Passes
Unverferth	117	48	13	14	36	6	.521
Chonko	2	1	0	1	0	0	.500
*Warfield	2	1	0	1	0	0	.500
Yonclas	12	4	0	2	3	3	.333
Barrington	3	0	0	0	2	1	.000
Totals	136	54	13	17	42	10	.493

SCORING

Player	Touchdowns Rush	Touchdowns Pass	Conversions Kick	Conversions Pass	Field Goals Made	Field Goals Att.	Total Points
*VanRaaphorst	0	0	10-11	0	8	14	34
*Snell	5	0	0	0	0	0	30
*Warfield	1	3	0	0	0	0	24
Lashutka	0	1	0	0	0	0	6
Unverferth	1	0	0	0	0	0	6
Sander	1	0	0	0	0	0	6
Barnett	0	0	0	1	0	0	2
(Safety)							2
Totals	8	4	10-11	1	8	14	110

TOTAL OFFENSE

Player	Plays	Rush	Pass	Total	Avg.	TD's
Unverferth	164	40	586	626	3.8	5
*Snell	134	491	0	491	3.7	5
*Warfield	64	260	25	285	4.4	1
Barrington	64	264	0	264	4.1	0
Harkins	30	168	0	168	5.6	0
Sander	41	143	0	143	3.5	1
Barnett	17	66	0	66	3.9	0
Yonclas	14	—9	73	64	4.6	0
Espy	13	31	0	31	2.4	0
Dreffer	8	23	0	23	2.9	0
Drenik	8	19	0	19	2.5	0
Chonko	7	12	7	19	2.7	0
*Bruney	2	0	0	0	0.0	0
Totals	566	1508	691	2199	3.9	12

PASS RECEIVING

Player	Caught	Dropped	Yards	TD's
*Warfield	22	8	266	3
Spahr	7	2	97	0
Harkins	5	0	74	0
*Ricketts	7	2	72	0
Kiehfuss	3	0	54	0
*Price	2	0	54	0
Barnett	5	1	36	0
Lashutka	2	0	32	1
Stock	1	0	6	0
Totals	54	13	691	4

PUNTING

Player	Number	Yards	Avg.
Dreffer	45	1785	39.7
Barrington	2	85	42.5
Totals	47	1870	39.8

KICKOFF RETURNS

Player	Number	Yards	Average	TD's
*Warfield	15	383	25.5	0
Harkins	2	34	17.0	0
Barrington	2	27	13.5	0
Dreffer	1	21	21.0	0
Chonko	1	20	20.0	0
*Snell	1	15	15.0	0
*Price	1	12	12.0	0
Barnett	1	10	10.0	0
Lashutka	1	0	0.0	0
Totals	25	522	20.9	0

PUNT RETURNS

Player	Number	Yards	Average	TD's
*Warfield	10	101	10.1	0
Barnett	2	33	16.5	0
Harkins	2	31	15.5	0
Chonko	4	22	5.5	0
Drenik	1	9	9.0	0
Totals	19	196	10.3	0

INTERCEPTION RETURNS

Player	Number	Yards	Average	TD's
Harkins	4	28	7.0	0
*Warfield	2	23	11.5	0
Chonko	2	0	0.0	0
Van Horn	1	7	7.0	0
Drenik	1	2	2.0	0
Bugel	1	0	0.0	0
Kiehfuss	1	0	0.0	0
Federle	1	0	0.0	0
Totals	13	60	4.6	0

OPPONENT FUMBLES RECOVERED

Player	Number	Player	Number
Kelley	2	*Stanley	1
*Snell	1	Kiehfuss	1
Spahr	1	*Warfield	1
*Jenkins	1	(Opponent fumble out of OSU end zone)	1
Chonko	1		

SCORE BY QUARTERS

	1	2	3	4	—T
Opponents	15	27	33	27	102
Ohio State	22	20	28	40	110

* not returning for 1964

1964 OHIO STATE FOOTBALL ROSTER
(Alphabetical)

No.	Name	Pos.	Wgt.	Hgt.	Age	Class	Home Town
21	Allen, Richard	QB	180	6-1	20	Jr.	Sidney
81	Anders, Billy	LE	186	6-2	19	So.	Sabina
57	Anderson, Kim	C	190	6-0	19	So.	Orrville
72	Anderson, Richard	LT	232	6-5	20	Sr.	Orrville
89	Anderson, Thomas	RE	197	6-1	21	Jr.	Lodi
61	Andrick, Theodore	LG	218	5-11	20	Jr.	Cuyahoga Falls
35	Baas, James	FB	200	6-1	19	So.	Columbus
14 **Barnett, Tyrone	RH	168	5-8	21	Sr.	Orrville
25 *Barrington, Thomas	QB	209	6-1	20	Jr.	Lima
16	Bodenbender, George	LH	182	6-0	21	Sr.	Bellefontaine
66 *Bugel, Thomas	LG	200	6-0	19	Jr.	W. Homestead, Pa.
76	Burgin, Asbury	RT	223	6-2	19	So.	Euclid
60	Cairns, Gary	LT	235	6-1	19	So.	Canton
23 **Chonko, Arnold	QB	204	6-2	21	Sr.	Parma
59	Cummins, Thomas	C	192	5-10	21	Sr.	London
73 *Davidson, James	LT	224	6-4	21	Sr.	Alliance
30 **Dreffer, Stephan	FB	206	5-9	21	Sr.	Montpelier
32 **Drenik, Douglas	RH	194	6-1	21	Sr.	Wickliffe
63	Eachus, William	LG	217	6-0	19	So.	Gallipolis
47 **Espy, Bennie	RH	177	6-0	21	Sr.	Sandusky
50 *Federle, Thomas	C	200	5-11	21	Sr.	Cincinnati
15	Fill, John	RH	174	5-9	21	So.	Cuyahoga Hgts.
52	Fitz, Thomas	LG	217	6-2	21	Sr.	Cuyahoga Falls
62	Funk, Robert	RG	221	6-1	20	Jr.	Lakewood
70	Green, Mark	LT	234	6-4	18	So.	Groveport
46 **Harkins, Donald	RH	188	6-1	21	Sr.	Urbana
79	Hill, Joseph	LT	233	6-1	19	So.	Columbus
84	Housteau, Joseph	RE	210	6-2	21	Jr.	Girard
92	Howman, Dennis	FB	212	6-1	21	Sr.	Wooster
36	Hudson, Paul	FB	205	5-11	20	So.	Coatesville, Pa.
71 *Kasunic, Gerald	LT	224	6-1	22	Sr.	Cleveland
27	Kaylor, Ronald	QB	190	6-3	21	Sr.	Canton
53 *Kelley, Dwight	C	218	5-11	20	Jr.	Bremen
88 **Kiehfuss, Thomas	RE	206	6-3	21	Sr.	Cincinnati
75	Kohut, William	RT	240	6-4	21	Sr.	Youngstown
87 *Lashutka, Gregory	RE	215	6-5	20	Jr.	Cleveland
49	Lindsey, Leon	LH	195	5-10	22	Sr.	Steubenville
94	Longer, Robert	RE	195	6-2	21	Sr.	Cleveland
48	Lykes, Robert	LH	177	6-1	20	Jr.	Akron
12	McCoy, John	RH	186	5-10	19	So.	Wooster
17	Meinerding, Wesley	LH	205	6-0	19	So.	Canton
58	Miller, Gary	RG	207	6-0	20	So.	Bellevue
91	Mobley, Ben	LE	208	6-2	22	Sr.	Montclair, N.J.
85	Nein, James	LE	196	6-2	19	So.	Middletown
20	Newcomer, Mark	QB	172	5-11	19	So.	Gibsonburg
56	Oates, James	C	226	6-0	20	Jr.	Dunkirk
77 *Orazen, Edward	RT	228	6-0	21	Sr.	Euclid
93	Orazen, Michael	RE	205	6-0	19	So.	Euclid
86	Palmer, John	RE	212	6-1	20	Jr.	Kettering
78 **Porretta, Doniel	RG	219	6-1	20	Sr	Clairton, Pa.
65	Pryor, Ray	LG	222	6-0	19	So.	Hamilton
45	Rein, Robert	RH	180	5-11	19	So.	Niles
44	Richley, Richard	LH	183	5-9	22	Jr.	Cincinnati
69 *Ridder, William	RG	221	5-10	19	Jr.	Springfield
33 *Sander, Willard	FB	212	6-2	20	Jr.	Cincinnati
64	Snyder, Larry	RG	200	6-2	21	Sr.	Wooster
82 **Spahr, William	LE	186	6-2	21	Sr.	Columbus
80	Stock, Robert	LE	207	6-1	21	Jr.	Washington, Pa.
11	Thomas, Will	RH	180	6-0	19	So.	Lima
54	Truster, Jerry	RG	204	6-0	21	Sr.	Columbus
26 *Unverferth, Donald	QB	208	6-3	20	Jr.	Dayton
68 *Van Horn, Douglas	RT	232	6-2	20	Jr.	Columbus
83	Walden, Robert	LE	182	6-0	19	So.	Middletown
67	Windle, Gary	RG	215	5-11	19	So.	Warren
97	Wortman, Robert	RT	240	6-2	21	Sr.	Cincinnati
22 *Yonclas, Nicholas	QB	177	5-10	20	Sr.	Delhi, N.Y.

* Indicates letter

1964
Captains: James Davidson
William Spahr
Thomas Kiehfuss

27	*Southern Methodist	8
17	*Indiana	9
26	Illinois	0
17	*Southern California	0
28	*Wisconsin	3
21	Iowa	19
0	*Penn State	27
10	*Northwestern	0
0	*Michigan	10
146		76

Won 7, Lost 2

U.P.I. POLL
1. Alabama
2. Arkansas
3. Notre Dame
4. Michigan
5. Texas
6. Nebraska
7. L.S.U.
8. Oregon State
9. OHIO STATE
10. Southern Cal.

A.P. POLL
1. Alabama
2. Arkansas
3. Notre Dame
4. Michigan
5. Texas
6. Nebraska
7. L.S.U.
8. Oregon State
9. OHIO STATE
10. Southern Cal.

Oct. 17

Unbeaten Bucks Top Trojans 17-0

COLUMBUS, Ohio (AP) — Ohio State's second-ranked Buckeyes shot down Southern California's air attack and sent fullback Willard Sander on a ground-eating rampage Saturday in defeating the Trojans 17-0 before 84,315 paying customers and a nationwide television audience.

It was Ohio State's fourth straight conquest, Southern California's first shutout in 25 games and the crowd was the third largest ever to make the Buckeye Stadium bulge at its seams.

The Ohioans, seeking to avenge last year's 32-3 loss to the Trojans, most one-sided defeat suffered by Coach Woody Hayes in his 14 years here, marched 64 yards in 15 plays for a score the first time they had the ball.

Sander, the 215-pound junior fullback from Cincinnati who gained 120 yards as he carried 29 times, plunged the last two yards for the counter.

In the second period, Don Unverferth passed 10 yards to Greg Lashutka for the second Ohio score after Tom Kiehfuss had recovered Mike Garrett's fumble on the 10. The Bucks put the icing on the cake with Bob Funk's 24-yard field goal, his sixth of the year, as a 75-yard drive was stalled.

Southern Cal's biggest threats were snuffed out by three pass interceptions and two fumbles and its nearest bid to score was erased by a peculiar penalty.

[1964]

Nov. 7

Penn State's Four-Time Losers Shock Powerful Ohio State, 27-0

COLUMBUS, Ohio (P) — Penn State's four-time losers turned Ohio State's second-ranked juggernaut into a stumbling, fumbling giant Saturday and beat the highly favored Bucks 27-0 in what must go into the books as the season's biggest upset.

The Nittany Lions in winning their fourth in four starts against the Bucks annihilated both the offense and the defense of Coach Woody Hayes' Big Ten Conference leaders.

With quarterback Gary Wydman guiding the Lions and fullback Tom Urbanik blasting the forward wall, Penn State scored in every quarter as it handed Ohio State its first shutout in 45 games and blasted any national championship hopes.

The victors went 65 yards in eight plays, 35 in five, 42 in seven and 64 in 10 for their touchdowns. Ohio State failed to reach enemy territory until the final minute.

Bucks Bewildered

The Bucks appeared battered and bewildered and were completely futile in the opening half as they failed to score a first down, and wound up with a minus 14 yardage.

It wasn't much better in the second half. Ohio State's initial first down came with 5:11 left in the third quarter, and it was on a penalty. The Bucks had only five first downs for the entire day, their lowest output in memory.

Kunit scored Penn State's last two touchdowns on runs of two and five yards. Quarterback Gary Wydman counted another on a three-yard option run, and Dirk Nye put over the opener when he recovered Urbanik's fumble in the end zone.

A crowd of 84,279 witnessed the contest, moving Ohio State's five-game gate to 415,530. It was Dad's Day and the fathers of most players were seated on the sideline for the humiliating defeat.

The only thing Ohio State won was the opening toss.

Nov. 21

Michigan Wolverines Top Buckeyes By 10-0 Score to Gain Rose Bowl Bid

COLUMBUS, Ohio (P) — Michigan's Wolverines frustrated Ohio State at every turn Saturday, defeating the Buckeyes 10-0 to win the Western Conference championship and the Rose Bowl berth.

The Wolverines capitalized on a break for their lone touchdown, added a fourth period field goal and then halted Ohio State's frantic passing attack to take it all.

It was Michigan's first Big Ten title and Rose Bowl trip since 1950.

Particularly distressing to Ohio Coach Woody Hayes was the fact that Ohio high school talent which got away came back to haunt him and hand him his first league loss of the year.

John Henderson of Dayton, Ohio, recovered a fumble on Ohio State's 20 in the second period and two plays later Bob Timberlake of Franklin, Ohio, passed 17 yards to Jim Detwiler of Toledo, Ohio, for a touchdown, and Timberlake booted the extra point.

Timberlake kicked a 27-yard field goal in the fourth period — so Ohio boys scored all of Michigan's points.

In the final period, after Ohio had surged twice into Wolverine territory, Richard Volk of Wauseon, Ohio, intercepted two passes to seal the shutout against the Bucks.

Coach Bump Elliott defeated Hayes in this big one after four straight losses to succeed his brother Pete of Illinois as conference champion and Rose Bowl representative, the first time a brother act has put the pair back to back.

1964 TEAM STATISTICS, BY GAME

	First Downs	Rush	Net Gain Pass	Total	Total Plays	Att.	Passing Comp.	Int.	Punting No.	Avg.	Fumbles No.	Lost	Yards Penalized	Points
SOUTHERN METHODIST	17	79	135	214	66	23	14	3	7	41.1	3	2	29	8
OHIO STATE	13	212	75	287	55	12	6	0	5	36.5	4	1	33	27
INDIANA	18	95	227	322	76	34	17	3	5	23.8	0	0	20	9
OHIO STATE	16	125	164	289	58	23	15	0	6	38.0	0	0	48	17
ILLINOIS	10	61	79	140	65	23	10	2	8	31.2	2	2	67	0
OHIO STATE	12	116	130	246	59	19	8	3	4	34.5	0	0	47	26
SOUTHERN CALIFORNIA	12	64	133	197	56	26	8	3	4	39.7	3	2	41	0
OHIO STATE	21	215	79	294	84	17	8	2	4	42.0	1	1	66	17
WISCONSIN	10	58	128	186	51	23	13	0	7	27.6	2	2	59	3
OHIO STATE	29	291	117	408	84	18	9	1	2	35.0	1	1	35	28
IOWA	18	94	221	315	72	33	17	3	4	32.5	2	1	32	19
OHIO STATE	12	79	110	189	60	16	6	1	5	33.8	4	3	56	21
PENN STATE	22	201	148	349	79	22	12	0	5	37.0	1	0	20	27
OHIO STATE	5	33	30	63	37	14	3	2	9	42.9	3	2	10	0
NORTHWESTERN	9	85	59	144	56	17	6	2	6	32.3	1	1	59	0
OHIO STATE	17	125	116	241	79	26	13	1	6	31.7	0	0	45	10
MICHIGAN	9	115	45	160	54	9	3	0	9	39.8	3	2	36	10
OHIO STATE	10	103	77	180	59	21	7	2	6	30.1	6	2	25	0
OPPONENTS	125	852	1175	2027	574	210	100	16	54	34.7	17	12	363	76
OHIO STATE	135	1299	898	2197	575	166	75	12	47	36.4	19	10	365	146

1964 OHIO STATE INDIVIDUAL STATISTICS

RUSHING

Player	Tries	Gain	Lost	Net	Avg.	TD's
Sander	147	628	2	626	4.2	7
Rein	73	309	28	281	3.8	2
Barrington	66	246	40	206	3.1	1
*Lindsey	13	109	2	107	8.2	0
McCoy	20	68	0	68	3.4	0
Hudson	13	46	0	46	3.4	0
*Barnett	7	19	0	19	2.7	0
Thomas	3	7	0	7	2.3	0
*Drenik	1	5	0	5	5.0	0
Lykes	1	3	0	3	3.0	0
*Espy	1	3	0	3	3.0	0
Meinerding	2	3	2	1	.5	0
*Bodenbender	1	1	0	1	1.0	0
*Kaylor	1	0	4	−4	−4.0	0
*Dreffer	2	3	10	−7	−3.5	0
*Yonclas	1	0	16	−16	−16.0	0
Unverferth	57	139	186	−47	−.8	2
Totals	404	1589	290	1299	3.1	12

FORWARD PASSING

Player	Att.	Comp.	Int.	Yards	Comp. Pct.	TD's
Unverferth	160	73	10	871	.456	4
*Yonclas	4	1	2	19	.250	0
*Chonko	1	1	0	8	1.000	0
Barrington	1	0	0	0	.000	0
Totals	166	75	12	898	.452	4

PASSING ANALYSIS

Player	Att.	Comp.	Had Dropped	Deflected	Out of Reach	Had Int.	% Well Thrown Passes
Unverferth	160	73	11	26	40	10	.525
*Yonclas	4	1	0	0	1	2	.250
*Chonko	1	1	0	0	0	0	1.000
Barrington	1	0	0	0	1	0	.000
Totals	166	75	11	26	42	12	.518

SCORING

Player	Rush	Touchdowns Pass	Int. Ret.	Extra Points	Field Goals	Total Points
Sander	7	0	0	0	0	42
Funk	0	0	0	17-18	7-14	38
Rein	2	1	0	0	0	18
Unverferth	2	0	0	0	0	12
*Spahr	0	0	1	0	0	6
Barrington	1	0	0	0	0	6
*Stock	0	1	0	0	0	6
Lashutka	0	1	0	0	0	6
*Dreffer	0	0	1	0	0	6
*Lindsey	0	1	0	0	0	6
Totals	12	4	2	17-18	7-14	146

KICKOFF RETURNS

Player	Number	Yards	Average	TD's
Barrington	8	223	27.9	0
Rein	10	203	20.3	0
*Barnett	1	11	11.0	0
Totals	19	437	23.0	0

PASS RECEIVING

Player	Caught	Dropped	Yards	TD's
Rein	22	2	320	1
*Stock	18	3	215	1
Lashutka	12	1	136	1
Barrington	8	1	64	0
*Davidson	2	0	37	0
Walden	3	0	36	0
Palmer	4	1	28	0
*Lindsey	2	2	28	1
*Barnett	3	1	27	0
Sander	1	0	7	0
Totals	75	11	898	4

PUNTING

Player	Number	Yards	Avg.
*Dreffer	46	1711	37.2
(Team)	1	0	00.0
Totals	47	1711	36.4

PUNT RETURNS

Player	Number	Yards	Average	TD's
Barrington	3	66	22.0	0
Rein	10	61	6.1	0
*Chonko	3	31	10.3	0
Bugel	1	9	9.0	0
*Barnett	1	3	3.0	0
*Stock	1	0	0.0	0
Totals	19	170	8.9	0

INTERCEPTION RETURNS

Player	Number	Yards	Average	TD's
*Chonko	7	72	10.3	0
Fill	2	48	24.0	0
*Dreffer	2	46	23.0	1
*Spahr	2	31	15.5	1
Bugel	1	18	18.0	0
Nein	1	8	8.0	0
Kelley	1	3	3.0	0
*Drenik	1	0	0.0	0
Totals	17	226	13.3	2

SCORE BY QUARTERS

	1	2	3	4	—T
Opponents	17	20	9	30	—76
Ohio State	51	40	28	27	—146

* Not returning for 1965

1965 OHIO STATE FOOTBALL ROSTER
(Alphabetical)

No.	Name	Pos.	Wgt.	Hgt.	Age	Class	Home Town
75	Adams, Thomas	RT	210	6-3	20	So.	Fairport
21	Allen, Richard	QB	177	6-1	21	Sr.	Sidney
18	Amlin, George	LH	165	5-10	20	So.	Tiffin
81	Anders, Billy	LE	191	6-2	20	Jr.	Sabina
57	*Anderson, Kim	LE	190	6-0	20	Jr.	Orrville
72	*Anderson, Richard	LT	238	6-5	21	Sr.	Lodi
61	*Andrick, Theodore	LG	212	5-11	21	Sr.	Cuyahoga Falls
35	Baas, James	LE	202	6-1	20	Jr.	Columbus
25	**Barrington, Thomas	FB	202	6-1	21	Sr.	Lima
66	**Bugel, Thomas	LG	208	6-0	20	Sr.	W. Homestead, Pa.
76	Burgin, Asbury	LT	232	6-2	20	Jr.	Euclid
90	Cairns, Gary	LG	238	6-1	20	Jr.	Canton
89	Calloway, Thomas	RE	186	6-0	19	So.	Troy
51	Cochran, Terrence	C	198	5-9	21	Sr.	Richwood
74	Current, Michael	RT	237	6-4	20	Jr.	Lima
88	Dillon, Dan	RE	185	6-0	19	So.	Springfield
82	Doles, Lonnie	LE	186	6-0	19	So.	West Milton
78	Dwyer, Donald	RT	218	6-2	19	So.	Lima
63	Eachus, William	LG	211	6-0	20	Jr.	Gallipolis
14	Elliott, Samuel	QB	176	6-0	19	So.	Akron
34	Farbizo, Thomas	FB	194	5-11	20	Jr.	New Philadelphia
73	Fender, Paul	LT	228	6-3	18	So.	Warren
15	*Fill, John	LH	177	5-9	22	Jr.	Cuyahoga Hgts.
23	Fontes, Arnold	QB	184	5-11	19	So.	Canton
62	*Funk, Robert	PK	222	6-1	21	Sr.	Lakewood
95	George, August	RT	222	6-0	20	Jr.	Kettering
70	Green, Mark	RT	242	6-4	19	Jr.	Groveport
46	Hamlin, Stanley	RH	190	6-1	19	So.	Monessen, Pa.
71	Himes, Richard	RT	235	6-4	19	So.	Canton
41	Hubbard, Rudy	LH	192	6-0	19	So.	Hubbard
36	*Hudson, Paul	FB	207	6-0	21	Jr.	Coatesville, Pa.
59	Hughes, Ralph	RG	226	5-9	19	So.	Pataskala
43	Jacobson, Howard	RH	192	5-10	19	So.	Freeport, N.Y.
80	Johnson, Robert	LE	210	6-1	19	So.	Logan
53	**Kelley, Dwight	C	216	5-11	21	Sr.	Bremen
77	Kelley, John	LT	215	6-0	19	So.	Englewood
84	Knight, Charles	RE	194	6-3	19	So.	Cincinnati
87	**Lashutka, Gregory	RE	219	6-5	21	Sr.	Cleveland
48	Lykes, Robert	LH	185	6-1	21	Sr.	Akron
12	*McCoy, John	FB	188	5-10	20	Jr.	Wooster
17	Meinerding, Wesley	RH	203	6-0	20	Jr.	Canton
58	*Miller, Gary	LT	216	6-0	21	Jr.	Bellevue
85	*Nein, James	RH	193	6-2	20	Jr.	Middletown
20	Newcomer, Mark	QB	175	5-11	20	Jr.	Gibsonburg
50	Newcomer, Robert	C	216	6-1	20	So.	Toledo
56	Oates, James	C	229	6-0	21	Sr.	Dunkirk
93	Orazen, Michael	RE	203	6-0	20	Jr.	Euclid
86	*Palmer, John	RE	208	6-1	21	Sr.	Kettering
30	Portsmouth, Thomas	RH	182	5-10	19	So.	Middletown
65	*Pryor, Ray	C	220	6-0	20	Jr.	Hamilton
38	Reed, Samuel	LE	183	5-8	19	Jr.	Garrettsville
45	*Rein, Robert	LH	182	5-11	20	Jr.	Niles
44	Richley, Richard	RH	183	5-9	23	Sr.	Cincinnati
69	**Ridder, William	RG	212	5-10	20	Sr.	Springfield
55	Rutherford, William	C	188	5-10	20	Sr.	Columbus
33	**Sander, Willard	FB	215	6-2	21	Sr.	Cincinnati
52	Sharp, Thomas	C	200	5-11	19	So.	Springfield
96	Smith, Larry	RT	209	5-10	21	Sr.	Amsterdam
64	Snyder, Larry	RG	198	6-2	22	Sr.	Wooster
11	Thomas, Will	RH	174	6-0	20	Jr.	Lima
26	**Unverferth, Donald	QB	208	6-3	21	Sr.	Dayton
68	**Van Horn, Douglas	RG	236	6-2	21	Sr.	Columbus
98	Vargo, Thomas	LG	190	5-10	20	Jr.	Columbus
83	*Walden, Robert	LE	180	6-0	20	Jr.	Middletown
24	Walker, Paul	QB	200	6-2	19	So.	Middletown

* Indicates letter

1965
Captains: Dwight Kelley, Gregory Lashutka

3	*North Carolina	14
23	Washington	21
28	*Illinois	14
7	Michigan State	32
20	Wisconsin	10
11	*Minnesota	10
17	*Indiana	10
38	*Iowa	0
9	Michigan	7
156		118

Won 7, Lost 2

FUNK BOOTS 17-YARDER
Three-Pointer Comes With 59 Seconds Left

Seattle, Oct. 2 — Bob Funk's slightly angled field goal from the 17-yard line with only 59 ticks left on the clock earned Ohio State a 23-21 football victory today over the Huskies of Washington.

The burly Buckeyes trying for their first 1965 triumph after a defeat by North Carolina last w marched from their own 20-yard line to get within kicking range in a fine display of coolness under pressure.

Washington had tried and missed a field goal from 20 yards out just before the Buckeyes' victory drive.

Statistics
First downs	14	16
Rushing yardage	160	197
Passing yardage	41	56
Passes	5-13	4-7
Passes intercepted by	0	1
Punts	4-37	3-29
Fumbles lost	0	2
Yards penalized	40	91

Ohio State .. 0 14 6 3—23
Washington . 7 6 8 0—21

Wash.—Medved, 1, run (Medved kick).
Ohio—Sander, 2, run (Funk kick).
Ohio—Darington, 1, run (Funk kick).
Wash.—Moore, 6, run (run failed).
Wash.—Moore, 3, run (Cramer, pass from Hullen).
Ohio—Fontes, 5, run (kick failed).
Ohio—F.G., 27, Funk.

[1965]

Front row, left to right: Snyder, Funk, Ridder, R. Anderson, Andrick, Van Horn, Unverferth, D. Kelley, co-captain; Lashutka, co-captain; Sander, Palmer, Barrington, Bugel, Richley, Adderly.

Second row: Cochran, Oates, Orazen, Anders, McCoy, Walden, Miller, Nein, Rein, Pryor, Fill, K. Anderson, Eachus, Smith, Lykes.

Third row: Allen, Elliott, Reed, Johnson, Portsmouth, Hudson, Fontes, Current, Dwyer, Himes, Thomas, Hamlin, Baas, Meinerding, Vargo.

Fourth row: Amlin, Sharp, J. Kelley, George, Dillion, Fender, Adams, Burgin, Hubbard, Walker, Cairns, Rutherford.

Back row: Head Coach Hayes, Assts. Strobel, Urick, McCullough, Catuzzi, Sarkkinen, Mrukowski, Ellison, Clark, Hindman; Athletic Director Larkins.

Michigan State Routs Buckeyes

EAST LANSING, Mich. (P) — Fourth-ranked Michigan State held Ohio State's traditional "cloud of dust and a first down" offense to a minus 22 yards rushing and the Spartans romped to a 32-7 Big Ten football victory over the Buckeyes Saturday.

It was the first time in Ohio State football history that the Buckeyes ended up on the minus side in rushing and marked the second straight Big Ten game in which the Spartans bottled up an opponent's rushing attack on the minus 38 yards rushing.

```
Ohio State            0  0  0  7—  7
Michigan State        7  0  5 20— 32
  MSU—Jones, 80 run (Kenney kick).
  MSU—FG, Kenney 35.
  MSU—Safety, Unverferth tackled in
end zone.
  OSU—Fontes, 36 pass from Unverferth
(Funk kick).
  MSU—Apisa, 1 run (Kenney kick).
  MSU—Lowther, 6 run (Kenney kick).
  Attendance: 75,288.
```

Ohio State Edges Gophers Before 84,359

COLUMBIA, Ohio (P) — Bob Funk booted an 18-yard field goal with only 1:17 left in the game Saturday, giving Ohio State a hard-fought 11-10 victory over Minnesota in a Big Ten struggle before 84,359.

The Buckeyes, keeping their slim hopes for a conference championship alive with their third victory in four starts, drove 89 yards on the passing of Don Unverferth to set up Funk's fifth three-pointer of the season.

Buckeyes 9-7

ANN ARBOR, Mich. (P) — Bob Funk's 27-yard field goal with 1:15 remaining—after Ohio State had gambled on fourth down deep in its own territory—gave the Buckeyes a 9-7 Big Ten football victory over Michigan Saturday.

[1965]

1965 TEAM STATISTICS, BY GAME

	First Downs Rush	First Downs Pass	First Downs Pen.	First Downs Total	Net Gain Rush	Net Gain Pass	Total	Total Plays	Passing Att.	Passing Comp.	Passing Int.	Punting No.	Punting Avg.	Fumbles No.	Fumbles Lost	Yards Penalized	Points
NORTH CAROLINA	5	9	0	14	181	127	308	51	16	11	1	4	40.0	4	2	13	14
OHIO STATE	8	10	1	19	66	178	244	82	35	19	2	4	36.5	1	1	14	3
WASHINGTON	10	3	3	16	197	56	253	55	7	4	0	3	29.3	3	2	91	21
OHIO STATE	11	1	4	16	160	41	201	69	13	5	1	4	38.0	0	0	40	23
ILLINOIS	9	5	0	14	207	81	288	73	24	7	1	7	37.4	3	1	67	14
OHIO STATE	12	4	0	16	252	92	344	70	11	4	0	5	37.6	5	2	35	28
MICHIGAN STATE	16	9	0	25	387	151	538	83	19	11	1	2	46.5	3	2	59	32
OHIO STATE	0	8	0	8	−22	174	152	46	29	14	2	7	39.9	0	0	20	7
WISCONSIN	10	7	1	18	128	111	239	71	26	12	1	4	31.2	5	3	20	10
OHIO STATE	7	4	0	11	153	46	199	61	12	6	0	8	33.2	3	1	20	20
MINNESOTA	7	6	0	13	97	128	225	63	21	10	1	7	37.4	2	0	38	10
OHIO STATE	11	10	0	21	142	196	338	73	25	14	2	5	35.4	3	3	27	11
INDIANA	6	6	1	13	95	140	235	64	27	12	3	6	37.3	3	1	40	10
OHIO STATE	7	7	1	15	141	131	272	64	24	12	2	5	43.8	1	0	15	17
IOWA	5	5	3	13	84	136	220	71	38	11	3	6	36.3	4	2	54	0
OHIO STATE	15	5	1	21	250	99	349	74	19	12	0	6	33.5	4	1	60	38
MICHIGAN	13	5	0	18	249	86	335	72	16	7	0	4	42.5	2	0	35	7
OHIO STATE	11	8	0	19	138	123	261	69	29	15	2	3	46.0	3	1	10	9
OPPONENTS	81	55	8	144	1625	1016	2641	603	194	85	11	43	37.2	29	13	417	118
OHIO STATE	82	57	7	146	1280	1080	2360	608	197	101	11	47	37.4	20	9	241	156

1965 OHIO STATE INDIVIDUAL STATISTICS

RUSHING

Player	Tries	Gain	Lost	Net	Avg.	TD's
*Barrington	139	580	26	554	4.0	6
*Sander	134	532	2	530	3.9	8
Rein	38	205	4	201	5.3	0
Fontes	32	99	29	70	2.2	1
*Adderley	9	25	5	20	2.2	0
Hudson	4	12	0	12	3.0	0
Meinerding	5	9	0	9	1.8	0
*Farbizo	1	3	0	3	3.0	0
Hubbard	1	2	0	2	2.0	0
Thomas	9	11	11	0	0.0	0
*Lykes	1	0	5	−5	−5.0	0
*Unverferth	38	34	150	−116	−3.1	0
Totals	411	1512	232	1280	3.1	15

FORWARD PASSING

Player	Att.	Comp.	Int.	Yards	Comp. Pct.	TD's
*Unverferth	191	99	10	1061	.518	4
Fontes	6	2	1	19	.333	0
Totals	197	101	11	1080	.512	4

PASSING ANALYSIS

Player	Att.	Comp.	Had Dropped	Deflected	Out of Reach	Had Int.	% Well Thrown Passes
*Unverferth	191	99	12	23	47	10	.581
Fontes	6	2	0	1	2	1	.333
Totals	197	101	12	24	49	11	.573

SCORING

Player	Touchdowns Rush	Touchdowns Pass	Extra Points Kick	Extra Points Run	Field Goals	Total Points
*Sander	8	0	0	0	0	48
*Funk	0	0	16–18	0	8–12	40
*Barrington	6	0	0	0	0	36
Fontes	1	1	0	1–1	0	14
*Adderley	0	1	0	0	0	6
Rein	0	1	0	0	0	6
Anders	0	1	0	0	0	6
Totals	15	4	16–18	1–1	8–12	156

SCORE BY QUARTERS

	1	2	3	4	—T
Opponents	38	23	23	34	—118
OHIO STATE	20	73	37	26	—156

* Not returning for 1966

PASS RECEIVING

Player	Caught	Dropped	Yards	TD's
Rein	29	2	328	1
Anders	25	2	244	1
*Lashutka	22	3	226	0
Fontes	6	1	111	1
*Sander	9	1	79	0
*Barrington	9	2	67	0
*Adderley	1	0	25	1
Current	0	1	0	0
Totals	101	12	1080	4

PUNTING

Player	Number	Yards	Avg.
*Kelley	5	192	38.4
*Barrington	42	1565	37.2
Totals	47	1757	37.4

KICKOFF RETURNS

Player	Number	Yards	Average	TD's
*Barrington	14	480	34.3	0
Rein	3	66	22.0	0
Fontes	3	44	14.7	0
*Adderley	1	26	26.0	0
Thomas	1	6	6.0	0
*Kelley	1	0	0.0	0
Totals	23	622	27.0	0

PUNT RETURNS

Player	Number	Yards	Average	TD's
Fill	11	53	4.8	0
Rein	3	9	3.0	0
Baas	1	0	0.0	0
Walden	1	0	0.0	0
Totals	16	62	3.9	0

INTERCEPTION RETURNS

Player	Number	Yards	Average	TD's
Johnson	2	15	7.5	0
Fill	2	11	5.5	0
*Bugel	2	3	1.5	0
*Kelley	1	8	8.0	0
Himes	1	1	1.0	0
McCoy	1	1	1.0	0
Portsmouth	1	1	1.0	0
*Lashutka	1	0	0.0	0
Totals	11	40	3.6	0

1966 Ohio State Football Squad Picture

Front row, left to right: Will Thomas, August George, Robert Walden, John McCoy, John Palmer, Paul Hudson, Michael Current (Capt.), Gary Miller, Ray Pryor (Capt.), James Baas, Robert Rein, William Eachus, John Fill (Capt.), Kim Anderson, Wesley Meinerding and Asbury Burgin. *Row two:* Head Coach Woody Hayes. Dan Dillon, George Amlin, Paul Fender, John Kelley, Sam Elliott, William Rutherford, Gary Cairns, Robert Johnson, Richard Himes, Billy Anders, James Nein, Thomas Portsmouth, Stanley Hamlin, Donald Dwyer, Rudy Hubbard and Arnold Fontes. *Row three:* Richard Timko, Ronald Coleman, Jaren Bombach, Jerome Tabacca, Terry Ervin, Nicholas Roman, Rufus Mayes, David Foley, Robert Smith, Joseph Jenkins, Albert Weber, Glenn Hodge, William Urbanik, Mark Stier, John Stowe and John Muhlbach. *Row four:* Assistant Coach Glenn Ellison, Assistant Coach Louis McCullough, Dirk Worden, Edward Bender, Merrill Phelan, John Ford, James Roman, Jules DiFederico, Michael Kafury, John Sobolewski, Michael Orazen, Thomas Petersen, William Powers, Assistant Coach Esco Sarkkinen and Assistant Coach William Mallory. *Back row:* Graduate Assistant John Derbyshire, Assistant Coach Larry Catuzzi, Assistant Coach Earle Bruce, Thomas Bartley, Victor Stottlemyer, Gerald Ehrsam, David Reynolds, Rudy Smith, William Long, John Krupko, Gary Roush, Leroy Peyton, Assistant Coach Hugh Hindman, Assistant Coach Harry Strobel and Graduate Assistant William Ridder.

[1966]

1966 OHIO STATE FOOTBALL ROSTER
(Alphabetical)

No.	Name	Pos.	Wgt.	Hgt.	Age	Class	Home Town
18	Amlin, George	S	166	5-10	21	Jr.	Tiffin
81	*Anders, Billy	LE	191	6-2	21	Jr.	Sabina
57	**Anderson, Kim	LB	186	6-0	21	Sr.	Orrville
35	*Baas, James	LE	202	6-1	21	Sr.	Columbus
33	Bartley, Thomas	LB	198	5-11	19	So.	Springfield
19	Bender, Edward	RH	175	6-0	19	So.	Akron
48	Bombach, Jaren	RH	197	6-1	18	So.	Dayton
76	*Burgin, Asbury	RG	228	6-2	21	Sr.	Euclid
90	Cairns, Gary	PK	229	6-1	21	Jr.	Canton
68	Coleman, Ronald	MG	193	6-0	19	So.	Toledo
74	*Current, Michael	LT	241	6-4	21	Sr.	Lima
66	DiFederico, Jules	RT	214	6-1	19	So.	Steubenville
88	Dillon, Dan	LE	184	6-0	20	Sr.	Springfield
78	*Dwyer, Donald	RT	226	6-2	20	Jr.	Lima
63	*Eachus, William	LG	218	6-0	21	Jr.	Gallipolis
28	Ehrsam, Gerald	QB	192	6-0	19	So.	Toledo
14	*Elliott, Samuel	QB	192	6-0	20	Jr.	Torrance, Calif.
75	Ervin, Terry	RT	222	6-2	18	So.	Wellston
73	Fender, Paul	RT	224	6-3	19	Jr.	Warren
15	**Fill, John	LH	178	5-9	23	Sr.	Cuyahoga Hgts.
70	Foley, David	RT	242	6-5	18	So.	Cincinnati
23	*Fontes, Arnold	RH	187	5-11	20	Jr.	Canton
67	Ford, John	RT	214	6-1	19	So.	Springfield
95	George, August	RT	222	6-0	21	Sr.	Kettering
46	*Hamlin, Stanley	RH	194	6-1	20	Jr.	Monessen, Pa.
71	Himes, Richard	RG	250	6-4	20	Jr.	Canton
47	Hodge, Glenn	LH	183	6-2	19	So.	Oberlin
41	*Hubbard, Rudy	LH	184	6-0	20	Jr.	Hubbard
36	**Hudson, Paul	FB	212	6-0	22	Sr.	Coatesville, Pa.
84	Jenkins, Joseph	RE	209	6-2	18	So.	East Cleveland
80	*Johnson, Robert	LB	208	6-1	20	Jr.	Logan
64	Kafury, Michael	MG	212	6-1	18	So.	Cambridge
62	Kelley, John	RG	217	6-0	20	Jr.	Englewood
24	Long, William	QB	173	6-1	19	So.	Dayton
72	Mayes, Rufus	LT	227	6-5	18	So.	Toledo
12	**McCoy, John	LB	192	5-10	21	Sr.	Wooster
17	*Meinerding, Wesley	RH	208	6-0	21	Sr.	Canton
58	**Miller, Gary	LT	219	6-0	22	Sr.	Bellevue
53	Muhlbach, John	C	188	5-10	19	So.	Massillon
85	*Nein, James	RH	194	6-2	21	Jr.	Middletown
93	Orazen, Michael	RE	209	6-0	21	Jr.	Euclid
86	**Palmer, John	LG	215	6-1	22	Sr.	Kettering
16	Peyton, Leroy	RH	175	5-8	19	So.	Lorain
30	*Portsmouth, Thomas	S	180	5-10	20	Jr.	Middletown
20	Powers, William	PK	176	6-1	19	So.	Bay Village
65	**Pryor, Ray	C	230	6-0	21	Sr.	Hamilton
45	**Rein, Robert	RH	182	5-11	21	Sr.	Niles
42	Reynolds, David	LH	196	5-11	20	Jr.	Lima
52	Roman, James	C	212	6-0	18	So.	Canton
89	Roman, Nicholas	LE	210	6-4	19	So.	Canton
59	Roush, Gary	LT	198	6-4	19	So.	Springfield
55	Rutherford, William	C	196	5-10	21	Sr.	Columbus
87	Smith, Robert	RE	226	6-4	19	So.	Lakewood
32	Smith, Rudy	FB	207	6-0	19	So.	Cincinnati
91	Sobolewski, John	RE	192	6-1	19	So.	Steubenville
54	Stier, Mark	LB	191	6-1	19	So.	Louisville
69	Stottlemyer, Victor	MG	208	6-0	19	So.	Chillicothe
92	Stowe, John	LE	214	6-2	19	So.	Columbus
94	Tabacca, Jerome	RE	212	6-2	19	So.	Warren
11	*Thomas, Will	LH	188	6-0	21	Sr.	Lima
79	Urbanik, William	LT	227	6-3	19	So.	Donora, Pa.
83	**Walden, Robert	LE	176	6-0	21	Sr.	Middletown
34	Weber, Albert	FB	210	6-0	20	So.	Dayton
56	Worden, Dirk	LB	195	6-0	19	So.	Dayton

* Indicates letter

1966
Captains: John Fill
Mike Current
Ray Pryor

14	*Texas Christian	7
22	*Washington	38
9	Illinois	10
8	*Michigan State	11
24	*Wisconsin	13
7	Minnesota	17
7	*Indiana	0
14	Iowa	10
3	*Michigan	17
108		123

Won 4, Lost 5

Oct. 15

MICHIGAN STATE 11, OHIO STATE 8

COLUMBUS, Ohio (AP) — Mighty Michigan State, stymied by rain, wind, and an inspired band of Buckeyes, rambled 83 yards on a fourth quarter touchdown drive Saturday and eked out an 11-8 Big Ten football victory over Ohio State before 84,282 fans.

The No. 1-ranked Spartans had to fight off a late Buckeye drive before posting their fifth straight conquest of the season while Ohio State was losing its third straight for the first time since 1943.

Michigan State 0 0 3 8—11
Ohio State 2 0 0 6— 8
OSU — Safety MSU center snap out of end zone
MSU — FG Kenny 27
OSU — Anders 47 pass from Long (kick failed)
MSU — Apisa 1 run (Wedemeyer pass from Kenny)
Attendance 84,282.

[1966] 195

OHIO STATE INDIVIDUAL STATISTICS

RUSHING

Player	Tries	Gain	Lost	Net	Avg.	TD's
*Rein	103	468	12	456	4.4	0
*Hudson	120	434	7	427	3.5	6
Hubbard	18	79	1	78	4.3	0
R. Smith	14	46	0	46	3.2	0
Long	96	196	163	33	.3	1
Ehrsam	11	42	11	31	2.8	0
*Fontes	7	32	2	30	4.3	0
Elliott	1	6	0	6	6.0	0
*Thomas	2	5	0	5	2.5	0
Totals	372	1308	196	1112	2.9	7

FORWARD PASSING

Player	Att.	Comp.	Int.	Yards	Comp. Pct.	TD's
Long	192	106	12	1180	.552	6
Ehrsam	10	2	1	15	.200	0
Totals	202	108	13	1195	.534	6

SCORING

Player	Touchdowns Rush	Touchdowns Pass	Extra Points Kick	Extra Points Run	Field Goals	Total Points
*Hudson	6	0	0	0	0	36
Cairns	0	0	11–12	0	5–11	26
Anders	0	2	0	1–0	0	14
*Rein	0	2	0	0	0	12
Long	1	0	0	0–1	0	6
*Fontes	0	1	0	0	0	6
Hubbard	0	1	0	0	0	6
(Safety)						2
Totals	7	6	11–12	1–1	5–11	108

PASS RECEIVING

Player	Caught	Dropped	Yards	TD's
Anders	55	3	671	2
*Rein	26	3	281	2
Hubbard	11	1	105	1
Mayes	11	2	95	0
*Fontes	4	0	33	1
*Walden	1	0	10	0
*Reynolds	0	1	0	0
Totals	108	10	1195	6

PUNTING

Player	Number	Yards	Avg.
*Current	38	1376	36.2
N. Roman	1	35	35.0
Totals	39	1411	36.1

KICKOFF RETURNS

Player	Number	Yards	Average	TD's
*Rein	11	207	18.8	0
*Thomas	4	154	38.5	0
*Fontes	4	51	12.7	0
*Peyton	1	36	36.0	0
Hubbard	3	33	11.0	0
*Reynolds	2	27	13.5	0
Ehrsam	1	22	22.0	0
Elliott	1	16	16.0	0
Totals	27	546	20.2	0

PUNT RETURNS

Player	Number	Yards	Average	TD's
*Fill	15	167	11.1	0
Ehrsam	4	34	8.5	0
*Fontes	1	3	3.0	0
*Rein	1	0	0.0	0
Nein	1	0	0.0	0
Totals	22	204	9.3	0

INTERCEPTION RETURNS

Player	Number	Yards	Average	TD's
*Fill	2	8	4.0	0
Muhlbach	2	6	3.0	0
Portsmouth	2	0	0.0	0
Nein	1	31	31.0	0
*Walden	1	20	20.0	0
Stier	1	0	0.0	0
Totals	9	65	7.2	0

SCORE BY QUARTERS

	1	2	3	4	—T
Opponents	10	40	38	35	—123
OHIO STATE	19	20	27	42	—108

* Not returning for 1967

1966 TEAM STATISTICS, BY GAME

	First Downs Rush	First Downs Pass	First Downs Pen.	First Downs Total	Net Gain Rush	Net Gain Pass	Net Gain Total	Total Plays	Passing Att.	Passing Comp.	Passing Int.	Punting No.	Punting Avg.	Fumbles No.	Fumbles Lost	Yards Penalized	Points
TEXAS CHRISTIAN	8	7	0	15	114	175	289	59	24	15	3	4	43.0	3	2	50	7
OHIO STATE	10	8	0	18	200	106	306	62	14	12	0	5	38.8	6	5	40	14
WASHINGTON	18	2	0	20	413	20	433	73	5	2	1	2	42.5	3	1	45	38
OHIO STATE	3	12	2	17	40	228	268	68	38	21	2	5	42.6	1	1	15	22
ILLINOIS	7	5	0	12	118	90	208	46	9	5	0	4	39.0	0	0	25	10
OHIO STATE	16	3	0	19	202	57	259	73	16	6	1	2	36.5	0	0	23	9
MICHIGAN STATE	8	6	1	15	93	121	214	70	16	6	1	6	41.8	7	1	45	11
OHIO STATE	2	5	2	9	39	144	183	43	18	11	3	7	31.8	3	1	30	8
WISCONSIN	5	12	0	17	96	207	303	70	32	18	1	2	32.5	3	2	25	13
OHIO STATE	10	11	1	22	177	160	337	72	24	15	0	3	33.0	3	1	14	24
MINNESOTA	14	0	0	14	264	3	267	61	4	1	0	4	34.5	2	1	53	17
OHIO STATE	8	6	2	16	114	127	241	68	26	11	2	2	42.0	2	2	0	7
INDIANA	10	3	0	13	143	123	266	66	25	12	1	6	39.0	2	0	54	0
OHIO STATE	4	8	2	14	93	116	209	61	17	11	1	6	40.0	3	0	35	7
IOWA	7	6	1	14	150	142	292	71	24	11	1	6	37.3	2	0	60	10
OHIO STATE	4	6	1	11	101	135	236	54	20	10	2	5	31.6	0	0	49	14
MICHIGAN	15	6	0	21	272	110	382	70	15	6	1	3	43.3	2	1	89	17
OHIO STATE	8	7	5	20	146	122	268	73	29	11	2	4	31.7	3	1	38	3
OPPONENTS	92	47	2	141	1663	991	2654	586	154	76	9	37	39.1	24	8	446	123
OHIO STATE	65	66	15	146	1112	1195	2307	574	202	108	13	39	36.1	21	11	244	108

THE OHIO STATE UNIVERSITY ROSTER

No.	NAME	POS.	WGT.	HGT.	AGE	CLASS	HOMETOWN
9	**Nein, James	LB	208	6-2	22	Senior	Middletown
11	Gillian, Ray	LH	182	5-11	19	Sophomore	Uniontown, Pa.
12	Brungard, David	LH	187	5-10	19	Sophomore	Youngstown
14	**Elliott, Samuel	RH	183	6-0	21	Senior	Torrance, Calif.
15	Polaski, Michael	RH	166	5-10	19	Sophomore	Columbus
16	Armstrong, Michael	RH	192	5-11	19	Sophomore	Springfield
17	Trapuzzano, Robert	RH	184	6-0	18	Sophomore	McKees Rocks, Pa.
19	Bender, Edward	S	172	6-0	20	Junior	Akron
20	Powers, William	PK	172	6-1	20	Junior	Bay Village
21	Burton, Arthur	LB	193	6-1	19	Sophomore	Fostoria
23	Rusnak, Kevin	QB	190	6-1	19	Sophomore	Garfield, N.J.
24	*Long, William	QB	180	6-1	20	Junior	Dayton
28	*Ehrsam, Gerald	QB	194	6-0	20	Junior	Toledo
30	**Portsmouth, Thomas	LH	181	5-10	21	Senior	Middletown
32	*Smith, Rudy	FB	203	6-0	20	Junior	Cincinnati
33	Bartley, Thomas	LB	191	5-11	20	Junior	Springfield
34	Huff, Paul	FB	217	6-3	19	Sophomore	Dover
35	Otis, James	FB	208	6-0	19	Sophomore	Celina
41	**Hubbard, Rudolph	RH	196	6-0	21	Senior	Hubbard
42	Jenkins, Joseph	RH	198	6-2	19	Junior	East Cleveland
43	Quilling, Richard	LH	189	6-1	19	Sophomore	Celina
44	Greene, Horatius	LH	173	5-11	19	Sophomore	Jersey City, N.J.
46	Provost, Ted	S	180	6-2	19	Sophomore	Navarre
47	McNeal, Charles	HB	185	5-10	19	Sophomore	Columbus
48	Bombach, Jaren	LB	198	6-1	19	Junior	Dayton
50	Smith, Robert G.	LB	221	6-1	19	Sophomore	Hamilton
51	Hackett, William	LB	204	6-0	19	Sophomore	London
52	*Roman, James	C	210	6-0	19	Junior	Canton
53	*Muhlbach, John	C	190	5-10	20	Junior	Massillon
54	*Stier, Mark	LB	208	6-1	20	Junior	Louisville
55	Radtke, Michael	LB	200	6-1	19	Sophomore	Wayne, N.J.
56	*Worden, Dirk	LB	197	6-0	21	Junior	Lorain
57	Backhus, Thomas	C	201	5-11	18	Sophomore	Cincinnati
58	Fertig, Dwight	LB	228	6-1	18	Sophomore	Ravenna
59	Roush, Gary	RT	198	6-4	20	Junior	Springfield
60	Tabacca, Jerome	LG	222	6-2	20	Junior	Warren
61	Jack, Alan	RG	215	6-0	19	Sophomore	Wintersville
62	*Kelley, John	LG	225	6-0	21	Senior	Englewood
63	Clark, Brian	MG	190	6-0	19	Sophomore	Sandusky
64	Kurz, Ted	E	222	6-2	19	Sophomore	Struthers
65	Hart, Randy	RG	220	6-1	19	Sophomore	Willoughby
66	Miller, William	C	165	5-11	19	Sophomore	Port Jefferson, N.Y.
68	*Stottlemyer, Victor	MG	200	6-0	20	Junior	Chillicothe
69	Jacobs, Paul	RG	194	6-0	20	Sophomore	Portsmouth
70	*Foley, David	RT	246	6-5	19	Junior	Cincinnati
71	**Himes, Richard	LT	243	6-4	21	Senior	Canton
72	Hutchison, Charles	RT	242	6-3	18	Sophomore	Carrollton
73	Fender, Paul	RT	237	6-3	20	Senior	Warren
74	Schmidlin, Paul	LT	221	6-1	18	Sophomore	Toledo
75	*Ervin, Terry	RT	232	6-2	19	Junior	Wellston
76	Crapser, Steve	T	260	6-1	19	Sophomore	Lockbourne A.F. Base
77	Nielsen, Brad	RT	222	6-3	19	Sophomore	Columbus
78	**Dwyer, Donald	LT	241	6-2	21	Senior	Lima
79	Urbanik, William	LT	238	6-3	20	Junior	Donora, Pa.
80	**Johnson, Robert	LB	210	6-1	21	Senior	Logan
81	**Anders, Billy	LE	194	6-2	22	Senior	Sabina
82	*Mayes, Rufus	RE	230	6-5	19	Junior	Toledo
83	Gentile, James	RE	210	6-2	19	Sophomore	Poland
84	Haer, Arthur	LE	180	6-2	19	Sophomore	North Canton
85	Pollitt, William	LE	215	6-2	19	Sophomore	Dayton
86	Aston, Daniel	RE	208	6-2	19	Sophomore	Cincinnati
87	Smith, Robert P.	RE	221	6-4	20	Junior	Lakewood
88	Whitfield, David	LE	182	6-0	19	Sophomore	Massillon
89	*Roman, Nicholas	RE	219	6-4	20	Junior	Canton
90	*Cairns, Gary	PK	212	6-1	22	Senior	Canton
91	*Sobolewski, John	RE	190	6-1	19	Junior	Steubenville
92	Stowe, John	RE	203	6-2	20	Junior	Columbus
93	Kaser, Daniel	LE	192	6-0	19	Sophomore	Sandusky
94	Fejes, Steve	E	212	6-2	19	Junior	Oregon
95	Shannon, James	C	196	5-10	19	Sophomore	Westerville

*Indicates letters won

1967
Captains: Billy Ray Anders
Samuel Elliott

7	*Arizona	14
30	Oregon	0
6	*Purdue	41
6	Northwestern	2
13	*Illinois	17
21	Michigan State	7
17	*Wisconsin	15
21	*Iowa	10
24	Michigan	14
145		120

Won 6, Lost 3

James Otis

35—OTIS, James, 19, 6-0, 200, sophomore ... from Celina ... was an all-Ohio fullback in high school ... won nine high school awards ... captained his high school football team ... the only boy in a family of four ... does construction work during the summer ... member of Sigma Chi fraternity ... a pre-dental student at Ohio State ... hobbies are hunting, fishing and boating ... admires Jim Brown and Jim Taylor ... has good speed and hits a hole quickly ... had an excellent spring practice moving up to a position of challenging for a starting berth ... probably the fastest fullback on the squad ... his top football thrill came in high school when his team, trailing 26-6 at halftime, scored 30 points to win 36-26 ... Otis carried 37 times for 238 yards in the second half of this game ...

Illinois, 17-13

COLUMBUS, Ohio (AP) — Halfback Dave Johnson crashed over the goal line with 34 seconds to play Saturday, bringing Illinois from behind in a 17-13 Big Ten football victory over Ohio State.

It spoiled a Buckeye homecoming day before a crowd of 83,928.

The fleet-footed Jackson, who has been out of action for two games because of an injury, earlier scored the Illini's first touchdown on a 14-yard run with 5:24 remaining in the first period.

BADGERS BOW 17-15
Buckeyes Draw 65,470, Fewest in 17 Years

COLUMBUS, Ohio (AP) — Quarterback Bill Long scrambled for two touchdowns Saturday, leading Ohio State to a 17-15 Big Ten football victory over stubborn Wisconsin before 65,470 rain-soaked fans.

The crowd was the smallest since 1950 when an estimated 50,000 watched Michigan and Ohio State in a blizzard.

Long, who got his first score on a 14-yard run in the second quarter, scampered four yards for the winning touchdown early in the fourth period.

It was the Buckeyes' first home victory of the season and boosted their record to 4-3 over-all and 3-2 in the conference.

Winless Wisconsin, which hasn't won in Columbus since 1918 took its seventh setback against a single tie.

The Badgers appeared headed for the victory when they scored nine points in the third quarter to take a short-lived 15-10 lead.

```
Wisconsin      6 0 9 0—15
Ohio State     3 7 0 7—17
OSU—FG Cairns 19
Wis—Reddick 4 pass from Boyajian
  (kick failed)
OSU—Long 14 run (Cairns kick)
Wis—FG Schinke 42
Wis—Schumitsch 51 pass from Boyajian
  (pass failed)
OSU—Long 4 run (Cairns kick)
Attendance 65,470.
```

STATISTICS
	Wis	O. State
First downs	16	20
Rushing yardage	70	198
Passing yardage	252	139
Return yardage	79	116
Passes	36-19-1	21-7-0
Punts	6-35	9-30
Fumbles lost	0	1
Yards penalized	59	20

TOTAL OFFENSE

Player	Plays	Rush	Pass	Total	Avg.	TD's
Long	157	59	563	622	3.9	7
Otis	141	530	0	530	3.7	2
Brungard	112	515	7	522	4.6	3
Huff	83	273	0	273	3.3	4
*Hubbard	41	219	0	219	5.3	3
Rusnak	34	23	119	142	4.2	1
Gillian	33	137	0	137	4.1	0
Ehrsam	48	44	83	127	2.6	0
Bombach	6	38	0	38	6.3	0
*R. Smith	12	26	0	26	2.2	0
Green	1	4	0	4	4.0	0
Totals	668	1868	772	2640	3.9	20

PASS RECEIVING

Player	Caught	Dropped	Yards	TD's
*Anders	28	1	403	3
*Hubbard	13	0	98	0
Brungard	6	0	90	0
Otis	7	0	48	0
Huff	3	0	46	0
Ehrsam	2	1	35	1
Gillian	3	0	23	0
Mayes	2	2	77	0
Rusnak	1	0	12	0
Totals	65	4	722	4

PUNTING

Player	Number	Yards	Avg.
*Portsmouth	52	1718	33.0
N. Roman	6	223	37.2
Totals	58	1941	33.5

* Not Returning for 1968

[1967]

OHIO STATE INDIVIDUAL STATISTICS

RUSHING

Player	Tries	Gain	Lost	Net	Avg.	TD's
Otis	144	541	11	530	3.7	2
Brungard	110	530	15	515	4.7	2
Huff	83	275	2	273	3.3	4
*Hubbard	41	230	11	219	5.3	3
Gillian	33	140	3	137	4.1	0
Long	55	163	104	59	1.1	5
Ehrsam	29	89	45	44	1.5	0
Bombach	6	38	0	38	6.3	0
*R. Smith	12	26	0	26	2.2	0
Rusnak	13	44	21	23	1.8	0
Greene	1	4	0	4	4.0	0
Totals	524	2080	212	1868	3.6	16

FORWARD PASSING

Player	Att.	Comp.	Int.	Yards	Comp. Pct.	TD's
Long	102	44	4	563	.431	2
Rusnak	21	11	0	119	.524	1
Ehrsam	19	9	2	83	.474	0
Brungard	2	1	0	7	.500	1
Totals	144	65	6	772	.451	4

PASSING ANALYSIS

Player	Att.	Comp.	Had Dropped	Deflected	Out of Reach	Had Int.	% Well Thrown Passes
Long	102	44	3	12	39	4	.461
Rusnak	21	11	1	4	5	0	.571
Ehrsam	19	9	0	5	3	2	.474
Brungard	2	1	0	0	1	0	.500
Totals	144	65	4	21	48	6	.479

SCORING

Player	Touchdowns Rush	Pass	Extra Points Kick	Pass	Field Goals	Total Points
Long	5	0	0	0-3	0	30
*Cairns	0	0	13-17	0	4-11	25
Huff	4	0	0	0	0	24
*Anders	0	3	0	0	0	24
*Hubbard	3	0	0	0	0	18
Brungard	2	0	0	0	0	12
Otis	2	0	0	0	0	12
Ehrsam	0	1	0	0	0	6
(Safety)						2
Totals	16	4	13-17	0-3	4-11	145

KICKOFF RETURNS

Player	Number	Yards	Average	TD's
Brungard	10	199	19.9	0
*Hubbard	6	103	17.1	0
Gillian	5	65	13.0	0
Otis	2	16	8.0	0
*R. Smith	1	14	14.0	0
*Anders	1	0	0.0	0
Mayes	1	0	0.0	0
Foley	1	0	0.0	0
Totals	27	397	14.7	0

PUNT RETURNS

Player	Number	Yards	Average	TD's
Polaski	28	238	8.5	0
*Portsmouth	1	9	9.0	0
Provost	3	6	2.0	0
Gillian	1	2	2.0	0
Worden	1	0	0.0	0
Totals	34	255	7.5	0

INTERCEPTION RETURNS

Player	Number	Yards	Average	TD's
Provost	7	55	7.7	0
*Portsmouth	4	16	4.0	0
*Elliott	3	29	9.6	0
*Nein	2	52	26.0	0
Worden	2	3	1.5	0
N. Roman	1	0	0.0	0
Totals	19	155	8.1	0

SCORE BY QUARTERS

	1	2	3	4	—T
Opponents	20	62	22	16	—120
OHIO STATE	57	23	25	40	—145

* Not Returning for 1968

1967 TEAM STATISTICS, BY GAME

	First Downs Rush	Pass	Pen.	Total	Net Gain Rush	Pass	Total	Total Plays	Passing Att.	Comp.	Int.	Punting No.	Avg.	Fumbles No.	Lost	Yards Penalized	Points
ARIZONA	7	4	1	12	171	59	230	71	13	5	3	10	31.1	2	0	61	14
OHIO STATE	8	3	2	13	104	118	222	69	26	7	0	8	38.2	4	2	43	7
OREGON	3	4	1	8	70	47	117	49	19	6	4	6	36.3	0	0	73	0
OHIO STATE	18	7	0	25	272	103	375	91	18	10	0	4	39.2	2	1	69	30
PURDUE	12	12	0	24	165	305	470	81	33	21	2	4	33.7	2	1	55	41
OHIO STATE	10	5	1	16	171	89	260	77	31	11	3	6	32.3	5	3	40	6
NORTHWESTERN	11	6	0	17	127	116	243	80	27	12	4	6	42.3	3	1	15	2
OHIO STATE	7	3	0	10	105	68	173	65	10	6	0	8	30.6	1	0	50	6
ILLINOIS	6	8	0	14	135	170	305	62	21	12	0	8	41.0	5	1	37	17
OHIO STATE	11	4	1	16	243	51	294	65	11	5	2	5	37.8	7	3	0	13
MICHIGAN STATE	6	5	0	11	98	94	192	55	14	6	3	6	35.0	4	2	18	7
OHIO STATE	11	6	0	17	208	129	337	78	11	9	0	7	31.6	2	2	30	21
WISCONSIN	5	10	1	16	70	252	322	70	36	19	1	6	34.8	2	0	59	15
OHIO STATE	12	5	3	20	198	139	337	75	21	7	0	9	30.1	3	1	20	17
IOWA	7	10	1	18	132	185	317	68	33	15	1	4	32.0	4	3	45	10
OHIO STATE	19	1	1	21	284	30	314	78	10	5	1	6	37.2	0	0	50	21
MICHIGAN	9	7	1	17	128	179	307	61	24	17	1	5	37.6	3	3	34	14
OHIO STATE	15	2	1	18	283	45	328	70	6	5	0	5	33.4	0	0	8	24
OPPONENTS	66	66	5	137	1096	1407	2503	597	220	113	19	55	36.0	25	11	397	120
OHIO STATE	111	36	9	156	1868	772	2640	668	144	65	6	58	33.5	24	12	310	145

1968 OHIO STATE FOOTBALL ROSTER
(Alphabetical)

No.	Name	Pos.	Wt.	Ht.	Age	Cl.	Home Town
63	Adams, Douglas	LB	215	6-0		So.	Xenia
85	Aldrin, Charles	ORE	207	6-3	19	So.	Glenview, Ill.
26	Anderson, Tim	DRH	194	6-0	19	So.	Follansbee, W.Va.
86	Aston, Daniel	DRE	208	6-2	20	Jr.	Cincinnati
57	*Backhus, Thomas	OLG	207	5-11	19	Jr.	Cincinnati
33	*Bartley, Thomas	LB	198	5-11	21	Sr.	Springfield
19	Bender, Edward	ORH	172	6-0	21	Sr.	Akron
48	*Bombach, Jay	ORH	201	6-1	20	Sr.	Dayton
42	Brockington, John	ORH	210	6-1	20	So.	Brooklyn, N.Y.
12	*Brungard, David	OLH	184	5-10	20	Jr.	Youngstown
21	Burton, Arthur	LB	193	6-1	20	Jr.	Fostoria
75	Cheney, David	OLG	230	6-3	19	So.	Lima
47	Coburn, James	DLH	190	5-11	19	So.	Maumee
36	Cunningham, Richard	FB	188	5-10	19	So.	Portsmouth
83	Debevc, Mark	DRE	210	6-1	19	So.	Geneva
78	Dombos, John	DLT	205	6-0	19	So.	Garfield Heights
66	Donovan, Brian	OLG	206	6-3	19	So.	Columbus
90	Ecrement, Thomas	DLE	195	6-0	19	So.	Canton
28	**Ehrsam, Gerald	S	194	6-0	21	Sr.	Toledo
70	**Foley, David (cc)	ORT	246	6-5	20	Sr.	Cincinnati
39	Gentile, James	LB	210	6-2	20	Jr.	Poland
11	*Gillian, Ray	OLH	194	5-11	20	Jr.	Uniontown, Pa.
44	Greene, Horatius	OLH	180	5-11	19	Jr.	Jersey City, N.J.
51	Hackett, William	LB	204	6-1	20	Jr.	London
65	Hart, Randy	ORT	220	6-2	20	Jr.	Willoughby
22	Hayden, Leophus	OLH	204	6-2	19	So.	Dayton
67	Holloway, Ralph	MG	222	6-1	19	So.	Oberlin
34	*Huff, Paul	FB	217	6-3	20	Jr.	Dover
72	*Hutchison, Charles	OLT	240	6-3	19	Jr.	Carrollton
61	*Jack, Alan	ORG	215	6-0	20	Jr.	Wintersville
82	Jankowski, Bruce	OLE	192	5-11	19	So.	Fair Lawn, N.J.
10	Kern, Rex	QB	180	6-0	19	So.	Lancaster
81	Kuhn, Richard	ORE	208	6-2	19	So.	Louisville
64	Kurz, Ted	ORG	222	6-2	19	So.	Struthers
24	**Long, William	QB	180	6-1	21	Sr.	Dayton
18	Maciejowski, Ronald	QB	186	6-2	19	So.	Bedford
73	**Mayes, Rufus	OLT	250	6-5	20	Sr.	Toledo
53	**Muhlbach, John	C	194	5-10	21	Sr.	Massillon
77	*Nielsen, Brad	DRT	222	6-3	20	Jr.	Columbus
76	Oppermann, James	OLT	240	6-4	18	So.	Bluffton
35	*Otis, James	FB	208	6-0	20	Jr.	Celina
15	*Polaski, Michael	DLH	170	5-10	19	Jr.	Columbus
46	*Provost, Ted	DLH	182	6-3	20	Jr.	Navarre
58	Qualls, Larry	C	190	6-0	19	So.	Dayton
43	Quilling, Richard	S	190	6-1	20	Jr.	Celina
55	*Radtke, Michael	LB	200	6-1	20	Jr.	Wayne, N.J.
52	**Roman, James	C	211	6-0	20	Sr.	Canton
89	**Roman, Nicholas	DRE	221	6-4	21	Sr	Canton
59	*Roush, Gary	ORT	200	6-4	21	Sr.	Springfield
23	*Rusnak, Kevin	ORH	190	6-1	20	Jr.	Garfield, N.J.
74	*Schmidlin, Paul	DLT	222	6-1	19	Jr.	Toledo
3	Sensibaugh, Michael	S	187	6-0	19	So.	Cincinnati
50	*Smith, Butch	DRT	224	6-2	20	Jr.	Hamilton
87	Smith, Robert	ORE	221	6-4	21	Sr.	Lakewood
91	*Sobolewski, John	DRE	192	6-1	20	Sr.	Steubenville
54	**Stier, Mark	LB	202	6-1	21	Sr.	Louisville
68	Stillwagon, James	MG	220	6-0	19	So.	Mt. Vernon
69	**Stottlemyer, Victor	MG	200	6-0	21	Sr.	Chillicothe
92	Stowe, John	OLE	200	6-2	20		Columbus
62	Strickland, Phillip	ORG	217	6-0			Cincinnati
32	Tatum, John	LB	204	6-0			Passaic, N.J.
17	Trapuzzano, Robert	DRH	187	6-0			Rocks, Pa.
71	Troha, Richard	ORT	227	6-3			Cleveland
79	*Urbanik, William	DLT	238	6-3			ora, Pa.
41	Wagner, Tim	DRH	175	5-10			Columbus
80	White, Jan	OLE	214	6-2			rg, Pa.
88	*Whitfield, David	DLE	184	6-0			Massillon
56	**Worden, Dirk (cc)	LB	198	6-0			Lorain
16	Zelina, Lawrence	ORH	195	6-0			Cleveland

* Indicates letter

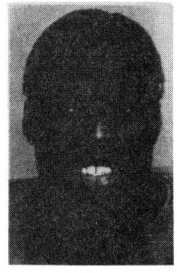

42—BROCKINGTON, John, 20, 6-1, 210, sophomore . . . from Brooklyn, New York . . . an all-Metropolitan and all-America fullback at Thomas Jefferson High . . . gained over 1,100 yards in one season . . . can play either fullback or halfback at Ohio State . . . will likely start at right halfback for the Buckeyes this season . . . has good speed and a deceptive running style . . . married . . . majoring in history . . . captained his high school football team . . . won only two high school letters, both in football . . . is a fine pass receiver . . . netted 180 yards in 25 carries in two freshmen games against Pittsburgh and Indiana last year . . . has break-away potential despite his size . . . admires Gale Sayers and Mickey Mantle . . . an excellent athlete . . .

John Brockington

10—KERN, Rex, 19, 6-0, 180, sophomore . . . from Lancaster . . . won all-America honors as a quarterback in high school . . . holds a rare distinction of winning all-Ohio honors in football, basketball, and baseball while at Lancaster High . . . underwent a spinal disc operation on June 19 . . . an unusually gifted runner in football with a deceptive style . . . quick and clever in the open field . . . netted 73 yards against Indiana and 116 with Pittsburgh in freshman games last year . . . one was a 77 yard run on an option pass-run play against Pitt . . . is an effective passer . . . has fine leadership, take-charge qualities . . . hobby is golf . . . wants to coach after graduation . . . works for a landscaping firm during the summer . . .

Rex Kern

68—STILLWAGON, James, 19, 6-0, 220, sophomore . . . from Mt. Vernon . . . attended Augusta Military Academy . . . won 14 letters in five sports . . . an outstanding prospect at middle guard . . . has the strength and quickness to become a topflight player . . . hobbies are hunting and fishing . . . in the College of Education . . . father is personnel director for an industrial firm . . . played center on offense and linebacker on defense at military school . . . from a family of three, all boys . . . was the number one middle guard from the opening of spring practice through the intra-squad game . . . will be the only sophomore to start on the defensive line . . . very hard to block . . . his top football thrill came when he was offered a tender by Ohio State . . .

James Stillwagon

32—TATUM, John, 19, 6-0, 204, sophomore . . . from Passaic, New Jersey . . . one of the most talented all-around backs on last year's strong freshman team . . . could play either halfback or fullback on offense and linebacker or halfback on defense . . . has been moved to the corner linebacking spot . . . made the switch easily in spring drills and should be a standout . . . has excellent speed and is strong physically . . . was an all-New Jersey and all-Metropolitan fullback in high school . . . from a family of five . . . father is a welder . . . will be 20 two days after the Iowa game . . . a history major in college . . . works in a plumbing supply plant in the summer . . . gained 1,421 yards as a high school senior . . .

[1968]

1968
Captains: David Foley
Dirk Worden

35	*Southern Methodist	14
21	*Oregon	6
13	*Purdue	0
45	*Northwestern	21
31	Illinois	24
25	*Michigan State	20
43	Wisconsin	8
33	Iowa	27
50	*Michigan	14
27	†Southern California	16
323		150

Won 10, Lost 0
Big Ten Champions
† Rose Bowl

A.P. POLL
1. OHIO STATE
2. Penn State
3. Texas
4. Southern Cal.
5. Notre Dame
6. Arkansas
7. Kansas
8. Georgia
9. Missouri
10. Purdue

U.P.I. POLL
1. OHIO STATE
2. Southern Cal.
3. Penn State
4. Georgia
5. Texas
6. Kansas
7. Tennessee
8. Notre Dame
9. Arkansas
10. Oklahoma

Ohio State Whips Michigan, 50-14

Nov. 23

COLUMBUS, Ohio (AP) — Unbeaten Ohio State, triggered by fullback Jim Otis' four touchdowns, soundly trounced Michigan 50-14 Saturday in a bruising Big Ten battle that decided the conference championship and swept the Buckeyes into the Rose Bowl game New Year's Day.

An all-time Ohio Stadium record crowd of 85,371 roared its approval as the No. 2 ranked Buckeyes exploded for 23 points in the final quarter to turn the title fray into a rout.

Otis, only a junior, smashed Michigan's line for 142 yards in 34 cracks, while teammates Rex Kern and Larry Zelina rambled for 96 and 92 yards, respectively.

Win Ninth of Season

The fired-up Buckeyes, winning their ninth of the season and 13th in a row over a two-year span, marked up their first perfect season since 1954.

A potent Ohio defense, spearheaded by a strong line, spoiled Michigan's bid for its first trip to Pasadena since 1965, but the Wolverines' outstanding tailback, Ron Johnson, broke two more Big Ten records and equaled another.

Johnson scored Michigan's two touchdowns to tie Leroy Keyes of Purdue with 15, but his 12 points gave him 92 on the season, eclipsing Keyes' mark of 90.

Johnson, who carried 21 times for 92 yards also broke the 996-yard season rushing record held by Illinois' Jim Grabowski. Johnson finished with 1,018 yards.

It was the worst beating Ohio has ever handed Michigan in the 65-year-old rivalry and equalled the Bucks' highest point output against the Wolves. Ohio walloped Michigan 50-20 in 1961.

Zelina, one of Hayes' standout sophomores, piled up his 92 yards in only eight carries. He took one kickoff 52 yards and had one brilliant punt return of 59 yards nullified by a clipping penalty.

It marked Hayes' fifth Big Ten championship in an 18-year career and the first for the Buckeyes since 1961.

The crunching ground game by the sophomore-studded Bucks netted 421 yards compared to Michigan's 140. The desperate Wolverines had to play catch-up football in the second half and ended up passing for 171 yards. The Bucks threw only three passes in the second half.

```
Michigan       7  7  0  0—14
Ohio State     7 14  6 23—50
Mich-Johnson 1 run Killian kick
OSU-Otis 5 run (Roman kick)
OSU-Kern 5 run (Roman kick)
Mich-Johnson 1 run (Killian kick)
OSU-Otis 2 run (Roman kick)
OSU-Zelina 6 run (kick failed)
OSU-FG Roman 32
OSU-Kern 3 run (Roman kick)
OSU-Otis 2 run (Roman kick)
OSU-Otis 1 run (pass failed)
A—85,371.
```

First Downs	17	28
Rushing Yardage	140	421
Passing Yardage	171	46
Return Yardage	160	162
Passes	14-24-3	6-9-1
Punts	5-39.8	2-30.5
Fumbles Lost	1	2
Yards Penalized	43	37

Oct. 26

Ohio State Rallies To Win 31-24

Buckeyes Score In Last Minute

CHAMPAIGN, Ill. (AP) — Undefeated and second-ranked Ohio State, on the threshhold of a season wrecking tie, rallied in the final minutes Saturday to hand underdog Illinois a 31-24 defeat.

A homecoming crowd of 56,174 hoping only for a good showing by the Illini, saw their winless favorites bounce off a 24-point deficit to tie the mighty Buckeyes with 4:38 left to play.

But the desperate Buckeyes, with quarterback Rex Kern leaving the field with an injury, struck quickly to dissolve the tie and hold a share of the Big Ten lead.

Ron Maciejowski on his first play from scrimmage, hit Larry Zelina with a 10-yard pass and then two plays later the same combination clicked for 44 yards down to Illini 4-yard line. Three plays later Jim Otis banged in from the 2 for the winning touchdown.

Ohio State Takes Rose Bowl, 27-16

Long Run By Simpson Not Enough

Throng Includes President-Elect

PASADENA, Calif. (AP) — Unbeaten Ohio State rebounded from a spectacular 80-yard touchdown run by O. J. Simpson in the second quarter and hammered out a 27-16 victory over No. 2-ranked Southern California in the Rose Bowl Wednesday and apparently wrapped up the national collegiate football championship.

A packed crowd of 102,063, including President-elect Richard Nixon, saw the hard-hitting champion Buckeyes from the Big Ten break a 10-10 halftime tie on a 25-yard field goal by Jim Roman.

Fourth-Quarter Spurt

Ohio State steamed ahead with two touchdowns in the final period of this 55th annual New Year's Day game.

It was the first defeat of the extended season for Southern Cal's Trojans, champions of the Pacific-8, who were tied by Notre Dame in the final game of the regular schedule.

A set of bruising backs, notably Jim Otis and Leophus Hayden, plus the alert play calling of sophomore Rex Kern, took advantage of errors by the stars of the USC backfield, quarterback Steve Sogge and Simpson, and turned them into a final two Buckeye touchdowns.

Kern, his first scoring strike virtually putting the game away for the Buckeyes, hit Hayden on a four yard play.

The last was a 16-yard bullet to Ray Gillian, all alone in the end zone.

Hayes Protests

Southern Cal collected its final touchdowns with 45 seconds remaining—and with it a protest from Ohio State Coach Woody Hayes, which drew the Buckeyes a 15-yard penalty.

Sogge led USC 52 yards in seven plays, the last a 19-yard pass to Sam Dickerson in the end zone. Dickerson and Buckeye Mike Polaski came down each with the ball in his grasp.

Officials gave the completion to the offensive team and Hayes stormed on to the field to protest the decision. By then, however, the over-all issue had long since been settled.

After a scoreless first period, the Trojans rolled for 10 points on a 21-yard field goal by Ron Ayala and Simpson's dramatic run.

Kept Sailing

The All-American halfback and Heisman Trophy winner broke to the left, cut back to the right, brushed off one try to stop him by Mike Sesibaugh at about the 40 and kept on sailing.

It was the second longest scoring run from scrimmage in Rose Bowl annals. Michigan's Mel Anthony raced 84 against Oregon in the 1965 game.

The stout Ohio State defense blunted the Simpson threat in the second half. O.J. carried the ball 18 times for 137 yards in the first half, but he wound up with 28 and 171 totals for this bright, warm afternoon, being limited to 34 yards in the second half.

Ohio State, after a devastating Simpson touchdown run, took the kickoff and marched 69 yards in 13 plays. Otis, whose initials J.O. are Ohio State's answer in reverse to USC's O.J., slammed over from the one.

The first of Roman's two field goals was from 26 yards and tied the score.

Roman had kicked only three field goals all season, but his second in this game, from 25, put Ohio State in front for the first time.

Poor Kick

The Buckeyes had pressured Trojan punter John Young into a poor, 26-yard kick. Then they moved on short but damaging blasts by Otis, Hayden and Gillian to the eight.

Kern, who was named the game's outstanding performer, began the finishing process early in the fourth period. Sogge was belted trying to pass and Vic Stottlemyer recovered for the Buckeyes on the Trojan 21. Five plays later, Kern passed to Hayden from the four.

It took one play from the 16 for Kern to finish off the Trojans after Simpson fumbled away a pass from Sogge. That play was thrown to Gillian.

The victory made it 10 in a row for Ohio State and most likely its first national championship since 1954. It was Hayes' third win in as many appearances at Pasadena's historic bowl.

Coach John McKay's Trojans, making their third consecutive appearance here, were the defending national champions as well as the rulers of the Pacific 8 Conference.

Final Vote

Big Ten champion Ohio State was voted No. 1 in The Associated Press poll at the end of the regular season. A final vote will be taken after the bowl games.

```
Ohio State              0 10 3 14—27
Southern California     0 10 0  6—16
USC—FG Ayala 21
USC—Simpson 80 run (Ayala kick)
OS—Otis 1 run (Roman kick)
OS—FG Roman 26
OS—FG Roman 25
OS—Hayden 4 pass from Kern (Roman kick)
OS—Gillian 16 pass from Kern (Roman kick)
USC—Dickerson 19 pass from Sogge (pass failed)
A—102,063.
```

	Ohio State	Southern Cal
First downs	21	19
Rushing yardage	280	177
Passing yardage	101	189
Return yardage	42	35
Passes	9-15-0	19-32-2
Punts	7-46	6-37
Fumbles lost	0	3
Yards penalized	53	51

1968 TEAM STATISTICS, BY GAME

	First Downs Rush	Pass	Pen.	Total	Net Gain Rush	Pass	Total	Total Plays	Passing Att.	Comp.	Int.	Punting No.	Avg.	Fumbles No.	Lost	Yards Penalized	Points
SO. METHODIST	5	21	1	27	50	437	487	98	76	40	5	3	42.0	4	3	51	14
OHIO STATE	13	5	0	18	227	145	372	80	17	9	0	11	36.5	3	1	61	35
OREGON	3	3	0	6	62	78	140	62	21	8	2	13	39.1	3	1	5	6
OHIO STATE	15	7	0	22	288	168	456	95	25	12	4	5	36.8	3	2	33	21
PURDUE	5	9	2	16	57	129	186	69	34	12	2	6	36.8	2	0	43	0
OHIO STATE	17	3	2	22	333	78	411	83	16	8	0	4	31.2	3	2	96	13
NORTHWESTERN	8	7	3	18	104	184	288	75	31	16	2	7	44.7	4	0	40	21
OHIO STATE	17	9	2	28	347	218	565	88	19	10	0	4	38.0	3	0	78	45
ILLINOIS	15	4	2	21	200	102	302	74	23	5	3	6	43.2	0	0	45	24
OHIO STATE	17	8	0	25	290	163	453	78	23	14	2	4	32.2	3	0	29	31
MICHIGAN STATE	9	7	2	18	134	137	271	74	15	9	3	5	38.6	5	4	26	20
OHIO STATE	13	10	1	24	214	215	429	80	26	16	1	7	37.3	2	1	71	25
WISCONSIN	5	3	0	8	88	99	187	60	15	6	1	9	32.3	3	3	76	8
OHIO STATE	17	8	2	27	301	167	468	86	25	15	1	3	41.7	4	1	25	43
IOWA	9	13	1	23	141	246	387	78	33	20	2	6	42.3	3	1	45	27
OHIO STATE	15	4	3	22	337	83	420	83	12	5	2	5	35.8	0	0	29	33
MICHIGAN	8	8	1	17	140	171	311	65	24	14	3	5	37.6	5	1	43	14
OHIO STATE	24	3	1	28	421	46	467	88	9	6	1	2	30.5	4	2	37	50
S. CALIFORNIA	8	10	1	19	177	189	366	74	32	19	2	6	36.7	3	3	51	16
OHIO STATE	16	5	0	21	260	101	361	82	15	9	0	7	45.7	1	0	53	27
OPPONENTS	75	85	13	173	1153	1772	2925	729	304	153	25	66	38.9	32	16	425	150
OHIO STATE	164	62	11	237	3018	1384	4402	844	188	104	11	52	37.2	26	9	512	323

RUSHING

Player	Tries	Gain	Lost	Net	Avg.	TD's
Otis	219	992	7	985	4.5	17
Kern	131	641	107	534	4.1	8
Zelina	39	339	1	338	8.7	1
Hayden	61	301	17	284	4.6	1
Brungard	66	266	5	261	3.9	1
Maciejowski	43	253	61	192	4.5	4
Brockington	45	204	17	187	4.1	1
Gillian	19	129	4	125	6.6	0
Huff	15	52	5	47	3.1	0
*Long	7	40	0	40	5.7	1
Greene	5	18	1	17	3.4	0
Coburn	2	8	0	8	4.0	0
White	1	2	0	2	2.0	0
Kuhn	1	0	0	0	0.0	0
Sensibaugh	2	7	9	−2	−1.0	0
Totals	656	3252	234	3018	4.6	34

FORWARD PASSING

Player	Att.	Comp.	Int.	Yards	Comp. Pct.	TD's
Kern	131	75	6	972	.572	7
Maciejowski	42	25	3	387	.595	3
*Long	14	4	2	25	.286	0
Brungard	1	0	0	0	.000	0
Totals	188	104	11	1384	.553	10

PASS RECEIVING

Player	Caught	Yards	TD's
Jankowski	31	328	3
Zelina	18	327	1
White	21	283	1
Brockington	7	104	0
Gillian	6	100	1
Otis	10	82	0
Hayden	4	41	1
Brungard	2	38	2
*Bender	1	37	1
Kuhn	2	29	0
Rusnak	1	10	0
*R. Smith	1	5	0
Totals	104	1384	10

PUNTING

Player	Number	Yards	Avg.
Sensibaugh	52		37.2

SCORING

Player	Touchdowns Rush	Pass	Extra Points Kick	Run	Pass	Field Goals	Total Points
Otis	17	0	0	0	0	0	102
Kern	8	0	0	0	0-1	0	48
*J. Roman	0	0	21-28	0	0-1	5-7	36
Maciejowski	4	0	0	0	0-1	0	24
Brungard	3	0	0	0	0	0	18
Jankowski	0	3	0	0	0	0	18
Zelina	1	1	1-2	0	1-1	0-2	13
Hayden	1	1	0	0	0	0	12
*Long	1	0	0	0-1	0-1	0	8
†Provost	0	0	0	0	0	0	6
White	0	1	0	0	0	0	6
*Bender	0	1	0	0	0	0	6
‡Polaski	0	0	0	0	0	0	6
Brockington	1	0	0	0	0	0	6
Gillian	0	1	0	0	0	0	6
*Merryman	0	0	6-9	0	0	0-4	6
Oppermann	0	0	0-1	0	0	0-1	0
(Safety)							2
Totals	36	8	28-40	0-1	1-5	5-14	323

† touchdown by pass interception
‡ touchdown by blocked kick

KICKOFF RETURNS

Player	Number	Yards	Average	TD's
Zelina	9	204	22.7	0
Hayden	3	58	19.3	0
Brockington	3	53	17.6	0
Brungard	3	43	14.3	0
Gillian	3	41	13.6	0
Otis	2	21	10.5	0
White	1	13	13.0	0
Kuhn	1	1	1.0	0
Jack	1	0	.0	0
Cheney	1	0	.0	0
*Roman	1	0	.0	0
Totals	28	434	15.5	0

PUNT RETURNS

Players	Numbers	Yards	Average	TD's
Sensibaugh	10	93	9.3	0
Zelina	9	61	6.8	0
Polaski	7	57	8.1	1
Otis	1	17	17.0	0
Tatum	1	17	17.0	0
Provost	2	0	.0	0
Totals	30	245	8.2	1

* Not Returning for 1969

Nov. 15

Buckeyes Pound Purdue

1969 OHIO STATE FOOTBALL ROSTER
(Alphabetical)

No.	Name	Pos.	Wgt.	Hgt.	Age	Class	Home Town
63	*Adams, Douglas	LB	214	6-0	20	Jr.	Xenia
26	*Anderson, Tim	DRH	194	6-0	20	Jr.	Follansbee, W.Va.
86	Aston, Daniel	DRE	206	6-2	21	Sr.	Cincinnati
57	**Backhus, Thomas	ORG	212	5-11	20	Sr.	Cincinnati
66	Betz, Steve	OLG	222	6-2	19	So.	Minerva
42	*Brockington, John	FB	216	6-1	21	Jr.	Brooklyn, N.Y.
12	**Brungard, David	OLH	186	5-10	21	Sr.	Youngstown
21	*Burton, Arthur	RB	194	6-1	21	Sr.	Fostoria
24	Campana, Thomas	OLH	185	5-11	19	So.	Kent
75	*Cheney, David	OLT	230	6-3	20	Jr.	Lima
47	Coburn, James	FB	190	5-11	20	Jr.	Maumee
54	Conroy, James	C	214	6-2	20	Jr.	Bay Village
94	Crapser, Steven	DLT	216	6-1	21	Sr.	Columbus
83	*Debevc, Mark	DRE	209	6-1	20	Jr.	Geneva
52	DeLeone, Thomas	C	214	6-2	19	So.	Kent
53	*Donovan, Brian	C	202	6-3	20	Jr.	Columbus
90	Ecrement, Thomas	DLE	197	6-0	20	Jr.	Canton
39	*Gentile, James	LB	218	6-2	21	Sr.	Poland
11	**Gillian, Ray	ORH	194	5-11	21	Sr.	Uniontown, Pa.
44	Greene, Horatius	OLH	177	5-11	20	Sr.	Jersey City, N.J.
51	Hackett, William	LB	202	6-1	21	Sr.	London
85	Harris, Jimmie	ORE	182	5-11	19	So.	Dayton
65	*Hart, Randall	ORT	234	6-2	21	Sr.	Willoughby
22	*Hayden, Leophus	OLH	206	6-2	21	Jr.	Dayton
67	Holloway, Ralph	DLT	227	6-1	20	Jr.	Oberlin
59	Houser, Thomas	MG	220	6-2	19	So.	Massillon
28	Howard, Harry	DLH	190	6-0	19	So.	Cincinnati
78	**Huff, Paul	OLT	234	6-3	21	Sr.	Dover
72	**Hutchison, Charles	ORT	242	6-3	20	Sr.	Carrollton
61	**Jack, Alan	OLG	218	6-0	21	Sr.	Wintersville
82	*Jankowski, Bruce	ORE	192	5-11	20	Jr.	Fair Lawn, N.J.
10	*Kern, Rex	QB	184	6-0	20	Jr.	Lancaster
81	*Kuhn, Richard	OLE	211	6-2	20	Jr.	Louisville
64	*Kurz, Ted	ORG	222	6-2	20	Sr.	Struthers
19	Lamka, Donald	QB	190	5-11	20	So.	Cleveland
87	Luttner, Kenneth	DRE	208	6-2	19	So.	Medina
18	*Maciejowski, Ronald	QB	186	6-2	20	Jr.	Bedford
69	Mason, Glen	LB	205	6-2	19	So.	Colonia, N.J.
33	Mountz, Gregory	LB	200	6-3	19	So.	Hummelstown, Pa.
77	**Nielsen, Brad	DRT	224	6-3	21	Sr.	Columbus
76	*Oppermann, James	OLT	237	6-4	19	Sr.	Bluffton
35	**Otis, James	FB	214	6-0	21	Sr.	Celina
15	**Polaski, Michael	DRH	168	5-10	20	Sr.	Columbus
97	*Pollitt, William	LB	218	6-2	21	Sr.	Dayton
46	**Provost, Ted	DLH	184	6-3	21	Sr.	Navarre
55	**Radtke, Michael	LB	198	6-1	21	Sr.	Wayne, N.J.
89	**Roman, Nicholas	DRE	226	6-4	22	Sr.	Canton
23	**Rusnak, Kevin	ORE	188	6-1	21	Sr.	Garfield, N.J.
74	**Schmidlin, Paul	DLT	224	6-1	20	Sr.	Toledo
3	*Sensibaugh, Michael	S	190	6-0	20	Jr.	Cincinnati
20	Sharp, William	S	170	5-10	19	So.	Lima
73	Simon, Richard	OLT	225	6-2	19	So.	Parma
14	Smith, Bruce	S	160	5-10	20	Jr.	Gallipolis
50	**Smith, Robert	DLT	222	6-2	21	Sr.	Hamilton
68	*Stillwagon, James	MG	216	6-0	20	Jr.	Mt. Vernon
62	*Strickland, Phillip	LB	219	6-1	20	Jr.	Cincinnati
32	*Tatum, Jack	RB	204	6-0	20	Jr.	Passaic, N.J.
17	Trapuzzano, Robert	DRH	192	6-0	20	Sr.	McKees Rocks, Pa.
71	*Troha, Richard	OLT	232	6-3	20	Jr.	Cleveland
79	**Urbanik, William	DRT	231	6-3	22	Sr.	Donora, Pa.
60	Vecanski, Milan	MG	227	6-1	20	So.	Harrisburg, Pa.
91	Wakefield, Richard	ORE	195	6-4	20	So.	Avon Lake
80	*White, Jan	OLE	216	6-2	20	Jr.	Harrisburg, Pa.
56	White, Stanley	LB	210	6-1	19	So.	Kent
88	**Whitfield, David	DLE	185	6-0	21	Sr.	Massillon
16	*Zelina, Larry	ORH	196	6-0	20	Jr.	Cleveland

* Indicates Letter

COLUMBUS, Ohio (AP) — A devastating Ohio State defense pressured Mike Phipps into five interceptions Saturday and the top-ranked Buckeyes clinched a Big Ten title share with a 42-14 pounding of Purdue.

Rex Kern scored twice and passed for a third touchdown in directing the versatile Ohio State attack that virtually killed Purdue's Rose Bowl hopes in snowy, 23-degree weather before a national television audience and 85,027 fans.

Ohio State equalled its own Big Ten winning streak record of 17 and prolonged its overall victory string to 22 games, six straight for the Buckeyes in the conference this season going into their showdown at Michigan next week.

Halfback Leo Hayden, who has played in the shadow of Kern and fullback Jim Otis in eight Buckeye victories this fall, led the crunching Ohio ground game with 130 yards in 14 carries and scored one touchdown.

Ted Provost and Mike Sensibaugh both picked off two Phipps passes and Tim Anderson snatched one as the Heisman Trophy candidate could complete only 19 of 45 passes for 203 yards and one score.

Purdue's only touchdown until Phipps' two-yard scoring pitch to Ashley Bell in the closing minutes was an electrifying 98-yard kickoff return in the second quarter by Stan Brown, the Big Ten leader in that department this season.

1969
Captains: David Whitfield
Alan Jack

62	*Texas Christian	0
41	Washington	14
54	*Michigan State	21
34	Minnesota	7
41	*Illinois	0
35	Northwestern	6
62	*Wisconsin	7
42	*Purdue	14
12	Michigan	24
383		93

Won 8, Lost 1
Big Ten Co-Champions

[1969]

Buckeyes Are Upset
Nov. 22

ANN ARBOR, Mich. (AP) — The Michigan Wolverines pulled one of the upsets of the decade, stunning No. 1 ranked Ohio State by taking a 12-point halftime lead and holding on to beat the Buckeyes 24-12 Saturday and clinch a Rose Bowl trip.

The victory in a game which saw all the scoring coming in the first half, snapped Ohio State's winning streak at 22 games and most likely will drop the Bucks from the top spot.

The Big Ten athletic directors Saturday selected Michigan, the conquerors of Ohio State, to represent the conference in the Rose Bowl on Jan. 1.

Michigan, meanwhile, captured a share of the Big Ten title with Ohio State and won the Rose Bowl bid without the necessity of a vote by conference athletic directors.

A crowd of 103,583, largest ever to watch a football game in Michigan, saw the Wolverines take a surprising 7-6 first quarter lead on a three-yard touchdown run by fullback Garvie Craw and an extra point kick by Frank Tias. It was the first time this season the Buckeyes had ever trailed.

An inspired Michigan defense continually held powerful Ohio State, forcing the Bucks to punt. It was a stunning 60-yard punt return by Barry Pierson that set up Michigan's third touchdown and gave the Wolves a little breathing room.

Pierson ran Mike Sensibaugh's punt to the OSU two and three plays later quarterback Don Moorhead went over from the two.

Ohio State drew first blood, scoring on a one-yard plunge by fullback Jim Otis at 7:22 of the first quarter.

The Buckeyes came back after Craw's first TD, with quarterback Rex Kern firing a 22-yard touchdown pass to Jan White. Stan White's extra point kick was good but the Bucks elected to take a Michigan penalty and try for a two-point conversion. But the hard rushing Michigan defense tackled Kern before he could get a pass off.

Moor had mixed his plays well, utilizing the running of sophomore tailback Billy Taylor and the fine pass catching of tight end Jim Mandich to full advantage.

Taylor set up Michigan's second touchdown with a 28-yard burst to the OSU five. Two plays later Craw dove over the goal line from the one.

Tim Killian added a 25-yard field goal in the second quarter. The Wolverine defense took over in the second half, successfully stopping the off tackle bursts of Otis and the option running of Kern.

Pierson intercepted three passes and Tom Curtis two after OSU got desperate and found it had to take to the air.

Curtis returned a Kern pass 26 yards late in the second quarter to give him 431 yards in 24 interceptions during his three-year career. That passed the old National Collegiate Athletic Association record of 410 yards set by Michigan State's Lynn Chadnois in the '40s.

Thousands of fans mobbed the artificially surfaced Michigan Stadium after the game, tearing down one of the bright yellow goal posts to the frantic cheering of supporters.

Choruses of "hail to the victors," Michigan's fabled fight song, filled the joyous stadium, with apparently only the dejected Ohio State fans filing out of the stands.

```
Ohio State       6  6  0  0  12
Michigan         7 17  0  0  24
OSU—Otis 1 run (kick failed)
Mich—Craw 3 run (Titas kick)
OSU—White 22 pass from Kern (run failed)
Mich—Craw 1 run (Titas kick)
Mich—Moorhead 2 run (Titas kick)
Mich—FG Killian 25.
A—103,588.
```

STATISTICS

	OSU	MICH.
First downs	20	21
Rushing yardage	222	266
Passing yardage	155	108
Return yardage	64	143
Passes	10-28-6	10-20-1
Punts	7-27	3-42
Fumbles lost	2	0
Yards penalized	5	36

In all the world there's only one!

Jai Lai Restaurant

1421 Olentangy River Road/Phone 294-5111/Open daily 9 a.m. to 1 a.m. Sundays 11:30 a.m. to 9 p.m.

[1969]

A.P. POLL	U.P.I. POLL
1. Texas	1. Texas
2. Penn State	2. Penn State
3. Southern Cal.	3. Arkansas
4. OHIO STATE	4. Southern Cal.
5. Notre Dame	5. OHIO STATE
6. Missouri	6. Missouri
7. Arkansas	7. L.S.U.
8. Mississippi	8. Michigan
9. Michigan	9. Notre Dame
10. L.S.U.	10. U.C.L.A.

SCORING

Player	Touchdowns Rush	Touchdowns Pass	Extra Points Kick	Extra Points Run	Extra Points Pass	Field Goals	Total Points
*Otis	15	1	0	0	0	0	96
Kern	9	0	0	0-1	0	0	54
S. White	0	0	39-52	0	0	1-5	42
Brockington	6	0	0	1-1	0	0	38
Jankowski	0	5	0	0	0	0	30
J. White	0	5	0	0	0	0	30
Campana	0	4	0	0	0	0	24
Hayden	3	0	0	0	0	0	18
#Zelina	0	0	0	0	1-1	0	14
Kuhn	0	2	0	0	0	0	12
Maciejowski	1	0	0	0	0	0	6
xDebevc	0	0	0	0	0	0	6
*Gillian	1	0	0	0	0	0	6
Coburn	1	0	0	0	0	0	6
Johnston	0	0	1-1	0	0	0	1
	36	17	40-53	1-2	1-1	1-2	383

\# scored two touchdowns on punt returns
x scored touchdown on intercepted pass
* not returning for 1970

1969 TEAM STATISTICS, BY GAME

	Rush	First Downs Pass	Pen.	Total	Rush	Net Gain Pass	Total	Total Plays	Att.	Passing Comp.	Int.	Punting No.	Punting Avg.	Fumbles No.	Fumbles Lost	Yards Penalized	Points
TEXAS CHRISTIAN	1	7	1	9	44	152	196	60	36	15	4	10	37.2	4	2	5	0
OHIO STATE	21	5	0	26	373	192	565	101	19	9	1	5	42.2	1	0	47	62
WASHINGTON	14	6	1	21	225	103	328	75	11	7	2	6	46.5	6	3	50	14
OHIO STATE	15	10	1	26	319	183	502	86	29	17	2	5	39.0	2	1	42	41
MICHIGAN STATE	3	8	1	12	82	218	300	57	21	10	2	8	44.6	5	1	114	21
OHIO STATE	13	11	6	30	167	233	400	93	30	16	1	3	34.3	2	1	44	54
MINNESOTA	9	14	2	25	139	304	443	91	47	26	1	4	33.5	5	5	82	7
OHIO STATE	17	5	2	24	288	141	429	84	17	8	0	5	31.8	1	1	18	34
ILLINOIS	4	3	1	8	70	86	156	59	15	5	1	10	41.2	5	4	55	0
OHIO STATE	20	10	1	31	355	209	564	101	32	14	1	5	37.8	2	1	60	41
NORTHWESTERN	4	12	3	19	−29	294	265	71	37	22	2	7	36.9	5	2	30	6
OHIO STATE	21	12	1	34	362	213	575	95	31	17	2	2	42.0	4	2	87	35
WISCONSIN	5	5	1	11	57	119	176	52	28	13	2	7	37.0	4	2	20	7
OHIO STATE	23	10	0	33	360	235	595	99	27	16	1	2	36.0	1	0	41	62
PURDUE	3	10	0	13	29	203	232	71	45	19	5	7	35.7	4	3	20	14
OHIO STATE	21	4	1	26	332	104	436	91	17	6	3	5	34.5	2	0	30	42
MICHIGAN	13	8	0	21	266	108	374	86	20	10	1	3	41.7	0	0	37	24
OHIO STATE	12	7	1	20	218	155	373	79	28	10	6	3	27.0	2	1	5	12
OPPONENTS	56	73	10	139*	883	1587	2470	622	260	127	20	62	39.4	38	22	413	93
OHIO STATE	163	74	13	250	2774	1665	4439	829	230	113	17	35	36.2	17	7	374	383

1969 OHIO STATE INDIVIDUAL STATISTICS

RUSHING

Player	Tries	Gain	Low	Net	Avg.	TD's
*Otis	225	1033	6	1027	4.5	15
Kern	109	717	134	583	5.3	9
Hayden	63	349	5	344	5.4	3
Brockington	72	337	3	334	4.6	6
Zelina	27	169	12	157	5.8	0
Maciejowski	36	194	60	134	3.7	1
Campana	19	73	0	73	3.8	0
*Rusnak	24	105	40	65	2.7	0
*Gillian	9	39	0	39	4.3	1
Coburn	9	31	0	31	3.4	1
Sensibaugh	2	18	0	18	9.0	0
J. White	1	1	0	1	1.0	0
*Greene	1	0	0	0	0.0	0
*Sharp	1	0	15	-15	-15.0	0
(Team)	1	0	17	-17	-17.0	0
Totals	599	3066	292	2774	4.6	36

FORWARD PASSING

Player	Att.	Comp.	Int.	Yards	Pct.	TD's
Kern	135	68	10	1002	.504	9
*Rusnak	54	28	3	417	.519	5
Maciejowski	40	16	4	228	.400	3
Sensibaugh	1	1	0	18	1.000	0
Totals	230	113	17	1665	.491	17

PUNTING

Player	Number	Yards	Avg.
Sensibaugh	24	895	37.4
*Sharp	5	198	39.6
Zelina	5	172	34.4
(Team)	1		0.0
Totals	35	1265	36.2

TOTAL OFFENSE

Player	Plays	Rush	Pass	Total	Avg.	TD's
Kern	244	583	1002	1585	6.5	18
*Otis	225	1027	0	1027	4.5	15
*Rusnak	78	65	417	482	6.2	5
Maciejowski	76	134	228	362	4.8	4
Hayden	63	344	0	344	5.4	3
Brockington	72	334	0	334	4.6	6
Zelina	27	157	0	157	5.8	0
Campana	19	73	0	73	3.8	0
*Gillian	9	39	0	39	4.3	1
Sensibaugh	3	18	18	36	12.0	0
Coburn	9	31	0	31	3.4	1
J. White	1	1	0	1	1.0	0
*Greene	1	0	0	0	0.0	0
*Sharp	1	-15	0	-15	-15.0	0
(Team)	1	-17	0	-17	-17.0	0
Totals	829	2774	1665	4439	5.3	53

KICKOFF RETURNS

Player	Number	Yards	Average	TD's
Zelina	11	195	17.7	0
Campana	6	97	16.2	0
*Gillian	2	29	14.5	0
Hayden	1	0	0.0	0
J. White	1	0	0.0	0
Totals	21	321	15.3	0

PUNT RETURNS

Players	Numbers	Yards	Average	TD's
Zelina	23	431	18.7	2
Campana	4	30	7.5	0
*Gillian	1	19	19.0	0
Totals	28	480	17.1	2

INTERCEPTION RETURNS

Player	Number	Yards	Average	TD's
Sensibaugh	9	125	13.9	0
*Provost	5	34	6.8	0
*Marting	1	18	18.0	0
Debevc	1	14	14.0	1
Anderson	1	6	6.0	0
*Polaski	1	0	0.0	0
Wakefield	1	0	0.0	0
*Roman	1	0	0.0	0
Totals	20	197	9.8	1

PASS RECEIVING

Player	Caught	Yards	TD's
Jankowski	23	404	5
J. White	23	308	5
Zelina	15	271	0
Campana	10	169	4
Kuhn	9	134	2
*Gillian	7	132	0
Hayden	4	79	0
*Otis	5	36	1
Wakefield	4	35	0
Brockington	6	29	0
*Wright	1	29	0
Harris	3	26	0
Burrows	2	18	0
*Backhus	1	-5	0
Totals	113	1665	17

* not returning for 1970

[1970]

1970 OHIO STATE FOOTBALL ROSTER

No.	Name	Pos.	Wgt.	Hgt.	Age	Class	Home Town (High School)	High School Coach
1	Schram, Fred	PK	174	5-10	20	Jr.	Massillon (Washington)	did not play in H.S.
2	Johnston, Paul	PK	172	5-10	20	Jr.	Cleveland (Cuyahoga Heights)	Bill Jacobs
3	**Sensibaugh, Michael	S	190	6-0	21	Sr.	Cincinnati (Lockland)	Ben Hubbard
4	Rice, Elliott	PK	164	6-0	19	So.	Jefferson (Jefferson)	Fred Colburn
5	Sivinski, Daniel	DRH	181	5-11	19	So.	Columbus (Watterson)	Ron Shay
6	Dale, Michael	DCB	174	5-10	21	Sr.	Erie, Pa. (Northeast)	Dave Hannah
7	Zeune, Roger	DLH	162	5-8	19	So.	Pataskala (Watkins Memorial)	Gary Mauller
10	**Kern, Rex	QB	184	6-0	21	Sr.	Lancaster (Lancaster)	Earl Jones
11	Cowman, Randall	DCB	190	6-0	19	So.	Dayton (Beavercreek)	Paul Martin
12	Moore, Ross	QB	188	5-11	19	So.	Allentown, Pa. (Dieruff)	John Bednarik
14	Smith, Bruce	S	162	5-10	21	Sr.	Gallipolis (Gallia Academy)	Terry Hansley
15	Zetts, Gary	QB	192	6-3	19	So.	Struthers (Struthers)	Bob Commings
16	**Zelina, Larry	ORH	196	6-0	21	Sr.	Cleveland (St. Benedictine)	August Bossu
17	Lucki, Martin	DRH	182	6-2	19	So.	Bridgeport (St. John)	Denny Bowman
18	**Maciejowski, Ronald	QB	192	6-2	21	Sr.	Bedford (Bedford)	Francis McBellie
19	*Lamka, Donald	LB	190	5-11	21	Jr.	Cleveland (South)	John Gentile
20	Kinsey, Marvin	DCB	195	6-2	19	So.	East Liverpool (East Liverpool)	Bob McNae
21	Andrulis, Frank	S	180	6-0	19	So.	Euclid (Euclid)	Ed Tekieli
22	**Hayden, Leophus	OLH	208	6-2	22	Sr.	Dayton (Roosevelt)	Dick Marquardt
23	Battista, Thomas	DLH	183	6-3	19	S.	Weirton, W.Va. (Weirton)	Charles Basl
24	*Campana, Thomas	OLH	185	5-11	20	Jr.	Kent (Roosevelt)	Thomas Campana, Sr.
25	Sloan, Gary	DRH	184	6-1	19	So.	Napoleon (Napoleon)	Charles Buckenmeyer
26	**Anderson, Tim	DRH	196	6-0	21	Sr.	Colliers, W.Va. (Follansbee)	Denny Williams
28	*Howard, Harry	DLH	190	6-1	20	Jr.	Cincinnati (Princeton)	Pat Mancuso
29	Conley, William	OLG	198	5-10	19	Jr.	Columbus (Pleasantview)	Don Eby
32	**Tatum, Jack	DCB	208	6-0	21	Sr.	Passaic, N.J. (Passaic)	John Federici
33	Galbos, Richard	FB	200	6-0	19	So.	Mentor (Mentor)	Dick Crum
34	Bledsoe, John	FB	210	6-1	19	So.	Westlake (Westlake)	Jim Janosek
35	Scannell, Michael	LB	210	6-2	19	So.	Sylvania (Central Catholic)	Jim Cordiak
36	Doll, John	FB	195	5-11	19	So.	Portsmouth (Portsmouth)	did not play in H.S.
37	Waugh, Charles	ORG	190	6-0	21	Sr.	Clinton (Clinton)	Ralph Beddow
38	Givens, Daniel	DLH	168	5-10	19	Jr.	Louisville (Louisville)	Virgil Roman
39	Ferko, Richard	LB	194	5-11	19	So.	Pittsburgh, Pa. (Montour)	Charles Connor
41	Seifert, Richard	S	182	6-1	19	So.	Cuyahoga Falls (Cuyahoga Falls)	Terry Ross
42	**Brockington, John	FB	216	6-1	22	Sr.	Brooklyn, N.Y. (Jefferson)	Moe Finkelstein
43	Evans, Frank	FB	185	5-10	19	So.	Columbus (North)	did not play in H.S.
44	Hughes, John	ORH	190	6-1	19	So.	Duquesne, Pa. (Duquesne)	Mike Kopolovich
45	Beecroft, Charles	DRT	225	6-3	19	So.	Dayton (Carroll)	Jim Spoerl
46	Breuleux, Jon	OLT	242	6-5	19	So.	Alexandria, Va. (Edison)	Dean Waddell
47	Coburn, James	FB	192	5-11	21	Sr.	Maumee (Maumee)	Don Prentiss
48	Burchinal, John	DRH	188	6-1	21	Sr.	Columbus (North)	Roger Hendrix
49	Harman, Timothy	C	205	6-1	20	Jr.	Uniontown (Lake)	Jim Smith

A.P. POLL
1. Nebraska
2. Notre Dame
3. Texas
4. Tennessee
5. OHIO STATE
6. Arizona State
7. L.S.U.
8. Stanford
9. Michigan
10. Auburn

U.P.I. POLL
1. Texas
2. OHIO STATE
3. Nebraska
4. Tennessee
5. Notre Dame
6. L.S.U.
7. Michigan
8. Arizona State
9. Auburn
10. Stanford

1970
Captains: Rex Kern
Jan White
James Stillwagon
Douglas Adams

56	*Texas A. & M.	13
34	*Duke	10
29	Michigan State	0
28	*Minnesota	8
48	Illinois	29
24	*Northwestern	10
24	Wisconsin	7
10	Purdue	7
20	*Michigan	9
17	†Stanford	27
290		120

Won 9, Lost 1
Big Ten Champions
† Rose Bowl

John Hicks

65—HICKS, John, 19, 6-3, 240, sophomore . . . from Cleveland . . . letters in three sports at John [ ] High . . . captained his high school football team . . . was a regular throughout spring practice . . . can play either guard or tackle but will likely be used at right guard . . . has an excellent attitude . . . is easy to coach . . . hobby is music . . . works in a steel mill during the summer . . . plays with great dedication . . . played offensive guard and defensive linebacker in high school . . . his top football thrill was in his first high school game when he intercepted a pass and returned it 60 yards . . . in the College of Education . . . wants to teach after graduation . . . considered top offensive lineman on last year's freshman team . . . admires Gene Hickerson and Jerry Kramer . . .

[1970]

No.	Name	Pos.	Wt.	Ht.	Age	Class	Hometown (High School)	Coach
50	Pitstick, Anthony	C	215	6-3	20	So.	Xenia (Xenia)	Don Middleton
51	Dixon, Kenneth	LB	203	6-3	19	So.	Wintersville (Wintersville)	Robert Kettlewell
52	*DeLeone, Thomas	C	214	6-2	20	Jr.	Kent (Roosevelt)	Thomas Campana, Sr.
54	*Conroy, James	C	214	6-2	21	Sr.	Bay Village (Bay)	Jack Llewellyn
55	Fletcher, Kevin	MG	218	6-1	19	So.	East Orange, N.J. (East Orange)	Tom Dean
56	Nixon, Thomas	C	218	6-2	19	So.	Mansfield (Mansfield Senior)	Gary Prahst
57	Houser, Thomas	ORG	217	6-2	20	Jr.	Massillon (Washington)	Bob Seaman
58	Bonica, Charles	OLG	242	6-3	21	So.	Waltham, Mass. (Waltham)	Fran Morelli
59	Pisanelli, Fred	LB	209	6-2	19	So.	Warren (Warren)	Richard Strahm
60	Vecanski, Milan	ORG	227	6-1	21	Jr.	Harrisburg, Pa. (Harris)	George Chaump
61	**Gentile, James	ORG	218	6-2	22	Sr.	Poland (Struthers)	Bob Commings
62	**Strickland, Phillip	LB	212	6-1	21	Sr.	Cincinnati (Taft)	Will Hundemer
63	**Adams, Douglas	LB	214	6-0	20	Sr.	Xenia (Xenia)	Jack Harbaugh
64	Rabatin, Thomas	OLG	211	6-0	19	So.	Wadsworth (Wadsworth)	Lorrell Mast
65	Hicks, John	ORG	240	6-3	19	So.	Cleveland (John Hay)	William Harris
66	Graf, Larry	OLG	212	6-1	19	So.	Akron (St. Vincent)	John Cistone
67	**Holloway, Ralph	DRT	227	6-1	21	Sr.	Oberlin (Oberlin)	Darel Goddard
68	**Stillwagon, James	MG	220	6-0	21	Sr.	Mt. Vernon (Augusta Mil. Acad.)	Edward Clymore
69	Mason, Glen	LB	210	6-2	20	Jr.	Colonia, N.J. (Colonia)	Joe Martino
70	Hasenohrl, George	DLT	240	6-1	19	So.	Garfield Heights (Garfield)	Cliff Foust
71	*Troha, Richard	ORT	232	6-3	21	Sr.	Cleveland (St. Joseph)	Bill Gutbrod
72	Cummings, John	OLT	250	6-2	19	So.	Cincinnati (St. Xavier)	Tom Ballaban
73	*Simon, Richard	ORT	226	6-2	20	Jr.	Parma (Valley Forge)	Jim Fritzsche
74	Long, David	ORT	222	6-1	20	Jr.	Delphos (Delphos)	Paul Krotzer
75	**Cheney, David	OLT	228	6-3	21	Sr.	Lima (Lima Senior)	Al Scrivner
76	Oppermann, James	DRT	237	6-4	20	Sr.	Bluffton (Bluffton)	Mark Covert
77	Stoudenmire, Malory	DLT	237	6-3	19	So.	Cleveland (Kennedy)	Vic Hanchuk
78	Wersel, Timothy	OLG	218	6-2	19	So.	Cincinnati (Roger Bacon)	Bron Bacevich
79	Williams, Shad	DRT	232	6-3	19	So.	Portsmouth (Portsmouth)	Carl Benhase
80	**White, Jan	OLE	212	6-2	21	Sr.	Harrisburg, Pa. (Harris)	George Chaump
81	**Kuhn, Richard	OLE	211	6-2	21	Sr.	Louisville (Louisville)	Paul Starkey
82	**Jankowski, Bruce	ORE	192	5-11	21	Sr.	Fair Lawn, N.J. (Fair Lawn)	Frank Devens
83	**Debevc, Mark	DLE	214	6-1	21	Sr.	Geneva (Geneva)	Tom Jennell
84	Marsh, Jack	DRE	219	6-2	21	Sr.	Elyria (Elyria)	William Barton
85	*Harris, Jimmie	ORE	182	5-11	20	Jr.	Dayton (Roth)	Ken Amlin
86	Cappell, Richard	DRE	204	6-0	21	Jr.	Dover (Dover)	Richard Haines
87	*Luttner, Kenneth	DRE	208	6-2	20	Jr.	Medina (Highland)	Phil Hahn
88	*White, Stanley	DLE	212	6-1	20	Jr.	Kent (Roosevelt)	Thomas Campana, Sr.
89	Mountz, Gregory	OLE	203	6-3	20	Jr.	Hummelstown, Pa. (Lower Dauphin)	Jim Seacrist
90	Teague, Mervin	DLE	214	6-5	20	So.	Youngstown (East)	Gus Hebory
91	*Wakefield, Richard	DLH	198	6-4	21	Jr.	Avon Lake (Avon Lake)	Al O'Neill
92	Burrows, Roger	ORE	192	6-2	21	Sr.	Brunswick (Brunswick)	John Armstrong
93	Brown, Jeffrey	DRE	195	6-4	19	So.	Chambersburg, Pa. (Chambersburg)	Thomas Carroll
94	Strong, Terry	DLE	189	6-3	18	So.	Weirton, W.Va. (Weirton)	Charles Basil
95	Lago, Gary	ORG	217	6-2	20	So.	Ashtabula (Edgewood)	David Six
96	Baxa, Thomas	ORT	245	6-5	19	So.	St. Clairsville (St. Clairsville)	Lewis Higginbotham
97	Jones, Kirk	DRE	200	6-3	19	So.	Wooster (Wooster)	Jack Peterson
98	Sapanero, Robert	DLT	226	6-2	20	Jr.	Mayfield Heights (Mayfield)	Charles Beach
99	Belgrave, Earl	DLT	233	6-5	19	So.	Brooklyn, N.Y. (Jefferson)	Moe Finkelstein

* indicates letter

Unbeaten Buckeyes Down Northwestern By 24 to 10

COLUMBUS, Ohio (AP) — Second-ranked Ohio State, its stuttering air game helping Northwestern to a 10-3 halftime lead, stuck to a powerful ground game in the second half Saturday and ground out a 24-10 Big Ten triumph.

The Buckeyes jumped on the inside track to the Rose Bowl with their fourth straight conference victory as Rex Kern scored twice and fullback John Brockington once in the second half comeback before a record Ohio Stadium crowd of 86,673.

Northwestern, bidding for its first Big Ten title in 34 years, dropped out of a share of the league lead after the aroused Wildcats picked off three of Kern's passes and used them to keep Ohio State from a touchdown in the first half.

Northwestern, now 3-1 in the league and 3-4 for all games, took the play away from the heavily-favored Buckeyes in the first half with fullback Mike Adamle outgaining the entire Buckeye team on the ground.

Adamle, who gained 102 yards to 83 for the Buckeyes in the first two quarters, scored on a one-yard run late in the first period.

Brockington, the 220-pound senior, carried 42 times for 161 yards on inside power plays. He scored from the eight-yard line to pull Ohio State ahead to stay 17-10 with four minutes left in the third period.

Buckeyes Handle Michigan, 20-9

Kern Leads Champs To Rose Bowl

COLUMBUS, Ohio (AP) — Behind Rex Kern's magical ball-handling and a miserly defense, Ohio State exploded for 10 points in the fourth quarter Saturday to master Michigan 20-9 and grab the Big Ten football crown and a spot in the Rose Bowl.

Tim Anderson blocked a Michigan placekick that kept the Wolverines from a 10-10 tie in the third quarter. Then Fred Schram kicked his second field goal for Ohio State and Leo Hayden scored on a four-yard run in the last period.

Perfect Record

The victory gave the fifth-ranked Buckeyes a final 9-0 record that included six straight triumphs in the conference, sending Ohio State to the Rose Bowl for the sixth time, this time against Pacific-8 winner Stanford. Michigan was ranked fourth in the latest Associated Press poll.

It also avenged a 24-12 loss to Michigan in the 1969 finale, Ohio State's only loss in its last 32 games. The Wolverines, who shared the Big Ten title with the Buckeyes last year, finished with a 9-1 over-all record and a 5-1 conference mark.

Scram and Michigan's Dana Coin each had field goals in the first half, both set up on breaks, before Kern found Bruce Jankowski for a 26-yard touchdown pass that sent the Buckeyes into a 10-3 halftime lead.

Harry Howard recovered a fumble by Michigan's Lance Scheffler on the opening kickoff at the Wolverine 25-yard line. Six plays later, Scram kicked a 28-yard field goal with less than three minutes gone before a record 87,331 Ohio Stadium fans.

Michigan safety Jim Betts intercepted a Kern pass and set up Coin's 31-yard field goal for a 3-3 tie just inside the second period.

A 23-yard Ohio State punt preceded the Wolverines' 50-yard touchdown drive in the third quarter. Don Moorhead capped the surge with a 13-yard scoring pass to Paul Staroba.

Ohio State's defense, anchored by All-Americans Jim Stillwagon and aJck Tatum, shut off the Michigan ground attack with only 31 yards and recovered two Wolverine fumbles.

	FIRST DOWNS				NET GAIN			Total	PASSING			PUNTING		FUMBLES		Yards	
	Rush	Pass	Pen.	Total	Rush	Pass	Total	Plays	Att.	Comp.	Int.	No.	Avg.	No.	Lost	Penalized	Points
TEXAS A. & M.	6	12	1	19	50	271	321	65	30	18	1	3	31.0	6	4	38	13
OHIO STATE	22	5	0	27	415	98	513	81	12	7	1	3	44.7	0	0	40	56
DUKE	8	7	2	17	136	113	249	72	24	12	2	6	36.7	1	1	45	10
OHIO STATE	18	6	3	27	397	84	481	87	14	6	0	1	36.0	3	2	50	34
MICHIGAN STATE	8	3	0	11	157	56	213	64	21	7	1	7	33.3	5	2	35	0
OHIO STATE	14	3	2	19	287	51	338	81	18	5	1	6	33.3	1	0	25	29
MINNESOTA	9	16	1	26	70	308	378	77	49	29	2	6	35.2	3	1	72	8
OHIO STATE	21	2	3	26	396	74	470	87	19	9	1	4	41.5	1	0	73	28
ILLINOIS	16	7	1	24	298	123	421	86	19	11	1	4	38.7	2	1	20	29
OHIO STATE	15	6	1	22	347	128	475	68	18	10	1	5	38.4	0	0	64	48
NORTHWESTERN	5	5	3	13	93	132	225	67	24	7	2	6	43.5	3	2	44	10
OHIO STATE	21	3	0	24	336	57	393	91	12	5	3	4	35.0	0	0	68	24
WISCONSIN	8	6	2	16	70	121	191	79	32	13	1	6	35.8	3	2	26	7
OHIO STATE	7	6	1	14	141	158	299	65	18	8	5	3	37.3	1	0	61	24
PURDUE	1	2	0	3	54	17	71	62	12	2	2	12	34.7	2	1	25	7
OHIO STATE	11	1	0	12	200	55	255	59	9	2	0	12	28.7	3	2	25	10
MICHIGAN	3	6	1	10	37	118	155	56	26	12	1	7	41.4	3	2	48	9
OHIO STATE	13	5	0	18	242	87	329	77	12	8	1	6	28.2	3	1	31	20
STANFORD	7	12	2	21	143	265	408	67	30	20	1	3	33.0	3	2	46	27
OHIO STATE	19	2	1	22	364	75	439	87	20	7	1	2	28.0	2	0	64	17
OPPONENTS	71	76	13	160	1108	1524	2632	695	267	131	14	60	37.2	31	18	399	120
OHIO STATE	161	39	11	211	3125	867	3992	783	152	67	14	46	33.8	14	5	501	290

1970 OHIO STATE INDIVIDUAL STATISTICS

RUSHING

Player	Tries	Gain	Lost	Net	Avg.	TD's
*Brockington	261	1150	8	1142	4.4	17
*Hayden	132	777	10	767	5.8	3
*Kern	112	691	94	597	5.3	7
Galbos	30	190	0	190	6.3	1
*Maciejowski	42	193	54	139	3.3	3
*Zelina	17	117	9	108	6.3	1
Campana	14	73	0	73	5.2	0
*Coburn	16	61	0	61	3.8	2
*Jankowski	2	41	0	41	20.5	0
*Smith	2	9	0	9	4.5	0
Bledsoe	2	7	0	7	3.5	0
Moore	1	0	9	—9	—9.0	0
Totals	631	3309	184	3125	4.9	34

FORWARD PASSING

Player	Att.	Comp.	Int.	Yards	Pct.	TD's
*Kern	98	45	8	470	.459	3
*Maciejowski	50	22	5	397	.440	1
Galbos	2	0	0	0	.000	0
Moore	2	0	1	0	.000	0
Totals	152	67	14	867	.441	4

SCORING

Player	Rush	Pass	Other	PAT Kick	FG	Total Points
*Brockington	17	0	0	0	0	102
Schram	0	0	0	33-36	7-13	54
*Kern	7	0	0	0	0	42
*Maciejowski	3	0	0	0	0	18
*Hayden	3	0	0	0	0	18
*Zelina	1	1	0	0	0	12
*Coburn	2	0	0	0	0	12
*J. White	0	2	0	0	0	12
Galbos	1	0	0	0	0	6
†Luttner	0	0	1	0	0	6
*Jankowski	0	1	0	0	0	6
Johnston	0	0	0	2-2	0	2
(Team)				0-1		
Totals	34	4	1	35-39	7-13	290

† Scored touchdown on a blocked punt.

TACKLES FOR LOSS (Leaders)

Player	No.	Yards	Player	No.	Yards
*Stillwagon	9	36	Luttner	3	12
Williams	8	78	S. White	3	9
*Adams	5	23	Howard	3	6
*Tatum	4	33	*Dale	2	18
*Debevc	4	33	Cappell	2	12
Hasenohrl	3	12	*Holloway	2	8

PASSES BROKEN UP

Player	No.	Player	No.
Howard	10	Ferko	1
*Adams	9	Hughes	1
*Anderson	8	Lamka	1
*Sensibaugh	3	Cappell	1
*Debevc	3	Battista	1
S. White	3	Williams	1
*Tatum	3		

PASS RECEIVING

Player	Caught	Yards	TD's
*Jankowski	12	235	1
*Zelina	13	212	1
*J. White	17	171	2
Campana	9	120	0
*Brockington	12	64	0
Harris	2	34	0
*Hayden	1	20	0
Galbos	1	11	0
Totals	67	867	4

PUNTING

Player	Number	Yards	Avg.
Lago	40	1357	33.9
*Zelina	3	125	41.7
*Sensibaugh	2	73	36.5
(Team)	1	0	00.0
Totals	46	1555	33.8

KICKOFF RETURNS

Player	Number	Yards	Average	TD's
*Brockington	6	160	26.7	0
*Jankowski	4	85	21.2	0
Harris	5	72	14.4	0
Galbos	4	41	10.2	0
Campana	2	32	16.0	0
*Hayden	2	28	14.0	0
*Zelina	1	26	26.0	0
Hicks	1	0	00.0	0
Simon	1	0	00.0	0
Totals	26	444	17.1	0

PUNT RETURNS

Player	Number	Yards	Average	TD's
*Anderson	10	72	7.2	0
Luttner	1	70	70.0	1
Campana	9	58	6.4	0
*Zelina	8	37	4.6	0
Galbos	2	19	9.5	0
Howard	2	18	9.0	0
*Holloway	1	4	4.0	0
Totals	33	278	8.4	1

INTERCEPTION RETURNS

Player	Number	Yards	Average	TD's
*Sensibaugh	8	40	5.0	0
S. White	2	21	10.5	0
Fletcher	1	32	32.0	0
*Adams	1	14	14.0	0
*Tatum	1	2	2.0	0
Howard	1	—2	—2.0	0
Totals	14	107	7.6	0

* Not returning for 1971

Stanford Stuns Buckeyes As Jim Plunkett Excels

PASADENA, Calif. (AP) — Quarterback Jim Plunkett of Stanford went into the Rose Bowl against undefeated Ohio State New Year's Day knowing that he was the leader of the Tribe and had the added burden of being the 1970 Heisman Trophy recipient.

The Buckeyes, who were to lose 27-17, had a record in this same game of restraining a previous Heisman winner, and Ohio's Coach Woody Hayes made a point of this as soon as he reached Pasadena.

Hayes noted the Plunkett had been chosen as the nation's outstanding player and reflected that Ohio State had "done quite well" in a similar situation two years before.

Obvious Inference

He didn't mention O.J. Simpson of the University of Southern California, but the inference was obvious. The Buckeyes did negate O.J.'s performance in winning 27-16.

The strategy did not work this time. Plunkett ushered the 11-point underdog Indians from behind in a fourth-quarter that seethed with excitement.

The result gave the undefeated Big Ten champion Buckeyes' hopes for the national championship a telling blow.

There was absolute bedlam from the 103,839 fans jammed into the historic old arena as Plunkett, the Heisman Trophy winner, ran and passed the Pacific 8 champions 80 yards for the go-ahead touchdown early in the final quarter.

Ohio State's brilliant quarterback, Rex Kern, went into a desperation aerial counterattack which abruptly misfired. Stanford's Jack Schultz, who grew up near the Rose Bowl, picked off a Kern pass and the Indians quickly swept 25 yards for the icing on the cake touchdown.

Surprising 10-0 Lead

Stanford, 8-3 in the regular season, got off to a surprising 10-0 lead, scoring a touchdown and a field goal before Ohio State got its offense going. The Buckeyes held a 14-10 lead at the half.

Ohio State dominated the game on the ball handling magic of Kern and his two punishing running backs, John Brockington and Leo Hayden. But Stanford was never too far back.

It was the first Rose Bowl appearance of the Indians from Palo Alto, Calif., since their loss to Illinois in 1952, 40-7, and their first victory here since they defeated Nebraska, 21-13, in 1941.

Ohio State entered this 57th New Year's Day classic knowing that Notre Dame was about to knock off No. 1 rated Texas. Ohio State was No. 2 in the Associated Press poll at the end of the regular season.

The mythical championship apparently is up for grabs as the final poll will be taken following the weekend bowl games around the country.

Brown Scores

Stanford's first touchdown came on a four yard run by Jackie Brown, the first of his two for the sunny, slightly chilly afternoon. It came after the Stanford defense, much stronger than it had been credited, stopped a Buckeye drive following the opening kickoff.

Stanford traveled 59 yards in six plays for the touchdown and added three more points on a 37-yard field goal by Steve Horowitz.

It was Horowitz who kicked a Rose Bowl record 48-yard field goal opening the third quarter, which narrowed the Indians' deficit to 14-13.

Brockington scored the first two Ohio State touchdowns, one in each of the first two quarters, with one-yard pops through the line, but it was Kern who engineered both scoring drives. The first went 65 yards, the second 55 and the red-haired senior seemed on his way to Player of the Game honors for the second time in his career. He won the honor in 1969 as a sophomore when the Bucks defeated Southern California 27-16.

Ohio State's other score came on a field goal of 32 yards by Fred Schram.

Completes 20 of 30

Plunkett completed 20 of 30 passes, with one meaningless interception, for a total of 265 yards and one touchdown. Kern, who has been more dangerous as a runner than a thrower, completed 4 of 13 with one interception for 40 yards.

Kern carried the ball 20 times for 129 yards.

The scoring surge that led to the winning touchdown began after Sanford stopped an Ohio State invasion. Brockington on fourth down had to make four inches. Stanford held and began the march from its 20. Plunkett passed successively to Demea Washington for 6 and 10 yards, ran for 2 and 10 on keeper plays and kept the ball moving with a 10-yard pass to Randy Vataha. A diversified attack continued with Brown and Hillary Shockley ripping off enough yardage to keep the Buckeye defense alert.

From Ohio State's 37, third and 16, Plunkett was given a big rush. He looked and looked, finally spotted Bob Moore, and unloaded a 35-yard pass which put the ball on the two.

Two plays later Brown, with great blocking, swept to the right into the end zone and it was Stanford 20-17.

Caps Career

Plunkett has enjoyed brilliant afternoons but this one, ending his college career, must have capped them all. Plunkett, who could have turned professional a year ago since his class was graduated, elected to continue at Stanford. He had one goal: the Rose Bowl.

Stanford staged a remarkable comeback after having lost to the Air Force and California in the final games of the season. Earlier the Indians lost to Purdue.

But Coach John Ralston and the Indians promised the comeback and pointed out that the losses came after they had wrapped up the Rose Bowl assignment.

This was the first Rose Bowl defeat for Buckeye Coach Woody Hayes, who previously had brought three winners here from Columbus.

Ohio State reeled off 87 offensive plays to 67 for the Indians.

```
Ohio State    7  7  3  0—17
Stanford     10  0  0 14—27
```

Stan—Brown 4 run (Horowitz kick)
Stan—FG Horowitz 37
OSU—Brockington 1 run (Schram kick)
OSU—Brockington 1 run (Schram kick)
Stan—FG Horowitz 48
OSU—FG Schram 32
Stan—Brown 1 run (Horowitz kick)
Stan—Vataha 10 pass from Plunkett (Horowitz kick)
A—103,839

	OSU	Stanford
First downs	22	21
Rushing yardage	364	143
Passing yardage	75	265
Return yardage	60	0
Punts	2-28	3-33
Passes	7-20-1	20-30-1
Fumbles lost	0	2
Yards penalized	64	46

[1971]

No.	Name	Pos.	Wgt.	Hgt.	Age	Class	Hometown
1	*Schram, Fred	PK	178	5-10	21	Sr.	Massillon
2	Johnston, Paul	PK	176	5-10	21	Sr.	Cleveland
4	Keith, Randal	FB	212	5-11	19	So.	Cincinnati
6	Thompson, Monty	DB	180	6-1	19	So.	Portsmouth
8	Cunningham, Dan	S	145	5-7	21	Sr.	Columbus
9	Murphy, Robert	DB	182	6-2	22	Jr.	Seattle, Wash.
11	Cowman, Randall	DCB	194	6-0	20	Jr.	Dayton
12	Moore, Ross	QB	188	5-11	20	Jr.	Allentown, Pa.
14	Kelly, Robert	DLH	194	6-1	19	So.	Butler, Pa.
15	Boyle, William	QB	178	6-0	19	So.	Columbus
16	Davis, Jeff	DLH	182	5-10	19	So.	Erie, Pa.
17	Baxter, Charles	OLE	222	6-2	19	So.	Painesville (Harvey)
18	Hare, Gregory	QB	198	6-3	19	So.	Cumberland, Md. (Ft. Hill)
19	**Lamka, Donald	QB	197	5-11	22	Sr.	Cleveland (South)
20	Kinsey, Marvin	CB	193	6-2	20	Jr.	East Liverpool (E. Liverpool)
21	Kern, Carl	DRH	184	6-0	19	So.	Dallas, Pa. (Lake-Lehman)
22	Gales, Richard	ORH	176	5-9	19	So.	Niles (McKinley)
23	Battista, Thomas	ORE	182	6-3	20	Jr.	Weirton, W. Va. (Weirton)
24	**Campana, Thomas	ORH	182	5-11	21	Sr.	Kent (Roosevelt)
25	Bradshaw, Morris	OLH	194	6-2	18	So.	Edwardsville, Ill. (Edwrdsvll)
26	Sharpp, Warren	DLH	194	5-11	19	So.	Akron (St. Vincent)
28	**Howard, Harry	CB	192	6-1	21	Sr.	Cincinnati (Princeton)
30	Mathis, Louis	CB	206	6-0	20	So.	Paterson, N.J. (Eastside)
32	Middleton, Richard	OE	211	6-3	19	So.	Delaware (Hayes)
33	*Galbos, Richard	OLH	196	6-0	20	Jr.	Mentor (Mentor)
34	*Bledsoe, John	FB	208	6-1	20	Jr.	Westlake (Westlake)
35	Rich, Rocco	MG	218	5-11	19	So.	Canton (McKinley)
36	Szabo, Thomas	DRT	227	6-1	18	So.	Elyria (Elyria)
37	Eggers, Patrick	FB	215	6-3	19	So.	Toledo (Central Catholic)
39	*Ferko, Richard	LB	198	5-11	20	Jr.	Pittsburgh, Pa. (Montour)
41	*Seifert, Richard	S	188	6-1	20	Jr.	Cuyahoga Falls (Cuy. Falls)
46	Gaffney, Michael	ORH	203	6-2	19	So.	South Euclid (Brush)
47	Lippert, Elmer	OLH	177	5-7	19	So.	Sandusky (Sandusky)
50	Pitstick, Anthony	OLG	212	6-3	21	Jr.	Xenia (Xenia)
51	Dixon, Kenneth	LB	206	6-3	20	Jr.	Wintersville (Wintersville)
52	**DeLeone, Thomas	C	227	6-2	21	Sr.	Kent (Roosevelt)
53	Gradishar, Randolph	LB	224	6-3	19	So.	Champion (Champion)
54	Meckstroth, James	C	215	6-0	19	So.	Wilton, Wis. (Royall)
55	*Fletcher, Kevin	MG	222	6-1	20	Jr.	E. Orange, N.J. (E. Orange)
56	*Nixon, Thomas	C	220	6-2	20	Jr.	Mansfield (Mansfield Senior)
57	Houser, Thomas	ORG	228	6-2	21	Sr.	Massillon (Washington)
58	*Bonica, Charles	ORG	254	6-3	22	Sr.	Waltham, Mass. (Waltham)
59	Pisanelli, Fred	LB	200	6-2	20	Jr.	Warren (Western Reserve)
60	*Vecanski, Milan	OLG	222	6-1	22	Sr.	Harrisburg, Pa. (Harris)
61	Husband, John	OLG	212	6-2	19	So.	Elyria (Elyria)
62	Koegel, Victor	LB	200	6-1	18	So.	Cincinnati (Moeller)
63	Kregel, James	ORG	227	6-2	19	So.	Toledo (Woodward)
64	*Conley, William	OLG	204	5-10	20	Sr.	Columbus (Pleasantview)
65	Wersel, Timothy	ORG	215	6-2	20	Jr.	Cincinnati (Roger Bacon)
67	Cutillo, Daniel	DLT	230	6-1	19	So.	Amityville, N.Y. (Amityville)
68	Cummings, John	OLT	260	6-2	20	Jr.	Cincinnati (St. Xavier)
70	*Hasenohrl, George	DLT	260	6-1	20	Jr.	Garfield Heights (Garfield)
71	Willard, Robert	OLT	232	6-2	19	So.	Chagrin Falls (Chagrin Falls)
72	Mountz, Gregory	OLT	214	6-3	21	Sr.	Hummelstown, Pa. (L. Dphin)
73	**Simon, Richard	OLT	228	6-2	21	Sr.	Parma (Valley Forge)
74	Long, David	OLT	225	6-1	21	Sr.	Delphos (Delphos)
75	*Teague, Mervin	OLE	216	6-5	21	Jr.	Youngstown (East)
76	Scott, Daniel	OLT	250	6-3	19	So.	Amityville, N.Y. (Amityville)
77	Belgrave, Earl	ORT	244	6-5	20	Jr.	Brooklyn, N.Y. (Jefferson)
78	Beecroft, Charles	ORT	221	6-3	20	Jr.	Dayton (Carroll)
79	*Williams, Shad	DRT	232	6-3	20	Jr.	Portsmouth (Portsmouth)
80	Pagac, Fred	OLE	205	6-1	19	So.	Richeyville, Pa. (Beth-Center)
81	Marendt, Thomas	DLE	206	6-1	19	So.	Indianapolis, Ind. (Howe)
82	Hazel, David	ORE	194	6-1	18	So.	Xenia (Xenia)
83	Scannell, Michael	DRE	204	6-2	20	Jr.	Sylvania (Central Catholic)
84	Jones, Scott	ORE	206	6-3	19	So.	Parma Heights (Valley Forge)
85	**Harris, Jimmie	ORE	176	5-11	21	Sr.	Dayton (Roth)
86	**Cappell, Richard	DLE	204	6-0	22	Sr.	Dover (Dover)
87	**Luttner, Kenneth	DE	206	6-2	21	Sr.	Medina (Highland)
88	**White, Stanley	LB	224	6-1	21	Sr.	Kent (Roosevelt)
91	**Wakefield, Richard	ORE	202	6-4	22	Sr.	Avon Lake (Avon Lake)
92	*Lago, Gary	P	222	6-2	21	Jr.	Ashtabula (Edgewood)
93	Brown, Jeffrey	DLE	198	6-4	20	Jr.	Chambersburg, Pa. (Cham.)
94	*Strong, Terry	DLE	190	6-3	19	Jr.	Weirton, W. Va. (Weirton)
96	Smurda, John	OLE	194	6-1	19	So.	Allentown, Pa. (Dieruff)
99	Baxa, Thomas	DLT	238	6-5	20	Jr.	St. Clairsville (St. Clairsville)

* indicates letter

1971
Captains: Harry Howard
Tom DeLeone

52	*Iowa	21
14	*Colorado	20
35	*California	3
24	Illinois	10
27	Indiana	7
31	*Wisconsin	6
14	Minnesota	12
10	*Michigan State	17
10	*Northwestern	14
7	Michigan	10
224		120

Won 6, Lost 4

Northwestern Stuns Ohio State

COLUMBUS, Ohio (AP)— Greg Strunk ran a kickoff 93 yards and Randy Anderson scored from one yard in the fourth period Saturday, giving Northwestern a 14-10 upset and knocking Ohio State from the Big Ten football title picture.

The home loss was the second in a row for Ohio State, giving the Buckeyes a 5-2 conference record to Michigan's title-clinching 7-0 mark.

Northwestern, despite five major errors in the first half that gave Ohio State all of its points, kept alive its hopes of finishing second.

The Wildcats are 5-3 in the Big Ten and 6-4 overall. Ohio State slipped to a 6-3 mark for all games.

Northwestern rolled 63 yards, twice clicking on key fourth down plays in Ohio territory for the deciding touchdown.

Maurie Daigneau sneaked one yard on a fourth down call at the Buckeye 25. Al Robinson picked up two yards on another fourth down play at the Ohio State three.

Spartans Slip By Ohio State

COLUMBUS, Ohio (AP) — Michigan State turned two Ohio State mistakes into touchdowns Saturday and knocked the ninth ranked Buckeyes from a share of the Big Ten football lead with a 17-10 upset.

Despite an off day and miserable weather conditions, Eric "The Flea" Allen notched touchdowns of five and one yards to drop Ohio State to a 5-1 record in the conference behind Michigan's 6-0 mark.

Allen's scores give him school records of 13 touchdowns and 80 points for one season.

Brad Van Pelt's fourth interception of the year of a Don Lamka pass set up Allen's first touchdown. That gave the Spartans a 10-7 lead in the second quarter.

Michigan State defensive end Doug Halliday recovered a fumble by Ohio State Halfback Morris Bradshaw at Buckeyes' 11-yard line late in the third period.

That paved the way for five-yard scoring scamper by Allen, who set an NCAA rushing record of 350 yards a week ago.

1971 OHIO STATE INDIVIDUAL STATISTICS

RUSHING

Player	Tries	Gain	Lost	Net	Avg.	TD's
Galbos	141	556	16	540	3.8	2
Bradshaw	65	381	41	340	5.2	4
*Lamka	107	416	108	308	2.9	8
Lippert	53	270	5	265	5.0	2
Bledsoe	61	265	0	265	4.3	2
Keith	66	217	1	216	3.3	4
Hare	25	153	69	84	3.4	2
Gales	13	57	2	55	4.2	0
Boyle	7	32	3	29	4.1	0
*Eggers	9	22	0	22	2.4	1
*Harris	1	0	8	—8	—8.0	0
Totals	548	2369	263	2116	3.9	26

FORWARD PASSING

Player	Att.	Comp.	Int.	Yards	Pct.	TD's
*Lamka	107	54	5	718	.505	2
Hare	59	25	5	299	.424	0
Boyle	2	1	0	9	.500	0
Totals	168	80	10	1026	.476	2

SCORING

Player	TD Rush	TD Pass	TD Other	PAT Kick	FG	Total Points
*Lamka	8	0	0	0	0	48
*Schram	0	0	0	27–27	7–13	48
Bradshaw	4	0	1	0	0	30
Keith	4	0	0	0	0	24
Bledsoe	2	0	0	0	0	12
Hare	2	0	0	0	0	12
Lippert	2	0	0	0	0	12
Galbos	2	0	0	0	0	12
Middleton	0	1	0	0	0	6
*Eggers	1	0	0	0	0	6
*Wakefield	0	1	0	0	0	6
*Campana	0	0	1	0	0	6
Johnston	0	0	0	2–2	0	2
Totals	25	2	2	29–29	7–13	224

* Not returning for 1972

	FIRST DOWNS Rush	Pass	Pen.	Total	NET GAIN Rush	Pass	Total	Total Plays	PASSING Att.	Comp.	Int.	PUNTING No.	Avg.	FUMBLES No.	Lost	Yards Penalized	Points
IOWA	4	14	1	19	31	216	247	67	38	25	0	7	40.6	4	2	35	21
OHIO STATE	24	3	0	27	402	60	462	77	8	5	0	4	36.2	5	2	55	52
COLORADO	15	4	0	19	285	97	382	59	9	4	2	4	39.7	2	1	59	20
OHIO STATE	11	12	1	24	145	299	444	90	34	21	0	6	38.5	0	0	47	35
CALIFORNIA	4	5	3	12	38	97	135	54	22	10	1	6	38.7	2	2	25	3
OHIO STATE	22	6	0	28	317	113	430	89	20	11	2	4	38.2	2	0	47	35
ILLINOIS	10	13	0	23	216	198	414	81	29	15	2	4	31.7	2	2	70	10
OHIO STATE	13	1	1	15	284	8	292	56	7	2	0	7	38.5	4	1	10	24
INDIANA	5	5	0	10	91	109	200	71	31	13	0	13	41.5	6	2	43	7
OHIO STATE	6	14	1	21	121	263	384	88	39	17	2	8	42.2	2	2	34	27
WISCONSIN	12	13	0	25	194	191	385	88	39	18	4	3	45.3	4	3	54	6
OHIO STATE	11	4	2	17	306	93	399	70	12	6	0	4	43.0	2	1	49	31
MINNESOTA	7	6	1	14	149	124	273	64	24	9	1	9	39.7	4	0	53	12
OHIO STATE	7	2	2	11	135	63	198	66	15	7	0	11	44.5	3	1	49	14
MICHIGAN STATE	10	1	1	12	180	19	199	71	7	1	1	9	40.2	2	0	25	17
OHIO STATE	10	0	1	11	175	10	185	66	15	2	3	6	37.5	3	1	10	10
NORTHWESTERN	12	4	0	16	174	85	259	75	15	7	3	5	42.4	2	2	5	14
OHIO STATE	7	3	0	10	153	57	210	63	8	4	1	8	41.5	2	0	20	10
MICHIGAN	16	2	2	20	289	46	335	81	10	2	0	8	44.4	2	2	49	10
OHIO STATE	3	2	2	7	78	60	138	51	10	5	2	8	35.4	2	1	64	7
OPPONENTS	95	67	8	170	1647	1182	2829	711	224	104	14	68	40.4	30	16	418	120
OHIO STATE	114	47	10	171	2116	1026	3142	716	168	80	10	66	40.0	25	9	385	224

KICKOFF RETURNS

Player	Number	Yards	Avg	TD's
Bradshaw	8		28.2	1
Lippert	9	153	17.0	0
*Campana	3	70	23.3	0
*Harris	2	54	27.0	0
Gales	2	16	8.0	0
Galbos	1	0	.0	0
Totals	25	519	20.8	1

PUNT RETURNS

Player	Number	Yards	Average	TD's
*Campana	37	447	12.1	1
Fletcher	1	25	25.0	0
Battista	2	9	4.5	0
Totals	40	481	12.0	1

INTERCEPTION RETURNS

Player	Number	Yards	Average	TD's
Seifert	4	0	.0	0
Koegel	3	44	14.7	0
*Howard	3	38	12.7	0
Davis	2	16	8.0	0
*Campana	2	0	.0	0
Totals	14	98	7.0	0

TACKLES (Leaders)

Player	Solo	Assists	Fumbles	Total
Koegel	61	65	5	126
*White	47	53	4	100
Gradishar	53	31	5	84
*Luttner	30	37	2	67
Hasenohrl	29	31	4	60
Seifert	39	18	1	57
Marendt	27	20	3	47
Davis	26	17	0	43
*Campana	28	6	0	34
Cutillo	14	14	2	28
*Howard	13	11	1	24
Williams	5	18	1	23
*Cappell	11	6	0	17
Fletcher	8	8	0	16
Beecroft	11	3	1	14
Ferko	8	5	4	13
Scannell	7	5	1	12

FUMBLES RECOVERED (Leaders)

Player	Defensive	Offensive	Total
*Lamka	0	3	3
Galbos	0	3	3
Marendt	2	0	2
Gradishar	2	0	2
*White	2	0	2
Bradshaw	0	2	2
*Vecanski	0	2	2
*DeLeone	1	1	2
Scannell	1	0	1
Fletcher	1	0	1
Koegel	1	0	1
Williams	1	0	1
Hasenohrl	1	0	1
*Luttner	1	0	1
Pisanelli	1	0	1
*Howard	1	0	1
Kern	1	0	1

TOTAL OFFENSE

Player	Plays	Rush	Pass	Total	Avg.	TD's
*Lamka	214	308	718	1026	4.8	10
Galbos	141	540	0	540	3.8	2
Hare	84	84	299	383	4.6	2
Bradshaw	65	340	0	340	5.2	4
Lippert	53	265	0	265	5.0	2
Bledsoe	61	265	0	265	4.3	2
Keith	66	216	0	216	3.3	4
Gales	13	55	0	55	4.2	0
Boyle	9	29	9	38	4.2	0
*Eggers	9	22	0	22	2.4	1
*Harris	1	—8	0	—8	—8.0	0
Totals	716	2116	1026	3142	4.5	27

PASS RECEIVING

Player	Caught	Yards	TD's
*Wakefield	31	432	1
Middleton	11	152	1
*Harris	9	200	0
Galbos	9	47	0
Pagac	5	59	0
Bradshaw	4	45	0
Bledsoe	4	10	0
Keith	3	11	0
Gales	2	34	0
*Campana	1	18	0
Lippert	1	18	0
Totals	80	1026	2

PUNTING

Player	Number	Yards	Avg.
Lago	63	2536	40.3
Gales	3	103	34.3
Totals	66	2639	40.0

TACKLES FOR LOSS (Leaders)

Player	No.	Yards	Player	No.	Yards
Marendt	7	40	Beecroft	5	22
Hasenohrl	6	50	*White	4	17
*Luttner	6	26	Davis	3	12
Koegel	6	16	Cutillo	3	11
Gradishar	5	30	*Cappell	1	11

PASSES BROKEN UP (Leaders)

Player	No.	Player	No.
Davis	4	*Campana	2
*White	4	Gradishar	2
*Howard	3	*Luttner	2

* Not returning for 1972

Ohio State University Football Roster

Name	Pos.	Wt.	Hgt.	Age	Class	Home Town (High School)
Wilkins, Dwight	LB	228	5-10	19	So.	Cincinnati (Taft)
Conway, Blair	PK	155	5-7	20	Jr.	Middleburg Hts.
Keith, Randall	FB	210	5-11	20	Jr.	Cincinnati (Moeller)
McBrayer, Tom	PK	185	6-0	19	So.	Hilliard
Thompson, Monty	CB	185	6-1	20	Jr.	Portsmouth (Portsmouth)
Ezzo, Billy	SE	146	5-8	19	So.	Canastota, N.Y.
Murphy, Robert	SE	197	6-2	23	Sr.	Seattle, Wash. (Odea)
Cowman, Randall	CB	191	6-0	21	Sr.	Dayton (Beavercreek)
Boyle, William	QB	180	6-0	20	Jr.	Columbus (Watterson)
Davis, Jeff	DLH	185	5-10	20	Jr.	Erie, Pa. (McDowell)
Morrison, Steve	QB	204	6-3	19	So.	Huntington, W. Va.
Hare, Gregory	QB	198	6-3	20	Jr.	Cumberland, Md. (Ft. Hill)
Purdy, David	QB	188	6-3	19	So.	Swanton
Colzie, Cornelius	DLH	194	6-0	19	So.	Coral Gables, Fla.
Kern, Carl	DRH	190	6-0	20	Jr.	Dallas, Pa. (Lake-Lehman)
Battista, Thomas	ORE	183	6-3	21	Sr.	Weirton, W. Va.
Parsons, Richard	S	184	5-11	19	So.	Cuyahoga Falls
Bradshaw, Morris	ORH	200	6-2	20	Jr.	Edwardsville, Ill.
DeFilippo, Joe	OLH	198	6-3	19	So.	Lancaster
Holycross, Timothy	OLH	188	5-11	19	So.	Bedford Heights (Chanel)
Plank, Douglas	DRH	185	5-11	19	So.	North Irwin, Pa. (Norwin)
Mathis, Lou	CB	207	6-0	20	Jr.	Paterson, N.J. (Eastside)
Middleton, Rick	LB	214	6-3	20	Jr.	Delaware (Hayes)
Galbos, Richard	ORH	211	6-0	21	Sr.	Mentor
Bledsoe, John	FB	212	6-1	21	Sr.	Westlake
Rich, Rocco	LB	222	5-11	20	Jr.	Canton (McKinley)
Bowers, Brian	LB	219	6-0	19	So.	Uniontown (Lake)
Henson, Harold	FB	225	6-4	19	So.	Ashville (Teays Valley)
Ferko, Richard	LB	204	5-11	21	Sr.	Pittsburgh, Pa. (Montour)
Seifert, Richard	S	186	6-1	21	Sr.	Cuyahoga Falls
Jones, Arnold	LB	222	5-11	19	So.	Dayton (Wayne)
Hughes, John	CB	194	6-1	21	Jr.	Duquesne, Pa.
Gaffney, Mike	ORH	203	6-2	20	Jr.	South Euclid (Brush)
Lippert, Elmer	ORH	183	5-7	20	Jr.	Sandusky
Pitstick, Anthony	ORG	223	6-3	21	Sr.	Xenia
Myers, Steven	C	234	6-2	19	So.	Kent (Roosevelt)
Gradishar, Randy	LB	238	6-3	20	Jr.	Champion
Fletcher, Kevin	LB	221	6-1	21	Sr.	East Orange, N. J.
Nixon, Thomas	C	221	6-1	21	Sr.	Mansfield (Senior)
Luke, Steven	C	195	6-2	19	So.	Massillon
Bonica, Charles	OG	256	6-3	21	Sr.	Waltham, Mass.
Belgrave, Earl	ORT	257	6-5	21	Sr.	Brooklyn, N. Y. (Jefferson)
Trepanier, Edwin	DT	250	6-4	19	Jr.	Rocky River
Husband, John	ORG	212	6-2	20	Jr.	Elyria
Koegel, Victor	LB	216	6-1	20	Jr.	Cincinnati (Moeller)
Kregel, James	ORG	234	6-2	20	Jr.	Toledo (Woodward)
Wiggins, Lawrence	OLG	229	6-0	19	So.	Columbus (Marion Franklin)
Wersel, Timothy	OLG	215	6-2	21	Sr.	Cincinnati (Roger Bacon)
Cutillo, Daniel	DRT	231	6-1	20	Jr.	Amityville, N.Y.
Cummings, John	OLT	254	6-2	21	Sr.	Cincinnati (St. Xavier)
Mack, Richard	OLG	215	6-0	19	So.	Bucyrus
Hasenohrl, George	DLT	262	6-1	21	Sr.	Garfield Heights
Cusick, Peter	DRT	242	6-2	19	So.	Lakewood
Schumacher, Kurt	ORT	244	6-4	19	So.	Lorain
Dannelley, Scott	ORT	229	6-3	19	So.	Williamsport, Pa.
Hicks, John	ORT	254	6-3	21	Jr.	Cleveland (Hay)
Teague, Mervin	OLT	221	6-5	21	Sr.	Youngstown (East)
Scott, Daniel	ORT	260	6-3	20	Jr.	Amityville, N. Y.
France, Doug.	OLT	265	6-6	19	So.	Dayton (Colonel White)
Beecroft, Charles	DLT	224	6-3	21	Sr.	Dayton (Carroll)
Williams, Shad	DRT	238	6-3	21	Sr.	Portsmouth
Pagac, Fred	OLE	208	6-1	20	Jr.	Richeyville, Pa. (Beth-Center)
Marendt, Thomas	DLT	220	6-1	20	Jr.	Indianapolis (Howe)
Hazel, David	DLT	188	6-1	20	Jr.	Xenia
Scannell, Michael	DLE	207	6-2	21	Sr.	Sylvania (Central Catholic)
Jones, Scott	SE	209	6-3	20	Jr.	Parma Heights (Valley Forge)
Smurda, John	TE	214	6-1	20	Jr.	Allentown, Pa. (Dieruff)
Donovan, Brendan	DLE	180	5-10	19	So.	Columbus (Upper Arlington)
Bartoszek, Michael	TE	206	6-4	19	So.	Erie, Pa. (McDowell)
DeCree, Van	DRE	216	6-1	19	So.	Warren (Western Reserve)
Powell, Theodore	TE	225	6-2	20	Jr.	Hampton, Va.
Straka, Mark	TE	220	6-5	20	Jr.	Elyria (Catholic)
Cope, James	DRE	205	6-2	19	So.	McKeesport, Pa. (S. Allegheny)
Lago, Gary	P	229	6-2	21	Sr.	Ashtabula (Edgewood)
Baxter, Charles	TE	222	6-2	20	Jr.	Painesville (Harvey)
Lillvis, Gary	DLT	230	6-2	19	So.	Ashtabula (Harbor)
Pisanelli, Fred	DLT	208	6-2	21	Sr.	Warren (Western Reserve)
O'Rourke, Larry	DT	230	6-0	19	So.	Yardley, Pa.

1972

Captains: Richard Galbos
George Hasenohrl

21	*Iowa	0
29	*North Carolina	14
35	California	18
26	*Illinois	7
44	*Indiana	7
28	Wisconsin	20
27	*Minnesota	19
12	Michigan State	19
27	Northwestern	14
14	*Michigan	11
17	†Southern California	42
280		171

Won 9, Lost 2

Big Ten Co-Champions

† Rose Bowl

A. P. POLL

1. Southern Cal.
2. Oklahoma
3. Texas
4. Nebraska
5. Auburn
6. Michigan
7. Alabama
8. Tennessee
9. OHIO STATE
10. Penn State

U.P.I. POLL

1. Southern Cal.
2. Oklahoma
3. OHIO STATE
4. Alabama
5. Texas
6. Michigan
7. Auburn
8. Penn State
9. Nebraska
10. L.S.U.

[1972]

GOLDEN ANNIVERSARY FOR OHIO STADIUM

Ohio Stadium, long a symbol of Ohio State University football and even of college football itself, celebrates its 50th anniversary this year.

The distinctive structure made possible by more than 13,000 people who gave gifts totalling $1,083,000, became a reality in 13 short months. The construction cost was $1,341,000 and the original capacity was 66,210.

Critics scoffed at the size and claimed it would never be filled. On the day of its dedication, October 21, 1922, 71,385 overflowed the stands and surrounded the playing field. And the fans have kept coming.

To date a total of 274 games have been played in the historic concrete horseshoe, with a total of 17,147,819 fans attending. This averages 62,576 each time the gates are opened, a remarkable record considering this era spans a world war, a major economic depression, gas rationing and various business recessions that have had adverse effects upon attendance at athletic events.

The Ohio Stadium has unusual design. It is a double-decked structure, built in the shape of a horseshoe, with towers on each of the open ends. The circumference is one-third mile and the ground area is 10 acres. The Stadium is 725 feet long and 596 feet wide and the height of the back wall is 98 feet.

Temporary field bleachers and south stands have added additional seats and minor changes have taken place within the Stadium itself to raise the capacity to 81,667.

A modern press box and two elevators have enhanced Ohio Stadium without materially changing its appearance or altering its architectural motif.

The latest addition is to the field itself with the installation of Astro-Turf for the 1971 season.

45—GRIFFIN, Archie, 18, 5-10, 185, freshman . . . from Columbus . . . was the 1971 "Ohio Back of the Year" in both the A.P. and the U.P.I. press polls . . . scored 170 points his senior year at Eastmoor as he averaged just under eight yards per carry . . . gained 1,737 yards in ten games his senior year . . . captained his high school football, track and wrestling teams . . . has three older brothers who played or are playing college football . . . seven boys and one girl in the family . . .

Griffin Sets School Mark With 239 Yards Rushing

STATISTICS OF THE GAME

	Ohio St.	N. Car.
First downs	24	11
Rushing yardage	66-430	48-174
Passing yardage	96	65
Passes	5-13	4-14
Interceptions by	2	1
Punts	4-25	9-39
Fumbles-lost	2-2	0-1
Penalties-yards	2-10	5-33

COLUMBUS, Ohio, Sept. 30 (AP)—Archie Griffin, a hometown freshman tailback carrying the ball for the first time in college, broke loose for a school record 239 rushing yards today, leading Ohio State to a 29-14 victory over North Carolina.

Griffin, a 5-foot-10-inch, 185-pounder, rushed 27 times and scored one touchdown, shattering the Buckeyes' one-game mark of 229 yards by Ollie Cline, a fullback, against Pittsburgh in 1945.

Griffin, who did not carry the ball once in an opening triumph against Iowa, also set up short touchdown runs by Randy Keith and Harold Henson and a 17-yard keeper by Greg Hare.

Blair Conway also booted a 22-yard field goal for the Buckeyes, handing North Carolina its first loss in four games with a relentless ground attack.

Ohio State, normally relying on its fullbacks, whipped the Tar Heels with Griffin and his alternate, Elmer Lippert, combining for 355 yards from the tailback spots.

Ohio State   3 6 14 6—29
North Carolina   7 0 0 7—14

N.C.—Bethesa, 37, pass from Vidnovic (Alexander, kick).
O.S.U.—F.G., Conway, 22.
O.S.U.—Hare, 17, run (kick failed).
O.S.U.—Keith, 11, run (Conway, kick).
O.S.U.—Henson, 1, run (Conway, kick).
O.S.U.—Griffin, 9, run (kick failed).
N.C.—Bethesa, 37, pass from Vidnovic (Alexander, kick).
Attendance—86,180.

Buckeyes Rose Bowl Bound

COLUMBUS, Ohio (AP) — Two brilliant goal line stands and the open field running of freshman Archie Griffin gave Ohio State a 14-11 victory over Michigan on Saturday. It gave the Buckeyes the Big Ten football co-championship with the Wolverines and a berth in the Rose Bowl.

The ninth-ranked Buckeyes matched Michigan's 7-1 conference record and will take a 9-1 over-all record against Southern California in the Rose Bowl on New Year's Day.

Griffin burst 30 yards for the clinching touchdown in the third quarter. His 18-yard gallop set up Champ Henon's one-yard plunge for the Buckeye's opening score.

An aggressive Ohio State defense led by tackles George Hasenohrl and Pete Cusick and linebackers Rick Middleton and Randy Gradishar made the two touchdowns standup.

The Buckeyes twice thwarted Wolverine scoring threats in the shadows of their goal posts—once in each dalf. Michigan had a first-and-goal at the Ohio State one just before halftime and first-and-goal at the five early in the fourth quarter, but was turned back both times.

A fumble by sophomore quarterback Dennis Franklin on fourth down at the two stymied the first bid.

Gradishor stopped Franklin's sneak at the one in the final period.

An Ohio Stadium throng of 87,040 and millions more on national television saw Michigan take a 3-0 lead on sophomore Mike Lantry's 35-yard field goal early in the seond qcarter.

The third-ranked Wolverines, suffering their first loss in 11 games, spent most of the dreary, rainy afternoon in buckeye territory but could score only one touchdown.

Fullback Ed Shuttlesworth bulled one yard with nearly five minutes to go in the third period for Michigan's lone touchdown.

Ohio State fans could not wait to celebrate the avenging of a 10-7 loss at Michigan last year. They tore down the south goalposts with 13 seconds to go while the Wolverines were trying to work into scoring position.

If Michigan had worked into field goal range, Ohio State officials had another set of goal posts ready to erect. They were being kept under the stands.

If the goals were needed by the Michigan team, the officials would have called time to erect the new goal posts.

A field goal could have given the Wolverines the three points to tie the Buckeyes and an undisputed hold on the Big Ten championship.

The Buckeye partisans poured onto the field, and the clock was halted with six seconds to play. When the field finally was cleared, the Ohio State defense stopped Franklin at the Buckeyes' 41, and the fans encircled the team at midfield as time ran out.

It was a frustrating afternoon for the Wolverines, favored by six points to earn their third Rose Bowl trip in four years.

They moved the ball into Ohio State territory nine of the 10 times they had possession, but mustered only 11 points.

```
Michigan     0  3  8  0—11
Ohio State   0  7  7  0—14
```
Mich—FG Lantry 35
OSU—Henson 1 run (Conway kick)
OSU—Griffin 30 run (Conway kick)
Mich—Shuttlesworth 1 run (Haslerig pass from Franklin)
A—87,040

	Michigan	OSU
First downs	21	10
Rushes-yards	60-184	41-175
Passing yards	160	17
Return yards	12	8
Passes	13-23-0	1-3-1
Punts	2-37	5-38
Fumbles-lost	1-0	0-0
Penalties-yards	6-40	3-35

includes Rose Bowl

1972 OHIO STATE INDIVIDUAL STATISTICS

RUSHING

Player	Tries	Gain	Lost	Net	Avg.	TD's
Griffin	159	888	21	867	5.4	3
Henson	193	795	0	795	4.1	20
Hare	87	415	50	365	4.2	4
Keith	92	345	1	344	3.7	4
Lippert	36	245	1	244	6.8	0
*Galbos	26	136	7	129	4.9	1
*Bledsoe	20	93	0	93	4.6	1
Morrison	9	52	0	52	5.8	1
Baschnagel	9	57	18	39	4.3	0
Bradshaw	12	42	7	35	2.9	0
*Gaffney	2	15	0	15	7.5	0
Elia	2	9	0	9	4.5	0
Purdy	7	15	6	9	1.3	0
Gales	1	7	0	7	7.0	0
Cramer	2	4	0	4	2.0	0
Greene	3	3	17	—14	—4.7	0
OSU Totals	660	3121	128	2993	4.5	34
Opp. Totals	542	2158	315	1843	3.4	10

FORWARD PASSING

Player	Att.	Comp.	Int.	Yards	Pct.	TD's
Hare	111	55	9	815	.495	3
Purdy	6	3	0	47	.500	2
Morrison	3	1	1	17	.333	0
Greene	1	0	0	0	.000	0
OSU Totals	121	59	10	879	.488	5
Opp. Totals	223	110	16	1537	.493	11

SCORING

Player	Touchdowns Rush	Pass	Conversions Kick	Other	FG	Total Points
Henson	20	0	0	0	0	120
Conway	0	0	26-35	0	5-9	41
Hare	4	0	0	0	0	24
Keith	4	0	0	0	0	24
Griffin	3	0	0	0	0	18
*Galbos	1	1	0	0	0	12
Powell	0	2	0	0	0	12
Bartoszek	0	1	0	0	0	6
Pagac	0	1	0	0	0	6
Morrison	1	0	0	0	0	6
*Bledsoe	1	0	0	0	0	6
Bradshaw	0	0	0	1-1	0	2
Klaban	0	0	1-2	0	0	1
Baschnagel	0	0	0	0	0	0
(Safety)						2
OSU Totals	34	5	27-37		9	280
Opp. Totals	10	11	17-17		16	171

* Not returning for 1973

TOTAL OFFENSE

Player	Plays	Rush	Pass	Total	Avg.	TD's
Hare	198	365	815	1180	5.9	7
Griffin	159	867	0	867	5.4	3
Henson	193	795	0	795	4.1	20
Keith	92	344	0	344	3.7	4
Lippert	36	244	0	244	6.8	0
*Galbos	26	129	0	129	4.9	1
*Bledsoe	20	93	0	93	4.6	1
Morrison	12	52	17	69	5.7	1
Purdy	13	9	47	56	4.3	2
Baschnagel	9	39	0	39	4.3	0
Bradshaw	12	35	0	35	2.9	0
*Gaffney	2	15	0	15	7.5	0
Elia	2	9	0	9	4.5	0
Gales	1	7	0	7	7.0	0
Cramer	2	4	0	4	2.0	0
Greene	4	—14	0	—14	—3.5	0
OSU Totals	781	2993	879	3872	4.9	39
Opp. Totals	765	1873	1537	3380	4.4	22

PASS RECEIVING

Player	Caught	Yards	TD's
*Galbos	11	235	1
Baschnagel	10	145	0
Pagac	8	68	1
Powell	7	129	2
Bartoszek	6	90	1
Griffin	6	71	0
Bradshaw	5	68	0
Holycross	2	37	0
Smurda	1	17	0
Keith	1	10	0
Henson	1	6	0
Lippert	1	3	0
Totals	59	879	5

PUNTING

Player	Number	Yards	Avg.
*Lago	48	1921	40.0
(Team)	2	0	00.0
Totals	50	1921	38.4

* Not returning for 1973

TACKLES FOR LOSS (Leaders)

Player	No.	Yards	Player	No.	Yards
DeCree	9	64	Gradishar	4	26
*Hasenohrl	8	39	Middleton	3	5
Cusick	7	27	*Scannell	2	12
*Williams	6	38	Mathis	2	8
*Beecroft	4	15	Cope	2	4

PASSES BROKEN UP (Leaders)

Player	No.	Player	No.
Gradishar	4	Middleton	3
Davis	4	Kuhn	2
Hughes	3	Plank	2

KICKOFF RETURNS

Player	Number	Yards	Average	Longest
Baschnagel	8	219	27.4	51
Griffin	10	196	19.6	25
Greene	3	56	18.7	28
Bradshaw	2	39	19.5	16
Keith	1	8	8.0	8
Pagac	1	0	0.0	0
Totals	25	518	20.7	51

PUNT RETURNS

Player	Number	Yards	Average	Longest
Baschnagel	22	139	6.3	35
Davis	6	36	6.0	11
Hughes	3	29	9.7	17
Colzie	3	4	1.3	2
Holycross	2	0	0.0	0
Fox	1	0	0.0	0
Totals	37	208	5.6	35

INTERCEPTION RETURNS

Player	Number	Yards	Average
Middleton	3	69	23.0
Colzie	3	31	10.3
Mathis	3	15	5.0
*Seifert	2	0	0.0
Kuhn	1	23	23.0
*Fletcher	1	14	14.0
Gradishar	1	10	10.0
Parsons	1	0	0.0
Plank	1	0	0.0
Totals	16	162	10.2

FUMBLES RECOVERED (Leaders)

Player	Offensive	Defensive	Total
Baschnagel	3	0	3
Parsons	1	2	3
France	2	0	2
Cope	0	2	2
Jones	0	1	1
DeCree	0	1	1
Davis	0	1	1
Plank	0	1	1
Keith	1	0	1
Purdy	1	0	1
Colzie	1	0	1
Cramer	1	0	1
Lippert	1	0	1
Kregel	1	0	1

* Not returning for 1973

USC Rips Buckeyes For National Crown

PASADENA, Calif. (AP) — "We didn't make any changes in strategy—we just kicked the pants off them," a happy Coach John McKay said Monday after his Southern California Trojans crushed Ohio State 42-17 in the 59th Rose Bowl football game.

McKay, in scoring his 100th collegiate victory with what he has termed the finest team of his career, said he was particularly pleased with the decisiveness of his triumph because there was still some doubt that the Trojans were worthy of their No. 1 rating.

"Is there anybody else The Associated Press wants us to play?" McKay said, referring to the traditional post New Year's Day poll by the wire service to determine national rankings.

"This is a satisfying victory because this wins the AP national championship."

A subdued Woody Hayes, veteran coach of the Ohio State Buckeyes who is seeking his 150th college triumph, doesn't qualify for the poll, but he gave his vote anyway.

Asked if he thought the 1972 Southern California team was best he ever played, the portly Ohio State veteran replied:

"Yes, I think so. Because of their tremendous balance. You can run on them some—as we proved—but in the second half they passed us right out of the park."

Southern California's Mike Rae completed 18 of 25 passes for 229 yards and the Trojans, with the flashy running of sophomore Anthony Davis, presented a one-two punch threat that the Buckeyes couldn't stop.

After being held to a 7-7 deadlock in the first half, McKay turned his quick, powerful legions lose in an awesome second half display, scoring three touchdowns in the third period and two in the fourth.

Four of the scores came on short plunges—actually headlong dives over the line—from less than two yards out by Sam "Bam" Cunningham, the 218-pound fullback who set a Rose Bowl scoring record.

The previous record of 18 points had been set by Elmer Layden, one of Notre Dame's Four Horsemen, against Stanford in 1925; Jack Weisenberger of Michigan against Southern Cal in 1948, and Mel Anthony of Michigan against Oregon State in 1965.

A record Rose Bowl crowd of 106,869 including Mrs. Richard Nixon, a Southern Cal alumna, saw the runaway victory.

Ohio State, while rushing for 285 yards, scored touchdowns early in the second period on a plunge by fullback Randy Keith, and in the closing seconds on a five-yard run by John Bledsoe. They aso got a third period 21-yard field goal by Blair Conway.

Asked why he used Keith in preference to Harold Henson, the nation's leading scorer, Hayes said simply:

"Keith looked better in practice."

The Trojans, propelled by Davis' running and the pinpoint passing of quarterback Mike Rae, who accounted for more than 200 of his team's yards, scored three touchdowns in that quarter after a 7-7 first-half standoff.

From then on, it was only a matter of how much mercy was left in Southern California hearts as the brute-strong defense of Woody Hayes' Buckeyes, strong enough to win the Big 10 conference with 9-1 record, collapsed.

The two final period scores by the Trojans were just frosting for a chill, blustery afternoon and a portion of revenge for John McKay, the Southern Cal coach who saw his Trojans beaten by Ohio State in the Rose Bowl in 1955 and 1969.

The victory was No. 100 as a college coach for McKay. The veteran Hayes will have to wait for his 150th. He now has 149.

It was the fourth straight Rose Bowl victory for the Pacific 8 champion in the series with the Big 10, which still maintains a 17-10 overall edge. It was McKay's fourth Rose Bowl triumph and the second loss for Hayes in five appearances.

The 42 points by Southern Cal matched the team's scoring total of 1963 when the Trojans beat Wisconsin 42-33.

Southern Cal's supremacy was reflected in the statistics, which gave the Trojans 451 yards, almost equally divided between passing and running, compared with 366 for Ohio State. The Buckeyes gained only 81 yards through the air.

Davis' 157 yards were gained on 23 carries, largely by strong sweeps behind deadly interference. He had a touchdown run of 20 yards.

```
Ohio State            0  7  3  7—17
Southern California   7  0 21 14—42
```
USC—Swann 10 pass from Rae (Rae kick)
OSU—Keith 1 run (Conway kick)
USC—Cunnigham 2 run (Rae kick)
OSU—FG Conway 21
USC—Davis 20 run (Rae kick)
USC—Cunnigham 1 run (Rae kick)
OSU—Bledsoe 5 run (Conway kick)
A—106,869

STATISTICS

	Ohio St.	USC
First downs	21	24
Rushes-yards	62-285	45-207
Passing yards	81	244
Returns yards	0	67
Passes	5-11-2	19-27-0
Punts	5-36.2	4-41.2
Fumbles-lost	2-1	2-1
Penalties-yards	2-7	6-48

INDIVIDUAL LEADERS

RUSHING—Ohio State, Griffin 20-95, Keith 15-59, Galbos 9-57. Southern California, Davis 23-157, Cunningham 11-38, McNeill 4-32.

RECEIVING—Ohio State, Holycross 2-37, Griffin 2-27. Southern California, Swann 6-108, Young 6-82, Davis 3-17.

PASSING—Ohio State, Hare 4-8-1, 64 yards; Morrison 1-3-1, 17. Southern California, Rae 18-25-0, 229; Haden 1-2-0, 15.

[1973]

No.	Name	Pos.	Wgt.	Hgt.	Class	Hometown
1	Thomas Skladany	P-PK	185	6-0	Fr.	Bethel Park, Pa.
2	Larry Molls	OHB	184	6-0	Fr.	Parma Heights
3	*Blair Conway	PK	157	5-7	Sr.	Middleburg Hts.
5	Tom McBrayer	PK	182	5-11	Jr.	Hilliard
5	Mike Keeton	P	168	6-0	So.	Caldwell
6	Monty Thompson	DHB	188	6-1	Sr.	Portsmouth
6	Thomas Klaban	PK	174	6-1	So.	Cincinnati
7	Cornelius Greene	QB	168	6-0	So.	Washington, D.C.
8	*Bill Ezzo	OE	154	5-7	Jr.	Canastota, N.Y.
8	Mike Mathis	DHB	170	6-0	Fr.	Pittsburgh, Pa.
9	Kenneth Thompson	QB	207	6-1	Fr.	Waverly
11	Max Midlam	DCB	180	5-10	Fr.	Marion
11	James Harrell	OHB	185	5-10	Fr.	Curtice
12	*Tim Fox	S	188	6-0	Fr.	Canton
13	*Morris Bradshaw	OHB	206	6-2	Sr.	Edwardsville, Ill.
14	Gary McCutcheon	SE	186	6-0	So.	Berwick, Pa.
14	*Robert Kelly	DE	207	6-1	Sr.	Butler, Pa.
15	James Pacenta	QB	185	6-3	Fr.	Akron
15	Steve Libert	OHB	194	6-0	Fr.	Dayton
16	*Jeff Davis	DHB	182	5-10	Sr.	Erie, Pa.
17	*Steven Morrison	QB	202	6-3	Jr.	Hntgtn., W. Va.
18	*Greg Hare	QB	202	6-3	Sr.	Cumberland, Md.
19	*David Purdy	QB	188	6-2	Jr.	Swanton
20	*Neal Colzie	DHB	196	6-2	Jr.	Coral Gables, Fl.
21	*Carl Kern	S	190	6-0	Sr.	Dallas, Pa.
22	Peter Souch	DHB	177	6-1	Jr.	Columbus
23	Craig Cassady	DHB	170	6-0	So.	Columbus
24	*Richard Parsons	S	190	5-11	Jr.	Cuyahoga Falls
25	Robert Gentry	DHB	197	6-3	Fr.	Sandusky
26	Leon Rodgers	DHB	188	5-11	Fr.	Columbus
27	*Tim Holycross	OHB	190	6-0	Jr.	Bedford Heights
28	*Douglas Plank	DCB	197	5-11	Jr.	North Irwin, Pa.
29	Jerome Davis	DHB	185	6-1	Fr.	Middletown
30	*Louis Mathis	DCB	204	6-0	Sr.	Paterson, N.J.
32	*Richard Middleton	LB	222	6-3	Sr.	Delaware
33	Pete Johnson	FB	227	6-1	Fr.	Long Beach, N.Y.
34	Dan Bembry	FB	198	6-1	Fr.	Utica, N.R.
35	*Rocco Rich	LB	230	5-11	Sr.	Canton
35	David Mazeroski	FB	204	6-1	So.	Cadiz
36	*Bruce Elia	LB	212	6-1	Jr.	Cliffside Pk., N.J.
37	Brian Bowers	LB	219	6-0	Jr.	Uniontown
37	Bob Hyatt	DHB	170	5-10	Fr.	LaGrange
38	*Harold Henson	FB	228	6-4	Jr.	Ashville
39	Howard Thornton	LB	220	6-3	Fr.	Columbus
41	Woodrow Roach	OHB	180	5-9	So.	Washington, D.C.
42	*Arnold Jones	LB	228	6-0	Jr.	Dayton
43	Bruce Ruhl	S	188	6-1	Fr.	Southfield, Mich.
44	*John Hughes	FB	196	6-1	Sr.	Duquesne, Pa.
45	*Archie Griffin	OHB	184	5-9	So.	Columbus
46	Steve Luke	DHB	194	6-2	Jr.	Massillon
47	*Elmer Lippert	OHB	180	5-7	Sr.	Sandusky
48	*Brian Baschnagel	OHB	192	6-0	So.	Pittsburgh, Pa.
49	Larry Kain	DE	212	6-2	Jr.	Dayton
50	Michael Datish	C	221	6-3	Fr.	Warren
50	Michael Sapp	LB	220	6-2	Jr.	Columbus
52	*Steven Myers	C	240	6-2	Jr.	Kent
53	*Randy Gradishar	LB	236	6-3	Sr.	Champion
54	*Kenneth Kuhn	LB	227	6-2	So.	Louisville
55	Dwight King	OT	312	6-4	Fr.	Toledo
55	Jeff Ferelli	DRH	182	5-10	Fr.	Columbus
56	Stephen Koegel	OT	218	6-3	So.	Cincinnati
56	Randy McEndree	C	215	5-11	So.	Cadiz
57	Mark Straka	C	210	6-4	Sr.	Elyria
58	Charles Baxter	OG	230	6-2	Sr.	Painesville
58	Jeffery Weiland	LB	214	6-2	So.	Englewood
60	Thomas Swank	OT	231	6-3	Jr.	Sandusky
61	John Husband	OG	220	6-2	Sr.	Elyria
62	*Victor Koegel	LB	214	6-1	Sr.	Cincinnati
63	*James Kregel	OG	234	6-2	Sr.	Toledo
64	William Lukens	OG	218	6-1	Fr.	Cincinnati
65	Barney Renard	OG	219	6-3	Fr.	Maumee
66	Larry Graf	OG	219	6-1	Sr.	Akron
67	*Dan Cutillo	DT	232	6-1	Sr.	Amityville, N.Y.
68	Louis Pietrini	OT	244	6-3	So.	Milford, Conn.
69	*Richard Mack	OG	218	5-11	Jr.	Bucyrus
70	Robert Willard	OT	240	6-2	Sr.	Chagrin Falls
71	*Peter Cusick	DT	244	6-2	Jr.	Lakewood
72	*Kurt Schumacher	OT	248	6-4	Jr.	Lorain
73	*Scott Dannelley	OT	246	6-3	Jr.	Williamsport, Pa.
74	*John Hicks	OT	258	6-3	Sr.	Cleveland
75	Nicholas Buonamici	DT	250	6-3	Fr.	Brentwood, N.Y.
76	*Dan Scott	OG	258	6-3	Sr.	Amityville, N.Y.
77	*Douglas France	OT	258	6-6	Jr.	Dayton
78	Robert Coan	OT	244	6-5	Fr.	Euclid
79	Craig Nemitz	DT	248	6-4	Fr.	Sandusky
80	*Fred Pagac	OE	210	6-1	Sr.	Richeyville, Pa.
81	*Thomas Marendt	DE	218	6-1	Sr.	Indianapolis, Ind.
82	*David Hazel	SE	188	6-1	Sr.	Xenia
83	Louis Williott	DE	212	6-1	So.	Youngstown
84	Robert Brudzinski	DE	210	6-4	Fr.	Fremont
85	*John Smurda	TE	212	6-1	Sr.	Allentown, Pa.
86	Don Coburn	DRE	195	6-1	Fr.	Wickliffe
87	*Michael Bartoszek	SE	210	6-4	Jr.	Erie, Pa.
88	*Van DeCree	DE	215	6-1	Jr.	Warren
89	*Ted Powell	OE	226	6-2	Sr.	Hampton, Va.
90	Patrick Curto	DE	209	6-2	So.	Groveport
91	*James Cope	DE	222	6-2	Jr.	McKeesport, Pa.
92	Marvin Battle	DT	247	6-4	Fr.	Brooklyn, N.Y.
93	Ronald Ayers	DE	227	6-4	Fr.	Columbus
94	Thomas Szabo	DT	227	6-4	Sr.	Elyria
94	John Federer	DRE	215	6-2	Jr.	Columbus
95	Richard Applegate	DT	252	6-3	Fr.	Cincinnati
96	Ernest Helms	DT	230	6-2	Sr.	Akron
96	Clarence Perry	DE	210	6-1	So.	Columbus
97	Ted Smith	LB	220	6-2	Fr.	Gibsonburg
98	James Cramer	LB	204	6-1	Fr.	Pittsburgh, Pa.
99	Lawrence O'Rourke	DT	248	6-3	Fr.	Yardley, Pa.

* Returning Lettermen.

1973
Captains: Greg Hare
Richard Middleton

56	*Minnesota	7
37	*Texas Christian	3
27	*Washington State	3
24	Wisconsin	0
37	Indiana	7
60	*Northwestern	0
30	Illinois	0
35	*Michigan State	0
55	*Iowa	13
10	Michigan	10
42	†Southern California	21
413		64

Won 10, Lost 0, Tied 1
Big Ten Co-Champions
† Rose Bowl

A.P. POLL
1. Notre Dame
2. OHIO STATE
3. Oklahoma
4. Alabama
5. Penn State
6. Michigan
7. Nebraska
8. Southern Cal.
9. Arizona State
10. Houston

U.P.I. POLL
1. Alabama
2. Oklahoma
3. OHIO STATE
4. Notre Dame
5. Penn State
6. Michigan
7. Southern Cal.
8. Texas
9. U.C.L.A.
10. Arizona State

Griffin Sets 2 Marks As Ohio State Romps

COLUMBUS, Ohio (AP) — Archie Griffin established two school rushing records and Bruce Elia scored four times Saturday to lead top-ranked Ohio State to a 55-13 Big Ten football mauling of winless Iowa.

The victory, Ohio State's ninth straight and seventh in a row in the conference, set the stage for the showdown for the Big Ten title and Rose Bowl berth at No. 4 Michigan next Saturday.

The Wolverines whipped Purdue Saturday, and both will carry unbeaten conference records into the nationally-televised title game.

Griffin, a 185-pound sophomore tailback, became the greatest one season rusher for the Buckeyes, carrying thirty times for 246 yards. That gave him 1,265 yards to break the school record of 1,142 yards set by fullback John Brockington in 1970.

Griffin, going over 100 yards for the ninth straight time this season, also broke his own one-game record of 239 yards last year against North Carolina.

Elia, a junior fullback, punched across twice from the three and twice from the one as Ohio State dealt the Hawkeyes their 10th straight loss in seven in a row in the Big Ten this season.

Iowa, however, snapped the Ohio State string of three state shutouts with two fourth-quarter touchdowns.

Butch Caldwell and Bill Schultz teamed on a 78-yard passing bomb. and Rod Wellington ran two yards for Iowa scores.

Cornelius Greene passed 41 yards to Dave Hazel and ran one yard for another touchdown before the slippery Ohio State quarterback was hurt in the third quarter.

Griffin ran an eight-yard run and Elmer Lippert, his understudy on a twelve-yard run, also scored for Ohio State in the romp before 87,447 Ohio Stadium fans.

Buckeyes, Wolverines Tie, 10 to 10

ANN ARBOR, Mich. (AP) — Dennis Franklin's 10-yard run in the fourth quarter lifted Michigan's Wolverines into a 10-10 tie with Ohio State Saturday in an exciting Big Ten contest which saw two last-minute field goal attempts by Michigan go wide.

The outcome left the perennial powers in a tie for the conference lead with 7-0-1 records. A decision on the Big Ten's Rose Bowl representative will be made Sunday after a vote of conference athletic directors in Chicago.

Michigan would likely go to Pasadena since Ohio State was the representative in last year's game against Pac-8 champion Southern California.

A national television audience and a record crowd of 105.223 saw Ohio State jump to a 10-0 lead in the second quarter on a 31-yard field goal by Blair Conway and a five-yard run by freshman fullback Pete Johnson.

After a scoreless third quarter, the Wolverines took command after stopping the Buckeyes at the Michigan 33. Michigan then drove 53 yards in 11 plays, with Mike Lantry booting a 30-yard field goal on the second play of the fourth quarter.

The Wolverines had the momentum and, after stopping the Buckeye offense, drove 51 yards in six plays with Franklin scoring on a fourth-and-one-inch play at the Ohio State 10.

Lantry's conversion kick was good, tying the score.

Michigan thwarted the Buckeye offense the rest of the way, and threated twice to win in the closing minute.

Lantry was wide on a 58-yard field goal attempt with 1:01 left and also missed on a 44-yard try with 24 seconds on the clock.

SCORING

Ohio State	0	10	0	0	—10
Michigan	0	0	0	10	—10

Ohio—FG Conway 31
Ohio—Johnson 5 run (Conway kick)
Mich—FG Lantry 30
Mich—Franklin 10 run (Lantry kick)
A—105,223

STATISTICS

	Ohio St	Michigan
First downs	9	16
Rushes-yards	49-234	56-204
Passing yards	0	99
Return yards	33	16
Passes	0-4-1	7-12-1
Punts	7-31	5-40
Fumbles-lost	1-0	1-1
Penalties-yards	0-0	4-37

INDIVIDUAL LEADERS

RUSHING—Ohio State, Griffin 30-163, Greene 8-32, P. Johnson 5-22; Michigan, Shuttlesworth 27-116, Chapman 19-58, Franklin 4-17.

RECEIVING—Ohio State, None; Michigan, Haslerig 5-64, Seal 1-27, Shuttlesworth 1-8.

PASSING—Ohio State, Hare 0-4-1, 0 yards; Michigan, Franklin 7-11-1, 99 yards.

33—JOHNSON, PETE, 18, 6-1, 227, freshman . . . from Long Beach, New York . . . an especially gifted athlete who played fullback and linebacker at Long Beach High one year . . . attended Peach County High in Georgia before moving to New York his senior year . . . has run a :10.1 hundred . . . considered one of top backs in greater New York City last year . . . combines power with break away speed . . . will be used at fullback for Ohio State . . .

[1973]

Big 10 Sending Buckeyes to Pasadena

CHICAGO (AP) — Top Ranked Ohio State, tied 10-10 by Michigan Saturday, was selected to represent the Big Ten in the Rose Bowl Sunday, drawing an angry response from Michigan Coach Bo Schembechler.

"This is the darkest day in my athletic career," said Schembechler, his voice quivering with anger. "I'm very bitter. It's a tragic thing for Big Ten football."

The decision was announced by Big Ten Commissioner Wayne Duke following a special balloting of conference athletic directors who gave the Buckeyes the nod.

Originally, the athletic directors had voted that the winner of the game between Ohio State and fourth-ranked Michigan would make the trip but that in a case of a tie a special vote would be taken.

Ohio State, with a 9-0-1 record and a title share with Michigan, goes up against Southern California, which has a 9-1-1 mark. The Trojans qualified for the Rose Bowl game with a 23-13 victory over rival UCLA Saturday.

Ohio State will be entrusted with breaking a four-game Big Ten losing streak in the Rose Bowl and the game will match up last season's foes in which Southern Cal rolled over the Buckeyes 42-17 to nail down the national championship.

The last Big Ten team to win in the Rose Bowl was Ohio State by a 27-16 score over Southern Cal in the 1969 contest. Since then Ohio State and Michigan each have lost twice in the New Year's Day classic.

Ohio State's selection came somewhat as a surprise but could very well have hinged on the fact that Michigan lost quarterback Dennis Franklin in the closing minutes of Saturday's game with a broken collarbone.

Hungry for a victory, the athletic directors apparently decided to go with the team which they figure has the best chance of winning. Without Franklin, Michigan would be at a disadvantage.

Schembechler, in his fifth year as Michigan head coach, criticized conference administration after the announcement of their decision. "Big Ten administration hasn't been very tough and it hasn't been very good," he said. "I would really like to know how those schools voted, and particularly how our sister school (Michigan State) voted."

Buckeye Hicks Wins Outland

OKLAHOMA CITY, Dec. 10 (AP)—John Hicks, Ohio State's outstanding offensive lineman, was named the recipient of the Outland Trophy Saturday by the Football Writers Association of America.

The Outland award goes annually to the guard or tackle—either on defense or offense—judged to be the best in the nation by the country's sportswriters.

Hicks, a 6-foot-3, 258-pound senior tackle, beat out Lucious Selmon, Oklahoma's noseguard.

The selection was announced by FWAA president Tom McEwen of the Tampa, Fla., Tribune.

Hicks, a native of Cleveland, is considered to be a top professional prospect because of his size and quickness. He figured heavily in the run-oriented Buckeyes' 9-0-1 season record and Rose Bowl invitation.

He was chosen by an eight-member committee after preliminary voting by the 1,100 members of the organization. Last year's winner was Rich Glover, Nebraska middle guard.

McEwen stressed that the writers pick players on college performance instead of professional potential.

Selmon, a 5-foot-11, 236-pounder, spearheaded the Oklahoma defense, which was given credit for Oklahoma's 10-0-1 record and No. 2 national ranking.

A senior, Selmon played between his two sophomore brothers, LeRoy and Dewey.

Buckeyes Pluck Trojans' Roses

From News Dispatches

PASADENA, Calif., Jan. 1—Formerly unknown freshman fullback Pete Johnson ripped off three touchdowns today as Ohio State left the University of Southern California wilted in the Rose Bowl, 42-21.

Ending four years of domination by the Pacific Eight over the Big 10 here, the Buckeyes stormed back under the quarterbacking of sophomore Cornelius Greene of Washington, D.C., for two touchdowns each of the last two quarters after trailing 21-14 early in the second half. The hard-driving Buckeyes avenged a 42-17 licking at the hands of the Trojans here last season.

Greene was named the game's most valuable player. Johnson, who carried the ball only 36 times this season, replaced starter Bruce Elia and scored on runs of 1, 1 and 4 yards. His effort was just one touchdown shy of Sam Cunningham's Rose Bowl record of four, set for USC last year.

A spectacular 56-yard punt return by Neal Colzie set up what proved to be Ohio State's winning touchdown. The runback gave the ball to the Buckeyes on the USC nine and they scored four plays later on a slick one-yard keeper by Greene at 12:48 of the third period, making the Ohio State lead 27-21.

After Greene's touchdown the Buckeyes became even more explosive. First came a 52-yard drive in five plays, a Greene-Brian Baschnagel pass gaining 25 and Archie Griffin running another 25 before Elia plunged over from the two. Greene ran in the conversion for two points.

Minutes later, Griffin broke loose on a 47-yard touchdown run.

Griffin, the fleet running ace of the Buckeyes, set a Big 10 season record as he pushed his total to 1,577 yards. He gained 149 today.

So the Buckeyes justified the vote of the Big 10 athletic directors who sent the club, ranked No. 4 nationally, to Pasadena instead of Michigan after the two undefeated clubs tied 10-10 in their final regular-season game.

The national-champion Trojans this year were ranked seventh nationally by the Associated Press with a 9-1-1 record. The Buckeyes came to Pasadena for this 59th renewal of college football's oldest postseason classic at 9-0-1.

Greene completed six of eight passes for 129 yards. His throwing proved decisive on several occasions, proving that Ohio State did indeed have an aerial game.

The Buckeyes gained 449 yards, 320 of them on the ground. Griffin gained his 149 in 22 carries, Johnson had 94 in 21 and Greene 45 in seven carries, some of them scrambles.

Southern California gained 406 yards with 239 passing. Haden completed 21 of 39 throws for 229 yards. Greene had one intercepted and Haden none.

Davis, a star high school quarterback, but a running star with USC, completed his first pass of this season with his 10-yard touchdown throw to McKay. On the ground, he gained 74 yards in 16 carries.

A free-for-all broke out in the final minute of the opening half when Ohio State defensive end Van DeCree slammed into Haden, who had run to the sidelines to stop the clock. Trojan tackle Booker Brown went after DeCree, other players quickly joined in, and coaches went into action to break up the melee. Hayes ran the full width of the field to help end the fight as a national television audience looked on.

	Ohio St.	USC
First downs	20	
Rushes-yards	59-320	42-
Passing yards	129	
Return yards	74	
Passes	6-8-1	22-40
Punts	3-41	3-
Fumbles-lost	1-0	
Penalties-yards	7-59	6-

Ohio State . . . . 7 7 13 15—
Southern California . . 3 11 7 0—

USC—Limahelu, 47, field goal.
OSU—Johnson (1, run); Conway (kick).
USC—Limahelu, 42, field goal.
USC—McKay (10, pass from Davis); McKay (pass from Haden).
OSU—Johnson (1, run); Conway (kick).
USC—Davis (1, run); Limahelu (kick).
OSU—Johnson (4, run); kick failed.
OSU—Greene (1, run); Conway (kick).
OSU—Elia (2, run); Greene (run).
OSU—Griffin (47, run); Conway (kick).
Attendance—105,267.

Individual Leaders

RUSHING—Ohio State, Griffin 22-149, Johnson 21-94, Greene 7-45, Elia 8-27. Southern Cal, Davis 16-74, Moore 8-32, McNeill 8-46.

RECEIVING—Ohio State, Pagac 4-49, Hazel 1-15, Raschnagel 1-25; Southern Cal, McKay 6-65, Swann 5-47, McNeill 4-39, Obradovich 2-28.

PASSING—Ohio State, Greene 6-8-1, 129 yards; Southern Cal, Haden 21-39-0, 229, Davis 1-1-0, 10.

1973 OHIO STATE INDIVIDUAL STATISTICS

RUSHING

Player	Tries	Gain	Lost	Net	Avg.	TD's
Griffin, tb	247	1611	34	1577	6.3	7
Greene, qb	126	823	103	720	5.7	12
Elia, fb	106	431	2	429	4.0	14
Roach, tb	33	211	0	211	6.4	0
Johnson, fb	55	206	1	205	3.7	6
*Lippert, tb	46	182	3	179	3.8	2
Baschnagel, wb	25	149	0	149	5.9	2
Henson, fb	27	107	0	107	3.9	4
*Bembry, fb	11	94	0	94	8.5	0
Holycross, wb	5	46	0	46	9.2	0
*Bradshaw, wb	5	49	4	45	9.0	0
Harrell, wb	5	36	0	36	7.2	0
Molls, tb	8	31	2	29	3.6	0
*Hare, qb	10	42	21	21	2.1	0
Williott, fb	4	19	0	19	4.7	0
Morrison, qb	8	18	2	16	2.0	0
*Hughes, fb	4	14	0	14	3.5	0
Purdy, qb	2	9	2	7	3.5	0
Hyatt, wb	1	4	0	4	4.0	0
OSU Totals	728	4082	174	3908	5.3	47
Opp. Totals	485	1755	297	1458	3.0	4

FORWARD PASSING

Player	Att.	Comp.	Int.	Yards	Pct.	TD's
Greene, qb	46	20	7	343	.434	2
*Hare, qb	30	11	2	224	.366	3
Purdy, qb	7	3	1	21	.429	0
Morrison, qb	4	1	1	15	.250	0
OSU Totals	87	35	11	603	.402	5
Opp. Totals	210	95	11	1004	.452	3

SCORING

Player	Touchdowns Rush	Pass	Ret.	Conversions Kick	Other	FG	Total Points
Elia, fb	14	0	0	0	0	0	84
Greene, qb	12	0	0	0	1-1	0	74
*Conway, pk	0	0	0	45-55	0	5-10	60
Griffin, tb	7	1	1	0	0	0	54
Johnson, fb	6	0	0	0	0	0	36
Colzie, dhb	0	0	4	0	0	0	24
Henson, fb	4	0	0	0	0	0	24
Baschnagel, wb	2	0	0	0	0	0	12
*Lippert, tb	2	0	0	0	0	0	12
*Pagac, te	0	1	0	0	1-1	0	8
*Bradshaw, wb	0	1	0	0	0	0	6
Ezzo, se	0	1	0	0	0	0	6
Fox, s	0	0	1	0	0	0	6
Hazel, se	0	1	0	0	0	0	6
Klaban, pk	0	0	0	1-1	0	0	1
OSU Totals	47	5	6	46-56		10	413
Opp. Totals	4	3	0	5-5			64

PASS RECEIVING

Player	Caught	Yards	Avg.	TD's
*Pagac, te	9	159	17.6	1
Griffin, tb	5	32	6.4	1
Hazel, se	4	121	30.2	1
Holycross, wb	4	76	19.0	0
Baschnagel, wb	3	43	14.3	0
*Smurda, te	2	42	21.0	0
*Bradshaw, wb	2	10	5.0	1
Ezzo, se	1	55	55.0	1
*Powell, te	1	22	22.0	0
*Lippert, tb	1	20	20.0	0
Bartoszek, se	1	15	15.0	0
Roach, tb	1	6	6.0	0
Elia, fb	1	2	2.0	0
Totals	35	603	17.2	5

KICKOFF RETURNS

Player	Number	Yards	Average	TD's	Longest
Griffin, tb	7	221	31.5	1	93
*Bradshaw, wb	2	63	31.5	0	32
Baschnagel, wb	4	59	14.7	0	18
Roach, tb	2	37	18.5	0	20
Holycross, wb	1	25	25.0	0	25
France, ot	1	3	3.0	0	3
Totals	17	408	24.0	1	93

PUNT RETURNS

Player	Number	Yards	Average	TD's	Longest
Colzie, dhb	40	679	16.9	2	78
Fox, s	2	44	22.0	1	24
Cassady, dhb	1	38	38.0	0	38
Plank, dhb	3	24	8.0	0	10
Baschnagel, wb	7	20	2.8	0	10
Totals	53	805	15.2	3	78

INTERCEPTION RETURNS

Player	Number	Yards	Average	TD's	Longest
Colzie, dhb	4	94	23.5	2	55
Fox, s	2	19	9.5	0	21
*Gradishar, lb	2	15	7.5	0	12
*Middleton, lb	2	2	1.0	0	2
Parsons, s	1	0	0.0	0	0
Totals	11	130	11.8	2	55

PUNTING

Player	Number	Yards	Avg.	Long.
Skladany	35	1252	35.7	56
Bartoszek	4	110	27.5	33
Keeton	2	82	41.0	46
Totals	41	1444	35.2	56

TACKLES FOR LOSS (Leaders)

Player	No.	Yards	Player	No.	Yards
Cope, de	8	54	Fox, s	4	17
Cusick, dt	7	27	Kain, de	3	27
*Gradishar, lb	6	13	*Koegel, lb	2	15
Jones, dt	4	31	Luke, dhb	2	5
DeCree, de	4	25	Buonamici, dt	1	9

PASSES BROKEN UP (Leaders)

Player	No.	Player	No.
Colzie, dhb	4	*Middleton, lb	2
*Gradishar, lb	4	Jones, dt	2
*Koegel, lb	4	Cope, de	2
Luke, dhb	3	Fox, s	2
DeCree, de	2	Ruhl, s	2

* Not returning for 1974

[1974]

No.	Name	Pos.	Wgt.	Hgt.	Class	Home Town
94	David Adkins	LB	197	6-2	Fr.	Xenia
22	Joseph Allegro	DHB	174	5-11	Fr.	W. Ptsbgh., Pa.
61	Richard Applegate	OG	252	6-3	So.	Cincinnati
59	Ronald Ayers	OG	229	6-4	So.	Columbus
62	Scott Baker	OG	220	6-1	Fr.	Willoughby
95	Douglas Bargerstock	DT	246	6-2	Fr.	Taylor, Mich.
87	*Michael Bartoszek	TE	218	6-4	Sr.	Erie, Pa.
48	*Brian Baschnagel	WB	190	6-0	Jr.	Pittsburgh, Pa.
67	Eddie Beamon	DT	245	6-2	Fr.	Cincinnati
37	*Brian Bowers	LB	232	6-0	Sr.	Uniontown
55	Aaron Brown	LB	222	6-2	Fr.	Warren
84	*Robert Brudzinski	DE	218	6-4	So.	Fremont
75	*Nicholas Buonamici	DT	238	6-3	So.	Brentwood, N.Y.
23	*Craig Cassady	DHB	174	6-0	Jr.	Columbus
20	*Neal Colzie	DHB	202	6-2	Sr.	Miami, Fla.
91	*James Cope	DE	235	6-2	Sr.	McKeesport, Pa.
78	Garth Cox	OT	242	6-5	Fr.	Wshngtn. Ct. Hs.
90	*Pat Curto	DE	225	6-2	Jr.	Groveport
96	Martin Cusick	DE	211	6-2	Fr.	Lakewood
71	*Pete Cusick	DT	250	6-2	Sr.	Lakewood
39	John D'Amato	LB	218	6-3	Fr.	Staten Isl., N.Y.
73	*Scott Dannelley	OT	240	6-3	Sr.	Williamsport, Pa.
50	Michael Datish	C	240	6-3	So.	Warren
29	*Jerome Davis	S	184	6-1	So.	Middletown
88	*Van DeCree	DE	218	6-1	So.	Warren
86	Joseph Dixon	DE	209	6-3	Fr.	Trenton, Mich.
36	*Bruce Elia	LB	219	6-1	Sr.	Cliffside Pk., N.J.
8	*Bill Ezzo	SE	150	5-7	Sr.	Canastota, N.Y.
58	Jeff Ferrelli	DHB	184	5-10	So.	Columbus
12	*Tim Fox	S	186	6-0	Jr.	Canton
80	*Douglas France	TE	260	6-6	Sr.	Dayton
25	Robert Gentry	DHB	200	6-3	So.	Sandusky
7	*Cornelius Greene	QB	170	6-0	Jr.	Washington, D.C.
45	*Archie Griffin	TB	182	5-9	Jr.	Columbus
44	Raymond Griffin	WB	174	5-9	Fr.	Columbus
11	James Harrell	WB	191	5-10	So.	Curtice
66	Tyrone Harris	DT	242	6-3	Fr.	Columbus
82	*David Hazel	SE	192	6-1	Sr.	Xenia
38	*Harold Henson	FB	231	6-4	Sr.	Ashville
27	*Tim Holycross	WB	190	6-0	Sr.	Bedford Heights
35	Robert Hyatt	WB	178	5-10	So.	Lagrange
13	Barry Johnson	TB	187	6-0	So.	Columbus
33	*Pete Johnson	FB	250	6-1	So.	Long Beach, N.Y.
42	*Arnold Jones	LB	240	6-0	Sr.	Dayton
49	Herman Jones	WB	196	6-3	Fr.	Miami, Fla.
98	Paul Jones	DE	206	6-2	Fr.	Dayton
92	Jeffrey Jurin	DE	197	6-0	So.	Newcomerstown
85	*Larry Kain	TE	221	6-2	Sr.	Dayton
3	Michael Keeton	P	172	6-0	Jr.	Caldwell
6	Thomas Klaban	PK	182	6-1	Jr.	Cincinnati
70	Steve Koegel	OT	217	6-3	Jr.	Cincinnati
54	*Kenneth Kuhn	LB	230	6-2	Jr.	Louisville
10	Mark Lang	LB	209	6-1	Fr.	Cincinnati
81	Robert Lillie	TE	222	6-3	Fr.	Dayton
51	Gary Lillvis	OG	230	6-2	Sr.	Ashtabula
34	Jeff Logan	TB	182	5-10	Fr.	North Canton
46	*Steve Luke	DHB	200	6-2	Sr.	Massillon
64	William Lukens	OG	226	6-1	So.	Cincinnati
69	*Richard Mack	OG	212	5-11	Sr.	Bucyrus
32	David Mazeroski	FB	209	6-1	Jr.	Cadiz
5	Tom McBrayer	PK	175	5-11	Sr.	Hilliard
14	Gary McCutcheon	SE	188	6-0	Jr.	Berwick, Pa.
21	Max Midlam	S	194	5-10	So.	Marion
2	Larry Molls	TB	184	6-0	So.	Parma Heights
17	*Steven Morrison	QB	188	6-3	Sr.	Huntington, W. V.
52	*Steve Myers	C	243	6-0	Sr.	Kent
68	James O'Rourke	DT	252	6-3	Fr.	Brooklyn, N.Y.
99	Larry O'Rourke	DT	252	6-2	Sr.	Yardley, Pa.
15	James Pacenta	QB	190	6-3	So.	Akron
24	*Richard Parsons	S	192	6-0	Sr.	Cuyahoga Falls
83	Clarence Perry	DE	219	6-0	Jr.	Columbus
74	Louis Pietrini	OT	242	6-3	Jr.	Milford, Conn.
28	*Douglas Plank	DHB	197	5-11	Sr.	North Irwin, Pa.
53	Douglas Porter	C	216	6-2	Fr.	Youngstown
18	Pete Prather	QB	182	6-1	Fr.	Glen Rock, N.J.
19	*David Purdy	QB	186	6-2	Sr.	Swanton
65	Barney Renard	C	228	6-3	So.	Maumee
41	*Woodrow Roach	TB	180	5-9	Jr.	Washington, D.C.
47	Bob Robertson	TB	205	6-0	Fr.	Barberton
26	Tom Roche	DHB	180	6-3	Fr.	Staten Isl., N. J.
16	Tony Ross	QB	190	5-10	Fr.	Pittsburgh, Pa.
43	*Bruce Ruhl	S	186	6-1	So.	Southfield, Mich.
97	Michael Sapp	LB	210	6-2	Sr.	Columbus
57	James Savoca	LB	226	6-2	Fr.	Solon
72	*Kurt Schumacher	OT	254	6-4	Sr.	Lorain
30	Charles Simon	LB	219	6-2	Fr.	Dublin
1	*Thomas Skladany	P-PK	194	6-0	So.	Bethel Park, Pa.
60	*Ted Smith	OG	236	6-1	Jr.	Gibsonburg
77	Gregory Storer	OT	217	6-5	Fr.	Cincinnati
76	Thomas Swank	OT	242	6-2	Sr.	Sandusky
9	Kenneth Thompson	LB	227	6-1	So.	Waverly
79	Christopher Ward	OT	268	6-4	Fr.	Dayton
63	Darryl Weston	OG	219	6-2	Fr.	Pittsburgh, Pa.
4	Louis Williott	FB	217	6-1	Jr.	Youngstown
89	Leonard Willis	SE	200	6-0	Jr.	Washington, D.C.
25	Scott Wolery	DHB			So.	Delphos

* indicates letters won

A.P. POLL
1. Oklahoma
2. Southern Cal.
3. Michigan
4. OHIO STATE
5. Alabama
6. Notre Dame
7. Penn State
8. Auburn
9. Nebraska
10. Miami (O.)

U.P.I. POLL
1. Southern Cal.
2. Alabama
3. OHIO STATE
4. Notre Dame
5. Michigan
6. Auburn
7. Penn State
8. Nebraska
9. N.C. State
10. Miami (O.)

1974
Captains: Steve Myers
Archie Griffin, Arnold Jones
Neal Colzie, Pete Cusick

34	Minnesota	19
51	*Oregon State	10
28	*Southern Methodist	9
42	Washington State	7
52	*Wisconsin	7
49	*Indiana	9
55	Northwestern	7
49	*Illinois	7
13	Michigan State	16
35	Iowa	10
12	*Michigan	10
17	†Southern California	18
437		129

Won 10, Lost 2

Big Ten Co-Champions
† Rose Bowl

Ohio State Rolls

COLUMBUS, Ohio, Oct. 19 (AP)—Archie Griffin of Ohio State became the greatest rusher in Big 10 history today, rolling for 146 yards and two touchdowns as the top-ranked Buckeyes thumped Indiana 49-9.

The junior tailback now has 3321 yards in his career, topping the conference record of 3,315 yards set by Purdue's Otis Armstrong two seasons ago.

A sellout Ohio Staduim crowd of 87,671, second largest in the school's history, gave Griffin a standing ovation while the Buckeyes mobbed him on the sidelines.

Meanwhile, quarterbak Carnelius Greene engineered the Buckeyes to their sixth straight victory of this season, prolonging their unbeaten streak to 17 games.

Greene piled up 331 total yards, running for one touchdown and passing for two as the Buckeyes pushed their league record to 3-0. Greene completed nine of 11 passes for 35 yards and ran for 96 yards in 11 carries.

With 16 straight regular-season games of more than 100 rushing yards, Griffin is one game short of the national record. Steve Owens of Oklahoma had 17 games in a row in 1968-69.

Unbeaten Ohio State Wins, 49-7

COLUMBUS, Ohio, Nov. 2 (AP)—Woody Hayes achieved his 200th college football coaching victory and Ohio State's junior sensation, Archie Griffin, set a national rushing record today in leading the top ranked Buckeyes to a 49-7 Big Ten victory over Illinois.

Cornelius Greene, Ohio State's quarterback, passed for two touchdowns and ran for another to engineer the triumph for Hayes, 61 years old, who has coached 200 victories, 60 defeats and 8 ties in his 29 college seasons.

Griffin piled up a 144-yard rushing day, his 18th consecutive 100-plus regular season performance, breaking the old major college record.

Griffin, who broke the record with a 22-yard touchdown run early in the third quarter, had shared the national mark with Steve Owens of Oklahoma, who established it for 1968-69.

The Buckeyes' running sensation also scored the opening touchdown on a 16-yard run in the first quarter.

Ray Griffin, the running star's brother, a freshman, also scored, teaming with substitute quarterback Steve Morrison on a 39-yard lateral play, for the Buckeyes, 8-0 on the year and 5-0-0 in the Big Ten.

| Ohio State | 7 | 4 | 14 | 14 | 49 |
| Illinois | 0 | 7 | 0 | 0 | 7 |

Ohio—A. Griffin, 16, run (Klaban kick).
Ill.—Johnson, 5, pass from Campbell (Beaver kick).
Ohio—Greene, 15, run (Klaban kick).
Ohio—France, 6, pass from Greene (Klaban kick).
Ohio—A. Griffin, 22, run (Klaban kick).
Ohio—Bartoszek, 8, pass from Greene (Klaban kick).
Ohio—R. Griffin, 39, lateral from Morrison (Klaban kick).
Ohio—Willis, 53, run (Klaban kick).
Attendance—87,813.

Top-Rated Ohio State Upset By Michigan State, 16 to 13

EAST LANSING, Mich., Nov. 9—Levi Jackson, a fullback, raced 88 yards for a touchdown with about three minutes left today and Michigan State upset top-ranked Ohio State, 16-13.

The game ended in tumult as many among the capacity crowd of 78,533 rushed onto the football field when the Buckeyes tried to get off a play from the Michigan State 1-yard line as the final gun sounded.

Both teams engaged in victory dances. Then it was announced that the Big Ten Wayne Duke, would rule on the outcome of the game after consulting with the officials, after a delay of 30 minutes. Duke ruled that the Michigan State victory stood.

The Spartans had scored just moments before Jackson's shocking dash on a 44-yard touchdown pass from Charlie Baggett to Mike Jones to bounce baack from on Ohio State touchdown and a 13-3 deficit.

The loss was the first regular-season defeat for Ohio tSate since the Spartans upset them here two years ago.

Ohio State saw its won-lost record drop to 8-1 over all and 5-1 in the Big Ten. The Spartens' record is five victories, three losses and a tie, 4-1-1 in the conference.

Ohio State Wins, But...

By Merrell Whittlesey
Star-News Staff Writer

COLUMBUS, Ohio — The Big Ten title game ended yesterday with the goal posts down, people on the field, both teams claiming victory, and a massive, king-sized problem today for the athletic directors who will vote on who goes to the Rose Bowl.

Tom Klaban, who escaped from behind the Iron Curtain 10 years ago with his mother, father and sister, kicked four field goals soccer-style to give Ohio State a 12-10 victory over Michigan, and set up more controversy in a conference that always is embroiled in family problems.

As far as winning Coach Woody Hayes is concerned, there is no problem. "We are tied for the conference title, and we beat the team we are tied with, what more logic?" he asked, spreading his hands for emphasis in the Ohio State clubhouse.

THE 10 ATHLETIC directors will meet before noon today at an undisclosed Chicago location, and Commissioner Wayne Duke will make the announcement at the Sheraton O'Hare near the airport about 1:30 p.m. Ohio State must receive six votes to win. A 5-5 vote would send the Wolverines because the Buckeyes went last year.

Both Ohio State and Michigan finished 7-1 in the conference, 10-1 over all, but Michigan has support because many think it should have gone last year when the teams tied 10-10 and finished unbeaten in 11 games.

Roughly 18 inches made today's vote necessary. With 16 seconds remaining, Michigan had the ball on the Buckeyes' 16-yard line. Mike Lantry, kicking with a strong wind from the open end of the stadium at his back, was barely wide and to the left on a 33-yard field goal try. If the kick had been good, only the formality of a telephone poll would have been necessary to send the Wolverines to Pasadena against the Pac-8 champion.

FOR A MOMENT there was pandemonium. The kick was so close the Michigan bench and fans in the record 88,243 thought it was good. They exploded. But after a long, close look, the officials signaled wide to the left and it became Ohio State's turn for a demonstration.

The players danced and punched each other and jumped and yelled, the goal posts at the closed end went down right away, thousands rushed onto the artificial turf field and the public address announcer pleaded with the fans to leave the field.

"It looked pretty good to me, if you ask me," a subdued Bo Schembechler said outside the Michigan clubhouse, after announcing that the players did not want to talk to the press.

"NAME ANOTHER team that could have kept Ohio State out of the end zone," Schembechler said. "Our great football team did it, but we lost the game." Asked if he would comment on the Rose Bowl vote, Schembechler, who was reprimanded by Duke for his comments last year, said "Not today." He was asked about tomorrow. "Tomorrow is not today," he said bluntly.

Hayes was not apologetic about winning without a touchdown. "Ohio State has a proud heritage of being a field goal team, since long before I came here," the 61-year-old coach said.

"That was the greatest exhibition of the kicking game I have ever seen. Not only the field goals, but the punting of Tom Skladany, and our great coverage. The name of the game of football is to win, and you win with the best weapons available on that day."

HAYES, NOTED for his tantrums when something goes against the Buckeyes, had only one flareup. He staged an arm-waving protest late in the third period when Greene threw a pass 60 yards in the air from his own six for Brian Baschnagel, who appeared to be bumped illegally by wingback Don Dufek. The officials disallowed the interference, however, and Hayes had to be restrained and pulled back to the bench by his assistants.

Asked about the play later, Hayes said he did not want to get involved in any more controversy with officials. Mindful of the vote, Hayes said, "I want to be the coach in the Rose Bowl."

Reprinted with permission of the Washington Star-News

OHIO STATE 12, MICHIGAN 10

	Michigan	Ohio St.
First downs	14	18
Rushes yards	54 195	57 195
Passing yards	96	58
Return yards	13	20
Passes	5 14 2	3 6 0
Punts	4 39	5 42
Fumbles lost	1 0	2 2
Penalties yards	1 16	3 45

Michigan	10 0 0 0—	10
Ohio State	0 9 3 0—	12

Mich — Chapman 42 pass from Franklin (Lantry kick)
Mich — FG Lantry 37
OSU — FG Klaban 47
OSU — FG Klaban 25
OSU — FG Klaban 43
OSU — FG Klaban 45
A — 88,243

INDIVIDUAL LEADERS
RUSHING — Michigan, Bell 25 114, Heater 15 56, Franklin 10 25, Lytle 3 19. Ohio State, A. Griffin 25 111, Greene 19 69, Johnson 10 24, Baschnagel 3 21.
RECEIVING — Michigan, Chapman 3 62, Smith 2 34. Ohio State, Hazel 2 43, France 1 15.
PASSING — Michigan, Franklin 5 14 2, 96 yards. Ohio State, Greene 3 6 0, 58.

Griffin Achieves Heisman, White Ninth in Voting

NEW YORK, Dec. 3 (AP) — Archie Griffin, Ohio State's record-smashing running back, won the Heisman Trophy as college football's No. 1 player today, but said he would rather have a national championship to share with his teammates.

Randy White, the University of Maryland defensive end who won the Outland Trophy as the nation's best lineman Monday, placed ninth in the Heisman voting.

"This trophy is not for me, it's for the team," said Griffin, a junior tailback.

"I'd love to win the national championship," he said, "and if trading this award for a win over Michigan State would mean being No. 1 . . . yes, I'd trade it. I'd rather have a national championship, to tell the truth."

Ohio State was No. 1 in the Associated Press rankings most of the season, but fell from the top by losing to Michigan State, 16-13, Nov. 9. The Buckeyes are currently ranked third with one game remaining, against Southern California in the Rose Bowl Jan. 1.

Griffin has 4,064 yards rushing in his college career, Ohio State and Big 10 records. More spectacular is his continuing NCAA record of having rushed for more than 100 yards in 22 consecutive games.

This year, as he led the Buckeyes to a 10-1 record and a third straight Rose Bowl, Griffin ran for 1,620 yards, the highest rushing figure in the nation.

Griffin became the fifth nonsenior to capture the Heisman, winning in a landslide over Southern California senior tailback Anthony Davis. The two will meet in the Rose Bowl for the third year in a row.

The 5-foot-9, 185-pound Griffin received 483 first-place votes—each worth three points—and 1,920 of a possible 2,547 points from a nationwide panel of 849 electors. He was named second on 198 ballots and third on 75. The votes were tabulated on a 3-2-1 point basis.

Davis received 120 first-place votes, 148 seconds and 163 thirds for 819 points.

Joe Washington, a junior halfback from Oklahoma, finished third with 87 first-place votes and 661 points. Then came Notre Dame quarterback Tom Clements and Nebraska quarterback David Humm.

USC Nips Ohio State in Rose Bowl

Underdogs Triumph By 18 to 17

PASADENA, Calif. (AP) — Pat Haden, Southern California's Rhodes scholar quarterback, fired a 38-yard touchdown pass to John McKay in the waning minutes of the game and followed with a two-point conversion pitch to Shelton Diggs to give the underdog Trojans an 18-17 Rose Bowl victory over the Ohio State Buckeyes Wednesday.

Just 2:03 remained in this 61st Rose Bowl football classic when Haden passed to McKay, his teammate since his high school days and the son of the Southern California coach.

USC decided to go for broke and not settle for a tie with an extra-point kick. The Trojans lined up in a regular formation, with the Haden rolling out to the right and threw over the outstretched hands of an Ohio State defender. Diggs snared the ball about a foot off the ground.

Both teams squandered most of their scoring chances during the first three quarters, which ended with Ohio State ahead 7-3.

But the action heated up for the final period with the Trojans scoring two touchdowns and the Buckeyes getting a touchdown and field goal.

The anticipated duel between Heisman Trophy winner Archie Griffin of Ohio State and runnerup Anthony Davis of USC failed to materialize. Griffin twice fumbled inside the USC 10 and for the first time in 23 games was held under 100 yards rushing. Davis suffered a chest injury in the first half and didn't see any action in the second half.

The first half was repleat with mistakes. In the first half on two occasions Southern Cal punter Jim Lucas failed to get his kicks away. The first time he picked the ball up behind the line of scrimmage and ran for a first down. The second was blocked by Tim Fox and recovered by Max Midlam at the Trojan 17.

```
Ohio State        0  7  0 10—17
Southern Cal      3  0  0 15—18
  USC—FG Limehelu 30 I
  OSU—Henson 2 run (Klaban kick)
  USC—Obradovich 9 pass from Haden
    (Limahelu kick)
  OSU—Greene 3 run (Klaban kick)
  OSU—FG Klaban 32
  USC—McKay 38 pass from Haden
    (Diggs pass from Haden)
  A—106,721
```

	Ohio St.	S. Cal
First downs	14	24
Rushes-yards	49-193	53-280
Passing yards	93	181
Return yards	21	5
Passes	8-14-1	12-22-2
Punts	3-48	2-15
Fumbles-lost	4-2	2-2
Penalties-yards	3-25	2-21

INDIVIDUAL LEADERS

RUSHING—Ohio State, Griffin 20-76, Greene 11-68, Johnson 10-33. Southern Cal, Davis 13-71, Carter 18-75, Farmer 7-67.

RECEIVING—Ohio State, France 2-28, Griffin 2-25, Bartoszek 2-22, Baschnagel 2-18. Southern Cal, McKay 5-104, Obradovich 4-75.

PASSING—Ohio State, Greene 8-14-1, 93 yards. Southern Cal, Haden 12-22-2, 181.

1974 TEAM STATISTICS
(Includes Rose Bowl)

	OHIO STATE	OPPONENTS
SCORING		
Total Points	437	129
Points Per Game	36.4	10.7
Touchdowns	59	15
PAT Kicks	56/58	9/10
PAT Passes	0/1	3/5
Field Goals	9/15	8/16
FIRST DOWNS	276	224
Average Per Game	23.0	18.7
By Rushing	220	139
By Passing	49	66
By Penalty	7	19
RUSHING		
Total Net Yards	4199	2304
Yards Per Game	350	192
Attempts	734	594
Yards Gained	4400	2671
Yards Lost	201	367
Touchdowns	48	6
PASSING		
Total Net Yards	1053	1458
Yards Per Game	87.7	121.5
Attempted	112	253
Completed	65	114
Had Intercepted	5	23
Touchdowns	9	9
TOTAL NET GAIN	5252	3762
Average Per Game	437.7	313.5
TOTAL PLAYS	846	847
Plays Per Game	70.5	70.6
PUNTS	34	56
Total Yards	1536	2158
Average Per Punt	45.1	38.5
PUNT RETURNS	23	20
Yards Returned	226	78
Average Per Return	9.8	3.9
KICKOFF RETURNS	30	49
Yards Returned	665	907
Average Per Return	22.2	16.5
Touchdowns	2	0
INTERCEPTION RETURNS	23	5
Yards Returned	214	27
Average Per Return	9.3	5.4
FUMBLES	25	25
Fumbles Lost	18	12
PENALTIES	47	31
Total Yards	414	282
SCORE BY QUARTERS		
Ohio State	103 131 110 93	— 437
Opponents	30 33 3 63	— 129

[1974]

1974 OHIO STATE INDIVIDUAL STATISTICS

RUSHING

Player	Tries	Gain	Lost	Net	Avg.	TD's
A. Griffin, tb	256	1705	10	1695	6.6	12
Greene, qb	155	951	109	842	5.4	9
*Henson, fb	88	433	0	433	4.9	12
Baschnagel, wb	37	357	2	355	9.5	3
Johnson, fb	80	324	4	320	4.0	6
R. Griffin, tb	43	249	26	223	5.1	3
Willis, wb	11	147	1	146	13.2	1
Roach, tb	16	81	0	81	5.0	0
*Morrison, qb	18	81	23	58	3.1	1
*Purdy, qb	7	22	9	13	1.8	0
Robertson, fb	6	13	0	13	2.1	0
Williott, fb	5	11	0	11	2.2	1
*Holycross, wb	3	5	0	5	1.6	0
Mazeroski, fb	1	5	0	5	5.0	0
Pacenta, qb	1	5	0	5	5.0	0
Hyatt, wb	2	4	0	4	2.0	0
Prather, qb	2	4	0	4	2.0	0
Logan, tb	1	3	0	3	3.0	0
Ross, qb	1	0	5	-5	-5.0	0
"Team"	1	0	12	-12		
OSU Totals	734	4400	201	4199	5.7	48
Opp. Totals	594	2671	367	2304	3.8	6

FORWARD PASSING

Player	Att.	Comp.	Int.	Yards	Pct.	TD's
Greene, qb	97	58	5	939	.597	9
*Morrison, qb	10	5	0	89	.500	0
*Purdy, qb	5	2	0	25	.400	0
OSU Totals	112	65	5	1053	.580	9
Opp. Totals	253	114	23	1458	.450	9

SCORING

Player	Rush	Pass	Ret.	Kick Conversions	Other	FG	Points Total
	Touchdowns						
Klaban, pk	0	0	0	52-53	0	9-12	79
A. Griffin, tb	12	0	0	0	0	0	72
*Henson, fb	12	0	0	0	0	0	72
Greene, qb	9	0	0	0	0	0	54
Johnson, fb	6	1	0	0	0	0	42
Baschnagel, wb	3	3	0	0	0-1	0	36
R. Griffin, tb	3	1	0	0	0	0	24
Willis, wb	1	0	2	0	0	0	18
*Bartoszek, te	0	2	0	0	0	0	12
*France, te	0	1	0	0	0	0	6
*Hazel, se	0	1	0	0	0	0	6
*Morrison, qb	1	0	0	0	0	0	6
Williott, fb	1	0	0	0	0	0	6
Skladany, pk	0	0	0	4-5	0	0-3	4
OSU Totals	48	9	2	56-58	0-1	9-15	437
Opp. Totals	6	9	0	9-10	3-5	8-16	129

TACKLES FOR LOSS (Leaders)

Player	No.	Yards	Player	No.	Yards
*Cope, de	8	51	*Elia, lb	5	25
*P. Cusick, dt	8	47	*DeCree, de	4	20
*A. Jones, lb	8	27	*Plank, dhb	3	17
Buonamici, dt	7	53	*Bowers, lb	3	12
Kuhn, lb	5	27	Fox, s	3	7

PASSES BROKEN UP

Player	No.	Player	No.
*Colzie, dhb	6	Buonamici, dt	2
*Luke, dhb	6	*Plank, dhb	2
Fox, s	5	Roche, dhb	1
*Elia, lb	4	*Cope, de	1
Kuhn, lb	4	*Davis, s	1
*DeCree, de	2	Midlam, s	1
		Thompson, lb	1

PASS RECEIVING

Player	Caught	Yards	Avg.	TD's	Long.
Baschnagel, wb	19	244	12.8	3	44
*Bartoszek, te	15	240	16.0	2	34
*Hazel, se	11	272	24.7	1	55
*France, te	8	140	17.5	1	26
A. Griffin, tb	5	77	15.4	0	27
R. Griffin, tb	2	23	11.5	1	18
Roach, tb	1	16	16.0	0	16
Johnson, fb	1	11	11.0	1	11
Lillie, te	1	11	11.0	0	11
Hyatt, wb	1	10	10.0	0	10
Kain, te	1	9	9.0	0	9
OSU Totals	65	1053	16.2	9	55

PUNTING

Player	Number	Yards	Avg.	Long.
Skladany	31	1416	45.6	63
Keeton	3	120	40.0	47
OSU Totals	34	1536	45.1	63

KICKOFF RETURNS

Player	Number	Yards	Average	TD's	Longest
Willis, se	16	420	26.2	2	97
Baschnagel, wb	5	93	18.6	0	26
A. Griffin, tb	4	71	17.7	0	36
Hyatt, wb	1	36	36.0	0	36
Roach, tb	1	16	16.0	0	16
Johnson, fb	1	12	12.0	0	12
*Holycross, wb	1	10	10.0	0	10
*France, te	1	7	7.0	0	7
Totals	30	665	22.1	2	97

PUNT RETURNS

Player	Number	Yards	Average	TD's	Longest
*Colzie, dhb	17	172	10.1	0	33
Fox, s	2	33	16.5	0	18
*Plank, dhb	3	11	3.7	0	6
Baschnagel, wb	1	10	10.0	0	10
Totals	23	226	9.8	0	33

INTERCEPTION RETURNS

Player	Number	Yards	Average	TD's	Longest
*Colzie, dhb	8	80	10.0	0	40
*Elia, lb	3	51	17.0	0	23
Ruhl, s	3	34	11.3	0	28
Fox, s	3	25	8.3	0	19
*Luke, dhb	3	24	8.0	0	24
*Plank, dhb	3	0	0.0	0	0
Totals	23	214	9.3	0	40

* Not returning for 1975

No.	Name	Pos.	Wgt.	Hgt.	Class	Hometown
94	*Adkins	LB	209	6-2	So.	Xenia
22	Allegro, Joe	S	177	5-11	So.	W. Pittsburgh, Pa.
5	Alles, Todd	DHB	185	5-10	Sr.	Columbus
69	Andria, Ernie	OG	238	6-3	Fr.	Wintersville
61	*Applegate, Rick	C	250	6-3	Jr.	Cincinnati
19	Archer, Mickey	WB	184	6-0	Fr.	Toledo
59	*Ayers, Ron	OG	236	6-4	Jr.	Columbus
95	*Bargerstock, Doug	FB	244	6-2	So.	Taylor, Mich.
48	*Baschnagel, Brian	WB	192	6-0	Sr.	Pittsburgh, Pa.
67	*Beamon, Eddie	DT	246	6-2	So.	Cincinnati
81	Bell, Farley	DE	222	6-4	Fr.	Toledo
55	*Brown, Aaron	MG	224	6-2	So.	Warren
27	Brown, Richard	LB	208	6-2	Fr.	Columbus
84	*Brudzinski, Bob	DE	228	6-4	Jr.	Fremont
75	*Buonamici, Nick	DT	242	6-3	Jr.	Brentwood, N.Y.
76	Burke, Tim	OT	252	6-4	Fr.	Wapakoneta
23	*Cassady, Craig	DHB	176	6-0	Sr.	Columbus
71	Cato, Byron	DT	248	6-2	Fr.	Lorain
93	Coburn, Don	DE	195	6-1	Jr.	Wickliffe
36	Cousineau, Tom	LB	220	6-3	Fr.	Fairview Park
78	Cox, Garth	OT	238	6-5	So.	Washington C. H.
90	*Curto, Pat	DE	227	6-2	Sr.	Groveport
73	*Dannelley, Scott	OT	252	6-3	Sr.	Williamsport, Pa.
37	Dansler, Kelton	LB	212	6-2	Fr.	Warren
50	Datish, Mike	C	235	6-3	Jr.	Warren
86	Dixon, Joe	DE	221	6-3	So.	Trenton, Mich.
24	Ferelli, Jeff	DHB	186	5-10	Jr.	Columbus
52	Fisher, John	MG	211	6-2	Fr.	Dayton
12	*Fox, Tim	S	186	6-0	Sr.	Canton
28	Garcia, Joe	LB	222	6-0	Fr.	LaPalma, Calif.
8	Gerald, Rod	QB	174	6-1	Fr.	Dallas, Texas
7	*Greene, Cornelius	QB	172	6-0	Sr.	Washington, D.C.
45	*Griffin, Archie	TB	182	5-9	Sr.	Columbus
46	Griffin, Duncan	DHB	184	5-11	Fr.	Columbus
44	*Griffin, Ray	S	177	5-9	So.	Columbus
42	Gordon, Lester	TB	186	6-1	Fr.	New Rochelle, N.Y.
11	Harrell, Jim	WB	190	5-10	Jr.	Curtice
66	*Harris, Tyrone	DT	242	6-3	So.	Columbus
13	Hemphill, Phil	SE	175	6-1	So.	Columbus
33	Hornik, Joe	DE	221	6-3	Fr.	North Olmsted
35	*Hyatt, Bob	WB	185	5-10	Jr.	Lagrange
87	Jaco, William	TE	251	6-5	Fr.	Toledo
13	Johnson, Barry	TB	181	6-0	Jr.	Columbus
33	*Johnson, Pete	FB	248	6-1	Jr.	Long Beach, N.Y.
49	Jones, Herman	SE	200	6-3	So.	Miami, Fla.
38	Jones, Paul	DE	200	6-2	So.	Dayton
3	Keeton, Mike	P	172	6-0	Sr.	Caldwell
85	*Kain, Larry	TE	232	6-2	Sr.	Dayton
6	*Klaban, Tom	PK	184	6-1	Sr.	Cincinnati
70	Koegel, Steve	OT	219	6-3	Sr.	Cincinnati
54	Kuhn, Ken	LB	231	6-2	Sr.	Louisville
10	Lang, Mark	MG	218	6-1	So.	Cincinnati
56	Laser, Joel	OG	236	6-2	Fr.	Akron
51	Lillvis, Gary	OG	234	6-2	Sr.	Ashtabula
34	*Logan, Jeff	TB	184	5-10	So.	North Canton
64	*Lukens, Bill	OG	231	6-1	Jr.	Cincinnati
32	Mazeroski, Dave	FB	217	6-1	Sr.	Cadiz
14	McCutcheon, Gary	SE	187	6-0	Sr.	Berwick, Pa.
62	McEndree, Randy	C	230	5-11	Sr.	Cadiz
21	*Midlam, Max	DHB	190	5-10	Jr.	Marion
20	Mills, Leonard	DHB	182	6-3	Fr.	Miami, Fla.
2	Molls, Larry	WB	184	6-0	Jr.	Parma Heights
99	Moore, Jimmy	TE	255	6-5	Fr.	Tempe, Arizona
68	O'Rourke, James	DT	253	6-3	So.	Brooklyn, N.Y.
15	Pacenta, James	QB	190	6-3	Jr.	Akron
93	Perry, Clarence	DE	224	6-1	Sr.	Columbus
74	*Pietrini, Lou	OT	244	6-3	Sr.	Milford, Conn.
53	*Porter, Doug	C	228	6-2	So.	Youngstown
65	Renard, Barney	OG	215	6-3	Jr.	Maumee
77	Rice, Dan	OT	223	6-3	Fr.	Cincinnati
41	*Roach, Woodrow	TB	182	5-9	Sr.	Washington, D.C.
47	Robertson, Bob	FB	212	6-0	So.	Barberton
62	Robinson, Joe	OT	243	6-5	Fr.	Paulding
26	*Roche, Tom	DHB	182	6-2	So.	Staten Is., N.Y.
16	Ross, Tony	QB	176	5-10	So.	Pittsburgh, Pa.
43	*Ruhl, Bruce	DHB	188	6-1	Jr.	Southfield, Mich.
25	Sales, Fred	S	184	6-0	So.	Fort Worth, Texas
24	Saunders, Keith	DHB	182	5-11	So.	Beaver Falls, Pa.
57	*Savoca, Jim	LB	228	6-2	So.	Solon
29	Schwertz, Jerome	FB	205	5-11	So.	Bethel Park, Pa.
1	Skladany, Tom	P-PK	190	6-0	Jr.	Bethel Park, Pa.
60	*Smith, Ted	OG	242	6-1	Sr.	Gibsonburg
80	Storer, Greg	TE	218	6-5	So.	Cincinnati
72	Sullivan, Mark	DT	242	6-4	Fr.	N. Bedford, Mass.
9	*Thompson, Ed	LB	220	6-1	Jr.	Waverly
97	Vogler, Terry	LB	198	6-2	Fr.	Covington
38	Vogler, Tim	FB	212	6-3	Fr.	Covington
79	*Ward, Chris	OT	270	6-4	So.	Dayton
58	Waugh, Thomas	OG	216	6-1	Fr.	Norwalk
88	Weiland, Jeff	MG	230	6-0	Sr.	Englewood
63	Weston, Darryl				So.	Pittsburgh, Pa.
4	*Willott,					Youngstown
89	*Willis,					Washington, D.C.
25	Wolery,					Delphos

*Denotes letterman

A.P. POLL
1. Oklahoma
2. Arizona State
3. Alabama
4. OHIO STATE
5. U.C.L.A.
6. Texas
7. Arkansas
8. Michigan
9. Nebraska
10. Penn State

U.P.I. POLL
1. Oklahoma
2. Arizona State
3. Alabama
4. OHIO STATE
5. U.C.L.A.
6. Arkansas
7. Texas
8. Michigan
9. Nebraska
10. Penn State

1975
Captains: Archie Griffin, Brian Baschnagel, Tim Fox, Ken Kuhn

21	Michigan State	0	24	*Indiana	14
17	*Penn State	9	40	Illinois	3
32	*North Carolina	7	38	*Minnesota	6
41	U.C.L.A.	20	21	Michigan	14
49	*Iowa	0	10	†U.C.L.A.	23
56	*Wisconsin	0		384	102
35	Purdue	6			

Won 11, Lost 1
Big Ten Champions
† Rose Bowl

JOHNSON SCORES RECORD FIVE TDs

COLUMBUS, Ohio. Sept. 27 (AP) — Pete Johnson scored a school record five touchdowns and Archie Griffin became the greatest yardage gainer in Ohio State history today, leading the second-ranked Buckeyes to their 500th college football victory, a 32-7 rout of North Carolina.

Johnson's inside power and Griffin's fluid runs helped Ohio State post a record 20th straight home triumph. The Buckeyes are 3-0 this season.

Griffin's 157 yards, his 24th straight regular-season game of over 100 yards, a continuing NCAA record, gave him a career total of 4,532 yards, bettering Rex Kern's school mark of 4,518 set in 1968-70.

Johnson scored on runs of 1, 5, 1, 2 and 3 yards. His performance broke the Buckeyes' record of four touchdowns in one game shared by eight players. The 248-pound junior fullback rambled for 148 yards.

More than 87,000 watched Ohio State run its record to 500-200-46 in its 86th season.

North Carolina, now 1-2, played the game without its leading rusher, Mike Voight, who had 131 yards rushing going into this week. Voight was suspended for what coach Bill Dooley called personal reasons.

The Tar Heels, however, became the first opponent this season to score a touchdown against the Buckeyes when quarterback Jimmy Paschall rifled a seven-yard pass to flanker Brian Smith early in the third quarter.

N. Carolina	0	0	7	0— 7
Ohio State	0	12	7	13—32

Ohio—Johnson 1 run (kick failed)
Ohio—Johnson 5 run (run failed)
NC—Smith 7 pass from Paschall (Biddle kick)
Ohio—Johnson 1 run (Skladany kick)
Ohio—Johnson 2 run (Skladany kick)
Ohio—Johnson 3 run (kick failed)
A—87,750

	N. Car.	Ohio St.
First downs	16	26
Rushes-yards	44-109	71-403
Passing yards	14	182
Return yards	40	68
Passes	8-18-2	7-9-0
Punts	8-47	4-46
Fumbles-lost	2-0	7-1
Penalties-yards	3-17	10-71

Buckeyes Conquer U.C.L.A.

LOS ANGELES, Oct. 4 (AP) — Cornelius Green, the quarterback, scored two touchdowns and set up three others tonight as Ohio State whipped U.C.L.A., 41-20, in a game that began with both teams unbeaten.

The Bruins, trailing by 38-7, tried vainly to overcome the big lead in the third quarter before a crowd of 55,482.

Pete Johnson, Ohio State's fullback, got his 10th and 11th touchdowns of the season, going over from 3 and 2 yards out. Greene ran 2 and 17 for his pair against the University of California, Los Angeles.

Archie Griffin, the 1974 Heisman Trophy winner, scored his first touchdown of 1975 and rushed for more than 100 yards in his 25th consecutive regular-season game. He gained 161 yards in 21 carries. Greene gained 120 in 23.

U.C.L.A. marched 73 yards the first time it controlled the ball, after a Griffin fumble, and scored on a 13-yard pass from John Sciarra to James Sarpy. Ohio State got the next 38 points.

Ohio State	7	21	10	3—41
U.C.L.A.	7	0	7	6—20

U.C.L.A.—Sarpy, 13, pass from Sciarra (White, kick).
O.S.U.—Greene, 2, run (Klaban, kick).
O.S.U.—Johnson, 3, run (Klaban, kick).
O.S.U.—Johnson, 2, run (Klaban, kick).
O.S.U.—Greene, 17, run (Klaban, kick).
O.S.U.—A. Griffin, 17, run (Klaban, kick).
O.S.U.—FG, Klaban, 34.
U.C.L.A.—Ayers, 2, run (White, kick).
U.C.L.A.—Ayers, 1, run (kick failed).
O.S.U.—FG, Klaban, 42.
Attendance—55,482.

Ohio State, 49-0

COLUMBUS, Ohio (AP) — Pete Johnson, the nation's leading scorer, rumbled for three touchdowns and Archie Griffin rushed for over 100 yards in his 26th regular-season game Saturday, powering top-ranked Ohio State to a 49-0 Big Ten football rout of winless Iowa.

The victory, a record 21st straight at-home for the 5-0-0 Buckeyes, was the 207th for Woody Hayes, tying the Ohio State coach for fourth place with former Rice mentor Jess Neely on the all-time list.

Johnson, a massive 245-pound junior fullback, barged across the goal line on runs of 4, 4 and 3 yards to run his touchdown total this season to 14.

Meanwhile, Griffin carried 21 times for 120 yards, extending his national record and helping the Buckeyes roll up their widest victory margin in 1975.

Griffin Runs 127 Yards, Bucks Roll

CHAMPAIGN, Ill. (AP) — Archie Griffin, Pete Johnson and Tom Skladany turned in record-shattering performances Saturday to lead top-ranked Ohio Sate to a 40-3 Big 10 football victory over Illinois.

Griffin gained 127 yards to surpass the 100-yard plateau for the 30th time. He ripped off a 30-yard touchdown run in the second quarter and hiked his regular-season career total to over 5,000 yards.

[1975]

Ohio State Pins Defeat On Purdue

By The Associated Press

WEST LAFAYETTE, Ind., Oct. 25—Archie Griffin of Ohio State set a National Collegiate rushing record today as the top-ranked Buckeyes defeated Purdue, 35-6, in a Big Ten game.

Griffin, held to 36 yards in the first half, finished with 130 yards on 20 carries to raise his career total to 4,730 yards. The previous record of 4,715, set by Ed Marinaro in 1969-71 at Cornell, fell midway through the fourth quarter when Griffin took a handoff from Cornelius Greene, the quarterback, and ran 23 yards up the middle.

It was the Heisman Trophy winner's final carry of the day. He also extended his streak of regular-season games of 100 yards or more rushing to 28.

Pete Johnson, the Buckeyes' fullback, scored on runs of 60 and 3 yards. That gave him 18 touchdowns this season, two short of the conference record set in 1972 by Champ Henson, also an Ohio State fullback.

Mike Pruitt of Purdue gained 127 yards on 24 carries. But despite two drives to the Ohio State 10-yard line, Purdue had to settle for a pair of first-half field goals by Steve Schmidt.

Ohio State, now with a 7-0 won-lost record over all, gained 355 yards rushing to 185 for Purdue.

As Griffin and Johnson were leading the Buckeyes' punishing ground game, Greene threw for touchdown passes of 41 yards to Lenny Willis and 22 yards to Brian Baschnagel. Greene also ran 28 yards for the Buckeyes' last touchdown.

Johnson's 60-yard scoring run came on Ohio State's first play from scrimmage, and his 3-yard touchdown came just seven plays after Griffin returned a kickoff 53 yards to the Purdue 37.

Win Clinches Trip to Bowl By Ohio State

Archie Griffin wins Heisman Trophy again

New York (AP)—Ohio State University's Archie Griffin, who gained 5,176 yards in his varsity career, overcame his lack of size, survived the taunts of 11 teams determined to ring his bell and became the first two-time winner of the coveted Heisman Trophy yesterday.

"There was a lot of pressure this year," the 5-foot-9, 184-pound senior tailback said after becoming the first Heisman repeater, succeeding where four others failed: Army's Doc Blanchard, Doak Walker of Southern Methodist, Ohio State's Vic Janowicz and Navy's Roger Staubach.

"Being tagged the Heisman winner, naturally guys on other teams were after me more this year. They all tackled me clean, but they might say a few things like, 'Get up, Heisman Trophy winner.'"

Griffin, who has rushed for 5,176 yards in four seasons, will wind up his collegiate career in a fourth consecutive Rose Bowl against the University of California at Los Angeles.

He captured the 1975 Heisman by a landslide over running backs Chuck Muncie of California and Ricky Bell of Southern Cal. Griffin received 454 first-place ballots, 167 seconds and 104 thirds from 888 sports writers and broadcasters across the country. On a 3-2-1 basis, that amounted to 1,800 points. Muncie (145-104-87) received 730 points to 708 for Bell (70-169-160).

COLUMBUS, Ohio (AP) — Top-ranked Ohio State, fired by the record running of Archie Griffin and Pete Johnson, clinched a trip to either the Rose or the Orange Bowl with a 38-6 Big Ten football victory Saturday over Minnesota.

The unbeaten Buckeyes will play Michigan at Ann Arbor, Mich. next week to decide the conference championship and accompanying Rose Bowl berth for the eighth straight season. The loser will go to the Orange Bowl.

After extending his national record to 31 straight regular season games of over 100 yards, Griffin was accorded a standing ovation by the crowd of nearly 88,000.

 # Ohio State Roster

No.	Name	Pos.	Wgt.	Hgt.	Class	Hometown
94	*Adkins, David	LB	214	6-2	Jr.	Xenia
22	*Allegro, Joseph	S	176	5-11	Jr.	West Pittsburgh, Pa.
69	*Andria, Ernest	OG	240	6-3	So.	Wintersville
19	Archer, Stewart	DB	191	6-0	So.	Toledo
59	*Ayers, Ronald	C	234	6-4	Sr.	Columbus
82	Barwig, Ron	TE	238	6-8	Fr.	Willoughby Hills
67	*Beamon, Eddie	DT	254	6-2	Jr.	Cincinnati
81	*Bell, Farley	DE	228	6-4	So.	Toledo
29	Blinco, Thomas	LB	225	6-2	Fr.	Lewiston, N.Y.
55	*Brown, Aaron	MG	228	6-2	Jr.	Warren
27	Brown, Richard	LB	205	6-2	So.	Columbus
84	*Brudzinski, Robert	DE	224	6-4	Sr.	Fremont
3	Budd, David	P	172	6-1	Fr.	Chester, N.J.
75	*Buonamici, Nicholas	DT	242	6-3	Sr.	Brentwood, N.Y.
76	Burke, Tim	OT	252	6-4	So.	Wapakoneta
63	Burris, Scott	OT	244	6-3	Fr.	Pt. Pleasant, W. Va.
38	Campbell, Paul	FB	218	6-1	Fr.	Ravenna
41	Caruso, Jim	DHB	196	6-0	Fr.	Wappingers Falls, N.Y.
7	Castignola, Greg	QB	181	6-2	Fr.	Trenton, Mich.
71	*Cato, Byron	MG	234	6-2	So.	Lorain
93	Coburn, Don	MG	195	6-1	Sr.	Wickliffe
36	*Cousineau, Thomas	LB	224	6-3	So.	Fairview Park
78	Cox, Garth	OT	248	6-4	Jr.	Washington Court House
88	Cox, Marc	SE	192	6-0	Fr.	London
96	Cusick, Martin	DE	214	6-2	Jr.	Lakewood
93	Dailey, Jed	PK	190	5-9	Jr.	Waverly
32	*Dansler, Kelton	DE	205	6-2	So.	Warren
50	Datish, Michael	C	235	6-3	Sr.	Warren
85	Diefenthaler, Dean	DT	255	6-2	Fr.	Curtice
86	*Dixon, Joseph	DE	221	6-3	Jr.	Trenton, Mich.
60	Dulin, Gary	OG	250	6-5	Fr.	Madisonville, Ky.
28	Durtschi, Herbert	DHB	190	5-9	Jr.	Galion
89	Ferguson, Bryan	SE	172	6-0	Fr.	Troy
4	Ferrelli, Jeff	DHB	181	5-10	Jr.	Columbus
56	Fritz, Kenneth	MG	232	6-3	Fr.	Ironton
8	*Gerald, Roderic	QB	173	6-1	So.	Dallas, Texas
42	Gordon, Lester	TB	192	6-1	So.	New Rochelle, N.Y.
46	*Griffin, Duncan	S	186	5-11	So.	Columbus
44	*Griffin, Raymond	S	179	5-9	Jr.	Columbus
12	Guess, Michael	S	173	5-11	Fr.	Columbus
54	Hall, Davis	OG	230	6-3	Fr.	Uniontown, Pa.
77	Harmon, William	OG	242	6-2	Fr.	Massillon
11	*Harrell, James	WB	186	5-10	Sr.	Curtice
66	*Harris, Tyrone	DT	246	6-3	Jr.	Columbus
95	Heilman, Philip	DE	218	6-2	Sr.	Defiance
83	*Hornik, Joseph	DE	219	6-3	So.	North Olmsted
24	Hunter, Charles	FB	212	6-2	Fr.	Newark, Delaware
35	*Hyatt, Robert	SE	175	5-10	Sr.	Lagrange
47	Jackson, Matthew	WB	210	6-3	Fr.	Fort Valley, Ga.
87	Jaco, William	TE	247	6-5	So.	Toledo
33	*Johnson, Pete	FB	247	6-1	Sr.	Long Beach, N.Y.
48	Johnson, Ricky	TB	194	6-0	Fr.	Santa Maria, Calif.
49	*Jones, Herman	SE	200	6-3	Jr.	Miami, Fla.
98	Kellum, Wendell	DT	212	5-8	So.	Columbus
51	*Lang, Mark	C	220	6-1	Jr.	Cincinnati
92	Laser, Joel	OG	232	6-2	So.	Akron
5	Laughlin, James	FB	208	6-2	Fr.	Lyndhurst
91	Lillie, Robert	TE	233	6-3	Jr.	Dayton
34	*Logan, Jeff	TB	182	5-10	Jr.	North Canton
64	*Lukens, William	OG	233	6-1	Sr.	Cincinnati
73	Mackie, Douglas	OT	250	6-4	Fr.	Saugus, Mass.
21	*Midlam, Max	DHB	192	5-10	Sr.	Marion
62	Mills, Edward	DT	250	6-7	Fr.	Columbus
20	*Mills, Leonard	DHB	190	6-3	So.	Miami, Fla.
2	Molls, Larry	FB	186	6-0	Sr.	Parma Heights
99	*Moore, Jimmy	TE	258	6-5	So.	Tempe, Arizona
15	*Pacenta, James	QB	190	6-3	Sr.	Akron
74	*Pietrini, Louis	OT	248	6-3	Sr.	Milford, Conn.
53	*Porter, Douglas	C	232	6-2	Jr.	Youngstown
65	Renard, Barney	OG	218	6-3	Sr.	Maumee
90	Robinson, Joseph	TE	255	6-5	So.	Paulding
26	*Roche, Thomas	DHB	190	6-2	Jr.	Staten Island, N.Y.
16	Ross, Paul	LB	224	6-1	So.	Fort Valley, Ga.
43	Ruhl, Bruce	DHB	187	6-1	Sr.	Southfield, Mich.
10	Saunders, Jeith	DHB	185	6-0	Jr.	New Brighton, Pa.
57	*Savoca, James	OG	228	6-2	Jr.	Solon
68	Sawicki, Tim	MG	206	6-0	Fr.	Mayfield
37	Schneider, Michael	FB	205	6-2	Fr.	Cincinnati
14	Schwartz, Brian	DHB	188	6-1	Fr.	Simi Valley, Calif.
17	Scudder, Al	TB	190	5-11	So.	Dayton
30	*Simon, Charles	LB	222	6-2	Jr.	Dublin
1	*Skladany, Thomas	P	192	6-0	Sr.	Bethel Park, La.
23	Springs, Ronald	TB	196	6-2	So.	Williamsburg, Va.
80	*Storer, Gregory	TE	224	6-5	Jr.	Cincinnati
39	Stover, Andrew	DHB	190	6-2	So.	Cleveland Heights
6	Strahine, Michael	QB	186	6-0	Fr.	Lakewood
72	*Sullivan, Mark	DT	245	6-4	So.	New Bedford, Mass.
9	*Thompson, Ed	LB	221	6-1	Sr.	Waverly
97	Vogler, Terry	DE	207	6-2	So.	Covington
85	Vogler, Tim	TE	232	6-3	So.	Covington
18	Volley, Ricardo	WB	210	6-0	Fr.	Lynchburg, Va.
79	*Ward, Christopher	OT	278	6-4	Jr.	Dayton
58	Waugh, Thomas	OG	242	6-1	So.	Norwalk
25	Wolery, Scott	S	170	5-10	Sr.	Delphos
13	Wolfe, Chris	FB	200	5-10	Sr.	Junction City
61	Wymer, Douglas	DT	240	6-3	Fr.	Findlay

*Denotes Letterman

[1976]

1976 RESULTS (9-2-1)

H—OSU 49,	Michigan State	21	86,509
A—OSU 12,	Penn State	7	62,503
H—OSU 21,	Missouri	22	87,936
H—OSU 10,	UCLA	10	87,969
A—OSU 34,	Iowa	14	59,170
A—OSU 30,	Wisconsin	20	79,759
H—OSU 24,	Purdue	3	87,898
A—OSU 47,	Indiana	7	39,663
H—OSU 42,	Illinois	10	87,654
A—OSU 9,	Minnesota	3	53,190
H—OSU 0,	Michigan	22	88,250
N—OSU 27,	Colorado	10	65,537

A.P. POLL
1. Pittsburgh
2. Southern Cal.
3. Michigan
4. Houston
5. Oklahoma
6. OHIO STATE
7. Texas A. & M.
8. Maryland
9. Nebraska
10. Georgia

U.P.I. POLL
1. Pittsburgh
2. Southern Cal.
3. Michigan
4. Houston
5. OHIO STATE
6. Oklahoma
7. Nebraska
8. Texas A. & M
9. Alabama
10. Georgia

Sept. 19

Ohio State 12, Penn State 7

```
Ohio St.        0 6 0 6—12
Penn State      0 0 0 7— 7
  OSU—Gerald 8 run (run failed)
  OSU—Hyatt 8 run (run failed)
  PS—M. Suhey 1 run (Bahr kick)
    A—62,503
```

Sept. 26

Missouri upset odds by sticking to plan

By SEYMOUR S. SMITH
Assistant Sports Editor of The Sun

When University of Missouri entered the third quarter of its game against No. 2 Ohio State University Saturday, trailing, 21 to 7, almost everyone expected the Tigers to come out throwing the ball, especially since the only Missouri touchdown came on a 31-yard pass. They did not, sticking to the their game plan as they came from behind to stun Ohio State, 22 to 21, in the closing 10 seconds.

"This was the greatest football game a Missouri team ever has played," winning coach Al Onofrio said in reviewing how his charges outscored Ohio State, 15-0, in the last 30 minutes, going 80 yards in the final five minutes in their decisive drive, and then winning on a 2-point conversion after the first attempt had misfired only to have Ohio State guilty of defensive holding.

"Our offense got stronger and stronger as the game went on," Onofrio said. Woody Hayes, Ohio State's unhappy mentor, agreed. "They weren't doing a lot differently in the second half. We thought they were a good team and we were especially aware of it after the first half. You want me to say something about those penalties. You just want me to to make an alibi. Well, nuts!"

Missouri's offense revolved around a substitute quarterback, Pete Woods, who rallied his team-mates after workhorse fullback Pete Johnson had guided Ohio State in front with three touchdown plunges. Woods culminated the pay-off march with a pass to Leo Lewis, but overthrew the same target on the conversion. Ohio State was caught holding and Woods, given another chance, rushed into the end zone.

Reprinted with permission from the **Baltimore Sunpapers**

Buckeyes Unveil Logan, Rout Mich. State, 49-21

COLUMBUS, Ohio, Sept. 11 (AP)—Jeff Logan, the tailback heir to Archie Griffin, scored three touchdowns and had a fourth nullified by a penalty today as Ohio State routed Michigan State, 49-21, in a Big Ten football opener.

Logan, a 184-pound junior from North Canton, Ohio, ran 75, 68 and 3 yards for his touchdowns. The penalty cost him a 71-yard score.

Logan gained 112 yards, and he formed a punishing backfield with the fullback, Pete Johnson, and the quarterback, Rod Gerald. They combined for 315 yards and six touchdowns rushing. Logan's 68-yard score was on a punt return. Johnson, a 247-pound senior and the nation's leading scorer last fall, raised his career touchdown total to 41 with scores of 1 yard and 58 yards.

Debut Ruined for Rogers

The Buckeyes posted their 25th consecutive home victory and ruined the conference coaching debut of Darryl Rogers of Michigan State.

Woody Hayes, the Ohio State coach, bitter over a series of Michigan State campus newspaper articles that accused him of recruiting violations, called three straight timeouts in the last 30 seconds of the first half. The Buckeyes had the ball and led, 35-0, at the time. When Michigan State scored its second touchdown with less than 15 minutes to play, Hayes ordered his No. 1 offensive unit back into the game.

```
Michigan St      0  0  7 14—21
Ohio State      21 14  7  7—49
  Ohio—Gerald 17 run (Skladany kick)
  Ohio—Johnson 1 run (Skladany kick)
  Ohio—Gerald 12 run (Skladany kick)
  Ohio—Johnson 58 run (Skladany kick)
  Ohio—Logan 3 run (Skladany kick)
  Ohio—Logan 75 run (Skladany kick)
  MSU—Gibson 4 pass from Lawson (Nielsen kick)
  MUS—Gibson 82 pass from Lawson (Nielsen kick)
  Ohio—Logan 68 punt return (Skladany kick)
  MSU—Radelet 28 pass from Robinson (Nielsen kick)
    A—86,509
```

	Michigan St.	Ohio State
First downs	14	17
Rushes-yards	34-85	61-475
Passing yards	259	36
Returns yards	18	67
Passes	16-36-1	1-2-0
Punts	9-36	6-43
Fumbles-lost	2-2	2-1
Penalties-yards	1-5	8-64

INDIVIDUAL LEADERS
RUSHING—Michigan St., Baes 13-30, Jackson 11-21, L. Williams 3-9. Ohio State, Logan 7-12, Gerald 10-104, Johnson 12-99.
RECEIVING—Michigan St., Gibson 3-93, Byrd 3-49, DeRose 3-25. Ohio State, Harrell 1-36.
PASSING—Michigan St., Lawson 14-32-1, 212 yards; Robinson 2-3-0, 47; Willingham 0-1-0, 0. Ohio State, Logan 1-1-0, 36; Pacenta 0-1-0, 0.

[1976]

Ohio State 10, U.C.L.A. 10

COLUMBUS, Ohio, Oct. 2 (AP)—Tom Skladany kicked a 25-yard field goal in the fourth quarter today to give Ohio State a 10-10 tie with the University of California, Los Angeles.

The deadlock ended the Bruins' seven-game winning streak.

In the closing minutes, both sides apparently played for a tie, running the ball instead of going to the air.

The Buckeyes (2-1-1) drew a chorus of boos when they ran seven successive running plays and punted, instead of trying a long-range field goal in the last minute.

Skladany punted to the Bruins' 7 and U.C.L.A. (3-0-1) ran out the clock with three rushing plays.

The Buckeyes, beaten by U.C.L.A., 23-10, in the 1976 Rose Bowl, struck for a 7-0 lead on Pete Johnson's 4-yard run midway in the second quarter. Frank Corral booted a 47-yard field goal to cut the deficit to 7-3 midway through the third quarter and the Bruins took a 10-7 lead on Jeff Dankworth's 1-yard quarterback sneak with 13 minutes to go.

U.C.L.A., averaging more than 480 yards a game, could muster only 288 against the Buckeyes' veteran defensive platoon. Ohio State, averaging 364 yards a contest, settled for 221.

Ohio State was particularly effective defensively in the first half as U.C.L.A. penetrated midfield only twice.

U.C.L.A. 10, Ohio State 10

```
UCLA          0 0 3 7—10
Ohio State    0 7 0 3—10
  Ohio—Johnson 4 run (Skladany kick)
  UCLA—FG Corral 47
  UCLA—Dankworth 1 run (Corral kick)
  Ohio—FG Skladany 25
  A—87,969
                    UCLA    Ohio State
First downs          16         13
Rushes-yards       54-205     48-180
Passing yards        83         41
Return yards          5         49
Passes             8-14-0     3- 8-0
Punts               6-47       6-42
Fumbles-lost        3-2        1-1
Penalties-yards     3-25       1- 5
```

Ohio State 24, Purdue 3

COLUMBUS, Ohio, Oct. 23 (AP)—Ohio State lost its starting quarterback to an injury today, but Jeff Logan scored on runs of 11 and 29 yards to lead the ninth-ranked Buckeyes to a 24-3 Big Ten victory over Purdue.

The quarterback, Rod Gerald, a sophomore from Dallas, suffered three broken ribs late in the first quarter and will be out for the season. His replacement, Jim Pacenta, who had played only 19 minutes in four previous games, engineered three touchdown marches in the last 16 minutes of the game.

Ohio State 24, Purdue 3

```
Purdue       0 0 3 0— 3
Ohio State   0 3 7 14—24
  OSU—FG Skladany 27
  Pur—FG Supan 31
  OSU—Logan 11 run (Skladany kick)
  OSU—Johnson 4 run (Skladany kick)
  OSU—Logan 29 run (Skladany kick)
  A—87,898
```

Ohio State 34, Iowa 14

IOWA CITY, Iowa, Oct. 9 (AP)—Pete Johnson set a Big Ten Conference career scoring record today as he ran for three touchdowns to help Ohio State to a 34-14 conference victory over Iowa.

The Buckeyes scored on their first three possessions, with Rod Garald getting the first on a 17-yard run to cap an 82-yard drive. Tom Skladany, the nation's leading punter the last two years, kicked four extra points and field goals of 26 and 46 yards in the contest dominated by the Buckeyes.

Johnson tied the conference scoring record of 46 touchdowns in Ohio State's second possession when he plunged over from the 1. He set the record on another 1-yard run in the next series, set up when Eddie Beaman recovered a Hawkeye fumble on Iowa's 20.

Ohio State 34, Iowa 14

```
OSU    21 3 10 0 —34
Iowa    0 0  0 10—14
  OSU — Gerald 17 run (Skladany kick)
  OSU — Johnson 1 run (Skladany kick)
  OSU — John 1 run (Skladany kick)
  OSU — FG Skladany 26
  OSU — FG Skladany 46
  OSU — Johnson 3 run (Skladany kick)
  Iowa — Sheeler 5 run (Quartaro kick)
  Iowa — Caldwell 3 run (Quartaro kick)
  A — 59,170
                    Ohio State    Iowa
First Downs            15          17
Rushes Yards         54-201      60-188
Passes Yards           73          39
Return yards           39           3
Passes              4-8-2       6-14-3
Punts                2-41        3-38
Fumbles lost          3-2         3-1
Penalties yards      4-61        5-45
```

Ohio State 47, Indiana 7

BLOOMINGTON, Ind., Oct. 30 (AP)—Pete Johnson scored two touchdowns after Indiana fumbles and Ray Griffin raced 65 yards with an intercepted pass for a score today as Ohio State trounced the Hoosiers, 47-7, in the Big 10.

Indiana held Ohio State without a first down until late in the second quarter. And the Hoosiers took a 7-6 lead when Scott Arnett connected with George Edgar on a 15-yard touchdown pass on the first play in the second period. But Indiana errors put the Buckeyes back on top in the closing seconds of the half, and Ohio State broke the game open in the third period.

Ohio State 47, Indiana 7

```
Ohio St    6 6 14 21—47
Indiana    0 7  0  0— 7
  OSU—R. Griffin 65 run (lateral from
    Buonamaici who intercepted at five (run
    failed)
  Ind—Edgar 15 pass from Arnett (Freud
    kick)
  OSU—Johnson 3 run (pass failed)
  OSU—Johnson 1 run (Skladany kick)
  OSU—Harrell 59 pass from Pacenta
    (Skladany kick)
  OSU—Logan 10 run (Skladany kick)
  OSU—Springs 13 run (Skladany kick)
  OSU—Springs 62 run (Skladany kick)
  A—39,663
                  Ohio St.   Indiana
First downs         16         10
Rushes-yards      53-292     53-99
Passing yards       98         56
Return yards       120          —
Passes            6-8-0     5-16-3
Punts              4-32       9-44
Fumbles-lost       4-3        5-4
Penalties-yards    4-48       4-31
```

Oct. 16

Ohio State 30, Wisconsin 20

MADISON, Wis. (AP)—Jeff Logan rushed for 113 yards in 19 carries, setting up two touchdowns apiece by Rod Gerald, quarterback and Pete Johnson, fullback, to power Ohio State past Wisconsin, 30-20, today in Big Ten college football.

The 247-pound Johnson added 44 yards rushing, while boosting his Big Ten career record for touchdowns to 49 as the Buckeyes raised their record to 4-1 won-lost-tied and 3-0 in the Big Ten. Wisconsin is 2-4 over all and 0-3 in the conference.

Ohio State 30, Wisconsin 20

```
Ohio St.     0 20 7 3—30
Wisconsin    7  0 7 6—20
  Wis-Pollard 1 run, Lamia kick
  OSU-Gerald 12 run, Skladany kick
  OSU-Johnson 1 run, Skladany kick
  OSU-Johnson 2 run, kick failed
  OSU-Gerald 29 run, Skladany kick
  Wis-Matthews 2 run, Lamia kick
  OSU-FG Skladany 25
  Wis-Rodriguez 13 pass from Carroll,
    pass failed
  A-79,579
                    Ohio St.   Wisconsin
First downs           21          25
Rushes-yards        60-311      55-266
Passing yards         53         150
Return yards          33           7
Passes              3-6-1      11-26-2
Punts                2-36        2-41
Fumbles-lost         3-0         0-0
Penalties-yards      1-5         0-0
```

Ohio State 42, Illinois 10

COLUMBUS, Ohio, Nov. 6 (AP)—Pete Johnson, fullback, scored four times, becoming the fifth player in National Collegiate history to score 50 career touchdowns, as he led Ohio State to a 42-10 rout of Illinois that gave the Buckeyes first place in the Big Ten.

Johnson scored from the 1, the 2, the 4 and the 1, bringing his regular-season total of touchdowns to 53. The 247-pound senior, from Long Beach, L.I., joins Glenn Davis of Army, Steve Owens of Oklahoma, Ed Marinaro of Cornell and Anthony Davis of Southern California on the select list. Davis is the leader, with 59 touchdowns

Ohio State 42, Illinois 10

```
Illinois     0  3  0  7—10
Ohio State   7 14 14  7—42
  Ohio—Thompson 81 interception return
    (Skladany kick)
  Ohio—Johnson 1 run (Skladany kick)
  Ohio—Johnson 2 run (Skladany kick)
  Ill—FG Beaver 31
  Ohio—Johnson 4 run (Skladany kick)
  Ohio—Johnson 1 run (Skladany kick)
  Ohio—Adkins 19 interception return (Skla-
    dany kick)
  Ill—Friel 17 pass from McCray (Beaver
    kick)
  A—87,654
                   Illinois   Ohio State
First downs          18          23
Rushes-yards       40-81       64-271
Passing yards       246         101
Return yards         2          136
Passes            14-33-5     7-11-1
Punts               5-37        2-39
Fumbles-lost        2-1         3-2
Penalties-yards     6-37        2-20
```

Nov. 13

Ohio State Nips Gophers

MINNEAPOLIS (AP) — A vaunted Ohio State defense, which has allowed only two touchdowns in its last four games, stopped two Minnesota scoring drives in the second half and the Buckeyes hung on behind Jim Pacenta's four-yard touchdown run for a 9-3 Big Ten football victory over the Gophers Saturday.

The nationally-ranked Buckeyes maintained sole possession of the Big Ten lead with their seventh straight conference victory and improved their season mark to 8-1-1.

Pacenta broke a 3-3 tie with his TD run in the second period. Tom Skladany's 39-yard field goal for Ohio State and Paul Rogind's 49-yarder were the only other scores in the game.

Minnesota, now 6-4 in all games and 4-3 in the conference, reached the Ohio State 22 in the third quarter and drove to the Buckeye 27 in the final period. But both drives were stopped.

Defensive tackle Nick Buonamici rambled 42 yards with an interception, which killed Minnesota's third-period threat.

Minnesota quarterback Tony Dungy, who completed 16 of 38 pass attempts for 201 yards, was hit while trying to pass and Buonamici gathered in the football and moved it to the Minnesota 23.

Another Gopher threat died in the final period, when Dungy threw an incompletion under a heavy rush.

Minnesota failed to contain the Buckeyes late in the game, losing a golden opportunity when Jeff Logan picked up 14 yards and a first down at the Buckeye 38. Ohio State faced a third-and-13 situation and caught the Gophers geared for the pass, which allowed Logan's critical smash up the middle.

The 5-foot-10, 182-pound Logan, who spent the past two seasons on the Buckeye bench behind Archie Griffin, rushed for 116 yards in 30 carries and boosted his season total to 1,106.

Ohio State managed only 42 yards offensively in the second half, while Dungy was able to move Minnesota through the air. However, the Gophers gained only 46 yards rushing in the game.

Nov. 20

Michigan, USC Head for Rose Bowl

Wolverines Zip Ohio State, 22-0

COLUMBUS, Ohio (AP) — Russell Davis knifed across for a pair of three yard touchdown runs in the third period as fourth-ranked Michigan ended four years of frustration and won its way to the Rose Bowl with a 22-0 victory over arch-rival Ohio State Saturday.

The triumph lifted the Wolverines into a share of the Big Ten football championship with eighth-ranked Ohio State. Although both teams finished with 7-1 conference records, Michigan earned its first trip to Pasadena in five seasons by taking the showdown it had to win.

A record Ohio Stadium of 88,250—the 50th consecutive sellout—plus a national television audience saw the Buckeyes suffer their worst defeat at home since a 41-6 loss to Purdue early in the 1967 campaign.

And the embarrassing shutout ended Ohio State's near-record string of scoring 122 consecutive games, just one short of the record set by Oklahoma from 1946-57. The last team to blank the Buckeyes was Michigan by a 10-0 count in the 1964 finale.

Rob Lytle put the icing on Michigan's cake with a three-yard scoring plunge at 6:47 of the final period, three plays after Jerry Zuver intercepted a pass from Jim Pacenta at the Ohio State 28, and returned it to the 15.

Although Michigan shared the Big Ten title with Ohio State in 1972, 1973 and 1974, the Buckeyes went to the Rose Bowl each time, twice by a vote of conference athletic directors and once by winning the head-to-head meeting.

Michigan finished the regular season with a 10-1 record, the only blot a 16-14 loss to Purdue two weeks ago.

Ohio State wound up 8-2-1. The Buckeyes, however, did manage at least a piece of the Big Ten crown for a record fifth year in a row.

The Wolverines marched 80 and 52 yards on their first two possessions of the third quarter after a scoreless and frustrating first half to give Coach Bo Schembechler, a one-time Ohio State assistant, his first victory in four tries at Columbus.

With slick quarterback Rick Leach deftly running the option, Michigan took the second half kickoff and stuck it to the Buckeyes with a scoring drive that consumed six minutes and 11 seconds.

The march included runs of 15, 11 and nine yards by Lytle, Michigan's all-time rushing leader, and a key 20-yard burst by Leach on a busted third-down play.

Davis cracked over from the three, and the rout was on.

Michigan, the nation's top rushing team, was running its option attack to perfection now, while its defenders had little trouble stopping Ohio's stodgy, conservative offense.

The Wolverines struck again after Jim Smith returned a punt to his 48. Lytle romped for 16 yards on the first play and, following a near-costly procedure penalty, Smith galloped 16 yards to the nine on a wingback reverse.

Davis scored again three plays later, and a gambling two-point conversion run by Zuver off a fake kick made it 15-0.

Ohio State's lone first-half threat ended with a leaping end zone interception by Jim Pickens in the final 90 seconds, and the Buckeyes coughed the ball up two more times in the fourth period.

Ohio State rallies to beat Colorado

MIAMI — (AP) — Woody Hayes, the iron-fisted ruler of Ohio State football, was in a good mood Saturday night — thanks to a domineering defense and an offensive explosion ignited by his sophomore quarterback, Rod Gerald.

That combination enabled the 11th-ranked Buckeyes to overcome a 10-0 deficit and record a 27-10 Orange Bowl decision over No. 12 Colorado.

"I feel a lot better than I did a year ago," said Hayes, thinking back to a Rose Bowl loss to U.C.L.A. that cost his team a national championship and irked him so much that he refused to be interviewed after the game.

He kept writers waiting only 15 minutes this time and answered all questions cordially.

"OUR DEFENSE did a fabulous job," Hayes said. "They only got 10 points and they are usually a high-scoring team," he said of Colorado. "Our offense set up their points.

"We played them like an accordian. We pushed them in and we stretched them out."

Gerald, a 173-pounder, triggered the comeback, sprinting 17 yards on his first play late in the opening quarter before sending Jeff Logan 36 yards for a touchdown in a two-play drive. Before that, Ohio State's offense had netted minus-20 yards.

Logan, a tailback who became Ohio State's fifth 1,000-yard rusher in history, moved into the fullback slot against the Buffaloes and Hayes said that the change contributed to the victory.

"They weren't ready for that kind of speed," he said.

The move left Pete Johnson, 240-pound fullback, on the bench for a time. Johnson, Ohio State's all-time touchdown leader, scored his 58th against the Buffaloes shortly before halftime and put the Buckeyes ahead to stay at 17-10.

"I'm not much on losses," said Colorado's coach, Bill Mallory, a former assistant to Hayes at Ohio State. "We didn't play as well as we can."

MALLORY CITED the kicking game as a major difference with Ohio State's Tom Skladany booting two field goals, booming kickoffs consistently to the end zone and punting well on the rare occasions when the Buckeyes were forced to kick.

Johnson's touchdown came on a three-yard run. Skladany's field goals covered 28 and 20 yards. The Buckeyes got their final score with only 45 seconds left on a four-yard keeper by Gerald following a pass interception deep in Colorado territory.

The Buckeyes (9-2-1) surged into the lead on a 99-yard drive shortly before halftime and dominated play from the second quarter on with a ball-control attack.

Colorado, which jumped to a quick 10-0 lead on Mark Zetterberg's 26-yard field goal and Emery Moorehead's 11-yard scoring catch from Jeff Knapple, got good field position only once in the second half when it recovered a fumble at the Buckeye 26.

That was erased two plays later when Tom Cousineau intercepted a pass with 11 minutes left in the third quarter, and the Buffaloes (8-4) never threatened again.

THE BUCKEYES probably could have turned the game into more of a rout but missed on several scoring opportunities in the second half, taking over five times from near midfield or closer and producing only 10 points.

O.S.U.'s starting senior quarterback, Jim Pacenta, had trouble getting the Buckeyes untracked despite two long kickoff returns in the opening minutes of the game, 39 yards by Matt Jackson and 49 yards by Logan.

It was a fumble by Pacenta that set up Colorado's first score, the 26-yard field goal by Zetterberg. With Pacenta attempting to pass, Mark Haynes knocked the ball from his hands and Randy Westendorf, a defensive end from Kent, Wash., recovered on the Ohio State 43.

The Buffalo touchdown drive covered 80 yards and featured a 20-yard pass from Knapple to Moorehead and a 40-yard reverse by Billy Waddy.

Ohio State's 99-yard scoring drive came in the final six minutes of the half and turned the game around, giving the Buckeyes a 17-10 halftime advantage.

A tackle, Nick Buonamici, was credited with blocking Zetterberg's field-goal attempt that went out of bounds on the one.

Colorado appeared to have stopped the Buckeyes' inside the 10, but a piling-on infraction gave Ohio State a first down at the 23. Gerald kept the drive on the ground, reaching the Colorado 35 where he quickly sprinted 17 yards on a pass-option and then hit Jim Harrell on a 15-yard pass to the three, setting up Johnson's touchdown run with only 24 seconds left in the half.

Colorado   10 0 0 0 — 10
Ohio State   7 10 3 7 — 27

Colo — FG, Zetterberg 26.
Colo — Moorehead, 11 pass from Knapple (Zetterberg kick).
O.S.U. — Logan, 36 run (Skladany kick).
O.S.U. — FG, Skladany 28.
O.S.U. — Johnson, 3 run (Skladany kick).
O.S.U. — FG, Skladany 20.
O.S.U. — Gerald, 4 run (Skladany kick).
Attendance — 65,537.

	Colo.	Ohio St.
First downs	12	21
Rushes-yards	40-134	71-271
Passing yards	137	59
Return yards	5	39
Passes	8-23-2	2-7-0
Punts	7-35	3-42
Fumbles-lost	1-0	4-4
Penalties-yards	8-60	4-37

INDIVIDUAL LEADERS

RUSHING — Colorado, Reed 22-58, Kelleher 11-26, Waddy 1-40. Ohio State, Springs 23-98, Gerald 14-81, Logan 14-80.
RECEIVING — Colorado, Moorehead 4-68, Reed 2-51, Hasselbeck 2-18. Ohio State, Harrell 2-59.
PASSING — Colorado, Knapple 8-22-2, 137 yards. Ohio State, Gerald 2-6-0, 59.

Final 1976 Ohio State Football Statistics
(Won 9, Lost 2, Tied 1)

	OHIO	OPP.		OHIO	OPP.
Total First Downs	216	205	Punt Returns	26	30
By Rushing	176	122	Yards Returned	223	237
By Passing	31	76	Kickoff Returns	23	28
By Penalty	9	7	Yards Returned	475	414
3rd Down Efficiency	79-169	76-170	Misc. Returns-Yards	0-0	1-3
Net Yards Rushing	3101	1865	Interceptions	25	7
Attempts	714	567	Yards Returned	399	51
Average per Game	258.4	155.4	Punts	53	67
Rushing Touchdowns	36	10	Total Yards	2252	2710
Net Yards Passing	693	1553	Average per Punt	42.4	40.4
Attempted	97	283	Fumbles	30	23
Completed	44	117	Lost	17	12
Intercepted	7	25	Penalties	44	44
Average per Game	57.7	129.4	Yards	410	351
Passing Touchdowns	1	9	Score by Quarters		
Total Net Gain	3794	3418		1 2 3 4	Total
Average per Game	316.1	284.8	OPPONENTS	17 20 42 70	149
Total Plays	811	850	OHIO STATE	65 110 62 68	305

RUSHING	ATT	NET	AVG	TD	LG
Logan	218	1248	5.7	6	75
*P. Johnson	186	724	3.8	19	58
Gerald	116	465	4.0	7	32
Springs	72	389	5.4	2	62
Campbell	29	112	3.8	0	33
*Pacenta	62	68	1.0	1	30
Castignola	3	20	6.6	0	10
R. Johnson	4	17	4.2	0	8
Jackson	7	16	2.5	0	5
*Harrell	5	11	2.2	0	7
*Hyatt	1	8	8.0	1	8
Schneider	2	8	4.0	0	5
Strahine	4	5	1.2	0	8
Hunter	3	5	1.6	0	2
*Molls	1	4	4.0	0	4
Gordon	1	1	1.0	0	1

PASSING	PA	PC	PI	YDS	PCT	TD	LG
*Pacenta	54	28	3	404	.518	1	59
Gerald	40	14	4	245	.350	0	44
Logan	1	1	0	36	1.000	0	36
Castignola	2	1	0	8	.500	0	8

RECEIVING	NO.	YDS	AVG	TD	LG
*Harrell	14	288	20.5	1	59
Storer	11	161	14.6	0	25
Logan	5	44	8.8	0	23
*P. Johnson	4	41	10.2	0	12
Jones	3	64	21.3	0	39
Jaco	3	53	17.6	0	36
*Hyatt	2	26	13.0	0	15
Campbell	1	8	8.0	0	8
Jackson	1	8	8.0	0	8

SCORING	TD	E-1	E-2	FG	TP
*P. Johnson	19	0	0	0	114
*Skladany	0	35-37	0-2	8-23	59
Logan	7	0	0	0	42
Gerald	7	0	0-1	0	42
Springs	2	0	0	0	12
Adkins	1	0	0	0	6
R. Griffin	1	0	0	0	6
*Harrell	1	0	0	0	6
*Hyatt	1	0	0	0	6
*Pacenta	1	0	0-1	0	6
*Thompson	1	0	0	0	6

PUNTING	NO.	YARDS	AVG.	LG
*Skladany	53	2252	42.4	63

RETURNS	K.O.	PUNT	INT.	TD
Logan	9-179	8-92		1
R. Griffin	17-131	1-76#		1
Springs	9-158			0
Jackson	4-116			0
*Thompson			3-103	1
*Brudzinski			4-68	0
*Buonamici			3-64	0
Guess			2-22	0
*Harrell		1-22		0
Cousineau			2-30	0
Adkins			1-19	1
Schwartz			1-14	0
Roche			4-3	0
Dansler			2-0	0
D. Griffin			1-0	0
*Ruhl		1-0	1-0	0

*Indicates Senior

#73 yards off lateral